Something about
the Author *was named
an "**Outstanding
Reference Source,**"
the highest honor given
by the American
Library Association
Reference and Adult
Services Division.*

SOMETHING ABOUT THE AUTHOR®

ISSN 0276-816X

SOMETHING ABOUT THE AUTHOR®

**Facts and Pictures about Authors
and Illustrators of Books for Young People**

volume 120

GALE GROUP

Detroit
New York
San Francisco
London
Boston
Woodbridge, CT

STAFF

Scot Peacock, *Managing Editor, Literature Product*
Mark Scott, *Publisher, Literature Product*

Katy Balcer, Sara L. Constantakis, Kristen A. Dorsch, Lisa Kumar, Thomas McMahon, Colleen Laine Tavor, *Editors;* Shayla Hawkins, Motoko Fujishiro Huthwaite, Thomas Wiloch, *Associate Editors;* Alana Foster, Jennifer Kilian, *Assistant Editors,* Joshua Kondek, *Technical Training Specialist*

Alan Hedblad, *Managing Editor*
Susan M. Trosky, *Literature Content Coordinator*

Victoria B. Cariappa, *Research Manager;* Tracie A. Richardson, *Project Coordinator;* Maureen Emeric, Barbara McNeil, Gary J. Oudersluys, Cheryl L. Warnock, *Research Specialists;* Tamara C. Nott, *Research Associate;* Nicodemus Ford, Tim Lehnerer, Ron Morelli, *Research Assistants*

Maria L. Franklin, *Permissions Manager;* Margaret Chamberlain, *Permissions Associate*

Mary Beth Trimper, *Composition Manager;* Dorothy Maki, *Manufacturing Manager;* Stacy Melson, *Buyer*

Michael Logusz, *Graphic Artist;* Randy Bassett, *Image Database Supervisor;* Robert Duncan, *Imaging Specialist;* Pamela A. Reed, *Imaging Coordinator;* Dean Dauphinais, Robyn V. Young, *Senior Image Editors;* Kelly A. Quin, *Image Editor*

iccrz

Library of Congress Catalog Card Number 72-27107

ISBN 0-7876-4708-X
ISSN 0276-816X

Printed in the United States of America

10 9 8 7 6 5 4 3 2 1

Contents

Authors in Forthcoming Volumes vii
Introduction ix
Acknowledgments xi

A

Ahlberg, Allan 1938- 1

Ahlberg, Janet 1944-1994 8

Armstrong, Jennifer 1961-

Autobiography Feature 13

B

Barunga, Albert 1912(?)-1977 24

Baskin, Leonard 1922-2000 24

Biggar, Joan R(awlins) 1936- 29

Bishop, Kathleen Wong 1954- 31

Bishop, Kathy

See Bishop, Kathleen Wong 32

C

Carle, Eric 1929- 33

Chapman, Gillian 1955- 40

Christelow, Eileen 1943-

Autobiography Feature 43

Cole, Joanna 1944- 61

Cooke, Ann

See Cole, Joanna 68

Coy, John 1958- 68

Crilley, Mark 1966- 69

Crossley-Holland, Kevin (John William) 1941- . . . 70

Currie, Robin 1948- 80

D

Denny, Diana 1910-2000

Obituary Notice 82

Dessen, Sarah 1970- 82

Doyle, Malachy 1954- 86

E-F

Ellestad, Myrvin H. 1921- 89

Fisher, Leonard Everett 1924- 90

Forest, Heather 1948- 101

Fox, Paula 1923- 103

G

Gri

See Denny, Diana 82

Gurney, James 1958- 110

H

Hathorn, Libby 1943- 113

Heimann, Rolf 1940- 118

Hillman, John 1952- 119

Hindley, Judy 1940- 120

Holm, Jennifer L. 19(?) 123

K

Kane, Bob 1916-1998 124

Kay, Verla 1946- 127

Kerr, Bob 1951- 128

Kuroi, Ken 1947- 129

L

Laird, Christa 1944-

Autobiography Feature 130

Lamensdorf, Len

See Lamensdorf, Leonard 140

Lamensdorf, Leonard 1930- 140

Laminack, Lester L. 1956- 141

Lawrence, Margery (H.) 1889-1969 142

Lesinski, Jeanne M. 1960- 143

Lewis, Anthony 1966- 145

Lidz, Jane 147

Lindgren, Barbro 1937- 148

Lofo

See Heimann, Rolf 153

Long, Sylvia 1948- 153

M

Marley, Louise 1952- 157

May, Elaine T(yler) 1947- 158

Mitchell, B(etty) J(o) 1931- 160

Moses, Will 1956- 161

Mosher, Richard 1949- 162

Munsch, Robert N(orman) 1945- 164

N

Norman, Lilith 1927- 171

P

Palmer, Jessica 1953- 174

Patent, Dorothy Hinshaw 1940- 175

Platt, Richard 1953- 181

Pokeberry, P. J.

See Mitchell, B(etty) J(o) 160

Priceman, Marjorie 19(?) 183

Purdy, Carol 1943- 187

Purnell, Idella 1901-1982 188

R

Richardson, Andrew (William) 1986- 191

Rodowsky, Colby 1932- 191

Ross, Diana

See Denney, Diana 82

Royston, Angela 1945- 196

S-T

Sabuda, Robert (James) 1965- 202

Schneider, Christine M. 1972(?)- 204

Sloan, Glenna (Davis) 1930- 204

Smith, Jos(eph) A. 1936- 205

Soto, Gary 1952- 209

Stobbs, William 1914-2000

Obituary Notice 215

Stone, Idella Purnell

See Purnell, Idella 188

Stone, Ikey

See Purnell, Idella 188

Svendsen, Mark (Nestor) 1962- 215

Tchen, Richard 19(?) 217

Trahey, Jane 1923-2000

Obituary Notice 217

W

Walsh, Vivian 1960- 218

Walsh, V. L.

See Walsh, Vivian 219

Weber, Bruce 1942- 219

Winer, Yvonne 1934- 221

Wood, June Rae 1946- 222

Z

Zalben, Jane Breskin 1950- 228

Authors in Forthcoming Volumes

Below are some of the authors and illustrators that will be featured in upcoming volumes of *SATA*. These include new entries on the swiftly rising stars of the field, as well as completely revised and updated entries (indicated with *) on some of the most notable and best-loved creators of books for children.

Yvonne Ashby: Ashby was encouraged by her family to pursue a career in drawing. The Australian native is now an award-winning illustrator and has designed pictures for several books, including the "Solo Bush Babies" series.

Charles Butler: Born in the English countryside, Butler is a young adult novelist whose main subjects are magic and the supernatural. Butler's approach to the fantasy genre is unique, because he prefers his magical elements to be grounded in reality. Butler took time to perfect his craft before writing his first book, *The Darkling*, which was published in 1997.

*Beverly Cleary: One of the most beloved authors of children's literature, Cleary has been writing books for young people for over fifty years, a period during which her popularity, critical acclaim, and relevance have held steady, if not increased. Cleary has won almost every honor created for a children's book author, including the prestigious Newbery Award. Cleary has written in a number of genres, but is most famous for her "Ramona Quimby" book series.

Alan Durant: Durant is an English writer whose style and subject matter have been greatly influenced by the births of his three children. Although Durant's early writing efforts included the teen novels *Blood* and *Hamlet, Bananas, and All That Jazz*, he has more recently focused on picture books for younger readers, including *Angus Rides the Goods Train*, *Mouse Party*, and *Snake Supper*.

*Patricia Reilly Giff: A prolific author, Giff specializes in writing humorous books for middle-grade readers. In many cases, even the titles of Giff's books, such as *Fish Face*, *Pickle Puss*, and *Poopsie Pomerantz, Pick Up Your Feet*, are comical. Giff has been writing for young readers for almost thirty years and attributes her success to her sincere love of both books and children.

Katherine Holubitsky: Published in 1999, Holubitsky's first book, *Alone at Ninety Foot*, was cited by the American Booksellers Association, American Library Association, Canadian Library Association, and the New York Public Library as one of the best young adult novels of the year. Holubitsky also works as a library technician in her hometown of Edmonton, Alberta, Canada.

Barbara Kimenye: Kimenye is a journalist who lives in England and writes for the African newspaper *Uganda Nation*. As a children's author, however, she is best known for her "Moses" series, whose protagonist is a mischievous but kindhearted young boy.

Marybeth Lorbiecki: Lorbiecki is a proficient writer in several genres of children's literature, including easy readers, young adult novels, and nonfiction books that tackle tough social problems. Lorbiecki's titles include *The Children of Vietnam* and *Just One Flick of a Finger*. For *Sister Anne's Hands*, a book about a child's first encounter with racism, Lorbiecki won several honors, including Bank Street College's Best Books of the Year award.

Bernie Monagle: Monagle is an Australian writer and high school teacher whose books explore such universal social dilemmas as teenage pregnancy. His first book, *Blue Girl, Yella Fella*, was published in 2000. Monagle is also employed as a drama consultant.

*Neal Shusterman: A critically acclaimed author of young adult fiction, Shusterman has won numerous awards, including the New York Public Library's Best Book for the Teen Age citation for *Speeding Bullet*. Shusterman's other books include *The Eyes of Kid Midas* and *Downsiders*.

Josef Vondra: Vondra is a European-born Australian journalist who began his literary career writing for adults, but he now creates stories for adolescents. His first young adult novel, *No-Name Bird*, was published in 2000.

Introduction

Something about the Author (*SATA*) is an ongoing reference series that examines the lives and works of authors and illustrators of books for children. *SATA* includes not only well-known writers and artists but also less prominent individuals whose works are just coming to be recognized. This series is often the only readily available information source on emerging authors and illustrators. You'll find *SATA* informative and entertaining, whether you are a student, a librarian, an English teacher, a parent, or simply an adult who enjoys children's literature.

What's Inside SATA

SATA provides detailed information about authors and illustrators who span the full time range of children's literature, from early figures like John Newbery and L. Frank Baum to contemporary figures like Judy Blume and Richard Peck. Authors in the series represent primarily English-speaking countries, particularly the United States, Canada, and the United Kingdom. Also included, however, are authors from around the world whose works are available in English translation. The writings represented in *SATA* include those created intentionally for children and young adults as well as those written for a general audience and known to interest younger readers. These writings cover the entire spectrum of children's literature, including picture books, humor, folk and fairy tales, animal stories, mystery and adventure, science fiction and fantasy, historical fiction, poetry and nonsense verse, drama, biography, and nonfiction.

Obituaries are also included in *SATA* and are intended not only as death notices but also as concise overviews of people's lives and work. Additionally, each edition features newly revised and updated entries for a selection of *SATA* listees who remain of interest to today's readers and who have been active enough to require extensive revisions of their earlier biographies.

New Autobiography Feature

Beginning with Volume 103, *SATA* features three or more specially commissioned autobiographical essays in each volume. These unique essays, averaging about ten thousand words in length and illustrated with an abundance of personal photos, present an entertaining and informative first-person perspective on the lives and careers of prominent authors and illustrators profiled in *SATA*.

Two Convenient Indexes

In response to suggestions from librarians, *SATA* indexes no longer appear in every volume but are included in alternate (odd-numbered) volumes of the series, beginning with Volume 57.

SATA continues to include two indexes that cumulate with each alternate volume: the Illustrations Index, arranged by the name of the illustrator, gives the number of the volume and page where the illustrator's work appears in the current volume as well as all preceding volumes in the series; the Author Index gives the number of the volume in which a person's biographical sketch, autobiographical essay, or obituary appears in the current volume as well as all preceding volumes in the series.

These indexes also include references to authors and illustrators who appear in Gale's *Yesterday's Authors of Books for Children, Children's Literature Review,* and *Something about the Author Autobiography Series.*

Easy-to-Use Entry Format

Whether you're already familiar with the *SATA* series or just getting acquainted, you will want to be aware of the kind of information that an entry provides. In every *SATA* entry the editors attempt to give as complete a picture of the person's life and work as possible. A typical entry in *SATA* includes the following clearly labeled information sections:

- *PERSONAL:* date and place of birth and death, parents' names and occupations, name of spouse, date of marriage, names of children, educational institutions attended, degrees received, religious and political affiliations, hobbies and other interests.

- *ADDRESSES:* complete home, office, electronic mail, and agent addresses, whenever available.

- *CAREER:* name of employer, position, and dates for each career post; art exhibitions; military service; memberships and offices held in professional and civic organizations.

- *AWARDS, HONORS:* literary and professional awards received.

- *WRITINGS:* title-by-title chronological bibliography of books written and/or illustrated, listed by genre when known; lists of other notable publications, such as plays, screenplays, and periodical contributions.

- *ADAPTATIONS:* a list of films, television programs, plays, CD-ROMs, recordings, and other media presentations that have been adapted from the author's work.

- *WORK IN PROGRESS:* description of projects in progress.

- *SIDELIGHTS:* a biographical portrait of the author or illustrator's development, either directly from the biographee—and often written specifically for the *SATA* entry—or gathered from diaries, letters, interviews, or other published sources.

- *BIOGRAPHICAL AND CRITICAL SOURCES:* cites sources quoted in "Sidelights" along with references for further reading.

- *EXTENSIVE ILLUSTRATIONS:* photographs, movie stills, book illustrations, and other interesting visual materials supplement the text.

How a SATA Entry Is Compiled

A *SATA* entry progresses through a series of steps. If the biographee is living, the *SATA* editors try to secure information directly from him or her through a questionnaire. From the information that the biographee supplies, the editors prepare an entry, filling in any essential missing details with research and/or telephone interviews. If possible, the author or illustrator is sent a copy of the entry to check for accuracy and completeness.

If the biographee is deceased or cannot be reached by questionnaire, the *SATA* editors examine a wide variety of published sources to gather information for an entry. Biographical and bibliographic sources are consulted, as are book reviews, feature articles, published interviews, and material sometimes obtained from the biographee's family, publishers, agent, or other associates.

Entries that have not been verified by the biographees or their representatives are marked with an asterisk (*).

Contact the Editor

We encourage our readers to examine the entire *SATA* series. Please write and tell us if we can make *SATA* even more helpful to you. Give your comments and suggestions to the editor:

BY MAIL: Editor, *Something about the Author,* The Gale Group, 27500 Drake Rd., Farmington Hills, MI 48331-3535.

BY TELEPHONE: (800) 877-GALE

BY FAX: (248) 699-8054

Acknowledgments

Grateful acknowledgment is made to the following publishers, authors, and artists whose works appear in this volume.

AHLBERG, ALLAN. From a cover of *The Jolly Pocket Postman*, by Janet and Allan Ahlberg. William Heinemann, 1995. Copyright © 1995 by Janet and Allan Ahlberg. Reproduced by permission of Reed Books. / Ahlberg, Allan. From an illustration in *Monkey Do!* by Allen Ahlberg. Illustration © 1998 Andre Amstutz. Reproduced by permission Candlewick Press, Inc., Cambridge, MA, on behalf of Walker Books Ltd., London. / Ahlberg, Allan. From an illustration in *The Bravest Ever Bear,* by Allen Ahlberg. Illustration © 1999 Paul Howard. Reproduced by permission of Candlewick Press, Inc., Cambridge, MA, on behalf of Walker Books Ltd., London. / Ahlberg, Allan. From an illustration in *The Mysteries of Zigomar,* by Allen Ahlberg. Illustration © 1997 John Lawrence. Reproduced by permission Candlewick Press, Inc., Cambridge, MA, on behalf of Walker Books Ltd., London.

AHLBERG, JANET. From an illustration in *The Baby's Catalogue,* by Janet and Allan Ahlberg. Copyright © 1982 by Janet Ahlberg and Allan Ahlberg. Reproduced by permission of Little, Brown and Company. / Ahlberg, Janet. From an illustration in *The Jolly Christmas Postman,* by Janet and Allan Ahlberg. Copyright © 1991 by Allan Ahlberg and Janet Ahlberg. Reproduced in U.S. by permission of Little, Brown and Company. In the U.K. by permission of Penguin U.K.

ARMSTRONG, JENNIFER. All photographs reproduced by permission of the author.

BASKIN, LEONARD. From an illustration in *A Book of Flies Real or Otherwise,* by Richard Michelson. Marshall Cavendish, 1999. Illustrations copyright © 1999 by the Estate of Leonard Baskin. Reproduced by permission of R. Michelson Galleries. / Baskin, Leonard, illustrator. From an illustration in *Did You Say Ghosts?*, by Richard Michelson. Macmillan, 1993. Illustrations copyright © 1993 by Leonard Baskin. / Baskin, Leonard, illustrator. From an illustration in *Moon-Whales and Other Moon Poems,* by Ted Hughes. Illustration copyright © 1976 by Leonard Baskin. Reproduced in the U.S. by permission of Viking Penguin, an imprint of Penguin Putnam Books for Young Readers, a division of Penguin Putnam, Inc. In the U.K. by permission of Leonard Baskin, Inc.

BIGGAR, JOAN R(AWLINS). From a cover of *Missing on Castaway Island*. Concordia Publishing House, 1997. Cover illustration by Matthew Archambault. Copyright © 1997 by Concordia Publishing House. Reproduced by permission.

BISHOP, KATHLEEN WONG. From a cover of *Fables from the Garden,* by Leslie Ann Hayashi. A Kolowalu Book, University of Hawaii Press, 1998. © 1998 University of Hawaii Press. Reproduced by permission.

CARLE, ERIC. From an illustration in his *Draw Me a Star.* The Putnam & Grosset Group, 1992. Copyright © 1992 by Eric Carle. Reproduced by permission of The Putnam & Grosset Group, a division of Penguin Putnam Inc. / Carle, Eric. From an illustration in his *Hello, Red Fox.* Copyright © 1998 Eric Carle Corporation. Reproduced in the U.S. by permission of Simon & Schuster Books for Young Readers, an imprint of Simon & Schuster Children's Publishing Division. In the U.K. by permission of the Eric Carle Studio. / Carle, Eric. From an illustration in his *The Very Clumsy Click Beetle.* Philomel Books, 1999. Copyright © 1999 by Eric Carle. Reproduced by permission of Eric Carle Studio. / Carle, Eric, photograph. Reproduced by permission of Eric Carle.

CHAPMAN, GILLIAN. From an illustration in her *The Egyptians.* Fernleigh / Heinemann, 1997. Copyright © 1997 by Fernleigh Books. Reproduced by permission. / Chapman, Gillian, photograph. Reproduced by permission of Gillian Chapman.

CHRISTELOW, EILEEN. All photographs reproduced by permission of the author.

COLE, JOANNA. From an illustration in her *The Magic School Bus in the Time of the Dinosaurs.* Scholastic Inc., 1994. Illustrations copyright © 1994 Bruce Degen. Reproduced by permission. / From a photograph in *My New Kitten*, by Joanna Cole. Morrow Junior Books, 1995. Photographs copyright © 1995 by Margaret Miller. Reproduced by permission of Morrow Junior Books, a division of William Morrow and Company, Inc.

COY, JOHN. Photograph. Reproduced by permission of John Coy.

CRILLEY, MARK. Photograph by Mary Moylan. Reproduced by permission of Mark Crilley.

CROSSLEY-HOLLAND, KEVIN (JOHN WILLIAM). From an illustration in *Beowulf,* retold by Kevin Crossley-Holland. Oxford University Press, Oxford, 1987. Illustrations © Charles Keeping 1982. All rights reserved. Reproduced by permission of Oxford University Press. / Crossley-Holland, Kevin. From an illustration in his *The World of King Arthur and his Court: People, Places, and Legend, and Lore*. Illustrations copyright © 1998 by Peter Malone. Reproduced in the U.S. by permission of Dutton, a division of Penguin Putnam, Inc. In the U.K. by permission of Orion Children's Books, Ltd./ Crossley-Holland, Kevin, photographs reproduced by permission of the author.

CURRIE, ROBIN. From an illustration in *Baby Bible Stories about Jesus.* Chariot Victor Publishing, 1996. Illustrations by Cindy Adams. Copyright © 1996 by Cook Communications Ministries. Reprinted Reproduced by permission.

SOMETHING ABOUT THE AUTHOR

AHLBERG, Allan 1938-

Personal

Born June 5, 1938, in England; married Janet Hall (an illustrator), July, 1969 (died 1994); children: Jessica. *Education:* Certificate in education, Sunderland College of Education, 1966.

Addresses

Home and office—20 Nether Hall Ln., Birstall, Leicester LE4 4DT, England. *Office*—c/o Penguin Books Ltd., 27 Wrights Ln., London W8 5TZ, England.

Career

Worked as letter carrier, grave digger, soldier, plumber's helper, and teacher; full-time children's writer, 1975—.

Awards, Honors

Commendation, Library Association (Great Britain), 1977, for *Burglar Bill;* Kate Greenaway Medal, Library Association (Great Britain), 1979, citation, Notable Children's Book Committee of the Association for Library Service to Children, 1979, and citation on honor list for illustration in Great Britain, International Board on Books for Young People, 1980, all for *Each Peach Pear Plum;* Other Award, Children's Rights Workshop, 1980, for *Mrs. Plug the Plumber;* Best Books of the Year award, *School Library Journal,* 1981, and Silver Paint Brush award (Holland), 1988, both for *Funny-*

bones; citation, Notable Children's Book Committee of the Association for Library Service to Children, 1981, and Best Book for Babies award, *Parents* magazine, 1985, both for *Peek-a-Boo!;* commendation, Library Association (Great Britain), 1982, Best Books of the Year award, *School Library Journal,* 1983, Children's Books of the Year award, Library of Congress, 1983, Teacher's Choice award, National Council of Teachers of English, 1983, and citation, Notable Children's Book Committee of the Association for Library Service to Children, 1983, all for *The Baby's Catalogue;* Emil/Kurt Mashler Award, Book Trust (Great Britain), commendation, Library Association (Great Britain), and award, Federation of Children's Book Groups, all 1986, Golden Key (Holland), 1988, and Prix du Livre pour la Jeunesse (France), all for *The Jolly Postman; or, Other People's Letters;* Signal Poetry Award, 1990, for *Heard It in the Playground;* Kate Greenaway Medal, Library Association (Great Britain), 1991, for *The Jolly Christmas Postman;* runner-up, British Book Awards, 1989, 1991.

Writings

CHILDREN'S BOOKS; WITH WIFE, JANET AHLBERG

Here Are the Brick Street Boys (part of "Brick Street Boys" series), Collins, 1975.
A Place to Play (part of "Brick Street Boys" series), Collins, 1975.
Sam the Referee (part of "Brick Street Boys" series), Collins, 1975.
Fred's Dream (part of "Brick Street Boys" series), Collins, 1976.

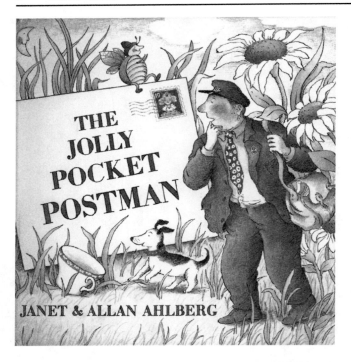

In Janet and Allan Ahlberg's "Jolly Postman" titles, children are offered a collection of missives from one classic storybook character to another, slipped into the pages of the book for readers to open and savor.

The Great Marathon Football Match (part of "Brick Street Boys" series), Collins, 1976.

The Old Joke Book, Kestrel Books, 1976, Viking, 1977.

The Vanishment of Thomas Tull, Scribner, 1977.

Burglar Bill, Greenwillow, 1977.

Jeremiah in the Dark Woods, Kestrel Books, 1977, Viking, 1978.

Cops and Robbers (verse), Greenwillow, 1978.

Each Peach Pear Plum: An "I Spy" Story (verse), Kestrel Books, 1978, Viking, 1979.

The One and Only Two Heads, Collins, 1979.

Two Wheels, Two Heads, Collins, 1979.

Son of a Gun, Heinemann, 1979.

The Little Worm Book, Granada, 1979, Viking, 1980.

Funnybones, Greenwillow, 1980.

Peek-a-Boo! (verse), Viking, 1981, published in England as *Peepo!,* Kestrel Books, 1981.

The Ha Ha Bonk Book, Penguin, 1982.

The Baby's Catalogue (see also below), Little, Brown, 1982.

Yum Yum (part of "Slot Book" series), Viking Kestrel (London), 1984, Viking Kestrel (New York), 1985.

Playmates (part of "Slot Book" series), Viking Kestrel (London), 1984, Viking Kestrel (New York), 1985.

The Jolly Postman; or, Other People's Letters, Little, Brown, 1986.

The Cinderella Show, Viking Kestrel, 1986.

The Clothes Horse and Other Stories, Viking Kestrel (London), 1987, Viking Kestrel (New York), 1988.

Starting School, Viking Kestrel, 1988.

Bye-Bye, Baby: A Sad Story with a Happy Ending, Little, Brown, 1989, published as *Bye-Bye, Baby: A Baby without a Mommy in Search of One,* 1990.

The Jolly Christmas Postman, Little, Brown, 1991.

The Bear Nobody Wanted, Viking, 1992.

It Was a Dark and Stormy Night, Viking, 1993.

The Jolly Pocket Postman, Little, Brown, 1995.

See the Rabbit, Doll and Teddy, Baby Sleeps, and *Blue Pram* (board books adapted from *The Baby's Catalogue*), Little Brown, 1998, Viking, 1998.

"HAPPY FAMILIES" SERIES

Mr. Biff the Boxer, illustrated by J. Ahlberg, Puffin, 1980, published in "Wacky Families" series, Golden Press, 1982.

Mr. Cosmo the Conjuror, illustrated by Joe Wright, Puffin, 1980.

Miss Jump the Jockey, illustrated by Andre Amstutz, Puffin, 1980.

Master Salt the Sailor's Son, illustrated by A. Amstutz, Puffin, 1980, published in "Wacky Families" series, Golden Press, 1982.

Mrs. Plug the Plumber, illustrated by J. Wright, Puffin, 1980, published in "Wacky Families" series, Golden Press, 1982.

Mrs. Wobble the Waitress, illustrated by J. Ahlberg, Puffin, 1980, published in "Wacky Families" series, Golden Press, 1982.

Miss Brick the Builder's Baby, illustrated by Colin McNaughton, Puffin, 1981, published in "Wacky Families" series, Golden Press, 1982.

Mr. Buzz the Beeman, illustrated by Faith Jaques, Puffin, 1981, published in "Wacky Families" series, Golden Press, 1982.

Mr. and Mrs. Hay the Horse, illustrated by C. McNaughton, Puffin, 1981, published in "Wacky Families" series, Golden Press, 1982.

Mr. Tick the Teacher, illustrated by F. Jaques, Puffin, 1981.

Mrs. Lather's Laundry, illustrated by A. Amstutz, Puffin, 1981, published in "Wacky Families" series, Golden Press, 1982.

Master Money the Millionaire, illustrated by A. Amstutz, Puffin, 1981.

Master Bun the Baker's Boy, illustrated by Fritz Wegner, Puffin, 1988.

Miss Dose the Doctor's Daughter, illustrated by F. Wegner, Puffin, 1988.

Mr. Creep the Crook, illustrated by A. Amstutz, Puffin, 1988.

Mrs. Jolly's Joke Shop, illustrated by C. McNaughton, Viking Kestrel, 1988.

Miss Dust the Dustman's Daughter, illustrated by Tony Ross, Viking, 1996.

Mrs. Vole the Vet, illustrated by Emma Chichester-Clark, Viking, 1996.

Ms. Cliff the Climber, illustrated by F. Wegner, Viking, 1997.

Master Track's Train, illustrated by A. Amstutz, Viking, 1997.

"HELP YOUR CHILD TO READ" SERIES

Bad Bear, illustrated by Eric Hill, Granada, 1982 (also see below).

Double Ducks, illustrated by E. Hill, Granada, 1982 (also see below).

Fast Frog, illustrated by E. Hill, Granada, 1982 (also see below).

Poorly Pig, illustrated by E. Hill, Granada, 1982, Rand McNally, 1984 (also see below).

Rubber Rabbit, illustrated by E. Hill, Granada, 1982 (also see below).

Silly Sheep, illustrated by E. Hill, Granada, 1982 (also see below).

Hip-Hippo-Ray, illustrated by A. Amstutz, Granada, 1983, Rand McNally, 1984.

King Kangaroo, illustrated by A. Amstutz, Granada, 1983.

Mister Wolf, illustrated by A. Amstutz, Granada, 1983.

Spider Spy, illustrated by A. Amstutz, Granada, 1983.

Tell-Tale-Tiger, illustrated by A. Amstutz, Granada, 1983.

Travelling Moose, illustrated by A. Amstutz, Granada, 1983.

Fast Frog and Friends: Help Your Child to Read Collection (first six volumes of series), illustrated by E. Hill, Dragon, 1984.

"DAISYCHAINS" VERSE SERIES

Ready Teddy Go, illustrated by J. Ahlberg, Heinemann, 1983.

Summer Snowmen, illustrated by J. Ahlberg, Heinemann, 1983.

That's My Baby!, illustrated by J. Ahlberg, Heinemann, 1983.

Which Witch, illustrated by J. Ahlberg, Heinemann, 1983.

Monster Munch, illustrated by A. Amstutz, Heinemann, 1984.

The Good Old Dolls, illustrated by A. Amstutz, Heinemann, 1984.

Rent-a-Robot, illustrated by A. Amstutz, Heinemann, 1984.

Clowning About, illustrated by A. Amstutz, Heinemann, 1984.

One True Santa, illustrated by J. Ahlberg, Heinemann, 1985.

"FOLDAWAYS" SERIES; ILLUSTRATED BY C. McNAUGHTON

Families, Granada, 1984.

Monsters, Granada, 1984.

Zoo, Granada, 1984.

Circus, Granada, 1984.

"RED NOSE READERS" SERIES; ILLUSTRATED BY C. McNAUGHTON

Jumping, Walker, 1985.

So Can I, Walker, 1985.

Big Bad Pig, Random House, 1985.

Bear's Birthday, Walker, 1985.

Help!, Random House, 1985.

Fee Fi Fo Fum, Random House, 1985.

Happy Worm, Random House, 1985.

Make a Face, Walker, 1985.

One Two Flea!, Walker, 1986.

Tell Us a Story, Walker, 1986.

Blow Me Down, Walker, 1986.

Look Out for the Seals!, Walker, 1986.

Shirley Shops, Random House, 1986.

Me and My Friend, Random House, 1986.

Crash, Bang, Wallop!, Random House, 1986.

Push the Dog, Random House, 1986.

Who Stole the Pie, Walker, 1996.

Put on a Show!, Walker, 1996.

"FUNNYBONES" SERIES; ILLUSTRATED BY A. AMSTUTZ

The Pet Shop, Greenwillow, 1990.

The Black Cat, Greenwillow, 1990.

Mystery Tour, Greenwillow, 1991.

Dinosaur Dreams, Greenwillow, 1991.

Bumps in the Night, Greenwillow, 1991.

Give the Dog a Bone, Greenwillow, 1991.

Skeleton Crew, Greenwillow, 1992.

The Ghost Train, Greenwillow, 1992.

"FAST FOX, SLOW DOG" SERIES; ILLUSTRATED BY A. AMSTUTZ

Chicken, Chips, and Peas, Viking, 1999.

Fast Fox Goes Crazy, Viking, 1999.

Ahlberg presents something of a hybrid in **The Mysteries of Zigomar,** *part story collection and part verse collection.* (Illustrated by John Lawrence.)

A spirited little money lets himself out of his cage at the zoo and spends an adventurous day, recounted in Ahlberg's rhyming text. (From Monkey Do!, *illustrated by Andre Amstutz)*

The Hen House, Viking, 1999.
Slow Dog Falling, Viking, 1999.
Slow Dog's Nose, Viking, 2000.

OTHER

The History of a Pair of Sinners: Forgetting Not Their Ma Who Was One Also (verse), illustrated by John Lawrence, Granada, 1980.
Ten in a Bed (fiction), illustrated by A. Amstutz, Granada, 1983.
Please, Mrs. Butler (verse), illustrated by F. Wegner, Kestrel Books, 1983.
Woof! (fiction), illustrated by F. Wegner, Viking Kestrel, 1986.
The Mighty Slide (verse), illustrated by Charlotte Voake, Viking Kestrel, 1988.
Heard It in the Playground (verse), Viking Kestrel, 1989.
Mrs. Butler Song Book (based on poems from *Please, Mrs. Butler* and *Heard It in the Playground*), music by Colin Matthews, illustrated by F. Wegner, Viking, 1992.
The Giant Baby, illustrated by F. Wegner, Viking, 1994.
The Better Brown Stories, illustrated by F. Wegner, Viking, 1995.
Janet's Last Book: Janet Ahlberg 1944-1994 (biography), Penguin, 1997.
The Mysteries of Zigomar, illustrated by J. Lawrence, Walker, 1997.
Mockingbird, illustrated by Paul Howard, Walker, 1998.
Monkey Do!, illustrated by A. Amstutz, 1998.
The Bravest Ever Bear, illustrated by Paul Howard, Walker, 1999.
My Brother's Ghost, illustrated by F. Wegner, Viking, 2000.
The Snail House, illustrated by Gillian Tyler, Candlewick Press, in press.

Also author of the stage play, "The Giant's Baby."

Adaptations

A number of Allan and Janet Ahlberg's books are available on audiocassette, including *A Place to Play, Fred's Dream,* and *Each Peach Pear Plum.*

Sidelights

Allan Ahlberg is an award-winning British writer of children's stories, verse, picture books, and short novels. He is known for his irreverent wit and unfailing ability to make the commonplace quite extraordinary. Ahlberg manages to imbue simple reading books with a tongue-in-cheek humor that keeps kids turning the pages. In series such as the "Red Nose Readers," "Funnybones," and the ever-popular and zany "Happy Families," Ahlberg sets nonsense rhymes at play and teases inspiration out of academic reading schemes. Reviewing the "Happy Families" series, Jeff Hynds of *Books for Keeps* wondered: "How was it that Allan Ahlberg could write books like those in reading schemes and yet, unlike the schemes be so entertaining?" Hynds answered his own question, "... This is Ahlberg in satirical vein—Ahlberg the arch-parodist.... 'Happy Families' is not a reading scheme but a wonderful parody of one."

From the outset of his writing career, in collaboration with his wife, Janet, an illustrator, Ahlberg enjoyed such self-referential parodies. His first series, the "Brick Street Boys," was a send-up of the old "Dick and Jane" readers, in comic book style. Since the mid-1970s, Ahlberg has worked with his wife and other illustrators, including Andre Amstutz, Eric Hill, Colin McNaughton, and Fritz Wegner, to create hundreds of titles, each bearing the distinctive Ahlberg humor, light-heartedness, and exaggeration. Such a formula has obviously worked: his "Happy Families" series has sold two and a half million copies in the U.K. in the twenty years since it was first published. Ahlberg has also won such prestigious awards as the Kate Greenaway Medal for his seemingly effortless labors.

Born in 1938, Ahlberg was educated at Sunderland Teacher Training College in England where he met his future wife, Janet Hall. In 1969 the two married and Ahlberg went on to work at a variety of jobs, including teaching. His wife, meanwhile, was pursuing a career in the graphic arts. By the mid-1970s they had set up a collaborative effort producing picture books, a joint effort that began with the "Brick Street Boys," and carried them through twenty years and over forty titles, including the popular and award-winning *Each Peach Pear Plum* and the "Jolly Postman" books. (For a detailed account of this collaborative effort, see the entry on Janet Ahlberg.)

Ahlberg created numerous picture books during the years of collaborative effort with his wife, and after her death in 1994 from cancer, he has continued to blend his sardonic humor and often-times wacky view of the world with the illustrations of a wide range of talented artists. The "Happy Families" series, twenty books strong and growing, features the antics of a variety of families from *Mr. Biff the Boxer,* the first title in 1980, to *Ms. Cliff the Climber,* in 1997. "To the uninitiated," remarked Hynds, "they might seem like simple stories in simple language, but those who think like this are missing the parody and underestimating the linguistic tricks that Ahlberg plays continually with his readers." There are silly jokes and puns galore, and parodies of the prescribed word repetition for beginning readers, as well as a "consistently excellent interplay ... between text and illustrations," according to Hynds. Some of the stories also involve rather complex themes, such as the competing needs of work and family when divorce breaks up a family as in *Mrs. Vole the Vet.* Liz Waterland, reviewing the classroom use of the "Happy Families" books in *Books for Keeps,* noted that "sophisticated and mature readership skills" were needed for these books, despite their simple vocabulary. Waterland went on to call the series a "delight," offering "little gems of entertainment." Reviewing *Master Bun the Baker's Boy* and *Miss Dose the Doctor's Daughter, Growing Point*'s Margery Fisher concluded, "Simple jokes and expressive, dramatically active coloured pictures should confirm the popularity of a favourite series, conducted with the utmost expertise in word and line." Reviewing several titles in the series, including *Miss Dose the Doctor's Daughter,* a writer for *Books for Keeps* commented on Ahlberg's "resourceful and ambitious" female character who saves her whole town. The same reviewer concluded, "I have no idea how the Ahlbergs do it but everything they do is magic and these ... books by Allan Ahlberg are winners all over again." Jill Bennett, writing in *Books for Keeps,* praised a 1997 addition to the series, *Master Track's Train,* as a "homage to Oscar Wilde which will amuse adult readers in this multi-layered story which is told through many voices." In this tale, young Toby gives chase to would-be train robbers, the Creeps, who also have their own book in the series.

Another popular series from Ahlberg, working with illustrator Colin McNaughton, is the "Red Nose Readers," a "brilliant ... collaboration," according to Pat Triggs in *Books for Keeps.* In a *School Library Journal* review of four early titles in the series, *Big Bad Pig, Fee Fi Fo Fum, Happy Worm,* and *Help!,* Louise L. Sherman described this quartet as "zany word and concept books whose bright droll illustrations and amusing situations will tickle the funnybones of children just beginning to read." A writer for *The Junior Bookshelf* noted that Ahlberg's *One Two Flea!* "appeals to the irreverence which lurks within the best behaved infants," and presents nursery reading "which is neither condescending nor over-earnest." Reviewing the same title as well as seven others in the series, a contributor for *Books for Keeps* noted that the series "has a lot of young fans" and employs "jokey illustrations and bubble talk." The same reviewer concluded that the "Red Nose Readers" "are a good bet for school bookshops and very good value ...." Some of the most popular scenes from the series are collected in two 1996 titles, *Who Stole the Pie?* and *Put on a Show!,* welcome revisitings of these "zany"

stories, according to a *Books for Keeps* reviewer. "Both books present words in imaginative ways likely to amuse children of infant age," commented a writer for *The Junior Bookshelf.*

Yet another popular series is "Funnybones," featuring a cast of skeletons in the usual crazy and downright silly situations that are the Ahlberg trademark. Reviewing the first two in the series, *The Black Cat* and *The Pet Shop,* Ruth Smith of *School Library Journal* described the books with their "[c]artoonlike layout, repetitive language, and situational humor" as a "good choice for beginning readers." Reviewing *Dinosaur Dreams* and *Mystery Tour* in *School Library Journal,* Leslie Barban remarked that these "crazy and wacky" books are "more funnier-than-spooky entries for an audience often looking for good material in this genre." A *Books for Keeps* contributor, reviewing reprints of *Mystery Tour* and *The Black Cat,* noted that "[f]ew beginning readers can resist the sheer silliness of these stories and few teachers can resist the brilliance with which Allan Ahlberg writes stories which are full of repetition, so easy to read and yet are quirky, witty and original."

Ahlberg maintains such brilliance, as well as his witty and quirky storylines in his non-series, stand-alone picture books and verse for younger readers. Working with his wife, Janet, Ahlberg created some amusing and charming fairy tale pastiches with *Jeremiah in the Dark Woods, Each Peach Pear Plum,* and the "Jolly Postman" books. Working with Amstutz, he wrote *Ten in a Bed,* about a little girl who finds a different fairy tale character in her bed each night: the Three Bears, the Big Bad Wolf, and the Cat from "Hey Diddle, Diddle," among others. Each time, the girl is able to get rid of the intruder by telling her own version of the fairy tale they inhabit. Critiquing this title in *Books for Your Children,* J. Tweedie commented that, "the stories are ideal for children at the stage when fantasy and reality are still interchangeable." Tweedie concluded that the stories "are racy and humorous and bound to become familiar favourites." More postmodern wit is presented in *The Bravest Ever Bear* in which well known fairy tale characters such as Red Riding Hood and the Big Bad Wolf tell their stories from their own perspective and create new endings for old tales. The characters also encounter each other as their tales overlap in a sort of tag-team narrative structure. A *Publishers Weekly* reviewer felt this was a "kid-tickling, episodic narrative that mixes familiar and never-before-seen characters ..., plot twists and hustling watercolors and pencil art into a silly and satisfying stew."

Writing expressly for middle grader readers, Ahlberg has turned his humorous talents to novels with *Woof!* and *The Giant Baby,* and to short stories with *The Better Brown Stories.* With *Woof!,* Ahlberg creates a Kafkaesque scenario when young Eric Banks suddenly turns into a Norfolk terrier one morning. Eric gets a dog's eye view of things until he becomes Eric once more, but he never knows when this change will occur again. Kathleen Brachman noted in *School Library Journal* that the book "is told in an understated manner with delightfully quiet, tongue-in-cheek humor." A reviewer for *Books for Keeps* called the novel a "good book ... thoroughly recommended for mid-juniors."

With *The Giant Baby,* Ahlberg again pushes the bounds of reality when a giant baby arrives on Alice's doorstep one day. Though the young girl longs for a baby brother, this is rather too much for her at first. But soon, she and her parents become attached to the large infant and they get into all sorts of predicaments trying to keep the foundling out of foster families. "Fast-paced, tightly plotted, and packed with excitement and humor, this tale is destined to take its place with the very best novels for this age group," wrote Ruth Semrau in a *School Library*

Journal review of *The Giant Baby.* Comparing Ahlberg's prose to that of Roald Dahl, Semrau further commented that Ahlberg's "wry wit makes his book as appealing to adults as to children." A contributor to *Books for Keeps* concluded, "Humour, huge attention to the practical and emotional implications, an instinctive interest in any abandoned baby, plus Ahlberg's personal writing style make this absolutely riveting."

Ahlberg presents characters who rebel against their creator in *The Better Brown Stories.* Miffed with the stories that are shaping their lives, the members of the Brown family seek out the writer responsible and give him a piece of their communal mind. Christina Dorr,

Well-known fairy tale characters tell the stories from their own perspectives and create new endings for the old tales, encountering each other as the stories progressively overlap in Ahlberg's humorous picture book. (From The Bravest Ever Bear, *illustrated by Paul Howard.)*

writing in *School Library Journal,* called the book a "clever collection of short stories that's sure to be a hit." *Booklist*'s Hazel Rochman concluded that if American readers did not quite get the British references, "everyone will enjoy the mischief and the wry characters that suddenly move from the mundane to the marvelous." A writer for *Books for Keeps* remarked, "Picking up a book by Allan Ahlberg is always exciting, for children and adults. There is a feeling that one is going to be both entertained and challenged, and this new title certainly lives up to that expectation."

With *The Mysteries of Zigomar,* Ahlberg presents something of a hybrid, part story collection and part verse collection. *Books for Keeps* contributor Annabel Gibb wrote that she "very much preferred the poems to the prose pieces," and indeed Ahlberg has written a variety of popular poetry collections for young readers, including *Cops and Robbers, Each Peach Pear Plum,* and *Peepo!* in collaboration with his wife, and other humorous volumes, including *Please, Mrs. Butler, Heard It in the Playground,* illustrated by Wegner, *Mockingbird,* with illustrations from Paul Howard, and *Monkey Do!,* illustrated by Amstutz. *Hear It in the Playground* serves up "[s]erious situations for the young ... treated lightly but shrewdly in rhymed stanzas or freer verse-lines," according to Fisher in *Growing Point.* Fisher went on to conclude, "A judicious and expert mixture of real life and that eternal wish-dream when school momentarily becomes really entertaining."

In *Mockingbird,* Ahlberg plays off the old song lyrics, "Hush little baby don't say a word / Mama's gonna buy you a Mockingbird." In this adaptation, an adoring family and friends promise the baby in question all sorts of presents. "Ahlberg's variation on a familiar theme turns that beloved old nursery song ... into a newly realized birthday lullaby," wrote Janice M. Del Negro in a *Bulletin of the Center for Children's Books* review. Valerie Coghlan, reviewing the same title in *Books for Keeps,* felt the book would "undoubtedly appeal to a market for nostalgia with its almost familiar words and the careful details of Howard's pictures." *Booklist*'s Carolyn Phelan urged, "Even if you have every other picture-book version of the song, make room for this beguiling edition." In *Monkey Do!* an adventurous and rather mischievous monkey escapes from the zoo and its exploits are recounted in rhyming verse by Ahlberg. Pat Mathews noted in *Bulletin of the Center for Children's Books* that "there are plenty of monkey shenanigans in this picture-book offering." A reviewer for *Magpies* featured the book in a roundup of picture books, calling it a "cheeky story told with great flair and perfect to read aloud." Linda Perkins, writing in *Booklist,* concluded, "this appealing story will tickle and delight."

Whether producing whimsical series readers or stand-alones with tongue-in-cheek wit, Allan Ahlberg has proven to be one of the most popular picture book authors on either side of the Atlantic. Collaborating with his wife and with other illustrators, Ahlberg has created a body of work that has won awards, critical acclaim, and legions of readers in the United States and his native

Great Britain. Yet the author is supremely understated about his achievement. "It's play," he once told Victoria Neumark in the *Times Literary Supplement.* "It's farce, it's the neatness of the plot."

Biographical and Critical Sources

BOOKS

Children's Books and Their Creators, edited by Anita Silvey, Houghton Mifflin, 1995.
Children's Literature Review, Volume 18, Gale, 1989.
St. James Guide to Children's Writers, 5th edition, edited by Sara Pendergast and Tom Pendergast, St. James Press, 1999.

PERIODICALS

Booklist, May 1, 1994, p. 1606; January 1, 1996, Hazel Rochman, review of *The Better Brown Stories,* p. 832; December 1, 1997, p. 61; April, 1998, Linda Perkins, review of *Monkey Do!,* p. 1328; September 15, 1998 Carolyn Phelan, review of *Mockingbird,* p. 228; January 1, 1999, p. 784.
Books for Keeps, January, 1988, Pat Triggs, "Editor's Page," p. 3; January, 1988, review of *Woof!,* p. 17; May, 1988, review of *One Two Flea!,* et al, p. 12; September, 1988, review of *Miss Dose the Doctor's Daughter,* et al, p. 8; March, 1993, review of *Mystery Tour,* et al, p. 10; July, 1996, review of *The Giant Baby,* p. 12; November, 1996, Jeff Hynds, "Master Allan the Ahlberg," pp. 4-5; November, 1996, Liz Waterland, review of "Happy Families," p. 5; November, 1996, review of *Who Stole the Pie?,* et al, p. 8; January, 1997, review of *The Better Brown Stories,* p. 23; September, 1997, Jill Bennett, review of *Master Track's Train,* p. 21; January, 1998, Annabel Gibb, review of *The Mysteries of Zigomar,* p. 19; January, 1999, Valerie Coghlan, review of *Mockingbird,* p. 18.
Books for Your Children, Spring, 1991, J. Tweedie, review of *Ten in a Bed,* p. 17.
Bulletin of the Center for Children's Books, April, 1998, Pat Mathews, review of *Monkey Do!,* pp. 272-73; October, 1998, Janice M. Del Negro, review of *Mockingbird,* p. 51.
Carousel, summer, 2000, Pat Tate, review of *My Brother's Ghost,* p. 25.
Growing Point, September, 1988, Margery Fisher, review of *Master Bun the Baker's Boy* and *Miss Dose the Doctor's Daughter,* p. 5049; January, 1990, M. Fisher, review of *Heard It in the Playground,* p. 5283.
Horn Book, July-August, 1993, p. 456; September-October, 1996, pp. 590-91; May-June, 1999, p. 354.
Junior Bookshelf, August, 1987, review of *One Two Flea,* p. 158; April, 1996, review of *Who Stole the Pie?,* et al, pp. 64-65.
Magpies, May, 1998, review of *Monkey Do!,* p. 5.
New York Times Book Review, April 10, 1977; April 22, 1979; April 29, 1979; May 20, 1979; March 1, 1981.
Observer, July 19, 1981; December 6, 1981; December 7, 1997, p. 17.
Publishers Weekly, November 2, 1990, p. 73; August 9, 1991, p. 56; January 25, 1993, p. 87; February 28, 1994, p. 88; November 27, 1995, p. 70; October 13,

1997, p. 75; January 31, 2000, review of *The Bravest Ever Bear,* p. 106.

School Library Journal, April, 1986, Louise L. Sherman, review of *Big Bad Pig,* et al, p. 67; February, 1987, Kathleen Brachman, review of *Woof!,* p. 76; March, 1991, Ruth Smith, review of *The Black Cat,* et al, p. 166; July, 1991, Leslie Barban, review of *Dinosaur Dreams,* et al, p. 52; July, 1995, Ruth Semrau, review of *The Giant Baby,* p. 76; February, 1996, Christina Dorr, review of *The Better Brown Stories,* p. 100.

Teacher Librarian, November, 1998, pp. 42, 44.

Times Educational Supplement, November 23, 1979; January 18, 1980; March 7, 1980; June 20, 1980; November 21, 1980; January 2, 1981; July 24, 1981; November 20, 1981; November 19, 1982; March 11, 1983; June 3, 1983; September 30, 1983; November 7, 1997, p. 2; December 5, 1997, p. 17; January 2, 1998, p. 23; November 20, 1998, p. 10; March 19, 1999, p. 25.

Times Literary Supplement, June 20, 1980, Victoria Neumark, "A Marriage of Words and Pictures," p. 42.*

—Sketch by *J. Sydney Jones*

*   *   *

AHLBERG, Janet 1944-1994

Personal

Born October 21, 1944, in Huddersfield, England; died of cancer, November 15, 1994, in Leicester, England; daughter of Eric (a lecturer in fine art) and Katherine (a teacher; maiden name, Crossley) Hall; married Allan Ahlberg (a writer), July, 1969; children: Jessica. *Education:* Sunderland College of Education, teaching diploma, 1966; Leicester Polytechnic, Dip. A.D. (first class), 1969.

Career

Worked as a layout artist for *Woman* magazine and as free-lance designer, 1969-72; illustrator, 1972-94.

Awards, Honors

Commendation, Library Association (Great Britain), 1977, for *Burglar Bill;* Kate Greenaway Medal, Library Association (Great Britain), 1979, citation, Notable Children's Book Committee of the Association for Library Service to Children, 1979, and citation on honor list for illustration in Great Britain, International Board on Books for Young People, 1980, all for *Each Peach Pear Plum;* Best Books of the Year award, *School Library Journal,* 1981, and Silver Paint Brush award (Holland), 1988, both for *Funnybones;* citation, Notable Children's Book Committee of the Association for Library Service to Children, 1981, and Best Book for Babies award, *Parents* magazine, 1985, both for *Peek-a-Boo!;* commendation, Library Association (Great Britain), 1982, Best Books of the Year award, *School Library Journal,* 1983, Children's Books of the Year award, Library of Congress, 1983, Teacher's Choice award, National Council of Teachers of English, 1983, and citation, Notable Children's Book Committee of the Association for Library Service to Children, 1983, all for *The Baby's Catalogue;* Emil/Kurt Mashler Award, Book Trust (Great Britain), commendation, Library Association (Great Britain), and award, Federation of Children's Book Groups, all 1986, Golden Key (Holland), 1988, and Prix du Livre pour la Jeunesse (France), all for *The Jolly Postman; or, Other People's Letters;* Kate Greenaway Medal, Library Association (Great Britain), 1991, for *The Jolly Christmas Postman;* runner-up, British Book Awards, 1989, 1991.

Writings

CHILDREN'S BOOKS; WITH HUSBAND, ALLAN AHLBERG

Here Are the Brick Street Boys (part of "Brick Street Boys" series), Collins, 1975.

A Place to Play (part of "Brick Street Boys" series), Collins, 1975.

Sam the Referee (part of "Brick Street Boys" series), Collins, 1975.

Fred's Dream (part of "Brick Street Boys" series), Collins, 1976.

The Great Marathon Football Match (part of "Brick Street Boys" series), Collins, 1976.

The Old Joke Book, Kestrel Books, 1976, Viking, 1977.

The Vanishment of Thomas Tull, Scribner, 1977.

Burglar Bill, Greenwillow, 1977.

Jeremiah in the Dark Woods, Kestrel Books, 1977, Viking, 1978.

Cops and Robbers (verse), Greenwillow, 1978.

Each Peach Pear Plum: An "I Spy" Story (verse), Kestrel Books, 1978, Viking, 1979.

The One and Only Two Heads, Collins, 1979.

Two Wheels, Two Heads, Collins, 1979.

Son of a Gun, Heinemann, 1979.

The Little Worm Book, Granada, 1979, Viking, 1980.

Funnybones, Greenwillow, 1980.

Mr. Biff the Boxer (part of the "Happy Families" series), Puffin, 1980, Western Publishing, 1982.

Mrs. Wobbles the Waitress (part of the "Happy Families" series), Puffin, 1980, Western Publishing, 1982.

Peek-a-Boo! (verse), Viking, 1981, published in England as *Peepo!,* Kestrel Books, 1981.

The Ha Ha Bonk Book, Penguin, 1982.

The Baby's Catalogue, Little, Brown, 1982.

Yum Yum (part of "Slot Book" series), Viking Kestrel (London), 1984, Viking Kestrel (New York), 1985.

Playmates (part of "Slot Book" series), Viking Kestrel (London), 1984, Viking Kestrel (New York), 1985.

The Jolly Postman; or, Other People's Letters, Little, Brown, 1986.

The Cinderella Show, Viking Kestrel, 1986.

The Clothes Horse and Other Stories, Viking Kestrel (London), 1987, Viking Kestrel (New York), 1988.

Starting School, Viking Kestrel, 1988.

Bye-Bye, Baby: A Sad Story with a Happy Ending, Little, Brown, 1989, published as *Bye-Bye, Baby: A Baby without a Mommy in Search of One,* 1990.

The Worm Book, Collins, 1989.

The Jolly Christmas Postman, Little, Brown, 1991.

The Bear Nobody Wanted, Viking, 1992.
It Was a Dark and Stormy Night, Viking, 1993.
The Jolly Pocket Postman, Little, Brown, 1995.

ILLUSTRATOR; "DAISYCHAINS" VERSE SERIES; WRITTEN BY A. AHLBERG

Ready Teddy Go, Heinemann, 1983.
Summer Snowmen, Heinemann, 1983.
That's My Baby!, Heinemann, 1983.
Which Witch, Heinemann, 1983.
One True Santa, Heinemann, 1985.

ILLUSTRATOR

Bernard Garfinkle, *My Growing Up Book,* Platt and Munk, 1972.

Night, Macdonald, 1972.
Sheila Mary Lane, *Lucky Charms,* Blackie and Son, 1973.
Ivy Eastwick, *Providence Street,* Blackie and Son, 1973.
Leslie Foster, *Toyshop Maths,* Macdonald, 1973.
Felicia Law, *Junk,* Collins, 1974.
F. Law, *Card,* Collins, 1974.
Making Music, Macdonald, 1974.
Vincent F. O'Connor, *Mathematics in the Toy Store,* Raintree, 1978.

Sidelights

Janet Ahlberg was a highly respected illustrator of children's books whose works in collaboration with her writer husband, Allan Ahlberg, were praised for their

Books

In **The Baby's Catalogue,** *Janet and Allan Ahlberg present a catalog version of a day in the lives of five families and their babies, featuring common articles and events of the twenty-four-hour period.*

Like its predecessor **The Jolly Postman, The Jolly Christmas Postman** *features facsimile letters from famous storybook characters for young readers to open and enjoy. (Written by Allan Ahlberg and illustrated by Janet Ahlberg.)*

humor and warmth. Ahlberg, who died in 1994, was known for such acclaimed series as the "Brick Street Boys" and the "Jolly Postman" series, as well as stand-alone titles such as *Each Peach Pear Plum*. Working closely together, husband and wife generally referred to themselves as picture book "makers," offering up a version of the world "that offers an absolutely uncomplicated sense of security," according to Eric Hadley in an entry in *Twentieth-Century Children's Writers*. The duo created works for preschoolers as well as for reluctant older readers, working in picture book genres from fantasy to informational to toy book. Though Janet worked primarily as the illustrator, and her husband Allan as the writer, of their forty-plus books, the ultimate Ahlberg product was a team effort with thoroughly integrated words and pictures. Their entertaining stories generally have happy endings and some lesson to be learned.

Born in Huddersfield, England in 1944, Janet Ahlberg was the daughter of parents involved in education and the arts, a fitting beginning for someone who would spend her creative life blending the two forms. She attended the Sunderland College of Education, where she met her future husband, and received a teaching diploma in 1966. Ahlberg earned a further degree from the Leicester Polytechnic in 1969. That same year she married Allan Ahlberg; the couple had one child. For several years, Ahlberg worked as a free-lance designer and illustrator while her husband worked as a teacher. In the mid-1970s she convinced Allan to write a children's story for her to illustrate.

The result was the first of dozens of collaborative efforts over the years, and inaugurated the "Brick Street Boys" series. The five lively books in this series are laid out in comic book fashion and relate the adventures of a rambunctious group of multiracial kids living in an urban setting replete with working class factories and alleyways. Reviewing the first three titles in the series, *Here Are the Brick Street Boys, A Place to Play,* and *Sam the Referee,* a critic for *Signal* magazine commented, "All those people who worry about the hard-core non-reading boys (and girls too) in primary school ought to welcome the 'Brick Street Boys'." The same reviewer called the books "fun to look at, fun to read," and the "kind of thing that can help make readers." *Growing Point*'s Margery Fisher wrote that the Ahlbergs succeeded in their attempts to entice reluctant readers with these initial titles in the series with "the minimum of fuss and polemic and the maximum of good humour," and concluded that the books were a "real triumph." Reviewing two further installments in the series, *Fred's Dream* and *The Great Marathon Football Match,* Fisher described the adventures as "zany, grotesque, [and] rainbow-colored .... These are books right on a young wave-length."

Joke books also figure in the Ahlberg scheme of things with *The Old Joke Book, Funnybones,* and *The Ha Ha Bonk Book.* For *The Old Joke Book,* Allan Ahlberg collected over 2000 jokes while Janet provided suitable illustrations to catch the whimsy. "This is an entirely successful production," wrote a *Books for Your Children* contributor in a review of *The Old Joke Book.* The same writer called special attention to the illustrations which "are beguiling comic strips in full color." Christopher Williams, reviewing *The Old Joke Book* in the *Times Literary Supplement,* remarked on the "vivid and lively drawings" which "ensure a groan if not an actual chuckle." Williams also noted that some of the jokes are "purely visual and put many newspaper cartoons to shame." Reviewing *The Ha Ha Bonk Book,* a writer for *Publishers Weekly* noted that it "abounds in merriment" and is illustrated by the "Ahlbergs' inimitable ink drawings."

The Ahlbergs also delighted in lighthearted tales with moral lessons and happy endings. The archetype of such a story is *Burglar Bill,* in which the protagonist steals such commonplace items as a toothbrush and a can of beans until one day he is robbed himself. Seeing how unpleasant it is to have things stolen, Bill changes his ways. Elaine Moss, writing in the *Times Literary Supplement,* commented that with *Burglar Bill* the Ahlbergs "extend their considerable talents for off-beat humour in a picturebook with a long text that turns out to be as moral as it is entertaining." Crime does not pay either in the 1978 *Cops and Robbers,* a "rollicking little Christmastime adventure," according to M. Hobbs writing in *The Junior Bookshelf.* In this story, a roving band of Christmastime thieves steal all the toys Santa leaves, and are brought to justice. In *The Vanishment of Thomas Tull,* the main character begins to shrink away until a puff on the pipe of a retired Apache medicine man reverses the process, with alarming results. Reviewing a 1988 reprint of this title, a contributor to *Books for Keeps* called the book a "classic," and noted that the Ahlbergs "are at their imaginative best with a gallery of eccentric characters and transcontinental action." The same writer concluded that the book was a reminder of "the immense contribution" the two made in bringing reluctant readers to books.

One notable Ahlberg convention is to include classic fairy-tale characters like the Three Bears and Little Red Riding Hood in some of their stories. The boy detective in *Jeremiah in the Dark Woods* embarks on a journey that introduces him to Three Bears and takes him past a field of giant beanstalks. Reviewing this title in the *Times Literary Supplement,* Myra Barrs commented that "[n]owhere in this splendidly eclectic tale is there any sense of a forced inventiveness." Barrs also praised Janet Ahlberg's "cozy and colourful illustrations," which "enrich the text without competing with it."

In *Each Peach Pear Plum,* one of the Ahlbergs' most enduringly popular titles, preschoolers can scan the vibrant, detailed illustrations to find such celebrated figures as Jack and Jill, Little Bo Peep, Tom Thumb, and Robin Hood. The book, which features nursery rhyme and an "I Spy" approach to discovering the fairy tale characters hidden within intricate pictures, won the Library Association of Great Britain's Kate Greenaway Medal for illustration. Reviewing the book in the *School Librarian,* Gabrielle Maunder called it a "most inventive collection of familiar nursery characters" and a book "that will delight children's thirst for puzzles and make an ideal introduction for the pre-reader to what books are for." Writing in *Signal,* Celia Berridge noted that *Each Peach Pear Plum* "has affection, humour, a perfect interweaving of words and pictures as simple as plaiting hair." Berridge concluded that the Ahlbergs' book was "an extremely skillful creation." Reviewing the U.S. edition in the *New York Times Book Review,* Harold C. K. Rice called it "a lovely small book, well-conceived and very well drawn, gentle, humorous, unsentimental." Twenty years after initial publication, the book is still popular with young readers and critics alike, being featured on numerous "bests" lists and earning praise for

a 1997 reprinting from a *Books for Keeps* contributor as a "beautifully thought out, well executed picture book."

More fairy tale and nursery rhyme resonance is served up in *The Jolly Postman,* a rhyming story inspired by the Ahlbergs' delight in watching their daughter Jessica open letters as a two-year-old. The book features a postman delivering mail to famous characters like Cinderella, the Big Bad Wolf, and Goldilocks. Tucked inside the volume are envelopes containing real letters that readers can open and enjoy. This book has been especially popular with readers and critics alike, as reflected in Chris Powling's comments in *Books for Keeps:* "Once in a while a picture-book arrives that's so brilliant, so broad in its appeal, it seems to be a summation of the state-of-the-art. For me, *The Jolly Postman* is just such a book. As a matching of word and image it's a virtuoso performance; as a feat of design it's without a flaw . . . ." Kate Flint, writing in the *Times Literary Supplement,* concluded, "The Ahlbergs' book succeeds in making the familiar new, even surprising. In its inventiveness and immaculate execution, it is a delight to read." Janet Ahlberg won a second Greenaway Medal in 1986 for *The Jolly Postman,* a book that has sold more than one million copies.

The Jolly Christmas Postman was published in 1991. Like its predecessor, it too is a toy book with facsimile letters of the ones the postman is delivering. Humpty Dumpty gets a jigsaw puzzle in the mail; Red Riding Hood gets a game from the Wolf. Each of the letters bears a holiday message, and the book would be "guaranteed a warm welcome," according to a reviewer for *The Junior Bookshelf.* The postman makes a further appearance in *The Jolly Pocket Postman,* a miniaturized version of the letter game, and the last book Janet Ahlberg illustrated before her death in 1994. Julia Eccleshare, reviewing the third postman book in *Books for Keeps,* commented that *The Jolly Pocket Postman* "has all the warmth and immediacy of the original but . . . also plays clever games with the idea of narrative."

The Ahlbergs' books are noted for originality of conception and design. In *The Baby's Catalogue,* they present a catalog version of twenty-four hours in the lives of five families and their babies. There are dozens of stories to be found in the book's pages, as well as jokes and games. Janice Prindle, writing in the *New York Times Book Review,* commented that the volume "has an antipasto eye appeal" with page after page of "intricate, colorful items." *The Little Worm Book* is a "hilarious parody on the solemn information book," according to Virginia Makins, writing in the *Times Literary Supplement,* with sections on Pet Worms, History of Worms and other spoof-like renderings. With *Peepo!* the Ahlbergs present a story as told from the limited vantage point of a baby. Readers can view along with the baby through a peephole cut in the pages. Judith Sharman, writing in *Books for Keeps,* called *Peepo!* a "true classic."

Other notable titles from the Ahlbergs' collaborative pen include *Bye-Bye Baby,* in which a parentless baby goes in search of a care-giver, *The Bear Nobody Wanted,* about a bear with an inflated ego, and *It Was a Dark and Stormy Night,* in which a kidnapped boy outwits his captors with his storytelling skills. In all of Janet Ahlberg's illustrations the reader is presented with "beauty and humor," as Eccleshare noted. Combining those qualities with her husband's ironic, tongue-in-cheek storytelling, the couple created dozens of books that "show how quality ... can be most creatively united," according to Eccleshare. In an interview with Victoria Neumark in the *Times Literary Supplement,* Janet Ahlberg insisted that she and her husband were after freshness and invention in their books. "The thing which does drive us on is an urge not to do the exact same thing again." The illustrator went on to note that her collaborative work with her husband held "no deep philosophies," but that doing the books was "enormous fun." It is this fun which Janet Ahlberg shared with an entire generation of young readers.

Biographical and Critical Sources

BOOKS

Fifth Book of Junior Authors and Illustrators, H. W. Wilson, 1983.
Hadley, Eric, *Twentieth-Century Children's Writers,* 4th edition, St. James Press, 1995, pp. 9-11.

PERIODICALS

Booklist, May 1, 1994, p. 1606.
Books for Keeps, January, 1987, Chris Powling, review of *The Jolly Postman,* pp. 4-5; January, 1988, review of *The Vanishment of Thomas Tull,* p. 17; November, 1995, Julia Eccleshare, review of *The Jolly Pocket Postman,* p. 32; March, 1997, review of *Each Peach Pear Plum,* p. 7; November, 1997, Judith Sharman, review of *Peepo!,* p. 19.
Books for Your Children, Winter, 1976, review of *The Old Joke Book,* p. 10.
Growing Point, October, 1975, Margery Fisher, review of *Here Are the Brick Street Boys,* et al, p. 2726; May, 1976, M. Fisher, review of *Fred's Dream,* et al, pp. 2888-89.
Horn Book, March-April, 1983, pp. 157-58; May-June, 1990, pp. 316-17; November-December, 1991, pp. 719-20; July-August, 1993, p. 456.
Junior Bookshelf, December, 1978, M. Hobbs, review of *Cops and Robbers,* p. 292; December, 1991, review of *The Jolly Christmas Postman,* p. 247.
New York Times Book Review, April 29, 1979, Harold C, K. Rice, review of *Each Peach Pear Plum,* p. 46; May 29, 1983, Janice Prindle, review of *The Baby's Catalogue,* p. 18; August 5, 1984, p. 14; August 14, 1988, p. 28; December 1, 1991, p. 34.
Publishers Weekly, November 5, 1982, review of *The Ha Ha Bonk Book,* p. 71; May 24, 1985, p. 227; July 25, 1986, p. 186; March 13, 1987, p. 82; January 29, 1988, p. 430; July 26, 1991, p. 11; August 9, 1991, p. 56; January 25, 1993, p. 87; February 28, 1994, p. 88.
School Librarian, June, 1979, Gabrielle Maunder, review of *Each Peach Pear Plum,* p. 127.
School Library Journal, May, 1983, p. 31; June-July, 1987, p. 75; April, 1988, p. 77; December, 1988, p. 78; August, 1990, p. 126; October, 1991, p. 26; September, 1993, p. 248.
Signal, September, 1975, review of *Here Are the Brick Street Boys,* et al, pp. 146-47; September, 1981, Celia Berridge, "Taking a Good Look at Picture Books," pp. 152-58.
Times Literary Supplement, December 10, 1976, Christopher Williams, "Knock, Knock," p. 1557; March 25, 1977, Elaine Moss, "Solace for Spring," p. 355; November 18, 1977, Myra Barrs, "Comic Horrors," p. 32; November 23, 1979, Virginia Makins, "A Laugh a Minute," p. 30; June 20, 1980, Victoria Neumark, "A Marriage of Words and Pictures," p. 42; November 28, 1986, Kate Flint, "Forms of Address," p. 1345.
Wilson Library Bulletin, June, 1994, p. 129.

Obituaries

PERIODICALS

Los Angeles Times, November 22, 1994, p. A24.
New York Times, November 19, 1994, p. 31.
School Library Journal, January, 1995, p. 23.
Times (London), November 17, 1994, p. 21.
Washington Post, November 21, 1994, p. B4.

—Sketch by J. Sydney Jones

Autobiography Feature

Jennifer Armstrong

1961-

Part I—Me? Suffer?

When my father was a small boy, he would play beneath the ironing board while my grandmother, who was a high school English teacher, recited Shakespeare to make the chore of ironing more pleasant. This image, the child beneath the ironing board, the mother reciting from *Hamlet* and *Measure for Measure,* is one I used in a novel of mine, *Black-Eyed Susan.* I admit I took it from my father, as I have taken many things from both my father and my mother.

Of course, it is an author's job to take things, ingredients, ideas, images, and use them and make meaning with them. Although I would not have defined the work of an author this way when I was in first grade, I still knew— way back then—that I was going to be one.

When I was in first grade, when I was learning to read and write, I told my family that I was planning to become an author. We lived in Switzerland at the time, and my small school practiced "whole language," even though it hadn't been invented yet. I had beautiful blue notebooks with smooth blank white paper for each subject: science, spelling, nature, reading, and so on. Each book was supposed to be filled up with stories, reports, pictures, and observations. One of my first literary triumphs was a story about Simba the baby elephant. (I found out much later that *Simba* is Swahili for lion, but at least I knew it was an African name.) Simba is in the jungle one day when a leopard jumps down on him from a tree. Simba's screams bring his mother charging to the rescue, and the leopard is flung to the ground and stomped to death. The end. This now strikes me as the story of a confident and happy child. No matter what wicked biting toothy creatures lived in the jungle, there was a capable parent within earshot all the time to bail out the kid.

Now, it occurs to me that there is a popular cliche in our culture: for there to be Real Art, there must be Suffering. Yet I never suffered at all really. (Careful readers notice here I am assuming my work is Real Art.) My childhood was a very happy one. I spent all of it (aside from the year in Switzerland) in the same big comfortable house in the country; I had lots of books and my own room; I had a big sister who beat me up and bossed me around just the right amount; my parents were industrious and interesting, and they believed kids should have pets and music lessons and summer camp and go to museums and travel; I was blessed with intelligence and quick wits; my dad read Shakespeare with us; I had a best friend who lived on a lake and was good with frogs and four-leaf clovers; and I didn't at all mind being alone.

I hasten to say that I did have *some* suffering. I dropped a large rock on my bare foot once, and to this day I have a deformed toenail as a result; I learned very late how to ride a bike, and until I did, my inability caused frequent attacks of horrific embarrassment; I was unable to hang

Jennifer Armstrong

onto nice things without wrecking or staining or ruining them; my mother would not let me pierce my ears until I was sixteen; I was held at bay by a large, fierce, barking dog once as I walked to my piano lesson until Liz Yoars's mom passed in her station wagon and rescued me. But these are small things really. They do not qualify as the kind of Suffering uniquely designed to produce Real Art.

There was even a period in college when I thought that I would not be able to become a writer because I was too happy, too well adjusted, too untouched by tragedy or failure. I got involved in a troublesome romantic relationship, probably out of a sick wish to make a catastrophic mistake. Eventually, however, I came to realize that it is not necessary to suffer to become a writer, it is only necessary to have sympathy and an imagination.

My imagination was always an unwieldy one, and I had a dreamy, romantic temperament even as a child. So I developed a routine very early in life called "TV show," which was a melodramatic mixture of the *Wonderful World of Disney* movies I watched on Sunday nights after my bath and Mutual of Omaha's *Wild Kingdom.* The way I played this solitary game was this: I went off by myself into the endless backyard and farm fields behind the house and pretended to be the hero or heroine of a dramatic saga. I made up a mournful theme song for the show and practiced those fake-surprised expressions that used to be common in the opening credits of TV programs in the 1960s. Then I would proceed to have adventures, taking all the parts, breaking into more melancholy songs, pretending to be shot or stabbed or deathly ill, and stopping to catch tadpoles or take thistle spines out of my bare feet or look for monarch butterfly caterpillars, as the season dictated. I never tried to entice anyone else into my TV game: it was strictly a one-girl show.

This story is not meant to show how I wanted to grow up to be a television actor or scriptwriter. Television was just one of a number of ways I knew of to tell stories, and it was a good one since it had thrilling music. The point here is that I was entranced with storytelling. I liked to play outside, and when I was rambling around the countryside it was easier to act out stories than it was to write them. In this way I could have my cake and eat it too.

When I was in fourth grade, I learned another technique for storytelling. This was when I first read *Harriet the Spy,* and of course I had to get a black-and-white marbled spy notebook. I spent months and months keeping detailed notes on what drippy things my sister had said, or what homework I had, or how hard and continuously Mrs. Blodgett polished her glasses with a tissue. Unlike Harriet, I did not live in the city and I had no near neighbors I could spy on from a dumbwaiter or skylight. I had to be content with the people immediately around me, and most of the time that was my sister. She eventually got her hands on the spy notebook and read it—at least read the parts about her, which was easy because I kept a cumulative index—and that was the end of my spy notebook days.

In fifth, sixth, and seventh grades, I became an expert at the discursive note. My best friend, Kirsten, and I talked on the telephone all the time, but we also wrote voluminous letters to each other every day. These letters could sometimes be six, seven, eight pages long, and we would trade them in the mornings before Attendance and the Pledge and spend the day reading them, and then beginning to compose our next letters. I saved shopping bags full of these letters until after college, when I had to admit to myself that whatever delightful prose they contained must be lost forever, because I could not bear to read through pounds and pounds of paper on such subjects as braces, gym class, who had gotten her period, who had picked his nose in class, and dinner.

And by high school I discovered poetry. I made strenuous attempts to write as though I was suffering greatly, but I don't think I pulled it off. I was always hopelessly in love with one boy or another, and depressed about it, so that counted as Suffering, but even then I realized it was an amateur suffering, not really full-fledged tragedy. I listened to a lot of Joni Mitchell albums and imagined myself truly suffering someday like Joni.

Through all these years, and through college, I still held to the firm resolve I had made in first grade to become a writer. I wasn't really sure what I was going to write about: I was still expecting all this Suffering to happen, and since it hadn't happened yet, the Real Art would have to wait. So in the meantime, after college, while I was waiting patiently for the Suffering to commence, I took a job in New York City.

My mother had tirelessly drummed into my head that I should learn to type. For high school graduation I had been given an electric typewriter, and eventually I sat myself down to learn touch-typing. Of course, I told myself—as I practiced *asdfg and ;lkjh*—I didn't really need to know how to type, because I was going to an elite college and was going to have a super-important job.

When you enter publishing right after college, you enter as an editorial assistant, and you strive mightily to tell yourself that you are not a secretary. However, no amount of wishful thinking changes the fact that that is what you are, a secretary, in spite of the optimistic title. I typed letters. I filed things. I called for bicycle messengers and hired cars. I got lunch. I made appointments. Secretary stuff.

Little by little, however, by osmosis, I learned about publishing. And I was given projects to shepherd, and I did sit in on production meetings, and I did learn all kinds of jargon. Most fortuitously, the company I worked for produced both adult and juvenile titles. Midway through 1985, after a year and a half in publishing, I felt I was ready to retire and begin my career as a writer.

Part II—Some Philosophy

It sounds ridiculously overconfident, put that way. But you see, the Suffering had never happened, so I wasn't conditioned to expect things to go wrong. I was conditioned to expect things to go right. They did go right. Within a year I was actually earning a living as a ghostwriter for some very popular mass-market juvenile series. I began in juvenile books, writing for my former colleagues. Naturally I had vague ideas of eventually writing some grand important Opus—for adults. When you are just out of college, the thought of writing books for children as your Career is hard to swallow. At twenty-three, a writer is desperately anxious to be thought of as grown-up, mature, sophisticated. At twenty-three, I considered the writing I was doing for kids to be a temporary thing, something to do *until I got good enough to write for adults.*

I want to slap myself now for having thought that way, because now when I encounter this assumption, that writing children's books is somehow preparatory to something larger and more important, I want to slap the person who has suggested it. I have come to realize that there is a hypocritical bias, in our youth-enchanted culture, against children; anyone who works for children—primary school teachers, pediatricians, children's book authors—must be doing it out of some lack of ambition, some failure of will or fortitude.

But I did not understand this when I was at the start of my career. As I say, I was a ghostwriter of mass-market series books, and because I was writing juvenile and young adult books, the ideas that I was coming up with for my own stories were turning out to be juvenile and young adult book ideas.

In my experience, there are two broad categories of writers for children. There are those who write for children because they have a teaching agenda, and there are those who write for children because they are writers and children's books are what they happen to write. There are certainly many fantastic writers in the first category, and there are certainly many lousy writers in the second category. But I would like to make a case for the second category being the more genuinely literary category. Literature is the art of using words to shape meaning. Art enriches our lives, feeds our spirits, strengthens the ties between one human being and all others. Children should be allowed to participate in the experience of art equally with adults. Children obviously can learn from this experience, but art does not have a didactic soul. Art has an artistic soul. I become enraged when people ask whether I think of the moral first before I write a story, as though the exclusive function of writing for children is a teaching one. In spite of the total failure of all that Suffering to appear in my life, I do want to create Real Art. I don't want to be a teacher. It happens that my chosen medium of expression is literature for children, but that does not make me a teacher.

So much for my writing philosophy and how I arrived there.

Part III—Some of My Dogs

I haven't mentioned yet exactly where and when I grew up, or any specific family details like names, jobs, or where I live now, and so on. I grew up in South Salem, New York, which is a small, formerly rural hamlet in northern Westchester County, about fifty miles north of New York City. I was born in 1961, the younger child of John and Elizabeth Armstrong. My sister, Sarah, was (and still is) two years older than I.

Our first dog was named Xanthippe (the name of Socrates' wife). She developed an unfortunate habit of napping on the road; it was her downfall, of course. But before she died she did eccentric things, like chasing airplanes. Once when there was a circus across the fields from us at the firehouse she followed us there and barked at the elephants until they almost panicked. Our dog causing an elephant stampede! That was a great honor, to say the least. Our second dog was officially *my* dog, and I picked him out and named him and fed him every day. He was

Jennifer with sister, Sarah, and their father in Switzerland, 1968.

called Jerry, and he was not allowed in the house, and so he never really became part of the family, I am sorry to say. He lived a very solitary life, and when I remember him now, I feel bad. When I chose him at the pound, I thought he was a husky; he had a curly tail, but he never turned into anything so noble. He was just a small, curly-tailed dog. When he shed every year, the birds nesting in the giant cherry tree in our yard would claim clumps of his thick fur to line their nests.

During my years at Smith College, I involved myself with a man much older than me. We acquired two black Lab crosses one summer, and we named them Margo and Hannah. Margo was big and dumb, and Hannah was smaller and very cunning. We lived in upstate New York, in a very wooded country area, and Hannah fell victim to a hunter's bullet one fall. Keeping the dogs inside during hunting season had been a terrible chore, and one day they went nuts and bounded out the door; Hannah never returned. When this relationship broke up (I was two years out of college), I lost custody of Margo, and I consoled myself by buying a Shetland sheepdog whom I named Minch.

Minch has been with me for the duration of my literary career. He is here right now, very cranky, very barky. We've moved several times, but now we live in a house in Saratoga Springs, New York, a small 1820s cottage which I bought when I was thirty. Shelties are one-person dogs, and they do not like to share their person, but poor Minch has been made to put up with cats and other dogs, and I think this has made him neurotic. I volunteered to raise a puppy for Guiding Eyes for the Blind a few years ago. Wheaton, a yellow female Lab who was slightly larger than my two fists when I got her, proved to be as amiable as Labs are supposed to be, and as smart. She now works in Tucson, Arizona. When she retires in a few years, she'll come back to live with us. Minch never did like her very much, especially once she outweighed him by fifty pounds.

And two years ago, Chloe entered our lives. She is a brown, muttley thing, about Minch's size with a crooked back and pelvis from being run over by a pickup truck when she was a pup in the Adirondacks. The person who ran her over was my husband, James Howard Kunstler, and by running over Chloe, he rescued her from an uncertain life as a hunting dog and provided for her a life of sleeping on the couch, running every day, and eating Flava-Snacks, which have developed her jaw muscles so much that she looks a little like Don Corleone. Jim is also a writer—a journalist, novelist, essayist, and screenwriter—and it has been immeasurably useful to have another professional word-whacker so close to hand.

We hope to get another dog very soon.

Part IV—Some Books

The first trade novel (i.e., hardcover book) that I wrote was in large part a reaction to the mass-market series books I had been writing in the mid-1980s. I was eager to write something meatier, something more challenging, something with more meaning. The original spark of an idea for *Steal*

Her first author photo at age nine, 1970.

Away is lost somewhere in the murk of my memory, but I do remember that I wanted very much to write an adventure story about girls. I also wanted to write a historical novel. In musing about what kind of adventure a girl could have in an American history setting, I eventually hit upon the idea of a white girl and a black slave girl running away together. I had an abolitionist-minded girl from Vermont, Susannah, orphaned and sent to Virginia. There, she was to be given a slave, a girl her own age named Bethlehem. These two girls would become friends and run away to the North together.

In the beginning, this was a very simple idea. I began by writing it in Susannah's voice, but that didn't work. I then tried alternating chapters between Susannah's voice and Bethlehem's, and that didn't work either. I was struggling for a way to tell this story, and unconsciously, I think, struggling for a way to make it a bigger story.

Along about this time, I happened to read a great novel by Wallace Stegner, *The Angle of Repose,* and had to read it thoroughly many times, because I was the leader of the public library's book discussion group and this book was next. In *The Angle of Repose,* Stegner moves the story back and forth in time, switching from a narrator reconstructing his grandmother's life to this same narrator commenting on the current failures and disappointments of his own life.

As I read this novel, I reflected on the story I was struggling with but could not write. It eventually occurred to me that what I needed was a way to narrate the story that would magnify its meaning. I added a third voice to the two I already had: Susannah's granddaughter, forty-some years after the adventure. When I created the prissy Mary listening to two grown women recount the adventure of their girlhood, I had a foil for Susannah and Bethlehem, and I felt I now knew how to write my book. I wrote forty or so pages as a sample and sent it to my agent, Susan Cohen at Writers House.

Sue loved it and asked where I wanted her to send it. I figured I might as well start at the top of my list, so I asked her to send it to Richard Jackson at Orchard Books. Dick liked it very much, but he asked me some very searching questions and listened to my answers before he agreed to take on *Steal Away.* He wanted to know if I intended to give the book a happy ending. He wanted to know if I planned to dump on Mary throughout the book. I was able to answer the first question readily: no, it was not going to have a happy ending, because a happy ending would be historically impossible. The second question was harder. I had to think through why I wanted Mary to act as the foil for Susannah and Bethlehem.

This eventually brought me to an understanding of what I wanted to write—not just in *Steal Away* but in all my historical novels. I wanted to write about how we understand history, how we tell it, how hearing an adventure forty years old can change our lives today, how storytelling is an active, dynamic process rather than a passive or static one. I needed Mary in my novel to show that Susannah and Bethlehem's story mattered to more people than just them. I needed Mary to show that history and stories affect us every day, that when we hear a story we are acted upon and transformed.

Understanding my novel was one thing; writing it was another. It was very hard to write, and I became very anxious about writing in Bethlehem's voice. I was writing this novel when the first signs of political correctness were rearing their ugly mugs, and I was sure someone was going to jump on me for writing as a black slave. So I did exhaustive research, even going so far as to study language patterns of West Africa; I took reams of notes; I haunted the library. Finally Dick Jackson called me and said, "Just write it." So I put down the books and steeled myself to face the computer. And I wrote *Steal Away.*

Very often I felt as though I was in the circus act where a clown keeps half a dozen plates spinning and balanced at the tops of bamboo canes. Because I had three narrators and two time periods, and because I wanted to show that although Susannah and Bethlehem lived the same adventure they understood their stories differently, and because I wanted the narration to affect Mary as it went along, I had a lot of plates to keep spinning. Periodically one or another would come crashing down. Then I'd go pay attention to that one for a while, getting it spinning again, and then listen for the next crash.

When I was done, I felt very smug. I huffed on my fingernails and polished them against my shirt. Dick read the manuscript and said I had a lot of work to do. A terrific editor makes all the difference of course, and Dick's meticulous editing and hard questions helped me get this novel into shape. When it finally came out, the reviews were almost universally excellent and went straight to my head.

Coincidentally, the same week I sold this first trade novel, I sold my first picture book. Simon Boughton had recently moved from Simon & Schuster to Crown Books, and he liked *Hugh Can Do* very much. It too required a lot of editing, but since it was only six pages rather than two hundred, it didn't make me wince so much. However, it did take six or seven drafts ultimately, and a year or so on the rewrites. The book was illustrated beautifully by Kimberly Bulcken Root, and when it came out (at the same time as *Steal Away,* more or less), it also got very fine reviews. So my first two trade books were highly praised, and I began to think that I could do no wrong. The last line of *Hugh Can Do,* by the way, is, "And Hugh knew for certain his fortune was made." This sums up my own feelings at the time; I was sure I was headed for the big leagues in short order.

Part V—On Trees

Trees have come and gone in my life, just as dogs have. Where I grew up, we were surrounded by pastureland and recently abandoned farm fields. These fields were soon to sprout a bumper crop of expensive homes, but when I was a kid, they were wonderfully vacant but not overgrown. In one of them there was an enormous tree on its side. It must have been an oak, a giant oak, because although long dead, even resting on its branches and tipped-up roots the huge trunk was ten or twelve feet from the ground. This tree was a favorite with the children in the area, and we had all kinds of crow's nests, secret caves, the hard way up, the easy way up, the poison ivy part, the blackberry part, and so on. It was a tree that provided play space for at least eight or nine of us, and from the best crow's nest there was a lordly view of our domain, stretching into wooded hills, stone walls, distant farmhouses. It was superb, and I spent a lot of time on it, in it, and under it. If our parents knew what we were up to, they

didn't try to stop us, thank goodness. This tree later caught fire when someone (I won't say who) was a teenager and had either a candle or a cigarette or a joint or some combination of such burning things. Much of the tree was destroyed, and it had rotted significantly anyway. This was the effective end of the tree as a playground. Besides, by then we were all too old for it, and the developers' bulldozers were rumbling in the next pasture.

Another good tree was the cedar that grew at the corner of our kitchen porch. My bedroom window opened onto the flat roof of this porch, and it was possible to climb down and up this tree, using it as a secret escape route. The one problem with this tree was that it was of a species armed with very short, very sharp needles, and since I was usually barefoot and in shorts and sleeveless shirts in the summer, using the secret escape route was horribly painful. The fact that no one prevented me from using the stairs and the kitchen door was beside the point. If you have a secret escape route, you are obligated to use it. I endured countless stabs and punctures doing so, but that was a small cost for such a tree.

We had a magnificently tall cherry tree with shiny, dark gray, splitting bark which oozed a semi-clear goo like rubber cement. The tree swarmed with birds when the cherries were ripe, and the ground was littered with pits. What with the gummy sap and the cherries, this was also a good tree to have. When it finally met its match in a hurricane and came down, my father had the wood salvaged and a beautiful wardrobe made with it, a glorious piece of cabinetry. When I later read about the origin of the wardrobe in C. S. Lewis's *The Lion, the Witch, and the Wardrobe,* I wished desperately that our cherry tree had had some similar mythical beginnings. I halfheartedly climbed into my father's wardrobe, even though I knew it had no fur coats hanging in it, and even though if I could have gone through to the other side it would only have led to the bathroom.

Part VI—More Books and a Really Helpful Editor

After my heady success with *Steal Away* and *Hugh Can Do,* my editor at Crown, Simon Boughton, bought another picture book from me, *Chin Yu Min and the Ginger Cat.* This story, about a cat that catches fish with his tail and the greedy, proud woman who takes him in, was inspired in this way: A number of years previously, I had found myself at a picnic and there met a Chinese man who was visiting friends in upstate New York for the summer. His English was not good, but we struck up a conversation and somehow ended up speaking of animals or pets or just cats, I'm not sure. He then proceeded to tell me that one day, while strolling through the park in his hometown, he happened to see a cat sitting at the edge of an ornamental goldfish pool. The cat was daydreaming, as cats do, and its tail drifted out behind it onto the surface of the pond. One of the fish there must have mistaken the cat for a caterpillar, because it swam up and bit the cat's tail. Leaping around, the very startled cat discovered an even more startled fish clinging to its tail. The cat ate it.

Now, although this is a charming anecdote, it is not in itself a whole story. I thought about it for a long time, wondering how I could use it. When at last I knew what the story should be, I decided to set it in China, as a way of acknowledging the man who gave me the idea. By the time I wrote the story, I could not remember his name, and so this was the only way I could think to thank him. The illustrator of this book, Mary Grandpre, later took some hits for what some critics thought was chinoiserie—old-fashioned stereotypes of Chinese people. I am convinced that if either of us had been Chinese, the critics would have agreed wholeheartedly that this was a wonderful book with fabulous pictures. As it was, the writing was praised, but many people took issue with the art. I, and many others, consider Mary's illustrations for this book to be magnificent. They are highly stylized, to be sure, but this is what gives them their life.

As I feared when I wrote part of *Steal Away* in a slave's voice, I have learned that some critics will not allow writers to be writers. By that I mean there is a widely held belief that only an African American can write the African American experience, only a Native American can retell Native American tales, and so on. There were people who thought that *Chin Yu Min and the Ginger Cat* was some kind of scam—as though we had tricked people into believing it was an authentic Chinese folktale. I made up a story, and I set it in China; it didn't occur to me that I should be limited to setting my stories in the Westchester County, New York, of the 1960s and 1970s. When I encounter this prejudice—that only members of Group X are authorized to write about Group X—I am stupefied with indignation. Taken to the extreme, this prejudice would force us all into writing autobiography, and while that is important for the *Something about the Author* series, it is deadly to creative fiction. If I am not allowed to imagine anything beyond my own experience, you will simply have to put up with more stories from me about my dogs and favorite trees.

This prejudice would also preclude historical fiction. Since I have not lived in any period other than my own, presumably I shouldn't be allowed to write about any period other than that of my own lifetime. Isn't that ridiculous? There are many ways to study history, and writing fiction about it is a very important and useful way to study it. I wrote *Steal Away* in part as an examination of the way we remember and retell history. I still have many things to say on this subject.

My editor at Crown, although very fond of my picture books (judging by the fact that he's bought five of them), kept urging me to write more novels. Dick Jackson had declined a book proposal I sent him when I finished *Steal Away*. Simon read the proposal and wanted it, and also urged me to turn a flawed picture-book manuscript into a novel. So Simon wanted two novels from me, which was very nice and encouraging, but I told him pointedly over lunch one day that I couldn't make a living on trade novels, and he knew it very well. The advances on juvenile trade novels are on the smallish side.

So Simon showed his true colors as a Really Helpful Editor. Crown and Knopf, of which he is the publishing director, are part of the Random House group, and they do many things in concert. He suggested to one of the Random House juvenile books editors that I do some mass-market work for them. The mass market pays better, which would allow me to write trade books for Crown and Knopf and still stay with the same publisher, Random House. Every-

one was very nice, everyone agreed, everyone was very supportive, and I got my nice deal. More on the Random House books later.

Part VII—Riding in the Car

I consider myself very fortunate in not having to commute to work. My office is in my house, and so when I finish my breakfast and take a shower and dress, I commute from the dining room into my office, and there I do my work. I also live in a town where most daily errands can be carried out on foot or by bicycle. So it is possible to go for long periods of time without getting in the car. That suits my political ideals very well, which is also very gratifying. I didn't always think cars were unavoidable irritations. When we lived in Switzerland, for instance, we had a red VW Beetle that I loved. We drove all over Europe in that car, and for most of those trips, I occupied the "way back." There was the back, where my sister sat, but I liked the way back, the little well behind the backseat and over the engine. (I was much smaller than I am now, naturally). The ceiling of the car was pockmarked with a regular pattern of tiny dots: I could stare at them and enter a trancelike state, a very youthful kind of Zen freak-out thing that I got a big bang out of.

And then, years later when I and my high-school friends became licensed to drive—well, stand back, that was freedom. Living in the suburbs means that there is almost nothing that a teenager wants that is accessible by bike or on foot. It should go without saying that teenagers love cars, but it's something I try to keep fresh in my mind, how paralyzed and cooped up kids are if they don't have wheels. (It forces them to stay confined at home trying to find pornography on the Internet.) When you are a teenager with wheels, it's another whole kind of Zen freak-out thing just to know you can go somewhere, and that is why teenagers like to get in the car and just go somewhere, anywhere, it doesn't matter at all.

It was not until I drove from western Minnesota to New York with a good friend that I discovered the truly great thing about driving in a car. When you are driving in a car alone, or with a friend who understands if you don't wish to talk—you can think. At home, the phone rings, the dogs bark, the laundry needs doing, there are a hundred and one distractions even on a good day, and so concentrating is always hard. But in the car, you can look out the window, and no one will call you, and you can think. For a writer, this is the food of the gods.

Furthermore, if you are driving on a long trip, you are seeing new sights. Seeing the Great Plains was a tremendous thrill. Having grown up in the wooded, hilly, city-covered Northeast, I was unaccustomed to the horizon and the sky of western Minnesota. I had read many books and accounts of the pioneers. But until I saw the prairie, I had no idea what it was. The geography itself became a character in my next novel, *Black-Eyed Susan*.

As I write this, I have just returned from a 2,400-mile drive from Saratoga Springs to western Pennsylvania to Charleston, South Carolina, and home again. And once again, I was able to think for long hours at a time and resolve a very difficult problem in the book I am now writing.

But I'm taking my bike in for a spring tune-up this weekend. I hope not to have to take any long drives for a while. I hope I won't need to, that my work will be going well and I won't be going crazy trying to think. If I find myself in a hole again with my work, however, I'll have to go on a long drive.

Part VIII—More Books

Black-Eyed Susan came out of this drive from Minnesota and out of an article I chanced upon in *Audubon* magazine. The article was about a little-known fact of pioneer history: the settlers on the plains were so lonesome for the sweet songbirds of the eastern states that they took to importing and nurturing canaries. Accompanying this article was a photograph of a sodhouse, a glorified hole in the ground really, and in the window of this primitive dwelling was a delicate cage with a single canary. Such a picture is not easily forgotten. I imagined a woman trying to keep house in a hole in the ground and taking the time from this difficult battle to shelter this fragile creature. And I had seen the plains, I had seen where this happened, and I said, *yes, yes, this is a story.*

I began it this way: "The low wind slowed outside our sodhouse door, then rolled over the buffalo grass, bowling down into hollows and up over mounds, blowing the dust before it."

The story began as a picture book, the story of a little girl whose mother is sick with lonesomeness. The little girl, Susie, goes out in search of a color or a sound to bring some life back to her mother's imagination, and she encounters a passing family of Icelanders, who give her a canary. This is the story which my editor said should be a novel, and after a few moments of being taken aback, I agreed.

Now, my usual style of operating on a novel is to lay careful plans, outline thoroughly, figure out what I'm getting at. I decided that one of the things *Black-Eyed Susan* was about was the geography of the prairie, and its power to uplift or crush a human soul. So I mapped out the book into three pieces: The Prairie, The Town, and The Icelanders. The first part would explore isolation, openness, and different ways of being alone. The second part would explore different aspects of social structures, both good and bad. And then the third would integrate social structure with the vast, isolating prairie.

I also decided that I wanted to set myself a particular challenge—to write a novel whose action spanned only twenty-four hours. I had recently read a novel of my husband's, called *The Halloween Ball,* which covered just one Halloween day and evening. I thought—if he can do it, I can do it.

But three people all alone on a big empty prairie . . . . I wasn't sure just what all could be happening that would fill a whole novel with just twenty-four hours. And furthermore, there was this idea that I had a reason to write historical fiction, that there was something more about how we tell history that I wanted to explore.

So I found a solution. The novel is made up of stories told by Susie and by other characters. This structure allowed me to break out of the confines of my twenty-four hours on the prairie and go to some other places and some other times. And the characters' histories are revealed by

The author's childhood home in South Salem, New York.

the stories they choose to tell. It worked, I think. It was here that I used my father's story about sitting under the ironing board, and I used it to reveal the desire for enclosure and security that Susie's mother has:

> I would hide under the ironing board while my mother pressed. The sheets would drape down on both sides at the ends of the board like a tent, and I'd crawl in under there to hide. It was always warm and steamy and smelled of starch, and the light was white and soft, like being in a cloud.

My mother liked to recite Shakespeare when she ironed, although I didn't know at the time what she was saying. I only knew that it made a lovely sound. And the iron would thump-thump, thump-thump over my head like a beating heart, and I could hear my mother's voice not talking to me but knowing I was there. No one could see me, hidden under the ironing board.

Susie's job in this novel is literally to help her mother be born, or to resurrect her, to bring her up out of the hole in the earth where she is hiding and let her take the wide world into her arms. Susie actually does it, I am glad to say, with the help of the Icelanders and the canary, who come along just in time.

When I finished this book, it was time to write the next one, the other book that Simon told me he wanted to buy. (He had actually given me contracts for both these books, so I had to write this one next whether I wanted to or not.) This next book proved to be the most challenging one I have yet written, and I am still trying to recover from the experience.

This book was *The Dreams of Mairhe Mehan.* The genesis of the book is very clear to me. While I was finishing *Steal Away*, Ken Burns's epic documentary on the Civil War was airing on public television, and I thought I'd died and gone to heaven. There was so much fantastic material collected in that program that I filled pages and pages with scribbled notes. Two things jumped out at me while I watched *The Civil War.* One was that the U.S. Capitol was being fitted with a new dome. The physical symbol of the Union was being rebuilt *even as the Union itself was being pulled to pieces.* If that is not fodder for the imagination, I don't know what is. The second item that jumped out at me during the documentary was this: there were regiments on both sides of the war composed entirely of Irish immigrants. The Irish were the largest single immigrant group in the country at the time, and because of their own political history, they were passionately divided on the issues of the American Civil War. The image of Irish soldiers blasting away at one another on American soil for ideals which were also Irish ideals—this too was intriguing stuff.

And so I had the essential pieces of a story: Irish laborers working on behalf of the Union either constructively, by rebuilding the Capitol dome, or destructively, by killing fellow Irishmen.

I also knew from the outset that this would be a violent book, because you cannot write about war and killing without violent emotions. Other things about how the book should work came to me gradually. It would be fragmentary, a broken narrative to mirror the breaking of lives and of the Union. It would have the characteristics of a very bad dream, scattered and uncertain. It would make connections between Irish history and American history, and so would have an Irish voice. And it would be an unreliable narrative, because who can safely aver the truth about something so complex and schizophrenic as a nation warring against itself? And ultimately, it would be about becoming American, and about America becoming itself.

In describing it, I realize I make it sound very straightforward, but it was not straightforward at all. It was very painful, very difficult, very tortured.

This is the story: Mairhe Mehan, an Irish barmaid, has one foot in Ireland and one foot in America. On one side of her is her beloved older brother, Mike, a laborer at the Capitol and a Union supporter. On the other side of her is her father, a broken-down, broken-hearted Irishman who cannot stop himself from pining for his lost land and wants nothing to do with America's troubles. Mairhe, in the midst of the turmoil that is 1863 Washington, cannot make the choice for herself, and when her brother joins the federal troops, she can think only of getting him *out,* not of why he would make such a decision. And pestering her all the time to make a choice is Walt Whitman, fortuitously met, that most American of poets spending the war as a nurse in the army hospitals.

Mairhe's narrative is a series of dreamlike fragments, some actual dreams, some myths, some projections of Mike's actions, some firsthand reporting. Everything she sees is falling into fragments, and her frantic attempts to keep all things together is breaking her heart. She realizes the impossibility of knowing anything for sure, even her own experience, so it is her (and my) assumption that even dreams and myths can tell us something true. She says, "So is history to be found in the heart and the memory and the imagination, not in the photographer's glass plate or the journalist's wired message to the editor. So these dreams are true, I tell you, as true as anything else. And if I tell you I kept my brother alive by dreaming of him, that is true, too."

Writing novels is itself an assumption that dreams and myths can tell us something true, and I do believe it is a fair way to study history. I don't claim that this novel

represents the universal experience of the Civil War. But then nothing can, can it?

In writing *The Dreams of Mairhe Mehan,* I did Suffer at last! I suffered so much I felt physically sick every day as I worked on it: I had a sensation of choking and breathlessness, I wanted to cry. It was so hard to write, and I suffered so much that I could not help thinking: at last, this must be Real Art. Of course, there was also a nagging voice that said, "Maybe you feel sick because it's so lousy." In order to recover from writing this book, I had to take a train to Hudson Bay to look for polar bears.

And on the way, I thought of a sequel.

Part IX—Series or Serious?

When I was a young reader, I loved Nancy Drew. I loved her so much, I can't begin to tell you. She was so admirable, so chic, she had a *roadster.* Owning a roadster was the dream of my heart for many years. For many children, I suspect, the experience of reading is entered so wholeheartedly, so willingly, that they forget that this is not real. Although I knew that I was going to be an author, and that authors make up stories, Nancy was so real to me that somewhere along the way I forgot that she was made up. In fact, I found myself thinking once, "That Nancy, she has this incredible timing. She takes riding lessons and boom—there's a mystery at the stables. She goes on a trip to Mexico and boom—there's a mystery." You see, I did not see the hand of "Carolyn Keene," the Stratemeyer syndicate, manipulating Nancy like a puppet. She was real, and she was amazing. To have a whole series of books about this paragon with Titian hair was heaven.

There were other series, some mass-market, some trade, i.e., serious. "The Chronicles of Narnia," "Encyclopedia Brown," the "Maida" books, "The Dark Is Rising" trilogy, "The Wizard of Earthsea" trilogy, the Hardy Boys, and so on. In our family, the tradition we kept for years and years was to go to the public library on Saturday mornings. We chose our own books and came back the next week for more. I found all kinds of things on my own, and I am embarrassed to say I rarely paid attention to the names of the authors. But I think it was because I believed in books so wholeheartedly. Becoming an author must obviously have been a somewhat abstract thing. It is possible for kids to believe in contradictory things; it was certainly possible for me to believe in this contradiction: (a) I am going to be an author, and (b) books are not written by people, they just are there, mysteriously and autonomously, like God.

But if the book was part of a series, I paid enough attention to the author so that I could find additional books. Although, on reflection, I realize that I remembered where on the shelf I found a book. I went to that section of the shelf and looked at titles most of the time.

When I began my writing career, it was in series books. My very first book was for a paperback romance series called "Sweet Dreams." These were the first generation of teen romances a la Harlequin or Silhouette romances. I wrote two of these under the pseudonym Julia Winfield. The first was called *Private Eyes* (about a girl who wants to be a detective, a homage to Nancy D.), and a few years later I was able to spin it off into a miniseries, the three books of the "Private Eyes" series.

In the meantime, however, I landed the all-time best freelance job for a young writer. I became, for several years, one of the regular ghostwriters of the "Sweet Valley High" series. I came in on book number 33. It had become clear by that time that the series was a run-away smash-hit boffo success, and that it was necessary to have a couple of writers who could be depended upon to know the characters, plots, vicissitudes, series style, and so on. I wrote book after book under the series pseudonym, Kate William.

Many students—and adults for that matter—ask me how I could bear to work so hard on books that did not bear my name. I tell them that this job was a remarkable apprenticeship for me. I learned scene and dialogue, I learned pacing, I learned plot and chapter structure, and most of all, I learned to write fast. Not infrequently I had to write a 130-page book in four weeks. It was like being trained on a daily newspaper. I learned speed and efficiency, neither of which are bad things for a writer. After twenty or so books, I also lost all fear of "writing a book." I could write books at the drop of a hat, and so when I was ready to take on trade fiction with *Steal Away* and *Hugh Can Do,* I was undaunted.

The series was remarkably successful, presaging the later successes of such series as "Babysitters' Club" and "Goosebumps." It was spun off into a series for younger readers called "Sweet Valley Twins," and then again into a series for even younger readers called "Sweet Valley Kids." I ended up writing the first thirty-five or so of the "SVK" books and discovered what a delight it is to write chapter books for young readers. I had a wonderful time writing those books, and that, too, was part of my training.

Writing mass-market series books was fraught with critical peril, of course. As is always the case with this kind of book, there are more than enough people ready to turn up their noses. It was easy for people to dismiss what I did as formulaic and trivial, if not actually detrimental to quality literature. I myself was sometimes ambivalent about what I was writing. It certainly did not represent my ambitions as a writer. However, popular series books have been with us for generations, and I have not noticed a corresponding decline in the quality of literature written for kids. On the contrary, the last few years have seen some remarkable trade novels published for children and young adults. Those people who dislike the very notion of series books, and the series they love to hate, will always be with us.

I did create some series of my own. The first was called "Pets, Inc.", a four-book series about girls who take care of neighborhood pets. It was fun to write, and I set it in a town called Indian Springs, which was only a thin disguise for my town of Saratoga Springs. It never sold that well, competing as it did with fifty other series on the bookstore shelves.

After the critical success of *Steal Away,* I was able to sell a historical series to Bantam Books, a six-book project called "The Wild Rose Inn." These books, all historical romances, were the stories of six girls in a single family over three centuries. The setting for the books was a family-run tavern in the town of Marblehead, Massachusetts, a very very old town on the coast. Keeping to the same family, the same house, and the same town, while changing historical periods, was an interesting writing job. I was able, over the course of the six books, to follow

individual families, particular objects, houses, the town, and give them their own narrative lifespan which was larger than the lifespan of each book. This is one of the great attractions of writing series books—although the books stand on their own, the whole can be greater than the sum of the parts.

Finally, to support my trade novels at Crown/Knopf, my Very Helpful Editor arranged for me to be offered a series in Random House's "First Stepping Stone" line of early chapter books. The publisher explained that I could make the series anything I wanted, but since I was creating a name for myself in historical fiction, it would be great if I wanted to do a series of historical chapter books. Additionally, if I wanted to do historical chapter books, it would be really great, the publisher said, if I wanted to write about immigrants.

Both ideas sounded swell to me. Creating a series, however, is a tricky thing. I had to figure out how the whole series would work, rather than simply thinking about individual books. I thought at first that I would follow one popular series convention: create a gang. In this case, it would be an ethnically and racially mixed gang of kids in one neighborhood, and I could write stories about each of them, exploring the experiences of their different immigrant groups.

This plan had the drawback of confining the books to one place and one time. The same would obviously be true if I built the series around a single character, with the added problem of confining it to a single immigrant group.

In order to give the series as much range as possible, I came up with the Fourth of July as the unifying principle. All the stories would take place on or around Independence Day. The stories wouldn't necessarily be *about* Independence Day, but that would be when they occurred. This, I felt, was subtle and nice. It wasn't until I wrote the first book, however, that the second unifying principle of the series became clear to me. In each book, a folktale or myth or legend of the country of origin would be told to the main character. Then, unconsciously, the main character would reenact that tale in the context of the new American setting. So in a book about a brave Norwegian girl, Lili Alesund,

With sister Sarah (left), Niagara Falls, 1989.

the heroine is regaled with spook stories about Nifelheim, the mythical land of mists where the Viking heroes must go to conquer trolls in feats of courage. On the steamship that takes her and her family to America, Lili must conquer her own fears to rescue her little brother from what they believe is a troll. She herself becomes a Viking hero. This book is called *Lili the Brave*.

Patrick Doyle Is Full of Blarney is about an Irish kid living in Hell's Kitchen in 1915. He and his pals have a great baseball field in a paddock behind Gilhooley's Brewery, and they are sitting pretty until the day the Copperheads, a gang of street toughs, show up. This story replays the legend of Saint Patrick driving the snakes from Ireland, which is typically referred to as a green field. *Foolish Gretel* takes the form of the classic Grimms' simpleton tale, with a family of three girls living in Galveston, Texas, in 1854. The youngest, foolish Gretel, passes three tests because she and she alone is of good heart, and she wins out over her mean and selfish older sisters to win a place at the castle, the grand hacienda of a wealthy widow in need of a companion.

Having designed the series in this way, I find that there are limitless possibilities for books. World folklore and mythology are full of stories, and reading them in conjunction with the immigration history of different nationalities almost gives me these stories ready-made. It is a delight to write them.

Part X—Many Rooms

The old house in which I grew up was a large farmhouse on two acres. When we first moved into it, it had six separate entrances and five porches. It had, and still has, two attics. One of these was the third floor of the house, full of wasps and cardboard boxes of old clothes. The other attic was on the second floor, with its own staircase by the side-hall door: a farmhand's dormitory. This sunny attic, also filled with wasps, was where we kept camping equipment and Christmas ornaments. The basement was divided into separate areas: coal cellar, root cellar, the part where the outside steps were, the part where the inside stairs were, the place we kept half-empty cans of paint, and so on. This basement was damp and spidery, prone to flooding, mysteriously lit with only two or three bare light bulbs. On one wall hung a dartboard falling to pieces from the damp. In another corner stood an enormous telescope, filmed over with mildew.

The house itself, the daylight parts of the house, changed shape and layout over the years. When we first moved in, it had a kitchen (with hand pump), a dining room, a laundry room, a living room, a library, an office, a TV room, a side hall, and a bathroom. This was just downstairs. Upstairs were four bedrooms and a bath, a couple of halls, and a large closet, which later turned into a bathroom. This large closet, before it was converted, contained (among other things) a large, almost life-sized doll's head on a high shelf. The light from the hall would penetrate only so far into this closet; always there, dimly lit in the far reaches of this hall, would be the staring Head, with medium brown hair in a flip. Perhaps I thought it looked a little bit like me. It filled me with dread, but I never asked about it. I accepted it as one of the terrible

things of life and made myself look at it from time to time, like a Romantic poet gazing upon a tomb.

Beyond the walls of the house, our property boasted a number of outbuildings. There was the garage with its peeling, scaly paint and many years' worth of old New York State license plates nailed to the wall. There was a corncrib with mummified relics of corncobs long since nibbled clean by raccoons. There was a chicken shed, still redolent of chicken poop, where occasional downy feathers still floated on sunny currents of air. There was an outhouse, which we actually used on a few occasions when the well went dry. There was a woodshed, a tiny house just perfect for a small child to climb around in. There was also the empty barn, a world unto itself.

And beyond our yard there were the old farm fields, set apart and outlined by stone walls and rusting gates and old tractor paths. Each of these fields had its own characteristics: the giant rabbit warren, the fallen oak tree, the rock pile, the raspberry canes, the big rock. And beyond these fields and our yard were other yards and other houses and other garages, into which we children ran freely and carelessly. Many of these places were dangerous in their own ways: nails and splinters stabbed bare feet, prickers scratched hands, poison ivy flashed around the corners, rocks tumbled suddenly. These dangers were dangers I accepted as the price I had to pay for access to all these places, for access to their hidden delights.

My world, as a child, was a world of many rooms, each of which held its mysteries and its secrets, its splendid treasures and its terrors. My nightmares often placed me in endless series of dark attic-like rooms, one opening onto another, onto a cellar, onto another cellar and another attic, each dim and dusty, each vaguely frightening but exciting. My dreams exaggerated what I lived during the days, endlessly exploring the many many rooms.

Does physical shape give shape to the imagination? Did the generous dimensions and sprawling layout of my childhood domain imprint their counterparts in my mind? I was a collector of spaces as a child, and I find I still collect them. I love stories about underground caves and hidden rooms and secret passages. I love long lists of contents and components, the many strange objects in a cupboard, the varieties of furniture and furnishings in a house, the ingredients of spells, the many names of dogs and horses. There was a lot of room where I grew up. I learned early how to spread out and encompass many things.

My head is filled with attics, closets, sheds, and cellars. I expect I will be stung by wasps, drive splinters into my fingers, find grotesque surprises, but there are many wonders and marvels there, and I want to find them.

Writings

PICTURE BOOKS

Hugh Can Do, illustrated by Kimberly Bulcken Root, Crown, 1992.

Chin Yu Min and the Ginger Cat, illustrated by Mary Grandpre, Crown, 1993.

Little Salt Lick and the Sun King, illustrated by Jon Goodell, Crown, 1994.

That Terrible Baby, illustrated by Susan Meddaugh, Tambourine, 1994.

The Whittler's Tale, illustrated by Valery Vasiliev, Tambourine, 1994.

King Crow, illustrated by Eric Rohmann, Crown, 1995.

Wan Hu Is in the Stars, illustrated by Barry Root, Tambourine, 1995.

EASY READERS

The Snowball, illustrated by Jean Pidgeon, Random House, 1996.

Sunshine, Moonshine, Random House, 1997.

Audubon, Random House, forthcoming.

CHAPTER BOOKS

Patrick Doyle Is Full of Blarney, illustrated by Krista Brauckmann-Towns, Random House, 1996.

Foolish Gretel, illustrated by Bill Dodge, Random House, 1997.

Lili the Brave, illustrated by Uldis Klavins, Random House, 1997.

MIDDLE-GRADE BOOKS

Steal Away, Orchard, 1992.

Black-Eyed Susan, illustrated by Emily Martindale, Crown, 1995.

FOR YOUNG ADULTS; FICTION

The Dreams of Mairhe Mehan, Knopf, 1996.

Mary Mehan Awake, Knopf, 1997.

B

BARUNGA, Albert 1912(?)-1977

Personal

Born c. 1912, in Port George, Australia; died, 1977; son of Pullarud ("Charlie") and Giyambi ("Maude") Barunga; married, wife's name, Pusdiwola; children: Gibson, Gordon, Jane, Jennifer, Francis, Nelson, Victor.

Career

Writer and promoter of Australian Aboriginal culture. Aboriginal Theatre Foundation, served as regional chairperson; Aboriginal Cultural Foundation, founding member; Australia Council, founding member of Aboriginal Arts Board. Worked as a civilian for the Australian Navy during World War II.

Writings

About This Little Devil and This Little Fella, Magabala Books (Broome, Australia), 1999.

*   *   *

BASKIN, Leonard 1922-2000

Personal

Born August 15, 1922, in New Brunswick, NJ; died of kidney failure, June 3, 2000, in Northampton, MA; son of Samuel (a rabbi) and May (maiden name, Guss) Baskin; married Esther Tane (a writer), November 26, 1946 (marriage ended); married Lisa Unger, October, 1967; children: (first marriage) Tobias Isaac; (second marriage) Hosea Thomas, Lucretia Manya. *Education:* Attended New York University, 1939-41, and Yale University, 1941-43; New School for Social Research, A.B., 1949, D.F.A., 1966; graduate study at Academie de la Grande Chaumiere, 1950, and Academia di Belle Arti, 1951; Clark University, L.H.D., 1966; University of Massachusetts, D.F.A., 1968.

Career

Graphic artist and sculptor, professor, illustrator, and printer. Worchester Museum, MA, art teacher, 1952. Worked as an instructor, associate professor, and professor at Smith College, Northampton, MA, beginning 1953. Gehenna Press, Northampton, MA, operator and co-owner, 1962-2000. *Military Service:* U.S. Naval Reserves, 1943-46, air corps; Merchant Marines, gunner. *Exhibitions:* Numerous one-man shows, including those at the Glickman Studio, New York City, 1939, Numero Galleria d'Arte, Florence, Italy, 1951, Museum Boymans-van Beuningen, Rotterdam, Holland, 1961, Royal Watercolor Society, London, England, 1962, National Collection of Fine Arts, Washington, DC, 1970, Jewish Museum, New York City, 1974, Kennedy Gallery, New York City, 1975. Contributor to retrospective and group shows, and to permanent collections in numerous institutions, including Metropolitan Museum of Art, Museum of Modern Art, Library of Congress, National Gallery of Art, Art Institute of Chicago, Fogg Museum of Harvard University, Pennsylvania Academy of Fine Arts, Princeton University, Brandeis University, Detroit Institute of Art, Chase Manhattan Bank, Bezalele Museum (Jerusalem). *Member:* American Academy of Arts and Sciences, American Institute of Graphic Artists, National Institute of Arts and Letters.

Awards, Honors

Louis Comfort Tiffany Foundation Fellowship for sculpture, 1947; Guggenheim Fellowship, 1953; Mrs. A. W. Erickson Prize from the Society of American Graphic Artists for sculpture and print making, 1953; Ohara Museum Prize for graphic art in the Tokyo biennial of prints at the Japanese National Museum, 1957; international prize in engraving from the Sao Paulo Biennial in Brazil, 1961; Alonzo C. Mather Prize from the Art Institute of Chicago, 1961; Medal of Merit from the American Institute of Graphic Arts, 1965; Gold Medal from the Pennsylvania Academy of Fine Arts, 1965; Medal of Merit from the American Academy of Arts and Letters, 1968; Gold Medal from the National Institute of

Leonard Baskin contributed evocative pen-and-ink drawings to Ted Hughes's collection of poems about imaginary lunar inhabitants and vegetation. (From Moon-Whales and Other Moon Poems.*)*

Arts and Letters, 1969; American Institute of Graphic Arts Children's Book Show selection, 1971-72, American Institute of Graphic Arts Fifty Books of the Year selection, 1972, *New York Times* Choice of Best Illustrated Children's Books of the Year, 1972, Caldecott Honor Book, 1973, and Brooklyn Art Books for Children Citation from the Brooklyn Museum and the Brooklyn Public Library, 1975, all for *Hosie's Alphabet;* Children's Book Showcase Selection from the Children's Book Council, 1976, for illustration of Ted Hughes's *Season Songs; New York Times* Best Illustrated Children's Books of the Year, and Parents' Choice, both 1983, for *Leonard Baskin's Miniature Natural History: First Series; New York Times* Notable Book, and Parents' Choice Picture Book award, both 1987, for illustrations for Lore Segal's *The Book of Adam to Moses.*

Writings

FOR CHILDREN; SELF-ILLUSTRATED

(With Hosea, Tobias, and Lisa Baskin) *Hosie's Alphabet,* Viking, 1972.

(With Tobias, Lucretia, Hosie, and Lisa Baskin) *Hosie's Aviary,* Viking, 1979.

(With Tobias, Lucretia, Hosie, and Lisa Baskin) *Hosie's Zoo,* Viking, 1981.

Leonard Baskin's Miniature Natural History: First Series, Pantheon, 1983, Simon and Schuster, 1993.

Imps, Demons, Hobgoblins, Witches, Fairies and Elves, Pantheon, 1984.

(With Hosie Baskin) *A Book of Dragons,* Knopf, 1985.

ILLUSTRATOR

Ted Hughes, *Season Songs* (poems), Viking, 1975.

T. Hughes, *Moon-Whales and Other Moon Poems,* Viking, 1976.

T. Hughes, *Under the North Star* (poems), Viking, 1981.

Lore Segal, *The Book of Adam to Moses,* Knopf, 1987.

James Baldwin, *Gypsy and Other Poems,* Gehenna Press, 1989.

Norton Juster, *Alberic the Wise,* Picture Book Studio, 1992.

Richard Michelson, *Did You Say Ghosts?,* Simon and Schuster, 1993.

Cathy Fishman, *On Passover,* Macmillan, 1994.

R. Michelson, *Animals That Ought to Be: Poems about Imaginary Pets,* Simon and Schuster, 1996.

R. Michelson, *A Book of Flies Real or Otherwise* (poems), Cavendish Children's Books, 1999.

FOR ADULTS, ILLUSTRATED BY LEONARD BASKIN

Esther Baskin, *Creatures of Darkness,* Little, Brown, 1962.

The Iliad of Homer, translated by Richard Lattimore, University of Chicago Press, 1962.

Aristotle, *Politics and Poetics,* translated by Benjamin Jowett and S. H. Butcher, Heritage Press, 1964.

Joseph Pulitzer, *A Tradition of Conscience: Proposals for Journalism,* St. Louis Press, 1965.

E. Baskin, *The Poppy and Other Deadly Plants,* Delacorte Press, 1967.

Figures of Dead Men, University of Massachusetts, 1968.

Baskin: Sculpture, Drawings, and Prints, Braziller, 1970.

The Graphic Work, 1950-1970, Far Gallery, 1970.

Beowulf, translated by Burton Raffe, University of Massachusetts Press, 1971.

T. Hughes, *Selected Poems 1957-67,* Harper, 1973.

William Shakespeare, *Othello* and *Titus Andronicus,* Gehenna Press, 1973.

A Passover Haggadah, edited by Herbert Bronstein, Grossman Publishers, 1974.

Appolodorus, *Gods and Heroes of the Greeks: The Library of Appolodorus,* translated by Michael Simpson, University of Massachusetts Press, 1976.

T. Hughes, *Cave Bird: Poems,* Scholar Press, 1975, Viking, 1978.

R. B. Morris, *The Framing of the Federal Constitution,* U.S. Government Printing Office, 1979.

Chosen Days: Celebrating Jewish Festivals in Poetry and Art, text by David Rosenberg, Doubleday, 1980.

The Raptors and Other Birds, preface by S. Dillon Ripley, commentary by Jose Yglesias, Pantheon, 1985.

Iconologia, Harcourt Brace Jovanovich, 1988.

Baskin also illustrated the works of many other authors and poets both for his own Gehenna Press and other publishers, including D. H. Lawrence, Herman Melville, Sylvia Plath, E. A. Poe, William Blake, James Baldwin, and Conrad Aiken. He also produced numerous limited editions of his own etchings and woodcuts.

Sidelights

Leonard Baskin was "one of America's most distinguished artists," according to Mary Lystad, writing in *St. James Guide to Children's Writers.* Excelling in sculpture and graphic arts, Baskin also created a noted career in watercolors, calligraphy, engraving, and graphic design, publishing scores of titles through his own Gehenna Press. A widely revered figurative sculptor and graphic artist, he commenced in 1962 a distinguished career in book illustration with his artwork for a translation of *The Iliad,* and from that time became a renowned contributor to the field of children's book illustration, winning a Caldecott Honor award for *Hosie's Alphabet.* In addition to two more "Hosie" books in collaboration with his wife and children, Baskin also illustrated several volumes of juvenile poetry by the English poet Ted Hughes and by the poet Richard Michelson.

Noted for his fanciful and sometimes surreal approach to the everyday world, Baskin created an amazing gallery of animal and human forms in his illustrations, working mostly in black and white. Part monster, part human, many such forms reflect a medieval sensibility, and indeed, Baskin's art was early affected by a sojourn in Italy and the study of thirteenth-century artists. "I consider myself an ordinary person," Baskin once commented in a *Newsweek* interview. "I've tried hard in my work to make the ordinary person heroic through the fact of his humanity—my figures 'are the fat guys you see in the subway and on the bus.'"

Baskin's chilling illustrations enhance the spooky tone of Richard Michelson's cumulative text, in which a parent uses a child's fear of night noises to create a game in which one monster frightens the next. (From Did You Say Ghosts?.)

Born in New Brunswick, New Jersey, in 1922, Baskin was brought up in a devout Jewish household. Baskin's father was a rabbi, and at age seven Baskin also began attending a Jewish parochial school, preparing to become a rabbi himself. But a visit to a craft exhibition at Macy's department store when he was fourteen proved to be an epiphany for the young boy. There he saw a sculptor molding a head in clay, and he continued watching the artist into the evening. He took several pounds of clay home with him that night, and by the next year Baskin was seriously studying art.

From 1937 to 1939 he studied with Maurice Glickman in New York. Sculpting became his whole life; before he was eighteen, Baskin won an honorable mention in a Prix de Rome competition. In 1940 he entered Yale, studying at the School of Fine Arts, but found that his method and the curriculum of that institution were at odds. He left Yale and enlisted in the Navy during the Second World War, and with the close of the war used the GI Bill to further his art studies in New York and then in Europe, both in Paris and in Florence. A trip to Pisa to see the carvings of the Pisan school was a revelation for Baskin, and proved a new beginning in his work.

Returning to the United States in 1952, Baskin set about making a name for himself in the art world with sculptures, engravings, and woodcuts. In 1953 he began a long and distinguished career as an art instructor at Smith College, and in the early 1960s established the Gehenna Press where he blended all his artistic interests in the publication of rare books in limited editions, most of them illustrated by himself. With such productions, Baskin involved himself in all aspects of the publishing process, from book design, choice of paper and binding, to typeset, and, of course, artwork. In 1962 his illustrations for Richard Lattimore's translation of *The Iliad* established him as a world-class book illustrator.

Baskin became involved in illustration for children's books when his three-year-old son, Hosea, asked him to draw an alphabet. Such a request soon turned into a family project, with text ultimately written by Baskin's second wife, Lisa, along with sons Hosea and Tobias. Baskin's watercolor illustrations accompanied this bestiary alphabet in a book that is not the typical children's alphabet book. In Baskin's edgy and whimsical world, the letter "D", for example, "is for demon", while "V" is "The cadaver-haunted vulture," "P" is "A primordial protozoa," and "G" is "A ghastly garrulous gargoyle." According to a contributor for *Children's Books and Their Creators,* Baskin, "with sometimes spirited, sometimes mystic, always creative, imaginative paintings, brought an exciting, edgy quality to the art in children's books: he created an art that demands attention and reaction, that is professionally astute and visually memorable." Mary Lystad, writing for *St. James Guide to Children's Writers,* remarked that the illustrations for *Hosie's Alphabet* "far exceed in graphic design and color those of most picture books for children," and drew special attention to the "amazonian armadillo, bumptious baboon, and carrion crow", which "are incredible in their physical characteristics and in their interpretation of psyche." Lystad concluded, "One would be tempted to frame the pictures in this book individually."

Hosie's Alphabet was named a Caldecott Honor Book in 1973, and the welcome reception of the book by critics and public alike inspired further collaborative efforts. *Hosie's Aviary,* a collaboration with his two sons and daughter Lucretia, in addition to Lisa Baskin, highlights Baskin's love of birds, illustrations of which are featured in many of his other works as well. *Hosie's Zoo,* third in the series, was published in 1981. Another all-family collaboration, the book expresses in "pithy, image-rich poems" the feelings of each family member about the animals portrayed in Baskin's "wonderful paintings," according to a reviewer for *Publishers Weekly.* The reviewer also called Baskin "one of America's foremost artists" and prophesied that *Hosie's Zoo* was destined to "be cited as a monumental contribution to picture books for all ages," just as were the first two volumes in the series. *Horn Book*'s Celia H. Morris concluded that the book was "an impressive combination of fine art and poetic imagery."

Baskin collaborated with his son, Hosie, on *A Book of Dragons,* "an enthralling gallery of beastly horrors that have niches in folklore throughout the world," according to a critic for *Publishers Weekly.* Baskin portrays an assortment of twenty dragons that have captured mankind's imagination through the ages, and which have found a place in mythology, fantasy, legend, epic, folk tale, and even the Old Testament. These include Grendel, who was killed by Beowulf, and the monster that fought with St. George, among a gallery of others. The *Publishers Weekly* critic also praised Baskin's paintings with "starkly contrasting dark and fiery colors." *Horn Book*'s Ethel L. Heins remarked that the dragons "appear highly individualized in expressionist paintings filled with brilliant jewel like color—often a kind of chromatic geometry—that interpret the full fury of the snarling, writing, pouncing creatures."

Going solo, Baskin contributed both text and illustrations to *Imps, Demons, Hobgoblins, Witches, Fairies and Elves,* another catalogue of the bizarre and strange. Baskin includes characters from fairy tales and nursery rhymes such as the Three Billy Goats Gruff and Rumplestiltskin, as well as the Black Dog and the Imp of the Perverse and other "unearthly beings," as *Horn Book*'s Ann A. Flowers described the creatures in the book. Flowers concluded, "The artist's great talent is expressing the inexpressible; his unique vision, at times sympathetic and at times delighting in the grotesque, is altogether arresting." More of Baskin's takes on the natural world around him are found in *Leonard Baskin's Miniature Natural History.*

Regarding this "grotesque" element in his work, Baskin once told Brian O'Doherty in an interview for *Art in America* that the "world of art is full of paintings of landscape, flowers, still life's, ripening grapes, young buxom ladies, dressed and undressed, and one has this entire world to choose from." Baskin took another course in his art, as he went on to explain. "Why can't one, single, obscure, isolated artist be morbid, gruesome and decadent—although I don't agree that I am any of these things. I keep seeing the gaping hole, the bleeding wound. The rest of the body may be healthy, but the wound that bleeds is what concerns me."

Baskin also illustrated three juvenile books of poetry for the well-known British poet, Ted Hughes. In *Season Songs,* "Baskin carried on his uncompromising approach with dramatic illustrations, his paintings growing out of the poem's moods and the qualities and possibilities of watercolor as a medium," according to the contributor for *Children's Books and Their Creators.* His line drawings for Hughes's 1976 *Moon-Whales and Other Moon Poems,* "presented powerful images in black-and-white," according to the same writer. And for *Under the North Star,* a 1981 collection from Hughes, Baskin helped to "celebrate the wonders of the animal kingdom," according to Richard C. Bartlett in a review for *Horn Book.* He goes on to say, "Quality tells, talent shines. When a publisher has a perceptive, gifted poet working in tandem with a graphic artist of great stature . . . the result is bookmaking as an art . . . . This book is enriching and full of wonderful experiences for children." A *Publishers Weekly* writer commented that Baskin and Hughes "have created a charming and handsome new book," and that Baskin's "expressive color drawings" complement Hughes's "touching and playful poems about animals existing in a land under the North Star." The same reviewer concluded, "Baskin evokes the animals with striking colors and original forms."

Additionally Baskin produced illustrations for works from the Old Testament in *The Book of Adam to Moses,* and on Jewish holidays in *On Passover,* as well as artwork depicting a Renaissance world in *Alberic the Wise.* For Lore Segal's retelling of the first five books of the Old Testament, Baskin created abstract black-and-white illustrations which "will give those who otherwise would hesitate at biblical reading a glimpse of the oft-mentioned mysteries of the age-old tradition," according to Diane Roeback of *Publishers Weekly.* For a new edition of Norton Juster's classic *Alberic the Wise,* the story of a Renaissance-age man's search for wisdom and knowledge, Baskin contributed "bold, expressionist watercolors" in "rich, earthy tones," as a contributor for *Publishers Weekly* remarked.

In the 1990s, Baskin collaborated with another poet, Richard Michelson, on several picture books: *Did You Say Ghosts?, Animals That Ought to Be: Poems about Imaginary Pets,* and *A Book of Flies Real or Otherwise.* The first title is a "good-humored picture book," according to a reviewer for *Publishers Weekly,* told in a rhyme that "hurtles along," in which a parent uses a child's fear of noises in the night to create a game. "Oversize watercolors, which combine an effective mix of somber grays and splashes of bright paint, are both eerie and exotic, and convey—spiritedly—the giddy intrigue of the text," concluded the same reviewer. A

Mixing poetry and prose Richard Michelson describes various details about thirteen insects while Baskin depicts them in witty drawings. (From A Book of Flies Real or Otherwise.)

contributor for *Entertainment Weekly* wrote, "Witty reflections on creatures that go bump in the night accompany Baskin's creepy watercolors," while Lolly Robinson, writing in a review for *Horn Book,* remarked that Baskin's "deliciously scary watercolor illustrations, using his signature rich color combinations with patches of textured paper showing through, epitomize each creature."

More Michelson/Baskin collaborative work is served up in *Animals That Ought to Be,* a catalogue of imaginary beasts such as the Nightnoise Gladiator and the Channel Changer. *Booklist*'s Hazel Rochman felt that "Baskin's full-page watercolor creatures facing each poem are mysterious enough to leave space for children's own imaginings," while *Horn Book*'s Mary M. Burns noted that Baskin's "brilliant expressionistic paintings" capture the feeling of the fourteen ghoulish oddities in Michelson's poems. A third collaborative effort appeared in 1999, *A Book of Flies Real or Otherwise,* a book full of "whimsy and humor," according to a writer for *Publishers Weekly,* which focuses on thirteen insects. Nine such insects are actual flies, of the order Diptera, while four more, such as the firefly or fruit fly are popularly called flies but belong to different orders. "The off-beat aggregate of facts and fictions, the splendid illustrations and the sly wit of both drawings and text will make this a book that both children and adults can enjoy together," concluded the *Publishers Weekly* reviewer. *Horn Book*'s Burns praised Baskin's "brilliantly colored, painstakingly executed illustrations" that are "imaginative, somewhat surreal interpretations" of the accompanying verse explanations.

Baskin's work in children's books was only one part of a much larger canvas of work, but his contributions were nonetheless significant. His children's book illustrations have been praised for their artistic quality and their imaginative intensity. Whether working in collaboration with his own family members, on his own, or together with poets of repute, Baskin's drawings for children's books established, according to the writer for *Children's Books and Their Creators,* "the highest standards for uncompromising quality and exceptional vision." His death on June 3, 2000, ended a career noted for continual questioning of the human condition though art that is both groundbreaking and compassionate.

Biographical and Critical Sources

BOOKS

American Artists, edited by Les Krantz, Facts on File, 1985.

Baskin, Leonard, *Hosie's Alphabet,* with Hosea, Tobias, and Lisa Baskin, Viking, 1972.

Children's Books and Their Creators, edited by Anita Silvey, Houghton Mifflin, 1995, p. 48.

Contemporary Artists, 4th edition, edited by Joann Cerrito, St. James Press, 1996.

Lystad, Mary, "Baskin, Leonard," *St. James Guide to Children's Writers,* 5th edition, edited by Sara Pendergast and Tom Pendergast, St. James Press, 1999, pp. 73-74.

PERIODICALS

Art in America, summer, 1962, Brian O'Doherty, "Leonard Baskin."

Atlantic, November, 1988, p. 100.

Booklist, January 15, 1993, p. 908; September 1, 1993, p. 69; October 15, 1996, Hazel Rochman, review of *Animals That Ought to Be,* p. 427; November 15, 1996, p. 567.

English Journal, October, 1985, p. 81.

Entertainment Weekly, October 1, 1993, review of *Did You Say Ghosts?,* p. 69.

Horn Book, April, 1982, Celia H. Morris, review of *Hosie's Zoo,* pp. 153-54; January-February, 1985, Ann A. Flowers, review of *Imps, Demons, Hobgoblins, Witches, Fairies and Elves,* p. 42; March-April, 1986, Ethel L. Heins, review of *A Book of Dragons,* pp. 189-90; November-December, 1986, Richard C. Bartlett, review of *Under the North Star,* pp. 710-11; March-April, 1994, Lolly Robinson, review of *Did You Say Ghosts?,* p. 192; November-December, 1996, Mary M. Burns, review of *Animals That Ought to Be,* p. 754; September, 1999, M.M. Burns, review of *A Book of Flies Real or Otherwise,* p. 620.

Library Journal, October 1, 1984, p. 1844; February 15, 1986, p. 174; November 1, 1988, p. 91.

Newsweek, October 22, 1962, "They Frighten People;" December 7, 1981, pp. 98, 101; December 5, 1983, p. 112.

New York Times Book Review, November 15, 1981, p. 60; February 2, 1997, p. 18.

Publishers Weekly, February 6, 1981, review of *Under the North Star,* pp. 365-66; December 11, 1981, review of *Hosie's Zoo,* p. 63; November 15, 1985, review of *A Book of Dragons,* p. 57; October 30, 1987, Diane Roeback, review of *The Book of Adam to Moses,* p. 71; August 26, 1988, p. 73; November 30, 1992, review of *Alberic the Wise,* p. 55; August 2, 1993, review of *Did You Say Ghosts?,* p. 81; September 23, 1996, pp. 76-77; August 2, 1999, review of *A Book of Flies Real or Otherwise,* p. 82.

School Library Journal, February, 1985, p. 70; January, 1986, p. 62; December, 1987, pp. 39, 97; March, 1993, p. 198; November, 1993, p. 87; September, 1996, p. 199; October, 1999, pp. 172-73.

Obituaries

PERIODICALS

Los Angeles Times, June 6, 2000, p. B6.
New York Times, June 6, 2000, p. A29.
Times (London), June 7, 2000.
Washington Post, June 6, 2000, p. B6.

—*Sketch by J. Sydney Jones*

*   *   *

BIGGAR, Joan R(awlins) 1936-

Personal

Given name is pronounced Jo-*Ann;* born October 18, 1936, in Olympia, WA; daughter of Delbert R. (a logger and repairer of sewing machines) and Marie (a nurse and homemaker; maiden name, Schmidt) Rawlins; married Robert W. Biggar, Jr., March 31, 1962 (died May 13, 1994); married Hendrick L. Husby (a safety officer), June 3, 2000; children: (first marriage) Robert W. III, Lenora Rose. *Education:* Everett Junior College, A.A.S., 1956; Seattle Pacific College (now University), B.A., 1958; also attended Western Washington State College (now Western Washington University) and University of Alaska, Fairbanks. *Politics:* Independent. *Religion:* Church of the Nazarene.

Addresses

E-mail—Questwriter@cs.com.

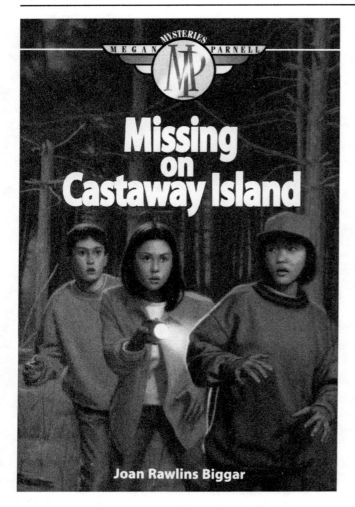

In Joan R. Biggar's adventure novel, sixteen-year-old Megan Parnell finds she must cooperate with her new stepbrother to uncover the identity and whereabouts of a boy hiding in the woods near their campground. (Cover illustration by Matthew Archambault.)

Career

Teacher at elementary schools in Everett, Marysville, and Langley, WA, and in Fairbanks, AK, 1958-65 and 1966-68; substitute teacher in Everett and Marysville, 1984-97.

Awards, Honors

First place award, creative nonfiction category, International Literary Contest, Klondike Gold Rush Centennial Committee of Washington State, for an article, "Untangling a Wilderness: The Abercrombie Trail, All-American Route to the Gold Fields."

Writings

"ADVENTURE QUEST" SERIES; WITH TEACHER'S GUIDES

Treasure at Morning Gulch, illustrated by Kay Salem, Concordia (St. Louis, MO), 1991.
Danger at Half Moon Lake, illustrated by Salem, Concordia, 1991.

Shipwreck on the Lights, illustrated by Salem, Concordia, 1992.
High Desert Secrets, illustrated by Salem, Concordia, 1992.

"MEGAN PARNELL" MYSTERY SERIES; WITH TEACHER'S GUIDES

Missing on Castaway Island, Concordia, 1997.
Mystery at Camp Galena, Concordia, 1997.
Trouble in Yakima Valley, Concordia, 1998.
Trapped at Haunted Canyon, Concordia, 1998.

OTHER

Work represented in anthologies, including *Devotions Day by Day,* Judson (Valley Forge, PA), 1988; *Beanie Baby Stories,* Starburst Publishers, 1999; and *God's Abundance for a More Joyful Life,* Starburst Publishers, 1999. Contributor to periodicals.

Work in Progress

A teen fantasy novel; a historical saga for adults; a biography of Alaskan explorer William Ralph Abercrombie; a family history project.

Sidelights

Joan R. Biggar told *SATA:* "Books were my close companions when I was growing up in the Cascade Mountains of Washington State. I loved the ones that featured lively characters leading lives of adventure in interesting places. In books I found heroes after whom to model my life. Books gave me windows on the world. I dreamed of someday traveling to faraway places myself.

"I grew up and became a schoolteacher. I found great joy in sharing reading adventures with my students. My dream expanded to writing books for young people, set in those interesting places I would visit.

"Then I met and married a young man from Alaska. We moved to Alaska. There I wrote my first book, set in the Washington valley where I'd grown up. Twenty years and many submissions later, the book connected with a publisher who shared my dream. Concordia Publishing House wanted to give young people books whose characters learn to live their faith while facing problems readers themselves face.

"In each of the eight books Concordia has published, the story starts with an interesting setting somewhere in the Pacific Northwest (except for *Trapped in Haunted Canyon,* which is set in Arizona). Mostly these are areas where my husband's jobs took us. Because plot and settings are closely woven together, readers pick up information about history, geography, natural science, and ways of living.

"In the 'Megan Parnell' series, the challenges of today are treated in a sensitive fashion. Sixteen-year-old Megan and her stepbrother Peter struggle to get along in their newly blended family. All of the stories deal with multiculturalism in some form. In some stories, racial prejudice and peer relationships are issues. In others,

Megan and her friends learn about caring for the ecology, dealing with sexual misconduct, and handling philosophies that contradict what the Bible teaches. While being entertained and informed, readers also learn that Christian faith is a practical necessity for successfully navigating the shoals of adolescence.

"Oh, yes. Somewhere along the way, I realized that my dream had come true. I was writing the kind of books I loved to read, with the kind of people and places I loved to read about."

*   *   *

BISHOP, Kathleen Wong 1954-
(Kathy Bishop)

Personal

Born September 11, 1954, in Honolulu, HI; daughter of Kai Fong (an engineer) and Dorothy (a teacher; maiden name, Wee) Wong; married David Jones Bishop (in retail), July 20, 1980; children: Lisa, Daniel, Rachel. *Education:* Stanford University, B.S., 1976. *Religion:* Christian.

Addresses

Office—P.O. Box 15462, Phoenix, AZ 85060. *E-mail*—Wongerooo@aol.com.

Career

Housing developer in Washington, DC, 1976-80; city planner in Phoenix, AZ, 1980-87; Christian educator in Phoenix, 1995—; illustrator, 1996—. Vice-president of local neighborhood association, 1985-95.

Awards, Honors

Excellence in Illustration Award and Award of Merit, children's books category, both Hawaii Publishers Association, 1999.

Illustrator

Leslie Hayashi, *Fables from the Garden,* University of Hawaii Press (Honolulu, HI), 1998.
Hayashi, *Fables from the Sea,* University of Hawaii Press, 2000.

Some work appears under the name Kathy Bishop.

Work in Progress

Illustrating *Fables from the Deep* and *The Chinese Temple,* completion of both expected in 2002.

Sidelights

"Do you believe in dreams?" Kathleen Wong Bishop asked *SATA.* "When I was seven, my best friend, Leslie Hayashi, told me she would write a book for me to illustrate, and our dream came true! I learned to paint because Leslie kept sending me stories to illustrate.

"An abundance of gifts has flowed from this. Our friendship has blossomed. I discovered the joy of painting and the beauty of the world when you take the time to really see it. Our first book, *Fables from the Garden,* was well received.

"Our books benefit society by teaching morals and an appreciation of nature. I love learning more through research and painting challenges. All this and more—with my best friend Leslie!

"Dragonflies have become very meaningful to me. This was my first good painting in 1996. I was excited to discover a new gift hidden in me. Becoming an artist has been like the incredible change a dragonfly goes through, from an ugly bug under the water to a beautiful, shimmering, flying creature. Leslie liked my dragonfly painting so much that she wrote a story for it, 'Dragonfly's Heart,' which is in our first book."

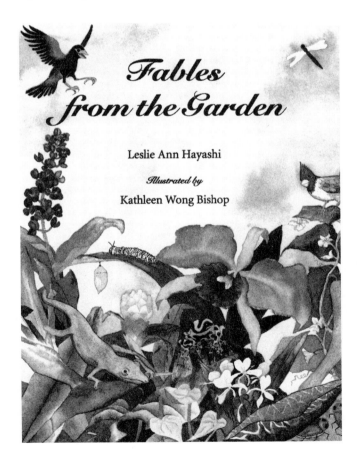

Through colorful illustrations and charming fables, Kathleen Wong Bishop and author Leslie Ann Hayashi introduce young readers to the plants and animals of Hawaii. (Cover illustration by Bishop.)

Biographical and Critical Sources

PERIODICALS

Honolulu Star Bulletin, August 7, 1998, interview with Kathleen W. Bishop and Leslie Hayashi.
Honolulu Weekly, December 1, 1998, review of *Fables from the Garden.*
MultiCultural Review, March, 1999, review of *Fables from the Garden.*

ON-LINE

Amazon.com, www.amazon.com/ (August 26, 2000).
University of Hawaii Press, www.uhpress.hawaii.edu/.

* * *

BISHOP, Kathy
See BISHOP, Kathleen Wong

C

CARLE, Eric 1929-

Personal

Born June 25, 1929, in Syracuse, NY; son of Erich W. (a civil servant) and Johanna (maiden name, Oelschlaeger) Carle; married Dorothea Wohlenberg, June, 1954 (divorced, 1964); married Barbara Morrison, June, 1973; children: (first marriage) Cirsten, Rolf. *Education:* Graduated from Akademie der bildenden Kuenste, Stuttgart, Germany, 1950.

Addresses

Home—P.O. Box 485, Northampton, MA 01060.

Career

U.S. Information Center, Stuttgart, Germany, poster designer, 1950-52; *New York Times,* New York City, graphic designer, 1952-56; L. W. Frohlich & Co., New York City, art director, 1956-63; free-lance writer, illustrator, and designer, 1963—. Guest instructor, Pratt Institute, 1964. *Military service:* U.S. Army, 1952-54. *Member:* Authors Guild.

Awards, Honors

New York Times Ten Best Illustrated Books of the Year award, 1969, for *The Very Hungry Caterpillar,* and Outstanding Children's Books of the Year selection, 1974, for *My Very First Library;* Deutscher Jugendpreis, for *1, 2, 3 to the Zoo!* and *The Very Hungry Caterpillar,* both 1970, and 1972, for *Do You Want to Be My Friend?;* first prize for picture books, International Children's Book Fair, 1970, for *1, 2, 3 to the Zoo!,* 1972, for *Do You Want to Be My Friend?,* and for *Papa, Please Get the Moon for Me;* Children's Book of the Year awards, Child Study Association, 1977, for *Do You Want to Be My Friend?, The Very Busy Spider,* and *The Very Lonely Firefly;* American Institute of Graphic Arts (AIGA) award, both 1970, for *Pancakes, Pancakes* and *The Very Hungry Caterpillar;* Selection du Grand Prix

des Treize, 1972, for *The Very Hungry Caterpillar,* and for *Do You Want to Be My Friend?* and *Have You Seen My Cat?,* both 1973; Nakamori Reader's Prize, 1975, for *The Very Hungry Caterpillar;* AIGA certificate of excellence, 1981, for *The Honeybee and the Robber;* silver medal from the city of Milan, Italy, awarded 1989 for *The Very Quiet Cricket;* Heinrich-Wolgast prize, German Education and Science Union, 1996, for *My Apron;* Medallion award, University of Southern Mississippi, 1997; best book award, 1997, for *From Head to Toe,* and platinum book award, 1999, for *You Can Make a Collage,* both from Oppenhein Toy Portfolio; Regina Medal, Catholic Library Association, 1999; Literary Lights for Children award, Boston Public Library, 2000;

Eric Carle

Japan Picture Book Awards translation winner, 2000, for *Hello, Red Fox*. Also recipient of numerous other awards, including awards from New York Art Directors Show, New York Type Directors Show, Society of Illustrators Show, Best Book Jacket of the Year Show, and the Carnegie Award for Excellence in Video for Children.

Notable citations, including Child Study Association citation, 1970, for *Pancakes, Pancakes;* American Library Association (ALA) notable book, for *The Very Busy Spider,* and 1971, for *Do You Want to Be My Friend?;* 100 Titles for Reading and Sharing selection, for *The Very Quiet Cricket,* and Gift List selections, 1971, for *Do You Want to Be My Friend?,* and 1972, for *Secret Birthday Message,* all from the New York Public Library; ALA notable book, for *The Very Busy Spider,* and 1971, for *Do You Want to Be My Friend?;* Brooklyn Museum of Art citation, 1973, for *The Very Hungry Caterpillar;* Outstanding Science Trade Book for Children, *A House for Hermit Crab;* National Children's Trade Book in the field of social studies, 1977, for *The Grouchy Ladybug;* Children's Choices award, Children's Book Council, for *The Very Lonely Firefly,* 1984, for *Brown Bear, Brown Bear* (both with the International Reading Association) and 1987, for *Papa, Please Get the Moon for Me;* Parents Choice award, 1986, for *Papa, Please Get the Moon for Me,* and 1988, for *The Mixed-Up Chameleon* (paperback); Jane Addams Children's Book Honorary Award, 1987, for *All in a Day;* ALA/Booklist Children's Editor's Choices award, for *Animals, Animals,* and Best Books of the 80s pick, for *The Very Busy Spider,* both 1989; *Parenting Magazine* certificate of excellence, 1989, for *Animals, Animals;* California Children's Book and Video award, 1990, for *The Very Quiet Cricket* (picture book category); *Redbook* top ten children's books of the year, 1989, for *Animals, Animals,* and 1990, for *The Very Quiet Cricket;* *Parents Magazine* Best Kid's Books award, 1989, for *Animals, Animals,* and 1995, for *The Very Lonely Firefly;* Buckeye Children's Book Award, Ohio Council of the International Reading Association, 1993, for *The Very Quiet Cricket;* Association of Booksellers Children Bookseller's Choices award, 1995, for *The Very Hungry Caterpillar* board book; David McCord Children's Literature citation, Framingham State College and Nobscot Reading Council of the International Reading Association, 1995; National Parenting Publications award, 1998, for *You Can Make a Collage;* Bank Street College Best Books award, 1998, for *Hello, Red Fox;* numerous titles selected for American Bookseller's Pick of the List. Additional awards for *The Very Busy Spider* include Library of Congress Advisory Committee recommended title; Best Books for Children selection, R.R. Bowker and Co.; Children's Editor's choice, Booklist; *Horn Book* Fanfair title; California Reading Initiative title. *The Very Hungry Caterpillar* was named Book of the Year by the California Reading Initiative, and was named among England's best books in 1971. *Papa, Please Get the Moon for Me* was awarded the gold medal during the Bratslavia Biennial of Illustration. *The Very Lonely Firefly* was named a Kansas City Reading Circle selection in 1996.

Writings

SELF-ILLUSTRATED

The Say-with-Me ABC Book, Holt, 1967.

1, 2, 3 to the Zoo, World Publishing, 1968.

The Very Hungry Caterpillar, World Publishing, 1969.

Pancakes, Pancakes, Knopf, 1970.

The Tiny Seed, Crowell, 1970 (published in England as *The Tiny Seed and the Giant Flower,* Nelson, 1970).

Do You Want to Be My Friend?, Crowell, 1971.

The Rooster Who Set Out to See the World, F. Watts, 1972, published as *Rooster's Off to See the World,* Picture Book Studio, 1987.

The Secret Birthday Message, Crowell, 1972.

The Very Long Tail (folding book), Crowell, 1972.

The Very Long Train (folding book), Crowell, 1972.

Walter the Baker: An Old Story Retold and Illustrated by Eric Carle, Knopf, 1972.

Have You Seen My Cat?, F. Watts, 1973.

I See a Song, Crowell, 1973, Scholastic, 1996.

My Very First Library, Crowell, 1974.

All about Arthur (an Absolutely Absurd Ape), F. Watts, 1974.

The Mixed-Up Chameleon, Crowell, 1975.

Eric Carle's Storybook: Seven Tales by the Brothers Grimm, F. Watts, 1976.

The Grouchy Ladybug, Crowell, 1977 (published in England as *The Bad-Tempered Ladybird,* Hamish Hamilton, 1977).

(Reteller) *Seven Stories by Hans Christian Andersen,* F. Watts, 1978.

Watch Out! A Giant!, Philomel, 1978.

Twelve Tales from Aesop: Retold and Illustrated, Philomel, 1980.

The Honeybee and the Robber: A Moving Picture Book, Philomel, 1981.

Catch the Ball, Philomel, 1982, Scholastic, 1998.

Let's Paint a Rainbow, Philomel, 1982, Scholastic, 1998.

What's for Lunch?, Philomel, 1982, Scholastic, 1998.

The Very Busy Spider, Philomel, 1985.

All around Us, Picture Book Studio, 1986.

Papa, Please Get the Moon for Me, Picture Book Studio, 1986.

A House for Hermit Crab, Picture Book Studio, 1987.

Eric Carle's Treasury of Classic Stories for Children, Orchard Books, 1988.

Eric Carle's Animals, Animals, edited by Laura Whipple, Philomel, 1989.

The Very Quiet Cricket, Philomel, 1990.

Eric Carle's Dragons, Dragons, edited by Whipple, Philomel, 1991.

Draw Me a Star, Philomel, 1992.

Today Is Monday, Philomel, 1993.

My Apron: A Story from My Childhood, Philomel, 1994.

The Very Lonely Firefly, Philomel, 1995.

Little Cloud, Philomel, 1996.

The Art of Eric Carle, Philomel, 1996.

The Very Special World of Eric Carle, Penguin Putnam, 1996.

From Head to Toe, HarperCollins, 1997.

Flora and the Tiger: Nineteen Very Short Stories from My Life, Philomel, 1997.

Hello, Red Fox, Simon and Schuster, 1998.

Carle's self-illustrated Draw Me a Star, *set in his childhood home of Germany, relates a creation story in which an artist invents objects based on the requests of his other drawings.*

You Can Make a Collage, Klutz, 1998.
The Eric Carle Library, HarperCollins, 1998.
The Very Clumsy Click Beetle, Putnam, 1999.
Does a Kangaroo Have a Mother, Too?, HarperCollins, 2000.
Dream Snow, Putnam, 2000.

"MY VERY FIRST LIBRARY" SERIES; SELF-ILLUSTRATED

My Very First Book of Colors, Crowell, 1974.
My Very First Book of Numbers, Crowell, 1974.
My Very First Book of Shapes, Crowell, 1974.
My Very First Book of Words, Crowell, 1974.
My Very First Book of Food, Crowell, 1986.
My Very First Book of Growth, Crowell, 1986.
My Very First Book of Heads and Tails, Crowell, 1986.
My Very First Book of Homes, Crowell, 1986.
My Very First Book of Motion, Crowell, 1986.
My Very First Book of Sounds, Crowell, 1986.
My Very First Book of Tools, Crowell, 1986.
My Very First Book of Touch, Crowell, 1986.

ILLUSTRATOR

Sune Engelbrektson, *Gravity at Work and Play,* Holt, 1963.
Engelbrektson, *The Sun Is a Star,* Holt, 1963.
Bill Martin, *If You Can Count to Ten,* Holt, 1964.
Aesop's Fables for Modern Readers, Pauper Press, 1965.

Louise Bachelder, editor, *Nature Thoughts,* Pauper Press, 1965.
Lila Perl, *Red-Flannel Hash and Shoo-Fly Pie: America's Regional Foods and Festivals,* World Publishers, 1965.
Samm S. Baker, *Indoor and Outdoor Grow-It Book,* Random House, 1966.
Bachelder, editor, *On Friendship,* Pauper Press, 1966.
Martin, *Brown Bear, Brown Bear, What Do You See?,* Holt, 1967.
Carl H. Voss, *In Search of Meaning: Living Religions of the World,* World Publishers, 1968.
Nora Roberts Wainer, *The Whale in a Jail,* Funk, 1968.
William Knowlton, *The Boastful Fisherman,* Knopf, 1970.
Martin, *A Ghost Story,* Holt, 1970.
Eleanor O. Heady, *Tales of the Nimipoo from the Land of the Nez Pierce Indians,* World Publishing 1970.
Aileen Fisher, *Feathered Ones and Furry,* Crowell, 1971.
George Mendoza, *The Scarecrow Clock,* Holt, 1971.
Vanishing Animals (posters), F. Watts, 1972.
Fisher, *Do Bears Have Mothers Too?,* Crowell, 1973 (published in England as *Animals and Their Babies,* Hamish Hamilton, 1974).
Isaac Bashevis Singer, *Why Noah Chose the Dove,* translated by Elizabeth Shub, Farrar, Straus, 1974.
Norma Green, reteller, *The Hole in the Dike,* Crowell, 1975.

Norton Juster, *Otter Nonsense,* Philomel, 1982.

Hans Baumann, *Chip Has Many Brothers,* Philomel, 1983.

Richard Buckley, *The Foolish Tortoise,* Picture Book Studio, 1985.

Buckley, *The Greedy Python,* Picture Book Studio, 1985.

Alice McLerran, *The Mountain That Loved a Bird,* Picture Book Studio, 1985.

Mitsumasa Anno, *All in a Day,* Dowaya (Tokyo), 1986.

Arnold Sundgaard, *The Lamb and the Butterfly,* Orchard Books, 1988.

Martin, *Polar Bear, Polar Bear, What Do You Hear?,* Holt, 1991.

Martin, *Brown Bear, Brown Bear, What Do You See?,* Holt, 1992.

Peter Martins, *Tributes,* Morrow, 1998.

Glassman, Peter, editor, *Oz: The Hundredth Anniversary Celebration,* HarperCollins, 2000.

Sidelights

Eric Carle "is one of the most beloved illustrators of children's books," according to *Booklist*'s Ilene Cooper. The author/illustrator of over seventy books, most of them bestsellers and many award-winners, Carle has had his work translated into more than thirty languages with sales in the millions. Known as a pioneer of the novelty book, Carle has developed innovative picture books for very young readers which include pages that grow larger as a ladybug meets ever larger animals, which have holes in them bored by a ravenous caterpillar, or which contain computer chips that provide the chirping of a cricket and the flashing lights of a firefly—books which bridge the gap between touchable book and readable toy. As Ethel Heins noted in *Horn Book,* "Almost from the start [Carle] has worked in collage—brilliantly painted tissue paper, cut and layered for nuances in color and texture." Even as a child, Eric Carle was fascinated by drawing, and he first displayed this playfully artistic approach to picture books with his 1969 *The Very Hungry Caterpillar,* a book that is still in print around the world and as popular as ever. Carle blends simple, primary-colored cut-paper art depicting mostly small animals and insects with direct and repetitive text, a winning formula for his legion of very young readers.

"Until I was six years old I lived in Syracuse, N.Y., where I went to kindergarten. I remember happy days with large sheets of paper, bright colors and wide brushes!" the author once told *Something about the Author (SATA).* Just after Carle started first grade, his family moved to Stuttgart, Germany, his father's original home. There Carle grew up in Hitler's Germany, a country gearing for war. His strict schooling was counterpoised with encouragement from an art teacher who praised the young boy's drawings. He also quickly made friends and was made to feel secure in the warm circle of a large extended family. But when war came in 1939, Carle's world changed. His father was absent from the family for eight years—first in the German army and then in a Soviet prisoner of war camp. Along with other children his age, Carle was a loyal German citizen, following news of the war and each of Hitler's victories. When the fortunes of war began to change, Carle and his family would spend nights in the local air raid shelter. Finally he was removed to the country to be safe from the bombing raids.

With the end of the war, Germany slowly recovered. Carle's father returned to his family in 1947; Carle entered the fine arts academy and was soon designing posters for the American information center in Stuttgart. Finally, in 1952, Carle felt confident enough in his art to take his portfolio and return to the United States. Soon after arriving, however, he was drafted into the U.S. Army and was stationed back in Stuttgart. There he met his first wife. After Carle's discharge the couple moved back to New York; they eventually had two children together, but separated in 1964. During this time, Carle worked as a designer and art director. In 1963, Carle quit his full-time company job to begin working as a freelance artist. As he related in his *Something about the Author Autobiography Series (SAAS)* essay, "I had come to the conclusion that I didn't want to sit in meetings, write memos, entertain clients, and catch commuter trains. I simply wanted to create pictures."

Carle first became interested in children's literature when he was asked to do illustrations for a book by Bill Martin. "I found Bill's approach to the world of the preschool and first grade child very stimulating; it reawakened in me struggles of my own childhood," Carle commented to Delores R. Klingberg in *Language Arts.* Remembering his difficult early schooldays in Germany, Carle added that the conflicts from that time "remained hidden until the opportunity and insight presented themselves. Through my work with Bill Martin, an unfinished area of my own growing up had been touched."

"I didn't realize it clearly then, but my life was beginning to move onto its true course," Carle said in the *SAAS* essay. "The long, dark time of growing up in wartime Germany, the cruelly enforced discipline of my school years there, the dutifully performed work at my jobs in advertising—all these were finally losing their rigid grip on me. The child inside me—who had been so suddenly and sharply uprooted and repressed—was beginning to come joyfully back to life."

"It was then that I met Ann Beneduce (then editor with World), and with her kind help and understanding I created my first two books: *1, 2, 3 to the Zoo* and *The Very Hungry Caterpillar,*" Carle told *SATA.* "A mixture of negative and positive influences had led to a fruitful expression." Both of Carle's first books contain bold, collage pictures and feature many different animals. The author recalled in a *Books for Keeps* article that his early years with his father taught him about nature. "We used to go for long walks in the countryside together, and he would peel back tree bark to show me what was underneath it, lift rocks to reveal the insects. As a result, I have an abiding love and affection for small, insignificant animals."

1, 2, 3 to the Zoo was published in 1968 and follows several animals on their train trip to live in a zoo, with a tiny mouse observing each car. The book is full of "superb paintings of animals, bold, lively, handsome, spreading over big double-spread pages," Adele McRae of the *Christian Science Monitor* wrote. "His elephant is all magnificent power, his giraffes a precision of delicacy, his monkeys a tangle of liveliness. This is a book to grow with its owner. The tiny mouse lurking in every picture may remain invisible to the smallest reader and, as the title implies, the book is waiting to teach the art of counting." Carle's award-winning book *The Very Hungry Caterpillar* was published in 1969. "I was just playfully punching holes in a stack of paper," the author told Molly McQuade of *Publishers Weekly*, "and I thought to myself, 'This could've been done by a bookworm.' From that came a caterpillar." *The Very Hungry Caterpillar* "tells the story of a caterpillar's lifecycle, from egg to butterfly," as John A. Cunliffe described it in *Children's Book Review*. The caterpillar "eats through a great many things on the way—one apple on Monday, two pears on Tuesday, and so on, to a list of ten exotic items on Saturday." Cunliffe went on to note "the book's delight, and originality, lie in the way in which these cumulative items are shown . . . . The text is brief and simple, and has a satisfying cumulative effect that neatly matches the pictures, which are large and bold, in brilliant colours and crisp forms set against the white page, mainly achieved by the use of collage."

Not only does *Caterpillar* contain brightly colored shapes designed to appeal to young children, it also has holes in the pages that match the path of the caterpillar. As Carle explained in *Books for Your Children,* the holes in *Caterpillar* "are a bridge from toy to book, from plaything, from the touching to understanding . . . . In the very young child the thought travels mightily fast from fingertips to brain. This book has many layers. There is fun, nonsense, colour, surprise. There is learning, but if the child ignores the learning part, let

Little Frog explains several optical illusions to his mother, allowing young readers to play with the effects themselves. (From Hello, Red Fox, *written and illustrated by Carle.)*

him, it's OK. Someday he'll hit upon it by himself. That is the way we learn." Carle's approach in *Caterpillar* has proved so popular that the book has sold millions of copies and been translated into over thirty languages.

Do You Want to Be My Friend? is another innovative picture book filled with bright and colorful animals. The only words in the story are the title question "Do you want to be my friend?" spoken by a lonely mouse, and a joyful "yes" from the new friend he finally discovers. Calling it "a perfect picture book for a small child," *Washington Post Book World* contributor Polly Goodwin added that *Do You Want to Be My Friend?* "offers a splendid opportunity for a pre-reader, with a little initial help, to create his own story based on the brilliantly colored, wonderfully expressive pictures." *The Rooster Who Set Out to See the World,* later published as *Rooster's Off to See the World,* is another "brilliantly colored picture story that does double duty as a counting book," Lillian N. Gerhardt said in *Library Journal.* The story follows a rooster who decides to travel and see the world. As he travels, he adds friends in twos, threes, fours, and fives. "The sums are presented pictorially in the corners of the page," Marcus Crouch of *Junior Bookshelf* noted, but this doesn't distract from Carle's "exquisitely drawn coloured pictures. Mr. Carle is still the best of all artists for the very young," Crouch concluded.

Carle introduced another innovation in his 1977 book *The Grouchy Ladybug:* the pages grow in size as larger and larger animals appear on them. The story follows a bad-tempered ladybug as she challenges different creatures, starting with other insects and ending with the whale whose cutout tail slaps her back to her home leaf. While Carle presents such instructive concepts as time and size, "this book is chiefly a pleasure to read and to look at," Caroline Moorhead wrote in the *Times Educational Supplement,* "with its cross and good-natured ladybirds . . . and its deep-toned illustrations of animals."

The Very Busy Spider follows a spider that spends her day spinning a web, which grows larger with each page. Although she is interrupted by a number of farm animals, the spider continues her work until the web is finished and she catches the fly that has been bothering the other animals. Because the web and fly are raised above the page so that they can be felt, the book "is obviously of value to the visually handicapped," as Julia Eccleshare commented in the *Times Literary Supplement.* Denise M. Wilms agreed, writing in *Booklist* "this good-looking picture book has just the ingredients" to become an "instant classic."

More of these "Very" insect books have followed. *The Very Quiet Cricket* tells the tale of a cricket who wants to find someone to talk to. He desperately wants to be able to rub his wings together and make a sound to return the greetings of other insects, and finally, after much labor, he gets his wish. The cricket's sound is reproduced via a battery-aided computer chip on the final page of the book. "Carle has created yet another celebration of nature," declared Starr LaTronica in a *School Library Journal* review of the book. LaTronica further noted, "Typical of Carle's style, the language is simple, with rhythm, repetition, and alliteration to delight young listeners. Painted collage illustrations are lavish and expressive." A *Books for Keeps* reviewer called the same book "perfect," remarking that "the lyrical text illustrated in Carle's individual and immediately recognisable style, moves to a moment of pure astonishment that touches every young reader."

The Very Lonely Firefly presents another lovable insect in search of love, a firefly that goes out into the night in search of others like itself. In its quest for illuminated buddies, it mistakes headlights, fireworks, even a flashlight for other fireflies before it finally finds its own kind on the final page of the book, with battery-powered twinkling lights. Roger Sutton, writing in *Bulletin of the Center for Children's Books,* noted that "toddlers will appreciate the predictability and rhythm of the text and the bold shapes of the firefly and other figures set against the streaky blue-black sky." Reviewing this supposed final book in the series, Christina Dorr concluded in *School Library Journal,* "This is a compelling accomplishment that will leave readers and listeners alike wishing Carle would turn the quartet into a quintet. A guaranteed winner as a read-aloud or read-alone." In the event Dorr, and thousands of young fans, were rewarded with a fifth entrant in the series in 1999, *The Very Clumsy Click Beetle,* about this peculiar insect which must learn to jump in the air in order to move once it has fallen on its back. Julie Corsaro called the book a "winning addition to Carle's oeuvre," in a *Booklist* review.

Carle has produced another series of books that deal with numbers, letters of the alphabet, tools, and a plethora of other activities and subjects for the very young. The "My Very First Book" series is designed in a "Dutch-door" style, each page split in half with separate illustrations on top and bottom halves so that the young reader can mix and match images. Again, such images are designed from brilliantly vibrant bits of collage tissue paper. Additionally, Carle has also written his own versions of familiar children's works, such as Grimm's fairy tales, Aesop's fables, and Hans Christian Andersen's stories. Reviewing *Eric Carle's Treasury of Classic Stories for Children,* a compilation of his retellings, LaTronica noted in *School Library Journal* "Carle's distinctive style of bright watercolor and collage illustration provides an excellent complement to the lively text."

Poems for young readers—from haiku to Kipling—were adapted for two popular picture books for the young reader, *Eric Carle's Animals, Animals* and *Eric Carle's Dragons, Dragons.* Susan Schuller, reviewing the first named in *School Library Journal,* observed, "Carle's distinctive tissue paper collages bring brilliance and verve to this excellent anthology of poems which conveys the wonder and diversity of the animal world." Betsy Hearne commented in the *Bulletin of the Center for Children's Books* that *Eric Carle's Animals, Animals*

provided a "splendid showcase for Carle's dramatic double image." Reviewing *Eric Carle's Dragons, Dragons,* a contributor to *Kirkus Reviews* called it a "well-chosen, gorgeously illustrated collection of poetry."

Carle has also produced many stand-alone titles that both delight and educate very young readers. *Today Is Monday* takes the young reader on a song-journey through the days of the week and the foods eaten every day. "Lovely to look at; delightful to know," concluded Trevor Dickinson in a *Books for Keeps* review. In *Little Cloud,* Carle tells of the "whimsical world of ever-changing shapes in the sky," according to Kathy Mitchell in *School Library Journal.* The cloud in mention delights in changing its shape into a lamb or airplane or shark, finally joining the others in one large rain cloud. "Children will enjoy the simple text and the colorful illustrations," Mitchell concluded. Dickinson, reviewing *Little Cloud* in the *School Librarian,* felt that the book was a "delight in its own artistic right," and would "encourage close and interested observation of the wider world."

Carle's 1997 *From Head to Toe* presents animals and multiethnic children demonstrating various body movements. "Keeping both text and graphics to a minimum, Carle proves once again just how effective simplicity can be," wrote a reviewer for *Publishers Weekly.* The same contributor concluded that children will "eagerly clap, stomp, kick and wriggle their way through these pages from start to finish." *Booklist*'s Cooper observed, "Carle's signature strong collages are put to good use in this book about movement." In *Hello, Red Fox,* "Carle asks readers to engage in optical illusions to view his illustrations for a story that becomes an unforgettable lesson in complementary colors," according to a *Kirkus Reviews* critic. After staring at a picture of the fox in green, for ten seconds, the reader then shifts focus to a pure white facing page and the fox appears in red as an after image. A reviewer for *Publishers Weekly* felt that Carle once again proved the old adage that "Less is more" with a "straightforward, repetitive text and minimalist cut-paper art." *Booklist*'s Linda Perkins commented that this "playful starting point for science discussions at home or at school" would be "sure to intrigue children."

Carle has used his childhood in Germany for several other books, including his award-winning *Draw Me a Star,* the autobiographical *My Apron: A Story from My Childhood,* and his only book for older readers, *Flora and Tiger: Nineteen Very Short Stories from My Life.* In *Draw Me a Star,* he harks back to memories of his German grandmother and links it to a dream that parallels the story of Creation. A reviewer for *Books for Keeps* called this a "splendid book for its colour, its richness and its potential for thought and imagination." *School Library Journal*'s Eve Larkin thought *Draw Me a Star* was an "inspired book in every sense of the word." *My Apron: A Story from My Childhood* tells of a young boy whose aunt makes him an apron so that he can help his uncle plaster the chimney. In this novelty book, a child-size apron is included for young readers.

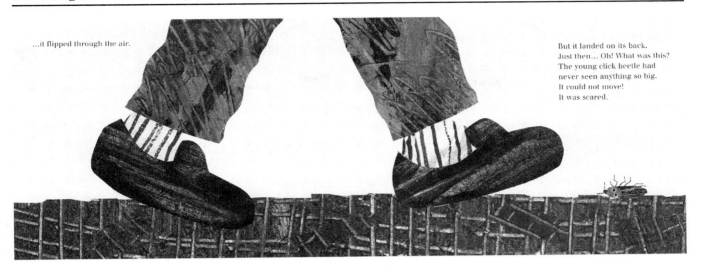

...it flipped through the air.

But it landed on its back.
Just then... Oh! What was this?
The young click beetle had
never seen anything so big.
It could not move!
It was scared.

Teaching young readers the value of perseverance, Carle penned the tale of a young click beetle who must try repeatedly to land on his feet. Clicking sounds from an electronic chip add to the climax of the tale. (From The Very Clumsy Click Beetle, *written and illustrated by Carle.)*

Flora and Tiger: Nineteen Very Short Stories from My Life presents "spare autobiographical vignettes that take place from [Carle's] childhood to the present," according to *Booklist*'s Hazel Rochman. Jane Claes noted in *School Library Journal* that these "sketches are sometimes moving, sometimes funny, and sometimes uplifting" and are a "super addition to any study of Carle or his work."

Such work continues into the new millennium. With his 2000 title, *Does a Kangaroo Have a Mother, Too?*, Carle asks this question about ten other animals, to show that all animals have mothers. Reviewing the title in *Booklist*, Tim Arnold noted, "Almost no author/illustrator over the past 30 years has played a more prominent role in the literary lives of preschoolers than Eric Carle." Arnold further commented, "His large, inviting graphic animals have consistently delighted and taught children during early stages of development. This latest effort is no exception." Whatever their topic, all of Carle's works are educational tools that interest children with their bold, imaginative drawings and whimsical presentations. "We underestimate children," Carle said in a 1982 *Early Years* interview. "They have tremendous capacities for learning." Such a belief in the inquisitiveness of the child has not altered in Carle over the years. In his web page, the author/illustrator responds to frequently asked questions about himself. Under "hobbies" he notes, "I would have to say my work is my hobby. And my hobby is my work. Even when I'm not working in my studio, I might be thinking about future books. I will probably never retire from creating books."

Carle devotes a multi-layered artistic sensibility to this "hobby." As Donnarae MacCann and Olga Richard claimed in *Wilson Library Bulletin*, "Eric Carle is like a half dozen creative people rolled into one." Because of Carle's skill in writing for pre-schoolers, his "innovativeness and artistic discipline," and his ability to turn a book into a toy, the critics concluded, "a child reared on such books will blossom into a confirmed bibliophile."

Biographical and Critical Sources

BOOKS

Children's Books and Their Creators, edited by Anita Silvey, Houghton Mifflin, 1995, pp. 120-21.
Children's Literature Review, Volume 10, Gale, 1986.
Famous Children's Authors, edited by Shirley Norby and Gregory Ryan, Denison, 1988, p. 18.
Something about the Author Autobiography Series, Volume 6, Gale, 1988, pp. 33-51.
St. James Guide to Children's Writers, 5th edition, edited by Sara Pendergast and Tom Pendergast, St. James Press, 1999, pp. 204-05.

PERIODICALS

Booklist, June 1, 1985, Denise M. Wilms, review of *The Very Busy Spider,* p. 1398; September 15, 1996, Ilene Cooper, review of *The Art of Eric Carle,* p. 253; April 15, 1997, I. Cooper, review of *From Head to Toe,* p. 1431; December 15, 1997, Hazel Rochman, review of *Flora and Tiger,* p. 692; April, 1998, Linda Perkins, review of *Hello, Red Fox,* p. 1329; October 1, 1999, Julie Corsaro, review of *The Very Clumsy Click Beetle,* p. 360; January 1, 2000, Tim Arnold, review of *Does a Kangaroo Have a Mother, Too?,* p. 930.
Books for Keeps, May, 1985, Eric Carle, "Authorgraph No. 2: Eric Carle," pp. 14-15; November, 1987, p. 4; May, 1994, Trevor Dickinson, review of *Today Is Monday,* p. 33; March, 1995, p. 25; July, 1995, review of *Draw Me a Star,* p. 6; December, 1996, p. 82; January, 1997, p. 18; March, 1997, p. 7; June, 1997, p. 352; November, 1997, review of *The Very Quiet Cricket,* pp. 5-6; January, 1998, p. 156.
Books for Your Children, Spring, 1978, Eric Carle, "From Hungry Caterpillars to Bad Tempered Ladybirds," p. 7.

Bulletin of the Center for Children's Books, October, 1989, Betsy Hearne, review of *Eric Carle's Animals, Animals,* p. 47; November, 1990, p. 56; July-August, 1995 Roger Sutton, review of *The Very Lonely Firefly,* pp. 379-80.

Children's Book Review, February, 1971, John A. Cunliffe, review of *The Very Hungry Caterpillar,* p. 14.

Christian Science Monitor, May 1, 1969, Adele McRae, "Crayoned Morality Plays," p. B2.

Early Years, April, 1982, "Eric Carle's Children's Books Are to Touch," p. 23.

Horn Book, March-April, 1997, Ethel Heins, review of *The Art of Eric Carle,* pp. 215-16.

Junior Bookshelf, October, 1972, Marcus Crouch, review of *The Rooster Who Set Out to See the World,* pp. 301-02; January, 1994, p. 14; June, 1994, p. 93; October, 1995, p. 167.

Kirkus Reviews, July 1, 1989, p. 988; July 15, 1991, review of *Eric Carle's Dragons, Dragons,* p. 940; June 1, 1995, p. 778; August 1, 1996, p. 1159; April 1, 1997, p. 551; February 1, 1998, review of *Hello, Red Fox,* p. 194.

Language Arts, April, 1977, Delores R. Klingberg, "Eric Carle," p. 447.

Library Journal, June 15, 1973, Lillian N. Gerhardt, review of *The Rooster Who Set Out to See the World,* pp. 1992-93.

Los Angeles Times Book Review, April 11, 1999, p. 6.

Magpies, July, 1996, p. 26.

Publishers Weekly, September 29, 1989, Molly McQuade, "Ballyhooing Birthdays: Four Children's Classics and How They Grew," pp. 28-29; February 17, 1997, review of *From Head to Toe,* p. 219; January 26, 1998, review of *Hello, Red Fox,* p. 91; October 18, 1999, p. 86; January 10, 2000, p. 66.

School Arts, May, 1999, p. 18.

School Librarian, August, 1997, p. 130; November, 1997, Trevor Dickinson, review of *Little Cloud,* p. 184; Autumn, 1998, p. 129.

School Library Journal, April, 1988, Starr LaTronica, review of *Eric Carle's Treasury of Classic Stories for Children,* p. 94; November, 1989, Susan Schuller, review of *Eric Carle's Animals, Animals,* p. 101; December, 1990, S. LaTronica, review of *The Very Quiet Cricket,* p. 72; October, 1992, Eve Larkin, review of *Draw Me a Star,* p. 80; November, 1992. p. 133; April, 1993, p. 109; November, 1994, p. 73; February, 1995, p. 126; August, 1995, Christina Dorr, review of *The Very Lonely Firefly,* pp. 120-21; May, 1996, Kathy Mitchell, review of *Little Cloud,* p. 85; December, 1996, p. 46; April, 1997, p. 120; February, 1998, Jane Claes, review of *Flora and Tiger,* p. 113; July, 1998, p. 71; November, 1999, p. 112.

Times Educational Supplement, February 3, 1978, Caroline Moorhead, "Animal/Animal, Animal/Human," p. 45.

Times Literary Supplement, March 29, 1985, Julia Eccleshare, "Following the Thread," p. 351.

Washington Post Book World, Part II, May 9, 1971, Polly Goodwin, review of *Do You Want to Be My Friend?,* p. 4.

Wilson Library Bulletin, January, 1989, Donnarae MacCann and Olga Richard, "Picture Books for Children," pp. 90-91.

ON-LINE

The Official Eric Carle Web Site, www.eric-carle.com/ (August 9, 2000).

—Sketch by J. Sydney Jones

*   *   *

CHAPMAN, Gillian 1955-

Personal

Born April 18, 1955, in London, England. *Education:* Harrow School of Art, higher diploma in illustration, 1977.

Addresses

Home and office—Brantwood House, Afton Rd., Freshwater Bay, Isle of Wight, P040 9TT, United Kingdom. *E-mail*—brantwood@freeuk.com

Career

Designer, illustrator, and writer of children's books.

Writings

My First Picture Dictionary, Ward Lock, 1985.
Little Bear Tales, Smithmark Publishers, 1987.

Gillian Chapman

(With Pam Robson) *Making Books: A Step-by Step Guide to Your Own Publishing,* Millbrook Press (Brookfield, CT), 1992

(With Robson) *Making Shaped Books: With Patterns,* Millbrook Press (Brookfield, CT), 1993.

(With Robson) *Making Maps and Mazes: A First Guide to Mapmaking,* Millbrook Press, 1993.

The Noisy Jungle, Campbell Books (London), 1994.

Pretty Parrots, Campbell Books, 1994.

The Noisy Farmyard, Campbell Books, 1994.

Chirpy Chicks, Campbell Books, 1994.

(With Robson) *Art from Fabric: With Projects Using Rags, Old Clothing, and Remnants,* Thomson Learning (New York), 1995.

(With Robson) *Art from Paper: With Projects Using Waste Paper and Printed Materials,* Thomson Learning, 1995.

(With Robson) *Art from Rocks and Shells: With Projects Using Pebbles, Feathers, Flotsam and Jetsam,* Thomson Learning, 1995.

(With Robson) *Art from Wood: With Projects Using Branches, Leaves, and Seeds,* Thomson Learning, 1995.

(With Robson) *Exploring Time,* Millbrook Press, 1995.

(With Robson) *Making Masks for Children,* Macdonald Young (Hove, England), 1996.

(With Robson) *Art from Sand and Earth: With Projects Using Clay, Plaster, and Natural Fibres,* Raintree Steck-Vaughn (Austin, TX), 1997.

(With Robson) *Art from Packaging: With Projects Using Cardboard, Plastics, Foil, and Tape,* Raintree Steck-Vaughn, 1997.

The Aztecs, Heinemann Interactive Library (Des Plaines, IL), 1997.

The Egyptians, Heinemann Interactive Library, 1997.

The Greeks, Heinemann Interactive Library, 1998.

The Romans, Heinemann Interactive Library, 1998.

Spring, Raintree Steck-Vaughn, 1998.

Summer, Raintree Steck-Vaughn, 1998.

Autumn, Raintree Steck-Vaughn, 1998.

Winter, Raintree Steck-Vaughn, 1998.

Vikings, Heinemann Interactive Library, 2000.

Art from the Past, Heinemann (Des Plaines, IL), 2000.

Santa's Workshop, Fernleigh Books, 2000.

Mice's Toy Box, Fernleigh Books, 2000.

Here Comes Christmas, Fernleigh Books, 2000.

Illustrator for several books by Myrna Daitz and Dorothy Savage.

Sidelights

British artist Gillian Chapman has written or collaborated on dozens of engaging books for children that provide "how-to" instructions for a variety of craft projects. Often, Chapman's books delve into a particular theme—the ancient culture of the Aztecs, for instance, or wintertime celebrations around the world—and her illustrations and photographs show readers how to make relevant art projects, based on these cultures, from simple household materials.

The ancient Egyptians loved fresh fruit and grew pomegranates, figs, dates and grapes in their gardens and vineyards, but not citrus fruit.

Decorate the ends of the fruit boat with strips of coloured paper.

4. Keep the longer bundles to the outer sides to form the boat shape. When they are all sewn together, bind lengths of string around each end.

5. Paint the dowels and leave to dry. Decorate the box with scraps of coloured paper. Glue the dowels to the four corners of the box.

6. Attach the box to the boat by pushing the dowels in-between the reed bundles. Glue them in place with PVA and leave to dry.

In her self-illustrated book **The Egyptians,** *Chapman discusses the everyday and religious art of the ancient culture, and then shows how to make one's own version of various artifacts.*

For many years, Chapman illustrated children's books written by others; she had also built up a steady commercial client base for her images since leaving the Harrow School of Art with a higher diploma in 1977. One of the earliest works for which she received author credit was *My First Picture Dictionary,* a 1985 title aimed at preschoolers. The pages each contained a letter of the alphabet, and offered Chapman's renderings of several common objects or animals that began with the particular letter. Though a rather simple format for the age group, Chapman's imaginative mettle showed in the interesting juxtapositions she tried to create—a magician with mice, for instance, or a dolphin adjacent to a figure in diving gear. Margery Fisher, reviewing the work in *Growing Point,* praised its "lively illustrations and a splendid choice of subjects," which she believed added to the book's educational appeal.

Most of Chapman's other works, however, are geared toward elementary-age children. As she told *SATA:* "My research for the first craft books led me into a number of schools and I asked Pam Robson, a primary teacher, to collaborate with me. The success of the series took us into many schools and libraries in England and Wales, where we showed both children and teachers how to make projects in our practical workshops." One of the first titles from this collaboration, which began in the early 1990s, was *Making Books: A Step-by Step Guide to Your Own Publishing.* Here, the author/illustrator duo explain a bit about the history of bookmaking and bookbinding, discuss the different types of books—such as rag and pop-up—and describe the materials traditionally used. Their activity pages show readers how to sew and bind a work, through easy instructions, photographs, and Chapman's drawings.

Chapman and Robson also wrote the 1993 title, *Making Maps and Mazes: A First Guide to Mapmaking,* which distinguishes the many different kinds of maps, such as grids, aerial views, and linear diagrams. The authors also explain, through the text and illustration, how these various kinds of guides are related to mazes and labyrinths. That same year, they also put forth *Making Shaped Books: With Patterns,* which prompted *School Library Journal* reviewer Melissa Gross to remark, "the layout is attractive and the illustrations are good-quality, full-color photographs." They also earned praise for a 1995 title, *Exploring Time,* designed to help readers aged eight to ten move beyond telling time and into the realm of life spans, solar time, and lunar time. Charts, illustrations and a glossary of new words enhance this work's educational value. "This attractively formatted title is a winner," wrote *School Library Journal* writer Susan Chmurynsky.

In *Making Masks for Children,* published in 1996, Chapman and Robson chronicle the history of masks in human civilization over the ages, and how they are still an integral part of ceremony and society in some parts of the world. They provide examples of different types of masks—a medieval helmet designed to protect, for instance, or a Japanese Noh mask used for traditional theater—and then show readers how to make their own versions. "The spreads are dominated by vividly colourful, sharply photographed masks," noted Kevin Steinberger in a *Magpies* review.

Chapman has also penned a series of "Seasonal Crafts" books that were published in England in 1997, and by a Texas publisher the following year. Directed at the early-elementary-age reader, *Autumn, Winter, Spring,* and *Summer* discuss each particular season's festivities in various parts of the world, and then include related craft projects. Another series, "Art from the Past," appeared around the same time. In *The Egyptians,* Chapman discusses the everyday and religious art of the ancient culture, and then shows how to make one's own version of scarab jewelry and other artifacts—even a catlike mummy. *The Aztecs* features projects for do-it-yourself mosaics, a textile, and a wheeled toy. All the learning activities, noted Marcia Hupp in a review of both titles for *School Library Journal,* "are attractive, often ambitious, and generally reflective of the culture."

Chapman won praise for *The Greeks* and *The Romans,* two other entrants in the "Art from the Past" series that appeared in 1998. Readers can learn how to craft papier-mâché pottery based on Greek urns, and even make a "Roman Ruin Desk Organizer" modeled after the Forum. After giving a brief history and art lesson about the particular culture, Chapman moves on to the craft projects, and includes safety tips and definitions of unfamiliar terms. "These titles offer sophisticated-looking crafts that children will want to try," remarked Wendy Lukeheart in a review of both for *School Library Journal.*

Chapman told *SATA:* "I enjoy all the aspects of my work. The different stages in the creative process are so diverse—from researching and developing projects and trying to make them fun, to illustrating how to make the projects, and finally organising the photo shoots of the finished craftwork. From my experience of working in schools and libraries with children of all ages and abilities I try to make all the practical projects achievable for the age group I'm working with.

"My husband and I moved from London to the Isle of Wight (just off the south coast of England) six years ago. We enjoy every aspect of our life here—we have a large garden, surrounded by beautiful countryside, close to the sea. My personal interests include gardening, photography, needlecrafts and many other craft activities that can be related to my professional work. I am also very interested in keeping up with information technology."

Biographical and Critical Sources

PERIODICALS

Growing Point, November, 1985, Margery Fisher, review of *My First Picture Dictionary,* pp. 4511-4512.
Junior Bookshelf, February, 1992, review of *Making Books,* pp. 26-27.
Magpies, March, 1996, Kevin Steinberger, review of *Making Masks for Children,* pp. 41-42.
School Librarian, November, 1993, Frances Ball, review of *Maps and Mazes,* p. 158; August, 1997, Joyce Banks, review of *Autumn* and *Winter,* p. 150.
School Library Journal, September, 1992, Susan H. Patron, review of *Making Books,* p. 265; March, 1993, Susan Chmurynsky, review of *Exploring Time,* p. 202; December, 1995, Melissa Gross, review of *Making Shaped Books,* p. 95; January, 1996, Susan Chmurynsky, review of *Art from Fabric,* p. 116; March, 1998, Starr LaTronica, review of *Autumn* and *Winter,* p. 194; April, 1998, Marcia Hupp, review of *The Aztecs* and *The Egyptians,* p. 142; February, 1999, Wendy Lukeheart, review of *The Greeks* and *The Romans,* p. 114.

Autobiography Feature

Eileen Christelow

1943-

The story I remember is my parents met in Washington, D.C., courted over bowls of fresh strawberries, and married in 1942. But when I called my mother to check a few details, she said, "Strawberries? I don't remember anything about strawberries."

"But I remember a story about strawberries!" I said.

"I remember that your father liked my air-conditioned apartment and my car," said my mother. "But I don't remember strawberries."

If my father were still alive, he might verify the strawberry story. Perhaps it was his. Or perhaps the strawberry story materialized out of my childhood imagination. What follows are my memories of growing up and becoming an adult. Fact or myth? I'm sure it's fact; but possibly that could be disputed.

I was born in Washington, D.C., in 1943. World War II must have dominated the lives and thoughts of everyone around me; but I was oblivious to it. The war ended when I was only two, and the consciousness of most two-year-olds does not extend much beyond the boundaries of home, which, at that time, was a ground-floor apartment in Fairfax, Virginia.

Both of my parents worked in Washington. My father, Allan Christelow, was an Englishman who worked with the U.K. British Treasury delegation. My mother, Dorothy Beal Christelow, was (and still is) an economist, who then worked with the U.S. Government Office of Price Administration. I was looked after at home by a woman whom I knew as "Johnsy."

Sometimes I speculate with friends about how far back into our childhood we can actually remember. I'm sure I remember sitting in a highchair. So perhaps I can remember being younger than two, although most of my friends are skeptical of that claim! But I have many memories of my first four years, living at the Park Fairfax apartments. I can remember coming home from having my tonsils out, and being given a doll with blinking brown eyes. I named her Candy. I remember the horror and embarrassment of falling into the toilet when I was watching my father shave. I remember sitting under a table at a party, eating a huge bowl of popcorn, staring out at the legs of the adults standing near the table.

And I remember reading books.

Every evening when my parents came home from work, we had "coat time." When I was ready for bed, in nightgown and bathrobe (my coat), we would all sit on the couch and we would read picture books. *The Tall Book of Mother Goose,* illustrated by Feodor Rojankovsky, was a favorite.

Once, when I was three or four, I had to forgo our reading ritual for a week. I had somehow set the lock on my parents' bedroom door, unintentionally locking them out of their bedroom. The only way they could get into their bedroom, until the locksmith came, was to climb through the window. My parents were not pleased! They had to think of a punishment that would fit my terrible

Eileen Christelow

Eileen, age three, with doll, Candy.

crime. "No bedtime stories for a week!" they said. A week without books was worse than a spanking. It was agony. It seemed like a year.

Although there was plenty of land around the Park Fairfax apartments, we were not allowed to plant our own garden. I suppose the managers of the apartments wanted the landscaping to be uniformly bland. For people, like my mother, who liked to garden, this must have been frustrating.

I think her frustration must have been infectious. One afternoon I decided, in spite of the rules, I was going to plant a garden, a secret garden. I went outside, checked and double-checked to make sure that no one was watching, and then ducked behind the bush by our front door. I quickly dug a hole in the soil with a spoon. Then I planted a few tiny pebbles.

For the rest of that day and the next, I waited for something to grow. With anticipation, I checked my garden several times a day. When no one was looking, I poured cups of water on it. Then suddenly, it occurred to me: what if the flowers grew so big that someone noticed them? My garden would no longer be a secret! I began to worry. A few weeks earlier, an older neighborhood boy, six or seven years old, had told me about policemen putting people in jail when they did bad things. Would I be put in jail? I wondered. I thought maybe I should dig up the pebbles before they sprouted.

But before I had a chance, a woman wearing a blue uniform knocked on our door. I was terrified! I was certain she was from the police. I was certain someone had told her about my secret garden. I knew she was going to take me

away from my parents and put me in jail. My life was ruined, and I was only four!

My mother didn't seem at all concerned. In fact, she seemed pleased to see the woman in the blue uniform. To my dismay, she even offered her tea. I tried to stay hidden behind the couch, hoping everyone would forget about me. "Come say hello!" urged my mother. I was uncharacteristically silent.

The woman left a couple of hours later, and she didn't haul me off with her. "Are you feeling okay?" asked my mother. "What is wrong with you?" I just couldn't explain. Later, when my mother was busy in the kitchen, I raced out the front door, ducked behind the bush, and unplanted my pebbles. I went to bed that night, relieved not to have to worry anymore about being hauled off to jail, leaving my parents forever.

I value these snapshot memories of my childhood and try to keep that knee-high perspective in mind when I'm working on picture books. Somewhere in my files I even have an unfinished story about a girl who plants pebbles.

When I was four, two things happened within months of one another. My parents rented a house in Alexandria, Virginia—which was then "out in the country"—where we could have all the gardens we wanted. (Now Alexandria is a densely packed suburb of Washington, D.C.)

A couple of months later, my brother, Allan, was born. Although I was looking forward to having a younger sibling, I thought he would be at least as much fun as my doll, Candy. But he wasn't. He was scrawny, wrinkled, and not at all like those cute babies on the Gerber baby food jars. He cried a lot, and I was not allowed to play with him. The adults seemed to think I would break him or give him some terrible disease. I didn't understand; if I was such a good mother to my baby dolls, why did I have to stay away from him? It took a few months for my parents to relax and for Allan to become a cute baby. In the meantime, I had to adjust to not being the only child.

The other big change was that my mother stopped working. Johnsy had refused to come to our house in the woods. It was too isolated for her. So, although I had to share my mother with a new brother, I saw more of her than I did when she was working.

Johnsy was correct; the house was isolated. There were no neighborhood children to play with. And a few odd things happened. My mother found a strange old lady wandering through our house one day. I have no memory of how she got there or where she went after my mother discovered her. Also, someone burned down a little stable in the woods behind our house. I don't remember being very fearful about these events, but it was enough to make my mother decide not to go back to work. She didn't feel comfortable leaving her children with a new babysitter for long periods of time in such an isolated spot.

The Alexandria house came with a well-stocked library. A favorite discovery was *Kings and Queens* by Eleanor and Herbert Farjeon. I asked my parents to read it to me again and again. Today, when I look at the flat pen-and-ink illustrations, each colored with red, yellow, blue, and green, I wonder why I liked the book so much. But then I remember the story of Henry VIII and the fate of his six wives, or the story of the two young princes imprisoned in the Tower of London. I realize my imagination filled in what the pictures lacked.

After two years in the country, we moved to Washington, D.C. We lived in a neighborhood with kids across the street and kids down the alley. It didn't take long to get to know them. We played hide-and-go-seek all over the neighborhood. I learned to ride a two-wheeler bike. We had a tepee in the backyard. I went to day camp and learned to swim.

The neighbors across the back alley had the first TV I ever saw. I became acquainted with Howdy Doody and Charlie Chan. My parents weren't at all interested in buying a TV. They didn't think that Howdy Doody and Charlie Chan were interesting enough to pay hundreds of dollars for a TV. Besides, we had books!

At the back of the house was my father's study. The walls were lined with bookshelves. The living room was filled with books. I could not wait to learn to read by myself! I often had a dream that I could read: entire newspapers, the books in my father's study, my picture books . . . . But always when I woke up, I found I still could not read.

Finally, when I was old enough for first grade, I expected that I would suddenly, magically, learn to read within the first few days. But it was not that easy. The books we were supposed to learn to read were not nearly as interesting as my picture books at home. There was a red book, a blue book, and a yellow book. They were about Dick and Jane and their dog Spot and their cat Puff. Dick, Jane, Spot, and Puff ran and jumped, and as far as I can remember, they did nothing else. They were boring and tedious books. But I was determined that I was going to learn to read.

After what felt like a very long time, I was able to read the red book. I brought it home to demonstrate my new skill to my mother. I wanted her to hear the entire story. It seemed like I read for the whole afternoon. We even had to take a break for a snack. But I finally reached the end. My mother stuck with me all the way. By the summer, I was a real reader. I could read all of my picture books.

A favorite book was *Madeline* by Ludwig Bemelmans, which my parents gave me when I had my appendix out in the second grade. I read it again and again, identifying completely with Madeline. Not only was she rushed to the hospital to have her appendix out, she could see pictures in cracks on the ceiling! I thought I was the only person in the world who did that!

The summer of second grade, my mother bought me my first chapter book to read. Since we were about to go to the seashore for a short vacation, she bought *The Bobbsey Twins at the Seashore.* My first chapter book! I felt I had reached a milestone. I started reading as soon as we got home. The first few pages were a terrible disappointment! But then I came to Chapter One. Chapter One? What had I just been reading? It turned out to be a foreword—a note to parents. With Chapter One, the action began. I couldn't put the book down. Two days later I was eager to buy another Bobbsey Twins book.

After several more trips to the bookstore, my mother introduced me to the Georgetown library. Upstairs there was an entire room filled with books for children. We could borrow a pile of books each week and they did not cost a penny! Every Saturday morning, there was a story hour, where the librarian introduced us to new books. I discovered Lois Lenski, Kate Seredy, and the famous American

Childhood series, with their orange covers and black silhouette illustrations: stories about George Washington, Martha Washington, the Wright brothers, Abe Lincoln, Juliette Lowe. There were probably fifty or sixty books in the series. I spent many hours in my growing-up years slouched in an armchair, legs hooked over one arm, reading book after book.

To my surprise, reading was not the only thing we were supposed to learn in elementary school. The teachers expected us to learn to add and subtract numbers. I suppose I knew how to count, but adding and subtracting? I'd never considered such a thing. And I wasn't certain I wanted to learn. But I had a mother who loves math, and I was going to a school where you had to learn to add and subtract whether you wanted to or not. I had to add and subtract until I could do it in my sleep. I even had to do pages of arithmetic in the summer.

My lack of comprehension about why anyone would want to add, subtract, multiply, or divide continued into the third grade. At one point, while I was laboring over a column of figures, my teacher said, jokingly, "You are as slow as molasses in January!" "What does that mean?" I asked.

"You've never heard that expression before?" asked my teacher.

"No."

"Well, what do you think molasses does in January?" I had no idea.

My teacher sighed. "It's cold in January, right?"

"Right."

"So do you think it would be easy to pour molasses when it's cold?"

"I don't know," I said. "I've never tried to pour molasses, ever."

"You really are as slow as molasses in January, aren't you?" laughed my teacher.

Suddenly, I thought I understood what she was saying. I felt embarrassed, stupid, and slow—slow as molasses thickened by the January cold. But I didn't see how that could be true. I didn't have much use for numbers, but I was one of the best readers in the class! My exasperated teacher probably thought she was being humorous, but she did not do much to increase my confidence with numbers. All through school I continued to excel at subjects I liked

With parents, Dorothy (Beal) and Allan Christelow, at the Beal family farm, Windsor, Vermont, about 1945.

and to be less diligent about applying myself to subjects I didn't like.

There were other surprises at Beauvoir Elementary. The playground became a war zone at recess—particularly in third grade. The wars were between the boys and the girls. We always started recess by lining up under a big leafy tree, the boys in one line, the girls in another. The gym teacher, Mr. Butts, an ex-marine, would bark out commands: "Attention!" We all stood rigid, looking straight ahead with our arms straight down, pressed to our sides.

"Right dress!" We snapped our heads to the right and our left hands to our hips. "Left dress!" We reversed the procedure. That was followed by various calisthenics. By the time we were let loose on the playground, we were well primed to fight our wars between the sexes. Those battles became terrifyingly real. I wasn't always sure I was going to survive. I did, of course, but not without suffering and inflicting a few scrapes and bruises.

Some people know they want to be writers when they are very young. Because I loved to read so much, the idea had occurred to me. But my first attempts at writing did not hold much promise. In third grade our teacher asked us to write about what we had done over the summer. Compared to the Bobbsey Twins' summers, mine seemed pretty dull. I was staring at a blank sheet of paper, my pencil poised. What should I write about? I remembered a snakeskin my cousins and I had found in a stone wall when we were visiting our grandparents in Vermont.

I wrote an elaborate story. The snakeskin became a real snake, a poisonous snake. I became a hero. I killed the snake and rescued my cousins from mortal danger. The story was a page and a half long. I thought it was very exciting.

My teacher didn't seem to see it that way. "Is this absolutely true?" she asked.

I was faced with a dilemma. If I said "yes," I would be lying.

If I said "no," I would be admitting that I had already told a lie.

On the other hand, if I said "yes," I would be telling *two* lies.

My teacher was waiting for an answer.

"Err ... it's true," I said. "It really happened." I hoped she couldn't see the red flush I felt creeping from my cheeks out to my ears; but my story was a masterpiece and I didn't want to give it up!

How was this early attempt at authordom resolved? Did I have to write another story? Did the teacher accept my story? I don't really remember. I just know that my enthusiasm for writing stories diminished for some time after that.

One subject I loved was art. At Beauvoir, I made a brown clay horse with a black tail and mane made of clay squeezed through a screen. I made a wedding cake from scraps of wood and got married to a boy named Michael. I helped paint a volcano on the lunchroom wall. I would have been happy to spend every day in the art room.

About the same time I was discovering how much I liked clay and paints, my father was discovering pastels. He bought several boxes of big, soft pastels. One box had sixty colors—more colors than I ever knew existed. Although I was not invited to use those pastels, I loved to look at them.

At age seven, with brother, Allan Christelow, age three, in the backyard of their home, Washington, D.C.

My father drew portraits of my brother and me: my brother in his green snowsuit and me in a red plaid skating outfit. When they were finished he hung them over the fireplace in the living room.

I liked the portraits, but I hated sitting still while he drew. I was not enthusiastic when my father wanted to do a second portrait of me in my Easter bonnet. After several periods of sitting for what seemed like hours, but probably wasn't, I decided to run away. I got as far as the backyard before my courage failed me. I had no idea where I could go.

Somehow, my father managed to finish that portrait of his scowling daughter in her Easter best. I think he worked on only one more picture, a vase of flowers. They sat more patiently and didn't scowl. After that, he put the boxes of pastels away. I still have them.

At some point, my father discovered a magic store near where he worked. Every once in a while he would bring home a new trick: silk scarves, connecting rings, or red plastic cups with gray foam rabbits. To our amazement, he could stack all the red plastic cups together, putting the gray foam rabbit in the bottom one, and then, without our seeing how, make it move to another cup.... "Do it again!" we'd cry. He'd do it again and it was still a mystery. I thought about that time when I wrote *Olive and the Magic Hat* years later.

My father also brought home comic books—*Mickey Mouse, Donald Duck, Uncle Scrooge,* and later, *Pogo.* He paid for them, so he figured he should read them first. My brother and I hung over him in anticipation. Since he was often a tease, he could take a long time reading those comics!

My father read more than comics. He always had a stack of books by his red armchair—history, economics, mysteries. In the evening, after dinner, was his reading time. One year, during the Christmas season, he read Charles Dickens's *A Christmas Carol* aloud to all of us. He read the Christmas ghost story so convincingly that I became so frightened I could hardly bear to listen. But I also didn't want to miss a word.

My father loved bookstores. Whenever my brother or I were sick, he would come home from work with a book. "If you don't get better, I'm going to put you in a bag and shake you up," he'd say, as I unwrapped *The Five Little Peppers and How They Grew,* or *Little Women,* or *Black Beauty.* We got such treats when we were sick! When we could read for hours without interruption, who wanted to get better?

Playing croquet with her maternal grandmother, Alice Beal, and her younger cousin, Joannie Lawrence, at the farm, Windsor, Vermont, about 1952.

At the end of third grade, my friends and I graduated from Beauvoir Elementary and moved up the hill. The boys went to one school, the girls to another, the National Cathedral School for Girls.

I did not particularly like fourth grade at National Cathedral School. I liked my teacher. I liked my classmates. But it was a serious place. The halls seemed dark. We ate lunch in a large, dark, wood-paneled dining room where they served Welsh rarebit, a yellow cheesy dish I was certain was made with rabbits from Wales. The slightest twingey stomach or headache would be my excuse to stay home. I couldn't put my finger on it, but for some reason, I didn't want to be at that school.

My mother grew up in Springfield, Vermont, the eldest, of three daughters. Her parents, Harry and Alice Beal, who were Damma and Daddy Harry to their twelve grandchildren, eventually retired to a farm they bought in Windsor, Vermont. They encouraged their children and grandchildren to fill the eleven bedrooms in their rambling farmhouse. My brother and I were always eager to go, and each summer stayed there for at least a couple of weeks and often longer.

Days were filled with rides into town in the back of Daddy Harry's pick-up truck, where we spent our weekly twenty-cent allowances at the five-and-ten on Main Street. We went swimming in ponds and streams, hiking up Mount Ascutney, a line of grandchildren helping to carry picnic baskets for an early supper on Brownsville Rock. We went horseback riding, learned to milk the neighbor's cows, spent hours jumping from as high as we could climb in the barn into piles of loose hay in the hayloft. We collected eggs from my grandfather's chickens and watched in fascination and horror as he slaughtered those chickens for winter roasting. I sat for hours in a pen mothering a newborn calf, probably to the consternation of the mother cow. We went to country fairs and box suppers. We helped with the haying, freezing vegetables for the winter, and making jam from wild blackberries picked on the hill behind the barn. We swatted flies. Two flies were worth a penny.

If there were more than two or three young grandchildren visiting at one time, a teenage girl would be hired as a live-in babysitter. Those girls endured innumerable pranks from the high-spirited Beal grandchildren. But they knew how to get even. If we short-sheeted their beds, they short-sheeted our beds. In part, these memories inspired my picture book *Jerome the Babysitter.*

We had projects. One summer, we found a place about half a mile down the hill from the farm where several of us cousins decided to build our own house. It was going to be a place where we could live on our own, away from the adults. The only available building material was large stones. We laid out all of the rooms in stones and then started to pile up the walls. It was hard work. The walls never grew higher than a foot before we were on to another project, but those walls, the foundation for big dreams, remained in those woods by the side of the road for years. Every time I went to visit, even into my twenties, I would always check.

My father was a Yorkshire man who first came to this country from England on a graduate fellowship to study at the University of California in Berkeley. He taught for two years at Princeton, and then, when England became

Maternal grandfather, Daddy Harry Beal, harvesting vegetables from his garden, Windsor, Vermont, about 1960.

embroiled in World War II, he went to work at the British Treasury in Washington, D.C., where he met and married my American mother.

Although I had never been to England, I felt proud to be part English. I loved my father's English accent. I loved to read about Elizabeth and Margaret, the two voting English princesses. I liked to read about palaces and castles, kings and queens and knights.

When I was in fourth grade, a year before she became queen, Princess Elizabeth visited Washington and came to the National Cathedral. All of us little schoolgirls stood in the crowd and waved to her. I fantasized that she would see that I was half English and single me out of the hundreds of people; but of course she didn't.

The summer after fifth grade, our family went to England. It was the first time my brother and I would meet our English grandparents, aunt, uncle, and cousins. We sailed there and back on the Cunard line, which had ships with names like *Mauritania* and *Coronia*. Those ships were floating resort hotels with swimming pools and glossy dark wood paneling. In the fifties it was much more common to travel across the Atlantic on ships. The trip took a week each way. The first day on the ship, although the ocean was glassy calm, I felt bilious. I couldn't even look at any of the lavish meals, or the tiny tea cakes. I just sat in bed with my

head at the open porthole, breathing in the sea air, and wondering why this was supposed to be fun. By the second day, my stomach recovered. Although we went through storms the whole trip back, I wasn't seasick again. I wanted to live on ocean liners forever. There were other kids to play with. We had free range of the ship. Our parents didn't seem to worry that we'd get lost or fall overboard.

Three days out, a stowaway was discovered. A woman had hidden away on the ship, hoping to make her way to Ireland. When she was discovered by the crew, she was held until another ship came by, headed to New York. Both ships stopped, mid ocean, and our crew lowered a lifeboat and rowed her over to the other ship, which took her back to New York. I bought an autograph book in the ship gift shop with a plaid fabric cover and started to keep a journal of our trip, which seemed to promise much to write about.

When we docked in England, I couldn't bear to leave the ship. I pouted for at least the first twenty-four hours we were in London. I wrote in my journal, "I pine for the *Mauritania.*" No wonder my parents, up to this point, had traveled to England without us!

My brother and I had been reading stories about King Arthur and the Knights of the Round Table. For weeks, in anticipation of our trip to England, we'd played Knights of the Round Table with the rest of the neighborhood kids. We'd held court in our barn at our not-so-round table built from castoff house shutters.

In England, we explored several castles, not King Arthur's, but it didn't matter. These were real castles, where all the stories of knights and kings and queens had played out hundreds of years before. And now we were walking in their footsteps. If only there had been such a thing as time travel!

The other highlight of our trip was getting to know our relatives in Heckmondwike, Yorkshire. My grandparents still lived in the house where my father grew up, a small two-story row house at the end of a narrow street. My grandfather worked in the spinning mills. He was silent, speaking with a heavy Yorkshire accent when he did speak. He had a shiny, bald head and very blue eyes. My grandmother was warm and friendly and loved to do jigsaw puzzles.

My cousins lived up the street. Philip was my age. Bernard was four years older. After all initial shyness, we got along fine. It turned out that they and all their friends had two expectations about their American cousins: they thought that we would wear cowboy hats and boots and that we ate lots of jelly beans.

Tea time was very different from the pot of tea with cookies that we were accustomed to at home. "Tea" was a big meal. The whole family sat down together and ate many courses along with a pot of tea. Afterwards, my cousin Philip played his accordion. He'd been taking lessons. My cousin Bernard was taking lessons in speech/declaiming—a little like storytelling. So he told us the story of "Albert and the Lion"—the story of young Albert Ramsbottom who goes to the zoo and is swallowed whole by a lion—popularized by Stanley Holloway. We howled with laughter. It was a genre of story that I love to this day.

We stayed in Heckmondwike for five or six days, learning about cricket, eating fish and chips, walking on the moors, giving some texture to my father's boyhood stories, matching faces and voices to relatives whom we had only known, up to then, through letters and my father's descriptions.

In 1953, my father took a new job with Standard Vacuum Oil Company. We moved to New Canaan, Connecticut, which was a small country town, rapidly changing to a bedroom community to New York City. Our new house had a few acres of land around it, stone walls, a field nearby, and a very small barn/garage. It seemed like Vermont in miniature.

There were neighbors with children the same age as my brother and me. Life in Connecticut seemed promising. There was a rope swing hanging from a tree. My father helped me build a tree house in the branches above the swing.

Life in New Canaan had its good and bad points. We lived partway down a steep country lane. In the winter when it snowed, all the kids in the neighborhood spent hours sledding down that hill, inventing faster and longer routes, trying daredevil tricks. The town was filled with ponds where we could go skating. In the summer, we spent hours on bicycles. In the fall, we played kickball and jumped in piles of leaves. There was a swamp behind our neighbor's house that we explored, looking for treasures.

New Canaan had a wonderful library. I worked my way through the children's room and eventually grew into the adult book section where I started in the fiction section with authors whose names began with *A*. I read books that looked interesting, letter after letter. Adult books portrayed a more complicated world—there was love, romance, sex, jealousy, murder. My parents never restricted what I read.

Although most of my friends had a TV, we were all readers. In fifth grade, we read our way through all the Nancy Drew mysteries we could find, and then discovered the Hardy Boys. There was one boy in the fifth grade who owned all the Hardy Boy mysteries and was willing to lend them in exchange for Nancy Drew mysteries. Most of the boys thought Nancy Drew was a sissy because she was a girl. They wouldn't be caught dead reading Nancy Drew. "Someday," I thought, "I'm going to be a detective, just like Nancy Drew." As a class project, my friend Pam Mitchell and I interviewed the town detective. He was not at all like Nancy Drew or the Hardy Boys. It didn't sound like he had any adventures. He just sat around in his office. My enthusiasm for a career as a detective died then and there.

When I was twelve, my parents bought a TV. They immediately established the rule that my brother and I were allowed to watch an hour and a half of TV during the week and no more than an hour and a half over the weekend. I think that they stuck to that regimen themselves because the TV was not on much in our house, and everybody still had their stacks of books.

We chose which programs we wanted to watch with care. My father loved comedy. Through him, we discovered Laurel and Hardy, the Marx brothers, *Life with Father,* and *The Honeymooners.* TV introduced us to British films like *The Lavender Hill Mob* and *The Bells of Saint Trinions.* It was an introduction to really good slapstick humor. If my father had lived to see them, he would have loved *Monty Python, Fawlty Towers,* and, most recently, *Wallace and Gromit.*

The downside of New Canaan was represented by dancing school. New Canaan was a town where many

With paternal grandmother, Louisa Christelow, in Yorkshire, England, 1953.

children were headed, like it or not, for debutante balls. Perhaps not their own debutante balls, but they were sure to be invited to someone else's. My parents made it clear, much to my relief, that a debutante ball was not in my future. But, that didn't mean I shouldn't go to dancing school. So, by sixth grade, I and most of my friends were enrolled in Miss Johnson's School of Dance. The girls dressed in party dresses, short white socks, patent leather Mary Janes, and white gloves. The boys wore suits, ties, and white gloves. The girls lined up in one line, the boys in another, and we were paired according to height. Problem number one: I was taller than most of the boys in sixth grade.

We learned the box step first. "Rest your left hand lightly on the boy's shoulder," purred Miss Johnson, "and your right hand lightly in his left hand." My partners and I moved stiffly, as far apart as possible, often stepping on each other's toes. I was sure I was the only girl who felt gawky and awkward. Some girls seemed to be in their element, dancing easily, chatting and smiling. I found I didn't know what to say to those boys and they didn't know what to say to me. But I kept going, week after week, hoping that I would suddenly learn to be socially adept, that I would magically transform into a social butterfly. After two years, it occurred to me, and several other kids, that we didn't have to go to Miss Johnson's School of Dance—that we might survive in the world without wearing white gloves.

In eighth grade, I had a wonderful English teacher named Mr. Harris. He was demanding. He worked us hard, and I discovered that I liked to write. We didn't use textbooks and workbooks. We read William Saroyan, J. D. Salinger. We wrote essays and short stories. He asked us to write a short story in which we had to describe how to make something. It seemed impossible until I placed my story on a beach and intertwined my plot with the building of a sand castle. Mr. Harris read my story to the class, and I started to think of myself as a decent writer.

I also knew that I liked to draw and to make things, but art classes were sporadic, once a week if we were lucky. Whatever art I did was mostly done out of school. I won a prize from the local garden club for making a giraffe out of a squash. At Halloween, the town sponsored a contest for kids to paint Halloween scenes on shop windows. In eighth grade, my friends and I teamed up and spent a blissful day executing a huge painting of ghosts and witches on a pharmacy window. I felt I would have been happy if I could have painted scenes on shop windows for the rest of my life.

When I came home, after painting the shop window, my parents announced that we were going to move to Japan for a year. Here on a day I had attained true happiness, I found out I was going to move away to JAPAN? I couldn't imagine what it would be like to live there! I didn't know anything about Japan. My father had been there several times. He'd given me a beautiful silk kimono. Did everyone wear kimonos? Did they have cars? Buses? Trains? Where would I go to school? Would I have any friends? Would anyone speak English? How would I learn to speak Japanese? Where would we live? I felt a combination of dread and excitement. I didn't want to leave my friends. I didn't want to miss out on the first year of high school. But this was an opportunity for adventure.

Eight months later, in 1957, we packed up our blue Ford station wagon and headed for San Francisco. The only four-lane highway we traveled on that trip was the New York State Thruway, which ended in Buffalo, our first overnight stop. This was the first time I had traveled west of the East Coast.

From Buffalo, we drove over miles and miles of flat, straight roads, through Ontario, Canada, Michigan, Wisconsin, South Dakota, and Wyoming, our car windshield covered with dead flying insects. We passed through miles of cornfields that dwarfed the cornfields we knew in Vermont. We passed through towns with populations of less than twenty, and through towns that sold foot-long hot dogs. We even drove for hours through an area in Wyoming that looked as I would have imagined the surface of the moon. It was sweltering hot as we traveled over those black ribbons of macadam. We stuck to the vinyl seats of our car. We kept the windows opened wide.

I'd read books about families traveling west a hundred years earlier. I wondered how they had survived. Did those siblings, riding in covered wagons, squabble as much as my brother and I did? At home we usually got along fine. But on that trip, after a few days of driving, somewhere in the Dakotas, we started to argue over quarter-inches in the back seat, and whose turn it was to read which comic. Was I really thirteen years old? Was he really nine?

My parents finally decided they'd had enough of our bickering. We stopped at a lodge in Sun Valley, Idaho. We didn't get back in the car for four or five days. I spent my days ice skating in the summer sun, a luxury I wouldn't have imagined a few days earlier. Thirty years later my brother would meet his wife at that same hotel.

The first leg of our trip to Japan ended in San Francisco, where we spent a few days exploring before boarding the *President Wilson,* the ship that took us across the Pacific.

We arrived in Yokohama, Japan, after ten days at sea and one day in Hawaii. As the ship docked, the pier was lined with Japanese school children on an excursion to the docks. They were about my age and all were dressed in black school uniforms. They stared and pointed and giggled at my brother and me as we walked down the gangplank. I suddenly realized that I was going to be an oddity in this country. I was taller than any of them, had brown hair (they all had black hair), and brown, round eyes. Was I going to be giggled at and pointed at for an entire year? Within hours I no longer cared. This country was so different from any place I had ever lived that curiosity overtook my feelings of awkwardness.

Tokyo was a city in motion. Cars darted in every direction, paying little attention to traffic lanes. Men pedaled bicycles, often pulling carts, moving among the cars. Trolley cars, crammed with people, made their way down the center of the major streets. People were everywhere, some dressed in kimonos, others in Western clothes. Students, elementary school through university, dressed in somber black school uniforms. People squatted on the sidewalks, waiting for trolleys. Women carried babies tied to their backs in velvet slings. People with colds wore white face masks. Interesting cooking smells wafted from small shops. Sounds ...

We lived in a contemporary stone and wood house. A block away were small shops, a silk gallery, and the shrine of the 47 Ronin. The trolley stopped by our gate.

It was a lifestyle to which we were not accustomed. The house came with a cook, two maids, and a chauffeur. If we had wanted, we need not have felt that we had left the

Paternal grandfather, Joseph Christelow, and cousin Phillip Wright playing his accordion, in Yorkshire, England, 1953.

United States. But that wasn't what we wanted. We wanted to explore. We walked often, all around our neighborhood, getting to know the little shops, the silk gallery, and the shrine. One Sunday, my father and I walked from our house into the center of Tokyo—perhaps an hour's walk stopping to look in shops: bookstores with books we couldn't read, noodle shops, curio shops, antique shops. My mother and I went to Kabuki and Noh performances. My mother studied Japanese, which was useful when we traveled to other parts of the country during school vacations.

Allan and I attended an American school, which was, in fact, very international. There were students from Japan, Taiwan, the Philippines, Indonesia, Eastern Europe, and some Americans. The style was America in the fifties— saddle shoes, bobby socks, cinch belts, crinolines, and Elvis mixed with an oddly contrasting worldliness. These were kids whose parents were missionaries, expatriates escaping repressive governments, foreign correspondents, embassy officials.... Most of them had lived in several different cultures. Many were at least bilingual. They moved easily through Tokyo, using its crowded subways and trolleys without trepidation.

The teachers were mostly Americans in transit. Some were on trips around the world and took on the job to make enough money to continue their trip. Some were spouses of people stationed with the American armed services in Japan. A few were fine teachers. Most were not. In English we read *Oliver Twist* twice, *Romeo and Juliet* once, and conjugated sentences. I started the year taking Japanese and French, but learning two new foreign languages at the same time seemed too much, so I had to choose. At that time, American high schools didn't even consider teaching Japanese. So if I concentrated on Japanese, a language that I could have put to good use then, I would have been behind in language credits when we returned to the United States. So I took French from a lousy French teacher while living in Japan. What a waste.

The following August we left Japan, planning to arrive back in Connecticut in time to start school. We stopped in Hong Kong for a few days and then flew on to Geneva, Switzerland, in a DC-3. The flight took thirty-six hours. Our plane stopped to refuel, disembark, and take on passengers in Bangkok, Calcutta, Karachi, Bahrain, and Cairo. DC-3s flew lower than today's large jets. We saw northern India, a lush green from monsoon season, people tending their gardens, a white Brahmin cow walking unchallenged through someone's garden. At midnight, we experienced the breathtaking desert heat of Bahrain. We saw the sun rise over the pyramids in Egypt. And finally, in Geneva, Switzerland, we staggered off the plane, grimy and exhausted, having glimpsed, in a very short period of time, places spread over half the globe.

I was planning to enter the New Canaan high school as a sophomore as soon as we arrived back in Connecticut. For some reason, many kids in New Canaan went away to boarding school in the tenth grade. I had thought about doing this, and had applied to Abbot Academy in Massachusetts. They accepted me, but after agonizing over the decision, I decided that I would prefer to go to the high school in New Canaan; I think, mostly, because I wasn't enthusiastic about leaving home. While we were in Geneva, a telegram arrived from my father, who was still in Tokyo.

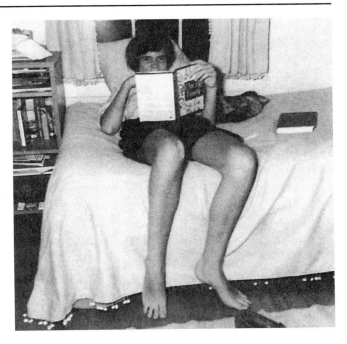

The author, age thirteen, reading in her customary fashion.

Through some confusion, he wrote, Abbot thinks that Eileen is going to be a member of their sophomore class.

I was shocked! How could that have happened? I suppose that we could have explained that they were confused, that perhaps they never received my rejection; but somehow, that isn't what happened.

After several more weeks in Europe, and perhaps ten days back in Connecticut, I found myself moving into a dormitory in a small New England girls' school. Three months earlier, I had been walking the streets of Tokyo by myself. Now I was at a school where we had to sign out in a book and have at least one other person with us if we wanted to walk into the village of Andover.

For a week I was unbearably homesick and miserable. I drafted a letter to my parents, telling them that this was a big mistake and I was coming home. I can't remember if I ever sent it. Our first weekend at Abbot we were taken to Crane's Beach. We spent an idyllic day, running in the waves, cooking hamburgers on the dunes. That evening we had a pep rally back in the school gym. I was startled to realize that I had not even thought about home all day. In fact, I was having a great time. "So why be miserable?" I thought. "It's too painful and this might be an okay place."

In retrospect, I think that you can get accustomed to almost anything. To be fair, for the most part, we received a good education at Abbot. By my junior year, with encouragement from a wonderful English teacher, Barbara Sisson, I discovered again that I liked to write. I had stories published in nearly every issue of the school magazine. I specialized in satirical essays with titles like "Them Picassas." Most of our classes were demanding. We wrote at least one essay a week and sometimes more. The classes were small. Most of the teachers were good. A few were excellent. A few were, unfortunately, using the school as a retirement home.

At Abbot there were rules. We had to wear leather lace-up shoes with good arch support. On Saturdays we could wear any shoes we wanted to. We had to dress for dinner: a good dress, one not worn to classes, stockings with seams down the back, and dress shoes. We had to be in bed with lights out by nine, and we were awakened by a loud bell at 6:45 every morning. We had to go to chapel every morning before classes, church on Sundays, and chapel on Sunday evenings.

Those of its who were inclined to rebel found small ways to do so. We stayed up late, reading under the covers or in closets. We wore the required stockings with the regulation seam up the back, but the rule books didn't say anything about no runs. By the end of the year, girls wore stockings that were in shreds, but still had the seam. It was a challenge to look as ragged as possible without breaking the rules that were intended to keep us "ladylike."

Romance was not encouraged. We had one chance each school year to meet "the boy of our dreams" at the school dance with Andover, the boys' school up the hill. We were paired off according to height, which did not necessarily guarantee instant compatibility. The event was too reminiscent of Miss Johnson's School of Dance, and I never found myself waltzing with "the boy of my dreams."

The preoccupation at Abbot was getting into a "good" college. The seven sister colleges—Smith, Wellesley, and so on—were considered preferable. As an average student in the middle of my class, I didn't stand much chance of admission to a "sister college," which was fine, because when I thought about it, I wasn't enthusiastic about going to another all-girl school, a larger version of Abbot.

I spent a lot of time pouring over college catalogues and applied to colleges in a haphazard fashion, not feeling any real enthusiasm for any of them. Then I found a yellow ocher catalogue, unusually well designed, with fine black-and-white photographs printed on a cream-colored paper. It felt good to the touch. It was interesting to read. No one from Abbot had ever gone to the University of Pennsylvania; but it sounded wonderful to me. It had thousands of students, including graduate students. Although Penn was an Ivy League school, it had been accepting women undergrads for at least twenty years. There were five or six men to every woman. It was in Philadelphia, an appealing change from small-town Andover. It had a huge course catalogue. It was everything Abbot wasn't. So I applied.

We had to wait for three or four months to hear from the colleges. In April letters started to appear in our mailboxes. Thin letters were usually rejections, a single piece of paper that said, *We are sorry to inform you. . . .* Thick letters usually meant acceptance. I received a lot of thin letters. None of them were from the University of Pennsylvania. I was beginning to worry. Then one night I dreamed that I received a thin letter from Penn. I opened it, thinking, "I'm in a real fix. I'm not going to college at all!" But then, I read the first line, *We are happy to inform you. . . .*

The next day my dream played itself out in exactly that way. I was accepted by the only college to which I really wanted to go. The acceptance came in a thin envelope.

My first days at the University of Pennsylvania, I felt like someone released from prison. I was living in a dormitory, but I could walk out the door, get on a bus, and head into the center of Philadelphia by myself. I didn't have to sign out. No one knew or cared what I did as long as I was back by midnight and didn't invite men into my rooms.

Not many of the students at Penn had spent their high school years in a boarding school. People came from all over the country from a wide variety of backgrounds (although there was a lack of racial heterogeneity). The university was huge. I was constantly meeting new people. Although Penn had a large number of courses from which to choose, I found one thing that I had overlooked when reading the course catalogue: they didn't offer any art courses to undergraduates. I had thought I would major in English, but after plowing through two dull years of required introductory English courses, I discarded that idea. It took a couple of years to figure out where I belonged at Penn.

The end of my freshman year at Penn, my parents moved back to Japan. I spent the summer with them in Tokyo, and twice a week took wood-block print lessons with a Japanese print master who did abstract prints. Most of his prints, and a series of more traditional prints, were printed by a printer, a man who sat in the corner of the studio, rubbing paper onto inked wood blocks. The studio was two rooms with tatami floors. I sat on the floor carving wood blocks with several other students, mostly Americans, all experienced artists and much older that I. Most of them were showing in galleries. I felt hopelessly inexperienced, but I loved the work. What I learned that summer enabled me to later understand how to do the color separations in my first books.

Several weeks after I arrived at Penn for my sophomore year, a telegram arrived from my mother. My father, who had had some health problems the year before, had a stroke. He was in intensive care in a Tokyo hospital. He was only fifty-three.

A month later, he was in Columbia Presbyterian Hospital in New York. I went up to meet my parents. As I talked to my father, I knew he was not the same father I had hugged goodbye a few weeks before in Tokyo. I think our whole family was numb as we tried to learn about this new person we were living with—my father most of all. He had the same wry sense of humor, the same intellect, the same warmth. He could still quote Shakespeare. He still read books piled by his chair. It took all of us time to realize what he couldn't do and probably would never be able to do. He couldn't find his way around the village of New Canaan, much less New York City. He couldn't button his shirt straight and he couldn't go back to work. For the last twelve years of his life, he faced up to his disability with courage and good humor—as did my mother.

It was obvious that my mother, at age forty-seven, after fifteen years away from work, needed to find a job. It took her some months and encouragement from friends to realize that she could go back to work as an economist. Although she had not worked for fifteen years after my brother was born, she had fortuitously gone back to Columbia University, to work on her Ph.D. in economics. She had also learned a lot about Japan when we lived there and could speak some Japanese. By the summer, she had been hired by the Federal Reserve Bank in New York as an economics specialist in international trade and finance. In midlife my mother suddenly found herself commuting daily from New Canaan to Wall Street. Although her new career was thrust upon her by tragic circumstances, it was a challenging and stimulating change.

My parents bought a small house in New Canaan. My brother and I were able to continue attending our schools, thanks to some insurance money. We all adjusted to a life with new circumstances. In certain ways things were turned upside-down: my brother and I, the children, were finding ourselves in the position of parent to our father. And we learned one of life's big lessons: *never take anything for granted.*

My sophomore year at Penn, I took some wonderful art history courses, and I discovered a life drawing course in the graduate school of fine arts. I talked the instructor into allowing me to take it. The two nights a week that I took that course, I noticed an interesting design studio that took place in the room next to ours. It was basic design for undergraduate architecture majors. I hadn't even known it was possible to major in architecture!

My junior year, I became an architecture major. But I had some catching up to do. Most of the students had spent their sophomore year drawing buildings while I had been drawing nudes. I spent the fall drawing buildings and being stimulated, delighted, and overwhelmed by the design course. I learned about color, line, form, space: basic principles of design. I completed projects, redid them, and redid them again.

The graduate school of architecture was an exciting place. Undergraduates could hang around the design studios and watch the grad students' critique sessions. Some of the country's top architects—Louis Kahn, Robert Venturi, and Aldo Guirgola—were practicing in Philadelphia and teaching at the university. The design studios were considering projects that were being planned for the city of Philadelphia—the airport, schools, housing projects. For the first time, I found a field of study that seemed to have some real relevance to the world outside our ivory towers. At the end of our junior year, ten or fifteen undergrads were allowed into the graduate program as seniors. The rest of us who did not make it had to cobble together a program for that final year. We could take any first-year graduate course but not the first-year graduate design studios. If I had been

older and more self-confident, I would have attended that design studio, done the assigned projects, and insisted that the professors consider them at the juries. But I wasn't older and I had little confidence about my design skills. A year later, a friend employed that tactic, and successfully worked her way into the graduate school.

In retrospect, my rejection was fortuitous, because as I looked around for other courses to take, I discovered the graduate school of fine arts, where I took design with a painter, Neil Welliver. I also discovered the darkroom in the graphics department where I learned to process black-and-white photographic prints and to make color separations and line shots with a darkroom camera.

With other students, I started working on a book about the fine arts building where we took most of our courses. It had been designed as the university library by Frank Furness, a well-known architect at the turn of the century. We photographed the gargoyles, the ornate ironwork, the leaded glass windows, the tile roofs, and the intricate spaces of the Furness Building from every angle, near and far, hanging from windows and lying on the ground.

A book designer came down from Yale and worked with us on dummies of the Furness book. All of the work I was doing in the graphics department was not part of any course; but what I learned about book design, color separation, photography, and darkroom technique was among the most valuable learning experiences I had in my four years at college.

As challenged as I was by the fine arts school, I could not let go of the idea of getting into the graduate school of architecture. I applied to Penn and to two other schools. I was accepted by one school, wait-listed by another, and rejected by Penn. I wanted to go to Penn and nowhere else. I was devastated, but only for a week or so. I started to think that it would be a relief not to go to school for a while. A few weeks later, the Penn fine arts graduate program offered me a full scholarship. Perhaps foolishly, I didn't take it.

So, in May of 1965, I had a B.A. and not the slightest idea what to do with it. Through the summer I continued to work in the darkroom at Penn. Everyone was on vacation and I had the place to myself. I began to take pictures of people instead of buildings. I met Ahren Ahrenholz, who was building vest-pocket parks in neighborhoods all over the city. I often went to sites with him, met the people he was working with, and took photographs.

He had grown up in Philadelphia, and he introduced me to a city I never knew existed: the Italian market, the Reading terminal farmers' market, baklava, grits and scrapple on South Street, jazz on Broad Street, canoeing on the Schuylkill River in Fairmount Park, Levis's hot dogs. Ahren lived in a 3,200-square-foot loft on the top floor of a factory building in north Philadelphia. His loft had windows on all four sides with an unobstructed panoramic view of the city.

Within a year we were married, and I moved into the loft with him. We had no hot water, no heat at night, two hot plates to cook on, and the best view in the city. The loft came with a freight elevator and a jeweler's safe, which I converted to a darkroom.

Eileen (left), age eighteen, with friend Libby Holloway, visiting a shrine in Kamakura, Japan.

The first winter was incredibly cold. The electric space heaters we turned on at night, when the heat went off, made no difference in a 3,200-square-foot space with twelve-foot ceilings and drafty windows. We reluctantly decided to move to a house in Chinatown. The house rented for forty dollars a month and was warm. It was small, with two staircases and two rooms on each floor, known in Philadelphia parlance as a "double father, son, and holy ghost." It was probably servants' quarters in the 1700s, and had most recently been a bail bondsman's office. It was two blocks from Skid Row and two doors from a police station. A good Chinese meal was a block away. Our neighbors were mostly recent arrivals from China and spoke little English.

We were constantly broke, and I needed to earn a living. Somehow I didn't feel that my B.A. degree offered me any opportunities at employment.

Having decided that I was not going to be an architect, I began to think about how I could sell my photographs. Ideally, I wanted to photograph for *Life* magazine. But I needed experience. I started by doing the rounds of offices of the architects who often needed their buildings photographed. Although my technical skills as a photographer were still lacking, I did know how to look at a building. The photos of the Furness Building made up my first portfolio. I found some work without much trouble. I hated calling people and making appointments to show my portfolio. But the thought of working nine to five in a cubicle office or behind a cash register made me lift the phone and call those architects.

I preferred photographing people to photographing buildings. I carried my two Nikon cameras wherever I went, looking at everyone and everything as a potential photograph. I developed two portfolios, one of buildings, one of photo essays about life in Philadelphia. I contacted a social services agency working on Skid Row and spent months, off and on, photographing life there, visiting flophouses with an ex-alcoholic. I was learning firsthand about people I had only seen from a passing car window. I was beginning to think that the architects and city planner at Penn had missed an important component of the process of designing for a city. They never asked their students to find out much about the lives of the people for whom they were designing buildings and spaces.

I photographed parades, playgrounds, people on the streets, children in schools. I photographed political demonstrations. This was the sixties. The country was in turmoil about the Vietnam War and about civil rights. I marched in Washington with my cameras, covering marches on the Pentagon and Resurrection City. I covered demonstrations, marches, draft-card burnings, and political rallies in Philadelphia. I packed hundreds of feet of Tri-X film, and Ahren and I took a couple of long trips, escaping cold, gray February days in Philadelphia driving to Mexico and California. I sold my photos to magazines and to textbook publishers.

Eighteen months after we moved to Chinatown, we heard that the owners of the factory building where we had lived before had decided that they had to keep the heat on twenty-four hours a day. They had had a bad experience with frozen water pipes. And we were having a bad experience living next to the police station in Chinatown. The often denied stories about police brutality were being

played out at our front door. We were often awakened by police roughing up apprehended suspects under our window. We reported them to the ACLU. The action on our doorstep stopped for almost eight months, but gradually picked up again. By that time, we were too politically jaundiced to believe that we could do anything about it.

With relief, we moved back to the loft on North Nineteenth Street eighteen months after we had left it. We found a few drawings we'd left behind, undisturbed. Our friends Laurie and Margie Cameron moved into the loft below us. Together, we scoured suburban newspaper ads for used stoves, sinks, and refrigerators. We bought a hot-water heater from Sears, some copper pipe, found bathtubs at a junkyard, and soon had functioning kitchens and bathing facilities. It was a big improvement over the living conditions that had driven us out of the loft before.

Laurie, among other things, was a photographer. In fact, we met at a photo show where we were both exhibiting. He set up a darkroom in his jeweler's safe, and I set up one in ours. Laurie knew how to make exquisite black-and-white photographic prints. Over the next few years, I learned a lot of darkroom skills from him.

Off and on, Ahren and I talked about moving out of Philadelphia; but we couldn't decide where we wanted to go. Ahren was beginning to make pots. Although we had lots of work space in our loft, it was not an ideal space for a kiln. The oil-fired kiln he used was unsafe and filthy, filling up our loft with black smoke and fumes every time he fired it. We began to think about living in the country; but I wasn't enthusiastic about leaving my photographic stomping ground or my sources of work.

In the spring of 1971, Ahren met the British potter Michael Cardew at a workshop in Bala Cynwyd. Ahren ended up giving Michael a ride to the train in Philadelphia. That evening, when Ahren arrived home, he said he'd been offered a chance to apprentice with Michael at his pottery in Cornwall, England. Only a few months earlier, Ahren had read about Michael Cardew in Bernard Leach's *A Potter's Book,* and he had shown me photos of his incredible pots. I didn't have to think more than a minute about whether I wanted to go. Neither did Ahren.

That summer we earned as much money as we could, and we sold almost everything we owned at the Englishtown flea market. By September, we were ready to take off. We had two round-trip tickets on Icelandic Air. We had money in the bank. We found lodging for our cat and lodging for our dog. But there was one thing we hadn't planned on. I was pregnant! But it never occurred to us to change our plans. Why couldn't we have a baby in England?

We arrived in Wenfordbridge, Cornwall, England, an eager apprentice and his four-months-pregnant wife. Luckily, the four-months-pregnant wife didn't faze Michael Cardew at all. After all, he was living with his dour German-Russian daughter-in-law, three young grandchildren, and another apprentice, a young Dane named Svend Bayer.

Wenfordbridge Pottery was once a pub and inn at a crossroads. The house was stone with well-worn bluestone slate floors and low-beamed ceilings painted white, glazed with years of smoke from the fireplaces. The largest room, just inside the front door, was where everyone gathered, around a long, dark wood, ancient table, for breakfast,

As a sophomore at the University of Pennsylvania, 1963.

lunch, tea, and dinner. The conversation was usually lively. The shelves behind Michael's place at the head of the table were filled with books that were often referred to as we discussed clay, politics, literature, Cornwall ....

For the first four months we rented a small apartment two miles up a country lane from the pottery. Ahren walked down there every morning to go to work. He soon discovered he had a lot to learn about making pots. And I soon discovered that I had nothing to do. I did some photography in nearby villages when I could get to them. I photographed at the pottery. I eventually found some small country schools where I photographed. But the lack of a proper darkroom made it difficult to really see what images I had. My creative life came to a screeching halt.

In March Michael Cardew left for a speaking tour of the United States.

A couple of weeks later, our daughter, Heather Christelow Ahrenholz, was born in Plymouth, Devon. Because she arrived three weeks before she was expected, she and I had to stay in the hospital for eight or nine days.

We brought Heather home to the pottery in the middle of a kiln firing. The big bottleneck kiln was being stoked with wood over a twenty-four-hour period. The house was full of helpers. Every surface of the room where we were living was piled high with baby paraphernalia that I hadn't had time to sort before being taken off to the hospital.

Somehow it seemed incongruous: the jump from nine days in a hospital where the focus was babies to a pottery full of people whose focus was getting a kiln up to temperature. But I was incredibly happy to be out of the hospital ... to be able to start to figure out how to be a mother without nurses hovering over me, each with a different theory about the care and feeding of babies. The biggest adjustment was to remember: "I am a mother!" I

had to remember when I was sitting around the table with all the people firing the kiln that the baby crying upstairs was our baby, that she wanted at least one of her parents ... now! Suddenly, I was responsible to someone else who was completely helpless and dependent on me.

We adjusted. And we fell in love with this tiny blue-eyed blonde who gradually started smiling, giggling, waving her hands in the air, kicking her feet. We were so in love with her and felt so incredibly lucky that the hours of washing "nappies," the interrupted sleep, the rocking, the burping, were an adjustment accepted without question.

In the tiny hamlet of Wenfordbridge, where the pottery was, there were not more than six or eight houses. So the birth of a baby was noted. Then a few days later, our neighbor Charley Marshall, who lead tours of the pottery, died of emphysema. Then two weeks later, our neighbors the Nottles had their third child, a son named Darren—after Bobby Darren. We had become an integral part of the rhythms of life at that tiny Cornish crossroads.

Luckily, by late May, when Michael Cardew arrived back at the pottery after his speaking tour, Heather was no longer colicky all evening. She was a happy, smiley, baby ... except in the middle of the night, when no one noticed except me. All Michael had to put up with was endless wash lines filled with drying terrycloth nappies.

In September, eleven months after we arrived as a family of two, we left Wenford—a family of three. We arrived in New York after a couple of weeks of house-sitting in London and visiting relatives in Yorkshire. We had fifty dollars left in the bank, a six-month-old baby, and not the slightest idea where we were going to live.

For four months, we lived with family and friends, working to build up our bank account. Then friends called from Berkeley, California. They were moving out of their rental house and wondered if we would like to take it over. The house had a large pottery studio and a low rent.

We moved to California, into the house on Colusa Avenue, a few months later. Ahren went to work building his pottery and doing odd carpentry jobs. I found some photo assignments.

Colusa Avenue was a real neighborhood—a mixture of ages, races, and incomes. There was a small grocery store half a block from our house. In the late afternoon, everyone strolled down there to buy something for supper. People stopped, talked, became friends. There were children everywhere. Heather was the youngest—for a while. She grinned at everyone, and everyone stopped to admire our happy "baby boy."

Ahren's studio building was zoned commercial, so he was able to open up a shop in the front. Very slowly, the pots found their buyers: Japanese who loved brown Temoku glazes, people who liked simple, well-thrown, straightforward, functional pots. Neighbors who had never thought much about pots walked in and bought a casserole or a mug and then came back to buy more. A priest walked in and wondered if Ahren could make a chalice cup. The local fire department came to examine the kiln and walked away with mugs. A department store wanted him to make plates, pitchers, and bowls.

I did not find it easy to find photographic jobs in California. I was also juggling being the mother of a toddler with rebuilding a career in a new and unfamiliar environment. Although I liked living in California, it was not a place that inspired my photographic eye the way Philadelphia had. I began to think about what other kinds of work I could do.

When we had lived in Philadelphia, my energy was mostly devoted to photography. But I loved picture books. Sometimes I visited the children's room at the Philadelphia library with the kids on our block. We read Maurice Sendak's *Alligators All Around* and *Where the Wild Things Are.* We read Don Freeman's *Corduroy.* Around that time, *Life* magazine published John Steptoe's *Stevie.* It was one of the few stories I'd ever seen that was about children whose lives were like the lives of my neighbors. I was inspired.

I tried to write a story using the photographs that I took in my neighborhood as illustrations. But I wanted to write fiction, and I decided that my photographs could not successfully illustrate fiction. So, occasionally, I put aside my cameras and pulled out some paintbrushes. But I needed a good story.

Then one day, when I was walking to our loft from the bus, I passed a couple of neighborhood boys who were pushing a grocery cart containing two young puppies. "Want to buy a dog?" they asked. They figured (correctly) that I was the sucker they were looking for. "Well, I don't think so," I said. But I didn't sound very convincing. Those young boys were born salesmen.

Several minutes later, I was carrying a tiny puppy up to our loft. "He was so cute!" I told Ahren. "Who knows what would have happened to him if I hadn't come along? He only cost a dime!"

It turned out that the puppy was not very cute at all! He smelled terrible, even after several baths. He had an incessant yippy-yappy little bark. We decided the dog had to go. Luckily, Irene, an eight-year-old girl who lived with her grandmother in an apartment across the street, had her heart set on owning a cute little dog. "Have we ever got the dog for you!" we said.

Irene and her grandmother took the smelly yippy-yappy puppy home. We held our breath. But they didn't march back across the street with the dog in tow. The word from the kids on the street was that Irene and her grandmother loved that dog. We never saw it again.

That experience inspired a story about a boy who is sent by his mother to the corner store to buy a box of soap; but he meets up with some friends who have a shopping cart full of puppies. My hero is as much of a sucker as I was.

I wrote the story. I made a dummy with color illustrations and put it away in a drawer and went back to my photography.

One day, four or five years later in Berkeley, with Heather clinging to my knees, I decided that I would try to write and illustrate another picture book. I figured that I could work on illustrations while she was playing around me, or while she was taking a nap, or after she went to bed. I set a goal. I would make one book dummy a week.

I started with an alliterative alphabet book. By the end of a week, I knew my goal was totally unrealistic. It took nearly two years to complete the alphabet book. Over the months, I learned about pens, ink, pencils, paper. I drew and redrew. Heather and I borrowed books from the library at least twice a week. I analyzed other illustrators' techniques.

With husband, Ahren Ahrenholz, 1967.

Heather was growing older. She wanted to be around other kids. And I needed some uninterrupted time to work.

We started with a neighborhood play group of three children. For three hours of caring for three children, I could have six hours to work. For four months that was a pretty good solution. But then our play group fell apart. When Ahren saw a sign advertising a woman in the neighborhood who was starting a very small day care, we decided to investigate.

Anna Stanislawski lived two blocks away on Colusa Avenue. To get to her house from the street, we climbed up several dozen stone steps through a thicket of scrub oak. Her house was a tiny white wooden structure with a porch and large windows looking out towards the San Francisco Bay. A huge lilac shaded the porch.

How to describe Anna? She was peaceful, calm, petite, wiry, had sparkling blue eyes and a reassuring smile spread over a face aging too quickly. She was a thirty-five-year-old flower child—a music graduate from Cal Berkeley who had no use for the competitive realities of the world outside her gate.

Her house was spare. There were cushions on the floor, a low child-height table, books, and a small slide and climber in one room and virtually no other furniture and no TV. Perhaps many people would have thought it was an eccentric place. But it looked a lot like our house. We also had cushions on the floor, and a dining table fifteen inches off the floor! Heather felt right at home.

Listening to Anna read to the two-year-olds snuggled up against her was a real revelation. When she read the Randall Jarrell translation of *Snow-White and the Seven Dwarfs,* illustrated by Nancy Ekholm Burkert, she always started with the illustration of the mirror on the title page. "Mirror, mirror, on the wall, who is the fairest of them all?" she would ask, holding the book so that each child could look at the picture of the mirror and imagine that they saw themselves reflected in it. When she read John Burningham's *Mr. Gumpy's Outing,* and Mr. Gumpy says, "You can get on my boat if you don't trample about," Anna and the children would put down the book and trample about the room. She showed the children and me how to jump into the illustrations and become a part of the stories.

I would deliver Heather to Anna's at nine, five mornings a week. Then I would race home and get to work, ignoring dishes, dirty floors, laundry, good novels. I had four hours to work. I learned to make those four hours count for more time than I had ever imagined possible.

I worked on the alphabet book. I started writing other stories. I found more photographic work. I started designing posters, then ads for small stores. Several bookstores, a children's clothing store, a department store, a glass factory, a science museum, and Ahren's Colusa Pottery became clients. I also started doing spot illustrations for textbooks.

I wasn't a trained graphic designer, illustrator, or photographer. I learned on the job, from typesetters, printers, other graphic designers, other illustrators, other photographers, and by constantly analyzing work that I liked. This is a daunting way to learn a skill, and I often felt like an impostor as I went around with my portfolio: a graphic designer without credentials, an illustrator without credentials. But I had some good instincts and ideas about helping clients to communicate. So no one seemed to notice that I was an impostor. After a few years, I stopped worrying.

While I worked on the alphabet book, I started writing other stories. The first was about a greased pole contest at a county fair. I spent months working on a dummy. When the dummy was completed, I asked Heather's nursery school teacher to read my story to her class. At the end of the day she reported that not all of the kids had walked away while she read. I knew I obviously had a lot to learn!

I tried again. I wrote a book about a messy room. I tried illustrating nursery rhymes. I wrote about a rabbit who painted himself with red stripes. I sent work out and received "encouraging" rejections: "Let us see what else you can do." The rejections were discouraging, but I loved working on those projects, and I had a notebook full of other ideas.

I took a course, "Writing for Children," at the University of California's extension program. It was taught by Betty Bacon, who had been an editor at Harper and Row in the forties and who wrote nonfiction for children. "Your rabbit story is good," she said. "But it's got too much of an Esalen message."

An Esalen message! That was a revelation. I hadn't seen the California "get your head together, you're OK, I'm OK" message; but she was right! My rabbit character, Henry, had painted red stripes on himself because he wanted to have stripes like his chipmunk friend, Max. After a harrowing run-in with a fox, Henry realizes why he is better off with his "plain brown fur." I was preaching "be content with who you are." It wasn't my intent to preach anything! I just wanted to tell an exciting and humorous story about a young rabbit's misadventures! The problem stewed at the back of my mind. Then one night, as I was about to fall asleep, I thought, "Henry painted himself with red stripes because he wanted to! Isn't that why most kids paint themselves?" I grabbed a piece of paper and jotted down ideas for a new beginning and a new ending.

"That's it!" said Betty Bacon. "This is a big improvement."

I stored the much-improved Henry Rabbit story away on a shelf. I was too busy to figure out which publisher to send it to. I was finding more and more graphic design and illustration work, and I was also working on a story about an inventor of wacky machines.

Our writing class was an enthusiastic class. About half of us didn't want it to end. We were in the middle of promising projects. So we continued to meet at Betty Bacon's house, once a week, for several months. By our last meeting, I had almost completed a dummy for *Mr. Murphy's Marvelous Invention.* Now I had two books, and I needed to face up to trying to find a publisher once again.

A few years earlier, Betty Bacon had taken a trip to Cuba with a group of children's book writers and editors. "You should show your books to Jim Giblin at Clarion Books," she suggested to me. "I met him on the trip to Cuba. I think he'd like quirky books like yours."

Ahren and I had decided to move back to the East Coast. Our house on Colusa Avenue was up for sale. We felt we couldn't afford to buy it, and the housing market in Berkeley was hyper-inflated. There was no place in Berkeley where we could afford to build another pottery. Besides, Ahren was sick of dealing with the laid-back Bay Area art scene.

From an auction, Ahren bought a big 1965 Ford truck, which had started its life as a tow truck. Sixteen years later, it was burdened with a ramshackle house on the back, and had been towed off the street for nonpayment of parking tickets. Abandoned and ownerless, the city of Berkeley put it up for auction. Ahren was the only bidder. He bought it for a hundred dollars. The house on the back was easily demolished and replaced with a flatbed. After some major engine rebuilding, the truck was ready to be loaded with pottery and some of our belongings. In June, Ahren headed east with our dog, Ladi.

We were fairly confident that the truck would make it to New England. We knew it wouldn't snow. But we never considered tornadoes in Kansas. Just before he and Ladi were about to climb into the truck after spending the night in a motel, a black, swirling twister hit town. They watched from the doorway of the motel. Our truck bounced up and down, careening into the car parked next to it, opening a large gash on the driver's door. But that was the only damage. The motel was left standing. But the doughnut shop where Ahren had stopped the night before was turned inside out.

Heather and I spent another two weeks in Berkeley, Heather finishing third grade, and I packing and labeling boxes of belongings to be sent to wherever we should happen to land. At the end of June we flew to New York City with an unhappy tiger cat in a cat carrier, a few suitcases, all of my photographic negatives, and two picture-book dummies. To our dismay, our unhappy tiger cat had to travel with the suitcases and a large unhappy dog. We didn't see him again until he came rolling out on the conveyer belt with the suitcases and the dog, whose carrier was upside down.

It took us three hellish months to decide where to send all those boxes of our belongings that I had left behind in Berkeley. We knew we didn't want to move back to Philadelphia. We thought maybe we could find a place outside of Boston. But it was difficult to find a place that felt as good as our life in Berkeley. We needed enough room for a kiln and studio for Ahren. We needed a good public school for Heather. I wanted to be near a place that might have use for a graphic designer/photographer/illustrator. And this place had to be affordable.

We stayed with friends and family in Connecticut, New Jersey, Boston, southeastern Massachusetts, and Brattleboro, Vermont. Vermont felt good. Rental housing was relatively affordable. Schools seemed to be promising. But it looked like a difficult place to earn a living.

In August, we decided to take a break from looking for a place to live. I decided that I would try to sell my two books. "Thousands of people want to publish children's books," advised a friend. "But few people ever find publishers." I knew that! But I had two books. Why not try to find a publisher? I was accustomed to rejections and I could certainly deal with more. I also thought it would be a good chance to meet editors and art directors, and possibly find an illustration job ... or something—anything!

With that discouraging advice ringing in my ears, I called Jim Giblin at Clarion Books, the editor Betty Bacon had recommended. I made seven or eight other appointments, scheduled over two days. Jim Giblin was my first appointment. He looked at the Henry Rabbit book first.

"I'd like to buy this," he said.

"Err ... okay," I said. I was stunned. I wasn't going to have to wait for months and months to hear whether he would accept my book?

He looked at my inventor book. He chortled. "This is very funny. I might like to buy this one, too," he said.

"But I have seven more appointments!" I said. "I need to be able to show the other editors something!"

"Well, why don't you take this around," he said. "But, I'd like the right of first refusal."

"Okay," I said. What had I just agreed to? What was "right of first refusal"?

I went to seven more appointments and met seven other editors who were interested in my inventor story. I explained about Jim Giblin's right of first refusal.

"Well, if he does refuse it, send it to us."

A few day later, I called Jim. "I'll buy that book, too," he replied.

Fifteen or so books later, I'm still working with Jim. Over the years I've learned how much one can learn from a good editor. I was very lucky he was my first appointment on my quest to sell my two books.

Suddenly life was looking up. Children's picture-book author/illustrators don't get paid much for their first books, but those two book contracts gave me the courage to think we could at least give life in Vermont a try.

We rented a house in Marlboro, Vermont, and moved in on October 1.

The next day, a month late, Heather started fourth grade at Marlboro Elementary, raising the population of the K-8 school to forty-nine students.

Marlboro, Vermont, has one convenience store, a post office, and a population of approximately six hundred. It is home to Marlboro College, a tiny liberal arts college with two-hundred-plus students. In the summer, the Marlboro Music Festival takes over the college. The largest nearby town, Brattleboro, Vermont, is ten miles away and a thousand feet lower, in the Connecticut River Valley.

We soon learned that our higher elevation meant colder weather, more snow, and more ice. We were not prepared. The main source of heat in the house we rented was a woodstove. We didn't have any wood, but we did

have an old chain saw. We soon learned the wisdom of the adage, "He who cuts his own wood gets warm twice," although we would have been warmer if the wood had been drier!

I set up my work table in the living room, close to the woodstove, and started to work on my two books, dressed in many layers of sweaters and tights. Ahren found some carpentry work and started to build a kiln; but winter closed in before he could complete it.

The next six months were unusually snowy, even for Vermont. There was a blizzard on April 10, and we didn't see the last of the snow until well into May. In January, our little Honda Civic station wagon died after a dose of gas tainted with water. It would not have taken much convincing to get me to pack my bag and head back to Berkeley.

But in the midst of adjusting to rural life in the middle of winter, we found a lot that we liked: world-class concerts performed in small churches attended by people in jeans and hiking boots, good bookstores and foreign films in Brattleboro, a music school and dance school for Heather. We met other people who had moved to Vermont because they liked the trees, hills, rivers, mountains, the quiet and the lack of city angst. There were many urban refugees who were all learning how to cut firewood, how to plant a vegetable garden, how to earn a living where conventional jobs were as scarce as year-round housing.

In twelve months we moved four times, finally finding a house we could rent year-round. Three years later, we bought twelve acres on a hillside in Dummmerston, six miles from Brattleboro, in the Connecticut River Valley with less snow and less cold weather than Marlboro.

On October 1, a cold, rainy day, five years after we moved to Vermont, we moved into a very unfinished six-level house we were in the process of building. There was no plumbing, insulation, interior doors, or sheetrock; but it was our house and no one could ask us to move. Our first night, our gray cat, Maude, spent the night racing through the house, catching mice. Outside in the woods, the owls welcomed us with hair-raising shrieks.

Two days after we moved in, the roofers drove down from Thetford to install a standing seam metal roof. By Thanksgiving, Ahren had installed a bathroom, a rudimentary kitchen, most of the insulation, and a lot of the sheetrock. It took five years to finish the house, working on it in fits and starts. We couldn't spend all of our time banging nails and painting; we had to earn a living. And Ahren had to build himself a studio.

When we moved in, I was working on *Olive and the Magic Hat,* my sixth book. I set up my drafting table in the middle of packing boxes and pink insulation in my own spacious, light-filled studio. And that is where I've worked for the last ten years. Today, my studio is sheetrocked and painted. I have shelves for a huge collection of picture books, drawers for paints, drawers for pencils, and large flat drawers for watercolor paper, all built by Ahren.

As an author/illustrator, I wear two hats. For weeks and months I scribble on pads, sit at my computer in my office, a tiny room looking out into the tops of trees, and I'm a writer. Then I spend months downstairs in my studio with paints and brushes and pens and ink, and I'm an illustrator. Sometimes it is difficult to make the transition between the two jobs: to remember how to turn on my computer after months of telling stories with color and line, or to remember how to use my brushes after months of telling stories with words.

Being an author/illustrator is a wonderful job. But there is one disadvantage. We always work alone. I need a lot of peace and quiet while I work, but I also like to see people. Every morning I drive seven miles to the town of Brattleboro to have a cup of coffee, read the paper, and do errands before I go back home to work. I need to make sure that the world still exists outside of my home and studio.

Shortly after my first book, *Henry and the Red Stripes,* was published, the State of Vermont Department of Libraries mounted a traveling exhibit of illustrations by Vermont illustrators of children's picture books. There were approximately twenty of us represented. I quickly realized that there were many writers and illustrators of children's books living and working in Vermont's green mountains. And so did Sam and Emily Bush, who lived in Norwich, Vermont. They decided to build a gallery in their home to exhibit and sell art from children's picture books. Over the years that their gallery was open, there were many show-opening parties at which illustrators from Vermont, New Hampshire, and further afield had a chance to meet, to become friends, and to look at each other's work. Although the gallery is no longer open, the parties have become a tradition—a way for people who are always working alone to get together once or twice a year.

Another way to combat isolation is to form a writers' group, which is what Liza Ketchum, Karen Hesse, Bob McLean, and I did twelve years ago. We meet almost every week. We read and discuss each other's work. We encourage each other. We talk about the trials, tribulations, and joys of publishing. We have become friends. Although we write very different types of books, thinking about their writing problems has taught me to look at my own work with a more critical eye.

When I am working on the finished illustrations for my books, I find that it is easy to lose perspective. One day I think my illustration is wonderful. The next day I wonder how I could do such an embarrassingly bad piece of art. I redo the illustration—sometimes many times. Recently, I've started getting together every other month with a few other Vermont children's book illustrators. We offer each other an experienced, but fresh perspective. We can tell each other, "Stop worrying! It's a terrific illustration," or, "That doesn't work because . . ."

When I speak at schools or conferences, people always ask me, "Where do you get your ideas?"

"Ideas seem to pop up at the most unexpected moments!" I always answer. And they do: in hot steamy baths, in the dentist's chair, in the car, in a hotel dining room while reading the newspaper. A few examples:

When I was visiting schools in Iowa, I read a newspaper story headlined "Hog Wild Day on the Road." It was about a farmer whose hogs escaped on the way to the auction yard. He later found them running around town and managed to catch them all and deliver them to their fate.

The proverbial lightbulb flashed in my brain.

"That's a picture book!" I thought. "But the story needs a different ending." A few weeks later, I started to write *The Great Pig Escape.*

The idea for *The Five-Dog Night* was inspired by a story I heard on the radio about an old Vermonter who relied on his five dogs to keep him warm through the most frigid winter nights. The image of an old codger, snoring in bed, buried deep under his five dogs while the cold winter winds howled around his cabin, appealed to my sense of humor as we learned to deal with our first Vermont winter. I jotted down a few notes, filed them away, and five or six years later, wrote my story.

The Robbery at the Diamond Dog Diner was inspired by a diner in Whatley, Massachusetts. We often stopped there on our way to New York. Everything was green, the countertops, the stools, the booths, the walls; and there was a singing waitress. I drew pictures of people sitting at the counters while we waited for our food and thought, "I'd like to write a story about this place." What kind of a story should it be? I thought perhaps it would be a good setting for a mystery. I remembered some dogs I tried to write about back in Berkeley. Those dogs had been cooks, so the diner was a good place for them. But what was the mystery? Robbers? What would they steal? A favorite recipe? Money? Diamonds? Diamonds in a diner?

Dogs and diamonds in a diner? The diamond dog diner? It was a wonderful alliteration. It sounded totally ridiculous. It sounded like fun. I needed a hero. Another dog? What about a chicken? Why not? So Glenda Feathers drove into the scene, delivering eggs to the diner in a yellow Volkswagen, becoming the witless player who eventually saves the day.

I have file folders filled with ideas: notes, newspaper clippings, scraps of overhead dialogue, nursery rhymes. I

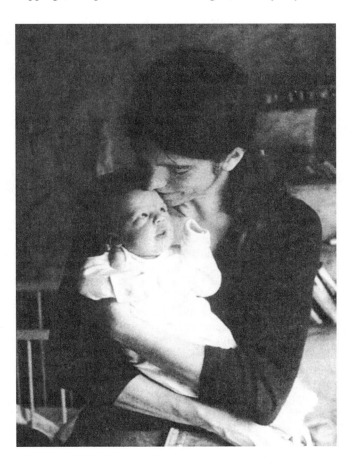

With newborn daughter, Heather, in their room at Wenfordbridge Pottery, Cornwall, England, 1972.

have other folders filled with unfinished stories looking for beginnings, middles, or endings: stories waiting for inspiration.

At one point, when I was working on several stories that wouldn't come together, I looked through my "book idea" folders and came across some rhymes that I had collected from my daughter, Heather, when she was little and running around the house chanting, "Five little monkeys sitting in a tree," and, "Five little monkeys jumping on the bed."

Eight years later, I decided to see if I could make the "monkeys jumping on the bed" rhyme into a full thirty-two-page picture book. I quickly realized that I did not want to start the book with the monkeys jumping on the bed. I needed to introduce them first. I thought about *Madeline* by Ludwig Bemelmans. I remembered how much Heather, at eighteen months, loved to look at the twelve little girls in two straight lines, brushing their teeth and going to bed. So, I had my monkeys take a bath, put on their pajamas, brush their teeth, and when they say goodnight to Mama, we know the hijinks are about to begin.

Before the monkey book was printed and bound, I read the dummy to a group of kindergartners. When I turned to page 5, where the monkeys start jumping on the bed, I opened my mouth to read the next lines; but the kids took over. They couldn't actually read but they knew the words, which they enthusiastically shouted as I mutely turned the pages. When we got to page 32, with the picture of stressed out Mama jumping on the bed, they howled with laughter—a good omen. That book became popular, and three more monkey books have followed.

All of my early stories were anthropomorphic. It wasn't that I didn't want to write about human characters, but for some reason, they seemed to put constraints on the story line. *Jerome the Babysitter* started with human characters. Then Jerome became an alligator babysitting human children. But that idea didn't work because I didn't think the children would misbehave around an alligator. If the children didn't misbehave, there wouldn't be a story! So the children became a family of ten obstreperous little alligators. Then the plot began to unfold.

I decide, by some subliminal process, what sort of animal my character is going to be: a dog, cat, alligator, pig, chicken, rabbit, opossum. Some types of animals seem to me to personify certain human personalities better than others. Also, I like to draw some animals better than others. I do not like to draw horses or unicorns!

My animal characters are caricatures of people. Anthropomorphism gives me license to exaggerate, and the freedom to expand the realms of possibilities in the world I am creating. My chicken character, Glenda Feathers, hides diamonds in the eggs and casts spells that open bank vaults. Gertrude, the bulldog detective, captures her robbers by sewing them into their seats in a movie theater.

Many of my anthropomorphic characters are drawn from the animals who have lived with us at one time or another—although we have never lived with an alligator, or, for that matter, a chicken! I don't start out with the intention to write *about* my animals; but if my character is a dog or a cat, I tend to draw the dogs or cats from our past or present menagerie.

My black-and-white dog, Ophelia, was the real star, having had roles in four books. In my book *Not Until Christmas, Walter!,* Ophelia plays the part of Walter. Just as I finished the book, Ophelia passed away. The book feels like a fitting memorial to an old pal.

Human characters first found their way into my books when I wrote *The Five-Dog Night*. My story about old Ezra and his five dogs was based on a tale about an actual person. My character had to be human. I didn't even think about turning him into an alligator! Other stories with human characters have followed: *The Great Pig Escape* and *Not Until Christmas, Walter!,* both of which are stories based loosely on real events.

For me, the process of writing a picture book is like hitting together the pieces of a jigsaw puzzle. When I get stuck with the writing, I draw. I draw the characters to get to know them better. I draw the action of the story in comic-book scenes, which often helps me to figure out what is going to happen next.

My eyes and ears are always tuned in search of a prospective story. My challenge to myself is to constantly experiment, to try to write different types of stories, and to explore different ways to illustrate them. But there is a common thread in my books. I am happiest when looking at the world with a comic, slapstick perspective, drawn with a quick and simple line.

Often, when I am interviewed about my books I am asked what moral message I'm trying to teach children. I always have to grit my teeth. Why do so many people assume that books for children must preach? My answer is I have no overt messages. I write about characters who are resourceful and self-reliant, with quirks and flaws like the rest of us. I want to tell a good story, hopefully with humor and a good dose of silliness. My aim is enjoyment: mine when I am writing and illustrating, and later my readers', when they sit down with my books. If I am teaching children anything, hopefully it is that reading can be a lot of fun. I cannot imagine a childhood without hours spent slouched in a comfortable armchair with a good book.

Writings

FOR CHILDREN; SELF-ILLUSTRATED; PUBLISHED BY
CLARION

Henry and the Red Stripes, 1982.
Mr. Murphy's Marvelous Invention, 1983.
Henry and the Dragon, 1984.
Jerome the Babysitter, 1985.
The Robbery at the Diamond Dog Diner, 1986.
Olive and the Magic Hat, 1987.
Jerome and the Witchcraft Kids, 1988.
(Reteller) *Five Little Monkeys Jumping on the Bed,* 1989.
Glenda Feathers Casts a Spell, 1990.
Five Little Monkeys Sitting in a Tree, 1991.
Gertrude, the Bulldog Detective, 1992.
Don't Wake Up Mama: Another Five Little Monkeys Story, 1992.
The Five-Dog Night, 1993.

The Great Pig Escape, 1994.

What Do Authors Do? 1995.

Five Little Monkeys with Nothing to Do, 1996.

Not Until Christmas, Walter!, 1997.

Jerome Camps Out, 1998.

What Do Illustrators Do?, forthcoming.

BOOKS ILLUSTRATED

(With others) Diane Downie, *Math for Girls and Other Problem Solvers,* University of California Press, 1981.

Barbara Dana, *Zucchini,* Harper and Row, 1982.

Sue Alexander, *Dear Phoebe,* Little, Brown, 1984.

Thomas Rockwell, *Oatmeal Is Not for Mustaches,* Holt, 1984.

Barbara Steiner, *Oliver Dibbs and the Dinosaur Cause,* Simon and Schuster, 1986.

Steven Kroll, *Annie's Four Grannies,* Holiday House, 1986.

Jim Aylesworth, *Two Terrible Frights,* Atheneum, 1987.

Joy Elizabeth Handcock, *The Loudest Little Lion,* A. Whitman, 1988.

Barbara Steiner, *Oliver Dibbs to the Rescue!,* Avon Books, 1988.

Myra Cohn Livingston, compiler, *Dilly Dilly Piccalilli: Poems for the Very Young,* McElderry Books, 1989.

Mary Elise Monsell, *The Mysterious Cases of Mr. Pin,* Atheneum, 1989.

Mary Elise Monsell, *Mr. Pin: The Chocolate Files,* Atheneum, 1990.

Jim Aylesworth, *The Completed Hickory Dickory Dock,* Atheneum, 1990.

Peggy Christian, *The Old Coot,* Atheneum, 1991.

Barbara Steiner, *Dolby and the Woof-Off,* Morrow, 1991.

Jan Wahl, *Mrs. Owl and Mr. Pig,* Lodestar, 1991.

Mary Elise Monsell, *Mr. Pin: The Spy Who Came North from the Pole,* Atheneum, 1993.

Jennifer Brutschy, *Celeste and the Crabapple Sam,* Lodestar, 1994.

Maryann Macdonald, *Secondhand Star,* Hyperion, 1994.

Mary Elise Monsell, *Mr. Pin: A Fish Named Yum,* Atheneum, 1994.

Maryann Macdonald, *No Room for Francie,* Hyperion, 1995.

Eve Bunting, *The Pumpkin Fair,* Clarion, 1997.

Darleen Bailey Beard, *The Flim-Flam Man,* Farrar, Straus, 1998.

OTHER

Christelow's photographs have appeared in *Progressive Architecture, Colloquy, Ford Foundation, Home, Media and Method, New York Times Book Review, Pennsylvania Gazette, Youth,* and *Teacher* and in various textbooks. She is also the creator of posters for the Children's Book Council.

COLE, Joanna 1944-
(Ann Cooke)

Personal

Born August 11, 1944, in Newark, NJ; daughter of Mario and Elizabeth (maiden name, Reid) Basilea; married Philip A. Cole (an artist and retired psychotherapist), October 8, 1965; children: Rachel Elizabeth. *Education:* Attended University of Massachusetts at Amherst and Indiana University—Bloomington; City College of New York (now of the City University of New York), B.A., 1967.

Addresses

Office—c/o Scholastic, Inc., 555 Broadway, New York, NY 10012-3999.

Career

New York City Board of Education, New York City, elementary school librarian and instructor, 1967-68; *Newsweek,* New York City, letters correspondent, 1968-71; Scholastic, Inc., New York City, associate editor of See-Saw Book Club, 1971-73; Doubleday & Co., Garden City, NY, senior editor of books for young readers, 1973-80; full-time writer, 1980—. *Member:* Authors Guild, Authors League of America, Society of Children's Book Writers and Illustrators, American Association for the Advancement of Science.

Awards, Honors

All of Cole's science books have been named Outstanding Science Trade Books for Children, National Science Teachers Association/Children's Book Council; Child Study Association of America's Children's Books of the Year, 1971, for *Cockroaches,* 1972, for *Giraffes at Home* and *Twins: The Story of Multiple Births,* 1973, for *My Puppy Is Born* and *Plants in Winter,* 1974, for *Dinosaur Story,* 1975, for *A Calf Is Born,* and 1985, for *Large as Life: Daytime Animals, Large as Life: Nighttime Animals,* and *The New Baby at Your House;* Children's Book Showcase selection, Children's Book Council, 1977, for *A Chick Hatches;* New York Academy of Sciences Children's Science honor book, 1981, and Children's Choice selection, International Reading Association/Children's Book Council (IRA/CBC), 1982, both for *A Snake's Body;* Golden Kite Honor Book Award, Society of Children's Book Writers and Illustrators, and Notable Children's Book selection, Association for Library Service to Children, both 1984, both for *How You Were Born;* Irma Simonton Black Award for Excellence in Children's Literature, 1986, for *Doctor Change;* Boston Globe-Horn Book Honor Book for Nonfiction, 1987, for *The Magic School Bus at the Waterworks;* IRA/CBC Children's Choice award, 1990, for *The Magic School Bus inside the Earth;* Eva L. Gordon Award, American Nature Study Society, 1990, for body of science and nature writing; *Washington Post*/Children's Book Guild Award for Nonfiction,

1991, for body of work; David McCord Children's Literature Citation, Framingham (MA) State College and the Nobscot Council of the International Reading Association, 1994, for significant contribution to excellence in children's literature.

Recipient of state children's book awards, including Colorado Children's Choice Award and Washington State Children's Choice Award, both 1989, both for *The Magic School Bus at the Waterworks,* and the Garden State Award for non-fiction, 1992, for *The Magic School Bus inside the Human Body,* and 1993, for *The Magic School Bus Lost in the Solar System.* Many of Cole's books have received best or notable book citations from the American Library Association, *Horn Book,* and *School Library Journal.*

Writings

NONFICTION FOR CHILDREN

Cockroaches, illustrated by Jean Zallinger, Morrow, 1971.

(Under pseudonym Ann Cooke) *Giraffes at Home,* illustrated by Robert Quackenbush, Crowell, 1972.

(With Madeleine Edmondson) *Twins: The Story of Multiple Births,* illustrated by Salvatore Raciti, Morrow, 1972.

Plants in Winter, illustrated by Kazue Mizumura, Crowell, 1973.

Fleas, illustrated by Elsie Wrigley, Morrow, 1973.

Dinosaur Story, illustrated by Mort Kunstler, Morrow, 1974.

Saber-Toothed Tiger and Other Ice-Age Mammals, illustrated by Lydia Rosier, Morrow, 1977.

Cars and How They Go, illustrated by Gail Gibbons, Crowell, 1983.

How You Were Born, Morrow, 1984, revised edition, photographs by Margaret Miller, 1994.

The New Baby at Your House, photographs by Hella Hammid, Morrow, 1985, revised edition with photographs by Miller, Morrow, 1998.

Cuts, Breaks, Bruises, and Burns: How Your Body Heals, illustrated by True Kelly, Crowell, 1985.

Large as Life: Daytime Animals, illustrated by Kenneth Lilly, Knopf, 1985.

Large as Life: Nighttime Animals, illustrated by Lilly, Knopf, 1985, published as *Large as Life Animals in Beautiful Life-Size Paintings,* 1990.

A Dog's Body, photographs by Jim and Ann Monteith, Morrow, 1985.

Hungry, Hungry Sharks: A Step Two Book, illustrated by Patricia Wynne, Random House, 1986.

The Human Body: How We Evolved, illustrated by Walter Gaffney-Kessell and Juan Carlos Barberis, Morrow, 1987.

Evolution, illustrated by Aliki, Crowell, 1987.

Asking about Sex and Growing Up: A Question-&-Answer Book for Boys & Girls, illustrated by Alan Tiegreen, Morrow, 1988.

A Gift from Saint Francis: The First Creche, illustrated by Michele Lemieux, Morrow, 1989.

Your New Potty, illustrated by Miller, Morrow, 1989.

Your Insides, illustrated by Paul Meisel, Putnam, 1992.

You Can't Smell a Flower with Your Ear!: All about Your Five Senses, illustrated by Mavis Smith, Putnam, 1994.

(With Stephanie Calmenson) *Crazy Eights and Other Card Games,* illustrated by Tiegreen, Morrow, 1994.

My New Kitten, photographs by Miller, Morrow, 1995.

Spider's Lunch: All about Garden Spiders, illustrated by Ron Broda, Grosset and Dunlap, 1995.

Riding Silver Star, photographs by Miller, Morrow, 1996.

(With Calmenson) *The Rain or Shine Activity Book: Fun Things to Make or Do,* illustrated by Tiegreen, Morrow, 1997.

(With Calmenson) *The Any Day Book,* Morrow, 1997.

(With Calmenson and Michael Street) *Marbles: 101 Ways to Play,* illustrated by Tiegreen, Morrow, 1998.

(With Calmenson and Street) *Fun on the Run: Travel Games and Songs,* illustrated by Tiegreen, Morrow, 1999.

Potty Book about a Boy, Morrow, 1999.

My Big Girl Potty, Morrow, illustrated by Maxi Chambliss, 2000.

My Big Boy Potty, Morrow, illustrated by Maxi Chambliss, 2000.

Card Games, Morrow, 2000.

Hopscotch and Sidewalk Game, Morrow, 2000.

NONFICTION FOR CHILDREN; PHOTOGRAPHS BY JEROME WEXLER

My Puppy Is Born, Morrow, 1973, revised edition, photographs by Miller, 1991.

A Calf Is Born, Morrow, 1975.

A Chick Hatches, Morrow, 1976.

A Fish Hatches, Morrow, 1978.

(With Wexler) *Find the Hidden Insect,* Morrow, 1979.

A Frog's Body, Morrow, 1980.

A Horse's Body, Morrow, 1981.

A Snake's Body, Morrow, 1981.

A Cat's Body, Morrow, 1982.

A Bird's Body, Morrow, 1982.

An Insect's Body, photographs by Wexler and Raymond A. Mendez, Morrow, 1984.

"MAGIC SCHOOL BUS" NONFICTION SERIES; ILLUSTRATED BY BRUCE DEGEN

The Magic School Bus at the Waterworks, Scholastic, 1986, special edition, Scholastic/New York City Department of Environmental Protection, 1990.

The Magic School Bus inside the Earth, Scholastic, 1987.

The Magic School Bus inside the Human Body, Scholastic, 1989.

The Magic School Bus Lost in the Solar System, Scholastic, 1990.

The Magic School Bus on the Ocean Floor, Scholastic, 1992.

The Magic School Bus in the Time of the Dinosaurs, Scholastic, 1994.

The Magic School Bus inside a Hurricane, Scholastic, 1995.

The Magic School Bus Gets Baked in a Cake, Scholastic, 1995.

The Magic School Bus Plants Seeds, Scholastic, 1995.

The Magic School Bus Briefcase, Scholastic, 1995.

The Magic School Bus Meets the Rot Squad, Scholastic, 1995.

The Magic School Bus Hello Out There, Scholastic, 1995.

The Magic School Bus in the Haunted Museum, Scholastic, 1995.

The Magic School Bus Hops Home, Scholastic, 1995.

The Magic School Bus Gets All Dried Up, Scholastic, 1996.

The Magic School Bus Wet All Over, Scholastic, 1996.

The Magic School Bus inside a Beehive, Scholastic, 1996.

The Magic School Bus out of This World, Scholastic, 1996.

The Magic School Bus Gets Eaten, Scholastic, 1996.

The Magic School Bus Blows Its Top, Scholastic, 1996.

The Magic School Bus Ups and Downs, Scholastic, 1997.

The Magic School Bus and the Electric Field Trip, Scholastic, 1997.

The Magic School Bus Goes Upstream, Scholastic, 1997.

The Magic School Bus Gets Planted, Scholastic, 1997.

The Magic School Bus Shows and Tells: A Book about Archaeology, Scholastic, 1997.

The Magic School Bus in a Pickle, Scholastic, 1997.

The Magic School Bus Plays Ball, Scholastic, 1998.

The Magic School Bus in the Arctic, Scholastic, 1998.

The Magic School Bus in the Rain Forest, Scholastic, 1998.

The Magic School Bus Explores the Senses, Scholastic, 1999.

The Magic School Bus Sees Stars, Scholastic, 1999.

The Magic School Bus Answers Questions, Scholastic, 1999.

The Magic School Bus Taking Flight, Scholastic, 1999.

The Magic School Bus Going Batty, Scholastic, 1999.

The Magic School Bus Gets Ants in Its Pants, Scholastic, 1999.

Ms. Frizzle's Adventures in Egypt, Scholastic, 2000.

FICTION FOR CHILDREN

Cousin Matilda and the Foolish Wolf, A. Whitman, 1970.

The Secret Box, Morrow, 1971.

Cole's immensely popular "Magic School Bus" books combine science and imaginative fun into the stories of Ms. Frizzle and her students, who travel through space and time, changing size if need be, to enjoy a close-up study of various phenomenon, such as prehistoric creatures. (From The Magic School Bus in the Time of the Dinosaurs, *illustrated by Bruce Degen.)*

Fun on Wheels, illustrated by Whitney Darrow, Morrow, 1976.

The Clown-Arounds, illustrated by Jerry Smath, Parents Magazine Press, 1981.

The Clown-Arounds Have a Party, illustrated by Smath, Parents Magazine Press, 1982.

Golly Gump Swallowed a Fly, illustrated by Bari Weissman, Parents Magazine Press, 1982.

Get Well, Clown-Arounds!, illustrated by Smath, Parents Magazine Press, 1982.

The Clown-Arounds Go on Vacation, illustrated by Smath, Parents Magazine Press, 1983.

Aren't You Forgetting Something, Fiona?, illustrated by Ned Delaney, Parents Magazine Press, 1983.

Bony-Legs, illustrated by Dirk Zimmer, Four Winds, 1983.

Sweet Dreams, Clown-Arounds, illustrated by Smath, Parents Magazine Press, 1985.

Monster Manners, illustrated by Jared Lee, Scholastic, 1986.

This Is the Place for Me, illustrated by William Van Horn, Scholastic, 1986.

Doctor Change, illustrated by Donald Carrick, Morrow, 1986.

Monster Movie, illustrated by Lee, Scholastic, 1987.

Norma Jean, Jumping Bean, illustrated by Lynn Munsinger, Random House, 1987.

Mixed-Up Magic, illustrated by Kelly, Scholastic, 1987.

(With husband, Philip Cole) *Hank and Frank Fix up the House,* illustrated by Van Horn, Scholastic, 1988.

Animal Sleepyheads: One to Ten, illustrated by Jeni Bassett, Scholastic, 1988.

The Missing Tooth, illustrated by Marilyn Hafner, Random House, 1988.

(With P. Cole) *Big Goof and Little Goof,* illustrated by M. K. Brown, Scholastic, 1989.

Who Put the Pepper in the Pot?, illustrated by R. W. Alley, Parents Magazine Press, 1989.

It's Too Noisy!, illustrated by Kate Duke, Crowell, 1989.

Buster Cat Goes Out, illustrated by Rose Mary Berlin, Western Publishing, 1989.

Bully Trouble: A Step Two Book, illustrated by Hafner, Random House, 1989.

Monster Valentines, illustrated by Lee, Scholastic, 1990.

Don't Call Me Names!, illustrated by Munsinger, Random House, 1990.

Don't Tell the Whole World!, illustrated by Duke, Crowell, 1990.

How I Was Adopted: Samantha's Story, illustrated by Chambliss, Morrow, 1995.

(With Stephanie Calmenson) *The Gator Girls,* illustrated by Munsinger, Morrow, 1995.

Monster and Muffin, illustrated by Karen Lee Schmidt, Grosset and Dunlap, 1996.

(With Calmenson) *Rockin' Reptiles,* illustrated by Munsinger, Morrow, 1997.

(With Calmenson) *Bug in a Rug: Reading Fun for Just Beginners,* illustrated by Alan Tiegreen, Morrow, 1996.

I'm a Big Brother, illustrated by Chambliss, Morrow, 1997.

I'm a Big Sister, illustrated by Chambliss, Morrow, 1997.

(With Calmenson) *Get Well, Gators!,* illustrated by Munsinger, Morrow, 1998.

Liz Sorts It Out, Scholastic, 1998.

Liz Looks for a New Home, Scholastic, 1998.

(With Calmenson) *Gator Halloween,* Morrow, 1999.

Jump Rope Rhymes, Morrow, 2000.

Street Rhymes, Morrow, 2000.

EDITOR OF CHILDREN'S ANTHOLOGIES

(And author of introduction) *Best-Loved Folktales of the World,* illustrated by Jill K. Schwarz, Doubleday, 1982.

A New Treasury of Children's Poetry: Old Favorites and New Discoveries, illustrated by Judith Gwyn Brown, Doubleday, 1983.

(With Calmenson) *The Laugh Book,* illustrated by Hafner, Doubleday, 1986.

(With Calmenson) *The Read-Aloud Treasury: Favorite Nursery Rhymes, Poems, Stories & More for the Very Young,* illustrated by Ann Schweninger, Doubleday, 1988.

Anna Banana: 101 Jump Rope Rhymes, illustrated by Tiegreen, Morrow, 1989.

(With Calmenson) *Miss Mary Mack: And Other Children's Street Rhymes,* illustrated by Tiegreen, Morrow, 1990.

(With Calmenson) *Ready . . . Set . . . Read! The Beginning Reader Treasury,* illustrated by Anne Burgess, Doubleday, 1990.

(With Calmenson) *The Scary Book,* illustrated by Chris Demarest, Morrow, 1991.

(With Calmenson) *The Eentsy, Weentsy Spider: Fingerplays and Action Rhymes,* illustrated by Tiegreen, Morrow, 1991.

(With Calmenson) *Pat-a-Cake and Other Play Rhymes,* illustrated by Tiegreen, Morrow, 1992.

(With Calmenson) *Pin the Tail on the Donkey and Other Party Games,* illustrated by Tiegreen, Morrow, 1993.

(With Calmenson) *Six Sick Sheep: One Hundred Tongue Twisters,* illustrated by Tiegreen, Morrow, 1993.

(With Calmenson) *Give a Dog a Bone: Stories, Poems, Jokes, and Riddles about Dogs,* illustrated by John Speirs, Scholastic, 1994.

(With Calmenson) *Why Did the Chicken Cross the Road?: And Other Riddles Old and New,* illustrated by Tiegreen, Morrow, 1994.

(With Calmenson) *A Pocketful of Laughs: Stories, Poems, Jokes, and Riddles,* illustrated by Hafner, Doubleday, 1995.

(With Calmenson) *Ready, Set, Read—and Laugh!: A Funny Treasury for Beginning Readers,* Doubleday, 1995.

(With Calmenson) *Yours Till Banana Splits: 201 Autograph Rhymes,* illustrated by Tiegreen, Morrow, 1995.

OTHER

The Parents Book of Toilet Teaching, Ballantine, Morrow, 1983.

(With Calmenson) *Safe from the Start: Your Child's Safety from Birth to Age Five,* Facts on File, 1990.

(With Wendy Saul) *On the Bus with Joanna Cole: A Creative Autobiography,* Heinemann, 1996.

Also contributor of articles to *Parents.*

Adaptations

An animated series for PBS-TV based on the "Magic School Bus" books began in 1994 and features the voices of Lily Tomlin, as Ms. Frizzle, Robby Benson, Carol Channing, and Malcolm-Jamal Warner; the series is also available in a CD-ROM version by Microsoft Home and Scholastic, Inc. The "Magic School Bus" series was used as the basis of the American Library Association's 1994 reading program, "Reading Is a Magic Trip." Cassette recordings have been made for *Bony-Legs,* Random House, 1985, and *Monster Movie* and *Dinosaur Story,* both for Scholastic, 1989.

Sidelights

Joanna Cole is the author of over a hundred children's books on subjects as varied as any young reader's interests. Cole's fertile imagination has produced first readers with jokes and puzzles, humorous tales of the Clown-Around family, retellings of folk tales and myths, and books about science that dazzle, inspire, and inform. The winner of numerous awards from the American Library Association, the National Science Teachers Association/Children's Book Council, and various state reading associations, Cole follows her own widespread interests to write about the life cycle of an insect, to field questions on sex, to talk about potty training, or to take a trip to the stars in a Magic School Bus. Cole has introduced the fascinating world of science to young readers in her stand-alone titles and in several series, including the hugely popular "Magic School Bus" books, the latter of which has spawned a television spin-off. A thorough researcher, the author has been praised by critics for her scientific accuracy, but her books are most effective because of her humor and frank and easily understood explanations that bring complicated, technical subjects within reach of younger audiences.

Cole first discovered the pleasures of writing when she was in grade school. "I discovered in the fifth grade what I liked to do; write reports and stories, make them interesting and/or funny and draw pictures to go along with the words," she once told *Something about the Author (SATA).* "Except for the pictures, I still do that. I remember grade school very clearly when I sat at my desk, happily interested in whatever subject I was writing about. Science was my favorite. Our teacher, Miss Bair, would assign us to read a science trade book every week. And each week, she would choose one student to do an experiment and report on it to the class. I would have done an experiment every week if she had let me. Grade school was very important to me, much more influential than my later education. Maybe that's why as an adult I ended up writing books for children."

After receiving her bachelor's degree from the City College of New York, Cole pursued her interest in books by working variously as a librarian, teacher, and editor. It was during her first job at an elementary school that she was inspired by an article about cockroaches in the *Wall Street Journal.* Realizing that this was a subject she had never read about in school, Cole decided to write about it herself. The first publisher she submitted her manuscript to rejected the idea, but the author had more luck when she sent her book to the publishing house of William Morrow, where editor Connie C. Epstein helped Cole hone her skills in science writing. Since the time of that debut book, Cole has written both nonfiction and fiction books for younger readers, and in 1980, after a decade of editing children's books, she went full time as a writer.

Many of Cole's nonfiction works focus on the life sciences. In her series, "Animal Bodies," Cole introduces young readers to the anatomy of such animals as horses, frogs, dogs, birds, cats, and snakes. Reviewing *An Insect's Body* in *Horn Book,* Sarah S. Gagne commented, "If it is possible for Joanna Cole to improve on the unparalleled series of books about animal bodies that she has written over the years, she has now done so." Using the cricket as a representative insect, Cole examined its body structure and how this corresponds to its environment. *Booklist*'s Ilene Cooper, reviewing the same title, remarked, "anyone whose curiosity is intact cannot help but be captivated by this fascinating work." This series concludes with *The Human Body: How We Evolved,* which explains how archaeologists have pieced together the evolutionary history of mankind and how human anatomy compares to that of apes, chimpanzees, gorillas, and others of our primate cousins. *Booklist*'s Cooper called this volume a "fine introduction to evolution that will go a long way toward answering children's questions about their origins," while Jason R. Taylor, writing in *Science Books and Films,* felt that it was "an excellent, extremely well-researched book."

In her science writing, Cole has always been aware of how children's feelings affect their reactions to factual material. In her series on animals' births, which includes *A Calf Is Born, My Puppy Is Born, How You Were Born,* and *My New Kitten,* the author explains the physiology of birth with candor and accuracy, and is careful to include the gentle care baby mammals need to grow, which mirrors children's own experience. Reviewing a revised edition of *How You Were Born,* Denise L. Moll noted in *School Library Journal* that "Cole relates the process of conception and birth in a personalized manner," and that while several other titles on the same subject are available, "Cole's book continues to set the standard." That standard was upheld in *My New Kitten,* a book that "promotes warm, fuzzy feelings and at the same time gives youngsters just a peek at the creatures' developmental stages," according to Margaret Chatham writing in *School Library Journal.*

Similarly, a number of Cole's books focus on child development. These titles—*The New Baby at Your House, Your New Potty, Asking about Sex and Growing Up, I'm a Big Brother, I'm a Big Sister,* and *How I Was Adopted: Samantha's Story*—help families share facts and feelings about key issues in children's lives. The first title deals with all topics involving the arrival of a new infant, including sibling rivalry. Martha Topol of *School Library Journal* felt that *The New Baby at Your House* "gives honest, practical advice on helping youngsters prepare for and cope with a new arrival." Such advice is furthered in the companion volumes, *I'm a Big Brother* and *I'm a Big Sister*. Dina Sherman, reviewing the books in *School Library Journal*, felt, "Familiar situations, as well as positive reinforcement of individuality and importance as part of the family, are good reasons to put this book into the hands of children who will soon be older siblings." Cole employed a question and answer format for her 1988 title on sex education for pre-teens, *Asking about Sex and Growing Up*, an "invaluable" book, according to a writer for *Kirkus Reviews*, and one that is "brief and to the point," as *Booklist*'s Denise M. Wilms pointed out, with "lots of information at a level younger children will appreciate." Adoption gets the Cole treatment in *How I Was Adopted: Samantha's Story*, about a young girl who tells her own story. A contributor for *Publishers Weekly* felt that this book presented a "cheerful, informative approach" to the subject. Stephanie Zvirin, writing in *Booklist*, noted, "Cole expertly negotiates a middle course that provides children with some excellent, age-appropriate background on adoption."

Of all her science books, however, it is her popular "Magic School Bus" series for which Cole is best known. All the books in the series combine science and imaginative fun into stories that have been warmly received by critics and readers alike. As a writer for *Children's Books and Their Creators* put it, "In recent years [Cole] has given the term nonfiction new meaning with the 'Magic School Bus' series. A masterly combination of scientific facts, humor, and fantasy, these books turn science class into story hour." Each book takes a class of school children led by their eccentric teacher, Ms. Frizzle, on some new adventure of discovery. The humorous illustrations by Bruce Degen and the unlimited possibilities for travel in a bus that can dig through the earth, shrink to microscopic size, or blast off into space result in lively reading. Each page is a combination of fact- and fun-filled text blending with and sometime competing for room with Degen's artwork. "Just as 'Sesame Street' revolutionized the teaching of letters and numbers by making it so entertaining that children had no idea they were actually learning something, so the 'Magic School Bus' books make science so much fun that the information is almost incidental," wrote Katherine Bouton in the *New York Times Book Review*. Bouton declared that these books offer "the freshest, most amusing approach to science for children that I've seen." Andrea Cleghorn, writing in *Publishers Weekly*, commented, "'The Magic School Bus' books serve science with a sizzle," and further noted that specialists in the field check all the books in the series for accuracy.

Cole based the character of the teacher, Ms. Frizzle, on her own favorite science teacher, Miss Bair, although, the author told *SATA*, "Miss Bair did not dress at all like Ms. Frizzle!" The kids in the "Magic School Bus" books may grumble a bit about the adventures they experience, but in their hearts they love Ms. Frizzle and are proud to be in her class. "In 'The Magic School Bus' books I use the same criteria as I do in all my science books," Cole

explained. "I write about ideas, rather than just facts. I try to ask an implicit question—such as, How do our bodies get energy from the food we eat? or How do scientists guess what dinosaurs were like? Then I try to answer the question in writing the book." The success of Cole's "Magic School Bus" books, which have sold in the millions worldwide, has carried over to television, where PBS has turned them into an animated series; Cole and illustrator Degen serve as consultants.

Adventures on the school bus take the students and Ms. Frizzle, as well as Mr. Wilde, the assistant principle, inside the human body, down to the waterworks, inside a dog's nose or beehive or hurricane, and back in time to the world of the dinosaurs or through space to the stars. "Climb aboard," John Peters encouraged readers in a *School Library Journal* review of *The Magic School Bus in the Time of the Dinosaurs*, "there's never a dull moment with 'the Friz' at the wheel!" Reviewing the 1999 addition to the series, *The Magic School Bus Explores the Senses*, Christine A. Moesch remarked in *School Library Journal* that it was "another fun, fact-filled adventure in the series." Commenting on *The Magic School Bus and the Electric Field Trip*, Blair Christolon noted in *School Library Journal* that the book "makes a complex subject fun to read about and simple to understand." The same could be said for all the titles in the series, books that mix a sense of humor with lucid explanations of scientific facts.

Although Cole is more often recognized for her science books, she is also the author of a number of stories for children, has compiled anthologies of children's literature, and has written books for adults on parenting and

In **My New Kitten,** *Cole presents information about the developmental stages of cats and stresses the gentle care baby mammals need to grow. (Illustrated with photographs by Margaret Miller.)*

child development. Early in her career Cole wrote a series of amusing easy-readers featuring the Clown-Arounds, a silly family who sleep in shoes and generally approach life from a goofy angle. Popular retellings of folk tales from Cole include *Bony-Legs,* "a bang-up read," according to Nancy Palmer writing in *School Library Journal,* and *Don't Tell the Whole World!,* an example of "fine storytelling," as a *Publishers Weekly* contributor noted.

Working with Stephanie Calmenson, Cole has produced both nonfiction anthologies as well as popular fiction titles, including "The Gator Girls" series. Together the two have dealt with riddles, card games, rhymes, and brainteasers. In their 1995 *Ready, Set, Read—and Laugh: A Funny Treasury for Beginning Readers,* Cole and Calmenson have compiled a combination of stories, poems, jokes, and games that according to *Booklist*'s Hazel Rochman, "will turn readers on to the fun of books." Rochman concluded, "Kids will delight in the word play and the nonsense, and they'll want to read more." Other popular titles include *Give a Dog a Bone, The Rain or Shine Activity Book, Marbles: 101 Ways to Play,* and *Bug in a Rug.* With their "Gator Girls" series, they present best reptilian friends Allie and Amy Gator in adventures from going to summer camp to getting over an illness. In the debut volume, *The Gator Girls,* the two girls want to cram all their summertime activities into the few days they have before going off to camp. *Booklist*'s Mary Harris Veeder thought that in this beginning chapter book "the joys of true-blue friendship are humorously realized." *Get Well, Gators!* sees the duo fighting swamp fever in time to take part in a local street fair. "Give this one to chapter-book readers looking for a funny book," advised Kay Weisman in a *Booklist* review. And in *Gator Halloween,* the girls "are up to their old tricks," according to Zvirin in *Booklist,* determined to win the best costume prize in the local Halloween parade. Zvirin called the book "fun, with a dash of over-the-top comedy and wonderful illustrations."

Whether sharing the antics of Ms. Frizzle and her dauntless crew in search of scientific knowledge, or having fun with rhymes and jokes, or making everyday developmental activities into a meaningful experience, Cole has proven that she has what it takes to hook a young reader and bring him or her back for more. "Always keeping mind the emotional level of her audience, Joanna Cole presents her information in a reassuring, caring tone, with great respect for children," concluded the critic for *Children's Books and Their Creators.* For Cole, being able to write for children is the fulfillment of a childhood dream; for her legions of contented readers it is a windfall.

Biographical and Critical Sources

BOOKS

Authors of Books for Young People, 3rd edition, Scarecrow Press, 1990.
Children's Books and Their Creators, edited by Anita Silvey, Houghton Mifflin, 1995, p. 154.

Children's Literature Review, Volume 5, 1983, Volume 40, Gale, 1996.

PERIODICALS

Appraisal: Science Books for Young People, spring, 1973; spring, 1975; spring, 1978; winter, 1980; winter, 1981; winter, 1982.
Booklist, June 15, 1984, Ilene Cooper, review of *An Insect's Body,* p. 1482; September 1, 1987, I. Cooper, review of *The Human Body,* p. 61; June 15, 1988, Denise M. Wilms, review of *Asking about Sex and Growing Up,* pp. 1733-34; April 15, 1995, Mary Harris Veeder, review of *The Gator Girls,* p. 1497; August, 1995, Stephanie Zvirin, review of *How I Was Adopted,* p. 1955; October 1, 1995, Hazel Rochman, review of *Ready, Set, Read—and Laugh!,* p. 329; October 15, 1997, p. 408; March 1, 1998, p. 1138; November 15, 1998, Kay Weisman, review of *Get Well, Gators!,* p. 590; September 1, 1999, S. Zvirin, review of *Gator Halloween,* p. 145; November 1, 1999, p. 534; January 1, 2000, p. 928.
Bulletin of the Center for Children's Books, July-August, 1986; November, 1986; February, 1987; January, 1988; March, 1988; June, 1988; December, 1992, p. 108; October, 1994, p. 40; October, 1996, p. 52; June, 1995, p. 340.
Horn Book, October, 1980; February, 1982; October, 1984, Sarah S. Gagne, review of *An Insect's Body,* p. 627; May-June, 1986, p. 347; September-October, 1986, p. 609; May-June, 1995, p. 348; January-February, 1998, p. 90; July-August, 1999, p. 480.
Kirkus Reviews, March 1, 1988, review of *Asking about Sex and Growing Up,* p. 361.
Los Angeles Times Book Review, March 22, 1987; February 28, 1988; July 30, 1989; December 17, 1989; September 30, 1990.
New York Times, April 23, 1999, p. E39.
New York Times Book Review, February 7, 1988, Katherine Bouton, p. 28.
Publishers Weekly, October 12, 1990, review of *Don't Tell the Whole World!,* p. 63; January 25, 1991, Andrea Cleghorn, "Aboard the Magic School Bus," pp. 27-28; April 18, 1994, p. 27; July 4, 1994, p. 63; October 2, 1995, review of *How I Was Adopted,* p. 74; August 23, 1999, p. 61.
School Library Journal, December, 1971; February, 1973; January, 1980; May, 1982; December, 1983, Nancy Palmer, review of *Bony-Legs,* p. 79; March, 1987, pp. 113-115; November, 1992, p. 38; December, 1992, p. 95; April, 1993, Denise L. Moll, review of *How You Were Born,* p. 110; September, 1994, John Peters, review of *The Magic School Bus in the Time of the Dinosaurs,* pp. 206, 226; April, 1995, Margaret Chatham, review of *My New Kitten,* p. 123; March, 1996, p. 188l; October, 1996, p. 111; April, 1997, Dina Sherman, review of *I'm a Big Brother* and *I'm a Big Sister,* pp. 96-97; November, 1997, Blair Christolon, review of *The Magic School Bus and the Electric Field Trip,* p. 106; April, 1998, Martha Topol, review of *The New Baby at Your House,* p. 114; May, 1998, p. 130; February, 1999, Christine A. Moesch, review of *The Magic School Bus Explores the Senses,* p. 96; October, 1999, p. 166.

Science Books and Films, January-February, 1988, Jason R. Taylor, review of *The Human Body,* pp. 174-75.

OTHER

Riding the Magic School Bus with Joanna Cole and Bruce Degen (videotape), Scholastic, 1993.*

—*Sketch by J. Sydney Jones*

*   *   *

COOKE, Ann
See COLE, Joanna

*   *   *

COY, John 1958-

Personal

Born August 9, 1958, in Minneapolis, MN; son of Richard (a professor) and Luanne (a teacher; maiden name, Kulas) Coy; married Fiona McCrae (a publisher), June 18, 1999; children: Sophie. *Education:* St. John's University, B.A. (summa cum laude), 1980; St. Mary's University, M.A., 1993. *Hobbies and other interests:* Basketball, yoga, travel, reading.

Addresses

Home—225 Cecil St., Minneapolis, MN 55414. *E-mail*—johncoy@uswest.net.

Career

Writer. Visiting author and writing teacher, 1994—, creator of the workshop, Basketball and Poetry, 1998—, participator in Page to Stage workshop, Children's Theater Company, Minneapolis, MN, 1999. Science Museum of Minnesota, collaborator on the Internet web site, Thinking Fountain, 1996—. *Member:* Society of Children's Book Writers and Illustrators, Minnesota Literature (vice-president of board of directors).

Awards, Honors

Selection as a "choice book of 1996," Cooperative Children's Book Center, Marion Vannett Ridgway Memorial Award, excellence in an author's or illustrator's first picture book, 1997, selection for Fanfare 1997, *Horn Book* Honor List, selection as "a best children's book of the year" by Children's Book Committee, Bank Street College of Education, 1998, and Seal of Quality, Family Channel Entertainment Guide, all for *Night Driving;* grant from the Loft, 1999; resident, Anderson Center for Interdisciplinary Studies, 2000; selection as "notable book for 2000," American Library Association, for "choices list," Cooperative Children's Book Council, and as a Notable Social Studies Trade Book for Young People, 2000, all for *Strong to the Hoop.*

John Coy

Writings

Night Driving, illustrated by Peter McCarty, Holt (New York), 1996.
(Editor) *A Special Stretch of Sky* (anthology of student writing), COMPAS, 1997.
Strong to the Hoop, illustrated by Leslie Jean-Bart, Lee & Low (New York), 1999.
Vroomaloom Zoom, illustrated by Joe Cepeda, Knopf/Crown (New York), 2000.

Librettist for *All Around Sound,* composed by Libby Larsen, 1999; writer and narrator for an orchestral piece based on the work of Aaron Copland, for Minnesota Orchestra, 2000.

Sidelights

John Coy told *SATA:* "Each summer when I was a boy, we took long car trips as a family. Because I was the oldest child, I sat up front with my dad as everybody else fell asleep. He would tell me stories, and we'd watch for animals and have the road to ourselves. These memories formed the basis for my first picture book, *Night Driving,* which was beautifully illustrated by Peter McCarty.

"Basketball is my favorite sport and it has become extremely popular with both boys and girls. I was surprised, however, to find that this was not reflected in picture book titles. Consequently I wrote *Strong to the Hoop,* which was illustrated in a striking style by Leslie Jean-Bart.

"For my third book, *Vroomaloom Zoom,* the illustrator was Joe Cepeda, who created bright colorful pictures that convey wonderfully the story about a girl who does not want to go to sleep. I have been fortunate to work with three such talented illustrators, who have produced three such distinct books.

"As a student I never had an author visit my school. I wonder if I had, if I would have considered writing stories an option for myself and started to do it sooner. This is one of the reasons I enjoy visiting schools and interacting with students so much.

"I feel lucky to be writing books that adults and children can enjoy together."

Biographical and Critical Sources

PERIODICALS

Booklist, September 1, 1996, Bill Ott, review of *Night Driving,* p. 141; December 15, 1999, Bill Ott, review of *Strong to the Hoop,* p. 784.
Bulletin of the Children's Center for Books, December, 1996, review of *Night Driving,* p. 131.
Children's Book Review Service, October, 1996, review of *Night Driving,* p. 14.
Horn Book, September-October, 1996, Roger Sutton, review of *Night Driving,* p. 574.
Horn Book Guide, spring, 1997, review of *Night Driving,* p. 574.
Hungry Mind Review, winter, 1996, review of *Night Driving,* p. 40.
Kirkus Reviews, September 1, 1996, review of *Night Driving,* p. 1320.
Los Angeles Times Book Review, December 8, 1996, review of *Night Driving,* p. 18.
New York Times, December 9, 1996, Christopher Lehmann-Haupt, review of *Night Driving,* p. B3.
New York Times Book Review, December 22, 1996, Sam Swope, review of *Night Driving,* p. 16.
Publishers Weekly, August 26, 1996, review of *Night Driving,* p. 97; September 27, 1999, review of *Strong to the Hoop,* p. 105.
School Library Journal, October, 1996, Lauralyn Persson, review of *Night Driving,* p. 91; October, 2000, Sheilah Kosco, review of *Strong to the Hoop.*

ON-LINE

John Coy's Web site, www.johncoy.com

CRILLEY, Mark 1966-

Personal

Born May 21, 1966, in Hartford City, IN; son of Robert H. and Virginia A. (Ruffin) Crilley; married Miki Hirabayashi (a teacher), May 2, 1998; children: Matthew Masayuki Robert. *Education:* Kalamazoo College, B.A., 1988. *Religion:* Presbyterian.

Addresses

Office—P.O. Box 71564, Madison Heights, MI 48071. *Agent*—Robb Horan, Sirius Entertainment, 264 East Blackwell, Dover, NJ 07801. *E-mail*—poogmail@earthlink.net.

Career

Young Men's Christian Association, Changhua, Taiwan, English teacher, 1988-90; Morioka English Academy, Iwate, Japan, English teacher, 1991-93; Young Men's Christian Association, Changhua, English teacher, 1993-94; Sirius Entertainment, Dover, NJ, creator and illustrator of the comic book series *Akiko,* 1995-.

Mark Crilley

Awards, Honors

Twelve nominations for Eisner Award, for the *Akiko* comic books.

Writings

SELF-ILLUSTRATED JUVENILE NOVELS

Akiko on the Planet Smoo, Delacorte (New York City), 2000.
Akiko in the Sprubly Islands, Delacorte, 2000.
Akiko and the Great Wall of Trudd, Delacorte, in press.

Work in Progress

Akiko in the Castle of Alia Rellapor (tentative), completion expected in 2001.

Sidelights

Mark Crilley told *SATA:* "I entered the world of children's books after having created the *Akiko* comic book series. Luckily one of my comics found its way into the hands of Lawrence David, an editor at Random House Children's Books. Though I had no experience in writing (apart from my own comic books), Lawrence felt confident that I would be able to create a series of four novels based on the first eighteen issues of my *Akiko* comics.

"The process of writing juvenile fiction has certainly been challenging for me, and even now I'm not quite convinced of my own competence as a writer! I think of myself as a storyteller really, and I simply do my best to entertain. I try to provide a quiet message in my books about the value of friendship and the great things a child can achieve when people really believe in her.

"I am fortunate to have both my *Akiko* comics and novels embraced by a small band of dedicated fans, without whom I'd never have made it to where I am today."

Biographical and Critical Sources

PERIODICALS

Booklist, March 1, 2000, Chris Sherman, review of *Akiko on the Planet Smoo,* p. 1243.
Entertainment Weekly, June 26, 1998, "Mark Crilley: Cult Cartoonist," p. 90.
Publishers Weekly, January 17, 2000, review of *Akiko on the Planet Smoo,* p. 57.
School Library Journal, February, 2000, Lisa Prolman, review of *Akiko on the Planet Smoo,* p. 92.

ON-LINE

Amazon.com, www.amazon.com/ (August 26, 2000).

CROSSLEY-HOLLAND, Kevin (John William) 1941-

Personal

Born February 7, 1941, in Mursley, Buckinghamshire, England; son of Peter Charles (a composer and musicologist) and Joan Mary (an MBE for services to the arts; maiden name, Cowper) Crossley-Holland; married Caroline Fendall Thompson, 1963 (marriage dissolved); married Ruth Marris, 1972 (marriage dissolved); married Gillian Cook, 1982 (marriage dissolved); married Linda Waslieu, 1999; children: (first marriage) Kieran, Dominic; (third marriage) Oenone, Eleanor. *Education:* St. Edmund Hall, Oxford, B.A., 1962. *Hobbies and other interests:* Music, archaeology, travel.

Addresses

Home—Clare Cottage, Burnham Market, Norfolk PE31 8HE, England. *Agent*—Rogers Coleridge and White, 20 Powis Mews, London W11 1JN, England.

Career

Author, editor, and translator; educator; broadcaster; and journalist. Macmillan, London, England, editor, 1962-71; Victor Gollancz Ltd., London, editorial director, 1972-77; Andre Deutsch Ltd., London, general editor, "Mirror of Britain" series, 1975—; Boydell and Brewer, Woodbridge, Suffolk, England, editorial consultant, 1983-91. Visiting lecturer, professor, or fellow at various colleges and universities, including Tufts-in-London Program, 1967-78, University of Leeds (Gregory Fellow), 1969-71, University of Regensburg, 1978-80, Winchester School of Art, 1983-84, St. Olaf College (Fulbright Scholar), 1987-88, University of St. Thomas (Endowed Chair in the Humanities and Fine Arts), 1991-95; visiting lecturer for British Council in Germany, Iceland, India, Malawi, Slovakia, and Yugoslavia. British Broadcasting Corp., London, talks producer, 1972; contributor to radio and television dramas, talks, features, and musical works. *Exhibitions:* Manuscripts, letters, artwork, and memorabilia from the Crossley-Holland archive exhibited as *Telling the Tides: A Writer's Life* at Brazen Head Gallery, Burnhamn Market, 1998, Aldeburgh Poetry Festival, 1998, and Leeds University Art Gallery, 1999. *Member:* Greater London Arts Association (Literature Panel, 1973-77), King's Lynn Festival (steering committee, 1977), Poetry Book Society (board of management, 1977-83), Eastern Arts Association (chairman, Literature Panel, 1986-89), Friends, Wingfield College, (trustee and chairman, 1989-98), American Composers Forum (board of directors, 1993-97), Poetry-next-the-Sea (co-founder and chairman, 1998—).

Awards, Honors

Arts Council Award for the best book for children, 1966-68, for *The Green Children;* Poetry Book Society Choice, 1976, for *The Dream-House;* Carnegie Medal,

Kevin Crossley-Holland

British Library Association, 1985, for *Storm;* Poetry Book Society Recommendation, 1986, for *Waterslain;* Oak Award, Nottinghamshire Libraries, 1999, for *Short!;* Smarties Prize, 2000, for *The Seeing Stone.* Elected as a Fellow of the Royal Society of Literature.

Writings

"WULF" SERIES; HISTORICAL FICTION

The Sea Stranger, illustrated by Joanna Troughton, Heinemann (London), 1973, Seabury (New York) 1974.

The Fire-Brother, illustrated by Troughton, Heinemann, 1974, Seabury, 1975.

The Earth-Father, illustrated by Troughton, Heinemann, 1976.

Sea Stranger, Fire-Brother, and Earth-Father (omnibus), Pan Books (London), 1979.

Wulf (revision of trilogy), illustrated by Gareth Floyd, Faber (London), 1988.

"WELSH FOLKTALES" SERIES; RETELLINGS, WRITTEN WITH GWYN THOMAS AND ILLUSTRATED BY MARGARET JONES

Tales from the Mabinogion, Gollancz (London), 1984, Overlook Press (Woodstock, New York), 1985.

The Quest for Olwen, Lutterworth Press (Cambridge), 1988.

The Tale of Taliesin, Gollancz, 1992.

"BRITISH FOLK TALES" SERIES; PICTURE BOOK RETELLINGS, EXCEPT AS NOTED

British Folk Tales: New Versions (collection), Orchard (London and New York), 1987.

Boo! Ghosts and Graveyards, illustrated by Peter Melnyczuk, Orchard (London and New York), 1988.

Dathera Dad: Fairy Tales, illustrated by Melnyczuk, Orchard (London and New York), 1988.

Piper and Pooka: Boggarts and Bogles, illustrated by Melnyczuk, Orchard (London and New York), 1988.

Small-Tooth Dog: The Wonder Tales, illustrated by Melnyczuk, Orchard (London and New York), 1988.

The Dark Horseman and Other British and Irish Folktales, illustrated by Melnyczuk, Orchard, 1995.

OTHER; FOR CHILDREN

Havelok the Dane, illustrated by Brian Wildsmith, Macmillan (London), 1964, Dutton (New York), 1965.

King Horn, illustrated by Charles Keeping, Macmillan, 1965, Dutton, 1966.

The Green Children, illustrated by Margaret Gordon, Macmillan, 1966, Seabury, 1968, picture book edition, illustrated by Alan Marks, Oxford University Press (London), 1994.

The Callow Pit Coffer, illustrated by M. Gordon, Macmillan, 1968, Seabury, 1969.

(With Jill Paton Walsh) *Wordhoard: Anglo-Saxon Stories,* Farrar, Straus (New York), and Macmillan, 1969.

(Translator) *Storm and Other Old English Riddles* (verse), illustrated by Miles Thistlethwaite, Farrar, Straus, and Macmillan, 1970.

The Pedlar of Swaffham, illustrated by M. Gordon, Macmillan, 1971, Seabury, 1972.

Green Blades Rising: The Anglo-Saxons (nonfiction), Deutsch (London), 1975, Seabury, 1976.

The Wildman, illustrated by C. Keeping, Deutsch, 1976.

The Dead Moon and Other Tales from East Anglia and the Fen Country, illustrated by Shirley Felts, Deutsch, 1982, Faber, 1986.

Beowulf, illustrated by C. Keeping, Oxford University Press (Oxford), 1982.

Storm (primary grade fiction), illustrated by A. Marks, Heinemann, 1985, Barrons (New York), 1989.

Axe-Age, Wolf-Age: A Selection from the Norse Myths, illustrated by Hannah Firmin, Deutsch, 1985.

(Reteller, with Susanne Lugert) *The Fox and the Cat: Animal Tales from Grimm,* illustrated by Susan Varley, Andersen (London), 1985, Lothrop (New York), 1986.

Under the Sun and over the Moon (poetry), illustrated by Ian Penney, Orchard (London), Putnam (New York), 1989.

Sleeping Nanna, illustrated by Melnyczuk, Orchard (London), 1989, Ideal (New York), 1990.

Sea Tongue, illustrated by Clare Challice, BBC Publications/Longman (London), 1991.

Tales from Europe, illustrated by Lesley Buckingham, Phyllis Malton, and Emma Whiting, BBC Publications, 1991.

Long Tom and the Dead Hand and More Tales from East Anglia and the Fen Country, illustrated by S. Felts, Deutsch, 1992.

Norse Myths, illustrated by Gillian McClure, Simon & Schuster (New York), 1993.

The Labours of Herakles, illustrated by Peter Utton, Orion (London), 1993.

The Old Stories: Folk-Tales from East Anglia and the Fen Country, illustrated by John Lawrence, Colt (Cambridge), 1997.

The King Who Was and Will Be: The World of King Arthur and His Knights, illustrated by Peter Malone, Orion (London), 1998, published in the United States as *The World of King Arthur and His Court: People, Places, Legends, and Lore,* Dutton, 1998.

(With Ivan Cutting) *The Wuffings: A Play,* Runetree (London), 1999.

The Seeing Stone (Volume 1 in *Arthur* trilogy), Orion Children's Books (London), 2000, Scholastic (New York), 2001.

Enchantment, illustrated by Emma Chichester Clark, Orion (London), 2000.

The Ugly Duckling, illustrated by Meilo SO, Orion (London), 2001, Random House (New York), 2001.

At the Crossing Places (Volume 2 in *Arthur* trilogy), Orion (London), 2001, Scholastic (New York), 2002.

EDITOR; FOR CHILDREN

Running to Paradise: An Introductory Selection of the Poems of W.B. Yeats, illustrated by Judith Valpy, Macmillan (London and New York), 1967.

Winter's Tales for Children: No. 3, Macmillan, 1967, St. Martin's Press (New York), 1968.

Winter's Tales 14, Macmillan, and St. Martin's Press, 1968.

The Faber Book of Northern Legends, illustrated by Alan Howard, Faber, 1977.

The Faber Book of Northern Folk-Tales, illustrated by Howard, Faber, 1980.

The Riddle Book, illustrated by Bernard Handelsman, Macmillan (London), 1982.

Northern Lights: Legends, Sagas and Folk-Tales, illustrated by A, Howard, Faber, 1987.

The Young Oxford Book of Folk Tales, Oxford University Press, 1998.

Short! A Book of Very Short Stories, Oxford University Press, 1998.

POETRY

On Approval, Outposts (London), 1961.

My Son, Turret (London), 1965.

Alderney: The Nunnery, Turret, 1968.

Confessional, Sceptre Press (Frensham, Surrey, England), 1969.

Kevin Crossley-Holland's East Anglian Poems (collection), illustrated by James Dodds, Jardine (Suffolk, England), 1988.

Norfolk Poems, illustrated by John Hedgecoe, Academy Editions (London), 1970.

A Dream of a Meeting, Sceptre Press, 1970.

More Than I Am, illustrated by Ralph Steedman, Steam Press (London), 1971.

The Wake, Keepsake Press (Richmond, Surrey), 1972.

The Rain-Giver (poetry collection), Deutsch, 1972.

Petal and Stone, Sceptre Press (Knotting, Bedfordshire), 1975.

The Dream-House and Other Poems (collection), Deutsch, 1976.

Between My Father and My Son, Black Willow Press (Minneapolis), 1982.

Time's Oriel and Other Poems (collection), Hutchinson (London), 1983.

Waterslain (poetry collection), Hutchinson, 1986.

The Wanderer, illustrated by James Dodds, Jardine (Colchester), 1986.

The Painting-Room (poetry collection), Century Hutchinson (London), 1988.

Oenone in January, illustrated by J. Lawrence, Old Stile Press (Llandogo, Wales), 1988.

The Seafarer, illustrated by Inger Lawrence, Old Stile Press, 1988.

New and Selected Poems: 1965-1990 (collection), Hutchinson, 1991.

Eleanor's Advent, illustrated by Alyson MacNeill, Old Stile Press, 1992.

The Language of Yes (poetry collection), Enitharmon (London), 1996, Dufour Editions (Chester Springs, PA).

Poems from East Anglia (selection), Enitharmon, 1997.

Selected Poems, Enitharmon (London), 2001.

EDITOR; FOR ADULTS

The Mirror of Britain, ten volumes, Seabury, 1974-79.

(With Patricia Beer) *New Poetry 2,* Arts Council of Great Britain (London), 1976.

(And translator) *The Anglo-Saxon World: An Anthology,* Boydell Press (Woodbridge, Suffolk), 1982, Barnes and Noble (Totowa, NJ), 1983, Oxford University Press, 1984.

Folk Tales of the British Isles, Folio Society, 1985, illustrated by Hannah Firmin, Faber, 1986, Pantheon, 1988.

The Oxford Book of Travel Verse, Oxford University Press (London and New York), 1986.

Medieval Lovers: A Book of Days, Century Hutchinson (London), Weidenfeld & Nicolson (New York), 1988.

Medieval Gardens: A Book of Days, Rizzoli, 1990.

TRANSLATOR

The Battle of Maldon and Other Old English Poems, edited by Bruce Mitchell, St. Martin's Press, and Macmillan, 1965.

Beowulf, illustrated by Brigitte Hanf, Farrar, Straus, and Macmillan, 1968, Brewer (Cambridge), 1977, Boydell (Woodbridge, England), 1987, illustrated by Heather O'Donoghue, Oxford University Press, 1998.

The Exeter Riddle Book, Penguin (London), 1969, illustrated by Virgil Burnett, Folio Society, 1978, as *The Exeter Book Riddles,* Folio Society, 1978, as *The Exeter Book of Riddles,* Penguin, 1979, revised edition, 1993.

The Old English Elegies, Folio Society, 1988.

OTHER; FOR ADULTS

Pieces of Land: Journeys to Eight Islands (nonfiction and poetry), Gollancz, 1972.

The Norse Myths: A Retelling, Pantheon and Deutsch, 1980, also published as *The Penguin Book of Norse Myths: Gods of the Vikings,* Penguin, 1993.

The Legends of Arthur, Pantheon, 1987.

The Stones Remain: Megalithic Sites of Britain (nonfiction), illustrated by Andrew Rafferty, Rider (London), 1989.

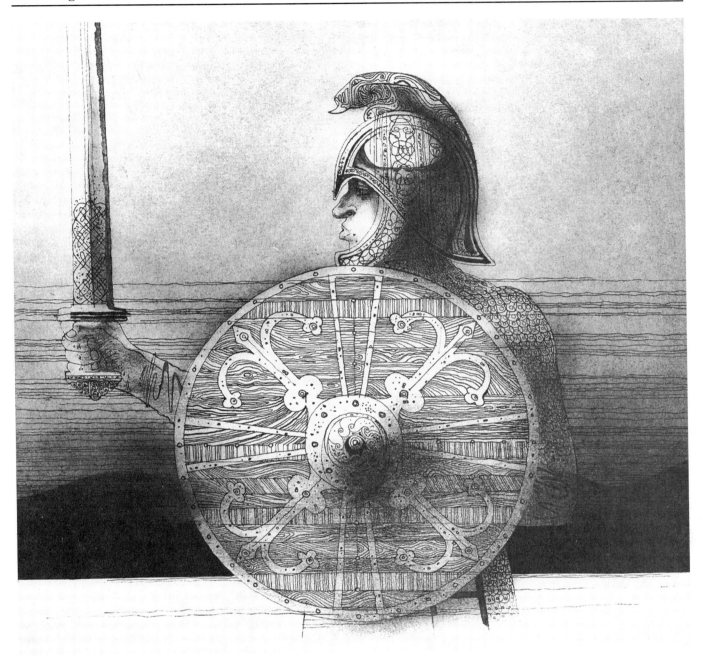

In his notably accessible retelling of the eighth-century Old English epic poem, Crossley-Holland depicts Beowulf, a brave young man who travels from Sweden to Denmark to vanquish two ferocious monsters, then returns home and rules his land peacefully for fifty years. (From Beowulf, *illustrated by Charles Keeping.)*

Different—But Oh How Like!, Daylight Press for the Society for Storytelling (London), 1998.

AUTHOR OF LYRICS

A Knot of Riddles, music by Sir Arthur Bliss (produced in Cheltenham, UK, 1964), Novello (London), 1964.

The Baltic Sprat, music by Albert Chatterly, Novello (London), 1964.

Riddles, music by William Mathias (produced in Vancouver, Canada, 1989), Oxford University Press (London and New York), 1992.

The Green Children, music by Nicola LeFanu (produced in the United Kingdom, 1990, and in St. Paul, MN, 1991), Novello (London), 1991.

The Dream of the Rood, music by James Callahan, produced in St. Paul, MN, 1994.

Listening for Your Name: Images of Childhood, music by Donald Betts, produced in St. Paul, MN, 1994.

The Wildman, music by N. LeFanu (produced in the United Kingdom, 1995), libretto, Boydell and Brewer (Cambridge), 1995, vocal and orchestral scores, Novello (London), 1995.

Soft Footfalls: Song of the Agnizes, music by Anne Kilstofte, produced in St. Paul, MN, 1995.

Four Advent Carols, music by Stephen Paulus, produced in St. Paul, MN, 1995.

Two Riddles, music by N. LeFanu, produced in Wilmslow, UK, 1996.

The Philosopher Bird, music by Peter Crossley-Holland, produced in Wilsmlow, UK, 1996.

Pilgrim Jesus, music by S. Paulus (produced in Cambridge, UK, 1996, produced in St. Paul, MN, 1997), European American Music Corporation (Pennsylvania), 1996.

The Nine Gifts, music by Steve Heitzig, produced in San Francisco, CA, 1998.

Crossing Places, music by S. Callahan, produced in St. Paul, MN, 1999.

The Earth's Embrace, music by Andrew Simpson, produced in Cheltenham, UK, 1999.

Author of introduction to *Peter Grimes: The Poor of the Borough* by George Crabbe, Folio Society, 1990. Editor, with Sarah James, of *A Winchester Folio: Ten Poems by People Who Have Given Readings at Winchester School of Art,* Winchester School of Art Press. Contributor of poems to poetry journals and of reviews to newspapers and periodicals, including the *Sunday Times* (London), the *Times Literary Supplement,* and the *Spectator.* Crossley-Holland's works have been translated into most European languages. A collection of Crossley-Holland's poetry notebooks, translations from Anglo-Saxon, and the manuscripts of recent children's books are housed in the Brotherton Collection at the University of Leeds. The manuscripts of his early children's books are housed in The Osborne Collection, Toronto; the Kerlan Collection, Minneapolis, MN, holds material relating to *Under the Sun and over the Moon.*

Work in Progress

King of the Middle March (Volume 3 in *Arthur* trilogy), for Orion Books (London), 2002, and Scholastic (New York), 2003.

Sidelights

An English author, reteller, translator, and editor, Kevin Crossley-Holland is acknowledged as an authority on European history and literature, as well as a gifted writer of prose and poetry. Marcus Crouch of the *Junior Bookshelf* called him "our leading interpreter of the Dark Ages and an eloquent writer too." Crossley-Holland is known for his preservation of traditional literature, as well as for his ability to bring the past to life for modern readers. Crossley-Holland is particularly noted for his retellings of British and Norse folktales—his collections are often considered definitive—as well as for his well-received translations of the Anglo-Saxon epic *Beowulf* and metaphorical riddles. He has often referred to the folktales and legends of East Anglia, and to the poetry of the Anglo-Saxons as the main influences on his work. As a poet, his main concern is with the power of the past, especially as it influences the present, and of place; in addition, he writes about such subjects as destiny, the passage of time, personal history and identity, and family life.

As a writer for children and young people, Crossley-Holland draws upon sources similar to those that inform his literature for adults. Most of his books for the young are retellings: for example, Crossley-Holland has produced volumes taken from Norse myths and medieval romances, as well as from the folktales of East Anglia. In addition, he has collaborated with Gwyn Thomas on retellings of the Mabinogion, a Welsh cycle of hero tales, and with Susanne Lugert on a collection of animal stories originally written by the Brothers Grimm. He has also retold the Greek myth about the labors of Herakles (Hercules) and has written a compendium of information, legend, and lore about King Arthur. Although he receives consistent praise for all of these works, Crossley-Holland is also well regarded for his historical fiction. His "Wulf" trilogy of young adult novels—*The Sea Stranger, The Fire-Brother,* and *The Earth-Father*—describe how an artistic, fatherless boy in seventh-century England becomes a monk after he gets to know the Northumbrian missionary Cedd, a real figure who brought Christianity to the East Saxons. Crossley-Holland later rewrote the trilogy as *Wulf,* a single-volume work. *Storm,* a Carnegie Medal-winning story for readers in the early primary grades, features a young girl who saves the life of her older sister with the help of a farmer's ghost.

Often lauded as a storyteller, Crossley-Holland is noted for investing his works with a poetic sense of language (his prose style has been called "lapidary English," which refers to the smooth, polished quality of a gemstone) and for bringing freshness, texture, and universality to his subjects. Although he is occasionally criticized for creating books that include some obtrusive contemporary dialogue and are more appealing to adult professionals than to children, Crossley-Holland is usually acknowledged as a talented, sensitive writer whose works show respect for the past while providing appeal for today's readers. Donna R. White of *St. James Guide to Young Adult Writers* concluded that Crossley-Holland's "true genius lies in retelling ancient myths, legends, and tales . . . . All of Crossley-Holland's best work combines his storytelling skills with his mastery of the poetic elements of language." Writing in *Twentieth-Century Children's Writers,* Charles Causley commented that, among his contemporaries, Crossley-Holland "has few rivals as an exponent of the traditional narrative re-told . . . . [I]n so much of his work, the people and moods of a period apparently remote in time are vitalized and gently brought near. In the writer, and by attrition, in the reader, past, present, and future meet. Such writing, to such effect, is a rare and notable achievement."

Born in Mursley, Buckinghamshire, England, Crossley-Holland is the son of Peter Crossley-Holland, a noted composer and ethnomusicologist, who taught at the University of California (Los Angeles) and contributed to such works as the *Encyclopaedia Brittanica* and *Grove's Dictionary of Music and Musicians.* His mother,

Joan Mary Cowper, was made a Member of the British Empire for her services to the arts; he has a younger sister, Sally. Before he was six, Crossley-Holland and his family lived in several parts of northwestern England. They returned to the house in which he was born, Crosskeys in the Chiltern Hills, in 1947. The next year, Peter Crossley-Holland joined the Music Division of the British Broadcasting Corporation (BBC). Joan Crossley-Holland, who had been a prominent potter and designer for the Doulton china-making company, began conducting social surveys for the Central Office of Information. Their jobs took both parents to London during the week. "But, at the weekends," Crossley-Holland wrote in *Something about the Author Autobiography Series (SAAS),* "until I was nine and went away to school, Crosskeys burst into life. In his study, my father played the piano and warbled as he worked on his own compositions; my mother, caught I think in a difficult marriage, filled the house with tides of friends—ours as well as hers—and filled the air with aromas from the Aga . . . . "

Crossley-Holland came from a musical family. He elected to learn the viola, and described his association with it in his essay in *Fourth Book of Junior Authors and Illustrators:* "Learning the viola was a purgatory, for me and for others . . . . Between the ages of ten and, say, eighteen, I doubt if I picked up more than half-a-dozen books! Notes, not words, seemed to me then and seem to me now to be the purest form of artistic expression." In addition to music, the Crossley-Holland household was filled with stories. Before bedtime, Peter Crossley-Holland, his son noted in *SAAS,* "sometimes came with his Welsh harp and sat by our bunk beds, and said-and-sang (as the Anglo-Saxons called it) folktales to Sally and me. Not only humans beautiful and ugly and rich and poor and ambitious and lazy and brave and cowardly (and most of us are a mixture of those) but seal-women and ghosts and dragons and boggarts visited that little room. Above all, though, my father loved the Celtic stories of fairy folk. In the gloom, I saw pookas and pipers, changelings, and the Banshee, dark horsemen, Tam Lin, and (my father's favourite), the bewitching lady who walked out of the lake up the mountain of Fan Fach. I haven't the slightest doubt that the seeds of my lifelong interest in folktale, legend, and myth were sown there, in the blue hour between day and night, waking and sleep."

As a boy, Crossley-Holland often accompanied his father on walking tours of archeological sites. "[F]rom that day to this," the author wrote, "I don't suppose I've walked past a molehill without kicking it over." Father and son found several artifacts from the Iron Age and medieval times, including two pieces of a Romano-British cooking pot that fit together. When they discovered a Roman coin with the head of the emperor Constantine on it, Crossley-Holland recalled, "I was electrified . . . . That was the place and moment at which I was first fully conscious of the presence of the past: that mysterious, challenging, enriching, shared dimension which has underpinned so much of my writing for adults and children." At the age of nine, Crossley-Holland had a letter printed in the London *Times* about

ancient coinage. With his father, Crossley-Holland cleared out a shed and created a museum for all of his treasures. The first visitor to the museum left the young proprietor half a crown—a fortune in those days; the visitor was the noted author Rumer Godden. Crossley-Holland stated, "That museum! How wonderful it was! . . . [O]f all the rooms I have ever stepped into, this is the one I return to most often."

Crossley-Holland's mother, the author wrote, "was eager for us to have not only as secure, but as rich and varied a childhood as possible." She arranged dancing, riding, golf, and cricket lessons and also paid for instruction in tennis; Crossley-Holland noted, "I came love the game dearly and to play competitive tennis in my teens and early twenties . . . . " Crossley-Holland attended a private day school, then went to Swanbourne House, a preparatory boarding school, at the age of nine and a half. At Swanbourne, Crossley-Holland met Latin teacher "Floppy" Wright, who showed the young student, as Crossley-Holland later recalled, "how Latin could underpin my knowledge of English and French. To him, I think, I owe part of my lifelong delight in language." Although he was not an avid reader, Crossley-Holland was enthralled by the book, *Our Island Story,* an account of key episodes in British history. He wrote, "Fired by this patriotic and highly-coloured book, and nothing if not ambitious, I decided at the age of eleven to embark on a major literary enterprise of my own, a History of the World which, somewhat later, and rather reluctantly, I scaled down to a History of Britain! I resumed work at the beginning of each holiday, and managed quite a number of chapters before eventually losing heart." Crossley-Holland also wrote what he called a "highly-derivative ghost story" at Swanbourne House. At fourteen, Crossley-Holland decided to become a priest, a vocation that he sustained until he entered Oxford University. At sixteen, Crossley-Holland wrote a poem in honor of his grandfather that he described as "a kind of psalm about life as a prelude to death." The fledgling poet wrote two additional poems, an impressionistic account of a concert and a sonnet about a windmill in Norfolk, within a few weeks; the sonnet was published in the *Bryanston Saga.* Crossley-Holland noted that "it was in drafting the three poems described above that I first felt excited by the risk and possibilities of imaginative writing." While working on a two-year project with his mother, he also wrote a descriptive inventory, *The Church Brasses of Buckinghamshire.*

Writing in *SAAS,* Crossley-Holland called the north coast of Norfolk "my imaginative heartland. The acres I walked and waded and rowed over, and so came to love as a boy, have become the ground—I think that's the right word—for much of my writing." Many of his early poems were inspired by what the author called "the fierce nature" of the place as well as by its history and inhabitants. Crossley-Holland also traveled to other parts of the world. As a boy, he went to France and Switzerland, experiences that had a profound effect on him. He noted, "It became natural to go abroad, and I was soon possessed of a great wanderlust." At seventeen, Crossley-Holland hitchhiked through Belgium,

Germany, Denmark, Sweden, and Finland; before he was twenty, he had visited nearly every country in western Europe. Later, Crossley-Holland traveled to India and Russia, lived and worked in Bavaria, and spent five years in Minnesota.

After graduating from Swanbourne House and Bryanston School, to which he went at the age of thirteen, Crossley-Holland entered Oxford University to study English literature. There, he wrote in *Fourth Book of Junior Authors and Illustrators,* "I met the Anglo-Saxons, and their world is one of the two mainsprings of my work. At first sight, their culture seemed so far removed from our own. Of course it is, yet their heroism and doggedness, their love of irony and understatement, their passion for the sea—these and other qualities seem to me as pertinent to the northern world now as they did then . . . . East Anglia is where I feel at home, and above all on the harsh uncompromising elemental north coast. My work's second mainspring has been a continuing fascination with that part of England." Crossley-Holland became drawn to old Anglo-Saxon poems like *Beowulf* and *The Battle of Maldon,* works that he would later retell or translate. He also continued to write poetry, and published his first book, the short pamphlet *On Approval,* in 1961. The next year, Crossley-Holland graduated from Oxford with a B.A. in the honors school of English language and literature. His first job was in the publicity department, and subsequently as an editor in the London publishing house of Macmillan, and he stayed with the company for nine years. He also became associated with "The Group," a gathering of English poets—Martin Bell, Peter Porter, Alan Brownjohn, Fleur Adcock, George MacBeth, and others—who met regularly to discuss each other's work. In 1963, Crossley-Holland married his first wife, Caroline Fendall Thompson; the couple had two sons, Kieran and Dominic. At around the same time, Crossley-Holland wrote an autobiographical novel, "Debendranath," that is as yet unpublished, as well as about fifty pages of a second novel.

In 1964, Crossley-Holland produced his first book for children and young people, the retelling *Havelok the Dane.* He discovered the original poem, a Middle English romance, and decided that it contained a compelling story that would work well in prose. In his narrative, Crossley-Holland outlines how young Havelok, the rightful king of Denmark, is forced to flee his homeland to escape death at the hand of his evil regent, Lord Godard. Havelok goes to England, where he meets Princess Goldborough, the rightful Queen of England; like Havelok, the princess has been deposed by her regent. Forced to marry as an indignity, Havelok and Goldborough fall in love and set about regaining their respective thrones. Havelok returns to Denmark and defeats Godard; he then returns to England and reinstates Goldborough. The king and queen live alternate years in Denmark and England and have fifteen children. Writing in the *Junior Bookshelf,* a reviewer queried, "What more can a reader ask, except the accurate and lively, colourful, dramatic transcription of the thirteenth century narrative romance by a youthful scholar—and, of course, Brian Wildsmith's drawings." Ethna Sheehan

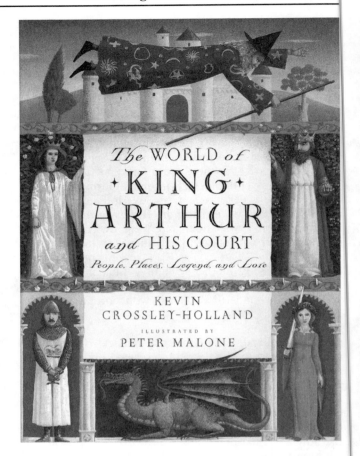

Crossley-Holland approaches the topic of the legendary king and his times by using myths and facts to discuss Merlin, the Crusades, knighthood, and several other related subjects. (Cover illustration by Peter Malone.)

of the *New York Times Book Review* observed that Crossley-Holland retold *Havelok the Dane* "with drama, horror, and fun. The author has carefully developed Havelok's likable personality and Goldborough's spirited nature." Writing in the *Horn Book Magazine,* Ethel L. Heins concluded, "This is a tale of ambition, bloody murder, loyalty, love, and the triumph of freedom over tyranny; the author has retold the original, rather long-winded narrative in a colorful, vigorous manner."

After the publication of *Havelok the Dane,* Crossley-Holland began to interweave his books for a youthful audience with original collections of poetry (often published by small presses in limited editions), translations from Anglo-Saxon, retellings of myth, and edited collections of tales, poems, and short stories. *The Green Children,* a retelling of a twelfth-century English legend, is one of his best known works for the young. In this book, Crossley-Holland describes how two siblings, a boy and a girl with green skin, are found in a chalk pit. The children do not speak English, eat only green vegetables, and are blinded by the sun. The boy dies of homesickness, but the girl adapts to her new life and learns to speak; she is able to tell the tale of how she and her brother strayed from their subterranean world. Although the girl gradually turns fairer and even marries, she never stops looking for the entrance to her lost home. Writing in *Growing Point,* Margery Fisher stated, "Though there is nothing solemn about the book, it is intensely moving. The author's unerring choice of words suggests antiquity...." Alice Low of the *New York Times Book Review* noted the "grace and authenticity of the text" before concluding that "modern children who give [the book] a chance should take to it." *The Green Children* was initially illustrated by Margaret Gordon, then republished, in a completely different form, as a monologue with illustrations by Alan Marks. The first edition won the Arts Council Award for the best book for children in the years 1966-69 and also inspired an opera of the same name, for which Crossley-Holland created the libretto and Nicola LeFanu the music.

Crossley-Holland received special acclaim for *Wordhoard: Anglo-Saxon Stories,* a collection of tales for young adults on which he collaborated with English author Jill Paton Walsh. Consisting of eight stories, four by each author, the volume includes tales about real people such as Bede, Aelfric, and William the Conqueror, as well as plots and quotes from Anglo-Saxon poetry. A critic in the *Junior Bookshelf* called the tales "a group as varied as they are intriguing," while Paul Heins of the *Horn Book Magazine* noted that the stories, "skillfully told and subtle in construction, form a unified historical sequence, and bring to life the rigorous splendors of the Old English period." Writing in *School Library Journal,* Bruce L. MacDuffie called *Wordhoard* the "first successful attempt to present a sensitive vision of Anglo-Saxon life to teens.... Teachers and librarians now have the means to bring the Anglo-Saxon experience alive for today's youth through stories worth having simply for themselves."

In 1970, Crossley-Holland produced *Storm and Other Old English Riddles,* translations of thirty-six riddles from the eleventh-century Anglo-Saxon manuscript, the *Exeter Book.* Noted for its variety of subject and mood, the collection includes riddles about such subjects as nature, everyday life, pagan attitudes, and Christian beliefs. Elizabeth Maslen of *Encounter* commented, "To cut through such tangles, retain a hint of the Old English alliterative line, and show the variety and appeal of subject matter and mood is quite a feat"; the critic concluded that Crossley-Holland "gives us the poetry, the teasing charm and above all the pleasure of the riddles—which is no small achievement." Alexander Taylor of *Children's Literature* added, "These are excellent translations. Mr. Crossley-Holland keeps the flavor of the four stress alliterative Anglo-Saxon line, but does not become a slave to it. Thus, the poems read as poems, rather than translations." At around the same time as the publication of *Storm and Other Old English Riddles,* Crossley-Holland became the editorial director of Victor Gollancz Ltd., a publishing house in London.

In 1972, Crossley-Holland married his second wife, Ruth Marris. He produced the first of his "Wulf" series of historical novels, *The Sea Stranger,* in the following year. The first of a trilogy set in Northumberland in

eastern England during the seventh century, the story centers on Wulf, a boy who is more interested in making carvings in wood and bone than he is in battles. When Cedd, a Christian missionary, spends the night with his family, Wulf is intrigued by the charismatic man and his message. Cedd leaves, but promises to return in the spring. When he comes back, it is to build a cathedral on land granted by King Ethelwald. At the end of the novel, Wulf is baptized, becomes Cedd's student, and decides to join his order of monks. A. R. Williams of the *Junior Bookshelf* stated, "Along the line, one gets an impression of fresh if astringent winds of change blowing through the East of England; some insight into the attitudes of contemporary rulers and their subjects to the largely welcome ideas of Christianity; a picture of family rural life and court organisation, possibly too simplified for the profound historian but adequate for the age group for whom the book is designed." Williams concluded by calling *The Sea Stranger* "a real children's book." Writing in the *Horn Book Magazine,* Paul Heins noted, "Wulf, the other members of his family, and Cedd are well-drawn, and the simple narrative is rich with historical, literary, and archeological details." The second volume of the series, *The Fire-Brother,* takes place a year after the conclusion of its predecessor. When their harvest is bad, some of the farmers blame the monks for convincing them not to sacrifice to their goddess Freya. In retaliation, Wulf's brother, Oswald, sets the monastery on fire before running away. Wulf, who is torn between the love for his family and his devotion to Cedd's teachings, is sent by Cedd—now a bishop—to find Oswald with a message of forgiveness and a plea to return home. Wulf finally finds his brother, reconciles with him, and coaxes him out of exile. Writing in the *Horn Book Magazine,* Paul Heins commented, "A nice balance is kept between the presentation of the purposeful, hopeful activities of monastic life and worship and the labors and tribulations of primitive land-cultivators...." In the final volume of the trilogy, *The Earth-Father,* Wulf is the only survivor of a plague that has killed all of the brothers in his monastery. In an attempt to be with Cedd before he dies, Wulf risks catching the plague himself. Cedd and Wulf are finally reunited; after Cedd's death, Wulf resolves to carry on his work.

In 1988, Crossley-Holland rewrote his trilogy in a single volume, *Wulf.* D. A. Young of the *Junior Bookshelf* stated, "The author's deep knowledge and love of this period enable him to bring alive the life and landscape of a dark and distant time." Juliet Townsend of the *Spectator* noted that *Wulf* "catches brilliantly the flavour of Anglo-Saxon imagery, expressed in simple modern English." The critic concluded by noting that the story "captures admirably the facts and feeling of this remote age." Writing in the *Times Literary Supplement,* Heather O'Donoghue stated, "[A]s one has come to expect from Kevin Crossley-Holland, there is a wonderfully evocative and accurate sense of time and place about the book." Margery Fisher of *Growing Point* concluded that the "dignified, simple narrative ... evokes the feeling of change and of a dedication to Christianity that takes practical and spiritual forms in the achievements of a young man whose life has been given a new direction by the incomer Cedd. The mixture of history and imagination is an entirely successful one."

In 1975, Crossley-Holland produced *Green Blades Rising: The Anglo-Saxons,* an informational book for young adults that describes the daily lives, beliefs, practices, art, and literature of the culture, as well as its influence on our own time. A critic in *Kirkus Reviews* noted that the author "has an eye for the beauty of an early sword or shield," before concluding, "When Crossley-Holland asks, 'Who were the Anglo-Saxons? What were they really like?' it is clear that the question has seized his own imagination; his answers ... might well fire others." Mary Columba of *Best Sellers* added that *Green Blades Rising* "gives a remarkable picture of the Anglo-Saxon life and its contributions to our own." The next year, Crossley-Holland produced *The Wildman,* a retelling of an East Anglian story that, like *The Green Children,* is considered one of his most memorable—and disturbing—works. The Wildman is a merman who tells of his capture, imprisonment, and torture during the reign of Henry II. Through his eyes, readers learn his impressions of human behavior. Finally, the Wildman becomes alienated from life on sea as well as on land. Nicholas Tucker of the *Times Literary Supplement* wrote that it would be "hard to imagine that anything in this book would appeal to most children." Marcus Crouch of the *Junior Bookshelf,* noting the book's picture-book format, queried, "Will older children, who might be receptive of its message, miss it for superficial physical reasons? If they do, they miss too a most moving experience." Donna R. White of the *Dictionary of Literary Biography (DLB)* concluded, "*The Wildman* represents the best of Crossley-Holland's work; it combines his poetic grasp of language and his storytelling abilities.... [It] is a moody, evocative piece, both haunting and sad." Crossley-Holland also wrote the libretto for an operatic version of *The Wildman* by Nicola LeFanu, which premiered at the Aldeburgh Festival in 1995.

In 1977, Crossley-Holland resigned his position at Gollancz in order to write full-time; however, he has continued to accept editorial commissions and to act as a visiting lecturer and college professor of English. Crossley-Holland has also produced a complete translation of *Beowulf* for adults, a work that was praised for its exceptional scholarship. Crossley-Holland married his third wife Gillian Cook in 1982; the couple have two daughters, Oenone and Eleanor. He retold *Beowulf* as a picture book for older children and young people in the same year as his marriage. Illustrated by noted artist Charles Keeping, the story outlines how Beowulf the Geat travels to Denmark to destroy the evil monster Grendel, who has been harassing his father's friends. After Beowulf kills Grendel, the monster's mother, an old sea-wolf, seeks revenge. Beowulf kills her and takes her head back to the king of the Danes. He rules over the Geats for fifty years and dies while courageously fighting a dragon; after his death, Beowulf is celebrated by his subjects. Although the retelling is considered especially graphic, it is credited with making *Beowulf* approachable for contemporary young readers, especial-

Crossley-Holland, as taken by his daughter Oenone.

ly through Crossley-Holland's strong prose and use of modern idioms. Margery Fisher of *Growing Point* concluded by calling *Beowulf,* "All in all, a remarkable new presentation of a hero-tale basic to our culture." Writing in *Junior Bookshelf,* G. Bott noted that Crossley-Holland's "vigorous prose narrative, a skillful and sensitive compression of ... the original, retains much of the unvarnished directness of the earlier version." Bonnie Saunders of *School Library Journal* concluded, "This retelling of the classic epic maintains much of the ancient storytelling tradition in its richly tapestried prose. It is told in a high, formal style worthy of an epic...."

In 1985, Crossley-Holland produced one his most popular books for children, *Storm,* a short work of fiction for readers in the early primary grades. This story (not to be confused with Crossley-Holland's riddle book of the same name) features small Annie, who lives in an isolated home in the East Anglian marsh. When her older sister goes into labor during a bad storm, it is up to Annie to help her. Annie is apprehensive about the ghost rider who haunts her village—a farmer who was killed when he confronted two highwaymen. However, Annie conquers her fears and heads into the storm. She meets a silent man on horseback who helps to get her to the doctor. Her companion, it turns out, is the ghost. Writing in the *Junior Bookshelf,* A. R. Williams commented, "A great deal of convincing drama is packed into so few pages without limiting character to cardboard cutout.... This is not strip-cartoon stuff." Donna R. White of *DLB* concluded, "The poetic cadence of the language lifts *Storm* above most tales of this sort." *Storm* was awarded the Carnegie Medal in 1985.

In 1985, Crossley-Holland produced *Folk Tales of the British Isles,* a collection directed to adults that helped to cement his reputation as an expert in the field. Two years later, Crossley-Holland produced *British Folk Tales: New Versions,* a collection of fifty-five stories and ballads for children. *British Folk Tales* includes hero tales, ghost stories, trickster tales, and works featuring fairies, goblins, selkies, and other supernatural creatures. Familiar favorites such as "Jack and the Beanstalk," "Goldilocks and the Three Bears," and "Tam Lin" appear with tales and verse that are less well known. In addition, the reteller provides some changes to his original sources, combining some tales and reframing others, shifting points of view, and turning narratives into poems. Calling Crossley-Holland "a fine story-teller with a poet's ear," Jennifer Westwood of the *Times Literary Supplement* stated that "this selection . . . is the most representative by a modern reteller." Westwood added, "Unlike most retellers, Crossley-Holland is no more afraid of the inconsequential snippet than he is of the fully developed narrative that gives scope for larger effects. What he makes of very slight tales such as 'Dathera Dad' is often a revelation." Writing in *Bulletin of the Center for Children's Books,* Betsy Hearne noted, "In its revealing and revitalizing of the traditional, this makes a long-lasting contribution to readers and story-tellers alike." Crossley-Holland called *British Folk Tales* "the book I have been working towards all my life" in an essay that he wrote for *Books for Your Children.* Throughout the rest of the 1980s and 1990s, Crossley-Holland produced selections from *British Folk Tales* as picture books illustrated by Peter Melnyczuk. Crossley-Holland is also well known for retelling the myths and legends of Scandinavian literature; his collection for adults, *The Norse Myths: A Retelling* was published in 1980, while his selection for children, *Norse Myths,* was published in 1993.

In 1999, Crossley-Holland married Linda Waslieu, and in 2000, he published only his second book of original fiction, *The Seeing Stone.* Set in England around the year 1200, a young boy, named Arthur, is given a "seeing stone," a piece of black obsidian, by Merlin. Using the stone, Arthur is able to visit the realm of King Arthur. The novel is first in Crossley-Holland's Arthur trilogy, with the remaining volumes in the series slated for publication in 2001 and 2002.

Crossley-Holland once stated that his work has its basis in "roots, the sense of the past embodied in present, the relationship of person to place." In a lecture at the University of St. Paul, Minnesota, Crossley-Holland stated, "A tale names, it expresses what children already instinctively know; it therefore helps them to understand their own thoughts and feelings." He added that the type of story that can foster understanding and tolerance for others makes "two apparently opposing points. Firstly it says, 'each one of us is *one,* is singular, completely and utterly different from any other one.' And then, in the same breath, the story says 'we are all the same, all of us, and together we are one, and only together are we one.'" In an essay that he wrote for *Books for Keeps,* Crossley-Holland commented that "a successful retelling depends . . . on the writer's depth of understanding and use of language. The writer working with folk-tale has access to an inherited word-bank, and needs to take account of the fact that he is working within a great tradition, but, for all that, his story must be told in language that is keen, quick, shining, resonant, and his own. Et nova et vetera! Both new and old. The writer asks himself: what does this story mean? And how am I to recast it? And in the end, the quality of his perceptions and narratives is defined by the very words that express them." Writing in *SAAS,* he said, "There is [a] saying stuck up on the wall behind my desk, the astonishing first sentence of St. John's Gospel; "In the beginning was the Word, and the Word was with God, and the Word was God." What does St. John mean? I think his seventeen words . . . express the nature of God in terms of sound and speech, and imply that the power of sound actually generated matter. It follows, doesn't it, that each artist (permitted one breath, one sip of this divine force) has a share in the process of constant renewal—a responsibility to sing this world to life."

Biographical and Critical Sources

BOOKS

Children's Literature Review, Volume 47, Gale, 1998, pp. 18-50.
Dictionary of Literary Biography, Volume 40: *Poets of Great Britain and Ireland since 1940,* Part 1, Gale, 1985, pp. 81-86.
Dictionary of Literary Biography, Volume 161: *British Children's Writers Since 1960,* Gale, 1996, pp. 103-08.
Fourth Book of Junior Authors and Illustrators, edited by Doris de Montreville and Elizabeth D. Crawford, Wilson, 1978, pp. 108-09.
St. James Guide to Young Adult Writers, 2nd edition, edited by Tom Pendergast and Sara Pendergast, St. James Press, 1999, pp. 34-36.
Something about the Author Autobiography Series, Volume 30, Gale, 1995, pp. 125-40.
Twentieth-Century Children's Writers, 3rd edition, edited by Tracy Chevalier, St. James Press, 1989, pp. 348-49.

PERIODICALS

Best Sellers, May, 1976, Mary Columba, review of *Green Blades Rising: The Anglo-Saxons,* p. 60.
Books for Keeps, November, 1990, Kevin Crossley-Holland, "Restraints and Possibilities," pp. 18-19; November, 1997, p. 24.
Books for Your Children, autumn-winter, 1987, K. Crossley-Holland, "Kings and Heroes, Horse dealers and Numbskulls," pp. 10-11.
Bulletin of the Center for Children's Books, January, 1988, Betsy Hearne, review of *British Folk Tales: New Versions,* pp. 86-87.
Children's Literature, Vol. 3, 1974, Alexander Taylor, review of *Storm,* pp. 199-200.
Encounter, September, 1971, Elizabeth Maslen, "Riddles," pp. 81-82.
Growing Point, November, 1966, Margery Fisher, review of *The Green Children,* p. 791; January, 1983, M.

Fisher, review of *Beowulf,* pp. 3998-99; March, 1989, M. Fisher, review of *Wulf,* p. 5116.

Horn Book Magazine, February, 1966, Ethel L. Heins, review of *Havelok the Dane,* p. 51; December, 1969, Paul Heins, review of *Wordhoard: Anglo-Saxon Stories,* p. 680; June, 1974, P. Heins, review of *The Sea Stranger,* pp. 280-81; December, 1975, P. Heins, review of *The Fire-Brother,* p. 591.

Junior Bookshelf, November, 1964, review of *Havelok the Dane,* pp. 307-08; October, 1969, review of *Wordhoard: Anglo-Saxon Stories,* p. 321; April, 1974, A. R. Williams, review of *The Sea Stranger,* p. 110; March, 1977, M. Crouch, review of *The Wildman,* p. 39; April, 1983, G. Bott, review of *Beowulf;* December, 1984, Marcus Crouch, review of *Tales from the Mabinogion,* p. 359; October, 1985, A. R. Williams, review of *Storm,* p. 215; December, 1988, D. A. Young, review of *Wulf,* pp. 288-89.

Kirkus Reviews, February 1, 1976, review of *Green Blades Rising,* p. 140.

Magpies, July, 1991; March, 1999, p. 44.

New York Times Book Review, November 14, 1965, Ethna Sheehan, review of *Havelok the Dane,* pp. 66-67; May 5, 1968, Alice Low, review of *The Green Children,* p. 47.

Publishers Weekly, November 1, 1999, p. 58.

School Librarian, spring, 1998, pp. 23-24; autumn, 1998, p. 136.

School Library Journal, February, 1970, Bruce L. MacDuffie, review of *Wordhoard: Anglo-Saxon Stories,* pp. 91-92; April, 1985, Bonnie Saunders, review of *Beowulf,* pp. 84-85.

Spectator, December 10, 1988, Juliet Townsend, review of *Wulf,* pp. 37-38.

Times Literary Supplement, December 10, 1976, Nicholas Tucker, "A Picture of Ugliness," p. 1550; November 13-18, 1987, Jennifer Westwood, "Tales within Tales," p. 1264; December 16-22, 1988, Heather O'Donoghue, "Actually Anglo-Saxon," p. 1406.

OTHER

Ronald M. Hubbs and Margaret S. Hubbs Lectures, number 1, University of St. Paul, 1992.

ON-LINE

Achuka, www.achuka.co.uk (August 1, 2000).

Amazon, www.amazon.co.uk (September 14, 2000).

—Sketch by Gerard J. Senick

*   *   *

CURRIE, Robin 1948-

Personal

Born August 25, 1948, in Peoria, IL; daughter of Robert (a circuit judge) and Dorothy (a homemaker) Hunt; children: Brian, Beth. *Education:* Western Illinois University, B.S., 1970; University of Iowa, M.L.S., 1983; Lutheran School of Theology at Chicago, M.Div., 1995.

Addresses

Home—2844 Windsor, No. 104, Lisle, IL 60532. *Office*—Grace Lutheran Church, 493 Forest Ave., Glen Ellyn, IL 60137; fax 630-469-1561. *E-mail*—rc2147@ aol.com.

Career

Ordained minister, Evangelical Lutheran Church in America, 1996; Corn Belt Library System, Normal, IL, state consultant for children's services, 1983-84; David C. Cook Publishing, Elgin, IL, associate editor of preschool materials, 1984-86; Palatine Public Library, Palatine, IL, head of youth services department, 1986-91; Anderson's Bookshop, Elmhurst, IL, manager of children's department, 1991-94; intern minister of Lutheran church in Lombard, IL, 1994-95; Grace Lutheran Church, Glen Ellyn, IL, pastor, 1996—. Addison Public Library, Addison, IL, reader's advisory librarian in adult services department, 1995-98, children's services librarian, 1998-2000. *Member:* Illinois Library Association (chairperson of IREAD program, 1985).

Awards, Honors

Achievement Award, Illinois Library Association, 1985; Quality Time Award, Iowa Library Association, 1993, for contributions to children's services in Iowa; named "Illinois Author," Children's Reading Round Table, 1995, for *Baby Bible Storybook* and *Mini Easter Activity Book;* Honor Resources Storytelling Time Award, International Reading Association, 1995, for *Straw into Gold.*

Writings

(With Carol Elbert) *Rainbows and Ice Cream,* Illinois State Library, 1983.

(With Jan Irving) *Mudluscious: Stories and Activities Featuring Food for Preschool Children,* illustrated by Robert B. Phillips, Libraries Unlimited (Littleton, CO), 1986.

(With Irving) *Glad Rags: Stories and Activities Featuring Clothes for Children,* illustrated by Tom Henrichsen, Libraries Unlimited, 1987.

(With Irving) *Full Speed Ahead: Stories and Activities for Children on Transportation,* illustrated by Karen Wolf, Libraries Unlimited, 1989.

Double Rainbows, Illinois State Library, 1989.

(With Irving) *Raising the Roof: Children's Stories and Activities on Houses,* illustrated by Marijean Trew, Teacher Ideas Press (Englewood, CO), 1991.

(With Irving) *From the Heart: Books and Activities about Friends,* illustrated by Susie Kropa, Teacher Ideas Press, 1992.

(With Irving) *Straw into Gold: Books and Activities about Folktales,* illustrated by Kropa, Teacher Ideas Press, 1993.

Mini Easter Activity Book, Lion Publications, 1993.

(With Irving) *Second Helpings: Books and Activities about Food,* illustrated by Kropa, Teacher Ideas Press, 1994.

The Baby Bible Storybook, illustrated by Cindy Adams, Chariot-Victor (Wheaton, IL), 1994.

Noah and the Big Boat, Chariot-Victor, 1995.

Zacchaeus, the Little Man, Chariot-Victor, 1995.

Baby Bible Stories about Jesus, illustrated by Adams, Chariot-Victor, 1996.

Eyewitness Animals: The Story of Easter, Standard Publishing (Cincinnati, OH), 1997.

My Bible Friends Read-and-Do Book, illustrated by Cecilia Washington Carr, Pauline Books and Media (Boston, MA), 1997.

Eyewitness Animals: The Story of Christmas, Standard Publishing, 1997.

Baby Bible: The Lord's Prayer, illustrated by Adams, Chariot-Victor, 1998.

Toddlers' Action Bible, illustrated by Bill Clark, Concordia (St. Louis, MO), 1998.

Peanut Butter Promises: Nap 'n' Snack Devotions, illustrated by Jack Kershner, Concordia, 1999.

More Baby Bible Stories, illustrated by Adams, Chariot-Victor, 2000.

Sidelights

Robin Currie told *SATA:* "Looking back as I begin the second half of life (and I plan to have another fifty years

In Robin Currie's book for the very young, stories about Christ are enhanced by simple activities the child can do and a short prayer related to the tale. (From Baby Bible Stories about Jesus, *illustrated by Cindy Adams.)*

at least!), I see the threads of events woven so that everything I have done comes together in who I am now. There have been three major loves that have governed my life choices: love of God, of children, and of books. At various stages I have paid more attention to one area than the others, but the most productive times of my life occurred when they were in balance.

"I finally gave in to the call of God to the ordained ministry after seven years of resisting. I loved children's library work and hated to give it up, especially storytelling. *The Three Pigs* and *Wild Things* were so much fun, and Bible stories for children seemed flat by comparison. Then I began to apply the storytelling techniques I had used in the library to Bible stories. Instead of having the children 'blow, blow, blow the house down,' I had them 'blow, blow, blow Noah's boat across the water.' I used the *Bear Hunt* story frame to recall the trip of the shepherds to Bethlehem to find the baby Jesus—through the field, swim the stream, slop through the mud, and tiptoe into the stable. Then run, run, run back through all the obstacles to tell everyone that Jesus is born.

"I write like I talk, which is why the signature trademark of all the children's books I have written is their interactive quality. Each line of text has an indicated body movement, suggested noise (I am partial to animals), or facial expression. This makes the books easy for group use as well as a bonding experience for families. The children, one on one or in a group, are kept involved in the story through this physical augmentation. Clapping, making 'frowny' faces, hugging someone they love involves them in the story and makes it memorable.

"I am not stopped on the street for my autograph, but once in a while a mother will tell me her child asks over and over for the 'come down' story of Zacchaeus, the little man in the tree who met Jesus. Then my joy is complete as an author, children's librarian, and minister of God."

Biographical and Critical Sources

PERIODICALS

School Library Journal, August, 1988, Tom Concannon, review of *Glad Rags,* p. 48.

D

DENNEY, Diana 1910-2000
(Diana Ross, Gri)

OBITUARY NOTICE —See index for SATA sketch: Born July 8, 1910, in Valetta, Malta; died May 4, 2000 in England. Illustrator, educator, author. Diana Denney was the illustrator and author of several books for children who also worked as a junior school general teacher and an art instructor during the 1930s. The author of thirty books, Denney illustrated four of them by herself, and used the pseudonym Gri on those occasions. Her written works might be classified as either nursery rhymes or of the fantasy genre; her first book, The World at Work, was published in 1939, and following was her 1941 Story of the Beetle Who Lived Alone. She wrote a number of books about a little red engine, which began as bedtime stories for her nephew; some of these include The Little Red Engine and the Rocket from 1956, and The Little Red Engine Goes Carolling from 1971. Her last book, I Love My Love with an A: Where Is He?, was published in 1972.

OBITUARIES AND OTHER SOURCES:

BOOKS

The International Authors and Writers Who's Who, 10th Edition, International Biographical Centre (Cambridge, England), 1986, p. 152.

PERIODICALS

London Times, May 13, 2000.

*   *   *

DESSEN, Sarah 1970-

Personal

Born June 6, 1970, in Evanston, IL. Education: University of North Carolina at Chapel Hill, B.A. (with highest honors) in creative writing, 1993.

Addresses

Home—Chapel Hill, NC. Office—Department of English, University of North Carolina at Chapel Hill, Chapel Hill, NC 27599. E-mail—dessen@email.unc.edu.

Career

Writer; lecturer at University of North Carolina at Chapel Hill, 1997—. Worked as a waitress during the early 1990s.

Awards, Honors

Best Books for Young Adults selection, American Library Association, 1997, for That Summer; Best Books for Young Adults selection and Quick Pick selection, both American Library Association, both for Someone Like You; American Library Best Books for Young Adults selection and Quick Pick selection, American Library Association, and Best Book of the Year selection, School Library Journal, all for Keeping the Moon.

Writings

That Summer, Orchard Books, 1996.
Someone Like You, Viking, 1998.
Keeping the Moon, Viking, 1999.
Dreamland, Viking, 2000.

Sidelights

"I always think that I get the best parts of myself from what my friends have taught me about strength and loyalty and spirit," Sarah Dessen reflected in Dream/ Girl Online Digest. Childhood and classmate friendships play an important role in Dessen's popular young adult novels. She is known for her coming-of-age stories featuring strong characterizations of true-to-life protagonists who face predicaments with which teen readers can relate. Dessen has quickly gained a loyal following in only a few years since her first published novel, That Summer, came out in 1996. "Why do we love Sarah

Sixteen-year-old Halley finds her friendship with Scarlett threatened as they cope with complex issues like death, pregnancy, and first love in Dessen's popular novel.

Dessen?" asked a *Dream/Girl* writer. "Because she remembers what it's like to be a teenager." Her stories, which also include *Someone Like You, Keeping the Moon,* and *Dreamland,* recognize that, as Nancy Tilly put it in *NewsBank* online, "although teens often want to be part of the 'in' crowd, adolescence, for most, is about being an outsider. It's a period of dizzying change and newness. Dessen suggests that if adults can accept the extremes of feeling and action typical of the age, they may encourage youngsters to chart paths to self-discovery and stability rather than losing themselves in the wild urge to rebel."

Dessen can recall vividly what it was like to be an awkward child and teenager. When she was young, she was a very shy girl at school, "but as I got older I tended to gravitate towards friendships with girls who were more outgoing than myself," she said in *Dream/Girl.* Never thinking of herself as being as pretty or as popular as her friends, she did not have the best self-esteem, but in her reading she was attracted to strong heroines. As a young girl, two of her favorite books were *Coming Attractions* by Fannie Flagg and *Gone with the Wind* by Margaret Mitchell. Both books feature assertive, lively female protagonists. Her mother challenged her reading abilities by giving her books that were slightly above her reading level; they were often written by Southern writers and had strong female characters in them. Dessen

not only liked to read, but she liked to write stories, too. As a child, she turned her dolls into the characters in her tales, and when she was a fifth grader her teacher turned her on to history, which led her to write a series of stories about the Revolutionary War.

Because of her love for writing, it wasn't a surprise when Dessen decided to study creative writing at the University of North Carolina at Chapel Hill. Her father was a professor there in the English department, and Dessen recalled in *NewsBank* how that was a somewhat awkward situation for her: "I struggled mightily not to be associated with my parents, even as I majored in my father's department. It is hard to be taken seriously when your professor jubilantly remembers how you were beaned in the head with a volleyball at a department picnic at the age of six." But she was an excellent student, graduating with top honors in 1993. The only problem was that, after finishing a degree that took her five-and-a-half years to earn, she wasn't sure what to do for a career. Her parents were a little concerned when she announced that, instead of sending out resumes and searching for a position in corporate America, she wanted to continue the job she had as a waitress and work on her writing. Luckily for her, her parents were as supportive as ever of her wish to try to make it as a writer. It was, they reasoned, better than the hairstylist career she had been considering, and less surprising than her brother's choice of spending three years as a Zen Buddhist in California after attending an expensive music school.

It turned out to be the right choice for Dessen, who, despite the low prestige of the job, greatly enjoyed her work. Being a waitress had two advantages for her: it gave her time to write in the afternoons before she went to the restaurant at night, and it gave her the chance to study a wide range of personalities who came there to eat. "On a typical night," she commented in a 1996 *NewsBank* article, "I overhear snippets of dialogue, bits and pieces of people's lives coming right to me as I pass.... As a server, you can be almost invisible, absorbing the color and characters around you. And as a writer, I benefit daily from what people do not even know they are giving me. My rudest customer ever, who slapped my hand when I tried to remove her empty salad plate, instantly earned a place in my third novel as a bitter nasty woman, dressed in the same green pant suit and with the same features, of course. I've learned that writing well can be the best revenge." The people with whom she worked also provided material. Many of the waiters and waitresses were fascinating people: some held graduate degrees, some were artists or nursing students, or had other interesting backgrounds. Dessen also drew on the stories her best friends would tell her. "I think all good fiction starts with some truth," she told a *Dream/Girl* interviewer. "The trick is to begin with what really happened, and then change it to what you wish had happened, or what you wished you'd said."

With time to write and her parents' encouragement, Dessen found success relatively quickly. Only three years after graduating from college, her first book, *That*

Summer, was published by Orchard Books. It is the story of Haven, an awkward fifteen-year-old girl who feels uncomfortable with being five feet, eleven inches tall. A lot of changes are going on in her life: her older sister, Ashley, is getting married to a guy Haven thinks is a big nerd, and is driving everyone crazy as she prepares for the wedding; Haven's father and mother are divorced, and her father is now married to annoyingly perky television weather girl, Lorna Queen; while her mother has joined a group of free-and-loose singles and has become friends with a woman Haven can't stand. Haven wishes things could be like they were four years ago, when her parents were still married and she didn't always fight with her sister. But then Ashley's former boyfriend, Sumner Lee, arrives in town, and the presence of this charming young man that Haven likes so much reminds her of the past. Sumner seems to understand what she's going through better than anyone, and Haven really likes him. But, as a *Horn Book* reviewer explained, "Haven's idealized little-girl view of him gradually changes, [and] she lets go of the past and begins to take a more active part in the present." By the end of the story, Haven has done a lot of growing up, and her feelings of awkwardness have virtually disappeared.

Many critics were impressed with Dessen's debut novel, enjoying this tale of teenage angst and growth spiced with humor and wry observations. "Dessen adds a fresh twist to a traditional sister-of-the-bride story," commented one *Publishers Weekly* contributor, "with her keenly observant narrative full of witty ironies." And Fran Lantz called Haven's maturation a "believable transformation" in a *Kliatt* article. But while many reviewers praised the book, others found some fault. *School Library Journal* critic Lucinda Lockwood, for example, found the situations cliched and the characters "forgettable"; and Hazel Rochman of *Booklist* thought that Haven's ability to accept her body and herself by the end of the book was a little too pat a resolution. However, Rochman felt this was a minor flaw that did not seriously detract from the book. "This first novel," stated the critic, "is written with such easy grace that you want to quote sentence after sentence." *Horn Book* contributor Nancy Vasilakis similarly complimented the "fresh, unselfconscious style" of the book." Vasilakis concluded, "This is a wise book about growing up that won't give teenage readers the feeling that they are being preached to."

While the friendship between Haven and Sumner is an important part of *That Summer,* the theme of friendship takes an even more central role in *Someone Like You.* The two friends here are high-school pals Halley and Scarlett. Dessen starts the novel off quickly with a phone call to Scarlett, who learns that her boyfriend has just been killed in a motorcycle accident. Up until that point, Scarlett had always been the stronger personality in their relationship, but this tragedy and the news that Scarlett is pregnant, quickly changes their roles. Halley now has to be strong and supportive of Scarlett, who wants to have the baby even though her mother says she needs to have it aborted. But this isn't Halley's only concern. She

is also falling in love with a boy named Macon Faulkner, who puts pressure on her to have sex. As these events progress in her life, Halley keeps them a secret from her mother. This is ironic because her mother is a psychologist and author who brags that she and her daughter have a perfect relationship, even as that relationship starts to fracture. Thus the book's themes center on how two young girls struggle towards womanhood as they deal with the issues of sex and the inevitable separation of daughters from their mothers, as well as how the sisterly friendship between Halley and Scarlett pulls them through these changes.

Critics, of course, compared *Someone Like You* with Dessen's first novel, and they did so favorably for the most part. Elizabeth Devereaux, writing in the *New York Times Book Review,* felt that Dessen tries to juggle too many plotlines: "She doesn't need to bustle so much; the best thing she has going is her own steady voice." Many other reviewers agreed that it is the author's writing that really makes the book. "Dessen has a unique talent for distilling character in a few biting words," asserted Nancy Vasilakis in *Horn Book,* "and she uses her sharp sense of humor to make her points without mawkishness." Hazel Rochman of *Booklist* further observed that Dessen's portrayal of the teens friendship is perfect: "The exciting center of the story is Halley's relationship with Scarlett: here Dessen gets it exactly right." And other critics also said that Dessen's portrait of life in suburbia for middle-class kids was well done. "Dessen deals accurately, sensitively, and smoothly with growing up in suburbia," wrote Gail Richmond in *School Library Journal,* adding that the author successfully gets her message across "without preaching."

With *Keeping the Moon,* Dessen set out to approach the theme of friendship from a different angle. Her main character, Nicole "Colie" Sparks, starts off as a loner and social reject but later finds strength in new friends. Colie, who was overweight until her mother, a fitness expert, managed to get her to lose forty-five pounds, is still rejected by her peers because of the way she dyes her hair a dark black and wears a lip ring. Colie is also deeply hurt by a classmate, who spreads rumors about her being a "slut," even though Colie hasn't slept with anyone yet. When her mother goes off to Europe on a tour to promote her fitness message, Colie is sent to spend time with her nutty Aunt Mira, who lives in the seaside town of Colby, North Carolina. Mira, who illustrates greeting cards for a living, is a wrestling fan and quite the oddball. She is a social reject like Colie, with one big difference: Mira doesn't care what other people think of her.

Drawing from her own experiences as a waitress, Dessen has Colie get a job at the Last Chance Cafe, where she meets two women in their twenties, Isabel and Morgan, who also work there. Even though they are several years senior to the fifteen-year-old Colie, the three waitresses become friends. An odd young man named Norman, who rents a room from Mira, also enters the scene. Norman is an artist who uses found objects, such as ash trays and bicycle parts, to create imaginative sculptures.

Isabel and Morgan give Colie a makeover and help bolster her self-confidence, while Colie's growing affection for Norman also has a powerful effect on her. By the end of the novel, Colie is ready to face her schoolmates again and even gets revenge on the nasty girl who gave her a bad reputation.

"Dessen has set herself quite a challenge in this third book," remarked Tilly: "how to make credible the salvation of a girl teetering on the brink of damaging isolation." According to many critics, the author succeeds in doing just that. As a *Bulletin of the Center for Children's Books* critic pointed out, the author helps make Colie's transformation realistic by balancing it with her interactions with other characters. Dessen points out, through Mira, that not everyone needs to feel accepted by the crowd. The book is also "honest in its assessment of the downside of transformation," according to the reviewer, who noted that "Colie almost leaves Norman behind in the dust" toward the story's end because she thinks she's too good for him. What is appealing about *Keeping the Moon,* according to some reviewers, are Dessen's characters, especially Isabel and Morgan. *School Library Journal* contributor Cindy Darling called the two friends "great characters and the workings of their friendship is smooth, insightful, and just fun to read." Lynn Evarts concluded in *Voice of Youth Advocates* that this story of the importance of friendship "will strike a chord with young adults who need a boost developing their own self-esteem."

Although Dessen's characters face a number of personal crises in her first three books, none of the roadblocks they break through are as dangerous as what Caitlin O'Koren must survive in *Dreamland.* Here, the author tackles the serious subject of physical abuse. The novel starts out somewhat like a typical Dessen story. Caitlin is jealous of her older, more popular sister, Cass, who gets good grades and has no problem snagging boyfriends. When Cass abruptly decides to follow her boyfriend to New York City, Caitlin has to deal with her parents' negative reactions. Caitlin tries to make the best of Cass's absence by being accepted into the cheerleading squad. When her parents are apathetic about this achievement, she searches for another way to obtain a sense of self-worth and finds Rogerson. Rogerson is a charismatic young man from a wealthy family. He drives a BMW, deals in marijuana, and has rebellious friends. Caitlin thinks that being with Rogerson brings out a new side of her that she likes, and she falls in love with him. Rogerson, however, has emotional problems that begin to emerge in wild mood swings that soon lead him to start hitting her. Confused and desperate, Caitlin doesn't know how to break off the relationship until Rogerson beats her right in front of other people. At this point, she is finally able to get help. Diane Masla, reviewing *Dreamland* in *Voice of Youth Advocates,* stated, "In examining the question of how much must be sacrificed to maintain a romantic relationship, Dessen has created a compassionate novel that examines how wrong love can go."

Dessen herself recalls a time in her life when she was attracted to a rebellious lifestyle, what her father called "my 'Dark Years,'" as the author recalled in *NewsBank.* It was a time "when I was not writing but instead hanging out on Franklin Street smoking cigarettes and behaving tormented." She later said, "I . . . remember so well what it was like, being that age. When everything was more intense, and I was focused only on what was going to happen that afternoon, that week, that moment." Dessen's ability to empathize so well with teenagers' lives, both the good and the bad sides, is what has made her writing so successful with young adults, and even parents, whose teens sometimes give them Dessen's books to read. Dessen, who grew up and still lives in Chapel Hill, North Carolina, feels that staying in the same town where she constantly runs into people from her past has also kept her in touch with her teenage years. "[My friends] make me laugh, still," she said in *Dream/Girl,* "and remind me where I've come from even as I'm so focused on where I'm going."

Biographical and Critical Sources

PERIODICALS

Booklist, October 15, 1996, Hazel Rochman, review of *That Summer,* p. 422; May 15, 1998, H. Rochman, review of *Someone Like You,* p. 1622; June 1, 1998, H. Rochman, review of *Someone Like You,* p. 1745; September 1, 1999, Michael Cart, review of *Keeping the Moon,* p. 123.

Bulletin of the Center for Children's Books, October, 1999, review of *Keeping the Moon,* pp. 49-50.

Horn Book, November-December, 1996, Nancy Vasilakis, review of *That Summer,* p. 742; July-August, 1998, N. Vasilakis, review of *Someone Like You,* p. 486.

Kirkus Reviews, August 15, 1999, review of *Keeping the Moon,* pp. 1309-1310.

Kliatt, November, 1998, Fran Lantz, review of *That Summer,* pp. 10, 12.

New York Times Book Review, September 20, 1998, Elizabeth Devereaux, review of *Someone Like You,* p. 33.

Publishers Weekly, September 2, 1996, review of *That Summer,* p. 132; May 18, 1998, review of *Someone Like You,* p. 80; September 20, 1999, review of *Keeping the Moon,* p. 89; September 4, 2000, review of *Dreamland,* p. 109.

School Librarian, winter, 1998, Ann G. Hay, review of *That Summer,* p. 215.

School Library Journal, October, 1996, Lucinda Lockwood, review of *That Summer,* p. 144; June, 1998, Gail Richmond, review of *Someone Like You,* p. 143; September, 1999, Cindy Darling, review of *Keeping the Moon,* p. 221; September, 2000, Gail Richmond, review of *Dreamland.*

Voice of Youth Advocates, August, 1998, Marcia Mann, review of *Someone Like You,* p. 200; December, 1999, Lynn Evarts, review of *Keeping the Moon,* p. 331; October, 2000, Diane Masla, review of *Dreamland,* p. 262.

ON-LINE

Dream/Girl Online Digest, www.dgarts.com/ (May 22, 2000).

NewsBank, http://archives.newsbank.com/ (May 22, 2000).

*   *   *

DOYLE, Malachy 1954-

Personal

Born June 30, 1954, in Carrickfergus, County Antrim, Northern Ireland; son of Conan Doyle (a sales representative) and Eileen (Dempsey) Doyle; married Liz Townsend-Rose (an administrator), August 6, 1977; children: Naomi, Hannah, Liam. *Education:* Bolton Institute of Technology, B.A. (with honors), 1975; earned postgraduate certificate in education from Shenstone New College, 1976. *Hobbies and other interests:* Walking, cycling, reading, theater and music.

Addresses

Agent—Celia Catchpole Ltd., 56 Gilpin Ave., East Sheen, London, SW14 8QY, United Kingdom. *E-mail*—malachydoyle@supanet.com.

Career

Rowntree Mackintosh, York, England, media controller, 1976-81; General Foods, Banbury, England, media controller, 1981-84; Highmead Special School, Llanybydder, Wales, care assistant, 1984-91; Aran Hall School, Dolgellau, Wales, deputy head, 1991-94; Coleg Powys, Newtown, Wales, lecturer in sociology and psychology, 1994-96; Coleg Ceredigion, Aberystwyth, Wales, lecturer in sociology, 1994-97; writer of children's books, 1994—. *Member:* Welsh Academy.

Awards, Honors

Welsh Council of Northern Ireland Literature Award, 1997.

Writings

Farewell to Ireland: A Tale of Emigration to America, illustrated by Greg Gormley, Franklin Watts, 1998.
The Great Hunger: A Tale of Famine in Ireland, illustrated by Greg Gormley, Franklin Watts, 1998.
Little People, Big People, illustrated by Jac Jones, Faber, 1998.
The Children of Nuala, illustrated by Amanda Harvey, Faber, 1998.
The Changeling, illustrated by Jac Jones, Pont, 1999.
The Great Castle of Marshmangle, illustrated by Paul Hess, Andersen Press, 1999.
Jody's Beans, illustrated by Judith Allibone, Candlewick Press, 1999.
12,000 Miles from Home, illustrated by Greg Gormley, Franklin Watts, 1999.

Malachy Doyle

Well, a Crocodile Can!, illustrated by Britta Teckentrup, Frances Lincoln, 1999, Millbrook Press, 2000.
Hungry! Hungry! Hungry!, illustrated by Hess, Andersen Press, 2000, Peachtree, 2001.
Owen and the Mountain, illustrated by Giles Greenfield, Bloomsbury, 2000.
Carrot Thompson, Record Breaker, illustrated by Leonard O'Grady, Poolbeg, 2000.
Just-the-Same Jamie, illustrated by Shane O'Meara, Poolbeg, 2000.
Hero, Toffer, and Wallaby, illustrated by Jan Nesbitt, Pont, 2000.
Cow, illustrated by Angelo Rinaldi, Simon & Schuster, 2001.
Tales from Old Ireland, illustrated by Niamh Sharkey, Barefoot Books, 2000.
Storm Cats, illustrated by Stuart Trotter, Simon & Schuster, 2001.
Sleepy Pendoodle, illustrated by Julie Vivas, Candlewick Press, 2001.
Joe's Bike Race, illustrated by Michelle Conway, Poolbeg, 2001.

"It's like a teepee," said Jody.

15

In Doyle's endearing picture book, young Jody learns about growing, harvesting, and cooking scarlet runner beans from her grandfather while, in a parallel plot, Jody's mother prepares for the birth of her new baby. (*From* Jody's Beans, *illustrated by Judith Allibone.*)

The Bold Boy, illustrated by Jane Ray, Candlewick Press, 2001.
Georgie, Bloomsbury, 2001.
Baby See, Baby Do!, illustrated by Britta Teckentrup, Penguin Putnam, 2001.

Sidelights

Since launching his career as a children's author in the 1990s, Malachy Doyle has enjoyed success in both the United Kingdom and the United States. His first works are instructive, entertaining presentations of Irish and British colonial history, while many others adapt Irish legends in a fresh retelling. He told *SATA:* "I was born in Carrickfergus, Northern Ireland, in 1954. My parents had recently moved up from Dublin and named me, their seventh child, after a local saint. We lived in Whitehead, a small town at the mouth of Belfast Lough, all my childhood—my father still lives there. I went to secondary school (St. Malachy's College) in Belfast, and then to Bolton, Lancashire, to take a degree in psychology.

"I taught in Leeds for a year, followed by six months packing Polo Mints. I then worked for seven long years in advertising, firstly for Rowntree Mackintosh in York

and later for General Foods in Banbury, before buying a smallholding in West Wales. To feed my wife, Liz, our three young children, Naomi, Hannah, and Liam, and numerous goats, pigs and chickens, I took a job as a care assistant in a local residential special school. For the next seven years I darned socks, patched jeans and generally looked after the children there, before being offered the post of deputy head at another special school. We moved to Machynlleth, a small town on the edge of the Snowdonia National Park, and three years later I began to write for children. I now write full-time, apart from visiting schools or escaping into the mountains, and my books are available in twelve different languages.

"It took me forty years to become a writer. Forty years of growing up, selling coffee, teaching, raising children, goats and pigs. From Ireland, through England, to Wales. I'm finally doing it—writing.

"I didn't know I was a writer. I knew I loved words, loved books. I knew I could tell stories, write the occasional soppy love poem, ramble on in long letters to my Dad back home in Ireland. But I didn't know I was a writer.

"And then, back in 1994, for want of a better way to while away the long Welsh winter, I enrolled in a creative writing evening class. 'Write about your childhood,' said Anna. 'Remember how it felt, how it smelt . . .' So I wrote a piece about my mother's button box. I brought it in the next week and read it out loud. Anna seemed to like it.

'Okay,' I thought. 'That's what I'll do. I'll pack in this teaching lark and become a writer, a writer for children.' And here I am.

"I write about things that matter to me. About relationships—children, parents, grandparents. About animals. I try to recapture some of the joy, the freedom, the curiosity, imagination and humour of my early childhood. I often draw on folk tale, because it's part of me—I was brought up on it."

In 1998, Doyle's retelling of a classic Irish folk tale appeared, *The Children of Nuala.* The story is one of misfortune: a stepfather finds a way to make his wife's children disappear, but then feels remorseful. His wife still loves him and her brood, however, and in the end the children return. "Although this is a melancholy tale it is well-written and contains a strong message without preaching," wrote Annette Dale-Meiklejohn in *Magpies.*

The 1999 picture book, *Jody's Beans* had a more universal appeal, and appeared in print in North America as well. The work begins with a visit by Jody's grandfather to her home, and together the two plant scarlet runner beans in the garden. Over the summer growing season, the two meet regularly, or speak on the phone about their project. To answer Jody's sometimes anxious inquiries, the grandfather likes to remind her, "Wait and see." Doyle manages to provide basic gardening lessons through this format, and when the beans are harvested, some cooking tips as well. A *Publishers Weekly* review commended "Doyle's winningly spare narration," and other reviewers remarked upon the nice parallel plot concerning Jody's mother, who is expecting a baby. "The cozy tale of everyday events," remarked *Horn Book* reviewer Margaret A. Bush, "... is very satisfying."

Doyle told *SATA:* "I'm passionate about books, about stories. I love going into schools, meeting children, encouraging them to read, encouraging them to write. Don't wait till you're forty, I say. Do it. Do it now!"

Biographical and Critical Sources

PERIODICALS

Booklist, July, 1999, Hazel Rochman, review of *Jody's Beans,* p. 1950.

Books for Keeps, May, 1999, George Hunt, review of *The Great Castle of Marshmangle;* September, 1999, Roy Blatchford, review of *Jody's Beans,* and Elizabeth Schlenther, review of *The Changeling.*

Books Ireland, September, 2000, review of *Carrot Thompson, Record Breaker.*

Bookseller, June 16, 2000, review of *Tales from Old Ireland.*

Cambrian News, July 2, 1998, reviews of *The Great Hunger* and *Farewell to Ireland;* November 12, 1998, reviews of *The Children of Nuala* and *Little People, Big People;* May 20, 1999, review of *The Changeling.*

Cambriensis, December, 1999, Lynne Walsh, review of *The Changeling.*

Carousel, September, 1999, Michael Thorn, reviews of *The Great Castle of Marshmangle* and *Jody's Beans,* and Jan Mark, review of *The Changeling.*

Children's Books in Ireland, June, 1999, Bronagh Naughton, review of *Little People, Big People.*

Children's Bookseller, March 19, 1999, reviews of *The Great Castle of Marshmangle* and *Jody's Beans;* September 8, 2000, review of *Tales from Old Ireland.*

Early Years Educator, November, 1999, review of *Well, a Crocodile Can!*

Guardian, May 25, 1999, Vivian French, review of *Jody's Beans.*

Horn Book, March, 1999, Margaret A. Bush, review of *Jody's Beans,* p. 187.

Irish Examiner, June 10, 2000, Brendan Malone, review of *Carrot Thompson, Record Breaker.*

Irish Times, May 22, 1999, Geraldine Whelan, reviews of *The Great Castle of Marshmangle* and *Jody's Beans.*

Kirkus Reviews, 1999, review of *Jody's Beans.*

London Parent's Guide (England), November, 1999, review of *Jody's Beans.*

Magpies, February, 1999, John Zahnleiter, review of *Jody's Beans;* March, 1999, Annette Dale-Meiklejohn, review of *Little People, Big People* and *The Children of Nuala,* p. 32.

Publishers Weekly, May 3, 1999, review of *Jody's Beans,* p. 74.

School Librarian, June, 1999, Teresa Scragg, review of *The Children of Nuala;* September, 1999, Carolyn Boyd, review of *Jody's Beans;* December, 1999, Ann Jenkin, review of *The Changeling.*

School Library Journal, June, 1999, Carolyn Jenks, review of *Jody's Beans,* pp. 92-93; March, 2000, Christine A. Moesch, review of *Well, a Crocodile Can!*

South China Morning Post, September 25, 1999, Katherine Forestier, review of *Jody's Beans.*

Sunday Tribune (Dublin), March 28, 1999, Mary Arrigan, review of *The Great Castle of Marshmangle;* May 2, 1999, M. Arrigan, review of *Jody's Beans;* August 1, 1999, M. Arrigan, review of *Well, a Crocodile Can!*

E–F

ELLESTAD, Myrvin H. 1921-

Personal

Born August 17, 1921, in Santa Maria, CA; son of Melvin (a teacher) and Myrtle (a teacher; maiden name, Dunton) Ellestad; married Lera Cotter; children: Bonney, Steven, Cynthia, Cheryl, Warren, Roger, Guy, Debbie. *Education:* University of California, Berkeley, A.B., 1943; University of Louisville, M.D., 1946. *Politics:* Conservative. *Religion:* Atheist.

Addresses

Home—6109 Costa del Rey, Long Beach, CA 90803. *Office*—2801 Atlantic Ave., Long Beach, CA 90801. *E-mail*—m.ellestad@memorialcare.org.

Career

Jersey City Medical Center, Jersey City, NJ, intern, 1946-47, resident, 1949-50; Seaside Memorial Hospital, Long Beach, CA, resident, 1950-51; San Francisco County Hospital, fellow in pathology and U.S. public health cancer trainee, 1951-52; Memorial Hospital, Long Beach, staff member at Children's Diagnostic Heart Clinic, 1952-70, senior attending physician at hospital, 1954—, director of Division of Clinical Physiology, 1957-80, chief of Department of Medicine, 1962-63, and Division of Cardiology at Medical Center, 1962—, vice-chief of staff at Medical Center, 1976-77, chief of staff, 1977-80, member of board of trustees, 1981—. University of California, Los Angeles, assistant clinical professor, 1955-63; University of California, Irvine, associate clinical professor, 1963-73, clinical professor, 1973—. Certified by American Board of Internal Medicine, 1955, and Sub-Specialty Board for Cardiovascular Disease, 1971; Harbor General Hospital, attending physician and member of cardiac catheterization team, 1955-63, chief of staff, 1961; U.S. Naval Hospital, Long Beach, cardiology consultant, 1966—; Federal Aviation Administration, cardiology consultant to Federal Air Surgeon, 1971—; consultant to Johnson Space Center and National Institute of Biological Sciences. *Military service:* U.S. Naval Reserve, active duty in Medical Corps, 1947-49; served in Cuba; became lieutenant junior grade. *Member:* American College of Cardiology (fellow), American Heart Association (fellow of Council of Clinical Cardiology), American Academy of Sports Physicians (member of board of governors, 1980), American College of Sports Medicine, American College of Chest Physicians (fellow), American Physiological Society, Royal Society of Medicine (fellow), California Society of Internal Medicine, Long Beach Society of Internal Medicine (president, 1954), Long Beach Heart Association.

Awards, Honors

Named "outstanding young man of the year," Long Beach Junior Chamber of Commerce, 1959; National Honors Achievement Award, Angiology Research Foundation, 1969.

Writings

JUVENILE

The World and Its Animals, illustrated by Joyce Robinson, Rivercross Publishing (Orlando, FL), 1998.

OTHER

(Compiler) *Stress Testing: Principles and Practice,* F. A. Davis (Philadelphia, PA), 1975, 4th edition, 1996.
(Contributor) E. B. Diethrich, editor, *Noninvasive Cardiovascular Diagnosis: Current Concepts,* University Park Press (Baltimore, MD), 1978.
(Contributor) Raskamm and Schmuziger, editors, *Coronary Heart Surgery,* Springer-Verlag (Berlin, Germany), 1979.

Contributor of more than 150 articles to medical journals. Member of editorial board, *Clinical Cardiology, Journal of Cardiac Rehabilitation, Annals of Sports Medicine, American Journal of Cardiology,* and *American Journal of Noninvasive Cardiology.*

Sidelights

Myrvin H. Ellestad told *SATA:* "I grew up in Auburn, California, a small town in the foothills of the Sierra Nevada mountains. As a child I spent time in the woods hiking and fishing, and in the winter skiing. My mother and father were both schoolteachers who encouraged me to pursue an education.

"As a child I was diagnosed as having rheumatic heart disease. When a new doctor came to town, he reassured my parents that my heart was normal. Dr. Dunovitz became a lifelong friend and mentor. Because of him I went to medical school. Although I have been in the private practice of cardiology for nearly fifty years, I have been active in a good deal of research and teaching, and I served as chief of a cardiology department at a large teaching hospital for many years.

"I started writing research papers early on, and then medical books. Since taking anthropology in college at Berkeley, I have always avidly followed the developments in both anthropology and archaeology. I have supplemented this knowledge by traveling to many famous anthropological locations, such as Egypt, Israel, Easter Island, and the Galapagos Islands. When my very bright granddaughter started asking many questions about life, I decided to write a children's book on evolution. My good friend, Joyce Robinson, who is an accomplished artist, agreed to illustrate the book.

"I believe it is important for books on science to be introduced to bright children early, so that they will become interested in the world around them, not just in the social whirl that so many young people believe is the center of the universe."

Biographical and Critical Sources

PERIODICALS

American Family Physician, May 1, 1997, Corey H. Evans, review of *Stress Testing,* p. 2359.
Journal of Occupational Medicine, November, 1983, Henry R. Herbert, review of *Stress Testing,* p. 791.
Physician and Sportsmedicine, April, 1981, John D. Cantwell, review of *Stress Testing,* p. 35.

*　　　*　　　*

FISHER, Leonard Everett 1924-

Personal

Born June 24, 1924, in the Bronx, NY; son of Benjamin M. and Ray M. (maiden name, Shapiro) Fisher; married Margery M. Meskin (a school librarian), 1952; children: Julie Anne, Susan Abby, James Albert. *Education:* Attended Art Students League, 1941, and Brooklyn College, 1941-42; Yale University, B.F.A., 1949, M.F.A., 1950.

Addresses

Home and office—7 Twin Bridge Acres Rd., Westport, CT 06880. *E-mail*—LeonardoE1@aol.com.

Career

Painter, illustrator, author and educator. Graduate teaching fellow, Yale Art School, 1949-50; Whitney School of Art, New Haven, CT, dean, 1951-53; faculty member, Paier College of Art, 1966-78, academic dean, 1978-82, dean emeritus, 1982—, visiting professor, 1982-87. Visiting professor, artist, or consultant at various universities and colleges, including Case Western Reserve University, Silvermine Guild School of the Arts, Hartford University School of Art, Fairfield University, and University of California. Designer of U.S. postage stamps for the U.S. Postal Service, 1972-77; design consultant, Postal Agent, Staffa and Bernera Islands, Scotland, 1979-82. Delegate to national and international conferences; member of arts councils and historical societies in Westport, CT, and Greater New Haven, CT; trustee, Westport Public Library Board of Trustees, 1982-85, vice-president, 1985-86, president, 1986-89. Lecturer and speaker at art institutes, academic seminars, education workshops and children's book programs nationwide. *Military service:* U.S. Army, Corps of Engineers, 1942-46; became technical sergeant; partici-

Leonard Everett Fisher

pated in topographic mapping of major invasion campaigns in European and Pacific areas. *Exhibitions:* Various one-man shows at museums, libraries, galleries, and universities in the United States, including Hewitt Gallery, NY; New Britain Museum (24-year retrospective), Everson Museum, University of Syracuse, NY; Kimberly Gallery, New York City; Museum of American Illustration, Society of Illustrators (50-year retrospective), New York City; Homer Babbidge Library, University of Connecticut (50-year retrospective); and special mini-exhibitions (including Smithsonian Institution, and Fairview Park Library, OH), all from 1952 to the present.

Work exhibited at various group shows at galleries, museums, and universities in the United States, including Brooklyn Museum, NY; Rockefeller Center, NY; Seligmann Galleries, NY; Eggleston Galleries, NY; Hewitt Gallery, NY; American Federation of Arts and Emily Lowe Foundation national tours; Whitney Museum, NY; National Academy (Audubon Artists), NY; New York Historical Society, NY; Society of Illustrators, NY; Yale Art Gallery, CT; and many others, all from 1939 to the present.

Work included in collections of various museums, libraries, and universities, including The Library of Congress, Washington, DC; Free Library of Philadelphia, PA; New Britain Museum of American Art, New Britain, CT; Museum of American Illustration, New York, NY; Universities of Connecticut, Oregon, Minnesota, Southern Mississippi, and Appalachian State; Fairfield University, CT; Brown University, Providence, RI; The Smithsonian Institution, Washington, DC; and miscellaneous public and private collections in Iowa, Massachusetts, Michigan, Delaware, Hawaii, Maryland, New York, New Jersey, Wisconsin, California, North Carolina, and Oklahoma. *Member:* PEN, Society of Children's Book Writers and Illustrators, Authors Guild, Society of Illustrators, Silvermine Guild of Artists (trustee, 1970-74), New Haven Paint and Clay Club (president, 1968-70; trustee, 1968-74), Westport-Weston Arts Council (founding member; director, 1969-76; vice-president, 1972-73; president, 1973-74; board chairman, 1975-76).

Awards, Honors

William Wirt Winchester traveling fellowship, Yale University, 1949; Joseph Pulitzer scholarship in art, Columbia University and the National Academy of Design, 1950; American Institute of Graphic Arts outstanding textbooks, 1958, outstanding children's books, 1963; Newbery Honor Award, 1960, for *America Is Born: A History for Peter* with text by Gerald W. Johnson; Spring Book Festival Older Honor Award, 1960, for *America Grows Up: A History for Peter* with text by Johnson; Newbery Honor Award, 1961, for *America Moves Forward: A History for Peter,* with text by Johnson; Ten Best Illustrated Books Award of the *New York Times,* 1964, for *Casey at the Bat;* New Haven Paint and Clay Club, Carle J. Blenner Prize for painting, 1968; premio grafico, Fiera di Bologna, 5a

Fiera Internazionale del Libro per l'Infanzia e la Gioventu, Italy, 1968, for *The Schoolmasters;* Mayor's Proclamation: Leonard Everett Fisher Day, Fairview Park, OH, opening National Children's Book Week, November 12, 1978; New York Library Association/School Library Media Section Award for Outstanding Contributions in the Fields of Art and Literature, 1979; Medallion of the University of Southern Mississippi for Distinguished Contributions to Children's Literature, 1979; Christopher Medal for illustration, 1981, for *All Times, All Peoples: A World History of Slavery;* National Jewish Book Award for Children's Literature, and Association of Jewish Libraries Award for Children's Literature, both 1981, both for *A Russian Farewell;* Parenting's Reading Magic Award, Time-Life, 1988, for *Monticello;* Children's Book Guild/*Washington Post* Nonfiction Award, 1989; nominee, Orbis Pictus Award for Outstanding Nonfiction for Children, National Council Teachers of English, 1989, for *The White House;* Parents' Choice Award, 1989, for *The Seven Days of Creation;* Regina Medal, Catholic Library Association, 1991, for "lifetime distinguished contributions to children's literature"; Kerlan Award, University of Minnesota, 1991, for "singular attainments in the creation of children's literature"; Arbuthnot Honor Lecturer, Association of Library Services to Children of the American Library Association, 1995.

Fisher's books have received numerous awards or special citations from the American Institute of Graphic Arts, the *New York Times, Booklist,* the American Library Association, the National Council of Social Studies, various state library and reading organizations in Utah, Kentucky, Oklahoma, and Texas, and the National Council of Social Studies, including all books in his "Colonial Americans" and "Nineteenth-Century America" series.

Writings

SELF-ILLUSTRATED CHILDREN'S BOOKS

Pumpers, Boilers, Hooks and Ladders, Dial, 1961.
Pushers, Spads, Jennies and Jets, Dial, 1961.
A Head Full of Hats, Dial, 1962.
Two If by Sea, Random House, 1970.
Picture Book of Revolutionary War Heroes, Stockpole, 1970.
The Death of Evening Star: The Diary of a Young New England Whaler, Doubleday, 1972.
The Art Experience, F. Watts, 1973.
The Warlock of Westfall, Doubleday, 1974.
Across the Sea from Galway, Four Winds, 1975.
Sweeney's Ghost, Doubleday, 1975.
Leonard Everett Fisher's Liberty Book, Doubleday, 1976.
Letters from Italy, Four Winds, 1977.
Noonan, Doubleday, 1978, Avon, 1981.
Alphabet Art: Thirteen ABCs from Around the World, Four Winds, 1979.
A Russian Farewell, Four Winds, 1980.
Storm at the Jetty, Viking, 1980.
The Seven Days of Creation, Holiday House, 1981.
Number Art: Thirteen 1, 2, 3's from Around the World, Four Winds, 1982.

In his self-illustrated The Great Wall of China, *Fisher commemorates the achievement of the Chinese people who erected the monument over two thousand years ago.*

Star Signs, Holiday House, 1983.

Symbol Art: Thirteen Squares, Circles and Triangles from Around the World, Four Winds, 1984.

Boxes! Boxes!, Viking, 1984.

The Olympians: Great Gods and Goddesses of Ancient Greece, Holiday House, 1984.

The Statue of Liberty, Holiday House, 1985.

The Great Wall of China, Macmillan, 1986.

Ellis Island: Gateway to the New World, Holiday House, 1986.

Calendar Art: Thirteen Days, Weeks, Months and Years from Around the World, Four Winds, 1987.

The Tower of London, Macmillan, 1987.

The Alamo, Holiday House, 1987.

Look Around: A Book about Shapes, Viking, 1987.

Monticello, Holiday House, 1988.

Pyramid of the Sun, Pyramid of the Moon, Macmillan, 1988.

Theseus and the Minotaur, Holiday House, 1988.

The Wailing Wall, Macmillan, 1989.

The White House, Holiday House, 1989.

Prince Henry the Navigator, Macmillan, 1990.

Jason and the Golden Fleece, Holiday House, 1990.

The Oregon Trail, Holiday House, 1990.

The ABC Exhibit, Macmillan, 1991.

Sailboat Lost, Macmillan, 1991.

Cyclops, Holiday House, 1991.

Galileo, Macmillan, 1992.

Tracks Across America: The Story of the American Railroad, 1825-1900, Holiday House, 1992.

Gutenberg, Macmillan, 1993.

David and Goliath, Holiday House, 1993.

Stars and Stripes: Our National Flag, Holiday House, 1993.

Marie Curie, Macmillan, 1994.

Kinderdike, Macmillan, 1994.

Gandhi, Atheneum, 1995.

Moses, Holiday House, 1995.

William Tell, Farrar, Straus, and Giroux, 1996.

Niagara Falls: Nature's Wonder, Holiday House, 1996.

The Gods and Goddesses of Ancient Egypt, Holiday House, 1997.

The Jetty Chronicles, Marshall Cavendish, 1997.

Anasazi, Atheneum, 1997.

To Bigotry No Sanction: The Story of the Oldest Synagogue in America, Holiday House, 1998.

Alexander Graham Bell, Simon and Schuster, 1999.

Gods and Goddesses of the Ancient Maya, Holiday House, 1999.

THE "COLONIAL AMERICANS" SERIES; SELF-ILLUSTRATED, PUBLISHED BY F. WATTS

The Glassmakers, 1964.

The Silversmiths, 1964.

The Papermakers, 1965.

The Printers, 1965.

The Wigmakers, 1965.

The Hatters, 1965.

The Weavers, 1966.

The Cabinet Makers, 1966.

The Tanners, 1966.

The Shoemakers, 1967.

The Schoolmasters, 1967.

The Peddlers, 1968.

The Doctors, 1968.

The Potters, 1969.

The Limners, 1969.

The Architects, 1970.

The Shipbuilders, 1971.

The Homemakers, 1973.

The Blacksmiths, 1976.

"NINETEENTH-CENTURY AMERICA" SERIES; SELF-ILLUSTRATED, PUBLISHED BY HOLIDAY HOUSE

The Factories, 1979.

The Railroads, 1979.

The Hospitals, 1980.

The Sports, 1980.

The Newspapers, 1981.

The Unions, 1982.

The Schools, 1983.

ADULT

Masterpieces of American Painting, Bison/Exeter, 1985.

Remington and Russell, W. H. Smith, 1986.

ILLUSTRATOR

Geoffrey Household, *The Exploits of Xenophon,* Random House, 1955, revised edition, Shoestring Press, 1989.

Florence Walton Taylor, *Carrier Boy,* Abelard, 1956.

Manley Wade Wellman, *To Unknown Lands,* Holiday House, 1956.

Roger P. Buliard, *My Eskimos: A Priest in the Arctic,* Farrar, Straus, 1956.

Richard B. Morris, *The First Book of the American Revolution,* F. Watts, 1956, revised edition published as *The American Revolution,* Lerner Publications, 1985.

L. D. Rich, *The First Book of New England,* F. Watts, 1957.

Kenneth S. Giniger, *America, America, America,* F. Watts, 1957.

Henry Steele Commager, *The First Book of American History,* F. Watts, 1957.

James C. Bowman, *Mike Fink,* Little, Brown, 1957.

Robert Payne, *The Splendor of Persia,* Knopf, 1957.

Morris, *The First Book of the Constitution,* F. Watts, 1958, revised edition published as *The Constitution,* Lerner Publications, 1985.

Jeanette Eaton, *America's Own Mark Twain,* Morrow, 1958.

Harry B. Ellis, *The Arabs,* World, 1958.

Robert Irving, *Energy and Power,* Knopf, 1958.

Estelle Friedman, *Digging into Yesterday,* Putnam, 1958.

E. B. Meyer, *Dynamite and Peace,* Little, Brown, 1958.

E. M. Brown, *Kateri Tekakwitha,* Farrar, Straus, 1958.

C. Edell, *Here Come the Clowns,* Putnam, 1958.

L. H. Kuhn, *The World of Jo Davidson,* Farrar, Straus, 1958.

Catharine Wooley, *David's Campaign Buttons,* Morrow, 1959.

Maurice Dolbier, *Paul Bunyan,* Random House, 1959.

Edith L. Boyd, *Boy Joe Goes to Sea,* Rand McNally, 1959.

Gerald W. Johnson, *America Is Born: A History for Peter,* Morrow, 1959.

Fisher penned a series of insightful short picture-book biographies, this one focusing on the famous inventor and advocate for the deaf. *(From* Alexander Graham Bell, *written and illustrated by Fisher.)*

Morris, *The First Book of Indian Wars*, F. Watts, 1959, revised edition published as *The Indian Wars*, Lerner Publications, 1985.

Elizabeth Abell, editor, *Westward, Westward, Westward*, F. Watts. 1959.

Phillip H. Ault, *This is the Desert*, Dodd, 1959.

Irving, *Sound and Ultrasonics*, Knopf, 1959.

Johnson, *America Moves Forward: A History for Peter*, Morrow, 1960.

Johnson, *America Grows Up: A History for Peter*, Morrow, 1960.

Irving, *Electromagnetic Waves*, Knopf, 1960.

Declaration of Independence, F. Watts, 1960.

Trevor N. Dupuy, *Military History of Civil War Naval Actions*, F. Watts, 1960.

Dupuy, *Military History of Civil War Land Battles*, F. Watts, 1960.

Edward E. Hale, *The Man Without a Country*, F. Watts, 1960.

Anico Surnay, *Ride the Cold Wind*, Putnam, 1960.

Natalia M. Belting, *Indy and Mrs. Lincoln*, Holt, 1960.

Belting, *Verity Mullens and the Indian*, Holt, 1960.

Morris, *The First Book of the War of 1812*, F. Watts, 1961, revised edition published as *The War of 1812*, Lerner Publications, 1985.

Emma G. Sterne, *Vasco Nunez De Balboa*, Knopf, 1961.

James Playsted Wood, *The Queen's Most Honorable Pirate*, Harper, 1961.

Harold W. Felton, *A Horse Named Justin Morgan*, Dodd, 1962.

Charles M. Daugherty, *Great Archaeologists*, Crowell, 1962.

Margery M. Fisher, *But Not Our Daddy*, Dial, 1962.

Robert C. Suggs, *Modern Discoveries in Archaeology*, Crowell, 1962.

Paul Engle, *Golden Child*, Dutton, 1962.

Jean L. Latham, *Man of the Monitor*, Harper, 1962.

Johnson, *The Supreme Court*, Morrow, 1962.

Harold W. Felton, *Sergeant O'Keefe and His Mule, Balaam*, Dodd, 1962.

Johnson. *The Presidency*, Morrow, 1962.

Jack London, *Before Adam*, Macmillan, 1962.

Eric B. Smith and Robert Meredith, *Pilgrim Courage*, Little, Brown, 1962.

E. Hubbard, *Message of Garcia*, F. Watts, 1962.

Charles Ferguson, *Getting to Know the U.S.A.*, Coward, 1963.

A. Surany, *Golden Frog*, Putnam, 1963.

Johnson, *The Congress*, Morrow, 1963.

Margery M. Fisher, *One and One*, Dial, 1963.

Andre Maurois, *The Weigher of Souls*, Macmillan, 1963.

London, *Star Rover*, Macmillan, 1963.

Helen Hoke, editor, *Patriotism, Patriotism, Patriotism*, F. Watts, 1963.

Gettysburg Address, F. Watts, 1963.

Johnson, *Communism: An American's View*, Morrow, 1964.

Smith and Meredith, *Coming of the Pilgrims*, Little, Brown, 1964.

Richard Armour, *Our Presidents*, Norton, 1964.

Meredith and Smith, *Riding with Coronado*, Little, Brown, 1964.

Robert C. Suggs, *Alexander the Great, Scientist-King*, Macmillan, 1964.

John F. Kennedy's Inaugural Address, F. Watts, 1964.

Suggs, *Archaeology of San Francisco*, Crowell, 1965.

Martin Gardner, *Archimedes*, Macmillan, 1965.

Florence Stevenson, *The Story of Aida* (based on the opera by Giuseppe Verdi), Putnam, 1965.

Lois P. Jones, *The First Book of the White House*, F. Watts, 1965.

Ernest L. Thayer, *Casey at the Bat*, F. Watts, 1965.

John Foster, *Rebel Sea Raider*, Morrow, 1965.

Surany, *The Burning Mountain*, Holiday House, 1965.

Martha Shapp and Charles Shapp, *Let's Find Out about John Fitzgerald Kennedy*, F. Watts, 1965.

Suggs, *Archaeology of New York*, Crowell, 1966.

Clifford L. Alderman, *The Story of the Thirteen Colonies*, Random House, 1966.

Foster, *Guadalcanal General*, Morrow, 1966.

Robert Silverberg, *Forgotten by Time*, Crowell, 1966.

Johnson, *The Cabinet*, Morrow, 1966.

Washington Irving, *The Legend of Sleepy Hollow*, F. Watts, 1966.

Surany, *Kati and Kormos*, Holiday House, 1966.

Surany, *A Jungle Jumble*, Putnam, 1966.

Meredith and Smith, *Quest of Columbus*, Little, Brown, 1966.

Madeleine L'Engle, *Journey with Jonah*, Farrar, Straus, 1967.

L. Sprague and Catherine C. De Camp, *The Story of Science in America*, Scribner, 1967.

Nathaniel Hawthorne, *Great Stone Face and Two Other Stories*, F. Watts, 1967.

Johnson, *Franklin D. Roosevelt*, Morrow, 1967.

George B. Shaw, *The Devil's Disciple*, F. Watts, 1967.

Surany, *Covered Bridge*, Holiday House, 1967.

Surany, *Monsieur Jolicoeur's Umbrella*, Putnam, 1967.

Irving, *Rip Van Winkle*, F. Watts, 1967.

Morris, *The First Book of the Founding of the Republic*, F. Watts, 1968.

Surany, *Malachy's Gold*, Holiday House, 1968.

Bret Harte, *The Luck of Roaring Camp*, F. Watts, 1968.

(With Cynthia Basil) J. Foster, *Napoleon's Marshall*, Morrow, 1968.

Gerald W. Foster, *The British Empire*, Morris, 1969.

Meredith and Smith, *Exploring the Great River*, Little, Brown, 1969.

Surany, *Lora Lorita*, Putnam, 1969.

Julian May, *Why the Earth Quakes*, Holiday House, 1969.

Victor B. Scheffer, *The Year of the Whale*, Scribner, 1969.

Scheffer, *The Year of the Seal*, Scribner, 1970.

Berenice R. Morris, *American Popular Music*, F. Watts, 1970.

Scheffer, *Little Calf*, Scribner, 1970.

Loren Eisely, *The Night Country*, Scribner, 1971.

May, *The Land Beneath the Sea*, Holiday House, 1971.

Isaac B. Singer, *The Wicked City*, Farrar, Straus, 1972.

Jan Wahl, *Juan Diego and the Lady*, Putnam, 1973.

Gladys Conklin, *The Journey of the Gray Whales*, Holiday House, 1974.

James E. Gunn, *Some Dreams are Nightmares*, Scribner, 1974.

E. Thompson, *The White Falcon*, Doubleday, 1976.

Milton Meltzer, *All Times, All Peoples: A World History of Slavery,* Harper, 1980.

Myra Cohn Livingston, *A Circle of Seasons,* Holiday House, 1982.

Richard Armour, *Our Presidents,* revised edition, Woodbridge Press, 1983.

Livingston, *Sky Songs,* Holiday House, 1984.

Livingston, *Celebrations,* Holiday House, 1985.

Livingston, *Sea Songs,* Holiday House, 1986.

Livingston, *Earth Songs,* Holiday House, 1986.

Livingston, *Space Songs,* Holiday House, 1988.

Livingston, *Up in the Air,* Holiday House, 1989.

Alice Schertle, *Little Frog's Song,* Harper, 1992.

Livingston, *If You Ever Meet a Whale,* Holiday House, 1992.

Eric A. Kimmel, editor, *The Spotted Pony: A Collection of Hanukkah Stories,* Holiday House, 1992.

David and Goliath: Retold from the Bible, Holiday House, 1993.

Kimmel, reteller, *The Three Princes: A Tale from the Middle East,* Holiday House, 1994.

Moses: Retold from the Bible, Holiday House, 1995.

Livingston, *Festivals,* Holiday House, 1996.

Kimmel, reteller, *The Two Mountains: An Aztec Legend,* Holiday House, 1999.

ILLUSTRATOR OF TEXT BOOKS AND LEARNING MATERIALS

Our Reading Heritage (six volumes), Holt, 1956-58.

Marjorie Wescott Barrows, *Good English through Practice,* Holt, 1956.

Don Parker, editor, *The Multilevel Reading Laboratory* (eight volumes), Science Research Associates, 1957-62.

M. W. Barrows and E. N. Woods, *Reading Skills,* Holt, 1958.

Dolores Betler, editor, *The Literature Sampler* (two volumes), Learning Materials, Inc., 1962, 1964.

How Things Change, Field Enterprise, 1964.

ILLUSTRATOR OF AUDIO-VISUAL FILMSTRIPS

Edgar Allan Poe, *Murders in the Rue Morgue,* Encyclopaedia Britannica, 1978.

Robert Louis Stevenson, *Dr. Jekyll and Mr. Hyde,* Encyclopaedia Britannica, 1978.

Bram Stoker, *The Judge's House,* Encyclopaedia Britannica, 1978.

A. B. Edwards, *Snow* (from *The Phantom Coach*), Encyclopaedia Britannica, 1978.

Poe, *The Tell-Tale Heart,* Encyclopaedia Britannica, 1980.

Also illustrator for *Cricket* and *Lady Bug* magazines. Many of Fisher's manuscripts, illustrations, drawings, and correspondence are housed at the Leonard Everett Fisher Archive, University of Connecticut, Storrs, the Kerlan Collection, University of Minnesota, Minneapolis, the de Grummond Collection, University of Southern Mississippi, Hattiesburg, the library of the University of Oregon, Eugene, and at the Postal History Collection, Smithsonian Institution, Washington, DC.

Adaptations

Filmstrips, all by Anico Surany and all produced by Random House: *The Golden Frog, The Burning Mountain, A Jungle Jumble, Monsieur Jolicouer's Umbrella, Ride the Cold Wind,* and *Lora Lorita.*

Work in Progress

Sky, Sea, the Jetty and Me, for Marshall Cavendish, 2001; *Gods and Goddesses of the Ancient Norse,* for Holiday House, 2001.

Sidelights

Prolific and diverse are adjectives often used to describe the work of Leonard Everett Fisher, a prominent author-illustrator of both fiction and nonfiction books for children, particularly books of American and world history. On his own, Fisher has published more than eighty books; he has illustrated over one hundred and sixty by authors as diverse as Washington Irving, Madeleine L'Engle, the poet Myra Cohn Livingston, and Eric Kimmel; he has also illustrated nearly twenty textbooks and learning tools.

Fisher's books of nonfiction are targeted at readers in the elementary and middle grades and present cogent and informative introductions to topics from world mythology, as in *The Olympians: Great Gods and Goddesses of Ancient Greece, Gods and Goddesses of Ancient Egypt,* and *Gods and Goddesses of the Ancient Maya,* to great moments in American history as revealed by buildings and institutions, such as *The Statue of Liberty, Ellis Island, The White House, Monticello,* and *Stars and Stripes.* Fisher's two historical series for young readers, "Colonial Americans," and "Nineteenth-Century America," also serve as introductions to the social history of the age, providing "accurate reflections of the period," according to Reba Pinney writing in *St. James Guide to Children's Writers.* Pinney further noted that these series books "are often witty and amusing" and clearly display Fisher's "desire to connect the reader with the institutions of the past." Fisher has also written numerous biographies, including *Galileo, Gutenberg, Gandhi, Marie Curie, William Tell,* and *Alexander Graham Bell;* short picture books that offer unique perspectives on the works and achievements of such famous people. Natural history gets the Fisher treatment as well, in works such as *Niagara Falls: Nature's Wonder,* and ancient civilization are illuminated by his pen in *Anasazi.*

Fisher is also the author of many works of fiction, several of them inspired by the writer's interest in the immigrant life, as in *Across the Sea from Galway, Letters from Italy,* and *A Russian Farewell.* The weird and fantastical also are deployed by Fisher in novels such as *The Warlock of Westfall, The Death of Evening Star,* and *Sweeney's Ghost,* while his childhood home at Sea Gate in Brooklyn serves as the setting for other tales, such as *The Jetty Chronicles.* In all of his work, Fisher accompanies text with powerful illustrations in a variety of media from pen-and-ink to acrylics. A

Fisher's interpretations of Greek mythology reveal another dimension of the artist, better known for his American historical subjects. (*From* Cyclops.)

renowned artist in his own right, Fisher brings to his illustrations the training and insight of a fine arts painter.

Fisher credits his father's love of art with his own decision to become an artist. The elder Fisher was a ship designer and draftsman who painted in his spare time. One of his paintings was still on the easel when two-year-old Leonard got hold of some india ink and a paintbrush and added his own embellishments to his father's work. The result was an unusable mess. But instead of being punished, Fisher was given his own little studio—a converted hall closet—complete with worktable, crayons, paper and pencils. "I was cozily in business," Fisher recalled in his article for *Something about the Author Autobiography Series* (*SAAS*), "ensconced in my first studio, lit from the ceiling by a naked bulb and about six steps from the kitchen."

While in school, Fisher began to win local art competitions, including several prizes sponsored by department stores. One of these was a float design for the Macy Thanksgiving Day parade. A pencil drawing was exhibited with the works of other high school students at the Brooklyn Museum. In addition to his schoolwork, Fisher also took art classes at Moses Soyer's art studio, at the Art Students' League, and at the Heckscher Foundation. His mother also made sure he visited the art museums of New York. After graduating from high school at the age of 16, Fisher studied art and geology at Brooklyn College for a time before entering the Army. He enlisted in 1942 and was assigned to become a mapmaker.

Fisher returned to college after his military service, earning two degrees from Yale University. "The Yale experience was memorable," Fisher explained in his *SAAS* article. "It prepared me for every artistic eventuality. It was up to me to discover those eventualities." Following graduation, Fisher traveled to Europe using money received from two fellowships. He visited the major art museums of London, Paris, Milan, Florence, Venice, Rome, and elsewhere in Italy. "I saw every painting I came to see and more," he remarked in *SAAS*. Returning to the United States, Fisher became dean of the Whitney School of Art. He had his first New York exhibition at the Edwin C. Hewitt Gallery in 1952. Although not one painting was sold, the critical reviews were favorable and Fisher, encouraged by the response, proposed to Margery Meskin, then a systems service representative with IBM. The couple was married later that year and eventually had three children.

Shortly after leaving the Whitney School of Art in 1953, Fisher began to illustrate books for children. His first was *The Exploits of Xenophon,* written by Geoffrey Household, which tells the story of an ancient Greek writer, historian, and military leader. Other projects soon followed, including the six-volume *Our Reading Heritage* and the *Multilevel Reading Laboratory,* an experimental concept in which 150 reading selections were printed with 150 suitable illustrations. Fisher did the illustrations for eight of the "laboratory" packages, more than 3,000 illustrations in all. In addition to illustrating educational materials, Fisher also illustrated a number of children's picture books, working for Holiday House and Franklin Watts. These books included both fiction and nonfiction titles, including many on American history, a subject close to Fisher's heart. "American history," he explained in *SAAS,* "had a strong presence during my growing years. To my parents, one an immigrant, the other the son of immigrants, the United States was heaven-sent."

Fisher has also written his own children's books, his first solo effort appearing in 1961. Many of these works have been about historical subjects. His "Nineteenth-Century America" series for Holiday House describes various aspects of American society, such as the growth of the railroads or the nation's most popular leisure-time activities, and is meant to provide a panoramic picture of the development of nineteenth century America. Fisher explained in *SAAS* that the books also "deal with my determination not to disconnect. In a culture like ours, wherein today's material gratification seems to deny any historical link, knowledge of the past is often and mistakenly brushed aside as irrelevant to our present and

future values, much less the course of our nation. I try to say otherwise."

Reviewing the first two titles in the series, *The Factories* and *The Railroads,* Shirley Wilton in *School Library Journal* remarked that the books "are characterized by excellent design, well-spaced, readable type, and Fisher's dramatic black-and-white scratchboard illustrations." Wilton further commented, "Lively writing, startling facts and striking illustrations make these books excellent supplements to standard historical coverage of industrial growth in America." Focusing on the human side of history, Fisher's books on nineteenth-century America follow the fortunes of various men and women who helped to build the country through newspapers, schools, hospitals, unions, and sports. Reviewing *The Sports,* a writer for *Publishers Weekly* noted that Fisher "writes briskly and authoritatively about competitive games and their social implications during American's early days." This same reviewer concluded, "Fisher

With the use of archeological clues discovered in the late 1800s, Fisher studies the ancient culture of the Anasazi, who inhabited the Four Corners region of Utah, Colorado, New Mexico, and Arizona before the arrival of the Europeans. (From Anasazi, *written and illustrated by Fisher.*)

describes the feats of legendary figures ... creating an exemplary document on an energetic age."

The "Colonial Americans" series from Franklin Watts (since republished by Marshall Cavendish) consists of nineteen books describing Colonial crafts, trades, and professions. Each begins with a brief history of the craft, trade, or profession in question and then proceeds to describe the actual techniques used by Colonial craftsmen. Fisher's illustrations for the books were done in a style reminiscent of old-time engravings to give them the proper feeling. The "Colonial Americans" series, according to Q. Mell Busbin in the *Dictionary of Literary Biography,* "has received wide use in classrooms throughout the United States, especially in the arts and social sciences." Over 500,000 copies of the series have been sold.

The American experience is also illuminated in Fisher's books about immigrants. *Across the Sea from Galway* tells the story of a group of Irish immigrants who flee famine and oppression in Ireland only to be shipwrecked off the Massachusetts coast. Cynthia Adams, writing in *School Library Journal,* felt the book was a "deft treatment of a survival theme as well as an accurate depiction of Irish life." *Letters from Italy* is the story of several generations of an Italian-American family, beginning with a grandfather who fought with Garibaldi for Italian independence and ending with a grandson who dies in World War II fighting Mussolini. *A Russian Farewell* traces a Jewish-Ukrainian family from their trials under the Czarist government to their decision to leave for America, while *Ellis Island* profiles the famous entry point for many immigrants to the United States. Reviewing *A Russian Farewell* in *School Library Journal,* Jack Forman noted that the tale is "broadly representative of the experiences of thousands of Russian Jews fleeing to the U.S.," and that "the story is given added force by the author's bleak and stark black-and-white sketches."

Other books were inspired by Fisher's childhood on the seashore. *The Death of Evening Star, Noonan, Storm at the Jetty,* and *The Jetty Chronicles* are all based on his recollections of living in the family house at Sea Gate in Brooklyn. Situated on the jetty of land where the Atlantic Ocean waters met the waters of Gravesend Bay, the family house had a magnificent view of passing ships, storms at sea, and the local lighthouse. *Storm at the Jetty* is a descriptive story of how a beautiful August afternoon on the seashore gradually transforms into a violent and ugly thunderstorm at sea. Barbara Hawkins called this "beautifully illustrated vignette of a summer storm" an "ode to the sea," in a *School Library Journal* review. *The Death of Evening Star* concerns a nineteenth century whaling ship from New England and the many tribulations of its final voyage. *The Jetty Chronicles* is based on Fisher's reminiscences of his life from 1934 to 1939, and is peopled by fictional characters including a geologist, an ex-convict, an Olympic hopeful, and a radical newspaper vendor. "This is a piece of Americana," wrote Marilyn Payne Phillips in *School Library Journal,* "an antidote to Normal Rockwell, portraying a

real place and time that no longer exists. A place of power and majesty reclaimed by nature."

Fisher has also commemorated the achievements of mankind around the world in the monuments and buildings of many cultures. He paid tribute to the human spirit in *The Great Wall of China,* an "impressive" book, according to *Booklist*'s Ilene Cooper, with "striking black-and-white acrylic paintings that spread over the pages and surround the text." In *The Tower of London* Fisher "sets a high standard in ... dramatic nonfiction," according to a reviewer for *Publishers Weekly.* Closer to home, Fisher has taken a look at many of the monuments of American history. *The Statue of Liberty* "offers one of the more eye-catching books on the subject," according to Deborah Vose in *School Library Journal,* while his *Ellis Island: Gateway to the New World* is "profusely illustrated," according to Zena Sutherland writing in *Bulletin of the Center for Children's Books,* offering "a detailed history of the island in Upper New York Bay that eventually came to be called Ellis Island." Fisher's award-winning *Monticello* is, as a *Kirkus Reviews* contributor noted, a "handsomely produced history of the house that Jefferson spent a lifetime working on in his spare time." Betsy Hearne, reviewing *Monticello* in *Bulletin of the Center for Children's Books,* called it a "prerequisite for any young reader's visit to Monticello, and an armchair tour for students who can't make the trip."

Fisher has acted as social and natural historian of the American experience, as well, in illustrated studies of other aspects of the culture and terrain. With the *Anasazi,* he took a look at the ancient culture, which once inhabited the Four Corners region of the Southwest. Darcy Schild remarked in *School Library Journal* that for this title Fisher "created unique and striking monochrome paintings to illustrate his interpretation of a historical event." However Schild found "some of the theories presented ... no longer considered correct." Fisher's *Stars and Stripes* tells the story of the American flag in a book "that makes every day Flag Day and the Fourth of July," according to Sylvia S. Marantz in *School Library Journal.* Marantz concluded that *Stars and Stripes* would be an "eye-catching addition to any collection." The Touro Synagogue in Newport, Rhode Island, completed in 1763, is the focus for *To Bigotry No Sanction: The Story of the Oldest Synagogue in America,* a book that details the struggle for Jewish religious freedom in America. *Booklist*'s Cooper concluded, "Although some may see this as the story of a particular group, it is also the story of religious freedom in the U.S." And with *Niagara Falls: Nature's Wonder,* Fisher turned his artist's eye to the natural history and wonders of North America, a blend of photographs old and new and a potpourri of facts and myths about the place.

Famous men and women worldwide provide the focus for a series of biographies from Fisher. His *Galileo* employed "spare prose and bold black-and-white illustrations" to bring that Italian astronomer to life, according to *Booklist*'s Cooper, who also felt that his *Marie Curie* "ably brings Curie to life and highlights the role of women in the sciences in particular and society in general." Kathleen Odean, writing in *School Library Journal,* called *Marie Curie* a "gripping introduction to the remarkable woman ...." Gutenberg, Gandhi, and even William Tell have received the Fisher biographical treatment, a mixture of spare text and black-and-white acrylic paintings. In *Alexander Graham Bell,* Fisher tackled the father of the telephone with "warm, storylike text" and "full- and double-page illustrations (in rather dark tones)" which provide, as a reviewer for *Horn Book* commented, "a good introduction to the subject." Carol Fazioli, reviewing *Alexander Graham Bell* in *School Library Journal,* felt that like Fisher's earlier biographies of Galileo and Gutenberg, "this title provides an overview of an individual's life without intimidating young readers."

Mythology, religion, and legend have also acted as catalysts for Fisher in a series of books on Greek, Egyptian, and Mayan deities and myths. Twelve deities of ancient Greece are served up in *The Olympians: Great Gods and Goddesses of Ancient Greece,* "a handsomely designed volume ideally suited for introducing the characters of Greek mythology," as *Booklist*'s Karen Stang Hanley commented. Thirteen gods and goddesses of Egypt appeared in his *The Gods and Goddesses of Ancient Egypt,* and in *Gods and Goddesses of the Ancient Maya* Fisher focuses on the principal figures in Mayan mythology. Reviewing the last-named title, *Booklist*'s Susan Dove Lempke called it a "visually striking edition." Fisher has also retold and illustrated individual takes of Greek mythology, including *Theseus and the Minotaur, Jason and the Golden Fleece,* and *Cyclops,* and has adapted tales from the Bible, such as *David and Goliath* and *Moses.* Reviewing *David and Goliath* in *School Library Journal,* Linda Boyles called the book "a vigorous retelling of an ancient story in an exciting picture book."

Collaborative efforts have also explored the world of myths and legends. Working with Eric A. Kimmel, Fisher illustrated *The Spotted Pony: A Collection of Hanukkah Stories, The Three Princes: A Tale from the Middle East,* and *The Two Mountains: An Aztec Legend.* Reviewing the latter title, a *Publishers Weekly* writer noted, "Fisher's acrylic paintings range from austere, boldly hued portraits of the warriorlike celestial residents to verdant landscapes of both heaven and earth." Such collaborative efforts have taken much of Fisher's creative energy, and some of the most successful blending of text and art occurred in Fisher's work with poet Myra Cohn Livingston. Peter Neumeyer, reviewing *A Circle of Seasons,* their first collaborative effort, in *School Library Journal,* called the teamwork in that book "the perfect blending of poetry and painting." Fisher and Livingston also worked together on *Sky Songs, Celebrations, Sea Songs, Earth Songs, Space Songs, Festivals,* and *Up in the Air.* Additionally, the ever-busy Fisher has led a full career as an artist, creating easel paintings, holding exhibitions of his work, and coordinating efforts to transpose his art into murals for such public buildings as the Washington Monument. In the early 1970s and 1980s he designed a number of postage stamps for the U.S. Postal Service, including a series of eight stamps on American craftsmen for the Bicentennial.

Writing in *Horn Book* about the place of art in contemporary children's nonfiction, Fisher offers these observations: "We have a tendency in children's nonfiction to respond only to the desires of curriculum and educators and to ignore the other needs .... The qualities of high art are hardly ever a factor for the judgment of nonfiction. What is important about me is the quality of my thinking, what drives me to do what I am doing; not the facts of my life—but the creative impulse behind that life. I am trying to make an artistic statement logically, and a logical statement to children artistically. I think the time has come for a stronger and more artistically expansive view of nonfiction." Such devotion to craft has made Fisher, as a writer for *Children's Books and Their Creators* summed up, "one of the most multifaceted creators in the field of children's literature."

Biographical and Critical Sources

BOOKS

Children's Books and Their Creators, edited by Anita Silvey, Houghton Mifflin, 1995, pp. 242-43.
Children's Literature Review, Volume 18, Gale, 1989.
Contemporary Authors, New Revision Series, Volume 77, Gale, 1999.
Daugherty, Charles M., *Six Artists Paint a Still Life,* North Light, 1977, pp. 10-29.
Dictionary of Literary Biography, Volume 61: *American Writers for Children since 1960: Poets, Illustrators and Nonfiction Authors,* Gale, 1987, pp. 57-67.
Fisher, Leonard Everett, *A Life of Art,* University of Connecticut Dodd Research Center, 1998.
Hopkins, Lee Bennett, *More Books by More People,* Citation, 1971, pp. 159-164, 316.
Munce, Howard, editor, *Magic and Other Realism,* Hastings House, 1979, pp. 56-59.
Something about the Author Autobiography Series, Volume 1, Gale, 1986, pp. 89-113.
St. James Guide to Children's Writers, 5th edition, edited by Sara Pendergast and Tom Pendergast, St. James Press, 1999, pp. 376-80.

PERIODICALS

American Artist, September, 1966, pp. 42-47, 67-70.
Booklist, October 1, 1984, Karen Stang Hanley, review of *The Olympians,* p. 246; March 15, 1986, Ilene Cooper, review of *The Great Wall of China,* p. 1082; September 1, 1996, p. 71; October 15, 1997, p. 397; November 1, 1997, p. 464; December 1, 1997, p. 618; December 1, 1998, I. Cooper, review of *Galileo* and *Marie Curie,* p. 680; February 1, 1999, I. Cooper, review of *To Bigotry No Sanction,* p. 971; March 15, 1999, p. 1326; October 1, 1999, p. 373; February 1, 2000, Susan Dove Lempke, review of *Gods and Goddesses of the Ancient Maya,* p. 1019.
Bulletin of the Center for Children's Books, December, 1986, Zena Sutherland, review of *Ellis Island,* pp. 65-

66; June, 1988, Betsy Hearne, review of *Monticello,* pp. 203-04; July, 1996, p. 370; April, 1999, p. 279.

Horn Book, May-June, 1988, Leonard Everett Fisher, "The Artist at Work: Creating Nonfiction," pp. 315-323; July-August, 1999, review of *Alexander Graham Bell,* p. 481.

Kirkus Reviews, May 15, 1988, review of *Monticello,* p. 760; March 15, 1996, p. 455; September 15, 1997, p. 1456; January 1, 1999, p. 65.

Language Arts, March, 1982, pp. 224-230.

Publishers Weekly, December 19, 1980, review of *The Sports,* p. 51; February 26, 1982, pp. 62-63; September 25, 1987, review of *The Tower of London,* p. 109; January 18, 1999, p. 340; November 29, 1999, p. 71; February 7, 2000, review of *The Two Mountains,* p. 84.

School Library Journal, January, 1976, Cynthia Adams, review of *Across the Sea from Galway,* pp. 52-53; November, 1979, Shirley Wilton, review of *The Factories* and *The Railroads,* p. 76; January, 1981, Jack Forman, review of *A Russian Farewell,* p. 60; October, 1981, Barbara Hawkins, review of *Storm at the Jetty,* p. 128; August, 1982, Peter Neumeyer, review of *A Circle of Seasons,* p. 118; December, 1985, Deborah Vose, review of *The Statue of Liberty,* pp. 86-87; June, 1993, Linda Boyles, review of *David and Goliath,* pp. 95-96; October, 1993, Sylvia S. Marantz, review of *Stars and Stripes,* pp. 117-18; July, 1996, p. 79; October, 1996, p. 132; December, 1996, Kathleen Odean, review of *Marie Curie,* p. 45; November, 1997, p. 106; December, 1997, Marilyn Payne Phillips, review of *The Jetty Chronicles,* p. 123; December, 1997, Darcy Schild, review of *Anasazi,* p. 108; March, 1999, Carol Fazioli, review of *Alexander Graham Bell,* p. 192; December, 1999, p. 149.

Voice of Youth Advocates, February, 1998, p. 384.

—Sketch by J. Sydney Jones

* * *

FOREST, Heather 1948-

Personal

Born September 19, 1948, in Newark, NJ; daughter of Manny (a teacher) and Fay (a nurse) Friedman; married Lawrence Foglia, September 27, 1981; children: Lucas, Laurel. *Education:* Douglass College, B.A. (art), 1970; East Tennessee State University, M.A. (storytelling), 2000. *Politics:* Democrat. *Religion:* Jewish.

Addresses

Home—47 Foxhurst Rd., Huntington Station, NY 11746. *E-mail*—heather@storyarts.org.

Career

Storyteller, beginning 1974; Story Arts Inc., Long Island, NY, executive director, 1975—. *Member:* National Storytelling Association.

Heather Forest

Awards, Honors

Notable Record Award, American Library Association, 1982, for *Songspinner;* Parents' Choice Gold Classic Award, 1993, for *Eye of the Beholder,* and Gold Award, 1994, for *The Animals Could Talk;* Storytelling World Anthology awards, 1996, for *Wonder Tales from around the World,* and 1997, for *Wisdom Tales from around the World;* Circle of Excellence Award, 1997, National Storytelling Association.

Writings

RETELLER

The Baker's Dozen: A Colonial American Tale, illustrated by Susan Gaber, Harcourt (New York City), 1980.

The Woman Who Flummoxed the Fairies: An Old Tale from Scotland, illustrated by Susan Gaber, Harcourt, 1980.

Earthsong, Joyful Noise (Norwich, VT), 1988.

Wonder Tales from around the World, illustrated by David Boston, August House (Little Rock, AR), 1995.

Wisdom Tales from around the World: Fifty Gems of Story and Wisdom from Such Diverse Traditions as Sufi, Zen, Taoist, Christian, Jewish, Buddhist, African, and Native American, August House, 1997.

A Big Quiet House: A Yiddish Folktale from Eastern Europe, illustrated by Susan Greenstein, August House, 1997.

Stone Soup, illustrated by Susan Gaber, August House, 1998.

RECORDINGS

Songspinner: Folktales and Fables Sung and Told, Weston Woods (Weston, CT), 1982.
Tales of Womenfolk, Weston Woods, 1985.
Sing Me a Story, A Gentle Wind (Albany, NY), 1986.
Tales around the Hearth, A Gentle Wind, 1989.
Eye of the Beholder, Yellow Moon Press (Boston), 1990.
The Animals Could Talk: Aesop's Fables, August House (Little Rock, AR), 1994.
Wonder Tales, August House, 1995.

Sidelights

Storyteller Heather Forest has entertained both young and old listeners for over 25 years with her delightful retellings of stories from around the world. Through recordings and such books for young children as *The Woman Who Flummoxed the Fairies, Stone Soup,* and *Wonder Tales from around the World,* she has expanded her audience even further, filling library story hours and "read me a story" bed times alike with tales that contain "phrasing and imagery [that] are consistently vivid," according to *School Library Journal* contributor Lee Bock.

Her written stories contain "the same smooth, appealing cadence that she uses in her live performances," added Susan Scheps in a review of *The Baker's Dozen* for *School Library Journal,* "with each comma and phrase carefully placed to create a musical whole."

While Forest has collected a number of tales into two large collections: *Wonder Tales from around the World* and *Wisdom Tales from around the World,* several of her books contain only a single story. In *The Baker's Dozen: A Colonial American Tale,* she explains the root of the 13-item "baker's dozen" in New York in the mid-1700s. A prominent baker who specializes in cookies shaped like St. Nicholas learns a bit about the Christmas spirit after he refuses to give one extra cookie to a mysterious customer who can only afford a dozen. When the customer returns the following year, a run of bad luck has made the baker realize what his stinginess has cost him; he gives her the 13th cookie free, completing the "baker's dozen."

In *Stone Soup,* published in 1998, two hungry travelers are refused food when they stop at a small village. Finally, they convince the less-than-generous villagers that they can make soup from a stone, and with contributions of various vegetables from curious onlookers, a wonderful collaborative soup is prepared and enjoyed by all. Forest's "simple, direct telling is enhanced by the addition of several folkloric-style rhymes," noted *Booklist* contributor Kay Weisman, while a reviewer for *Publishers Weekly* added that the author's "jolly prose simmers with energy . . . . Flavorful and nutritious, this classic tale is served up with a smile." Another stand-alone tale, *A Big Quiet House: A Yiddish Folktale from Eastern Europe* illustrates a clever

solution to the problem of a complaining spouse who finds the house too small. Slowly fill the home to overflowing with a host of noisy animals, then take the animals away and peace, quiet, and space are gained! In this version of the Yiddish tale "It Could Always Be Worse," Forest "hams up her telling with intermittent rhymes and refrains," noted a contributor to *Publishers Weekly,* who added that *A Big Quiet House* "invit[es] audience participation."

Forest became interested in storytelling while learning to play folk guitar as a teen. As she noted in an essay on her *Story Arts* Web site, she "especially enjoyed ballads because they had a plot," and when she began writing her own songs in her early twenties, she looked to the traditional ballad form for inspiration. She also turned to the folktale section of her local library for stories to set to music, and discovered that she "could wander the world reading plots from cultures around the globe and create songs out of them." From writing songs, she soon began to craft spoken tales, inspired by stories that contained "a sense of familiarity . . . as though it was really about something that happened to me. Or maybe there was something I needed to learn from the tale. Maybe it healed me. Maybe it made me face myself, by telling it again and again. There is a freeing anonymity

Forest collects twenty-seven ancient folk tales from diverse nations. On an audiocassette of the same title, she performs six of these tales with music she has composed. (Cover illustration by David Boston.)

and at the same time, a revealing vulnerability in telling a folktale."

Forest lives on a tree and perennial flower farm on Long Island, New York, with her husband and two children. "As well as writing books, I share stories with over 40,000 children each year in the Long Island area in schools and community settings," the author/storyteller explained to *SATA.* "I also travel to storytelling festivals and theaters throughout the United States to present my repertoire of world folk tales told in a minstrel style which interweaves original music, poetry, prose, and the sung and spoken word."

Forest began telling stories in 1974, and her invitations to tell have come from all over the country: "from concert halls to circus tents, to elementary school auditoriums," she told *SATA.* She has been a featured storyteller at Jonesborough, Tennessee's National Story-telling Festival several times, and has also appeared at the Smithsonian Institute, the Museum of Modern Art, Edinborough, Scotland's Festival Fringe, Austria's World Festival of Fairytales, and at Rio de Janeiro's "Telebration."

"As a storytelling artist, I am attracted to tell folk tales and fables from around the world that contain a kernel of wisdom passed down through the oral tradition," Forest explained. "Spanning time and place, these ancient tales have a universality which is fresh and relevant in modern times. Although the plots in Wisdom Tales come from diverse cultures, a common thread of joys, sorrows, hopes, dreams, and fears emerge as the colorful tapestry of human experience is presented in metaphor. In spite of our global differences, people everywhere share the same sky."

In addition to her many books and recordings, Forest has also created an educational and informative Web site that focuses on the art of storytelling. The site can be accessed at www.storyarts.org.

Biographical and Critical Sources

PERIODICALS

Booklist, May 15, 1995, Sandy Doggett, review of *The Animals Could Talk,* p. 1662; November 15, 1995, Janice Del Negro, review of *Wonder Tales from around the World,* p. 551; October 1, 1996, Hazel Rochman, review of *A Big Quiet House,* p. 353; March 1, 1997, Karen Morgan, review of *Wisdom Tales from around the World,* p. 1157; September 1, 1998, Kay Weisman, review of *Stone Soup,* p. 121.

Publishers Weekly, March 16, 1990, Diane Roback, review of *The Woman Who Flummoxed the Fairies,* p. 68; October 7, 1996, review of *A Big Quiet House,* p. 74; May 25, 1998, review of *Stone Soup,* p. 89.

School Library Journal, April, 1989, Susan Scheps, review of *The Baker's Dozen,* p. 96; June, 1990, Luann Toth, review of *The Woman Who Flummoxed the Fairies,* p. 112; April, 1996, Lee Bock, review of *Wonder Tales from around the World,* p. 144; November, 1996, Linda Greengrass, review of *A Big Quiet House,*

p. 97; April, 1997, Judy Sokoll, review of *Wisdom Tales from around the World,* p. 169; May, 1998, Kathleen Whalin, review of *Stone Soup,* pp. 131-32.

ON-LINE

Story Arts Web site, www.storyarts.org (February 29, 2000).

*   *   *

FOX, Paula 1923-

Personal

Born April 22, 1923, in New York, NY; daughter of Paul Hervey (a writer) and Elsie (de Sola) Fox; married Richard Sigerson in 1948 (divorced, 1954); married Martin Greenberg, June 9, 1962; children: (first marriage) Adam, Gabriel, Linda. *Education:* Attended Columbia University, 1955-58.

Addresses

Home—Brooklyn, NY.

Career

Author. Has worked in numerous occupations, including model, saleswoman, public relations worker, machinist, staff member for the British publisher, Victor Gollancz, reader for a film studio, reporter in Paris, France, and Warsaw, Poland, for the British wire service Telepress, English-as-a-second-language instructor, and teacher at the Ethical Culture School in New York City and for emotionally disturbed children in Dobbs Ferry, New York; University of Pennsylvania, Philadelphia, professor of English literature, beginning 1963. *Member:* PEN, Authors League of America, Authors Guild.

Awards, Honors

Finalist in National Book Award children's book category, 1971, for *Blowfish Live in the Sea;* National Institute of Arts and Letters Award, 1972; Guggenheim fellowship, 1972; National Endowment for the Arts grant, 1974; Newbery Medal, American Library Association, 1974, for *The Slave Dancer;* Hans Christian Andersen Medal, 1978; National Book Award nomination, 1979, for *The Little Swineherd and Other Tales; A Place Apart* was selected one of *New York Times*'s Outstanding Books, 1980, and received the American Book Award, 1983; Child Study Children's Book Award from the Bank Street College of Education and one of *New York Times*'s Notable Books, both 1984, Christopher Award and Newbery Honor Book, both 1985, and International Board on Books for Young People Honor List for Writing, 1986, all for *One-Eyed Cat;* Brandeis Fiction Citation, 1984; Rockefeller Foundation grant, 1984; *The Moonlight Man* was selected one of the *New York Times*'s Notable Books, 1986, and one of the Child Study Association of America's Children's Books of the Year, 1987; Silver Medallion, University of Southern Mississippi, 1987; *Boston Globe/Horn Book* Award for fiction and Newbery Honor Book, 1989, for *The Village by the Sea*. Empire State Award for children's literature, 1994.

Writings

FOR JUVENILES

Maurice's Room, illustrated by Ingrid Fetz, Macmillan, 1966.

A Likely Place, illustrated by Edward Ardizzone, Macmillan, 1967.

How Many Miles to Babylon?, illustrated by Paul Giovanopoulos, David White, 1967.

The Stone-Faced Boy, illustrated by Donald A. Mackay, Bradbury, 1968.

Dear Prosper, illustrated by Steve McLachlin, David White, 1968.

Portrait of Ivan, illustrated by Saul Lambert, Bradbury, 1969.

The King's Falcon, illustrated by Eros Keith, Bradbury, 1969.

Hungry Fred, illustrated by Rosemary Wells, Bradbury, 1969.

Blowfish Live in the Sea, Bradbury, 1970.

Good Ethan, illustrated by Arnold Lobel, Bradbury, 1973.

The Slave Dancer, illustrated by Eros Keith, Bradbury, 1973.

The Little Swineherd and Other Tales, Dutton, 1978, new edition illustrated by Robert Byrd, Dutton Children's Books, 1996.

A Place Apart, Farrar, Straus, 1980.

One-Eyed Cat, Bradbury, 1984.

(Author of introduction) Marjorie Kellogg, *Tell Me That You Love Me, Junie Moon*, Farrar, Straus, 1984.

The Moonlight Man, Bradbury, 1986.

Lily and the Lost Boy, Orchard Books, 1987, published in England as *The Lost Boy*, Dent, 1988.

The Village by the Sea, Orchard Books, 1988, published in England as *In a Place of Danger*, Orchard Books, 1989.

Monkey Island, Orchard Books, 1991.

(With Floriano Vecchi) *Amzat and His Brothers: Three Italian Tales*, illustrated by Emily Arnold McCully, Orchard Books, 1993.

Western Wind, Orchard Books, 1993.

The Eagle Kite, Orchard Books, 1995.

Radiance Descending, D.K. Inc., 1997.

FOR ADULTS

Poor George, Harcourt, 1967.

Desperate Characters, Harcourt, 1970, reprinted with an afterword by Irving Howe, Nonpareil, 1980.

The Western Coast, Harcourt, 1972.

The Widow's Children, Dutton, 1976.

A Servant's Tale, North Point Press, 1984.

The God of Nightmares, North Point Press, 1990.

Adaptations

Desperate Characters was adapted as a motion picture by Paramount, 1970; a cassette and a film strip accompanied by cassette have been produced of *One-Eyed Cat* by Random House.

Sidelights

Best known for her "uncompromising integrity," according to *Horn Book*'s Alice Bach, American writer Paula Fox has crafted distinguished careers in both children's books and adult fiction. Among the former are novels such as *The Slave Dancer, One-Eyed Cat, The Village by the Sea, Monkey Island, The Eagle Kite,* and *Radiance Descending*. In such juvenile and YA novels Fox pulls no punches; she deals with subjects from abandonment to the misery of AIDS and puts her youthful protagonists in difficult situations and exotic locales, from an island off the coast of northeastern America to an island in the Aegean. "Children know about pain and fear and unhappiness and betrayal," Fox once told *Authors and Artists for Young Adults*. "And we do them a disservice by trying to sugarcoat dark truths.... We must never, ever try to pull the wool over children's eyes by 'watering down' powerful stories."

"Paula Fox believes children have the right to know what to expect from life," Bach noted in her *Horn Book* overview of the author's works. "She acknowledges confusion. Nowhere in her books does she imply there are solutions to grief, abandonment, loneliness.... By admitting to the universality of fear, puzzlement, and foolish behavior, she invites the reader to scream, to snicker, to laugh, to admit pain." It is a formula that readers and critics alike have responded to positively, for her books prove to be popular many years after initial publication and have won numerous awards, including the prestigious Hans Christian Andersen Medal, the Newbery Medal, and the American Book Award for Children's Fiction Paperback.

In addition to her award-winning picture books, chapter books, novels for intermediate readers, and realistic fiction for young adults, Fox has also authored novels for adults, such as *Desperate Characters*, which was adapted for a motion picture. Fox has been described by *Nation* contributor Blair T. Birmelin as "one of our most intelligent (and least appreciated) contemporary novelists." Fox does not feel the need to distinguish between her adult and juvenile fiction, however. She commented in John Rowe Townsend's *A Sense of Story: Essays on Contemporary Writers for Children*, "I never think I'm writing for children, when I work. A story does not start *for* anyone, nor an idea, nor a feeling of an idea; but starts more for oneself." As *School Library Journal* contributor Linda Silver noted, "So few authors write equally well for children and adults that Paula Fox and Isaac Bashevis Singer (who do) should be noted." Silver went on to comment, "Fox's polished prose is so restrained that at times it is cryptic." And as Fox noted in her acceptance speech for the Hans Christian Andersen Medal, reprinted in *Bookbird*, she sees no general difference in the division between children's and adult literature. "The heart of the matter, I believe, is that the art of storytelling is, ultimately, the art of truth. In the imaginative effort that lies behind a good story, there is no difference between writing for children and for adults."

Fox spent her childhood moving from place to place and school to school. Her father was what Fox described as "an itinerant writer." Working in New York City, he earned a living by rewriting plays by other authors, as well as writing several of his own, and later he went to Hollywood and England to work for film studios. While her parents were traveling about, Fox was sent elsewhere. As she recalled in *Authors and Artists for Young Adults,* "As for me, my home for the first six years of my life was with a congregational minister who had been a newspaperman ... before he had found his vocation in the ministry. He was an ardent historian of the Revolutionary period in American history, particularly as it unfolded in the Hudson Valley, where he spent a large part of his life. Every morning he went to his study, and over the years there issued from his Remington typewriter sermons, items he wrote for a local newspaper ... essays ... [and] poems." Fox lived with the minister and his invalid mother in a Victorian house overlooking the Hudson River. With his active and curious mind, the minister had a profound influence on Fox. He taught her to read and to appreciate the works of authors such as Rudyard Kipling, Eugene Field, Mark Twain, Washington Irving, and Walt Whitman; and he also told her tales of the Revolutionary War and other historical events. All these stories inevitably rubbed off on the young Fox. "When I was 5, I had my first experience of being a ghost writer—of sorts," Fox related, recalling how the minister once accepted her suggestion to write a sermon about a waterfall. For "an instant," she later added, "I grasped consciously what had been implicit in every aspect of my life with the minister—that everything could count, that a word, spoken as meant, contained in itself an energy capable of awakening imagination, thought, emotion." It was this experience that first inspired Fox to become a writer.

When Fox was six years old, she left the minister's home to live in California for two years, and in 1931 she moved again, this time to live with her maternal grandmother on a sugar plantation in Cuba. Here, Fox quickly picked up Spanish from her fellow students while attending classes in a one-room schoolhouse. Three years after her arrival, the revolution led by Batista y Zaldivar forced Fox to return to New York City. By this time in her life, Fox had attended nine schools and had hardly ever seen her parents; she found solace and stability by visiting public libraries. "I learned young that public libraries are places of refuge and stability amid chaos and confusion," Fox said.

Fox worked several different jobs after finishing high school, ranging from machinist to working for a publishing company and a newspaper. "I knew I wanted to travel and was able to find jobs that would enable me to do so," Fox recalled. Her desire to travel led her to a position with a leftist British news service that assigned her to cover Poland after World War II. Later, she returned to the United States, married, and had children, but the marriage ended in divorce. Afterwards, Fox resolved to finish her education, attending Columbia University for four years, until she could no longer afford the expense and had to leave before receiving her diploma. Despite the lack of a degree, Fox's knowledge of Spanish helped her find a job as an English teacher for Spanish-speaking children. She also found other teaching positions, including one as a teacher for the emotionally disturbed.

In 1962, Fox married an English professor and moved to Greece for six months where her husband—recipient of a Guggenheim fellowship—studied and wrote. All this time, she had harbored hopes of one day becoming a writer, "but for a long time it remained a shining, but elusive, goal," she recalled. But with the trip to Greece, Fox was finally able to realize her dream, working full time as a writer.

Fox's first publication, *Maurice's Room,* appeared in 1966, and is, as Townsend noted in *A Sounding of Storytellers,* "a blessedly funny book." The story about a boy who is such an avid collector that only he and one friend can enter his room safely, *Maurice's Room* "is a hilarious, subversive book, full of casual joys," according to Townsend. The book was well received and was followed a year later by *A Likely Place,* the story of a young boy whose parents fuss over-much about him. His salvation comes about when he is left under the care of the yogurt and yoga-loving Miss Fitchlow, who gives the boy room to maneuver. Townsend dubbed this second book "dry" and "subtle."

Fox's third book, *How Many Miles to Babylon?,* is longer and more complex than the first two. James is a young black boy growing up in Brooklyn. With his father out of his life and his mother in the hospital, James is left in the care of three aunts and soon falls into the clutches of a juvenile gang of dog thieves. He travels with the gang to Coney Island, where they explore the deserted funhouse. While there, he is able to set the dogs free and escape back to his aunts where his mother, released from the hospital, is waiting for him. Townsend observed that on the surface this novel "is a straightforward story," but that there are symbolic undertones and an almost "dreamlike" quality to the book. Writing in *Horn Book,* Ruth Hill Viguers observed that the writing in *How Many Miles to Babylon?* is "subtle, making the understated story almost nightmarish in its excitement."

A similar journey of discovery comes in *The Stone-Faced Boy,* in which Gus, the middle child of five, ventures out into the snow one night to free a stray dog that has gotten caught in a trap. Once again, the youthful protagonist is able to prove himself. A dog again figures in the 1968 *Dear Prosper,* this time as the narrator of a memoir. The dog in question, it seems, is self-educated, and writes his memoir to Prosper, his next-to-last owner. Here he recounts his infancy in New Mexico, his time spent on a cattle ranch, and the course of events that led him from a life of pampered luxury in Boston to a circus and to abandonment in Paris. A contributor to *Kirkus Reviews* observed that the writing is "clipped" and "economical," and "puts people in perspective." Margaret F. O'Connell, praising the book in the *New York Times Book Review* for its "offbeat" approach, concluded the book made a dog's life seem "downright adventurous."

Overall, Fox's juvenile novels have a complexity and sincerity that make them popular with readers and critics alike. These books cover a wide range of subjects, including parental conflict, alcoholism, and death. Frequently, her young protagonists are emotionally withdrawn children who undertake a journey that is symbolic of their emotional development. In *Blowfish Live in the Sea,* for example, nineteen-year-old Ben travels from New York to Boston to see his estranged, alcoholic father after a twelve-year absence. Because of a past trauma involving a lie his father told him, Ben has withdrawn into himself to the point where he no longer speaks to anyone. His sister Carrie is the only family member who tries to reach out to Ben. The importance of Ben and Carrie's journey to Boston, explained a *Horn Book* reviewer, is that "each step ... relays something further in their tenuous gropings towards an understanding of themselves and of others."

Of all of her books, the controversial yet highly acclaimed *The Slave Dancer,* winner of the 1974 Newbery Medal, is the work for which Fox is best known. It is the story of a New Orleans boy who is kidnapped and placed on a slave ship bound for West Africa. The boy, Jessie Bollier, is chosen for his ability to play the fife; his task aboard ship is to "dance" the slaves so they can exercise their cramped limbs. Eventually, Jessie escapes when the ship's crew is drowned in a storm, but he is forever scarred by his experience. Despite the praise *The Slave Dancer* has received, a number of critics have complained that Fox's portrayal of the slaves made them appear to be merely dispirited cattle, and they accused the author of excusing the slave drivers as being victims of circumstance. Binnie Tate, for example, commented in *Interracial Books for Children:* "Through the characters' words, [Fox] excuses the captors and places the blame for the slaves' captivity on Africans themselves. The author slowly and systematically excuses almost all the whites in the story for their participation in the slave venture and by innuendo places the blame elsewhere." Albert V. Schwartz, also writing in *Interracial Books for Children,* felt that book promoted racist viewpoints because of the passive representation of the black victims. "The Black people are only pathetic sufferers," Schwartz commented. "No 'fight back' qualities whatever are found in these characters.... For them the author provides no balance."

Presenting more of a middle ground between condemnation and praise was Julius Lester, writing in the *New York Times Book Review.* "What saves [this] book from being a failure," wrote Lester, "is the quality of [the] writing, which is consistently excellent." However Lester also found problems with *The Slave Dancer.* "With such good writing, it is too bad that the book as a whole does not succeed." Lester felt that while the novel "describes" the horrors of such slave ships, it "does not re-create them, and if history is to become reality, the reader must live that history as if it were his own life."

Lester complained that readers of Fox's book were "spectators" rather than "fellow sufferers."

Other reviewers, however, regarded *The Slave Dancer* as a fair and humane treatment of a sensitive subject. In her *Horn Book* essay, Bach called the book "one of the finest examples of a writer's control over her material.... With an underplayed but implicit sense of rage, Paula Fox exposes the men who dealt in selling human beings." Writing in *Children's Book Review,* C.S. Hannabuss commented on Fox's "concise and carved style," and went on to note that "Fox once again gets into a child and looks out on a harsh and dangerous world. For the nightmare of the voyage is shown in the very moments of realisation, growing fear and panic and disgust gripping the reader too at deep levels of consciousness." Hannabuss concluded that *The Slave Dancer* "extends the belief that [Fox] is one of the most exciting writers practicing for children and young people today." In *Dictionary of Literary Biography,* Anita Moss wrote that *The Slave Dancer* "is historical fiction at its finest, for Fox has meticulously researched every facet of the slave trade and of the period." Comparing the book to Joseph Conrad's *Heart of Darkness,* Moss further observed that it "takes the reader on a voyage that reveals a haunting glimpse into the abyss of human evil.... *The Slave Dancer* is clearly Fox's masterpiece, and it is fast becoming a classic in American children's literature."

No other work by Fox has been quite as controversial as *The Slave Dancer,* though the author continues to deliver bittersweet messages to today's youth. Other award-winning children's novels by Fox, such as *A Place Apart, One-Eyed Cat,* and *The Village by the Sea,* are similarly concerned with relationships, strong characterization, and emotionally troubled protagonists. *A Place Apart* concerns Victoria Finch, a thirteen-year-old girl whose comfort and security are shaken when her father dies suddenly. Victoria's grief, writes *Washington Post Book World* contributor Katherine Paterson, "is the bass accompaniment to the story. Sometimes it swells, taking over the narrative, the rest of the time it subsides into a dark, rhythmic background against which the main story is played." Victoria must also come to terms with her infatuation with Hugh, a manipulative boy who "exerts ... a power over her spirit," according to Paterson. "This is almost an adult novel," remarked Zena Sutherland in a *Bulletin of the Center for Children's Books* review, "subtle and percipient in its relationships, mature in its bittersweetness; the characters are firmly drawn, and the style is grave and polished." Writing in the *New York Times Book Review,* novelist Anne Tyler complimented Fox on a "story without gimmicks or exaggerations." Tyler concluded, "[Fox] writes a honed prose, avoiding all traces of gee-whillikers tone, and her language is simple and direct. *A Place Apart* is a book apart—quiet-voiced, believable and often very moving."

One-Eyed Cat, declared *Dictionary of Literary Biography* contributor Moss, "is one of Fox's finest literary achievements." The title refers to a stray cat that the main character Ned accidentally injures with an air rifle.

The guilt Ned feels afterwards plagues him through most of the rest of the book, even making him physically ill at one point. He finally confesses his thoughtless act to his mother, who in turn confesses that she had once deserted Ned and his father when he was younger. Recognizing these flaws leads Ned to a reconciliation with his parents and with himself. Tyler, reviewing the novel in *New York Times Book Review,* felt that the book was "full of well-drawn, complicated characters," and that there was "integrity in the plot." Tyler went on to comment, "Most important, though, is what the story can teach young readers about grown-ups' expectations of them." *Horn Book*'s Ethel L. Heins observed, "The much-honored author writes with an artlessness that conceals her art, using the nuances of language to reveal the subtleties of human experience and to push back the frontiers of a young reader's understanding."

A typical Fox device is to put a main character in an unfamiliar and hostile setting. This occurs in *Lily and the Lost Boy,* in which three youngsters are visiting a Greek island, and again, in *The Village by the Sea.* In this book, a girl, Emma, is sent to live with her uncle and neurotic, alcoholic aunt for two weeks when her father has to go to the hospital for heart surgery. Unable to cope with her hateful aunt and troubled about her father's health, Emma finds some solace in creating a make-believe village on the beach. But, as Rosellen Brown relates in the *New York Times Book Review,* "Emma's miniature haven is ultimately beyond her protection. She can only cherish the building of it, and then the memory." Reviewing the novel in *School Library Journal,* Amy Kellerman observed that the "cancerous effect of envy and the healing properties of love and self-esteem are driven home poignantly and with a gentle humor that runs throughout the book." Kellerman concluded, "Fox has given readers another treasure for reading alone or reading aloud."

Continuing her practice of placing her young protagonists in difficult circumstances, Fox, in *Monkey Island,* examines the issue of homelessness and explores the more general childhood fear of abandonment. The story concerns an eleven-year-old middle-class boy named Clay Garrity. His father loses his job as a magazine art director and abandons his family. Because his mother is eight months pregnant and can't work, Clay fears the social services department will take him away and put him in a foster home. Clay decides to leave home and live on the streets, where he is befriended by two kindly homeless men. Finally, however, a bout of pneumonia brings Clay to the attention of the social services, and he is put in a foster home. By the end of the novel, the family is reunited, with Clay, his new baby sister, and mother moving into an apartment together after the mother has secured work. "The novel individualizes the problems of homeless people and puts faces on those whom society has made faceless," remarked Ellen Fader in a *Horn Book* review. Fader felt "readers' perceptions will be changed after reading the masterfully crafted *Monkey Island.*" Writing in the *New York Times Book Review,* Dinitia Smith called the novel "delicate and

moving," and a "relentless story that succeeds in conveying the bitter facts" of homelessness.

In *Western Wind,* Fox has been praised for taking a rather well-worn premise in children's literature—a lonely young girl is sent by her parents to live with an elderly relative who proves to be quite wise—and making it original and interesting. This is achieved mainly by Fox's depiction of the young heroine's grandmother, an eccentric painter who lives on a remote island off the coast of Maine in a house without indoor plumbing. Patricia J. Wagner in the *Bloomsbury Review* lauded Fox's literary skills and concluded that both "adult and junior fiction writers should study her work with care." Ilene Cooper, on the other hand, writing in *Booklist,* offered oblique criticism of this novel and much of Fox's writing: "Fox's work can be like a piece of fine lace. You admire its beauty and the delicate craftsmanship that went into its making, but you don't always know what to do with it. And sometimes you just get tired of so much lace." Betsy Hearne, however, reviewing *Western Wind* in the *Bulletin of the Center for Children's Books,* observed that Fox "uses an isolated situation, as she has done before, to delve into a child's deepening awareness." Hearne further commented, "Fox's style especially suits this taut narrative, into which she slips similes that are frequent but consciously plain to suit the setting."

Homosexuality and AIDS are the issues that Liam Cormac and his family must come to terms with in *The Eagle Kite.* Young Liam's father is dying from the HIV virus. His imminent death and the circumstances under which he contracted the disease cause the family almost unbearable grief; they also provide the narrative struggles through which some memorable characters are defined. Though his mother tells him that his father contracted AIDS from a bad blood transfusion, Liam now remembers seeing his father embrace a young man on the beach several years earlier. Coming to terms with this memory and with the present day reality is at the heart of this novel. Writing in *Voice of Youth Advocates,* W. Keith McCoy described the book as "a brief, but intense, portion of one young boy's life," and further noted that "Fox's spare prose enhances the emotions that are buffeting the Cormacs." In *The Washington Post Book World,* Elizabeth Hand called the book "beautifully written," and reviewing the novel in *Horn Book,* Nancy Vasilakis remarked on its "painstaking honesty." Vasilakis concluded, "This will be a hard novel for teens to absorb, but well worth the effort."

Such honesty is also displayed in Fox's 1997 novel *Radiance Descending,* the story of a boy struggling to ignore his brother who is suffering from Down's syndrome. Adolescent Paul Coleman is tired of his brother, Jacob. Having just moved to Long Island from New York City, Paul is eager to avoid the eternal laughter of his brother, and the way he messes up the table and Paul's room. Though Jacob idealizes Paul, Paul is also tired of the way his parents focus all attention on the lovable but simple younger brother. Slowly, however, Paul comes to realize that the mere fact of avoiding Jacob is still focusing on him, and that there may be a middle ground. Escorting Jacob to his Saturday morning allergy shots, Paul is forced into Jacob's world: into its slower pace and the loyal friends who inhabit it. "Older readers will find many layers of meaning in this novel," noted a reviewer for *Publishers Weekly.* "Younger readers may be put off by a few esoteric allusions ... but will still be able to recognize the gradual blossoming of Paul's compassion." Edward Sullivan, writing in *Voice of Youth Advocates,* felt that *Radiance Descending* "is a quiet, introspective novel told with great eloquence." Sullivan went on to write, "Fox's every word is chosen with care, and every sentence masterfully crafted," and concluded that the novel is "moving and touching." A contributor for *Kirkus Reviews* remarked that the story was "worthwhile" and "poignant" if for no other reason than the "authentic delineation of a loving family's coping with one member's special needs."

Fox's career has been long and distinguished. Though she has won less notoriety for her adult fiction than for her works for children, she has continued to contribute in the latter field, as well, with her popular *Desperate Characters,* and publishing *A Servant's Tale* in 1984 and *The God of Nightmares* in 1990. Such novels are, according to Linda Simon writing in *Commonweal,* "concerned with the cataclysmic moments of private lives, and the quiet desperation of ordinary people." But it is decidedly for her contributions in children's literature that Fox is deservedly best known. As Cathryn M. Mercier noted in an essay on Fox in *St. James Guide to Young Adult Writers,* "In every novel, Fox attributes significant capabilities to her readers. She pays tribute to their emotional, intellectual, and psychological abilities with layered, probing narratives, identifiable characters who achieve genuine illumination, and lucid, striking prose." Mercier further pointed out, "Although some critics occasionally label her work 'depressing,' most praise her integrity in writing honestly about relationships and emotional development. Her craft seems effortless; her vision essential and eloquent."

Biographical and Critical Sources

BOOKS

Authors and Artists for Young Adults, Volume 3, Gale, 1990, pp. 95-106.
Authors of Books for Young People, 3rd edition, edited by Martha E. Ward et al, Scarecrow Press, 1990.
Children's Books and Their Creators, edited by Anita Silvey, Houghton Mifflin, 1995.
Children's Literature Review, Volume 1, Gale, 1976, Volume 44, 1997.
Contemporary Literary Criticism, Gale, Volume 2, 1974, Volume 8, 1978.
Kingman, Lee, editor, *Newbery and Caldecott Medal Winners, 1966-1975,* Horn Book, 1975.
Mercier, Cathryn M., "Fox, Paula," *St. James Guide to Young Adult Writers,* 2nd edition, edited by Tom Pendergast and Sara Pendergast, St. James Press, 1999, pp. 292-93.

Moss, Anita, "Paula Fox," *Dictionary of Literary Biography,* Volume 52: *American Writers for Children since 1960: Fiction,* Gale, 1986.
Townsend, John Rowe, *A Sense of Story: Essays on Contemporary Writers for Children,* Lippincott, 1971.
Townsend, John Rowe, "Paula Fox," *A Sounding of Storytellers: New and Revised Essays on Contemporary Writers for Children,* Lippincott, 1979, pp. 55-64.

PERIODICALS

Bloomsbury Review, March-April, 1994, Patricia J. Wagner, review of *Western Wind.*
Bookbird, December 13, 1978, Paula Fox, "Acceptance Speech—1978 H. C. Andersen Author's Medal," pp. 2-3.
Booklist, March 15, 1993, p. 64; October 15, 1993, Ilene Cooper, review of *Western Wind,* p. 432; February 1, 1995, p. 1003; September 1, 1997, p. 124.
Bulletin of the Center for Children's Books, November, 1980, Zena Sutherland, review of *A Place Apart,* p. 52; September, 1993, Betsy Hearne, review of *Western Wind,* pp. 9-10.
Chicago Tribune, April 9, 1995, p. 7.
Children's Book Review, December, 1972; winter, 1974-75, C. S. Hannabuss, review of *The Slave Dancer.*
Commonweal, January 11, 1985, Linda Simon, review of *A Servant's Tale.*
English Journal, November, 1996, p. 132.
Horn Book, September-October, 1967, Viguers, Ruth Hill, review of *How Many Miles to Babylon?;* August, 1969; November-December, 1970, review of *Blowfish Live in the Sea;* August, 1974; September-October, 1977, Alice Bach, "Cracking Open the Geode: The Fiction of Paula Fox," pp. 514-21; October, 1978; April, 1984; January-February, 1985, Ethel L. Heins, review of *One-Eyed Cat,* pp. 57-58; September-October, 1991, Ellen Fader, review of *Monkey Island,* pp. 596-97; July-August, 1993, p. 468; March-April, 1994, p. 198; September-October, 1995, Nancy Vasilakis, review of *The Eagle Kite,* pp. 608-9; September-October, 1997, p. 569.
Interracial Books for Children, Volume 5, number 5, 1974, Albert V. Schwartz, review of *The Slave Dancer* and Binnie Tate, review of *The Slave Dancer.*
Kirkus Reviews, April 1, 1968, review of *Dear Prosper,* p. 393; September 1, 1997, review of *Radiance Descending,* p. 1389.
Los Angeles Times Book Review, September 25, 1988; July 16, 1995, p. 27.
Ms., October, 1984.
Nation, November 3, 1984, Blair T. Birmelin, review of *A Servant's Tale.*
Newsweek, March 16, 1970; September 27, 1976; December 1, 1980.
New Yorker, February 7, 1970; November 1, 1976.
New York Review of Books, June 1, 1967; October 5, 1972; October 28, 1976; June 27, 1985.
New York Times, February 10, 1970; September 22, 1972; September 16, 1976.
New York Times Book Review, July 21, 1968, Margaret F. O'Connell, review of *Dear Prosper,* p. 22; February 1, 1970; October 8, 1972; January 20, 1974, Julius Lester, review of *The Slave Dancer;* October 3, 1976;

November 9, 1980, Anne Tyler, "Staking Out Her Own Territory," p. 55; July 12, 1981; November 11, 1984, A. Tyler, "Trying to Be Perfect," p. 48; November 18, 1984; February 5, 1989, Rosellen Brown, review of *The Village by the Sea,* p. 37; July 8, 1990, p. 18; November 10, 1991, Dinitia Smith, "No Place to Call Home," p. 52; November 10, 1993, p. 52; April 10, 1994, p. 35.

Publishers Weekly, April 6, 1990; April 12, 1993, p. 64; August 23, 1993, p. 73; April 10, 1994, p. 35; February 20, 1995, p. 207; January 13, 1997, p. 36; July 27, 1997, review of *Radiance Descending,* p. 202.

School Library Journal, February, 1979, Linda Silver, "From Baldwin to Singer: Authors for Kids and Adults," pp. 27-29; August, 1988, Amy Kellerman, review of *The Village by the Sea,* p. 93; August, 1991, p. 164; April, 1992, p. 42; July, 1993, p. 90; December, 1993, p. 111; February, 1995, p. 63; April, 1995, p. 150; September, 1997, p. 216.

Voice of Youth Advocates, December, 1993, p. 290; June, 1995, W. Keith McCoy, review of *The Eagle Kite,* pp. 93-94; October, 1995, p. 210; February, 1998, Edward Sullivan, review of *Radiance Descending,* p. 383.

Washington Post Book World, February 8, 1981, Katherine Paterson, review of *A Place Apart;* May 7, 1995, Elizabeth Hand, review of *The Eagle Kite,* p. 14.*

—Sketch by J. Sydney Jones

G

GRI
See DENNEY, Diana

*   *   *

GURNEY, James 1958-

Personal

Born June 14, 1958; son of Robert Denison (a mechanical engineer) and Joanna (Mackay) Gurney; married Jeanette Lendino (an artist), April 24, 1983; children: Daniel, Franklin. *Education:* University of California, Berkeley, B.A., 1979; attended Art Center College of Design, 1980.

Addresses

Office—c/o Dinotopia, P.O. Box 391, Red Hook, NY 12571-0391.

Career

Writer and illustrator. Ralph Bakshi Productions, Burbank, CA, animation background artist, 1981; freelance illustrator for paperback science fiction and fantasy books, 1982-91; National Geographic Society, Washington, DC, historical and archaeological illustrator, 1983-99; U.S. Postal Service, illustrator for postal card issued 1988, and commemorative stamp series issued 1997. *Exhibitions:* Various group shows at museums, universities, and other venues, including the Cleveland Museum of Natural History; Delaware Art Museum; Society of Illustrators (New York); Park Avenue Atrium (New York City); Words and Pictures Museum; Bruce Museum (Connecticut); Explorer's Hall (Washington, D.C.); University of Maryland; Norman Rockwell Museum (Stockbridge, MA); Field Museum (Chicago, IL). *Dinotopia* solo shows in various locations, including the L.A. County Museum of Natural History; Cleveland, OH; Buffalo, NY; Albuquerque, NM; and Richmond, CT.

Member: Association of Science Fiction Artists, Authors Guild, Phi Beta Kappa.

Awards, Honors

Chesley Award, Association of Science Fiction and Fantasy Artists, 1991, 1992, 1995, 2000; Abby Award nomination, World Science Fiction Convention, 1992, and Hugo Award for best original artwork, World Science Fiction Convention, 1993, both for *Dinotopia;* Judges' Art Award, World Science Fiction Convention, 1993, for painting *Garden of Hope;* Locus Award, *Locus* magazine, 1993; World Fantasy Award, World Fantasy Association, 1993; Silver Medal, Society of Illustrators (New York), 1999.

Writings

(With Thomas Kinkade) *The Artist's Guide to Sketching,* Watson-Guptill Publications, 1982.

SELF-ILLUSTRATED

Dinotopia: A Land Apart from Time, Turner Publishing (Atlanta, GA), 1992.
Dinotopia: The World Beneath, Turner Publications, 1995.
(With Thomas Holtz) *The World of Dinosaurs,* Greenwich Workshop Press, 1998.
Dinotopia: First Flight, HarperCollins, 1999.

ILLUSTRATOR

Alan Dean Foster, *The Hand of Dinotopia,* HarperCollins, 1999.

The book, *James Gurney: The World of Dinosaurs,* by Michael Brett-Surman and Thomas R. Holtz, Jr., is based on Gurney's art commissioned for the Postal Service dinosaur stamp series.

Sidelights

Set in 1862, James Gurney's first book, *Dinotopia,* is the tale of Arthur Denison and his young son, Will, who are saved by dolphins after their ship is sunk. The dolphins bring them to the island of Dinotopia, where dinosaurs,

James Gurney

mammoths, and other prehistoric creatures have developed their own civilization, language, and culture. On Dinotopia, human beings—all shipwreck survivors like Arthur and Will—and dinosaurs peacefully co-exist. With a dinosaur named Bix as their guide, father and son explore the island. Arthur is intrigued by the hints he finds of the civilization that preceded the current utopia, and Will is immediately enamored by the romantic skybax pilots, who fly the winged Quetzalcoatlus dinosaurs. The first book was a popular success, spawning *Dinotopia* memorabilia such as mugs, stuffed toys, a calendar, a pop-up book, and several sequels.

Gurney has been fascinated with dinosaurs since the age of five, when he caught his first glimpse of an Allosaurus skeleton at a science museum. He majored in anthropology in college, and after graduating from the University of California he continued to study drawing and painting at the Pasadena Art Center College of Design. The inspiration for *Dinotopia* came from two of Gurney's paintings, *Dinosaur Parade* and *Waterfall City*. He drew a map of Dinotopia, and then began to develop characters and a story line. Gurney wanted both the story and the artwork to be as realistic as possible. He read nineteenth-century travel journals, studied current scientific literature on dinosaurs, traveled to the Smithsonian, and consulted noted paleontologists, so that both the plot and the illustrations emerged as equally important in the completed book.

Creating the artwork was a painstaking endeavor. "The process for doing the paintings is very much like doing a frame for a big-budget movie," Gurney told *Something about the Author.* He built models of dinosaurs and then brought them outside, onto the lawn of his Hudson Valley home. His wife, Jeanette—who is also an artist—designed period costumes. Neighborhood children then put on the costumes and acted out scenes from the book. Sometimes, Gurney's own two sons, Daniel and Franklin, would join them on the lawn. "They're the cheapest models," he joked. Gurney photographed the scenes, and then used the photographs as the basis for his paintings. "I don't think of [Dinotopia] as a fantasy world to escape to, but rather as a real world to participate in," Gurney says. "I try to make each painting so real that you feel you can step through the frame and disappear into it."

Critics reacted favorably to *Dinotopia,* predicting that the book would fascinate juvenile and adult readers alike. Cathryn A. Camper wrote in the *School Library Journal,* "Younger readers . . . will be enticed by the dramatic, full-color illustrations, which include both panoramic sweeps of the utopian cities and detailed sketches of Dinotopian contraptions." A reviewer for *Kirkus Reviews* called the book "a sweet, visually attractive utopian fantasy," and added that, "some adults—and children—will love it dearly." The book also won several awards for its artwork. The reaction to

Dinotopia pleased Gurney, who told *SATA:* "I've been absolutely delighted ... as a new author to have this incredible response."

Gurney's second book, *Dinotopia: The World Beneath,* takes off from Arthur Denison's fascination with the caverns beneath Dinotopia, whose mysteries are hinted at in the first Dinotopia book. While the text of *Dinotopia* took the form of journal entries written and illustrated by Arthur as he and his son discovered the unique island, *The World Beneath* has an omniscient third-person narrator, and thus a more conventionally structured plot. "Where *Dinotopia* is a leisurely ramble, *The World Beneath* is more of a melodrama, with a greedy sailor and the ever-ferocious meat-eating dinos providing the danger," remarked Donald Dale Jackson in *Smithsonian.* In both books, "story and pictures work together in a way reminiscent of a comic book," remarked Susan Dove Lempke in *Booklist,* though in neither is Gurney's artwork—universally described as lush, detailed, and romantic—"cartoonish," the critic added. Arthur and Will's explorations in *The World Beneath* reveal connections between the civilization of Dinotopia and the mythical worlds of Poseidon and Atlantis, as well as ancient China and Egypt. Though a reviewer for *Publishers Weekly* found Gurney's plot "trite," the book's fabulous illustrations "at once fanciful and precise, pull readers into an enchanting adventure that should capture the most skeptical, armor-plated heart."

In an interview with Andrew LeCount featured on the Dinotopia web page, Gurney talked about the third Dinotopia novel: "The first two books introduce Dinotopia's golden age. I set out to describe that idyllic universe as a peaceful garden for the imagination. At the time, my own kids were very young, and I wanted to make the books into a kind of sandbox they could play in. Now they're aged 10 and 12, and I find that my own interests have expanded along with theirs. I will be returning to the 19th Century Dinotopia, but lately I've been interested in exploring themes surrounding characters that grow from conflict and camaraderie. So I went back thousands of years to a time in Dinotopia's history where everything isn't perfect, and the future of the island hinges on the actions of a few individuals. *First Flight* is more in the spirit of classic adventure stories like Robin Hood and Treasure Island. It's an age of heroes."

Biographical and Critical Sources

PERIODICALS

Booklist, January 1, 1996, Susan Dove Lempke, review of *Dinotopia: The World Beneath,* p. 814; June 1, 1998, p. 1742.
Entertainment Weekly, June 18, 1993, p. 68A.
Highlights for Children, January, 1998, p. 12.
Kirkus Reviews, July 15, 1992, review of *Dinotopia.*
Life, October, 1992, "Living with Dinosaurs: Inside the Mind of a Man Who Makes Fantasy Seem Real."
Magpies, September, 1992, p. 8.
People, December 14, 1992, Paula China, and Tony Kahn, "Prehistoric Pals: In James Gurney's New Illustrated Fantasy, Dinosaurs Are Man's Best Friends."
Plays, March, 1999, p. 64.
Publishers Weekly, May 18, 1992, p. 32; August 10, 1992, p. 52; September 25, 1995, review of *Dinotopia: The World Beneath,* p. 45.
School Arts, February, 2000, p. 60.
School Librarian, February, 1996, p. 20.
School Library Journal, December, 1992, Cathryn A. Camper, review of *Dinotopia,* p. 110.
Smithsonian, September, 1995, Donald Dale Jackson, "Daring Deed, Bold Dreams, in a Land Removed from Time," p. 70.
U.S. Kids, March, 1997, p. 18.
USA Today, November 18, 1992, "Dinosaur Tale Lets Kids' Imagination Roam."

ON-LINE

Dinotopia, www.dinotopia.com (April 4, 2000).

H

HATHORN, Libby 1943-

Personal

Full name, Elizabeth Helen Hathorn; surname is pronounced "hay-thorn"; born September 26, 1943, in Newcastle, New South Wales, Australia.

Addresses

Agent—Tracey Adams, McIntosh and Otis, New York, NY.

Career

Teacher and librarian in schools in Sydney, Australia, 1965-81; worked as a deputy principal, 1977; consultant and senior education officer for government adult education programs, 1981-86; full-time writer, 1987—. Sydney University, part-time lecturer in English and children's literature, beginning in 1982; writer in residence at the University of Technology, Sydney, 1990, Woollahra Library, 1992, and at Edith Cowan University, 1992. Consultant to the Dorothea Mackellar National Poetry Competition/Festival for children, 1992-93; speaker for student, teacher, and parent groups.

Awards, Honors

The Tram to Bondi Beach was highly commended by the Children's Book Council of Australia, 1982; *Paolo's Secret* was shortlisted for the Children's Book of the Year Award and for the New South Wales Premier's Literary Awards, both 1986; *All about Anna* received an Honour Award from the Children's Book Council of Australia, 1987, and was shortlisted for the Kids Own Australian Literary Award (KOALA), 1988, and for the Young Australians Best Book Award (YABBA), 1989 and 1990; Literature Board of the Australia Council fellowships, 1987 and 1988; *Looking Out for Sampson* received an Honour Award from the Children's Book Council of Australia, 1988; *The Extraordinary Magics of Emma McDade* was shortlisted for the Children's

Book of the Year Award, 1990; Hathorn was highly commended in 1990 by the Society of Women Writers for the body of her work during 1987-89; *Thunderwith* was named Honour Book of the Year for older readers by the Children's Book Council of Australia, 1990, an American Library Association Best Book for Young Adults, 1991, was shortlisted for the Canberra's Own Outstanding List, KOALA, and YABBA, all 1991, and the Dutch translation received an award from Stichting Collectieve Propaganda van het Nederlands Boek (Foundation for the Promotion of Dutch Books), 1992; *So Who Needs Lotto?* and *Jezza Says* were both named Children's Book Council of Australia notable books, 1991; New South Wales Children's Week Medal for literature, 1992; Kate Greenaway Award, United Kingdom, 1995, for *Way Home;* Australian Violence Prevention Certificate Award, 1995; Notable Book citations from the Children's Book Council of Australia, 1993, 1996, and 1997.

Writings

FOR CHILDREN AND YOUNG ADULTS

Stephen's Tree (storybook), illustrated by Sandra Laroche, Methuen, 1979.

Lachlan's Walk (picture book), illustrated by Laroche, Heinemann, 1980.

The Tram to Bondi Beach (picture book), illustrated by Julie Vivas, Collins, 1981.

Paolo's Secret (novella), illustrated by Lorraine Hannay, Heinemann, 1985.

All about Anna (novel), Heinemann, 1986.

Looking out for Sampson (storybook), Oxford University Press, 1987.

Freya's Fantastic Surprise (picture book), illustrated by Sharon Thompson, Ashton Scholastic, 1988.

The Extraordinary Magics of Emma McDade (storybook), illustrated by Maya, Oxford University Press, 1989.

Stuntumble Monday (picture book), illustrated by Melissa Web, Collins Dove, 1989.

The Garden of the World (picture book), illustrated by Tricia Oktober, Margaret Hamilton Books, 1989.

Thunderwith (novel), Heinemann, 1989.

Jezza Says (novel), illustrated by Donna Rawlins, Angus & Robertson, 1990.

So Who Needs Lotto? (novella), illustrated by Simon Kneebone, Penguin, 1990.

Talks with My Skateboard (poetry), Australian Broadcasting Corp., 1991.

(Editor) *The Blue Dress* (stories), Heinemann, 1991.

Help for Young Writers (nonfiction), Nelson, 1991.

Good to Read (textbook), Nelson, 1991.

Who? (stories), Heinemann, 1992.

Love Me Tender (novel), Oxford University Press, 1992.

The Lenski Kids and Dracula (novella), Penguin, 1992.

Valley under the Rock (novel), Reed Heinemann, 1993.

The Way Home (picture book), illustrated by Greg Rogers, Random House, 1993.

Feral Kid (novel), Hodder & Stoughton, 1994.

Grandma's Shoes (picture book), illustrated by Elivia Salvadier, Little, Brown, 1994, reissued, illustrated by Caroline Magerl, Hodder, 2000.

What a Star (novel), HarperCollins, 1994.

The Wonder Thing (picture book), illustrated by Peter Gouldthorpe, Penguin, 1995.

Juke-box Jive (novel), Hodder, 1996.

The Climb (novel), Penguin, 1996.

Chrysalis (novel), Reed, 1997.

Rift (novel), Hodder Headline, 1998.

Sky Sash So Blue (picture book), illustrated by Benny Andrews, Simon and Schuster, 1998.

(With Gary Crew) *Dear Venny, Dear Saffron* (novel), Lothian, 1999.

Ghostop (novel), Headline, 1999.

The Gift, illustrated by Greg Rogers, Random House, 2000.

Also author of a libretto for a children's opera, composed by Grahame Koehne, based on *Grandma's Shoes,* that was performed at the Australian Opera Workshop.

Some of Hathorn's works have been translated into Greek, Italian, Dutch, German, French, Norwegian, Danish, and Swedish.

FOR ADULTS

(With G. Bates) *Half-Time: Perspectives on Mid-life,* Fontana Collins, 1987.

Better Strangers (stories), Millennium Books, 1989.

Damascus, a Rooming House (libretto), performed by the Australian Opera at Performance Space, Sydney, 1990.

The Maroubra Cycle: A Journey around Childhood (performance poetry), University of Technology, Sydney, 1990.

(And director) *The Blue Dress Suite* (music theatre piece), produced at Melbourne International Festival, 1991.

Adaptations

Thunderwith was produced as a "Hallmark Hall of Fame" television movie titled *The Echo of Thunder.* Several of Hathorn's works have also been adapted for interactive online storytelling.

Work in Progress

A young adult novel, *The Painter,* about a young boy's meeting with Vincent Van Gogh.

Sidelights

A multi-talented Australian writer, Libby Hathorn produces poetry, picture books, drama, novels, short stories, and nonfiction for children, young adults, and adults. Best known in the United States for her critically acclaimed novel *Thunderwith,* Hathorn has created works ranging from serious stories of troubled youth to lighthearted, fast-paced comedies. She writes of powerful females in her novels for junior readers, such as the protagonists in *All about Anna* or *The Extraordinary Magics of Emma McDade,* or of lonely, misunderstood teenagers in novels such as *Feral Kid, Love Me Tender,* and *Valley under the Rock.* As Maurice Saxby noted in *St. James Guide to Children's Writers,* "In her novels for teenagers especially, Hathorn exposes, with compassion, sensitivity, and poetry the universal and ongoing struggle of humanity to heal hurts, establish meaningful relationships, and to learn to accept one's self—and ultimately—those who have wronged us."

"I must have been very young indeed when I decided to become a writer," Libby Hathorn once commented. "My grandmother always kept my stories in her best black handbag and read them out loud to long-suffering relatives and told me over and over that I'd be a writer when I grew up." Though Hathorn started her career as a teacher and librarian, she did eventually become a writer. "Libby Hathorn knows exactly how today's children think and feel," observed Saxby in *The Proof of the Puddin': Australian Children's Literature, 1970-1990.* "She has an uncanny ear for the speech nuances of the classroom, playground and home.... [She] is always able to penetrate the facade of her characters and with skill and subtlety reveal what they are really like inside."

Hathorn grew up near Sydney, Australia, and recalled that at the time her parents did not own a car. "In fact, not many people on the street where I lived in the early 1950s owned cars. We had no television, either. We amused ourselves with storytelling and reading out loud and lots of games." Hathorn often read and told stories to her sisters and brother; she was encouraged by her parents, who "loved books" and had bookcases crammed with them. "Books were pretty central in our lives," she stated. "My father in particular read to us at night when he could get home in time. He was a detective and had long shifts at night that often kept him late. When he read we didn't interrupt, in fact we'd never dream of it as his voice filled the room because it seemed so obviously important to him—the ebb and flow of the language. My mother—who was very proud of her Irish ancestry—told us lots of true stories about the history of our family and also about her own girlhood."

As a child, Hathorn read "adventure books set in the Australian bush, like *Seven Little Australians,* as well as classics like *Black Beauty, The Secret Garden, Little Women,* and books by Emily and Charlotte Bronte," she once explained. She also read works by Australian authors "with considerable delight at finding Australian settings and people in print." Later, Hathorn would lend her own work an Australian flavor after noticing "the need for more books that told Australian kids about themselves."

Hathorn began writing her own stories and poems when she was still a young girl. Though she was often shy and quiet, Hathorn once noted that she could keep company "entertained with strings of stories that I made up as I went along." Her family encouraged her, and Hathorn "loved being at center stage—so I couldn't have been altogether a shy little buttercup." At school, she enjoyed reading and creative writing, and was disappointed in later years when "we had to write essays and commentaries but never, never stories or poems. I was extremely bored in my final years at school." Hathorn has also acknowledged that her high school years weren't all bad: "After all, I was introduced to the works of William Shakespeare, and particularly in my later years the poetic nature of his work touched me deeply. And best of all we studied the Romantic poets and I fell in love with John Keats and Samuel Coleridge as well as Percy Bysshe Shelley, Lord Byron, and William Wordsworth."

After graduating from high school, Hathorn worked in a laboratory and studied at night for a year before attending college full-time. Despite her parents' objections, she contemplated a career in journalism, hoping that she could learn "the art and craft of novel writing." "Anyway, my parents thought it important that I have a profession where I could earn a reasonable living—writers being notoriously underpaid," Hathorn remarked. "I was drawn to teaching; so after a year of broken specimen flasks and test tubes and discovering that my science courses did not enthrall me, I left the laboratory."

Hathorn attended Balmain Teacher's College (now the University of Technology, Sydney). "I must admit that I found the regulations of the place quite hard," she recalled. "Many of the lectures of those days seemed so dull to me that I wondered whether indeed I would last as a teacher for very long." Hathorn did enjoy her literature classes and was surprised to find that "when I came out of the rather dull years at college, I not only liked classroom teaching, but I also discovered that it was the most thrilling, absorbing, rewarding, and wonderful job anyone could have!"

After teaching for several years in Sydney, Hathorn applied for a position as a school librarian. "Although I was sorry to leave the intimacy of family that a classroom teacher has with her own class, the library was a new and exciting chapter for me," Hathorn once commented. "I had books, books, and more books to explore and the amazingly enjoyable job of bringing stories to every child in the school!" Her job as a librarian, the author added, "had a major influence on my decision to seriously try to publish my stories."

Hathorn's first book for children was *Stephen's Tree,* which was published in 1979. She followed this with two picture books: *Lachlan's Walk* and *The Tram to Bondi Beach.* In the genre of children's picture books, Hathorn discovered, as she explained, "such a scarcity of Australian material! I wanted to talk about our place, here and now, and have pictures that Australian children would instantly recognize. *Stephen's Tree* was a breakthrough in publishing. I had to fight with my publisher to have a gumtree on the cover. They wanted an ash or elm or oak so it would sell in England and Europe! Similarly, I was told *The Tram to Bondi Beach* should not mention Bondi. I won those fights and I must say *The Tram to Bondi Beach* has made its way onto the American market and American children didn't seem to have much trouble at all."

The Tram to Bondi Beach tells the story of Keiran, a nine-year-old boy who longs for a job selling newspapers to passengers on the trams that travel through Sydney. Keiran wants to be like Saxon, an older boy, who is an experienced newspaper seller. Reviewers commented on the nostalgic quality of the story, which is set in the 1930s. Marianne Pilla assessed the picture book in *School Library Journal,* pointing out its "smooth" narrative and "vivid" passages. *Times Literary Supplement* contributor Ann Martin called *The Tram to Bondi Beach* "a simple but appealing tale," and Karen Jameyson wrote in *Horn Book* that the book "will undoubtedly hold readers' interest."

Hathorn followed *The Tram to Bondi Beach* with *Paolo's Secret, All about Anna,* and *Looking out for Sampson.* As Hathorn once noted, *All about Anna,* her first novel, "is based on a wild, naughty cousin I had who drove her mother's car down the road at ten years of age and did other wild deeds—a perfect subject to write about." The book details the comic adventures of Lizzie, Harriet, Christopher, and their energetic, imaginative cousin, Anna. Lizzie, the narrator, explains that "I like being with Anna because somehow things always seem fast and furious and funny when she's around—and well, she's just a very unusual person."

Like *All about Anna, Looking out for Sampson* touches on family themes. In the book Bronwyn wishes that her younger brother, Sampson, were older so that she could have a friend instead of someone to babysit. And when Cheryl and her mother come to stay with Bronwyn's family, Bronwyn's situation worsens. A disagreeable girl, Cheryl hints that Bronwyn's parents must care more about Sampson, since they give the toddler so much attention. After Sampson is lost briefly at the beach, however, Cheryl and Bronwyn reconcile and Bronwyn's parents express their appreciation of her.

Around the time *All about Anna* was published in 1986, Hathorn decided to give up her job and become a full-time writer. "I wanted to be a full-time writer secretly all my life but when I began my working life as a teacher this dream seemed to recede," the author once explained. "And once I was married and with two children I felt I had to keep up my contribution to our lifestyle. My husband is also a teacher and I thought it would be unfair if he had to work every day while I was home writing. It was as if in the eyes of the world writing was not work! And I'm to blame for allowing myself to think like that too.

"I've changed my mind now and I wish I had had the courage to do so much sooner. While I loved teaching, after some years of it I was ready for change. I was already writing short stories but I was aching to tell longer stories, to produce a novel for older readers. This was very hard when I was working full-time and had young children—so the stories I chose to write at that time were for younger children and were either picture books or junior novels like *All about Anna* and *Looking out for Sampson*."

Among Hathorn's other books for young readers is *The Extraordinary Magics of Emma McDade*. The story describes the adventures of the title character, whose superhuman powers include incredible strength, the ability to call thousands of birds by whistling, and control over the weather. Another of Hathorn's books geared towards beginning readers is *Freya's Fantastic Surprise*. In it Miriam tells the class at news time that her parents bought her a tent, a surprise that Freya attempts to top by making up fantastic stories that her classmates realize are false. Freya eventually has a real surprise to share, however, when her mother announces that Freya will soon have a new sister. Published in the United States as well as Australia, *Freya's Fantastic Surprise* was praised by critics. Louise L. Sherman noted in *School Library Journal* that "Freya's concern about impressing her classmates ... is on target." In a *Horn Book* review, Elizabeth S. Watson called the book "a winner" and commented that "the text and pictures combine to produce a tale that proves truth is best."

Hathorn began writing her first novel for young adults, *Thunderwith,* after receiving an Australia Council grant in 1987. "At home writing for a year, I realized that this was to be my job for the rest of my life," Hathorn once remarked. "And since I have been able to give full-time attention to my writing it has certainly flowered in many new directions. I have begun writing longer novels for young adults and I have been able to take on more ambitious projects like libretti and music theatre pieces, which I enjoy tremendously."

Thunderwith, published in 1989, is the story of fourteen-year-old Lara, who begins living with the father she barely knows after her mother dies of cancer. Lara's new home is in the remote Wallingat Forest in New South Wales, Australia. Though Lara's relationship with her father develops smoothly, he is often away on business and Lara's stepmother is openly antagonistic towards her. Lonely and grief-stricken, Lara finds solace in her bond with a mysterious dog that appears during a storm. She names the dog Thunderwith and keeps his existence a secret; she only tells the aboriginal storyteller she has befriended at school. Eventually, Lara realizes that Thunderwith has filled the space that her mother's death created, enabling her to come to terms with her loss.

Lara is also able to slowly win over her stepmother and to adjust to her new home and family life.

The setting of *Thunderwith* is one with which Hathorn is intimately acquainted. As a child, she had relatives who lived in the Australian bush, and she spent many holidays in the country. "This was to prove very important to me," Hathorn once stated. "The bush weaves its own magic and it's something you cannot experience from a book or television show in a suburban setting. My holidays, especially those on my grandmother's farm in the Blue Mountains, created in me an enduring love for the Australian bush. As a writer, however, up until a few years ago the settings I chose to write about were in the hub of the family and quite often in suburbia."

Hathorn came upon the idea for *Thunderwith* after her brother bought land in Wallingat Forest. "During the first holiday there a huge storm blew up at about midnight and such was the noise and intensity of it we all rose from our beds to watch it," Hathorn once said. "You can imagine how vulnerable you'd feel way out in the bush with thunder booming and lightning raging and trees whipping and bending ... and in the midst of this fury suddenly I saw a dog. A huge dark dog dashed across the place where some hours earlier we'd had a campfire and eaten our evening meal under the stars—a lovely looking half-dingo creature.

"When I lay down again I had the image of the dog in my mind, against the landscape of the bush and storm. Again and again I saw the dog and a line of a poem seemed to fall into my head from the storm clouds above. 'With thunder you'll come—and with thunder you'll go.' What did it mean? What could it mean? By morning I had unraveled the mystery of the lines of poetry and I had a story about a girl called Lara whose mother dies in the first chapter and who comes to live on the farm in a forest with her dad and a new family."

The dog that Hathorn had seen became Thunderwith, "Lara's friend, her escape, and her link to her mother," as Hathorn explained. Lara's mother was modeled after Hathorn's friend Cheryl, who died of cancer before the book was finished. "I feel that Cheryl's spirit leaps and bounds all through it," the author once noted. "So you see for me there are many emotions through many experiences that weave themselves into my stories and into this story in particular—happiness in being together, the joy one feels in being surrounded by natural beauty, a dark sadness at loss, and the pain in hardships that must be endured. And the way people can change and grow even through dark and mystifyingly sad experiences. But you may be pleased to know that love and hope win out in *Thunderwith*. They have to—as I believe eventually they have to in life itself."

Thunderwith garnered praise as a sensitive, realistic, and engaging young adult novel. A *Publishers Weekly* reviewer commented that "Hathorn deftly injects a sense of wonderment into this intense, very real story." According to *Horn Book* contributor Watson, *Thunder-*

with possesses "a believable plot featuring a shattering climax and a satisfyingly realistic resolution." Robert Strang, writing in *Bulletin of the Center for Children's Books,* commended Hathorn's "especially expert weaving of story and setting." Similarly, *Magpies* contributor Jameyson noted that Hathorn's "control over her complex subject is admirable; her insight into character sure and true; her ear for dialogue keen." Jameyson added that the author's "nimble detour from the usual route will leave readers surprised, even breathless."

After the success of *Thunderwith,* Hathorn moved beyond novels and picture books to publish poems for children and a story collection for young adults. Her poetry book, *Talks with My Skateboard,* is divided into several sections and includes poems about outdoor activities, school, family life, cats, and nature. The poem "Skateboard" is written from a child's perspective: "My sister has a skateboard / and you should see her go ... She can jump and twirl / Do a twist and turn, / What I want to know / Is why I can't learn?" *Who?,* published in 1992, contains stories about ghosts, love and friendship, and mysteries, some of which are based on tales that Hathorn's mother told her. The collection includes "Who?," in which a pitiful ghost awakens a family from their beds; "An Act of Kindness," in which a family mysteriously loses their ability to remember the names of objects; and "Jethro Was My Friend," where a young girl attempts to save her beloved bird from rapidly rising floodwaters.

Hathorn published more novels, with the young adult book *Love Me Tender* and a comic work for junior readers, *The Lenski Kids and Dracula.* Hathorn once commented that "*Love Me Tender* was a story I circled for a few years. It drew on my girlhood experiences although it's about a boy called Alan. It's a gentle story set in the days of rock and roll." In the novel, Alan and his sister and brothers are abandoned by their mother and sent to live with various relatives. Alan is taken in by his bossy, unsmiling Aunt Jessie, and the story chronicles his "interior journey as hope fades that he will ever see his Mum and his family again," Hathorn explained. "Alan changes but more importantly he causes people around him—including his old aunt—to change too. Self-growth is a very important message for young people today—looking inside and finding that strength to go on." *Love Me Tender* is among Hathorn's favorite creations; the book "has a place in my heart," she once commented, because it captures the atmosphere of the author's girlhood in the 1950s.

A common thread in several of Hathorn's works is the author's belief in love, hope, and the resiliency of the human spirit. "With all the faults in the world, the injustices, the suffering, and the sheer violence that I am forced to acknowledge though not accept, I still have a great sense of hope," Hathorn once noted. "Human beings never cease to surprise me with their unexpectedness, their kindness, their cheerfulness, their will to go on against the odds. That's inspiring. And I feel a sense of hope should be nurtured in young people, for they are the hope of the world. My stories may sometimes have sad endings but they are never without some hope for the future."

In several books Hathorn has combined her interest in young people with her concerns about the environment, poverty, and homelessness. "My picture book *The Wonder Thing,* written after a visit to a rainforest to 'sing' about the beauty of the place, is also a plea for the survival of the earth's riches—trees, forests, mountains, and rivers," the author once explained. "There are only four to five words per page and it is a prose poem; I try to make those words the most delicately beautiful and evocative that I can. Both a recent picture book, *The Way Home,* and a recent novel, *Feral Kid,* take up the theme of the homelessness of young people. I feel strongly that we should *never* accept the fact of homeless children on our streets. A society that allows this sort of thing is not a responsible and caring society to my mind; I very much want people to look closely at stories like mine and begin asking questions about something that is becoming all too common a sight in all cities of the world."

Alan, the protagonist in Hathorn's 1996 novel, *Juke-box Jive,* is another homeless child,; his mother, who has gone to live with a new boyfriend, has abandoned him. Farmed out to his strict Aunt Jessie, Alan's life greatly improves when his aunt takes over a milk bar and installs the juke-box of the title. "This could so easily have been just a collection of cliches," remarked Mary Hoffman in a *School Librarian* review of the novel. "What raises it is Libby Hathorn's honesty about Alan's feelings for his mother and his aching realization that the family will never all live together again." Another abandoned adolescent figures in the 1998 novel, *Rift.* Vaughan Jasper Roberts is stuck with his grandmother in an isolated coastal town when his parents take off. "At times ponderous and confusing, this is a complex novel in which Hathorn explores human fragility and courage, manipulation and madness and the comfort of habit and ritual," noted Jane Connolly in a *Magpies* review.

Hathorn also teamed up with writer Gary Crew to produce an epistolary novel between two teenagers in *Dear Venny, Dear Saffron,* and has also experimented with online storytelling on her web site, adapting the novel, *Ghostop,* from that format. And with all this different activity, Hathorn has not neglected the picture books she began with. Her 1998 *Sky Sash So Blue* tells the story of young Susannah, from a slave household, who is willing to give up her one bit of ornament—her scrap of sky-blue sash, to ensure that her sister the bride has a lovely wedding dress. *Children's Book Review Service* called this picture book a "lovely story of hardship, perseverance and love," while reviewer Carol Ann Wilson pointed out in *School Library Journal* that Hathorn employed an article of clothing, as she did in *Grandma's Shoes,* "to symbolize the indomitable spirit of family." Wilson concluded, "Susannah's narrative makes human and accessible the poignant struggles of a people, a family, and one little girl."

Hathorn acknowledged that though her writings often contain messages, "I don't ever want to write didactic books that berate people, young or old, with messages. I don't think you can really write a successful book by setting out with a 'do-good' or any other kind of message in mind. I can only write what moves me in some way to laugh or to cry or to wonder. I don't know what I'll be writing about a few years hence. There is a great sense of adventure in this—and a sense of mystery about what will find me."

As for advice to aspiring young writers, Hathorn has said: "The more you write the better you write. It's as simple and as difficult as that. To write well you must develop an ease with the pen and paper or the word processor or whatever—but most of all an ease with words. To do this you must be immersed in words; they should be your friends and your playthings as well as your tools. So, young writers, write a lot and love what you write so much that you work over it and shine it up to be the best you can possibly do—and then SHARE IT WITH SOMEONE."

Biographical and Critical Sources

BOOKS

Hathorn, Libby, *All about Anna,* Heinemann, 1986.

Hathorn, Libby, "Skateboard," *Talks with My Skateboard,* Australian Broadcasting Corp., 1991.

St. James Guide to Children's Writers, 5th edition, edited by Sara Pendergast and Tom Pendergast, St. James Press, 1999, pp. 482-83.

Saxby, Maurice, *The Proof of the Puddin': Australian Children's Literature, 1970-1990,* Ashton Scholastic, 1993, pp. 219-21.

PERIODICALS

Australian Bookseller and Publisher, March, 1992, p. 26.

Booklist, February 15, 1998, p. 1019.

Books for Keeps, November, 1996, p. 10.

Bulletin of the Center for Children's Books, April, 1991, Robert Strang, review of *Thunderwith,* p. 194; May, 1998, pp. 322-23.

Children's Book Review Service, August, 1998, review of *Sky Sash So Blue,* pp. 164-65.

Horn Book, March-April, 1989, Elizabeth S. Watson, review of *Freya's Fantastic Surprise,* p. 199; July, 1989, Karen Jameyson, review of *The Tram to Bondi Beach,* p. 474; July, 1991, E. Watson, review of *Thunderwith,* p. 462; July-August, 1998, p. 472.

Junior Bookshelf, October, 1990, p. 232.

Magpies, March, 1990, K. Jameyson, review of *Thunderwith,* p. 4; March, 1993, p. 31; July, 1998, Jane Connolly, review of *Rift,* p. 38; November, 1999, pp. 10-13, 38.

Publishers Weekly, May 17, 1991, review of *Thunderwith,* p. 65; August 1, 1994, p. 79; December 18, 1995, p. 53; June 22, 1998, p. 91.

School Librarian, August, 1996, Mary Hoffman, review of *Juke-box Jive,* p. 105.

School Library Journal, July, 1989, Marianne Pilla, review of *The Tram to Bondi Beach,* p. 66; August, 1989, Louise L. Sherman, review of *Freya's Fantastic Surprise,* p. 120; May, 1991, p. 111; October, 1994, p. 123; March, 1996, p. 189; June, 1998, Carol Ann Wilson, review of *Sky Sash So Blue,* p. 108.

Times Literary Supplement, July 23, 1982, Ann Martin, "Encouraging the Excellent," p. 792.

Voice of Youth Advocates, June, 1991.

ON-LINE

Libby Hathorn Web site, http://www.libbyhathorn.com/.

* * *

HEIMANN, Rolf 1940- (Lofo)

Personal

Born May 9, 1940, in Dresden, Germany; immigrated to Australia, 1959; son of Hellmuth (a railway worker) and Annemarie (a homemaker; maiden name, Schoeffel) Heimann; married Lila Tuivasa, December 10, 1976; children: Elisapeta, Vincent. *Education:* Studied at graphic art studios in Frankfurt, Germany, 1956 and 1957. *Religion:* None. *Hobbies and other interests:* Languages, marine ecology.

Addresses

Home and office—170 Mills St., Albert Park 3206, Australia. *E-mail*—heimann@primus.com.au.

Rolf Heimann

Career

Writer, cartoonist, and illustrator. Worked in the fields of advertising, printing, and publishing; Unigraphic (graphic design studio), Melbourne, Australia, founder, 1968; also worked as a fruit picker, railway worker, and factory worker in the 1960s. *Member:* Australian Black and White Artists Association, Humanist Association of Australia.

Writings

FOR CHILDREN

(Illustrator) Robin Klein, *Junk Castle,* Oxford University Press (New York), 1983.
A City by a River, Oxford University Press, 1985.
For Eagle Eyes Only, Troll Communications, 1990.
Amazing Mazes: Mind Bending Mazes for Ages 6-60, Doubleday (New York City), 1990.
Preposterous Puzzles, Doubleday, 1991.
More for Eagle Eyes, Periscope Press, 1991.
Awesome Alpha Maze, Periscope Press, 1992, Troll Communications, 1996.
Bizarre Brainbenders, Doubleday, 1992.
Ultimaze, Doubleday, 1993.
Amazing Mazes II, Doubleday, 1995.
Ultimaze Book, Troll Communications, 1995.
Amazing Mazes 2, Troll Communications, 1996.
Bizarre Brain Benders, Troll Communications, 1997.
Mega Mind-Twisters, Troll Communications, 1997.
Totally Amazing Games and Puzzles, Troll Communications, 1997.
Amazing Mazes 3, Troll Communications, 1997.
Drain Your Brain, Troll Communications, 1998.
Brain-Baffling Picture Puzzles, Troll Communications, 1999.
Sydney through Time, Roland Harvey (Australia), 1999.
Day of the Dragon, Roland Harvey (Australia), 2000.

OTHER

The Fishbook, Mills & Ashworth, 1971.
Knocking on Heaven's Door, Friends of the Earth, 1978.
Unfair to Hipocrits (cartoons), Friends of the Earth, 1978.
No Emus for Antarctica (cartoons), privately printed, 1978.
(Editor) *No Fission: A Collection of Anti-Nuclear Cartoons,* Melbourne Bookworkers Press (Albert Park, Australia), 1983.
Wattle and Dope (novel), Angus & Robertson, 1986.

Also author of several books published by Roland Harvey. Editor and publisher, *Access,* 1980-85. Some works appear under the pseudonym Lofo.

Work in Progress

A children's book, *The World's Coolest Hat,* illustrated by John Spooner, completion expected in 2001.

Sidelights

Rolf Heimann told *SATA:* "I was born in Dresden in 1940 and escaped from communist East Germany to West Germany in 1955. I started a cabinet-making apprenticeship in Hamburg, moved to Frankfurt in 1956, went to evening art classes, and migrated to Australia in 1959.

"I worked as a fruit picker, on railways, and in factories throughout Australia, always sketching and writing. With improving knowledge of the English language, I started to do graphic and photographic work in printing, advertising, and publishing. I traveled around the world in 1965, stopping at the islands of the Pacific and the Caribbean. In 1968 I opened my own graphic design studio, Unigraphic, in Melbourne, and started to do cartoons and illustrations for books. In 1974 and 1975 I participated in protests against French nuclear testing on Muroroa, skippering the ketch *La Flor* to the nuclear testing zone. I spent two years sailing the Pacific, sometimes single-handedly. This trip resulted in the book *Knocking on Heaven's Door,* published by Friends of the Earth in 1978. I married a Samoan girl and had two children.

"From 1980 to 1985 I published and edited the alternative magazine *Access.* I published two collections of my own cartoons and co-published several cartoon anthologies. I published cartoons, articles, and short stories in a number of magazines. The novel *Wattle and Dope* was published in 1986. With the success of the first children's books, especially *For Eagle Eyes Only,* I concentrated more and more on writing and illustrating juvenile literature. More than twenty titles were published by Roland Harvey of Melbourne, many of which were translated into German, Danish, Spanish, and even Chinese. I have also participated in cartooning conferences in Hungary, France, Japan, and Cuba."

Biographical and Critical Sources

PERIODICALS

Magpies, May, 1991, Betty Klaosen, review of *More for Eagle Eyes,* p. 30; July, 1991, Kristina Lindsay, review of *Preposterous Puzzles,* p. 34; September, 1992, Shirley Dacey, review of *Awesome Alpha Maze,* p. 34.
Quill and Quire, September, 1990, review of *Amazing Mazes,* p. 22.

* * *

HILLMAN, John 1952-

Personal

Born August 16, 1952, in Grand Saline, TX; son of Royce Ezekiel (a farmer) and Inez (a homemaker; maiden name, Wilcox) Hillman; married Kathy Robinson (a college librarian), December 22, 1973; children: John Marshall, Michael Thomas, Holly Michelle-Marie. *Education:* Baylor University, B.B.A., 1974, M.B.A., 1987. *Politics:* Independent. *Religion:* Southern Baptist.

Addresses

E-mail—guardeen@aol.com.

Career

Self-employed certified public accountant, Waco, TX, 1978—. Southwest Texas State University, lecturer, 1990-95.

Awards, Honors

Named sportswriter of the year, Texas Association of Private and Parochial Schools, 1998.

Writings

(With wife, Kathy Hillman) *Devotions from the World of Sports,* Chariot Victor Publishing (Colorado Springs, CO), 1998.

(With Ace Collins) *Blackball Superstars: Legendary Players of the Negro Baseball Leagues,* Avisson Press (Greensboro, NC), 1999.

(With K. Hillman) *Devotions from the World of Women's Sports,* Cook Communications (Colorado Springs), 2000.

Sidelights

John Hillman told *SATA:* "I began writing in earnest after I left teaching to prepare for my eventual retirement from accounting. As I have experienced success as a writer, I try to devote three to four hours each day to the craft. My purpose in writing the sports devotional books was to illustrate how God's presence can be experienced through everyday events and the common bonds shared through sports. Victor Lee's on-line review at crosswalk.com gives an insightful view of our book."

Biographical and Critical Sources

PERIODICALS

Library Journal, July, 1998, Bernadette McGrath, review of *Devotions from the World of Sports,* p. 98.

School Library Journal, August, 1999, Tom S. Hurlburt, review of *Blackball Superstars,* p. 168.

ON-LINE

Amazon.com, www.amazon.com/ (August 26, 2000).

*   *   *

HINDLEY, Judy 1940-

Personal

Born December 24, 1940, in Lompoe, CA; daughter of Vernon Kelly (a lab technician) and Virginia Mae (Knight) Phelps; married Brian Hindley, February 11, 1961 (divorced 1982); children: John, Anna. *Education:* University of Chicago, B.A. (English, with honors), 1963. *Politics:* Radical green.

Addresses

Home and office—The Flat, 46 Kingsbury St., Marlborough, Wiltshire SN8 1JE, England.

Judy Hindley

Career

Writer. Usborne Publishing Ltd., London, former editor. Activist, involved in local, environmental, and human rights issues, 1990—. Member of management team, Results (lobby group), 1990—. *Member:* Survival International, U.N.A., Campaign against the Arms Trade.

Writings

(With Anabelle Curtis) *The Know-how Book of Paper Fun,* illustrated by Colin King, Usborne (London), 1975, Corwin (New York), 1976.

The Know-how Book of Spycraft, Usborne, 1975, published as *The Know-how Book of Codes, Secret Agents, and Spies,* Corwin (New York), 1976.

How Your Body Works, illustrated by Colin King, Usborne, 1975, new edition, 1995.

The Time-Traveler Book of Knights and Castles, illustrated by Toni Goffe, Usborne, 1976, published as *Knights Castles,* 1997.

(With Donald Rumbelow) *The Know-how Book of Detection,* illustrated by Colin King, Usborne, 1978.

The Good Spy Guide to Secret Messages, Usborne, 1978.

The Good Spy Guide to Tracking and Trailing, Usborne, 1978.

The Good Detective's Guide to Fakes and Forgeries, Usborne, 1979.

The Counting Book, Usborne, 1979.

Pete and Jim, illustrated by Colin West, Hardy/Clarke, 1985.

The Brave Explorers, Hardy/Clarke, 1985.

Polly's Dance, illustrated by Jill Bennett, Hardy/Clarke, 1985.

Jane's Amazing Woolly Jumper, illustrated by Jill Bennett, Hardy/Clarke, 1985.

The Animal Parade, Collins (London), 1985.

The Alphabet Game, illustrated by Colin West, Collins, 1985.

Isn't It Time?, Collins, 1985, illustrated by Nick Sharratt, Candlewick Press, 1996.

How Big? How Tall?, Collins, 1985.

The Big Red Bus, Collins, 1985, illustrated by William Benedict, Candlewick Press (Cambridge, MA), 1995.

The Little Yellow Truck, Collins, 1985.

If I Had a Car, Collins, 1985.

The Train Stops Here, Collins, 1985.

Once There Was a House: And You Can Make It!, illustrated by Robert Bartelt, Collins, 1986, Random House, 1987.

Once There Was a Knight: And You Can Be One Too!, illustrated by Robert Bartelt, Collins, 1987, Random House, 1988.

Make, Bake, Grow, and Sew, illustrated by Judy Bastyra, HarperCollins, 1989.

Mrs. Mary Malarky's Seven Cats, illustrated by Denise Teasdale, ABC, 1989, Orchard (New York City), 1990.

The Little Train, illustrated by Robert Kendall, ABC, 1989, Orchard, 1990.

The Tree, illustrated by Alison Wisenfeld, C. N. Potter (New York), 1990.

The Sleepy Book: A Lullaby, illustrated by Patrice Aggs, ABC, 1990, Orchard, 1991.

When a trusty bus gets one of its wheels stuck in a pothole, a traffic jam occurs, until a tractor, a truck, and a steamroller save the day. (Cover illustration by William Benedict.)

My Own Story Book, ABC, 1990.

Uncle Harold and the Green Hat, illustrated by Peter Utton, Farrar, Straus (New York), 1991.

How Many Twos?, illustrated by Steve Bland, ABC, 1991.

My Own Fairy Story Book, illustrated by Toni Goffe, Kingfisher, 1991.

(Contributor) *Bedtime Stories for the Very Young,* Kingfisher, 1991.

Soft and Noisy, illustrated by Patrice Aggs, Hyperion (New York), 1992.

Zoom on a Broom! Six Fun-filled Stories, illustrated by Toni Goffe, Kingfisher (New York), 1992.

What If It's a Pirate?, illustrated by Selina Young, ABC, 1992, published as *Maybe It's a Pirate,* Thomasson-Grant (Charlottesville, VA), 1992.

(Contributor) *The Crocodile Book,* Hutchinson (London), 1992.

A Piece of String Is a Wonderful Thing, illustrated by Margaret Chamberlain, Candlewick Press, 1993.

Robbers and Witches, illustrated by Toni Goffe, Kingfisher, 1993.

Giants and Princesses, illustrated by Toni Goffe, Kingfisher, 1993.

Feathery Furry Tales, illustrated by Toni Goffe, Kingfisher, 1993.

Into the Jungle, illustrated by Melanie Epps, Candlewick Press, 1994.

The Wheeling and Whirling-around Book, illustrated by Margaret Chamberlain, Candlewick Press, 1994.

Funny Walks, illustrated by Alex Ayliffe, BridgeWater (Mahwah, NJ), 1994.

One by One, illustrated by Nick Sharratt, Walker, 1994, Candlewick Press, 1996.

Little and Big, illustrated by Nick Sharratt, Walker, 1994, Candlewick Press, 1996.

(Contributor) *Animal Stories for the Very Young,* Kingfisher, 1994.

Crazy ABC, illustrated by Nick Sharratt, Walker, 1994, Candlewick Press, 1996.

Princess Rosa's Winter, illustrated by Margaret Chamberlain, Kingfisher, 1997.

A Song of Colors, illustrated by Mike Bostock, Candlewick Press, 1998.

Ten Bright Eyes, illustrated by Alison Bartlett, Peachtree (Atlanta, GA), 1998.

The Best Thing about a Puppy, illustrated by Pat Casey, Candlewick Press, 1998.

Eyes, Nose, Fingers, and Toes: A First Book All about You, illustrated by Brita Granstroem, Candlewick Press, 1999.

(Contributor) *Pirates,* Transworld, 1999.

Hurry, Scurry, Mousie, Reader's Digest, 1999.

Leap, Froggie, Leap!, Reader's Digest, 1999.

The Perfect Little Monster, illustrated by Jonathan Lycett-Smith, Walker, 2000, Candlewick Press, 2001.

Mama, Did You Miss Me?, Bloomsbury, 2001.

The Best Thing about a Kitten, Walker, 2001.

Dogs Are My Favorite Thing, Random House, 2001.

What's In a Baby's Morning?, Walker, 2001.

The Very Silly Duck, Walker, 2001.

Rosy's House, Walker, 2001.

Work in Progress

Mainstream adult novel "focusing on my relationship with money."

Sidelights

Judy Hindley is the author of numerous books for young children—from toddler books that teach such basics as color, shape, and size, to stories of the world we live in and its past. Enhanced by the illustrations of such artists as Nick Sharratt, Toni Goffe, and Margaret Chamberlain, Hindley's nonfiction books and story picture books are written in "a lean rhythmic prose," according to a *Kirkus* reviewer.

Many of Hindley's stories feature animal characters, as in *Mrs. Mary Malarky's Seven Cats*. In this tale, a "warm, cozy story," that *School Library Journal* contributor Susan Hepler noted should find a satisfied audience among "owners of cats, stuffed or real," a little boy quizzes his babysitter about the seven cats who have temporarily decided to share her home. On her next visit, Mrs. Malarky informs her quizzical charge that all the cats but one have moved on. The boy feels sorry for Mrs. Malarky, in her quiet, lonely house, until she shows him a picture of the remaining cat—and its litter of young kittens.

In *The Best Thing about a Puppy,* which was published in 1998, a young boy catalogues his puppy's good and bad points, but concludes, "The best thing is, a puppy is a friend." Praising Hindley's simple text, critic Maura Bresnahan noted in her appraisal for *School Library Journal,* that "Children will be charmed by the antics of a lovable pup" in an "inviting" tale. A *Kirkus* reviewer added that the author "masterfully captures the abundant energy and mischievousness" of the young dog as it becomes "the delight and exasperation of its new owner."

Into the Jungle, published in 1994, takes readers away from their comfortable relationships with docile pets and leads them on a walk on the wild side. "When you go into the jungle, go carefully," Hindley warns. In the story, two children walk through an imaginary jungle, surrounded by unseen beasts: chimps, tigers, crocodiles, and exotic birds. "The exuberance and the suspense and the wondering of what jungle creature to expect all combine to make this conversation book a delight," pronounced Cynthia Anthony in a review of *Into the Jungle* for *Magpies.*

While still featuring main characters of the four-legged variety, Hindley's *The Big Red Bus* and *The Little Train* focus on vehicles rather than animals. In *The Big Red Bus,* the trusty bus gets one of its wheels stuck in a deep pothole. Soon, a line of cars is stopped behind the bus, until a tractor helps the bus out of its predicament and a truck and steamroller repair the pothole. *School Library Journal* contributor Martha Topol deemed *The Big Red Bus* a story that "begs to be read aloud ... to toddlers who ... won't be able to resist participating." A *Books*

A group of toddlers discover multiple uses for various parts of their bodies in Hindleys' exuberant rhyming text. (Cover illustration by Brita Granstroem.)

for Keeps reviewer called Hindley's work "a clearly told, lively story" that is "ideal for storytelling time." Similarly, *The Little Train* was praised by *School Library Journal* reviewer Jeanne Marie Clancy for being "lyrically told in a language both simple and spare."

In addition to picture books, Hindley has put together several toddler "concept" books that showcase her abilities as a poet. In *A Song of Colors,* she focuses rhythmic verse on twelve different colors: blue for dragonflies, red for poppies and cherries, and the like. The concept of counting is introduced in both *One by One* and in *Ten Bright Eyes.* "The simple rhyming text works wonderfully with the eye-catching, childlike pictures," commented *School Library Journal* contributor Rachel Fox of the collaboration between Hindley and artist Alison Bartlett, that resulted in *Ten Bright Eyes.*

Among the most interesting of Hindley's books for young people are a group of books that inspire curiosity and encourage creativity. In *Once There Was a House,* Hindley and designer Gregg Reyes show young people how to construct a house—in fact, a whole town—out of discarded cardboard boxes, tape, plastic detergent bottles, old newspapers, and other cast-away materials easily found around the home. Praising the book as ideal for children with "bounce and initiative," *Growing Point* reviewer Margery Fisher similarly voiced approval for *Once There Was a Knight.* In Hindley and Reyes' companion volume, the authors introduce a boy and girl who create their own mini Renaissance Fair complete with jousting knights, a terrifying dragon, and a king and queen. "Illustrations ... show the busy young ... exercising imagination and ingenuity," commented Fisher, the critic adding praise for the historical accuracy of the crafts presented. Other idea books for young readers include *Make, Bake, Grow, and Sew,* which teaches basic skills for everything from sewing on a button to building simple wood furniture.

Biographical and Critical Sources

PERIODICALS

Booklist, August, 1994, Mary Harris Veeder, review of *Into the Jungle,* p. 2048; October 15, 1995, Hazel Rochman, review of *The Big Red Bus,* p. 411; November 1, 1998, Stephanie Zvirin, review of *The Best Thing about a Puppy,* p. 502; January 1, 2000, review of *Eyes, Nose, Fingers, and Toes,* p. 824.

Books for Keeps, November, 1986, review of *Once There Was a House,* pp. 20-21; May, 1993, review of *A Piece of String Is a Wonderful Thing,* p. 4; November, 1995, review of *Into the Jungle,* p. 6; March, 1996, review of *Crazy ABC,* p. 6; November, 1996, review of *The Big Red Bus,* p. 6; September, 1998, Judith Sharman, review of *The Best Thing about a Puppy,* pp. 19-20.

Books for Your Children, Margaret Carter, review of *Animal Parade,* spring, 1985, p. 14; autumn-winter, 1990, p. 23.

Bulletin of the Center for Children's Books, May, 1993, Betsy Hearne, review of *A Piece of String Is a Wonderful Thing,* p. 274; September, 1994, review of *The Wheeling and Whirling-around Book,* p. 14.

Growing Point, September, 1976, review of *How Your Body Works,* p. 2947; March, 1980, review of *The Counting Book,* p. 3663; September, 1986, review of *Once There Was a House,* p. 4685; November, 1987, Margery Fisher, review of *Once There Was a Knight,* p. 4891.

Junior Bookshelf, June, 1990, review of *Make, Bake, Grow, and Sew,* p. 135; October, 1990, review of *The Tree,* p. 221; December, 1994, review of *Crazy ABC,* p. 215.

Kirkus Reviews, August 15, 1995, review of *The Big Red Bus,* pp. 1188-89; August 1, 1998, review of *The Best Thing about a Puppy,* p. 1118; May 15, 1999, review of *Eyes, Nose, Fingers, and Toes,* p. 801.

Magpies, March, 1995, Cynthia Anthony, review of *Into the Jungle,* p. 21.

Publishers Weekly, February 9, 1990, Diane Roback, review of *Mrs. Mary Malarky's Seven Cats,* p. 59; November 9, 1992, review of *Maybe It's a Pirate,* p. 82; June 27, 1994, review of *Into the Jungle,* p. 76; March 2, 1998, review of *A Song of Colors,* p. 68; June 21, 1999, review of *Eyes, Nose, Fingers, and Toes,* p. 66.

School Library Journal, March, 1990, Susan Hepler, review of *Mrs. Malarky's Seven Cats,* p. 193; August, 1990, Jeanne Marie Clancy, review of *The Little Train,* p. 130; January, 1992, Lori A. Janick, review of *Uncle Harold and the Green Hat,* p. 90; May, 1992, Judith Gloyer, review of *The Sleepy Book,* p. 89; July, 1992, Nancy A. Gifford, review of *How Many Twos?,* p. 69; November, 1992, Jody McCoy, review of *Zoom on a Broom!,* p. 71; February, 1993, Nancy Seiner, review of *Soft and Noisy,* pp. 83-84; July, 1993, Patricia Pearl Doyle, review of *A Piece of String Is a Wonderful Thing,* p. 79; September, 1994, Patricia Pearl, review of *Funny Walks,* p. 186; January, 1995, Sandra Welzenbach, review of *The Wheeling and Whirling-around Book,* p. 104; January, 1996, Martha Topol, review of *The Big Red Bus,* p. 85; May, 1998, Lauralyn Persson, review of *A Song of Colors,* p. 113; October, 1998, Maura Bresnahan, review of *The Best Thing about a Puppy,* p. 102; November, 1998, Rachel Fox, review of *Ten Bright Eyes,* p. 86; July, 1999, Olga R. Barnes, review of *Eyes, Nose, Fingers, and Toes,* p. 73.

*   *   *

HOLM, Jennifer L. 19(?)

Personal

Daughter of William W. (a pediatrician) and Beverly A. (a pediatric nurse) Holm; married Jonathan Hamel. *Education:* Dickinson College, B.A.

Addresses

Agent—Jill Grinberg, Anderson/Grinberg, 266 West 34rd St., New York, NY 10011. *E-mail*—jholm@crowdedfire.com.

Career

Producer of television commercials, music videos, and promotional materials, New York City, 1990—.

Awards, Honors

Silver Award, *Parents' Choice,* and citation among the best books of the year, *Publishers Weekly,* both 1999, and Newbery Honor Award, ALA Notable Book, both 2000, all for *Our Only May Amelia.*

Writings

Our Only May Amelia (historical novel), HarperCollins (New York City), 1999.

Work in Progress

Another historical novel, *Boston Jane,* completion expected in 2001.

Biographical and Critical Sources

PERIODICALS

Booklist, September 1, 1999, Susan Dove Lempke, review of *Our Only May Amelia.*

Publishers Weekly, June 14, 1999, review of *Our Only May Amelia,* p. 71; November 1, 1999, review of *Our Only May Amelia,* p. 58.

School Library Journal, June, 1999, Cindy Darling Codell, review of *Our Only May Amelia,* p. 130.

ON-LINE

Amazon.com, www.amazon.com/ (August 26, 2000).

K

KANE, Bob 1916-1998

Personal

Born October 24, 1916, in New York, NY; died November 3, 1998, in Los Angeles, CA; son of Herman (an engraver for the *New York Daily News*) and Augusta Kane; married first wife, Beverly, 1949 (divorced, 1957); married Elizabeth Sanders (an actress), 1986; children: (first marriage) Deborah Majeski. *Education:* Attended Commercial Art Studio, Cooper Union, and Art Students League.

Career

Graphic artist. Freelance cartoonist with S. M. Iger's Studio, 1936-37, and Fiction House, 1937-39; DC Comics, Inc., New York City, cartoonist and creator of "Batman" comic, 1939-66. Worked in the garment industry, New York City, c. 1937; Fleischer Animated Film Studio, New York City, fill-in animator, inker, and painter, c. 1937. Creator of animated syndicated television series *Courageous Cat and Minute Mouse,* Trans-Artist, 1961, and *Cool McCool,* NBC-TV, 1966-69; creator of superhero Negative Man, c. 1989. *Exhibitions:* Galere Internationale (one-man show), New York City, 1969; Galere Michael, Beverly Hills, CA, "Batman Art Exhibitions," 1989; many other galleries and venues.

Writings

(With Tom Andrae) *Batman and Me,* Eclipse, 1989.
Peter Poplaski, editor, *Batman: The Dailies,* Kitchen Sink Press, Volume 1, *1943-1944,* 1990, Volume 2: *1944-1945,* 1990, Volume 3: *1946-1946,* 1991.

Adaptations

Film Adaptations: The Batman (15-episode movie serial), starring Lewis Wilson as Batman and Douglas Croft as Robin, Columbia, 1943; *Batman and Robin* (15-episode movie serial), starring Robert Lowry as Batman and John Duncan as Robin, Columbia, 1949; *Batman* (television series), starring Adam West as Batman and Burt Ward as Robin, American Broadcast Company (ABC-TV), 1966-68; *Batman* (film), starring West and Ward, Twentieth Century-Fox, 1966; *The Adventures of Batman* (animated television series), with Bud Collyer as Batman and Casey Kasem as Robin, produced by

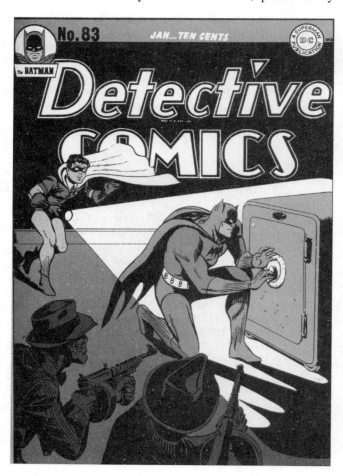

The "dynamic duo," Batman and Robin, conceived by Bob Kane in 1939, were immensely popular comic-book superheroes who dedicated themselves to fighting crime after their parents were murdered.

Filmation, Columbia Broadcast System (CBS-TV), 1968-69, rebroadcast as part of *The Batman-Superman Hour,* 1968-69; *The New Adventures of Batman* (animated television series), featuring West and Ward, produced by Filmation, CBS-TV, 1977-78; *Batman: Fortieth Anniversary Special,* National Broadcast Corp. (NBC-TV), 1979; *Batman* (film), starring Michael Keaton as Batman and Jack Nicholson as the Joker, Warner Bros., 1989; *Batman Returns* (film), starring Keaton, Warner Bros., 1992; *Batman Forever* (film), starring Val Kilmer as Batman, Warner Bros., 1995; *Batman & Robin* (film), starring George Clooney as Batman, Warner Bros., 1997.

Novels: Batman and the Fearsome Four (novelization of 1966 film), Signet, 1966; Winston Lyon, *Batman versus Three Villains of Doom,* Signet, 1966; *Batman versus the Joker,* Signet, 1966; *Batman versus the Penguin,* Signet, 1966.

Sidelights

The creator of the popularly dubbed "Dynamic Duo," cartoonist Bob Kane is remembered for creating a twentieth-century icon in the Batman. Inspired by the Superman character that was featured in *Action Comics* during the 1930s, Kane and writing partner Bill Finger decided to bring to comic-book life their own superhero drawn from the darker reaches of the American mythos: the inner city, with its crime bosses and mafia, and dark recesses. The result: the black-caped Batman.

Kane was born in 1916 in the East Bronx, the son of Herman Kane, an engraver for the *New York Daily News.* In his biography *Batman and Me,* he recalled what it was like living in a multi-ethnic neighborhood that embodied the "melting pot" characteristic of U.S. society during the early years of the twentieth century. "Often one nationality would be pitted against another," Kane wrote. "In order to survive, if one were a loner like myself, he would have to join his neighborhood gang for protection, believing in the old adage, 'safety in numbers.'"

Kane's father quickly realized that his son's obvious talent and interest in art could be channeled into a lucrative career; in fact, he saw cartoonists at the newspaper he worked for earning impressive salaries. Encouraging his young son's drawing habit, the elder Kane brought home books on drawing for his son to study. Upon reaching high school, Bob Kane also gained encouragement from several teachers who arranged a scholarship to the Commercial Art Studios for him. Beginning to approach publishers with his work while still attending classes, Kane was hired by fellow-cartoonist Will Eisner to draw humorous character strips on *Wow! What a Magazine* in 1936. Mimicking the popular style of Walt Disney, Kane drew several strips, including *Peter Pupp,* before quitting the job to find something more lucrative.

Although he made efforts to sell single-panel cartoon strips to magazines such as *Saturday Evening Post* and *Colliers,* Kane's work resulted in only a single sale. The hard economic times that were sweeping the nation in the 1930s soon forced the struggling artist to go to work for his uncle in New York's garment industry as a way to help support his parents. After nine months working for his uncle, Kane quit, determined to give cartooning another try. He got a regular job as an inker and painter at Fleischer Animated Film Studio, and worked on "Betty Boop" animated films. However, the job did not provide an outlet for Kane's own creativity, and when the studio moved to Florida in late 1937, Kane declined to follow them.

Kane's decision to remain in New York City proved to be a good one, as he soon found himself with a dream job: working for DC Comics, one of the top comic book publishers, illustrating his own comic strips. His move to DC coincided with a dramatic change in the comic book industry: the dawn of the age of the superhero in June of 1938, as DC launched *Action Comics* and introduced the Superman character created by Jerry Siegel and Joe Shuster. The mythic saga of Superman joined with such minor heroes as 1936's Phantom to crystalize comic books' Golden Age.

Quick to see the possibilities in creating his own superhero, Kane went to work. During a single weekend he developed the basic Batman character: a human detective who, after years of rigorous, disciplined study, determines to stem the rising tide of crime in his own town by acting in anonymity. Asked by *People* interviewer Michael Alexander to list the influences behind Batman, Kane cited three: the "Zorro" character he recalled from watching *The Mark of Zorro* as a child. "By day, like Bruce Wayne, he feigned being a bored, foppish count, the son of one of the richest families in Mexico," Kane told Alexander. "By night, he became a vigilante. He would disguise himself, wearing a handkerchief mask with the eyes slit out. He exited on a black horse from a cave underneath his home, and that's the inspiration for the Batcave and the Batmobile." The second influence was the drawing of a bat-winged flying machine Kane had seen in a published version of Leonardo DaVinci's *Notebooks.* And the third was the silent film *The Bat,* based on a novel by popular Gothic novelist Mary Roberts Rinehart, that featured a murderer who acted in the shadows, the shadow he himself threw on the wall as he attacked his victims. Other inspirations on Kane were the Shadow, comic book detective Dick Tracy, and adventure films such as *Robin Hood.*

Batman first appeared in *Detective Comics,* number 27, in May of 1939. A grim, ruthless crime-fighter, he wears a cowl mask that covers almost all his face, with sinister-looking slitted eye-holes and sharp, horn-like ears. With his face hidden from view, and his body covered by a black bodysuit and draped in a long black ribbed cape, the superhero's appearance certainly called into question which side of the battle between Good and Evil he was on. However, the caped crusader's fight for justice began with his very first case, "The Case of the Chemical Syndicate," in which Batman tracks down the killers responsible for the death of several partners in the

Apex Chemical Corporation. Not one to leave loose threads, Batman dispenses with the last of the killers by pushing him into a vat of acid. Such ruthless methods didn't endear Batman with the local Police Department, who, according to E. Nelson Bridwell in *Batman from the '30s to the '70s,* "resented this mystery man's taking the law into his own hands." But Batman acted in a manner typical for his era, reflecting the mythos of the American West. Noted Bridwell: "Many a superhero killed with no compunction if he felt the victim deserved it. No fooling around with habeas corpus or trial by jury or the fifth amendment. The heroes dealt out their own brand of justice quickly and efficiently."

In *Detective Comics,* number 33, published in November of 1939, Batman's history was laid out for growing numbers of fans. According to Kane's strip, young Bruce Wayne, after witnessing the murder of his wealthy parents, pledges to dedicate his life to flushing out the criminal element in the city of Gotham by leading a double life as Batman. By the following year—April of 1940—Batman was joined by Dick Grayson, alias Robin. Like Batman, Grayson lost his parents, circus trapeze performers, due to the orders of a crime boss who arranged for the couple to plunge to their deaths under the big top. Fearing nothing, Robin is willing to risk everything to join Batman to avenge his parents' death. With Robin by his side, Batman grew more relaxed and less sinister, according to Mark Cotta Vaz in his *Tales of the Dark Knight.* "Batman [now] had a lively pupil who seemed far more resilient in responding to the death of his parents than had the young, obsessed Bruce Wayne. Dick Grayson's enthusiasm helped bring a smile to Batman's lips. Robin helped make fighting crime FUN!"

Kane's "Batman" strip soon had a cast of regular characters: the Joker in the spring of 1940, Two-Face in August of 1942, and the Riddler in October of 1948. Together with the Penguin and the Catwoman, these dastardly criminals made their careers out of plotting to destroy the Dynamic Duo, but to no avail. During World War II, even the Nazis got involved in Batman and Robin's overthrow, only to have their efforts fail beneath Kane's pen. In the years following World War II, Batman and Robin entered a more peaceful era, replacing their crime-fighting fervor with a less serious, more civic-minded attitude as their retinue of arch enemies grew "less macabre and more zany," wrote Mark Waid in *The Greatest Joker Stories Ever Told.*

By the end of the 1950s Batman had joined the space race, traveling with Robin to other planets to seek out evil-doers. But the following decade found the Caped Crusader earthbound once more, and taking his traditional role of aiding the police in defending Gotham City. Although Batman's popularity began to decline by the mid-1960s, a popular—and campy—television series and several motion pictures would keep the Dynamic Duo in the public eye through the close of the twentieth century.

Batman in the Sixties *traces the superhero's surge in popularity during the 1960s and his alteration into an increasingly mysterious figure.*

Kane gave up artistic control of his creation in the mid-1940s, and resigned from his role as series advisor in the 1960s. After retiring from work on the "Batman" strip, he pursued other interests, among them painting. Watching his creation take on a life of its own, not only in television and films, but in novelizations and graphic novels, Kane was quoted in *Entertainment Weekly* as saying: "It's awesome and a little unbelievable. I wake up in the morning sometimes and say, 'Did I really do that?'" The cartoonist died in November of 1998, at the age of eighty-three, near his home in West Hollywood, California.

Biographical and Critical Sources

BOOKS

Authors and Artists for Young Adults, Volume 8, Gale, 1990, pp. 109-123.
Bridwell, E. Nelson, *Batman from the '30s to the '70s,* Crown, 1971.
Daniels, Lee, *Batman: The Complete History,* Chronicle Books, 1999.
Feiffer, Jules, *The Great Comic Book Heroes,* Bonanza, 1965, pp. 26-32.
The Greatest Joker Stories Ever Told, DC Comics, 1988, pp. 6-10.

Kane, Bob, and Tom Andrae, *Batman and Me,* Eclipse, 1989.

Vaz, Mark Cotta, *Tales of the Dark Knight: Batman's First Fifty Years, 1939-1989,* Ballentine, 1989.

PERIODICALS

Cinefantastique, November, 1989, pp. 48-62.
Economist, November 14, 1998, "Bob Kane," p. 98.
Entertainment Weekly, November 20, 1998, "Holy Heroes!," p. 20.
New York Times, November 7, 1998, "Cartoonist Bob Kane Dies at 83," p. B6.
People, July 31, 1989, interview with Michael Alexander.
Publishers Weekly, July 14, 1989, p. 51.

*   *   *

KAY, Verla 1946-

Personal

Born October 25, 1946, in California; daughter of Donald (a crop duster) and Norma (a homemaker) Deisenroth; married Terry Kay (a glazier; retired), April 18, 1965; children: Eric, Portia, Donn, Bruce. *Education:* Attended Institute of Children's Literature. *Hobbies and other interests:* Fishing, reading, sewing, playing pinochle, Nintendo and computer games.

Addresses

Home and office—P.O. Box 67, Soulsbyville, CA 95372. *Agent*—Curtis Brown Ltd., 10 Astor Pl., New York, NY 10003. *E-mail*—verlakay@aol.com.

Career

Children's writer, 1994—. Worked as teacher's aide, scout leader, church school teacher, and licensed day care provider; volunteer for story hours at a local library. Visits schools and writing classes, and works as a public speaker.

Awards, Honors

Named among "best books of the year," Bank Street College of Education, for *Gold Fever;* International Honor Book citation, Society of School Librarians, 1999, and cited among "notable social studies trade books for young people," Children's Book Council, 2000, both for *Iron Horses;* cited among "101 best web sites for writers," *Writer's Digest,* 2000, for web site www.verlakay.com.

Writings

Gold Fever (juvenile fiction), illustrated by S. D. Schindler, Putnam (New York City), 1999.
Iron Horses (juvenile fiction), illustrated by Michael McCurdy, Putnam, 1999.
Covered Wagons, Bumpy Trails (juvenile fiction), illustrated by S.D. Schindler, Putnam, 2000.

Work in Progress

Tattered Sails (illustrated by Dan Andreasen), for Putnam, publication expected in fall of 2001; *Rough, Tough Charley,* for Millbrook Press, 2001; *Broken Feather* (with illustrations by Stephen Alcorn) and *Homespun Sarah* (illustrations by Ted Rand), both for Putnam, 2002; *Orphan Train,* for Putnam.

Sidelights

Verla Kay told *SATA:* "Writing is the love of my life, which seems amazing to me because as a child, I not only hated to write, but was convinced that I was the world's worst writer. It wasn't until I was in my forties that I finally understood the reason I had such a hard time writing wasn't because I was a bad writer, but because I was a dedicated writer. I needed to revise over and over again before I was satisfied with what I'd written.

"Today I love writing and can't imagine my life without it. I enjoy everything about it, from the initial research on a subject, through the many drafts of a manuscript, to the thrill of a perfectly crafted story. I love all of the 'author' stuff, too—the workshops and speeches to other aspiring writers, the school visits, the book signing events.

"It's my fervent hope and desire to assist other aspiring writers to find their success in this business. That is why I created a web site with a chat room where writers of children's literature can gather and share information. I would hate someday to make it to the top and find myself totally alone. If I ever get there, I want all my writing friends there, too!"

Biographical and Critical Sources

PERIODICALS

Booklist, January 1, 1999, Lauren Peterson, review of *Gold Fever,* p. 888; June 1, 1999, Hazel Rochman, review of *Iron Horses,* p. 1842.
Childhood Education, fall, 1999, Penny Boepple, review of *Gold Fever,* p. 44.
Horn Book, March, 1999, Margaret A. Bush, review of *Gold Fever,* p. 192; July, 1999, review of *Iron Horses,* p. 456.
Kirkus Reviews, December 15, 1998, review of *Gold Fever,* P. 1798; May 15, 1999, review of *Iron Horses,* p. 802.
Publishers Weekly, January 11, 1999, review of *Gold Fever,* p. 71; June 21, 1999, review of *Iron Horses,* p. 67.
School Library Journal, March, 1999, John Sigwald, review of *Gold Fever,* p. 177; July, 1999, Steven Engelfried, review of *Iron Horses,* p. 74.
Teacher Librarian, December, 1999, Teri Lesesne, "Journeys Real and Imagined: Books to Take Us Places," p. 45.

ON-LINE

Amazon.com, www.amazon.com/ (August 26, 2000).
Verla Kay Web Site, www.verlakay.com/

KERR, Bob 1951-

Personal

Born March 17, 1951, in Wellington, New Zealand; son of Robert (an engineer) and Winifrid (a secretary) Kerr; married Hazel Armstrong (a trade unionist); children: Kathleen, Robin. *Education:* University of Auckland, degree (with honors).

Addresses

Home and office—56 Maidavale Rd., Roseneath, Wellington, New Zealand. *E-mail*—hazel.armstrong@paradise.net.nz.

Career

Writer and illustrator of children's books and fiction for teenagers.

Awards, Honors

Honor award and first book award, AIM Children's Book Awards, 1992, for *The Optimist;* Children's Choice Award, *New Zealand Post,* 1996, for *Mechanical Harry.*

Writings

AUTHOR AND ILLUSTRATOR

Lucy's Big Plan, Collins, 1977.
Lucy Loops the Loop, Collins, 1979.
The Optimist, Mallinson Rendel (Wellington, New Zealand), 1992.
The Paper War, Mallinson Rendel, 1994.
Mechanical Harry, Mallinson Rendel, 1996, Gareth Stevens, 1999.
Strange Tales from the Mall, Mallinson Rendel, 1998.
Mechanical Harry and the Flying Bicycle, Gareth Stevens, 1999.
After the War, Mallinson Rendel, 2000.

ILLUSTRATOR

Stephen Ballantyne, *Terry and the Gunrunners,* Collins, 1982.
Ballantyne, *Terry and the Yodeling Bull,* Finlayson Hill, 1986.
Ballantyne, *Terry and the Last Moa,* Hodder & Stoughton, 1990.
Joy Cowley, *The Day of the Rain,* Mallinson Rendel, 1993.
Cowley, *The Day of the Snow,* Mallinson Rendel, 1994.

OTHER

(Editor with Linda Mitchell) *For a Living,* Working Life Publications, 1991.

Work represented in anthologies, including *The Body in the Driveway,* Scholastic, 1995. Contributed to *Landfall,* Volume 186, spring, 1993.

Bob Kerr

Adaptations

The book *Terry and the Gunrunners* was adapted into a six-part television series and broadcast in New Zealand.

Sidelights

Bob Kerr told *SATA:* "I enjoy visiting schools to talk about books, and I enjoy reading the letters of thanks that classes often send after a visit. A recent letter from a boy named Simon said, 'Dear Mr. Kerr, Thank you for coming to our school to talk about your books. Even though I wasn't there I'm sure you were good.' Another favorite letter said, 'Dear Mr. Kerr, Thank you for coming to our school to talk about your work, I hope you will come back when you have improved.' To check out whether I need to improve, you will have to read my books."

Biographical and Critical Sources

PERIODICALS

Books for Keeps, March, 1995, review of *The Optimist,* p. 11.

Magpies, March, 1997, review of *Mechanical Harry,* p. 2; November, 1998, Frances Hoffmann, review of *Strange Tales from the Mall,* p. 8.

Tailspinner, number 11, 2000, interview with Bob Kerr.

*   *   *

KUROI, Ken 1947-

Addresses

Home—Japan.

Career

Illustrator.

ILLUSTRATOR

Setsuo Yazaki, *Little Bunny's Christmas Present,* Heian International Publishing, 1983.

Hisako Madokoro, *Buster and the Dandelions,* translated from Japanese by Patricia Lantier, Gareth Stevens (Milwaukee, WI), 1991.

Madokoro, *Buster and the Little Kitten,* translated by Lantier, Gareth Stevens, 1991.

Madokoro, *Buster Catches a Cold,* translated by Lantier, Gareth Stevens, 1991.

Madokoro, *Buster's Blustery Day,* translated by Lantier, Gareth Stevens, 1991.

Madokoro, *Buster's First Snow,* translated by Lantier, Gareth Stevens, 1991.

Madokoro, *Buster's First Thunderstorm,* translated by Lantier, Gareth Stevens, 1991.

Nancy White Carlstrom, *Swim the Silver Sea, Joshie Otter,* Philomel Books (New York City), 1993.

Carlstrom, *Midnight Dance of the Snowshoe Hare: Poems of Alaska,* Philomel Books, 1998.

Nankishi Niimi, *Buying Mittens,* translated from Japanese by Judith Carol Huffman, University of Hawaii Press (Honolulu, HI), 1999.

Goldilocks and the Three Bears, Heian International Publishing, 1999.

Adaptations

The book *Buster's First Thunderstorm* was adapted for CD-ROM by Media Vision.

Biographical and Critical Sources

PERIODICALS

Booklist, April 1, 1993, Julie Corsaro, review of *Swim the Silver Sea, Joshie Otter,* p. 1436.

Cyber News and Reviews, May, 1996, Howard Berenbon, review of CD-ROM version, *Buster's First Thunderstorm.*

School Library Journal, May, 1993, Mary Rinato Berman, review of *Swim the Silver Sea, Joshie Otter,* p. 82; June, 1998, Susan Lissim, review of *Midnight Dance of the Snowshoe Hare,* p. 128.

ON-LINE

Children's Literature, www.childrenslit.com/ (June 14, 2000).*

L

Autobiography Feature

Christa Laird

1944-

My mother used to say that my entry into the world was marked by a big bang. A V-2 rocket apparently exploded at the crucial moment in the next street, though to keep her calm the midwife told her it was only shooting practice at the nearby Knightsbridge Barracks. The time was December 1944; the place, central London.

But I was a war baby in more ways than one: my arrival took place less than three months after the death of my father at the Battle of Arnhem in September 1944. This was part of a major push to drive a corridor through Nazi-occupied northern Europe into Germany itself, and was also the first attempt on the part of the Allies to free Holland from Nazi occupation; as such it is seen by most Dutch people as one of the great heroic episodes of the war. By the English, it is more usually seen as a colossal example of mistiming and poor planning, of an over-ambitious attempt to go "a bridge too far." My father was one of the 17,000 Allied servicemen who were killed, wounded, or went missing as a result.

No doubt in common with many other posthumous children, or with those who have lost a parent before memory has captured them in some way, there has always been and there will always remain a space in my life where something should have been, but it is a space which is strictly reserved. The space next door contains a courageous hero who gave his life for a noble cause, who will never run to fat or make a mean remark, who left me his beautiful twin sisters as fairy godmothers and his ghost as a lifelong companion, at once elusive and exacting, insistent and inspiring.

Perhaps the most poignant aspect of my father's death is the fact that it was, in a very particular sense, unnecessary. He was German, born in Cologne to a successful German Jewish architect and his "Aryan" German wife, who had the good sense to leave Germany shortly after Hitler came to power. They settled in Holland, however, where of course the Nazi occupation eventually caught up with them, but by that time my father had been sent to the University of Oxford in England, from where in due course he graduated with a degree in law. He then volunteered to join the armed forces which, as an "enemy alien," he was not required to do; indeed, he had to be vetted for six months prior to admission in a specially established internment camp. Apparently he would afterwards refer to his period in "prison" with a certain glee, particularly in polite company. Later he volunteered for the Parachute Regiment, which is how he eventually came to be sent to Arnhem; ironically, my grandparents and aunts were watching as the greatest airborne offensive in history flew over their home in Amsterdam, jubilant at the promise of liberation and little suspecting that their beloved son and brother, not seen since war broke out five years earlier, might be among them.

Overshadowed though it was by my father's death, my childhood, like most, contained both joys and miseries, and in my case there were definitely more of the former. I was devoted to my young, lovely, and adoring mother and, in retrospect, jealous and put out when she married again when I was five. At that time, and for several years afterwards, the secret that I hated my stepfather was one I chose to share, like a sacrificial offering, with only the most special or coveted of friends. One of the most hurtful things anyone ever said to me was when I had explained to one such "friend" why my surname was different from that of my mother—a source of curiosity still in those far-off days. "Oh, that's all right, then," she said with the satisfaction of certainty, "you never knew your real dad so it doesn't matter."

Not that my stepfather was cruel or abusive in any way; distant, certainly, and unsure how to relate to children, with other more pressing things on his mind than how to

Christa Laird in Prague, 1996.

win over a resentful and probably rather self-opinionated little girl. In adulthood our relationship mellowed to one of real affection, tinged on my side by compassion and a sort of surprised respect on his. He outlived my mother by twenty-seven years and never remarried, living, except for the last three years, on his own. When he died, I was genuinely sad.

When I was eight and a half my brother, or more precisely my half-brother, was born. I remember the night distinctly. My grandmother and I had had a bet on the baby's gender, and my first reaction was that as it was a boy, I had therefore won! I think the stakes were worth, in today's currency, all of twenty cents. I had seen a lot of my indulgent and much-loved grandparents in recent weeks, as I had been suffering from German measles and had to be kept away from my mother in her pregnancy, no doubt for much longer than would be thought necessary today. But quarantine had its consolations—for on Coronation Day my grandparents had booked expensive seats outside the Savoy Hotel, right on the route of the procession, and I remember boasting to my mother afterwards that I had been close enough to see the Queen's blue eyes as she passed in her golden coach!

I have many other happy memories of my maternal grandparents, both of whom died in their sixties. My grandfather was a dear and endlessly patient man, who loved to play card and board games with me and to take me to London Zoo on Sunday mornings. I remember pestering him to test me on my general knowledge. "Ask me a question, Grandpa, ask me a question!" would be my standard greeting. My grandmother was a more irascible, indeed fiery, character, and I think my mother was always a little in awe of her even in adulthood. She would regularly fall out with people, but I was in the enviable position of being able to do absolutely no wrong in her eyes. Even now I cannot see a tin of Quality Street sweets (candy) without thinking of her and the "secret" place in the corner of her cupboard where she would keep a store for me, and later for my brother, too, to "steal" from.

Such little luxuries were comparatively rare in the post-war rationing period of my early childhood. I still remember the delight with which my mother and I greeted the arrival of huge food parcels from my father's family, who by then had emigrated to the United States. I can see us laughing gleefully on the kitchen floor, up to our elbows in the paper shavings which had protected all sorts of goodies on their long sea-journey across the Atlantic. My particular favourites were those little brown Hershey bars—there always seemed to be just one more lurking in the bottom of the box when we thought we had discovered everything.

My grandparents owned a cottage in North Devon in the southwest of England, an area of soft rounded hills, patchworked with the irregular shapes of some of the nation's greenest and richest fields. This is the country of famous clotted cream, but of so much else besides. White-washed villages nestling in wooded valleys; wide rolling expanses of moor, roamed by deer and ponies, in late summer purple with heather; narrow lanes, sometimes scarcely wide enough for one car, turned into tunnels by summer hedgerows atop banks bright with wild-flowers; golden sands washed by the high western tides, and steep rocky cliffs plunging into wicked currents where the Bristol Channel meets the Atlantic.

It was here that, at least until my early teens, I spent all my childhood holidays, when the days were always long and sunny and the hydrangea bushes in the cottage garden always in full bloom. A local farmer's wife used to take care of the place in my grandparents' absence and, when we arrived after the long journey from London—in those pre-motorway days two hundred miles could take at least seven hours—we would find tea laid out on a blue-and-white checked cloth: homemade scones and Devonshire clotted cream fresh from the farm, covered by a piece of muslin weighted at the edges by coloured beads—strange that a childish memory should retain such detail. There would be strawberry jam, and marigolds from the garden in a bulbous blue pottery jug to welcome us. And in the garden my swing would be waiting for me—from my vantage point several feet above the ground I would watch the sun set over the long low bulk of Lundy Island, which some ten miles away on the horizon separated the sky from the sea.

Lundy—whose name means "Isle of Puffins" in old Saxon—is a very special place. Over the centuries it has offered lonely, windswept sanctuary to birds, smugglers, pirates and even, in the Middle Ages, out-of-favour royals. My mother took my brother and me there on several occasions, and once we stayed two nights. The best moment then was when we stood watching the steamer depart with its cargo of day trippers, and we could begin to pretend that we had been shipwrecked and marooned, with only seabirds and wild deer and the ghosts in the ruined castle for company. In fact we had comfortable lodgings in the old manor house, a favourite haunt of writers and naturalists. My mother, who was fascinated by the history of the island, was herself writing a novel set there in the turbulent thirteenth century, when she died at the tragically young age of forty-six.

When I was eleven and three quarters, I went away to boarding school. I am always indignant when I hear parents of a certain social class in England accused of not loving their children because they sent them away to school. Although I believe that in the present generation that particular tradition has finally been broken, forty years ago it was still something that had to be gone through "for the sake of the children." My mother suffered torment, I know, and even more so when my little brother went away to "prep" school at the age of eight and a half. With hindsight that seems positively barbaric, but both she and my stepfather were convinced that what they were doing was in the long run the best thing for us. She had been sent away in her own time, to the same school as me, in fact. We even shared the same maths teacher, who could never decide which of us was the less numerate.

I cannot pretend for the sake of narrative interest that I was desperately unhappy at boarding school. I was certainly homesick for the first few days of each term, often near to tears as we stood in line every morning before breakfast to have our temperatures taken, in case we had brought back some dreaded infection from darkest London or Liverpool or Land's End or wherever our homes happened to be. I was standing in just such a line one bleak and homesick morning when sleepiness and misery were dispelled by a buzz of excitement from those girls whose mouths had not yet been stopped by a thermometer. "The Russians have put a sputnik in space, a sputnik in space . . . " I did not like to admit that I had no idea what on earth—or above earth for that matter—a sputnik was; everyone else seemed so fully informed that I passed on the news to the next person with equal self-importance. Nor did I admit that the rumour made me feel uneasy; the posthumous war baby was already the only one in the class who bothered to look up when yet another practising fighter plane thundered across the sky. I've often thought it strange that I was twenty-two before I met anyone else of my age whose father had been killed in action; such a companion in childhood might perhaps have shared my acute fear of renewed outbreak of war and helped me to be less ashamed of it. But all the same, I enjoyed both sports and academic work, so on the whole school was a positive experience; and several of the friends I made then are still my friends today.

At fifteen I made what was probably the first major mistake of my life. I decided that, although I was considered to be an able pupil with particular potential for languages, I had had enough of school and discipline and would not go on to university. My mother and step-father decided to send me instead to a school in Switzerland for a year; not, they assured me, a "finishing school," but one where I would study seriously to improve my French and

German. After that, they thought, I could return to London and do a bilingual secretarial course.

In the event Switzerland proved to be not much more than an enjoyable and fattening diversion! It was only when my mother collapsed with laughter when she met me at Christmas after the first term, that I realised what all that easy access to Swiss chocolate and the school craze for tubes of sweetened condensed milk had done to my shape. I did learn to ski, and the hours spent gazing across the lake to the mountains of the Haute Savoie beyond may well have had something to do with the fact that, many years later, my husband and I decided to invest for a period in a tiny property in those mountains, where we loved to walk in the summer as well as ski in the winter. My German and French improved to the extent that I changed my mind about university, but, at first reluctant to admit as much, I went through the charade of applying to the secretarial college as planned. It was hardly surprising that after the interview the principal commented in puzzlement to my mother on my "uncommitted and immature approach"!

I then had to work very hard cramming two years of A-level study into one year. I lived at home and attended several individual tutorials a week through a crammers, or, more elegantly put, a tutorial college in London. It was not ideal, particulary as no less than three of my teachers in that year succumbed to nervous breakdowns or other health-related problems—coincidence rather than consequence, I hope. But I did successfully achieve my A-levels and secured a place at the University of Bristol, where I was to spend three of the happiest years of my life.

But before beginning my studies in the autumn of 1963, I had five months to spare, so I used the opportunity to go out to California and get to know the American side of my family—my father's twin sisters, who had emigrated to the United States in 1947, married Americans, and produced two children apiece. Sadly, my paternal grandfather had died within a year of reaching the States, and my grandmother followed him within a few years. When I was a baby we had stayed with them in Holland and in France and apparently they doted on me. I must, I suppose, have been some solace to them then, but I shall carry a sense of guilt to the end of my days, that on the one occasion when my grandmother came to visit us in England and wanted to

North Devonshire coastline in southwestern England.

On a trip to the French Alps.

take me for a walk in the park, I, a little brat of four or five, threw a tantrum and refused. She had brought up three children of her own so I am sure she understood, but with adult hindsight I can see only too sharply how painful it must have been for her.

It was only some forty years later, when I had young adult sons of my own, that the realisation of what she and my grandfather must have gone through during those years of waiting and of loss finally assaulted me. In September 1994 I made a little pilgrimage to Arnhem on the fiftieth anniversary of the battle; I stayed with a wonderfully hospitable Dutch couple in their sixties, who still remembered with gratitude the day the sky went dark as thousands of Allied planes swept across the sun. I had never known exactly what happened, but thanks to some tireless investigations on the part of a member of my father's regiment, I now found the precise spot where he was killed; he had nearly made it, and was gunned down after nine terrible days in the final hours of the battle, aged twenty-four. Julian, my elder son who bears my father's second name, was to be twenty-four in two weeks' time. Never had I felt so close to the grandparents I hardly knew.

One of my uncles by marriage was William Castle, well-known producer of many horror films and thrillers, including *Rosemary's Baby,* and staying in his beautiful Beverly Hills home was a dizzying experience. Not because he had a particularly ostentatious life-style, by Beverly Hills standards, or socialised much with people in the movie world—despite genially extrovert behaviour in company, he much preferred to spend his time quietly with his wife and two daughters, to whom he was utterly devoted—but because of the luxury and scale and sheer abundance of material things. Beautifully landscaped swimming pool, colossal glasses of freshly squeezed orange juice for breakfast, huge sunken marble bathtubs, tender steaks which seemed to climb over the edges of your plate, weekend home overlooking the ocean at Malibu, with terrace right on the sands, ever-present and obliging domestic help, Charlton Heston sitting on the lawn of my cousin's school—it was all enough to spoil an impressionable eighteen-year-old for life!

But something about the mood or the character of LA made me uneasy; perhaps it was the constant emphasis on the desirability of longness and leanness, which to a still slightly overweight (I had fortunately shed most of my Swiss excess by then!) teenager of five foot one was a trifle discouraging, despite a naturally cheerful temperament! The greatest compliment you could pay a woman, it seemed, was that she looked seven feet tall and had a straight up-and-down figure. And apart from that the constant emphasis on looks in general—on whether you had a tan or a new hair style, had lost weight, or were wearing a flattering ("makes you look taller"!) outfit—always seemed tedious and irrelevant to a slob like me who could happily go a whole day without looking in the mirror to comb her hair. Fortunately I was cocooned by my family, who did not seem to share the general "looksamania," and whom I quickly came to adore.

My American family has remained very important to me throughout my life, and even though we will sometimes go years without seeing one another, we always pick up exactly where we left off. When the children were small we had two magical family holidays in California with them—my husband sometimes looks back on them and describes them as his only experience of fairyland. Our every whim, let alone need, was catered for, there was always someone to take care of the boys whenever we wanted to go out, and we were surrounded, as I had been when I was eighteen, by luxury and plenty. My aunts and cousins continued to view my boys as honorary grandsons and nephews while they were growing up, having them out to stay and sending them back spoilt beyond recognition; but it was a sin I readily forgave, delighted that they should have such a close tie with my father's side of the family, which, I am glad to say, continues to this day.

A perfect antidote to the vanities of LA is a trip to the Grand Canyon—something I have managed to do three times so far—and particularly a mule ride down to the tip of Tonto Plateau. With the brutal Arizona sun branding the back of your neck, dust scraping your eyeballs and sweat glueing shirt firmly to armpit, it would surely be hard for anyone, even a Hollywood starlet, to care about how they looked! There, where the trail winds down through vanished worlds of sea and desert lying shrivelled in fossil-inscribed lime- and sandstones, the silence is so pervasive, so profound, that the occasional calls of your companions do not so much as wrinkle its surface. From the plateau's tip you can peer down some fifteen hundred feet to where the Colorado River continues to gouge its course through some of the oldest exposed rocks on Earth, black with the mysteries of a billion years. Few other places have made such a deep and lasting impression on me.

Back in England in the autumn of 1963, I started my degree course at the University of Bristol, where on my very first day I met the man I was to marry. Not that it was love at first sight, exactly. Love works in mysterious ways, and it took a good many shared classes, enough cups of coffee to float a battleship, and several months of sitting around in various bars for me subtly to persuade Nigel to persuade me that he was the man who should share my life. Those three years at Bristol, which included extended stays in France and Germany, were blissful; I enjoyed the subjects I was studying, I thrived on the hectic social life, I relished living independently for the first time in a little apartment shared with my best girlfriend and, all importantly, I was in love. I lived in a constant state of exhilaration, willing the time to pass more slowly as the days slid inexorably into weeks, the weeks accelerated into months, and the terms rushed past out of control, before finally vanishing behind me into a blurred and rosy glow.

And suddenly it was time to decide what we should "do" with our lives. Nigel went off to teach for a year in Austria, in preparation for a long-term career as a schoolmaster teaching modern languages. I, on the other hand, harboured a desire, or perhaps a need, to "help" people. I needed to earn my living, but, at the same time, for some totally obscure reason, I had no particular interest in financial reward for its own sake; I wanted to make a useful contribution to society, but equally was not in the slightest bit ambitious, and had no vision of what I wanted to achieve for myself in the long-term. Nor, I am sure, did I ever stop to think how my own particular strengths and talents, such as they were, could be channelled to the best advantage, and I never seriously considered any career other than social work. Looking back, I realise I was not so much misguided as unguided at that time, and it may have been partly because I was still of the generation in which women's careers were generally considered less important, more a matter of making some money to live on in the short term, than of a lifelong commitment. I hope I am not in the habit of blaming other people for my mistakes, for I believe that it is important to acknowledge one's own share of responsibility when things go wrong as well as right, but I *do* regret not having had better career advice at that point. Nowadays that sort of advice is much more readily available, I am glad to say, and for what it is worth, my counsel to any young person leaving university, who is still in any doubt at all about what they want to do, is to talk to as many informed and interested people as possible, and to consider *all* their options.

I trained as a social worker at the University of Exeter, on the southern side of the county of Devon where I had spent all those childhood holidays. It was about this time that my mother became seriously ill, though no one seemed able to identify the cause of her breathlessness and general debility. The attacks were intermittent to start with, however, which allowed me to convince myself that she was not as seriously sick as I feared she was. But worry over her, and Nigel's absence in Austria, combined to make this period a less than happy one, particularly after the unalloyed delights of my undergraduate days. I sometimes wonder whether that accounts for the lasting ambivalence over my chosen career in social work.

After qualifying, I returned for my first job to Bristol, where Nigel was by now doing his post-graduate teaching qualification. I was what was then known as a "Child Care Officer"—a social worker with children and families. What stands out most clearly from that period were the arrangements for out of hours duty cover at which we all had to take a turn for a week at a time. We would be called out after hours if, for example, a child was abandoned or a teenager threatened a parent with a knife or an elderly confused person was found wandering, half-dressed, in the road.

From my point of view the major drawback was that I didn't have a phone and during one famous week the police, who had to act as intermediaries between the duty telephonist and myself, turned up at the house no less than three times in one evening alone! I often wondered what the neighbours thought, especially as once the police even

William Castle, uncle by marriage, Hollywood film producer, 1971.

bundled me into their car with them! There had been an attempted murder in a family with three small children, and it was felt that I needed protection while I made arrangements for them, but appearances cannot have been in my favour that night!

That was in 1968, and an extraordinarily eventful year it turned out to be. We were engaged on Leap Year Day (not, as tradition permits on that day, at my request, but the fact that I even bother with a disclaimer probably dates me!). My mother was delighted with the news, but she was by now seriously ill and in bed more often than not. For a while, a very short while, it gave her a new lease on life while she busied herself with plans, arrangements, outfits. It saddened her deeply not to be able to help me choose a wedding dress, but she sent my little brother Paul as her surrogate, and he rose admirably, aged fourteen, to the occasion. Perhaps in an act of defiance she ordered the most wonderful, most extravagant hat I have ever seen, and which I have never been able to part with, and she would undoubtedly have looked stunning—it was not to be. She died on May 18 1968, less than four months before the wedding and two months before my brother's fifteenth birthday, which must have been devastating for him. We kept the arrangements exactly as she had helped to plan them; to have changed to a different, more modest affair would have felt like excluding her altogether.

The first four years of married life were spent in Coventry, a city famous for its wholesale destruction in World War Two and for the remarkable new cathedral, built, in the spirit of reconciliation, alongside the shattered ruins of the old. For all that, the character of the city in the late '60s and early '70s was not so much spiritual as brash, vigorous, and materialistic, viewed by many people in less affluent parts of the country as the place where milk and honey as well as cars flowed out of the factories. Friday afternoons as a social worker were apt to be very depressing; often whole families, who had arrived penniless and homeless in search of their fortune, would find themselves at the end of the week not only without a job but also without accommodation and subsistence. Usually we had to give them the wherewithal to return whence they came, their trailing children bedraggled and disconsolate, their pride dented, their hopes dashed.

Looking back, I seemed to spend most of the two years in which I practised as a social worker in Coventry, chasing around England after delinquent adolescents who had absconded from care—there was one particular girl who broadened my horizons considerably, dragging me in her wake to all manner of dreary places I would never have dreamt of visiting, and more than once in the comparative luxury of police cars. It was rather fun seeing how other cars slowed down the moment we hove into view! I even remember the little thrill of power when the driver wanted to make better time, and so turned on the siren to clear a way through the traffic ahead!

But Coventry's real significance for me is that it is the city where both my sons were born.

Nothing quite prepares you for the shock of your first baby! I was the archetypal proud mum, totally convinced that my baby boy, with his wide startled blue eyes, as if being born was not really quite what he had expected, was by far the most beautiful in the entire world. I remember telling my visitors how sorry I felt for the other mothers in my ward who had failed to produce anything so perfect; it was only several weeks later when my mother-in-law showed me some pictures of Julian, which she had taken on her first visit, that I realised what a red wrinkled little soul he had actually been! But contrary to popular belief, the camera *does* lie and it is certainly the first image, of the little round-eyed Russian doll wrapped tight in his white blanket, that has stayed with me rather than the leathery-faced infant in the photo.

We had read some of the literature you are given at ante-natal classes and talked to plenty of other people who appeared to have survived the first weeks and months of parenthood and lived to tell the tale; no one, however, had thought to mention the terror you experience on that first evening when you have left the hospital and are at home on your own with a tiny, unfathomable, unpredictable creature, who is *totally* and *utterly* dependent on *you*. This is also the evening when you discover that not all the advice you have been treated to so liberally over the last few weeks is sound. "Don't use plastic pants, they cause nappy rash," one bright spark had volunteered; naturally anxious to avoid subjecting those perfect little buttocks to anything so horrific as a nappy rash, we religiously changed the damp cot sheets every time he wet his nappy, until we had reached the end of our supply. Not having the luxury of a dryer in our apartment, the realisation dawned very early on—within three hours of leaving the hospital to be precise—that our baby would have to suffer either the abuse of plastic pants or of sleeping on a bare mattress. It was our first major parental crisis.

I missed my mother terribly in those early days of motherhood and resented the tendency in my family for the generations to miss each other. It remains one of the great sadnesses of my life that my mother never knew my boys, and vice versa. But I have been extremely fortunate in the affection and support I have always received from my husband's parents, and it was hugely appreciated when my mother-in-law came to stay and help after both boys were born.

The first twenty months of motherhood were far from ideal. We lived at the top of a small block of flats overlooking a pleasant park, but the area was essentially without interest and suburban and, without access to a car during the week, I felt isolated and even, for the first time in my life, lonely. When I returned to social work I think I had a better understanding of the pressures which unsupported, lone mothers are under and of the consequent vulnerability of their children. "There but for the grace of God go I" was a phrase which sometimes sprang to mind. But the grace of God, as the saying goes, had blessed me with a good marriage and adequate material support; I adored my baby and enjoyed his company, but as my sole day-time companion he was not quite articulate enough at age one and a half to satisfy even my admittedly modest intellectual requirements. (Now, at twenty-seven, he has an intelligent, un-stereotyped thought about a wide range of subjects, and is one of the most stimulating companions I know!) So it was to fill a certain void that while he was taking his morning nap, I started to write my first novel.

The story was about an injured woman terrorist and the relationship which develops between her and the social worker who is charged with "minding" her in the hospital, to protect her from reprisals and over-zealous interrogation. Even now I think the idea was a good one, but I have no doubt it was clumsily handled and I expect the social worker was far too transparently "me"; it malingers to this day at the bottom of a drawer somewhere because last time I had a clear out I couldn't quite bring myself to throw it in the bin! I am mildly intrigued by this because I *have* succeeded in jettisoning manuscripts which have taken just as much time and effort to produce; perhaps it is because the idea of the "good" terrorist is one which continues to fascinate me, both from an ethical and an aesthetic point of view. It makes one consider the gulf between public and private virtue, which has always struck me as one of *the* most interesting moral issues of our day. Have you ever noticed that the people with the vision, creative energy and single-mindedness to make big differences in the world are often not those who make kind, considerate neighbors? Conversely, I have always been perhaps ghoulishly fascinated by the reputed fact that the commandant of Auschwitz and Treblinka death camps, Rudolf Hoess, was a kind and considerate father and husband, or that Himmler, head of Hitler's SS, was sentimentally fond of animals.

So evil and goodness both come in lots of different packagings, and sometimes the packaging obscures their true character, so that they are not always immediately recognisable. I can remember a time, not so very many years ago, when Nelson Mandela was written off by many people as a terrorist, associated with a violent cause, that of the overthrow of the regime in South Africa. The people who were quickest to condemn that cause were usually those who were slowest to condemn the institutional violence of apartheid; it is worth remembering that one person's terrorist is often another person's freedom fighter. If there are such things as moral absolutes, they are elusive creatures, and typically easier to identify on someone else's territory than on one's own. These are some of the questions that have preoccupied me over the years, and, having no answers which are remotely satisfactory, I have tried instead to work them in some way into my books.

It was while I was pregnant with my second son, Adam, that my husband applied for a post at a boys' independent school in Oxford, and we were both delighted when he was successful. The prospect of living among the "dreaming spires" was highly attractive, though the gloss dulled somewhat over that summer of 1972 when, just as we were attempting to buy our first house, prices soared as never before or since! Literally every week brought a dramatic increase; eventually, just when I was becoming resigned to living in a garage—anything to have a roof over my head after I had given birth—we found a pleasant, modern townhouse which, by counting every last penny, we could just about afford, within cycling distance of Nigel's work. Unlike our apartment in Coventry, this was the ideal place for a young family, as the houses were situated around a small courtyard, which served as a safe and sociable playground for the children and provided the opportunity for parents to meet as and when they wanted.

Thanks to this ideal environment, both boys learnt to ride two-wheel bicycles at a ridiculously young age—in Adam's case, desperate to keep up with his older brother, before his third birthday. Having been brought up in central London, it was a skill I had never learnt as a child, but equally it was one I quickly realised I had to master if I was to make the most of living in Oxford. My mother-in-law had recently made herself learn to drive a car at age sixty, in the aftermath of my father-in-law's first heart attack. I saw this as a challenge; surely I could learn to ride a bicycle at half that age! But it is certainly the boys who can take the credit for teaching me; they would ride along the pavement with total confidence, shouting encouragement and advice as I wobbled nervously, and perilously, along the kerbside! But master it I did, and now I cannot imagine what life would be like here without a bicycle. Another abiding image, which illustrates for me the community spirit of those four-and-a-half years in our little courtyard, is of Santa Claus approaching along the top of the boundary wall, a great spray of balloons billowing out behind him in the chilly starlight, the children crowding around in tense expectant silence, while we parents stood clutching our steaming glasses of mulled wine. It was Adam who later expressed surprise that Santa's watch had looked very like Daddy's!

In 1977 we moved to our present house, and the move heralded a new stage for me in particular with the boys now in nursery school. I had taken the conscious decision to stay at home while they were little, which in the early and mid-'70s was less controversial than it might be now; I was clear that during the period when they grow and change so rapidly I did not want to have to ask someone else "what did they learn today?" At the same time I was ready to meet a fresh challenge. Despite my foray into the social sciences in the course of training to be a social worker, my heart belongs much more to languages and literature, and for some time I had thought of returning to my degree subject, German, to do some literary research. Since my student days, where I had become one of the very early members of Amnesty International, I had also been fascinated by the subject of oppression and responses to it; the obvious solution seemed to be to combine these strands of interest

and to write a thesis on a specific aspect of the German literary response to Nazism.

I was lucky enough to be accepted as a post-graduate student by one of the colleges of the University of Oxford, and to be allocated a tutor who turned out to be the best teacher I have ever had. The degree, formerly known as a B.Litt though the title has since changed to M.Litt in line with research degrees at a similar level from other universities, demanded a fifty-thousand-word thesis after two years. There were no compulsory lectures or course work assignments and consequently, although I was officially studying full-time, I could set my own deadlines according to the varying demands of the family and other commitments; at the same time, I enjoyed the luxury of regular supervision with my immensely well-read and helpful tutor. My thesis, on fascist mentality as configured by two German novelists, Gunter Grass and Siegfried Lenz, proved to be a perfect antidote to toys, tears, and tea parties, and I look back on the period as one of the most balanced and fulfilled of my life. I was extremely fortunate to be so well placed here in Oxford with its extraordinary resources, though since then part-time and flexible opportunities for further study have of course become much more generally accessible.

After finishing my research degree I did a little literature teaching, mainly for undergraduates at a few of the Oxford colleges who were studying "my" authors as their special subject, and this continued sporadically until I returned to work full-time. I had always intended to return to social work in some capacity, not because I enjoyed it particularly but because we needed the extra income and it was, after all, what I had been professionally trained to do. But now, with hindsight, I once again have the sense that I drifted back into a sort of career with half a heart and no vision. I did not question whether it was really what I wanted to do with my life, perhaps because I assumed that it was by now too late for a change of direction and that my B.Litt in itself was in any case not enough to equip me for a serious alternative. Nowadays I observe young women around me whose careers, sometimes even from their schooldays, are mapped out with a clear focus and strategy, and my admiration is tinged with envy. I genuinely do not understand why I also recoil a little. Perhaps because, even today, women seem to pay a much higher price than men for ambition. Still, for all that, I recall with a little glow of pleasure the special Christmas presents I was able to buy for the boys that first year after returning to work. Adam's was a particular success—Paddington Bear, almost as big as six-year-old Adam himself, was to accompany us everywhere for years to come, even as far as Greece, where we once spent a lotus-eating summer in a remote part of the Pelopponese.

It was while I was doing my research degree that I came across a reference to an amazing man called Janusz Korczak, a Polish Jew. He was a pediatrician, writer, teacher, educational theorist, broadcaster, and social worker who ran orphanages throughout his life and who, when the Nazis sealed off the ghetto in Warsaw in 1940, was forced to take his two hundred children into its filthy, narrow confines. There he struggled against overwhelming odds not only to protect them from starvation and guarantee their physical survival, but also to retain for them some quality of life. It is said that when the Nazis were deporting the inhabitants of the ghetto to Treblinka death camp, and among them the children from Korczak's orphanage, they offered him personally the chance of reprieve. "Desertion," he is reputed to have replied, "is not in my vocabulary," and, accordingly, he accompanied his charges to their death. "There's a story there," I thought to myself, "which I'll return to when I have time." This I duly did, and in so doing discovered that the sacrificial manner of Korczak's death was but an extension of his entire way of life. There was indeed a story there, and eventually *Shadow of the Wall,* my first book, came into being.

They say that all works of fiction are essentially autobiographical, and my sons tease me that my three books are all about searching for a lost father, which I suppose, in a way, they are. Misha, in *But Can the Phoenix Sing?* does, after all, lose not just one but *three* father figures, so the reader must draw his or her own conclusions! But *Shadow of the Wall,* as well as its sequel *But Can the Phoenix Sing?* is also about courageous responses to oppression, about human resilience and different sorts of courage, all themes which have fascinated me since my teens, perhaps because of my own pre-history. I remain intensely proud of the fact that my aunts were active in the Resistance in Amsterdam, to the extent of carrying guns and helping to operate a clandestine telephone exchange; that Allied airmen and weapons were from time to time concealed in my grandparental house, despite the fact that my grandfather, archetypally Jewish to look at, lived in virtual seclusion at the top of the house and could ill-afford to run extra risks. I have often wondered how he came to survive the war at all, and understand it was because of my grandmother, who was "Aryan"—which would certainly not have been enough to save him in other parts of Europe, so a large slice of luck must also have been responsible.

Shadow of the Wall found its way to several publishers before it was eventually accepted—in fact by a publisher who had turned it down the first time, but thoughtfully, and with some suggestions, which I later re-worked into the manuscript. In a vague and visionless way, which by now any persevering reader will probably recognise as characteristic, I had always wanted to write. My mother wrote and published articles and short stories, mainly romantic ones for magazines, but she also had a couple broadcast on the BBC's *Morning Story,* a radio slot which used to be something of an institution in this country. She was, as mentioned above, trying her hand at a novel when she died. So the inclination to write was a maternal legacy, the subject matter, on the other hand, rather persistently paternal.

I had returned to a part-time social work job in 1978, and by the mid-'80s it had certainly begun to pall. When you make a habit of intervening in other people's lives at the moments of greatest stress and distress, which after all is what social workers by definition tend to do, there are bound to be some very bad moments indeed for all concerned, particularly when serious risk to children is involved. My worst one came when I was called upon to remove a baby from young parents who were grieving the loss of their other child, dead in unusual circumstances. In that particular situation, it was the only thing we could do, the right thing to do, later supported by a decision of the

court, but somehow, after that dark spring day, I never really had any heart for the job again.

But a year or two later, about the time that I started writing *Shadow of the Wall,* my career took an unexpected turn for the better. In a short pause during a day on duty, looking for a distraction from other people's crises, I idly picked up a newsletter advertising vacant posts within the organisation and noticed that they were looking for a locum training officer. Although the closing date had already passed, a quick telephone call ascertained that I could still submit an application, which I did without hesitation. That casual picking up of a publication which I very rarely saw turned out to be a really lucky break. I became a training officer and about three weeks into my new job something strange happened to me—I woke up one morning and realised that I was actually looking forward to going to work! And this despite the fact that, with the boys aged sixteen and fourteen respectively, I had now taken the plunge and returned to work full-time.

Perhaps because I was so happy at work at this time, I also managed to write more. Not much more than a year after the appearance of *Shadow of the Wall* in 1989, *The Forgotten Son* was published. This is the story of the fourteen-year-old son of the famous French medieval lovers, Abelard and Heloise, and his anguished enquiries into his early childhood when he had effectively been abandoned by his parents. They had both taken holy orders after their affair had been discovered and after Abelard, one of the greatest philosophers of the age, had been castrated in an act of revenge on the part of Heloise's guardian uncle. Once again, a search for lost parents, but also for a definition of identity this time, set against the picturesque backdrop of twelfth-century France. The fated love affair of Abelard and Heloise, brought to a wider audience in Britain through a famous novel, *Peter Abelard,* by medieval scholar Helen Waddell, had always fascinated my mother, and when I read the book in my early twenties I had been profoundly moved by it. The challenge for me was to find a fresh perspective on an ancient story, which has been retold by many writers and artists over the centuries, so the discovery that the lovers did actually have a son, about whom very little is known, was a gift. I have always found the "vertical" relationships between the generations, the

Laird with her husband, Nigel, and their two sons, Julian and Adam, about 1975.

complexities of parental and ancestral bonds, somehow more fascinating than those associated with romantic or sexual love, which I think are more usually the subject of fictional treatment.

My three published books have all had historical settings, which I find easier to work with than contemporary ones. Historical facts give you a sort of trellis around which to weave a story; I found when I tried to write a novel set in present-day England a year or so ago that I desperately missed the supports of that trelliswork, and the whole thing eventually collapsed! I loved writing *The Forgotten Son;* it is my favourite of the three books so far and, my family and I believe, the best, although it has done much less well in terms of sales than the others. Perhaps that is because the subject matter is less accessible or dramatic than the Holocaust—or perhaps our judgment is simply wrong.

Professionally, since the late '80s I have played several different roles within the Training Section of the Social Services Department, specialising for a short while in training staff on matters related to child abuse and child protection. I never returned to social work as such, and though that was through my own choice, after a while I realised that that very distance from the front line which at first I had so relished was taking its toll on my training. I was glad, therefore, when in the early '90s I was able to take on a managerial position, in which I could learn new skills. This was fine initially, naively oblivious as I was to the rumblings of a revolution about to shake the world of training to its foundations, and not only in the public sector.

I have a measure of how far that world has changed when I start talking about my work to family (rarely) and friends (hardly ever). I am met with polite (friends only) nods and a shifting gaze, as the jargon—competence-based qualifications, internal verification, performance criteria, value added evaluations, outputs and outcomes—pushes them from me as effectively as any fist. If I leave the jargon out, there is little left to say, which in itself probably says rather a lot. The technology-led mania for measurement which is sweeping the world has given us all a new robotic language, rich in impoverished imagery, which typically uses nouns for adjectives, ignores grammar, and abuses punctuation. It reminds me of a book I once read about the de-humanising properties of the corrupted Nazi version of the German language, in which nouns, and particularly compound nouns, served to obfuscate and generalise. Why bother with syntactical clarity—the computer will produce clear performance indicators regardless! And the worst thing about it is that in order to play the game, survive with the fittest, swim with the tide, I catch myself slipping into these habits as well.

I often wonder what my mother would make of the world if she were to return on a surprise visit; so much has changed so radically since 1968. She would need a dictionary to understand much of the vocabulary; would be terrified by the multi-lane highways, which can turn a minor navigational error into a major crisis; would puzzle over the strange screens on everyone's desk which seem to conjure up out of nowhere answers to any question with the speed of lightning; would be delighted by the way letters can be transmitted simultaneously to anywhere in the world for less than the cost of a telephone call ... surely no other generation in the entire history of mankind has seen so much technological change in its own lifetime?

After the publication of *Shadow of the Wall* and the sale of a number of translation rights, my publishers showed an interest in a sequel. I decided that a sequel should be aimed at adults and proceeded to write a story about Misha as an adult, with little reference, except through a few flashbacks, to his experiences after escaping from the ghetto. This was not at all what my publishers wanted, so I had to scrap what I had written—about a quarter of a novel—and start all over again. It was disheartening to begin with, but a sympathetic publisher who is actively encouraging you to write something is not a person to be ignored or disregarded, and I knew I could not afford to be obstinate. I soon set about re-writing the sequel, still from an adult perspective, but now with much more of a focus on Misha's wartime adventures after his escape from the ghetto, and sent my publishers a sample chapter. This they seemed to like, and within weeks I actually had a contract. I found this frightening and quickly secreted the down payment away, modest though it was, convinced that I would wake up one morning to find that my imagination had dried up overnight and that I would have to pay it back!

But Can the Phoenix Sing? was the eventual result. It was a difficult book to research because it covers many different aspects of the war—partisan activity in the forests of eastern Poland, courier activity in Warsaw, the Warsaw Uprising of 1944, prisoner-of-war camp in Germany, liberation, the Polish Army in Italy, the immediate post-war years in Britain. It was also a very grim story to research, as indeed *Shadow of the Wall* had been. I have seen all too many Amnesty International reports over the years to be surprised by the horrors I had to read about, but I am glad to say that I never lost my capacity to be shocked, which is something different. And always, to balance the atrocities, there would be the true stories of superhuman courage, resilience, or self-sacrifice.

I remain fascinated by the quality of courage in its thousand manifestations, and haunted by the question of

The author's American aunt, Ellen Castle, accepting the Janusz Korczak Award on her behalf for **Shadow of the Wall,** *New York, 1992.*

whether I could ever rise to the challenge, as my family did, of putting my own life at risk for the sake of others. At the end of *Shadow of the Wall,* I have written a brief outline of Korczak's life, and have gone on to say: "If these stories of love and horror have one message for those of us who live in happier circumstances, it is surely one of humility; for none of us knows the limits—good or evil, moral or physical—of which we are capable, until put to the test."

I have often been asked how I manage to write and at the same time hold down a demanding full-time job, whose hours are not flexible. The truth is that even if I had all day at my disposal I would probably not be able to produce more than I do, as I can only sustain the intensity of concentration demanded by writing for, at the most, three hours at a time. I am fortunate in having the understanding and support of my husband when I closet myself away for entire evenings, and I do have considerable reserves of energy which may of course evaporate as I grow older, but sometimes I resent the fact that it is my writing which gets what is left over at the end of the day. On the other hand it offers me a whole world into which to escape from the frustrations of working to please other people in a large and complex organisation, a world in which *I* am indisputably the boss! Except, that is, when certain characters decide to assert their identities and take over, which does happen from time to time.

What *is* difficult sometimes is managing the research in the allotted time, particularly when visits out of Oxford to interview someone or visit a particular archive become necessary. I was fortunate to find two very willing Polish survivors, both of whom lived in Oxford, who helped me with certain parts of *But Can the Phoenix Sing?* and of course I am lucky to live close to the most wonderful libraries. I do take the research for my books very seriously indeed—for me it is at once the greatest pleasure and the greatest pain of writing. I see it as a sort of responsibility to get the historical facts as accurate as possible, partly, in the case of the Holocaust stories, so as not to insult any survivors who might read them, but also, at the risk of sounding precious, out of a certain respect for the characters themselves. I think this only dawned on me when I was writing *The Forgotten Son.* Heloise, dead for more than eight centuries, would not have hurt feelings or write rude letters to the press, and yet she too deserved to have her case heard with fairness and understanding. She would have been a remarkable woman even today, but in the context of the twelfth century she was quite extraordinary; with her daunting intellect, her formidable scholarship, and her smouldering passion, she achieved distinction throughout France for the religious community she built up and led, even though her heart was never truly in it. And yet she abandoned her only son. That is the heartbreak which Peter, the son, has to come to terms with in the book.

Of course there can be plenty of artistic licence in the interpretation of historical facts—that is where the climbing plants around the trellis come in—but the trelliswork itself should not be made of rotten wood. One major research difficulty which, oddly enough, *The Forgotten Son* and *But Can the Phoenix Sing?* had in common, was that while the "hard," external facts were well documented—battle details, dates of Nazi raids on the forests, Abelard's movements around France, for example—the day-to-day details were not so easy to discover. There may be plenty of

The author (right) with her aunt Ellen, 1995.

reference books on costumes and architecture and weapons, but what is less easy to imagine are the sounds and smells, the little activities in which people passed their time, whether as partisans in the forests of Poland or lords and serfs on a remote manor in northwest France. I once heard Joseph Heller describe the historical novelist as something of a jackdaw; that image really rang a bell with me for that is exactly how I am when I am trying to piece together the jigsaw of an historical novel. A chance reference or a picture glimpsed perhaps while searching for something else will suddenly glint at me, a detail which might help to bring the story to life, to give to historical chronology the shine of real experience; it might be as small a thing as the picture of a medieval wheelbarrow or an ancient herbal recipe, a description of the flies in the forests of eastern Europe, an actual quoted remark, the goggles worn by the American liberators of a prisoner-of-war camp, an unusual sound—like that of the children's clogs on the hard road as they were marched to the cattle trucks on their way to Treblinka.

It is this jackdaw approach which crucially differentiates research for historical fiction from academic research, which must concern itself much more with context and consequence. The fiction writer can afford to dive in for the glittering object and ruthlessly leave the rest behind. The result is that although I learnt a good deal about the periods in which my novels are set, and retain a vivid picture in my mind of certain aspects of life at those times, I would not welcome being tested on the chronology or causation of events in those periods. It is mood and spirit which are all important to me, and which are often so difficult to capture. I was very aware, for example, when I was writing *The Forgotten Son,* that Peter's aunt, who is a spirited and outspoken character, could all too easily become a hybrid of twentieth-century emancipated ideas and opinions with twelfth-century manners and dress.

And so to the future I hope that there will be more novels, but inspiration can be strangely elusive and I must have an idea which excites me before I can commit the prodigious amounts of energy and effort which writing seems to require of me, especially now that my paid job is busier than ever. Fancifully, I think of the creative process rather like a river; it may often be traced to one small wellspring of an idea, discovered perhaps while the author is exploring the area for reasons best known to him or herself (the Nazi period in my case), but during its course the river is fed by many tributaries—the author's own feelings, ideas, experiences, acquaintances, observations— which may swell or quicken or divert or even dam up the flow. At times the current will run smooth and steady, at others it will meander around almost in circles; sometimes it disappears underground, perhaps forever, perhaps to re-emerge in a different form. And, to complete the image, I am even told that contrary to what I was taught many years ago in geography lessons at school, some rivers never actually reach the sea but instead peter out in desert or swamp.

Thanks to a sabbatical term granted to Nigel by his school, and a corresponding period of unpaid leave from my job, we have recently had the opportunity for some extensive travelling, which gave us our first glimpse of several parts of the world outside Europe and America. It remains to be seen whether some infant inspiration lies concealed beneath memories of a husband bent double with pain from acute appendicitis in a squalid roadside clinic in India; or of an Australian eucalyptus forest, where, as if in some parody of its own other-worldliness, kangaroos leap and ruby and emerald parrots flash among trees pale as ghosts.

For the moment, however, my personal river of creativity seems to have retreated some way below ground!

Writings

FOR YOUNG ADULTS; FICTION

Shadow of the Wall, Julia Macrae Books (London), 1989, Greenwillow Books (New York), 1990.
The Forgotten Son, Julia Macrae Books, 1990.
But Can the Phoenix Sing? Julia Macrae Books, 1993, Greenwillow Books, 1995.

*   *   *

LAMENSDORF, Len
See LAMENSDORF, Leonard

LAMENSDORF, Leonard 1930-
(Len Lamensdorf)

Personal

Born June 22, 1930; son of Maurice (a merchant) and Gertrude (Hellman) Lamensdorf; married Joyce Greenbaum, August 5, 1952 (divorced, October, 1974); married Barbara Witkowski, March 16, 1975 (divorced); married Erica Mamis (in public relations), May 4, 1997; children: (first marriage) Lauren, Mark. *Education:* University of Chicago, B.A. (with honors), 1948, J.D., 1952. *Hobbies and other interests:* Travel.

Addresses

Home and office—SeaScape Press Ltd., 1010 Roble Lane, Santa Barbara, CA 93103; fax: 805-963-8188. *E-mail*—llamensdor@aol.com.

Career

Harvard University, Cambridge, MA, research associate for American Law Institute Federal Tax Reform Project, 1952-53; attorney and real estate developer, beginning in 1953; SeaScape Press Ltd., Santa Barbara, CA, president. Builder, owner, and manager of stores, office buildings, and regional shopping centers throughout the United States, 1953-1986. California Polytechnic State University, adjunct professor. *University of Chicago Law Review,* served as managing editor between 1948 and 1952.

Awards, Honors

Image Award nominations, National Association for the Advancement of Colored People, for the film *Cornbread, Earl, and Me;* 2000 Benjamin Franklin Award for Juvenile/Young Adult Fiction, for *The Crouching Dragon,* Book I of the "Will to Conquer" series.

Writings

Kane's World (novel), Simon & Schuster (New York City), 1968.
In the Blood (novel), Dell (New York City), 1974.
(Author and executive producer) *Cornbread, Earl, and Me* (screenplay), released by American International Pictures, 1975.

AS LEN LAMENSDORF

The Crouching Dragon (young adult novel), interior maps by Bob Swingle, SeaScape Press (Santa Barbara, CA), 1999.
Gino, the Countess & Chagall, SeaScape Press, 2000.

Author of *The Guest House,* a full-length play, produced in Provo, UT, at Brigham Young University. Contributor to periodicals, including law reviews.

Leonard Lamensdorf

Work in Progress

The Raging Dragon (sequel to *The Crouching Dragon*), Book II of the "Will to Conquer" series; a novel, *The Stolen Scroll;* a screenplay, *Little Marvin: The Man Who Thought He Was Lindbergh;* a stage play, *The Survival Game.*

Sidelights

Leonard Lamensdorf told *SATA:* "When asked what I do, I sometimes say, 'I'm a lawyer by profession, a regional shopping center owner-builder by trade, and a writer by choice.' The fact is, who I am, what I am, and what I do are all the same: I am a writer. I have been one since my first-grade teacher, Mrs. Moore, sent me to the principal's office with a poem I had written. I have never wanted to be anything but a writer—of something. Across the years this has included school and college plays and musicals (words and music), law review articles, theatrical feature films, full-length plays, and novels. Especially novels. I do not favor any particular genre, but have assayed stories ranging from the college world to business, young adult fantasy-history to humor-satire, modern art to sports, mystery, adventure—you name it.

"The beauty of the modern technological revolution is that, although I have had publishers like Simon & Schuster and Dell in the past, I no longer have to whine and plead with agents, publishers, and the like—and eventually lose all control over my work because I'm neither Stephen King nor John Updike. For a remarkably reasonable sum of money, I can publish and promote my own works, as I am presently doing with my wife Erica, under the aegis of our SeaScape Press Ltd. I can work with a profound sense of joy and achievement. I still have no control over reviewers, distributors, or booksellers, but the Internet gives me the means to reach at least part of the market directly. There is no guarantee of success, but what fun it is!"

Biographical and Critical Sources

PERIODICALS

Booklist, September 1, 1999, Sally Estes, review of *The Crouching Dragon,* p. 124; October 15, 2000, Patty Engelman, review of *Gino, the Countess & Chagall.*
Kirkus Reviews, June 1, 1968, review of *Kane's World,* p. 618.
Library Journal, July, 1968, Paul Sarnoff, review of *Kane's World,* p. 2690; September 15, 1999, Jackie Cassada, review of *The Crouching Dragon,* p. 116.
Publishers Weekly, June 25, 1968, review of *Kane's World,* p. 62; October 16, 2000, review of *Gino, the Countess & Chagall.*
School Library Journal, December, 1999, Debbie Fuelner, review of *The Crouching Dragon,* p. 136.

*   *   *

LAMINACK, Lester L. 1956-

Personal

Born July 11, 1956; son of Jimmy R. (a welder) and Mary Jo (Thompson) Laminack; married Glenda Jo Anthony (a receptionist), November 28, 1974; children: Zachary Seth. *Education:* Jacksonville State University, B.S., 1977, and M.S., 1978; Auburn University, Ed.D., 1983. *Religion:* Methodist. *Hobbies and other interests:* travel, playing the saxophone, reading children's books and southern fiction.

Addresses

Office—Department of Elementary and Middle Grades Education, 246 Killian Bldg., Western Carolina University, Cullowhee, NC 28723. *E-mail*—laminack@ wcu.edu.

Career

Cleburn County Elementary School, first grade teacher, 1977-1981, reading teacher, 1981-82; Western Carolina University, Cullowhee, NC, professor of elementary and middle grades education, 1982—, and head of department and past member of board of governors of the Whole Language Umbrella and the North Carolina

Association for the Education of Young Children. Governing board member of the Center for Expansion of Language and Thinking (CELT); member of kindergarten, pre-K, and reading task forces of the North Carolina Department of Public Instruction. *Member:* International Reading Association, National Council of Teachers of English, National Association for the Education of Young Children, Literacy Volunteers of America, Inc.

Awards, Honors

Botner Superior Teaching Award, College of Education and Psychology, Western Carolina University, 1989; Chancellor's Distinguished Teaching Award, Western Carolina University, 1991; Joan Fassler Award, Association for the Care of Children's Health, 1998, for *The Sunsets of Miss Olivia Wiggins.*

Writings

Learning with Zachary, Scholastic Inc. (New York City), 1991.
(With Katie Wood) *Spelling in Use,* National Council of Teachers of English (Urbana, IL), 1996.
Trevor's Wiggly-Wobbly Tooth, illustrated by Kathi Garry McCord, Peachtree Publishers (Atlanta, GA), 1998.
The Sunsets of Miss Olivia Wiggins, illustrated by Constance R. Bergum, Peachtree Publishers, 1998.
Volunteers Working with Young Readers, National Council of Teachers of English, 1998.

Work in Progress

"Always working on a story."

Biographical and Critical Sources

PERIODICALS

Booklist, May 1, 1998, Susan Dove Lempke, review of *The Sunsets of Miss Olivia Wiggins,* p. 1521.
Horn Book Guide, fall, 1998, review of *The Sunsets of Miss Olivia Wiggins,* p. 297; spring, 1999, review of *Trevor's Wiggly-Wobbly Tooth,* p. 34.
Publishers Weekly, March 30, 1998, review of *The Sunsets of Miss Olivia Wiggins,* p. 82.
School Library Journal, July, 1998, Martha Topol, review of *The Sunsets of Miss Olivia Wiggins,* p. 78; February, 1999, Farida Shapiro, review of *Trevor's Wiggly-Wobbly Tooth,* p. 86.
Teacher Librarian, May, 1999, review of *Volunteers Working with Young Readers,* p. 41.

ON-LINE

Amazon.com, www.amazon.com (October 16, 2000).

*   *   *

LAWRENCE, Margery (H.) 1889-1969

Personal

Born August 8, 1889, in Wolverhampton, Staffordshire, England; died November 13, 1969, in London, England; married Arthur Edward Towle (died, 1948). *Education:* Attended art schools in Birmingham and London, England, and in Paris, France.

Career

Writer. Also worked as a book illustrator.

Writings

NOVELS

Red Heels, Hutchinson (London, England), 1924.
Fine Feathers, Curtiss (New York City), 1928.
Bohemian Glass: A Story of the Younger Set, Hurst & Blackett (London), 1928.
Drums of Youth, Hurst & Blackett, 1929.
The Madonna of Seven Moons, Hurst & Blackett, 1931, Bobbs-Merrill (Indianapolis, IN), 1933.
Silken Sarah, Hurst & Blackett, 1932.
Madame Holle, Jarrolds (London), 1934.
The Crooked Smile, Jarrolds, 1935.
Overture to Life, Jarrolds, 1937.
The Bridge of Wonder, R. Hale (London), 1939.
Step Light, Lady, R. Hale, 1942.
The Gilded Jar, R. Hale, 1948.
The Rent in the Veil, R. Hale, 1951.
Emma of Alkistan, R. Hale, 1953.
Evil Harvest, R. Hale, 1954.
Daughter of the Nile, R. Hale, 1956.
Spanish Interlude, R. Hale, 1959.
The Gate of Yesterday, R. Hale, 1960.
Skivvy, R. Hale, 1961.
Green Amber, R. Hale, 1962.
The Unforgetting Heart, R. Hale, 1963.
Dead End, R. Hale, 1964.
The Yellow Triangle, R. Hale, 1965.
The Tomorrow of Yesterday, R. Hale, 1966.
Bride of Darkness, R. Hale, 1967, Ace Books (New York City), 1969.
The Green Bough, R. Hale, 1968.
Over My Shoulder, R. Hale, 1968.
A Residence Afresh, R. Hale, 1969.
Autumn Rose, R. Hale, 1971.

STORY COLLECTIONS

Miss Brandt: Adventuress, Hutchinson, 1923.
Nights of the Round Table: A Book of Strange Tales, Hutchinson, 1926.
Snapdragon, Hurst & Blackett, 1931, Ash-Tree Press, 1998.
The Terraces of Night; Being the Further Chronicles of the Club of the Round Table, Hurst & Blackett, 1932, Ash-Tree Press, 1999.
The Floating Café and Other Stories, Jarrolds, 1936.
Strange Caravan, R. Hale, 1941.
Number Seven Queer Street, R. Hale, 1945, abridged edition, Mycroft & Moran (Sauk City, WI), 1969.
Cardboard Castle, R. Hale, 1951.
Master of Shadows, R. Hale, 1959.

OTHER

Songs of Childhood and Other Verses, Grant Richards (London), 1913.

Ferry over Jordan, R. Hale, 1944.
What Is This Spiritualism?, Spiritualist Press (London), 1946.
Fourteen to Forty-Eight: A Diary in Verse, R. Hale, 1950.

Adaptations

The novel *Red Heels* was adapted for the film *Das Spielzeug von Paris* in 1925; the novel *The Madonna of Seven Moons* was adapted as a film, 1944.

Biographical and Critical Sources

BOOKS

St. James Guide to Horror, Ghost, and Gothic Writers, St. James Press (Detroit, MI), 1998, pp. 349-50.

PERIODICALS

Books, April 30, 1933, George Conrad, review of *The Madonna of Seven Moons,* p. 11.
Magazine of Fantasy and Science Fiction, March, 1970, review of *Number Seven Queer Street,* p. 112.
New York Times, May 21, 1933, review of *The Madonna of Seven Moons,* p. 7.
New York Times Book Review, August 31, 1969, Allen J. Hubin, "Criminals at Large," p. 20.

*   *   *

LESINSKI, Jeanne M. 1960-

Personal

Born December 11, 1960, in Macomb County, MI; married to a biologist; children: three. *Education:* DePauw University, B.A., 1983. *Hobbies and other interests:* Gardening, music, cross-country skiing.

Addresses

E-mail—jmlesinski@alltel.net.

Career

Magazine writer, contributing author, and editor for reference works, author of nonfiction books for juveniles.

Writings

Exotic Invaders: Killer Bees, Fire Ants and Other Alien Species Are Infesting America!, Walker (New York), 1996.
MIAs: A Reference Handbook, ABC-CLIO (Santa Barbara, CA), 1998.
Bill Gates, Lerner Publications (Minneapolis, MN), 2000.

Contributor of articles to magazines, including *Garden, Deck, and Landscape, Garden Ideas and Outdoor Living, Perennials, Simply Perfect Garden Rooms,* and *Simply Perfect Perennials.*

Sidelights

From childhood Jeanne M. Lesinski entertained dreams of becoming a children's book author, a goal she achieved in 1996 with the publication of *Exotic Invaders: Killer Bees, Fire Ants and Other Alien Species Are Infesting America!* In this book for the scientifically inclined young person, Lesinski profiles five species that have been inadvertently or purposefully introduced into the United States with unforeseen results. The species examined are the sea lamprey, the fire ant, zebra mussels, European starlings, and African killer bees. For each species, Lesinski provides the scientific name, an account of its introduction into the United States, what it feeds upon, how its spread is being controlled, and maps showing geographic area of infestation. The author also includes information on what can be done to help impede the spread of these species, whose aggressivity is pushing out native species, and in the case of the lamprey and zebra mussels, is harming the national fishing and shipping industries. All told, *Exotic Invaders* "provides a well-written, informative, and interesting account of each exotic," averred John R. Conway in *Science Books and Films. School Library Journal* contributor Karey Wehner faulted the book's lack of a glossary, however, and noted that not all the scientific terms used in the book are explained in the text. But little information is available on any of these species

Jeanne M. Lesinski

except the killer bee, Wehner added, and thus, "despite minor omissions, *Exotic Invaders* provides timely data on these pests."

Lesinski told *SATA:* "I sold my *Exotic Invaders* book based on a sample chapter and book proposal, which is certainly the way to go for nonfiction. But before this happened, I had gone to a talk by an author who'd written about animals. After the talk, I spoke to him about my project. He told me I'd never see it published based on a proposal, so later I was very glad to prove him wrong! I learned a great deal writing that book because I did not only research for the text but photo research (always ask for a photo budget!). It has also been a fun book to talk about with children because one of the biologists I interviewed gave me a preserved sea lamprey, which children and adults exclaim over."

Lesinski is also the author of *MIAs: A Reference Handbook,* which provides a wealth of material on soldiers missing in action (MIA). It includes an overview of the MIA-prisoner-of-war controversy, a chronology covering the period from the Korean War to the present, statistics, source documents, and a directory of organizations. Mary Ellen Quinn, a reviewer for *Booklist,* noted that the book's resources section is "especially rich" in providing extensive information on non-book sources, including an annotated list of web sites on the Internet. "Publishers approached me about doings *MIAs* and *Bill Gates* after I sent them resumes," Lesinski recalled. "*MIAs* was a very difficult book to write because I spent months doing research and could have taken years to research more. My father was a Korean War veteran and a history teacher, so I dedicated the book to him. It was especially difficult reading so much about prisoners being tortured and killed, but in those difficult times I felt like my father was there, looking over my shoulder."

About her biography of the richest man in the world, Lesinski revealed, "Bill Gates was a fascinating subject for a biography. When I was in grade school I tried to read the entire biography section of the school library! So writing a biography was something I'd wanted to do for a long time. It was also fun to find out that Bill Gates likes to read biographies." In *Bill Gates* Lesinski introduced readers to the highlights of Gates's life and his challenges as the head of Microsoft. "I tried to show readers the best I could that despite his tremendous success—and all the negative publicity surrounding the antitrust trial and caricatures of his personality—Gates is still a real person who cried when his mother died and enjoys being a father to his two children." *Bill Gates* caught the attention of critics. Sandra L. Doggett, writing in *School Library Journal,* applauded Lesinski's objective treatment of the subject matter, while *Kliatt* reviewer Sherri Forgash Ginsberg deemed the work an "essential addition to any YA library."

Lesinski told *SATA:* "It might seem strange that someone would write a science book, a history book, and a biography, but variety is part of what I enjoy about writing. Sometimes it's hard to pull myself away from

In her book for the scientifically inclined young reader, Lesinski profiles five species that have been inadvertently or purposefully introduced into the U.S. with unforeseen results.

the research to get down to the writing because I think that children deserve up-to-date and accurate information. Writing has also allowed me to be home with my husband and children at important times in our lives." Lesinski was once asked about how the people closest to her felt about having a writer in the family: "They're pretty used to it by now," she replied. "In fact they probably take it a little for granted, until I remind them of an upcoming deadline and that 'Mom is a little stressed by the deadline coming up.' One day at the local library when we saw they'd acquired *Bill Gates* and it was on the new bookshelf, my son was happy to see it and wanted to check it out. I laughed and said that I have a whole box of them at home he could read. I also have to admit that some people who've seen me in my other roles, e.g. volunteer or on the ball fields with the kids, are surprised when they find out I'm a writer. They must not realize that writers are real people with families and varied interests. It makes me think of school children who think teachers have no lives outside of school!"

Lesinski continued: "I think that some people are just writers and they aren't happy if they can't write. I think that the time spent in creative endeavor is like athletes in the ZONE. It's a kind of all-engrossing effort that leaves you wondering how time passed so quickly. It's addictive in a positive way. There have been times when I had to work at other jobs to help support the family, but it was always the writing I did on the side that sustained me creatively. Some writing I do, though all I do is nonfiction or creative nonfiction, takes a lot more creativity than other writing. I like to try something new every so often to stretch, but I'm also a working writer who depends on a steady stream of projects for income."

"I talk to school children on occasion and I always show them corrections on my manuscripts that became a book because it's really hard to get children to understand that they have to revise, reread, revise. To adults I recommend the same thing, and of course to hone the craft. How can a reader become engrossed in a work if bad grammar and punctuation distracts him/her? Joining a writers' group can be very useful too. The other thing I recommend is to read avidly and analyze the style of writers you like. Look how they write dialog. Look at character development. Look at the broad strokes of the plot. How do they incorporate details that make the characters, setting, and situations seem real. In nonfiction, you can use fictional techniques to make the story more interesting."

Biographical and Critical Sources

PERIODICALS

Booklist, March 1, 1999, Mary Ellen Quinn, review of *MIAs: A Reference Handbook,* p. 1248.

Horn Book, fall, 1996, Kelly A. Ault, review of *Exotic Invaders,* p. 336.

Kliatt, July, 2000, Sherri Forgash Ginsberg, review of *Bill Gates,* p. 28.

School Library Journal, May, 1996, Karey Wehner, review of *Exotic Invaders,* p. 124; September, 2000, Sandra L. Doggett, review of *Bill Gates,* p. 251.

Science Books and Films, January-February, 1997, John R. Conway, review of *Exotic Invaders,* p. 19.

* * *

LEWIS, Anthony 1966-

Personal

Born December 8, 1966, in Chester, United Kingdom; son of Rodney (a building contractor) and Marjorie (Duncalf) Lewis; married Kathryn Caulfield (a graphic designer), July 26, 1997. *Education:* Attended Chester College, 1985-86, and Liverpool School of Art, degree in Graphic Design (first-class honors), 1989.

Addresses

Home—Weathertop, Nemos Close, Alvanley, Cheshire, UK. *Agent*—Rosemary Canter, Peters Fraser & Dunlop, London, UK, and Harriet Kasak, HK Portfolio, 666 Greenwich St., New York, NY 10012. *E-mail*—lewis. anthony@talk21.com.

Career

Freelance illustrator since summer, 1989. Has also illustrated many advertising campaigns, theatre posters, promotional and corporate brochures, and magazine articles in the United Kingdom.

Awards, Honors

Smarties Book Prize Gold Award, *The Owl Tree* (written by Jenny Nimmo), 1997; *Meet Me by the Steelmen* was shortlisted for the Sheffield Book Award, 1998.

Writings

My Book of Time, Leopard, 1994.
My Book of Weather, Leopard, 1994.

ILLUSTRATOR

John Mole, *Catching the Spider,* Blackie, 1990.
Kate Sinnett, *My Five Disguises,* Blackie, 1991.
Robina Beckles Willson, *Mozart's Story,* A & C Black, 1991.
Maggie Russell, *The Three Bears Christmas Party,* 1992.
Roger McGough, *My Dad's a Fire-Eater,* Puffin, 1992.
Margaret Nash, *The Haunted Canal,* Puffin, 1992.
Heather Maisner, *Alice's Magic Alice Band,* Heinemann (Oxford), 1992.
Mary Hoffman, *The Four-Legged Ghosts,* Orchard (London), 1992.
Mary Hoffman, *The Ghost Menagerie,* Orchard, 1992.
Kathy Henderson, *Second-Time Charley,* Walker, 1992.
Jon Blake, *The Ghost of Joseph Grey,* Simon & Schuster, 1992.
Anne Digby, *Mystery of the Missing Footprints,* Piccadilly, 1992.
Mary Norton, *Bonfires and Broomsticks,* Dent, 1993.
Mary Norton, *The Magic Bedknob,* Dent, 1993.
Roberto Piumini, *Mattie and Grandpa,* Puffin, 1993.
Beverly Cleary, *Muggie Maggie,* Puffin, 1993.
Rachel McAlpine, *Maria in the Middle,* Young Lions, 1993.
William Mayne, *The Egg Timer,* Heinemann, 1993.
Martin Waddell, *Herbie Whistle,* Puffin, 1993.
Douglas Hill, *The Voyage of Mudjack,* Methuen, 1993.
Harriet Graham, *Tom's Saturday Trousers,* Puffin (London), 1993.
Angela Sommer-Bodenburg, *The Little Vampire and the Wicked Plot,* Simon & Schuster, 1993.
Angela Sommer-Bodenburg, *The Little Vampire Gets a Surprise,* Simon & Schuster, 1993.
Angela Sommer-Bodenburg, *The Little Vampire in the Lion's Den,* Simon & Schuster, 1993.
Angela Sommer-Bodenburg, *The Little Vampire Learns to Be Brave,* Simon & Schuster, 1993.
Elizabeth Dale, *Spike's Specs,* Heinemann (London), 1994.
Ian Whybrow, *The Time Sailors,* Walker, 1994.
Alan Gibbons, *Not Yeti,* Orion (London), 1994.
Andre Gutelle, *Why Can't I See the Wind,* Timelife for Children, 1994.
Angela Sommer-Bodenburg, *The Little Vampire and the Christmas Surprise,* Simon & Schuster, 1994.
Angela Sommer-Bodenburg, *The Little Vampire and the School Trip,* Simon & Schuster, 1994.
Robert Leeson, *Swapper,* Heinemann, 1994.
Pippa Goodhart, *Flow,* Heinemann, 1994.
Leon Rosselson, *Save our Playground,* Collins, 1994.
Leon Rosselson, *Swim, Sam, Swim,* Puffin, 1994.
Charles Causley, *All Day Saturday and Other Poems,* Macmillan, 1994.

Angela Sommer-Bodenburg, *The Little Vampire Meets Count Dracula,* Simon & Schuster, 1995.

Claire Llewellyn, *Rivers and Seas,* Barron's Educational Series (Hauppauge, NY), 1995, published as *Why Do We Have Rivers and Seas?,* Heinemann, 1996.

Claire Llewellyn, *Rocks and Mountains,* Barron's Educational Series, 1995, published as *Why Do We Have Rocks and Mountains?,* Hienemann, 1996.

Claire Llewellyn, *Day and Night,* Barron's Educational Series, 1995, published as *Why Do We Have Day and Night?,* Heinemann, 1996.

Claire Llewellyn, *Wind and Rain,* Barron's Educational Series, 1995, published as *Why Do We Have Wind and Rain?,* Heinemann, 1996.

June Crebbin, *Cows Moo, Cars Toot,* Viking (London), 1995.

Annalena McAfee, *All the Way to the Stars,* Julia MacRae (London), 1995.

Margaret Joy, *The Little Troglodyte,* Viking, 1995.

Vivien Alcock and others, *Best Stories for Seven Year Olds,* Hodder Children's, 1995.

Helen Cresswell and others, *Best Stories for Six Year Olds,* Hodder Children's, 1995.

Frances James (compiler), *The Cambridge Big Book of Nursery Rhymes,* Cambridge University Press, 1996.

Federation of Children's Book Groups (compiler), *Simply the Best,* 1996.

Linda Jennings (compiler), *A Treasury of Pony Stories,* Kingfisher (New York), 1996.

Emma Fischel, *My Teacher the Ghost,* Macdonald Young (Hove), 1996.

Mary Hoffman, *Quantum Squeak,* Orchard, 1996.

Mary Hooper, *The Surprise Party,* Heinemann, 1996.

Jillian Harker, *Dan and Pip's Ship,* Ladybird, 1996.

Jillian Harker, *Peep's Asleep,* Ladybird, 1996.

Penelope Lively, *A Martian Comes to Stay,* Macdonald, 1996.

Claire Llewellyn, *Why Do We Have Deserts and Rainforests?,* Heinemann, 1996, published *Deserts and Rainforests,* Rigby Interactive Library (Crystal Lake, IL), 1997.

Mary Hoffman, *A Vanishing Tail,* Orchard, 1997.

Claire Llewellyn, *Towns and Cities,* Barron's Educational Series, 1997, published as *Why Do We Have Towns and Cities?,* Heinemann, 1997.

Rosie McCormick, *All Kinds of Animals,* Kingfisher, 1997.

Rosie McCormick, *Things That Go,* Kingfisher, 1997.

Linda Newbery, *Whistling Jack,* CollinsChildren's (London), 1997.

Chris Powling, *Kit's Castle,* Kingfisher, 1997.

Theresa Tomlinson, *Meet Me by the Steelmen,* Walker, 1997.

Jenny Nimmo, *The Owl Tree,* Walker, 1997.

Douglas Hill, *Fireball and the Hero,* Methuen, 1997.

Annalena McAfee, *Why Do Stars Come Out at Night?,* Julia MacRae, 1997.

Gari Fairweather, *10 Minutes a Day to Reading Success,* Houghton Mifflin, 1997.

Pat Thomson (compiler), *A Bedfull of Night-Time Stories,* Transworld, 1998.

Jamila Gavin, *Monkey in the Stars,* Mammoth (London), 1998.

Jamila Gavin, *Someone's Watching, Someone's Waiting,* Mammoth, 1998.

Pat Posner, *Guinea Pig's Adventure,* Hippo, 1998.

Jillian Powell, *Sports on Wheels,* Ginn (Aylesbury), 1998.

Francie Alexander and Nancy Hechinger, *Let's Go on a Museum Hunt,* Scholastic, 1998.

Rosie McCormick, *Me and My Body,* Kingfisher, 1998.

Rosie McCormick, *Me and My World,* Kingfisher, 1998.

Teddy Slater, *Max's Money,* Scholastic, 1998.

Jennifer Curry, *Young Hippo: Animal Poems,* Hippo (London), 1998.

Jasmine Brook, *Over the Moon Bear,* Barons, 1998.

Jasmine Brook, *Top to Tail Bear,* Barons, 1998.

Angel Nieto, *La Feria Escolar,* Scholastic, 1998.

Nancy Maria Grande Tabor, *La Gatita del Lago,* Scholastic, 1998.

Carolina Conde, *Las Abejas y la Miel,* Scholastic, 1998.

Graciela Vidal, *Gata Va al Rio!,* Scholastic, 1998.

Julie Bertagna, *Clumsy Clumps the Baby Moon,* Heinemann (London), 1999.

Geraldine McCaughrean, *Noah and Nelly,* Orchard, 1998.

Louis Weber, *So Much to Love,* Publications International Ltd., 1999.

Pat Thomson, *A Parcel of Stories for Five Year Olds,* Transworld, 1999.

Rosie McCormick, *Fun Finding out about Our World,* Kingfisher, 1999.

Wendy Cheyette Lewison, *Buzz, the Little Seaplane,* Grosset & Dunlap (New York), 1999.

L. J. Sattgast, *Steps to Jesus: A Child's Path to Faith in Christ,* WaterBrook Press (Colorado Springs, CO), 1999.

Sam Godwin, *Clockwise,* Macdonald, 1999.

Rose Impey, *Greedy Guts and Belly Busters,* Orchard, 1999.

Jenny Nimmo, *The Box Boys and the Bonfire Cat,* Hodder, 1999.

Jenny Nimmo, *The Box Boys and the Dog in the Mist,* Hodder, 1999.

Jenny Nimmo, *The Box Boys and the Fairground Ride,* Hodder, 1999.

Jenny Nimmo, *The Box Boys and the Magic Shell,* Hodder, 1999.

Rose Impey, *I-Spy, Pancakes and Pie,* Orchard, 1999.

Claire Llewellyn, *The Earth Is Like a Roundabout,* Macdonald, 1999.

Annalena McAfee, *Busy Baby,* Julia MacRae, 1999.

Helen Paiba (compiler), *Magical Stories for Six Year Olds,* Macmillan, 1999.

Carol Pugliano-Martin, *25 Mini Science Books,* 1999.

Hilary Robinson, *Email: Jesus@Bethlehem,* Macdonald, 1999.

Rosie McCormick, *Things That Go,* Kingfisher, 2000.

Michaela Morgan, *I Looked through My Window,* Rigby, 2000.

Justine Korman Fontes, *Bedtime for Little Monster,* Troll, 2000.

Janet Craig, *What's in the Piggy Bank?,* Troll, 2000.

Judith Bauer Stamper, *The Pony Express,* Scholastic, 2000.

Anne Schreiber, *Picnics on the Hill,* Scholastic, 2000.

Theresa Thomlinson, *Night of the Red Devils,* Walker, 2000.

Mary Hooper, *A Lamb for Lucy,* Macmillan, 2000.

Mary Hooper, *Lucy's Donkey Rescue,* Macmillan, 2000.
Mary Hooper, *Lucy's Badger Club,* Macmillan, 2000.
Mary Hooper, *A Stormy Night for Lucy,* Macmillan, 2000.
Mary Hooper, *Lucy's Wild Pony,* Macmillan, 2000.
Mary Hooper, *Lucy's Perfect Piglet,* Macmillan, 2000.
Jane Kemp and Clare Walters, *Rocket to the Rescue,* Collins, 2000.
Jane Kemp and Clare Walters, *The Piggy Race,* Collins, 2000.
Linda Newbery, *The Cat with Two Names,* Scholastic, 2000.
Enid Blyton, *More Wishing Chair Stories,* Egmont, 2000.
Helen Paiba (compiler), *Magical Stories for Five Year Olds,* Macmillan, 2000.
Helena Rigby, *Test Your Child's English,* Scholastic, 2000.
Ingrid Oliver, *Ideas for Pshe,* Scholastic, 2000.
Robert Munsch, *Love You Forever,* Hutchinson, 2000.

*　　*　　*

LIDZ, Jane

Career

Photographer, author, teaching fellow in architecture.

Writings

Rolling Homes: Handmade Houses on Wheels, A & W Visual Library (New York), 1979.
One of a Kind, A & W Publishers, 1982.
(Illustrator) Charles W. Moore, *Water and Architecture,* Harry N. Abrams (New York), 1994.
Zak: The One-of-a-Kind Dog, Harry N. Abrams, 1997.

Sidelights

Jane Lidz is a professional photographer whose first book, *Rolling Homes: Handmade Houses on Wheels,* was greeted as a quirky celebration of those adventurous folk who have transformed flatbed trucks or buses into custom-made homes that can be relocated on a whim. "This is a beguiling introduction to a new breed of American who's flourishing in Oregon and other West Coast states ..." began a reviewer in the *New York Times Book Review.* Though some detail is given about the methods and costs of building one of these homes on wheels, "mostly, [the book] is a visual curiosity," remarked Craig Shaw Gardner in *Kliatt.* Likewise, Douglas Birdsall, writing in *Library Journal,* contended: "Lidz's color photography has caught the delightful detail of handcrafted homes made mobile."

Lidz published a collection of black-and-white photographs of her dog, Zak, in 1982, under the title *One of a Kind.* When the small press book went out of print, Lidz was urged by her mother to find a way to make the book available again. Lidz hand-colored the original black-and-white photos, and the prestigious art publisher Abrams republished the book under the title *Zak: The One-of-a-Kind Dog,* in 1997. In Lidz's story, Zak is a mutt who wonders what kind of dog he is, since he's never seen another like himself, not even in a book of

Through a simple text and expressive hand-colored photographs Jane Lidz relates the story of her dog, a mutt named Zak, who embarks on a quest to find out what kind of dog he is. (From Zak: The One-of-a-Kind Dog.*)*

dog breeds. In her photos of Zak, Lidz "combines an eye for expressive dog antics with a delicate sense of color and strong, varied compositions," a reviewer for *Publishers Weekly* observed. Finally, Zak decides that he is unique—one of a kind—and turns to the reader to ask "What kind of person are you?" Reviewers contended that *Zak: The One-of-a-Kind Dog* was likely to prove irresistible to dog lovers among adults and children. Lidz's photos were the highlight of reviews of the book; a reviewer for *Children's Literature* claimed that coloring the black-and-white photos "gives a magical, otherworldly feel to the story." Although the reviewer for *Kirkus Reviews* complained that the story's message about self-acceptance is an example of the kind of "overly earnest curricula" offered children these days, Lidz's humorous photographs save the effort. Like other reviewers, John Peters of *School Library Journal* contended that the winsome personality of Zak shines through in Lidz's photos, and "will win over this generation of children as easily as it did the last."

Lidz's photographs illustrate Charles W. Moore's text in *Water and Architecture,* which celebrates the ways in which architects throughout human history have incorporated water into the very heart of cities and dwellings. Lidz shot her photographs in locations around the world, both renowned and relatively unknown, and the result is an "exquisite" photo-essay, according to a reviewer in *Publishers Weekly.* This critic continued: "Lidz's intuitive photographic vision seems perfectly attuned to this subject ...."

Biographical and Critical Sources

PERIODICALS

Booklist, April 15, 1998, p. 1452.
Children's Literature, review of *Zak: The One-of-a-Kind Dog.*
Horn Book, spring, 1998, p. 37.
Kirkus Reviews, November 15, 1997, review of *Zak: The One-of-a-Kind Dog,* p. 1709.
Kliatt, fall, 1979, Craig Shaw Gardner, review of *Rolling Homes,* p. 67.
Library Journal, July, 1979, Douglas Birdsall, review of *Rolling Homes,* p. 1444.
New York Times Book Review, June 3, 1979, review of *Rolling Homes,* p. 59.
Publishers Weekly, April 18, 1994, review of *Water and Architecture,* p. 53; October 6, 1997, p. 29; November 17, 1997, review of *Zak: The One-of-a-Kind Dog,* p. 60.
School Library Journal, March, 1998, John Peters, review of *Zak: The One-of-a-Kind Dog,* p. 182.*

*   *   *

LINDGREN, Barbro 1937-

Personal

Born March 18, 1937, in Stockholm, Sweden; daughter of George (a civil engineer) and Maja (an artist; maiden name, Loefstedt) Enskog; children: Andreas, Mathias. *Education:* Attended Konstfackskolan Art School, 1954-58, and Konstakademin Academy of Arts, 1959.

Addresses

Home—Brunnsgatan 4, 27231 Simrishamn, Sweden. *Agent*—Raben & Sjoegren, Box 2052, SE-10312 Stockholm, Sweden; Eriksson & Lindgren Books, Box 22108, 10422 Stockholm, Sweden.

Career

Author, artist, and designer.

Awards, Honors

Swedish Foundation of Authors Labor Scholarship, 1967; Literary Promotion Scholarship, 1967 and 1971; Swedish Foundation of Authors Scholarship, 1968-69; "Gramophone-70" Award, 1970, for children's song texts; Marsta Municipal Culture Prize, 1970; Swedish Foundation of Authors Five Year Labor Scholarship, 1971-1975; Literary Promotion Scholarship, 1971; *Expressen*'s Heffaklump Award (Sweden), 1971, for *Jaettehemligt;* Astrid Lindgren Award, 1973, for honorable authorship; Nils Holgersson-Plaketten from the Swedish Library Association, 1977, for *Lilla Sparvel;* Premio Europeo "Citta di Caorle" (picture book category), 1980, for *Sagan om den lilla farbrorn; The Wild Baby* was selected one of *School Library Journal*'s Best Books, 1981; *The Wild Baby Goes to Sea* was selected one of *School Library Journal*'s Best Books, 1983; Hans

Christian Andersen Award nomination, 1988; Lista d'Onore Narrativa del Premio Europeo di Letteratura Giovanile, for *Vems lilla moessa flyger,* 1989; Stockholms Stads Hederspris, and Litteraturframjandets Stora Pris, both 1991.

Writings

Mattias sommar, illustrated by Stan Tusan, Raben & Sjoegren (Stockholm), 1965, reissued, 1980, translation by Annabelle MacMillan published as *Hilding's Summer,* Macmillan, 1967.
Mera om Mattias (title means "More about Mattias"), Raben & Sjoegren, 1966, reissued, 1980.
Hej, hej Mattias (title means "Hi, Hi, Mattias"), Raben & Sjoegren, 1967, reissued, 1980.
I Vaestan Grind (title means "Westwind Gate"), illustrated by Monica Schultz, Raben & Sjoegren, 1968, reissued, 1980.
Loranga, Masarin och Dartanjang, (title means "Loranga, Masarin, and Dartanjang"), Raben & Sjoegren, 1969, reissued, 1980.
Loranga Loranga, Raben & Sjoegren, 1970, reissued, 1984.
Nu har Kalle faatt en liten syster (title means "Kalle Now Has a New Little Sister"), Raben & Sjoegren, 1970, reissued, 1976.
Jaettehemligt (title means "Giant Secret"), illustrated by Olof Landstrom, Raben & Sjoegren, 1971, reissued, 1985.
Goda goda: Dikter (title means "Good, Good: Poems"), Raben & Sjoegren, 1971, new edition, 1976.
Nu aer vi gorillor laassas vi, Raben & Sjoegren, 1971, translation by Suzanne Carlson published as *Let's Be Gorillas!,* illustrated by Susan Acker, Clamshell Press, 1976.
Vaerldshemligt (title means "World Secret"), Raben & Sjoegren, 1972, 4th edition, 1979.
Alban: Popmuffa foer smaa hunder (title means "Alban: A Muff Hat for Small Dogs"), Raben & Sjoegren, 1972, translation by Joan Tate published as *Alban,* A. & C. Black (London), 1974.
Bladen brinner (title means "Burning Pages"), Raben & Sjoegren, 1973, new edition, 1978.
Groengoelingen aer paa vaeg: Dikter foer barn och andra (title means "The Green Woodpecker Is on His Way: Poems for Children and Others"), illustrated by Katarina Olausson, Raben & Sjoegren, 1974, reissued, 1980.
Babros pjaeser foer barn och andra (title means "Barbro's Plays for Kids and Others"), Raben & Sjoegren, 1975, new edition, 1978.
Lilla Sparvel (title means "Little Sparrow"), illustrated by Andreas Lindgren and Mathias Lindgren, Raben & Sjoegren, 1976.
Vad tycker du? (title means "What Do You Think?"), Liber, 1976.
Stora Sparvel (title means "Big Sparrow"), Raben & Sjoegren, 1977.
(With L. Westman) *Hemliga laadans hemlighet* (title means "The Secret Box's Secrets"), Liber, 1978.
(With Westman) *Jag har en tam myra* (title means "I Have a Tame Aunt"), Liber, 1978.

(With Westman) *Kom ner fraan traedet* (title means "Come Down from the Tree"), Liber, 1978.

(With Westman) *Var aer mina byxor?* (title means "Where Are My Pants?"), Liber, 1978.

(With Westman) *Vaerldens laengsta korv* (title means "The World's Longest Hot Dog"), Liber, 1978.

(With Westman) *Laesa med varandra* (title means "Reading with Each Other"), Liber, 1978.

Garderobsbio (title means "The Movie Closet"), Raben & Sjoegren, 1978.

Bara Sparvel (title means "Only the Sparrow"), Raben & Sjoegren, 1979.

Sagan om den lilla farbrorn (title means "Story about a Little Man"), illustrated by Eva Eriksson, Raben & Sjoegren, 1979, reissued, 1985, translated by Steven T. Murray published as *The Story of the Little Old Man*, R & S Books, 1992.

Nils Pantaloni Penell, Raben & Sjoegren, 1980.

Fotograf Jag (title means "Me, the Photographer"), Liber, 1980.

Mamman och den vilda bebin, illustrated by E. Eriksson, Raben & Sjoegren, 1980, published as *The Wild Baby*, adapted from the Swedish by Jack Prelutsky, Greenwillow, 1981.

Den vilda bebiresan, illustrated by E. Eriksson, Raben & Sjoegren, 1982, published as *The Wild Baby Goes to Sea*, adapted from the Swedish by J. Prelutsky, Greenwillow, 1983, large print edition, Greenwillow, 1983, translation by Alison Winn published as *The Wild Baby's Boat Trip*, Hodder & Stoughton (London), 1983.

Max nalle, illustrated by E. Eriksson, Raben & Sjoegren, 1981, published as *Sam's Teddy Bear*, Morrow, 1982, published as *Sam's Teddy*, Methuen (London), 1984.

Max bil, illustrated by E. Eriksson, Raben & Sjoegren, 1981, published as *Sam's Car*, Morrow, 1982.

Max kaka, illustrated by E. Eriksson, Raben & Sjoegren, 1981, published as *Sam's Cookie*, Morrow, 1982, published as *Sam's Biscuit*, Methuen (London), 1984.

Max boll, illustrated by E. Eriksson, Raben & Sjoegren, 1982, published as *Sam's Ball*, Morrow, 1983.

Max lampa, illustrated by E. Eriksson, Raben & Sjoegren, 1982, published as *Sam's Lamp*, Morrow, 1983, published in England as *Bad Sam!*, Methuen, 1983.

Max balja, illustrated by E. Eriksson, Raben & Sjoegren, 1982, published as *Sam's Bath*, Morrow, 1983.

OBS! Viktigt! (title means "Please Note! Important"), illustrated by Dan Jonsson, Liber, 1983.

Sagan om Karlknut, illustrated by Cecilla Torudd, Raben & Sjoegren, 1985, published as *A Worm's Tale*, Farrar, 1988.

Vilda bebin far en hund, illustrated by E. Eriksson, Raben & Sjoegren, 1985, translation by A. Winn published as *The Wild Baby's Dog*, Hodder & Stoughton, 1986, published as *The Wild Baby Gets a Puppy*, adapted from the Swedish by J. Prelutsky, Greenwillow, 1988.

Max potta, illustrated by E. Eriksson, Raben & Sjoegren, 1986, published as *Sam's Potty*, Morrow, 1986.

Max dockvagn, illustrated by E. Eriksson, Raben & Sjoegren, 1986, published as *Sam's Wagon*, Morrow, 1986, published as *Sam's Cart*, Methuen, 1986.

Vems lilla moessa flyger, illustrated by E. Eriksson, Raben & Sjoegren, 1987.

Pellerell, illustrated by Johannes Schneider, Raben & Sjoegren, 1987.

Sunkan flyger, illustrated by Olof Landstrom, Raben & Sjoegren, 1989, translated by Richard Fisher published as *Shorty Takes Off*, R & S Books, 1990.

Korken flyger, illustrated by E. Eriksson, Raben & Sjoegren, 1990.

Stackars Alan, illustrated by Sven Nordqvist, Eriksson & Lindgren, 1990.

Pojken och stjarnan, illustrated by Anna-Clara Tidholm, Eriksson & Lindgren, 1991.

Titta Max grav, illustrated by E. Eriksson, Eriksson & Lindgren, 1991.

Jam Jam Ib-Ib, illustrated by Madeleine Pyk, Eriksson & Lindgren, 1992.

Stora syster lilla bror, illustrated by E. Eriksson, Eriksson & Lindgren, 1992.

Bra Borje, illustrated by Pija Lindenbaum, Raben & Sjogren, published as *Louie*, R & S Books, 1994.

Gomorron Gud, illustrated by M. Pyk, Eriksson & Lindgren, 1994.

Har ar det lilla huset, illustrated by E. Eriksson, Eriksson & Lindgren, 1994.

Max Napp, illustrated by E. Eriksson, Raben & Sjoegren, 1994.

Max Bloja, illustrated by E. Eriksson, Raben & Sjoegren, 1994.

Svempa vill ha manga nappar, illustrated by Fibben Hald, Eriksson & Lindgren, 1995.

Lilla lokomotivet Rosa, illustrated by E. Eriksson, Eriksson & Lindgren, published as *Rosa: Perpetual Motion Machine*, Publishers Group West, 1996.

Rosa flytta till stan, illustrated by E. Eriksson, Eriksson & Lindgren, 1996, translated by Jennifer Hawkins published as *Rosa Moves to Town*, Groundwood Books, 1997.

Nu ar vi gorillor, illustrated by Anna Hoglund, Eriksson & Lindgren, 1997.

Nu ar vi jobbarkaniner, illustrated by A. Hoglund, Eriksson & Lindgren, 1997.

Andrejs langtan, illustrated by E. Eriksson, Raben & Sjoegren, 1997, published as *Andrei's Search*, R & S Books, 2000.

Namen Benny, illustrated by O. Landstrom, Raben & Sjoegren, 1998, published as *Benny's Had Enough!*, R & S Books, 1999.

Per och Pompe, illustrated by E. Eriksson, Eriksson & Lindgren, 1998.

Rosa pa dagis, illustrated by E. Eriksson, Eriksson & Lindgren, 1999, published as *Rosa Goes to Daycare*, Groundwood Books, 2000.

Angeln Gunnar dimper ner, illustrated by Charlotte Ramel, Eriksson & Lindgren, 2000.

FOR ADULTS

Genom ventilerna (title means "Through the Ventilators"), Bonnier (Stockholm), 1967.

Felipe, Bonnier, 1970.

Eldvin (title means "Winefire"), Bonnier, 1972.

Molnens broeder (title means "The Celestial Brothers"), Bonnier, 1975.

Rapporter fraan marken: Dikter (title means "Reports from the Land: Poems"), Raben & Sjoegren, 1976.

Det riktiga havet (title means "The Real Ocean"), Bonnier, 1979.

En liten cyklist (title means "The Little Cyclist"), Raben & Sjoegren, 1982.

Elegi oever en doed raatta (poems; title means "Elegy Over a Dead Rat"), Raben & Sjoegren, 1983.

Hunden med rocken: prosadikter (title means "The Dog with the Overcoat: Prose and Poems"), Raben & Sjoegren, 1985.

Vitkind. I ett barns hjaerta (roman), hoesten (novel), Raben & Sjoegren, 1986.

Nu aer du mitt barn, illustrated by Katarina Olausson Saell, Raben & Sjoegren, 1988.

Jag sajer bara Elitchoklad, Raben & Sjoegren, 1993.

Kungsholmens Ros, Alfabeta, 1995.

Rosa pa bal, Alfabeta, 1997.

OTHER:

Loranga, Masarin och Dartanjang (CD-ROM), music by Mathias Lindgren and Andreas Lindgren, Rabenforlagen, 1997.

Also composed lyrics for *Goda Goda* (music by Jojje Wadenius); *Nu sjunger naktergalen* (music by Georg Riedel); and *Lilla ungen min* (music by Riedel).

Adaptations

"The Wild Baby" was adapted by Random House into a filmstrip.

Sidelights

"You have to experience sorrow and passion to be able to write well," asserted Barbro Lindgren in an interview with Marit Andersson in *Femina.* The author of many children's books, as well as books for young adults and adults, Lindgren draws stories from life experiences in which she describes the "unique" with understanding, sensitivity, love, and much humor. Lindgren has a clear recollection of her childhood, and in particular "the sounds, the scents, the feeling of security when you squeezed somebody's hand, the fear of dark corners. I recall this with happiness, sadness, and anxiety," the author told Lena Rydin in *Vi foraeldrar.* "My childhood was traumatic. There weren't any horrendous happenings causing this, rather, the insignificant treacherous moments.

"I was afraid of everything when I was little," Lindgren continued in the same source. "Some homes seemed unsafe to me, and I didn't want to stay in them, especially overnight. Some people seemed insecure and I didn't want to stay with them. I was scared of everything new. When my mother left me at nursery school for the first time, I huddled in the corner and stayed there until she returned. After that I didn't want to return to the school. Quite often thereafter when I attended my first class in anything, I never returned. At the same time I was also very curious and eager to learn."

Barbro Lindgren

"I [also] experienced childhood as an adventure. I had much freedom to make my own friends and to investigate the world on my own," Lindgren told Birgitta Fransson in *Opsis Kalopsis.* As it is with all children, school eventually became a reality for Lindgren as well. Her impressions were most vividly revealed in her *Jaettehemligt:* "Now I have been in school for a week, the fall is approaching more each day. The leaves are falling and you can smell smoke outside. I feel so sad inside and I don't know why, but it feels like I never want to laugh again. I think it began yesterday. I was sitting in the rear of the classroom, watching leaves fly through the window. The teacher was lecturing and suddenly there was a flock of blackbirds flying by.

"Thereafter it seemed I saw the classroom for the first time; how small it was, and how hopeless it seemed with the rasping sound from the pencils while everyone sighed. And I thought: here I must sit for the rest of my life, until I'm eighteen years old and study and listen to the blackbirds chirp! Then everything truly seemed hopeless. I couldn't stay there. I got up and started walking towards the door," Lindgren recounted to Fransson.

"I was afraid of death more than anything else. I was terrified that someone in my family would die and leave me. 'Don't bicycle so close to the edge!' I would scream at my parents when we were riding close to the edge of a pier. On a boat trip with my grandparents, I was convinced we would never reach the island alive. I was equally scared when I had my own family, worried something would happen to them, and was especially frightened when my children were ill. I was frightened to take their temperature when I knew they were burning up. If they were gone for too long, I would worry myself sick about cars, about them falling into wells. I was probably too worrisome to have a family in the first place. I have done a lot of writing about death, to get to know it and to bring it closer to life.

"I grew up during the 1940s, and I now meet women who seem to deal with the same feelings and conflicts. At that time adults were caught between their own upbringing which was very strict, highly moral with a heavy demand on obedience and the new thinking about a more liberal upbringing. So, they didn't know on which leg to stand. Just the same, this kind of upbringing produced a lot of 'split' children and I am one of them," the author told Rydin.

Lindgren's writings began in her childhood diaries. "I wanted to be famous at any price—to be a child genius on the front page of newspapers was my grandest dream. I submitted fairy tales to newspapers and publishers, but my work was rejected. One day when I was thirteen years old, however, *Daily News* printed one of my stories on the children's page. A great moment.

"The years rolled on and my writing slowed. A few more stories were published but things eventually came to a halt. I decided, instead, to concentrate more on drawing and painting and attended art school for four years, where I met the man I eventually married. I worked a few years in advertising and layouts. I tried writing again, but was again unsuccessful and stopped altogether. My writing was superficial. It was not until I realized that I must write about things with which I am familiar, drawing from my own experiences, that my writing took shape.

"Astrid Lindgren (no relationship) gave me some sound advice after reading my stories: 'Do not use too many characters—one or two is enough. Keep your characterizations shorter! It's enough to use a brief description here or there. Reduce excessive action which becomes exhausting for the reader. Instead, allow the story to build slowly to a climax and then let it slowly subside.'"

The following year *Mattias sommar* was published. Lindgren's first effort was autobiographical. "I really don't try to make up too much. I feel that real life is exciting enough." Her childhood is the subject of *Lilla Sparvel, Stora Sparvel, Bara Sparvel, Jaettehemligt, Vaerldshemligt,* and *Bladen brinner.* Her childhood reading habits were recounted in *The Key to My Childhood,* the conception of an editor at Bromberg's. "She suggested that I try to recollect which specific books I had read as a child and gather them all together with my own comments.

"I have tried to remember the very first stories. The ones I had heard before I started school.

"All children are drawn to fright, it's always been that way," Lindgren told Helena Ridelberg in *Foerfattarportratt,* as she recalled the part in *The Cat Trip* where the cat splits in two. "That was the worse thing I had experienced at three years old. But when the gruesome becomes pleasurable and deep inside you have the feeling that all will be fine (in this case the cat is sewn

back together at the bottom of the same page) then it becomes palatable."

After Lindgren's first books were published, she traveled to schools to discuss her writing. "I then noticed that what I thought was important when I grew up was, in fact, just as important now. We talked about life and death, sorrow and birth, sex and about being different—such things as I would have liked to have read as a child. So I went home and wrote about my experiences: about all those difficult things in life," Lindgren told Ridelberg.

"I identify with people who are at a disadvantage. Those who are oppressed. I react with fury towards injustice—people who are treated unfairly in the workplace and people who misuse their power," Lindgren told Ann Rudberg in *Vi maenskor.* "I have a longing to write and work with language. If children experience some relief in reading my books, it makes me happy. I pull together things that are burdensome and thorny and I peel away idyll, because that doesn't interest me .... I like to describe the best relationships between people, warm and friendly, but deep."

Lindgren's books deal with all ages from babies to pensioners and have a readership across the spectrum as well. "It's fun to change, it keeps things from becoming monotonous. You don't stiffen up and it's fun to improve oneself. I want to write in simple terms for all, but in the adult books I can include linguistic difficulties and such things that children have not acquired through experience and consequently don't understand. At the same time it's fun to write for children in an artistic way. Adult books require more nuances," Lindgren told Fransson.

Lindgren's personality is well-suited for the life of an author, but she feels slightly uneasy about the solitary nature that is demanded. "I liked being alone as a child. It seemed to make me strong. As an adult, however it has become a negative escape. I only had fun when I was alone in my own little fantasy world. Quite often I would become depressed and apathetic. On those days I refrained from making phone calls and talking with anyone. The wrong word would make me brood for months. I easily misunderstood a conversation and would become hurt because I was so focused on my own interests, not understanding the other person's situation.

"When there are many things that are not cleared up within you, you tend to feel insecure and fatalistic. I found it easier at those times to be with other children instead of my own. My own made too many demands on me," Lindgren told Rydin. Lindgren had to learn to deal with her anger, as well, which she regarded as a burden of her guilt. She recalled the day she became enraged because her children would not clean up after themselves. She flung open a window and threw all of their toys into the snow. The toys stayed outside in the snow for a few days. Later, Lindgren herself picked them all up. This genuine anger, she recalled, was deep within her. Psychoanalysis was the key that helped her unlock all of these disturbing feelings.

"I've become more and more anti-social through the years. I don't behave the way I *should* and I don't fit in at social gatherings. Once I attended a party for authors held by a publisher. I couldn't stand the crowd, so I decided to sit behind the switchboard alone," Lindgren told Rudberg. "'If anyone would like to talk to me, please tell them that I'll be sitting behind the switchboard,' I said. Food was delivered to me there. I didn't dare join the crowd and be friendly.

"Most people would behave that way if they had been used to a great deal of freedom. I have to be alone to be able to experience my freedom, or be with someone I know very well who feels the same way.

"I have to feel completely free when I start writing a book. I have a starting point after which I don't know where it will lead. Suddenly there will be twists and turns I had never thought of before. That is fun and adventure."

Lindgren's thrust in her writings is the search for elemental truth, she told Fransson. "Towards the origin, towards the 'seed' is what we all strive for. This is not easy, because we are not always honest with ourselves. Then we must start all over, like rolling yarn into a ball. It is too easy to be influenced by trends. At least I think that was the case when I was younger. Now it's easier for me to be truthful and as such I always have to be obstinate. I need tranquility and reflection .... I find tranquility in nature."

"There are certain of my books for which I have special feelings: *Felipe, Eldvin* and *Molnens broeder*. I wrote them in my own way with slowly evolving illustrations, where language and pictures blend.

"Writing captures everything for me: music, art, photography," Lindgren told Ridelberg. "What I may wish to paint, I instead translate into words. I can express myself more subtly with words, although nothing moves me as deeply as music. Mozart, Mahler, Pettersson. But I can always *listen* to music. I don't have to play it myself."

Lindgren's familiarity with feelings of loneliness and her trust that children are capable of taking an interest in a world that is not idyllic are at the heart of the picture book *The Story of the Little Old Man*. Here, the author tells the story of an old man who has no friends in the town until one day a dog befriends him, and he is finally happy. Then, the dog makes friends with a little girl, and the old man's heart is broken until he is made to realize that they can all be friends together. It's "an offbeat story," that exhibits the author's "droll humor," according to Carolyn Phelan in *Booklist*. *School Library Journal* contributor Rita Soltan called this "a simple yet profound story about an old man's search for companionship."

For *The Story of the Little Old Man,* Lindgren teamed up with illustrator Eva Eriksson, a partnership that had yielded a successful series of board books about a little boy named Sam. The team paired up again for *Rosa: Perpetual Motion Machine,* which tells the story of a puppy's young life as she chews on everything in sight, digs holes, and runs away when she is taken for a walk. Whether or not readers will find Rosa's antics humorous depends on their relationship with dogs, contended Susan Dove Lempke in *Booklist,* who nevertheless stated that "Lindgren captures the puppy stage with zesty humor." Joanne Schott remarked: "Anyone who has ever brought home a new puppy will know the non-stop Rosa is barely exaggerated." Readers learn more about Rosa in *Rosa Moves to Town,* which focuses on the young dog's adventures with eating everything in sight, including items that cause her to be taken to the hospital. "Lindgren renders the entire piece from a dog's view," remarked a critic for *Kirkus Reviews.*

Lindgren's offbeat sense of humor is the showcase in another picture book story, *Shorty Takes Off,* in which a little boy is so resentful of his short stature that he wishes he could grow wings and fly high above his world. When he wakes up one day to find his wish has come true, he promptly flies away for the day, finding the cat that ran away and a lost soccer ball, and coming home exhausted for dinner. Shorty's wings disappear as he grows up, and he eventually becomes a rock star.

Biographical and Critical Sources

PERIODICALS

Booklist, December 1, 1992, Carolyn Phelan, review of *The Story of the Little Old Man,* p. 680; June 1, 1996, Susan Dove Lempke, review of *Rosa: Perpetual Motion Machine,* pp. 1734-35.

Femina, September, 1981, Marit Andersson, "Barbro Lindgren: Man maaste ha upplevt sorg och passion foer att skriva bra."

Foerfattarportratt, March, 1986, Helena Ridelberg, "Barbro Lindgren: Jag aer en typisk bakvaegsmaenniska."

Horn Book Guide, July, 1990, review of *Shorty Takes Off.*

Kirkus Reviews, March 1, 1997, review of *Rosa Moves to Town,* p. 384.

Opsis Kalopsis, February, 1988, Birgitta Fransson, "Barbro Lindgren: Ocksaa en cyklist."

Publishers Weekly, October 12, 1990, review of *Shorty Takes Off,* p. 63.

Quill & Quire, March, 1996, Joanne Schott, review of *Rosa: Perpetual Motion Machine,* p. 76.

School Library Journal, February, 1993, Rita Soltan, review of *The Story of the Little Old Man,* pp. 75-76; July, 1996, Kathy Piehl, review of *Rosa: Perpetual Motion Machine,* p. 68.

Vaar bostad, 1986, Annika Rosell, "Barbro Lindgren: Bakom idyllen lurar moerkret."

Vi foraeldrar, 1977, Lena Rydin, "Minns du din barndom?" (amended by B. Lindgren).

Vi maenskor, 1982, Ann Rudberg, "Barbro Lindgren, Nu goer jag bara det jag vill!"

LOFO
See HEIMANN, Rolf

*   *   *

LONG, Sylvia 1948-

Personal

Born September 29, 1948, in Ithaca, NY; daughter of Frank J. Jr. (a soil scientist) and Marion (a homemaker; maiden name, Lyman) Carlisle; married Thomas Wayne Long (a physician), June 20, 1970; children: Matthew Thomas, John Charles. *Education:* Maryland Institute of Art, B.F.A., 1970. *Hobbies and other interests:* Bird-watching, jogging, filmgoing, hiking, country dancing.

Addresses

Office—c/o Chronicle Books, 85 2nd St., 6th Floor, San Francisco, CA 94105.

Career

Illustrator of books for children. *Exhibitions:* Long is represented by Suzanne Brown Galleries (Scottsdale, AZ), Elizabeth Stone Gallery (Birmingham, MI), and Every Picture Tells a Story (Los Angeles, CA). *Member:* Society of Children's Book Writers and Illustrators.

Awards, Honors

International Reading Association Children's Book Award, 1991, and California Book Award, both for *Ten Little Rabbits; Alejandro's Gift* was named a Reading Rainbow Book and bestowed with the CLASP award and Best Book of the Year for Latin American Studies; *Hawk Hill* was named a notable book of 1996 by *Smithsonian* magazine; *Hush Little Baby* was named one of *Child* magazine's best books for children of 1997; Reading Magic Award, *Parenting* magazine, 1999, for *Bugs for Lunch.*

Writings

Hush Little Baby, Chronicle Books, 1997.
My Baby Journal, Chronicle Books, 1998.
Sylvia Long's Mother Goose, Chronicle Books, 1999.
Deck the Hall, Chronicle Books, 2000.

ILLUSTRATOR

Virginia Grossman, *Ten Little Rabbits,* Chronicle Books, 1991.
Oliver Herford, *The Most Timid in the Land,* Chronicle Books, 1992.
Jonathan London, reteller, with Lanny Pinola, *Fire Race: A Karuk Coyote Tale,* Chronicle Books, 1993.
London, *Liplap's Wish,* Chronicle Books, 1994.
Richard E. Albert, *Alejandro's Gift,* Chronicle Books, 1994.

Sylvia Long

Matthew Long and Thomas Long, *Any Bear Can Wear Glasses: The Spectacled Bear and Other Curious Creatures,* Chronicle Books, 1995.
Suzie Gilbert, *Hawk Hill,* Chronicle Books, 1996.
Margery Facklam, *Bugs for Lunch,* Charlesbridge Publishing, 1999.

Some of the books Long has illustrated have been translated into French, German, Japanese, and Korean.

Work in Progress

Twinkle, Twinkle Little Star, for Chronicle Books, 2001.

Sidelights

Sylvia Long is an award-winning illustrator of several children's books, and both author and illustrator for several picture books for preschoolers. An established painter as well, Long has earned praise for her charming depictions of personality-rich animals, particularly rabbits, with which her readership can identify. "My passion headed toward children's books," she told Stephanie Balzer in the *Phoenix Business Journal* about her career shift into children's literature. "I feel like I can make a greater contribution that way."

After earning a degree from the Maryland Institute of Art, Long forged a successful career as a painter while married and raising two sons. As she told *SATA:* "During a relatively successful career as a fine artist, I created a children's book with a friend, just for fun.

Some years later, it was published and I found I had the opportunity to illustrate additional books for children, which became my primary interest." That work was Virginia Grossman's *Ten Little Rabbits,* published by Chronicle Books in 1991. A simple counting book, it featured rabbits costumed in Native American dress, and a new one appears on each page to create the educational aspect. The bunnies take part in traditional Native American rituals and subsistence activities. A *Publishers Weekly* review found *Ten Little Rabbits* in possession of "an unusual—and effective—balance between the real and the imaginary."

Long next illustrated a book by Oliver Herford, *The Most Timid in the Land,* which was a retelling of the poem "A Bunny Romance" that dated back to the early 1900s. Its story, set in a medieval realm, revolves around the rabbit Princess Bunita, whose kingly father has offered the hand of his daughter to the suitor who proves himself "the most timid in the land." All the eligible bachelor hares strive to outdo one another and, appropriately enough, when the day of the contest arrives, all flee in fear. The wise Princess Bunita waits for one to return. A *Publishers Weekly* review found that the "delightfully expressive faces" of the rabbits, combined with their "imaginative antics ... make this a splendid visual treat."

In 1993, Long provided the artwork for *Fire Race: A Karuk Coyote Tale,* a Native American myth retold by Jonathan London and Lanny Pinola. Here, a Northern California band of animals freeze because they do not yet know how to create fire. The mean Yellow Jacket sisters keep a vital flame to themselves on a mountaintop, and Coyote, the clever trickster, devises a plan to steal some of it from them. He sneaks about, pilfers a burning piece of oak, and is chased by the sisters. But the allied animals thwart their path, and the ember makes it to animals' land safely, where it is swallowed by willow tree. "Long creates impressively realistic animal characters with an inventive measure of whimsy," stated a *Publishers Weekly* review.

Alejandro's Gift, a story for readers aged six to ten from Richard E. Albert that Long illustrated for 1994 publication, won an award for Best Book of the Year for Latin American Studies. The title character is a solitary older man who lives in an adobe house out in the desert. Lonely, he tends to his gardens, with his burro as his sole friend. One day, a squirrel appears in Alejandro's garden and drinks from the furrows, or irrigation ditches; soon, a host of other creatures follow suit. At first welcoming of the intrusion, Alejandro then sees that they are there only for the water, not for his company, and so he digs a larger water hole for them, hoping that even larger creatures will come. When they fail to appear, he realizes that it was dug too close to the road, and so he digs it for them again, this time in a quieter spot. A lesson in the desert ecosystem is embedded within Albert's text, and Long's "polished paintings ... impressively recreate the muted colors and varied textures of the desert," observed a *Publishers Weekly* review. Graciela Italiano, reviewing the book for *School*

Library Journal, found that "Long's rich, detailed, and realistically rendered pictures provide the perfect visual setting" for Albert's empathetic story.

Long returned to the rabbit world with her illustrations for another work by London, *Liplap's Wish,* published in 1994. The title bunny builds a "snowbunny" when the first snow of the season arrives, but feeling sad over the passing of his grandmother, he gives the snowbunny a sad expression. That night, his mother tells him a bedtime story of how the first rabbits became stars that watch over the world below. They pick out a star that might be Liplap's departed grandmother, and when he arises the next day in a more optimistic mood, he replaces his snowbunny's frown with a carrot smile. The drawings here, wrote Martha Gordon in *School Library Journal,* "reflect the poignancy of the tale with soft colors and thoughtful expressions" on the faces of Liplap, his mother, and the others involved. The combination of Long's artwork and "London's impressively visual narrative," declared a *Publishers Weekly* review, "create an affecting work that will be especially meaningful to" readers who have recently lost a grandparent.

Long's son, Matthew, and her physician husband, Thomas Long, collaborated with her on a 1995 title, *Any Bear Can Wear Glasses: The Spectacled Bear and Other Curious Creatures.* Here, a host of animals with rather unusual names fill the pages, and help elementary-age readers learn about endangered species. The text states, for instance, that "any crab can make music" alongside an illustration of four crabs playing instruments, while the opposite page reads, "but there's only one fiddler

In Long's reworking of a classic lullaby, the bunny mother points out the wonders of nature at nightfall to her children, to remind them that it is time to retire for the day. (From Hush Little Baby, *written and illustrated by Long.)*

Margery Facklam's rhyming verse and Long's detailed illustrations describe the variety of animals, including human, that feast on bugs. (From Bugs for Lunch.*)*

crab." Long's images, noted Lisa Wu Stowe in *School Library Journal,* "do not sacrifice accuracy, even when being silly," and a *Publishers Weekly* review declared that the work's "lighthearted presentation successfully pulls youngsters into the crisply written text."

The instructive tale of Suzie Gilbert's *Hawk Hill,* published in 1996, was amplified by Long's skilled images of both birds and humans. The story, aimed at readers aged eight to ten, introduces a young boy, Pete, who finds his recent move with his family to a new town has yielded a certain despair for him. He loves birds of prey, however, and finds solace in watching a band of hawks circle a hilltop. One day, he comes across a hospital for injured birds run by a taciturn older woman named Mary. He begins helping out at the hospital, and learns much about these majestic creatures. Mary, despite her initial gruffness, becomes an important friend to Pete. Long's illustrations depict owls, falcons, osprey, and other birds of prey, but it was her images of Mary that *Booklist*'s Julie Corsaro commended. "Long presents a convincing physical portrait—wrinkles and all—of a compassionate elderly person," noted the critic.

Long's first solo work for young readers came in 1997 with *Hush Little Baby.* It was named one of *Child* magazine's best books for children of 1997, in part

because of its unique reworking of the classic children's nursery lullaby. Long found fault with the original, in which a mother promises a wealth of treats if her child will just fall asleep. In her text, Long's bunny mother substitutes the material goods for both natural wonders and more personal awards, like a song, or a shooting star. Across the pages, she points out the wonders of nature at nightfall to her children, to remind them that it is time to retire for the day. "Long's song is gracious," wrote a reviewer for *Publishers Weekly,* and her pictures "both soothing and diverting." *Kirkus Reviews* also praised the work, and mentioned Long's "trademark rabbits frequently depicted in warm embraces" as one of the book's charms.

Long also worked on, for 1999 publication, a title from Margery Facklam: *Bugs for Lunch.* Aimed at early readers, the rhyming verse describes the variety of animals that feast on bugs, such as bats, toads, other insects—and even a human—and which kinds they prefer. Long's illustrations show tarantulas, caterpillars, and their daily activities, as well as their natural foes. The artwork here, noted Kay Weisman for *Booklist,* "conveys a great deal of scientific information without ever appearing cluttered." Patricia Manning, writing in *School Library Journal,* termed it "an attractive, high-interest book with ... dramatic illustrations."

Long tackled the revision of a children's standard with her 1999 picture book, *Sylvia Long's Mother Goose.* Ink and watercolor drawings accompany the 82 verses from the original—but some have been reworked by Long to offer a more positive lesson. As she wrote in the book's introduction, she wanted to "make it unique," and to remove some of the scarier imagery in the traditional version. The approach won her laudatory reviews. In the Humpty Dumpty tale, for instance, the fall of this egg creature does not end with his complete destruction, but rather a duckling emerges from the cracked shell. When the bough breaks in another tale and sends a tree-tied cradle plummeting, a young bird is inspired to take his first solo flight. Patricia Pearl Dole, writing in *School Library Journal,* described Long's artwork here as "luminous" and "lively." A *Publishers Weekly* assessment declared that "Long conjures up winsome animal characters," and "links the rhymes inventively."

A resident of Scottsdale, Arizona, Long has shown her work at a gallery there and in previous cities. She told *SATA:* "I have been asked if it takes a lot of discipline to be self-employed, working in a studio in my home. For me, discipline is required to accomplish all the other responsibilities of life—laundry, cooking, etc.—rather than my work in the studio. I love what I do and don't think my life would change much if I won the lottery tomorrow."

Long hopes to bring her winsome, hugging bunnies to a wider audience with a line of furnishings for children's bedrooms and nurseries. As she told Balzer in the *Phoenix Business Journal,* Long believes the most rewarding part of her job is "making a difference. [For instance, w]hen I hear about or get a letter from someone who used the books as a vehicle for cuddling with their kids or made reading a special nightly ritual."

Biographical and Critical Sources

PERIODICALS

Booklist, April 15, 1994, Julie Corsaro, review of *Alejandro's Gift,* p. 1537; January 15, 1995, Janice Del Negro, review of *Liplap's Wish,* p. 937; November 1, 1996, J. Corsaro, review of *Hawk Hill,* p. 497; June 1, 1997, J. Corsaro, review of *Hush Little Baby,* p. 1708; February 1, 1999, Kay Weisman, review of *Bugs for Lunch,* p. 976.

Business Journal (Phoenix, AZ), December 3, 1999, Stephanie Balzer, "Picture Perfect," p. 21.

Child, December-January, 1998, Margot Slade, "Editor's Picks," p. 126.

Kirkus Reviews, March 15, 1997, review of *Hush Little Baby,* p. 464.

Parenting, December-January, 2000, "Reading Magic Awards," p. 94.

Publishers Weekly, February 8, 1991, review of *Ten Little Rabbits,* p. 56; April 13, 1992, review of *The Most Timid in the Land,* p. 52; April 19, 1993, review of *Fire Race,* p. 59; February 14, 1994, review of *Alejandro's Gift,* p. 87; October 3, 1994, review of *Liplap's Wish,* p. 68; October 30, 1995, review of *Any Bear Can Wear Glasses,* p. 60; October 7, 1996, review of *Hawk Hill,* p. 74; January 20, 1997, review of *Hush Little Baby,* p. 400; August 18, 1997, p. 29; January 11, 1999, review of *Bugs for Lunch,* p. 71; October 4, 1999, review of *Sylvia Long's Mother Goose,* p. 72.

School Library Journal, July, 1994, Graciela Italiano, review of *Alejandro's Gift,* p. 73; November, 1994, Martha Gordon, review of *Liplap's Wish,* p. 84; December, 1995, Lisa Wu Stowe, review of *Any Bear Can Wear Glasses,* p. 98; March, 1999, Patricia Manning, review of *Bugs for Lunch,* p. 192; December, 1999, Patricia Pearl Dole, review of *Sylvia Long's Mother Goose,* p. 122.

Skipping Stones, Autumn, 1994, review of *Fire Race,* p. 31.

M

MARLEY, Louise 1952-

Personal

Born August 15, 1952, in Ross, CA; daughter of Frank M. (a physician) and June (a teacher; maiden name, Bishop) Campbell; married Richard Marley (an engineer), August 31, 1975; children: Zachary Richard. *Education:* University of the Pacific, B.Mus.; University of Washington, Seattle, M.Mus. *Politics:* Independent. *Religion:* Roman Catholic.

Addresses

Agent—Peter Rubie Literary Agency, 240 West 35th St., New York, NY 10001. *E-mail*—LMarley@aol.com.

Career

Classical concert and opera singer in the Pacific Northwest for fifteen years; college music professor for eleven years; science fiction writer, 1995—.

Writings

SCIENCE FICTION NOVELS

Sing the Night, Ace Books (New York City), 1995.
Sing the Warmth, Ace Books, 1996.
Receive the Gift, Ace Books, 1997.
The Terrorists of Irustan, Ace Books, 1999.
The Glass Harmonica, Ace Books, 2000.

Work in Progress

Two novels, tentatively titled *Starhold* and *The Little Ones of Lan Shi.*

Sidelights

Louise Marley told *SATA:* "I'm intrigued by the fact that a significant number of my readers are young adults. This tells me as much about them, the readers, as it does about my work. All my books are adult novels. I think young adults want to read books in which the characters have ideals, have strong character, have discipline and ability and commitment. As a teacher (college level) for eleven years, I'm honored and delighted that my work appeals to such readers.

"An author can't, and mustn't, try to write to a specific audience. As with music, my other field, the artists must tell the stories that are theirs to tell, in voices that are uniquely theirs, and rejoice when their stories find a

Louise Marley

receptive audience. In my "Nevya" series, I wanted very much to write about just this, the drive of the artist to find his or her own path. Fortunately, Nevya is a fascinating place to be, and the characters and their interactions are great fun to watch. In *The Terrorists of Irustan* I wanted to tell the story of a strong woman in a repressed society where the strength of women is not valued; such a woman finds herself trapped by the very talents that make her unique. *The Glass Harmonica* is a story about musical prodigies and what their lives are like. Half of it takes place in the eighteenth century, a remarkable place to visit, and half in the very near future. There's a little mystery, a little secret, in the book, and I'm eager to see which of my readers will guess at it!

"Although not all my novels are musical, my musical life has a strong influence on my writing life. In years of musical study and experience, I learned about form, rhythm, color, pacing, the building and release of tension; these are all aspects of literary art as well as musical art. As an opera singer, I learned about character and scene and drama. What more could an author ask? I've been very lucky indeed."

Biographical and Critical Sources

PERIODICALS

Booklist, May 15, 1999, Karen Simonetti, review of *The Terrorists of Irustan,* p. 1682.
Kirkus Reviews, April 15, 1999, review of *The Terrorists of Irustan,* p. 580.
Kliatt Young Adult Paperback Book Guide, March, 1996, Karen S. Ellis, review of *Sing the Light,* p. 18; March, 1997, Susan Cromby, review of *Sing the Warmth,* pp. 18, 20; March, 1998, review of *Receive the Gift,* p. 19.
Publishers Weekly, May 24, 1999, review of *The Terrorists of Irustan,* p. 72.
Voice of Youth Advocates, February, 1998, Donna Scanlon, review of *Receive the Gift,* p. 394; April, 1998, review of *Receive the Gift,* p. 13.

*   *   *

MAY, Elaine T(yler) 1947-

Personal

Born September 17, 1947, in Los Angeles, CA; daughter of Edward T. (a physician) and Lillian (an art historian and family-planning educator; maiden name, Bass) Tyler; married Lary L. May (a historian and author), March 7, 1970; children: Michael Edward, Daniel David, Sarah Lillian May. *Education:* University of California, Los Angeles, A.B. (cum laude), 1969, M.A., 1970, Ph.D., 1975. *Politics:* Democrat. *Religion:* Jewish.

Addresses

Home—88 Arthur Ave. SE, Minneapolis, MN 55414. *Office*—American Studies Program, 104 Scott Hall,

University of Minnesota, Minneapolis, MN 55455. *E-mail*—mayxx002@umn.edu.

Career

U.S. Senate, Washington, D.C., research intern with Committee on Intergovernmental Relations, 1969; California State University, Fullerton, instructor in history, 1971-72; California State University, Los Angeles, instructor in history, 1972-73; Princeton University, Princeton, NJ, instructor, 1974-76, assistant professor of history, 1976-78; University of Minnesota, Minneapolis, assistant professor, 1978-81, associate professor of American studies, 1981-89, professor of American studies and history, 1989—, associate dean, College of Liberal Arts, 1987-92, chair, American studies program, 1992-96, member of women's studies governing council; Mary Ball Washington Professor of American History, University College, Dublin, 1996-97. Public speaker; humanities commentator for Minnesota Public Radio, 1981. *Member:* American Historical Association, Organization of American Historians, American Studies Association, American Association for the Advancement of the Humanities, National Organization for Women, Social Science History Association, Women Historians of the Midwest.

Awards, Honors

Research fellow at Princeton University, 1975-77, Princeton Inn fellow, 1976; Mellon Fellow at Harvard University, 1981-82; research scholar at Radcliffe College, 1982; American Council of Learned Societies fellowship, 1983-84; National Endowment for the Humanities grant, 1983, summer research stipend, 1983, travel-to-collections grant, 1984; Fulbright Distinguished Chair in Ireland, Rockefeller Foundation research grant, 1985-87; Bush Sabbatical Supplement Award, 1993-94; McKnight Research Award, 1993-96.

Writings

Great Expectations: Marriage and Divorce in Post-Victorian America, University of Chicago Press, 1980.
(Contributor) Michael Gordon, editor, *The American Family in Social-Historical Perspective,* 3rd edition, St. Martin's Press, 1983.
(Contributor) Stanley I. Kutler and Stanley N. Katz, editors, *The Promise of American History: Progress and Prospects,* John Hopkins University Press, 1983.
Homeward Bound: American Families in the Cold War Era, Basic Books, 1988.
(Contributor) Lary May, editor, *Recasting America: Culture and Politics in the Age of Cold War,* University of Chicago Press, 1989.
(Contributor) Steven Fraser and Gary Gerstle, editors *The Rise and Fall of New Deal Liberalism,* Princeton University Press, 1989.
Pushing the Limits: American Women, 1940-1961, Oxford University Press, 1994.
Barren in the Promised Land: Childless Americans and the Pursuit of Happiness, Basic Books, 1995.

(Editor, with Reinhold Wagnleitner) *Here, There, and Everywhere: The Foreign Politics of American Popular Culture,* University Press of New England, 2000.

Work in Progress

"Family Values": Politics and Private Life in Twentieth-Century America; Created Equal, a U.S. history textbook, with Peter Wood, Jacqueline Jones, Dan Usner, Vicki Ruiz, and Tim Borstelmann (Longman Press).

Sidelights

A scholar, historian, and professor of American studies at the University of Minnesota, Elaine T. May focuses her attention on the social fabric of the twentieth century, particularly as it relates to women. In addition to her books geared toward an academic readership, May has also authored *Pushing the Limits: American Women, 1940-1961.* Released in 1994, the book is part of "Young Oxford History of Women in the United States," a proposed ten-part series designed to "present ... American history with a social and cultural slant that emphasizes the roles of women," according to *Voice of Youth Advocates* contributor Florence H. Munat. Among the other volumes in the series is *Laborers for Liberty: American Women 1865-1890,* which focuses on the changing social landscape wrought by the industrialization of the northern United States.

Including such well-known women as Rosa Parks, Eleanor Roosevelt, and Rachel Carson, May's volume also explores the lives and contributions of many less well-known women between World War II and 1961. Middle-class, suburban housewives, abolitionists, suffragists, lawyers, immigrant women, prostitutes, migrant farm workers, and others are profiled, their lives brought to light through photographs, contemporary newspaper accounts, novels, letters, speeches, interviews, and other sources. "During the 1950s and the 1960s mom and apple pie were upbeat images," noted *Booklist* contributor Ilene Cooper, "but May does a fine job of chronicling the dark side of this phenomenon." The author "does not shirk tough issues such as lesbianism, abortion, the sexual double-standard, and racial discrimination" in her focus on women's changing role in both the workplace and society during this period, added Munat. Dubbing the volume "lively, fascinating, lucid, accessible, [and] balanced," a *Kirkus* reviewer called *Pushing the Limits* "a fine resource that belongs in every library."

May's interest in U.S. history emerged in 1968, while she was spending her junior year in college living in Tokyo, Japan. "I was taking courses in the history of Vietnam and the culture of Japan," she told *SATA,* "and planned to become an Asian Studies major. Along with many of my generation, I was thoroughly alienated from American government policies in Asia, and everything that the United States represented in the world. I tried very hard to shake my identity as an American. But it turned out to be impossible.

"Like it or not, I was an unwitting and unwilling representative of my country," May recalled. "My own personal background and experiences somehow linked me to American national identity. It did not matter that I protested against the Vietnam War, or that I demonstrated for Civil Rights. Everywhere I went, I faced the same questions: Why is your country fighting a war in Asia? Why are black people oppressed in your country, leader of the Free World? I began to realize that for all my opposition and political activism, I could not really answer those questions when my Japanese friends would confront me. I knew those things were true, but I did not really understand *why.* It became clear to me that I would never be able to understand another culture if I did not yet understand my own."

When May returned to the United States to complete her senior year at the University of California-Los Angeles, she enrolled in several courses in U.S. history. "By the time I graduated in the spring of 1969, all my plans had changed. I had been accepted to the Peace Corps in Madagascar, and I had also been offered a job in Japan as a guide at Expo '70, and the 1970 World's Fair. But I felt I had only just scratched the surface in my quest to comprehend the complexities of my own country. I decided that I was not yet well enough equipped to make a contribution abroad—first I needed a better understanding of what it meant to be an American." She scrapped her plans to go abroad and instead found a position as an intern in the U.S. Senate in Washington, D.C. "That experience convinced me that I would rather study the American political system than work in the midst of it," May recalled, "so I went straight into graduate school."

May recalled the 1970s as "heady years, politically and academically. Struggles for the rights of black Americans and other minorities, the rebirth of feminism, and the many movements for social justice fueled an explosion in the field of history, leading to the 'new social history' and many efforts to uncover and analyze the lives of ordinary Americans who had previously been left out of the historical record: women, immigrants, people of color, the working classes, the poor. It was a time when activists were discovering that 'the personal is political,' and I was discovering that, too. Coming of age and studying history at a time when the feminist movement was challenging time-honored assumptions about the proper roles and behaviors of women and men, I wondered why pundits and politicians blamed women's rights activists for destroying the family, and bringing down the nation with it. Eventually, it was the question of how the personal intersects with the political that sparked my curiosity, especially at a time when the very essence of American national identity seemed to be bound up with ideas about the family. That fundamental question has propelled most of my scholarly work since then."

Among May's other books is *Barren in the Promised Land: Childless Americans and the Pursuit of Happiness,* which she published in 1996. Focusing on the emotional, economic, and social aspects of childlessness from the seventeenth century to modern times, the volume "provides stimulating, even exciting, reading for sociologists, medical historians, feminists, and legal scholars," according to *Journal of the American Medical Association* contributor Jane E. Hodgson. The topic of infertility is of particular interest to May; her father, Edward Tyler, Jr., was a pioneer in infertility research during the 1950s.

Biographical and Critical Sources

PERIODICALS

Booklist, August, 1994, Ilene Cooper, review of *Pushing the Limits,* p. 2035; June 1, 1995, Patricia Hassler, review of *Barren in the Promised Land,* p. 1703.
Journal of the American Medical Association, February 21, 1996, Jane E. Hodgson, review of *Barren in the Promised Land,* p. 566.
Kirkus Reviews, January 1, 1994, review of *Pushing the Limits,* p. 72.
Voice of Youth Advocates, June, 1994, Florence H. Munat, review of *Pushing the Limits,* p. 111.
Women's Review of Books, October, 1995, review of *Barren in the Promised Land,* p. 21.

* * *

MITCHELL, B(etty) J(o) 1931-
(P. J. Pokeberry)

Personal

Born May 2, 1931, in Coin, IA; daughter of Edith McWilliams; married John Lewis Mitchell, 1951 (divorced, 1963). *Education:* Southwest Missouri State University, B.A.; University of Southern California, M.S., M.S.L.S.; American Management Association, certificate in business management; California Coast University, doctoral study; also attended University of California, Los Angeles. *Politics:* Democrat. *Religion:* "Mixed." *Hobbies and other interests:* Music, travel, hiking, painting.

Addresses

Home—PMB 400, 785 Tucker Rd., Suite G, Tehachapi, CA 93561.

Career

California State University, Northridge, assistant acquisitions librarian, 1967-69, assistant director for personnel and budget, 1969-71, associate director (dean) of libraries, 1971-81; Viewpoint Press, Tehachapi, CA, president, researcher, and writer, 1981-84; City of Santa Monica, CA, manager of information systems for city Rent Control Board, 1984-93; Viewpoint Press, president and writer, 1993—. Member of board of directors, San Fernando Valley Girl Scout Council, 1974-77, Empyrean Foundation, 1978-81, California State University, Northridge, Credit Union, 1978-81, BVS Town Forum, 1982, BVS Condo Owners Association, 1982-

B.J. Mitchell

83, and Tehachapi Community Orchestra, 1998—; Chamber of Commerce, member of planning group for Vision Hermosa, 1993-94; active in Democratic party politics. *Member:* Authors Guild, American Library Association, American Association of University Women, Association for Women in Computing (member of board of directors, 1987-89), Southwest Manuscripters, Book Publicists of Southern California.

Writings

(With Norman E. Tanis and Jack Jaffe) *Cost Analysis of Library Functions: A Total System Approach,* JAI Press (Greenwich, CT), 1978.
ALMS: A Budget Based Library Management System, JAI Press, 1983.
(With M. M. Dragoo) *How to See the U.S. on $12 a Day per Person, Double Occupancy,* illustrated by Danna Marshall Moore, Viewpoint Press (Tehachapi, CA), 1982.
(Under pseudonym P. J. Pokeberry) *The Secret of Hilhouse: An Adult Book for Teens,* illustrated by Peggy Mueller, Viewpoint Press, 1993.

Author of "Staff Development," a column in *Special Libraries,* 1975-76. Contributor to library journals.

Work in Progress

The Huckenpuck Papers: The Tale of a Family's Secrets and a Young Girl's Search for Self-Esteem; research on ethics for children and teenagers.

Sidelights

B. J. Mitchell told *SATA:* "I began my writing career late in life. After several years in cost accounting in Missouri, and following a divorce, I moved to California and earned the degree of Master of Science in Library Science from the University of Southern California. At that time there were few librarians with a background in business (particularly accounting), so immediately upon graduation I was appointed to the position of assistant director for personnel and finance at California State University, Northridge. This sparked a love of research and launched my writing career. While there, I developed a cost analysis program for libraries that eventually resulted in two library management books with an international distribution.

"Eventually, I began to write for the pleasure of writing instead of for the world of management. My love of travel led me on a ten-month trip around the United States and a book about how to travel on a shoestring. Reviewers were positive about the material presented in the book.

"The next book did not surface until several years later, and it was quite different. This book, titled *The Secret of Hilhouse,* was a fable that dealt with spiritual and values issues for young people. It was the first of a planned series dealing with the problems that children and teens face. It was written by P. J. Pokeberry, a 'possum that swings by her tail from tree limbs and peers into windows to observe the activities of humans. Once again, the reviews were positive.

"My interest in things spiritual resulted from some thought-provoking encounters with metaphysical phenomena and a deep friendship with a warm, loving, and very ethical psychic. Added to that mix were my undergraduate degree in the sciences and discussions with another friend who was deeply involved in the scientific aspects of spiritual thought. The decision to write from a spiritual perspective for a young readership came from memories of my own childhood questions that never seemed to be answered in a way that made sense to me. It was never enough for me to hear 'that's just the way it is.' I wanted to know *why* it was that way. That answer was rarely forthcoming. In *The Secret of Hilhouse,* I answer some of those nagging questions that all kids have. Why shouldn't I experiment with sex? Why shouldn't I drink alcohol? Why shouldn't I do this if all the other kids are doing it? What is God? If I ask God what to do, how do I know God is answering me? The answers are simple, but you have to think like a stubborn child to discover them.

"The first sequel to *The Secret of Hilhouse* is nearing the publication stage. Its title is *The Huckenpuck Papers: The Tale of a Family's Secrets and a Young Girl's Search for Self-Esteem.* The book deals with the difficult issues of family violence and teen pregnancy. The two are frequently related, and the lack of self-esteem often plays a major role in the pregnancy of young girls. This book presents a program that adults could put in place to help children deal with an abusive home environment. It also gives young girls a series of questions and answers to aid them in developing a healthy self-esteem.

"The series, to be titled 'Tree Limbs,' will continue to be written by 'possum P. J. Pokeberry, and it will be in fable format. The subject matter will remain focused on spiritual and ethical issues: the problems that all children (and most adults) face on a daily basis. The metaphysical frog Ribbit will continue to provide the wisdom of the universe, with Pokeberry adding her own particular brand of philosophy. Stay tuned."

Biographical and Critical Sources

PERIODICALS

American Reference Books Annual, Volume 10, 1979, G. Edward Evans, review of *Cost Analysis of Library Functions,* p. 128; Volume 15, 1984, H. Robert Malinowsky, review of *ALMS,* pp. 123-24.

Book Reader, summer, 1994, review of *The Secret of Hilhouse,* p. 29.

Library Quarterly, January, 1980, James Michalko, review of *Cost Analysis of Library Functions,* p. 155.

Portsmouth Herald, February 2, 1995, review of *The Secret of Hilhouse,* p. B1.

West Coast Review of Books, December, 1994, review of *The Secret of Hilhouse.*

Woman's Voice, December, 1994, review of *The Secret of Hilhouse,* p. 19.

* * *

MOSES, Will 1956-

Personal

Born January 7, 1956, in Cambridge, NY; son of Gerald Hugh (a farmer and machinist) and Lillian Elizabeth (a homemaker) Moses; married Sharon Andrew (a corporate administrator), October, 1977; children: Gerald, Lloyd, Georgianna. *Education:* Attended high school. *Politics:* "Free thinker." *Religion:* Protestant. *Hobbies and other interests:* Herbal studies, fishing, "giving advice."

Will Moses

Addresses

Home—58 Grandma Moses Rd., Eagle Bridge, NY 12057. *Office*—Mount Nebo Gallery, 60 Grandma Moses Rd., Eagle Bridge, NY 12057. *E-mail*—Will@ Willmoses.com.

Career

Mount Nebo Gallery, Eagle Bridge, NY, artist and publisher of art prints, cards, and posters, 1977—. Mount Nebo Farm, grower of livestock and Christmas trees and producer of maple syrup. Bennington Museum, member of board of directors, 1990—, chairperson of board, 1995-98; member of local town council, 1985-91; Mary McClellan Hospital, member of advisory board; Mary McClellan Foundation, member of board of directors.

Writings

(Reteller and illustrator) *The Legend of Sleepy Hollow* (based on the story by Washington Irving), Philomel Books (New York City), 1995.

(Author and illustrator) *Silent Night,* Philomel Books, 1997.

(Reteller and illustrator) *Rip Van Winkle* (based on the story by Irving), Philomel Books, 1999.

Work in Progress

Research on the life of John Chapman, for a book on Johnny Appleseed.

Sidelights

Will Moses told *SATA:* "I began painting when I was a little boy. My grandfather, Forest Moses, was a painter, as was my great-grandmother, Grandma Moses. My grandfather Forest had a studio nearby the home where I grew up, and naturally I spent a lot of time there painting with him. As a result, by the time I graduated from school I had been painting for quite a while and thought I would like to try to make a career out of art. I had been painting and publishing graphics for a number of years when the opportunity to illustrate and author children's books came along. This was not a line of work that I necessarily envisioned myself doing, but nevertheless it appealed to me. Having three children myself, I have had the opportunity to review many books for children. I found a wide range in terms of quality and subjects. I hope that my own books, which tend to be in the tradition of the illustrated storybook, will become family heirlooms, books which I hope will be read, kept, treasured, and handed down through the generations.

"I try to make books that I would want to read to my own kids. When I write or paint, I tend to be single-minded, focusing on the task at hand, bringing the book or painting through the creative process without too many deviations along the way. To date, I think my books seem to reflect traditional stories. I guess this is probably because of the association my art has with hearth and home values. I don't pay too much attention any more to what other authors and illustrators are doing. I don't want to be influenced by the work of others or possibly fall into doing what might be trendy at the moment. I do what I do. If people like it, and I hope they do, that's great."

Biographical and Critical Sources

PERIODICALS

Booklist, October 1, 1995, Carolyn Phelan, review of *The Legend of Sleepy Hollow,* p. 316; September 1, 1997, Ilene Cooper, review of *Silent Night,* p. 141A; November 1, 1999, Phelan, review of *Rip Van Winkle,* p. 530.

Children's Book Review Service, August, 1995, review of *The Legend of Sleepy Hollow,* p. 162.

Horn Book, March-April, 1996, Mary M. Burns, review of *The Legend of Sleepy Hollow,* p. 193.

Horn Book Guide, spring, 1996, review of *The Legend of Sleepy Hollow,* p. 56; spring, 1998, review of *Silent Night,* p. 63.

Kirkus Reviews, August 1, 1995, review of *The Legend of Sleepy Hollow,* p. 1112.

Publishers Weekly, July 24, 1995, review of *The Legend of Sleepy Hollow,* p. 65; October 6, 1997, review of *Silent Night,* p. 56.

Reading Teacher, November, 1998, review of *Silent Night,* p. 283.

School Library Journal, October, 1995, Kristin Lott, review of *The Legend of Sleepy Hollow,* p. 134; October, 1997, Jane Marino, review of *Silent Night,* p. 43; October, 1999, Ronald Jobe, review of *Rip Van Winkle,* p. 121.

*   *   *

MOSHER, Richard 1949-

Personal

Born April 24, 1949, in Mussoorie, India; immigrated to the United States; son of Arthur (a missionary) and Alice Wynne (Hall) Mosher; married Christine Tschida (a radio producer), 1996. *Education:* Antioch College, B.A. (elementary education), 1972. *Hobbies and other interests:* Travel, languages.

Addresses

Home—c/o Putnam Publishing Group, 345 Hudson St., New York, NY 10014.

Career

Worked as a tree trimmer in Bangor, ME, 1968, an auto worker in Detroit, MI, 1969, and a house builder in Brainerd, MN, 1972, and Menomonie, WI, 1972-73; Learning disabilities teacher in West Virginia, 1972-73; Chicago & Northwestern Railway, Minneapolis, MN, brakeman, 1973-78; cab driver in New York City, 1983-89; Grace Nursery School, Minneapolis, van driver for students, 1992-96; "The Writer's Almanac," St. Paul, MN, wrote scripts for entertainer Garrison Keillor, 1996-98; freelance writer.

Writings

The Taxi Navigator (young adult novel), Philomel (New York City), 1996.

Work in Progress

The Girl by the Water Gate, a novel.

Sidelights

Richard Mosher did not get a job driving a cab in order to use the experience in his fiction, but his first novel for young people does in fact include as a major character a New York City cab driver. *The Taxi Navigator,* aimed at middle-grade to junior high readers, tells the story of a nine year old named Kyle, who begins spending time with his cab-driving Uncle Hank when Kyle's parents become immersed in career and marital problems. One day Hank and Kyle meet Marcella, who calls herself a witch; she in turn introduces them to a girl named Ruby and to Ruby's mother, Lydia. The group becomes a sort of surrogate family for Kyle, a "delightfully off-center group," according to *Booklist* reviewer Ilene Cooper, "with a richness of spirit that will appeal to a wide age range." A *Publishers Weekly* reviewer offered similar praise for the novel, citing its emotional warmth and its "solemn and wise" core.

In an interview published online by the Putnam Berkley Group, Mosher explained that he did not draw heavily on real job experiences for *The Taxi Navigator.* "Kyle and the other characters are completely made-up," he noted, "as was most of the action." But he emphasized that the story is psychologically true. "During my years of cab-driving I did encounter enough children neglected by ambitious parents, and enough far-out oddballs, that I can promise you ... the fictional events of this story could easily have taken place in real life."

Though Hank is a fictional creation, he does share one characteristic with Mosher: he drifts from place to place and job to job. This, Mosher noted, is a strength, for it enables Hank to remain open to many different types of people. Mosher, too, has moved around a great deal and has worked at several different jobs. Born in India, he has lived in France, Costa Rica, Ireland, and the Dominican Republic. He has worked as a tree surgeon in Maine, an automobile worker in Michigan, a school teacher in West Virginia, and a house builder in Wisconsin and Minnesota. He drove a cab in New York City for five years, and worked as a brakeman on the Chicago & Northwestern Railroad. He relishes these experiences, he claims, because they buy him time to write, not because he's seeking raw material for his books. But in time, he says, the experiences do influence his writing.

Mosher feels *The Taxi Navigator* should appeal to adults as well as younger readers. Citing *The Wind in the Willows* as an example, he argues that "some of the most beautiful pieces of writing have been done for children." He told *SATA,* "My mother recently sent me a sample of some early writing of mine she'd come across in her lifetime of family boxes. In the blocky writing of a seven-year-old, I had laboriously penciled 'The Story of My Life,' which was as far as that attempt got—but clearly the impulse was in place. At twelve I extended it to actual hard work, taking the family typewriter into my tiny room and pecking away with one finger until I knocked out five stories—sixty pages in all—in two concentrated months of work. So I learned early that I had the stubbornness to be a writer, and I knew early that a kid has as much to say as anyone else, however frustrating his lack of tools or vocabulary.

"The writers who influence my work are the ones from whom I can feel 'the magic,' as F. Scott Fitzgerald called it, working. He was one it sometimes worked for and often didn't. Others among my favorites are Steinbeck (when he was young and not so serious), Graham Greene (almost always), Hemingway a good deal of the time, Willa Cather, Kenneth Grahame, Raymond Queneau, A. A. Milne, Flann O'Brien, Mikhail Bulgakov, Knut Hamsun, e. e. cummings, Edna O'Brien, and Philip Roth.

"My writing process is to wait until the well fills up—a process that can take months or years—then manage to free up a large block of time in which to write, and then *write,* every day, for as long as it feels fresh—sometimes two hours, sometimes seven—but best cut off sooner, especially when it feels brilliantly funny, which most often, on rereading, proves merely cute. When I have had things to say—enough things to comprise a real story—I've never felt blocked. I don't believe in the necessity of a writer writing every day, as is so often preached. When there's nothing to say, I contend, don't say it. When there *is,* get to work.

"My current work in progress is a novel in the voice of a nearly thirteen-year-old girl who lives in France and helps her grandfather run a lock in the canal system. It involves unconventional family relationships, racism, conflicting views on warfare, and a number of poems, short and long, written by the old man and granddaughter together, and then, as his brain fades, by her alone. I like to think of it as a modern fable about growing up in a complex world."

Biographical and Critical Sources

PERIODICALS

Booklist, September 15, 1996, Ilene Cooper, review of *The Taxi Navigator,* p. 242.
Children's Book Review Service, March, 1997, p. 95.
Horn Book Guide, spring, 1997, p. 72.
Kirkus Reviews, September 1, 1996, p. 1325.
Publishers Weekly, October 28, 1996, review of *The Taxi Navigator,* p. 82.
School Library Journal, January, 1997, p. 115.

MUNSCH, Robert N(orman) 1945-

Personal

Born June 11, 1945, in Pittsburgh, PA; emigrated to Canada; naturalized Canadian citizen, 1983; son of Thomas John (a lawyer) and Margaret (a homemaker; maiden name, McKeon) Munsch; married Ann Beeler (a university educator), January 22, 1973; children: Julie, Andrew, Tyya. *Education:* Studied for the Roman Catholic priesthood, Jesuit order, for seven years; Fordham University, B.A. (history), 1969; Boston University, M.A. (anthropology), 1971; Tufts University, M.Ed. (child studies), 1973. *Religion:* Raised Roman Catholic; currently listed in sources as both Unitarian Universalist and Agnostic. *Hobbies and other interests:* Reading, movies, geology, cycling, off-trail hiking.

Addresses

Office—Bob Munsch Enterprises, 15 Sharon Pl., Guelph, Ontario, Canada N1H 7V2.

Career

Author, storyteller, educator, and lecturer. Bay Area Childcare, Coos Bay, OR, teacher, 1973-75; University of Guelph, Guelph, Ontario, head teacher at Family Studies Laboratory Preschool and assistant professor, 1975-84. Full-time writer, 1984—. Founder of Bob Munsch Enterprises, Guelph, Ontario. Performer in storytelling concerts and at school visits, and speaker at keynote speaking engagements. *Member:* Association of Canadian Television and Radio Artists (ACTRA), Canadian Association of Children's Authors, Illustrators, and Performers, Writers Union of Canada.

Awards, Honors

Canada Council grant, 1982; Juno Award for best Canadian children's record, 1985, for *Murmel, Murmel, Munsch: More Outrageous Stories;* Ruth Schwartz Children's Book Award, Ontario Arts Council, 1986, and ELBA (Element Library Book Award), Grand Forks Public School, 1988, for *Thomas's Snowsuit;* Vicky Metcalf Award, 1987; North Dakota Children's Choice (Picture Book), 1989, and listed as the sixth of the top 100 favorite children's books as voted on by the members of the National Education Association, 1999, for *Love You Forever;* Author of the Year, Canadian Booksellers Association, 1991; Member of the Order of Canada, 1998; Arizona Young Readers Award, Arizona Library Association, 1999, for *Stephanie's Ponytail. The Paper Bag Princess* was named to the Greatest Books of the Century List, Vancouver Public Library, and was also named to the Cat-a-List for Reading by the National Education Association. *I Have to Go!* appeared on the Most Frequently Banned Books of the 1990s list.

Robert N. Munsch

Several of Munsch's books have been selected for the Children's Book Centre "Our Choice" lists of the Canadian Children's Books Festival and were designated Read America! Classics. In 1982 Canadian school children voted Munsch the writer that they would most like to visit their school during the National Book Festival.

Writings

FOR CHILDREN; PICTURE BOOKS

The Mud Puddle, illustrated by Sami Suomalainen, Annick Press (Toronto), 1979, revised edition, 1986.

The Dark, illustrated by Sami Suomalainen, Annick Press, 1979, revised edition, 1991, new edition illustrated by Michael Martchenko, 1997.

The Paper Bag Princess (also see below), illustrated by Michael Martchenko, Annick Press, 1980.

Jonathan Cleaned Up, Then He Heard a Sound; or, Blackberry Subway Jam (also see below), illustrated by Michael Martchenko, Annick Press, 1981.

The Boy in the Drawer, illustrated by Michael Martchenko, Annick Press, 1982.

Murmel, Murmel, Murmel (also see below), illustrated by Michael Martchenko, Annick Press, 1982.

Angela's Airplane (also see below), illustrated by Michael Martchenko, Annick Press, 1983.

David's Father (also see below), illustrated by Michael Martchenko, Annick Press, 1983.

The Fire Station (also see below), illustrated by Michael Martchenko, Annick Press, 1983.

Mortimer (also see below), illustrated by Michael Martchenko, Annick Press, 1983.

Millicent and the Wind, illustrated by Suzanne Duranceau, Annick Press, 1984.

Thomas's Snowsuit (also see below), illustrated by Michael Martchenko, Annick Press, 1985.

50 Below Zero, illustrated by Michael Martchenko, Annick Press, 1985.

I Have to Go! (also see below), illustrated by Michael Martchenko, Annick Press, 1986.

Love You Forever, illustrated by Sheila McGraw, Firefly Books (Scarborough, Ontario), 1986.

Moira's Birthday, illustrated by Michael Martchenko, Firefly Books, 1987.

(With Michael Kusugak) *A Promise Is a Promise* (also see below), illustrated by Vladyana Krykorka, Annick Press, 1988.

Pigs, illustrated by Michael Martchenko, Annick Press, 1989.

Giant; or, Waiting for the Thursday Boat, illustrated by Gilles Tibo, Annick Press, 1989.

Something Good (also see below), illustrated by Michael Martchenko, Annick Press, 1990.

Good Families Don't, illustrated by Alan Daniel, Doubleday Canada (Toronto), 1990.

Matthew and the Midnight Tow Truck, Firefly Books, 1991.

Show and Tell (also see below), illustrated by Michael Martchenko, Annick Press, 1991.

Get Me Another One! illustrated by Shawn Steffler, Doubleday Canada, 1992.

Purple, Green and Yellow (also see below), illustrated by Helene Desputeaux, Annick Press, 1992.

Wait and See, illustrated by Michael Martchenko, Firefly Books, 1993.

Where Is Gah-Ning?, illustrated by Helene Desputeaux, Firefly Books, 1994.

(With Saoussan Askar) *From Far Away,* illustrated by Michael Martchenko, Annick Press, 1995.

Stephanie's Ponytail (also see below), illustrated by Michael Martchenko, Annick Press, 1996.

Alligator Baby, illustrated by Michael Martchenko, North Winds Press/Scholastic, 1997.

Aaron's Hair, illustrated by Alan and Lea Daniel, Scholastic, 1998.

Andrew's Loose Tooth, illustrated by Michael Martchenko, Scholastic, 1998.

Get Out of Bed! illustrated by Alan and Lea Daniel, Scholastic, 1998.

Munschworks: The First Munsch Collection (contains *The Paper Bag Princess, David's Father, The Fire Station, Thomas's Snowsuit, I Have to Go!*), illustrated by Michael Martchenko, Annick Press, 1998.

Ribbon Rescue, illustrated by Eugenie Fernandes, Cartwheel Books, 1999.

Munschworks 2: The Second Munsch Treasury (contains *Pigs, Mortimer, Murmel, Murmel, Munsch, Something Good,* and *Purple, Green and Yellow*), illustrated by Michael Martchenko and Helene Desputeaux, Annick Press/Firefly, 1999.

We Share Everything! illustrated by Michael Martchenko, Scholastic, 1999.

Munschworks 3: The Third Munsch Treasury (contains *Stephanie's Ponytail, A Promise Is a Promise* (with Michael Kusugak), *Angela's Airplane, Jonathan Cleaned Up, Then He Heard a Sound; or, Blackberry Subway Jam,* and *Show and Tell*), illustrated by Michael Martchenko and Vladyana Krykorka, Annick Press, 2000.

Mmm, Cookies! illustrated by Michael Martchenko, Scholastic/Cartwheel, 2000.

RECORDINGS

(And narrator) *Munsch: Favourite Stories* (contains published and unpublished works), Kids' Records (Toronto), 1983.

(And narrator) *Murmel, Murmel, Munsch: More Outrageous Stories,* Kids' Records, 1985.

Love You Forever, Kids' Records, 1987.

Also recorded *Animation Videos* for CINAR Animation and reads *The Paper Bag Princess* on the Web site *Between the Covers.*

OTHER

A Promise Is a Promise, Holly Harris (play; for children), Dramatic Publishing (Woodstock, IL), 1995.

Collaborator, with Jinna Marton, on *Flores Para Mama/ Flowers for Mama.* Contributor of articles to periodicals, including *Journal of the Canadian Association for Young Children.* Munsch's works have been translated into several languages, including Cantonese, French, German, Spanish, and Swedish.

Adaptations

Jonathan Cleaned Up, Then He Heard a Sound; or, Blackberry Subway Jam was made into an animated film and released by the National Film Board of Canada, 1984; it also appears on the videotape *Children's Favourites: Three Canadian Stories,* released by the board; the videotapes *The Best of Robert Munsch* and *Robert Munsch's Favourite Stories* have also been released. In addition, Munsch is the subject of *Meet the Author: Robert Munsch,* a video by the School Services of Canada that was released in 1993. Some of Munsch's stories have been adapted for film and released as filmstrip and tape combinations by the Society for Visual Education. Several of Munsch's works are available on CD-ROM. *The Paper Bag Princess* was adapted into a play by Irene Watts. It also appears as part of the play *The Paper Bag Princess and Other Stories.* Theatrical compilations include *More Munsch* and *Murmel, Murmel, Mortimer, Munsch;* the latter is by Kim Selody.

Sidelights

Described as "our best-known spinner of yarns that stretch the truth in bizarre and hilarious ways" by Kit Pearson in *Quill and Quire,* Robert N. Munsch is an American-born Canadian author of picture books who is considered a publishing phenomenon. Canada's best-selling author, he has sold more than thirty million of his books internationally. Munsch directs his works to a preschool and early primary grade audience, although older children and adults also enjoy his books. A former teacher who is now a professional storyteller, Munsch has developed a style that draws on the oral tradition—he tells many of his stories for two or three years before writing them down. He uses humor, repetition, sound effects, surprise endings, and interactive participation to achieve his goal of providing pure entertainment for his audience.

Characteristically, Munsch depicts young children, both boys and girls, whose daily lives are thrown into chaos by unexpected, fantastic, and often absurd situations. The forces that interrupt each child's ordinary world—such as a tiny boy who lives in a little girl's sock drawer, a marauding mud puddle, and a giant fart—are calmed by the cool and resourceful behavior displayed by the protagonist. Munsch's main characters deal with these scary or irritating events by tackling them head on or by figuring out a way to defeat them. Munsch's portrayals of adults are generally less complimentary than those of the young; his grownups are usually characterized as more unimaginative and ineffectual than their youthful counterparts. The author has written a number of books that feature children who bring disorder into the adult world through their determined, even testy, behavior. For example, in *Thomas's Snowsuit* Munsch describes how a small boy's refusal to wear his snowsuit to school turns into a personal victory over educational authority. Munsch is also well known for writing gentler, less anarchic books. One of his best known works along these lines is *Love You Forever,* an internationally best-selling picture book depicting a mother's love for her son.

As a writer Munsch relies on an economical, rhythmic style that includes words and sounds designed to catch the attention of children, such as loud noises, funny voices, and hyperbole, among other elements. Munsch's books are often noted for being particularly good read alouds; in addition, their success is thought to be aided by their illustrations, which are often drawn by Michael Martchenko. Despite his irreverent and often audacious humor, Munsch is generally considered a moralist. Based on the feelings, perceptions, and emotional concerns of children, his works are underscored by such themes as fairness, equality, acceptance, independence, self-reliance, the nature of love, and, in the words of Sarah Ellis in *Horn Book,* "a jaunty belief in the power of children." He is also acknowledged for his playful reworkings of literary conventions—for example, the fairy tale, the tall tale, and the bedtime story—and for his abilities as a satirist.

Although Munsch is usually regarded as a delightfully inventive writer with a gift for nonsense who understands children and knows what appeals to them, he is also criticized for sometimes creating predictable, contrived, and formulaic stories. A few of his books have been banned by some Canadian schools and libraries for

Princess Elizabeth, using a large paper bag as a dress after a dragon burns her clothes, sets off to rescue her fiancee from the beast, only to find that the Prince is petty and shallow. (From The Paper Bag Princess, written by Munsch and illustrated by Michael Martchenko.)

their inclusion of inappropriate concepts and language. However, most reviewers consider Munsch an author beloved by children who leads them to reading while keeping them well entertained. Noting that Munsch's work "is now the object of something like a children's literature cold war," Janet McNaughton of *Quill and Quire* concluded that a "diet of nothing but Munsch might be about as nourishing to the developing literary soul as a diet of Kool-Aid. But Munsch is now as important to a whole generation of children as any television character. That is a remarkable accomplishment. And, if the search for Munsch books takes unwitting parents into the encampments of the other side (aka librarians and children's bookstores), children are the winners in this war."

Born in Pittsburgh, Pennsylvania, Munsch is the son of an attorney and a homemaker. The fourth of nine children, he was the middle child, which meant that, as he wrote on his official Web site, "I was attacked by both the younger coalition and the older coalition." Munsch has noted that he did badly in elementary school. He recalled that he "day-dreamed all the time, never learned how to spell, graduated from eighth grade counting on my fingers to do simple addition." However, he quickly discovered his gift for writing and created poetry all through elementary school. Munsch stated that he wrote "[f]unny poems, silly poems, all sorts of poems. Nobody thought that was very important." Munsch attended a Catholic high school in Pittsburgh. There, he recalled, "I didn't get along with anybody, read lots of books, and decided to be a

Catholic priest." Munsch studied to become a Jesuit for seven years. During this time, he majored in history at Fordham University in New York City, earning his bachelor's degree in 1969, and he studied anthropology at Boston University, earning his master's degree two years later. While preparing for the Jesuits, Munsch took a part-time job at a day-care center in order to, as he noted in his Web site, "escape from deadly classes in philosophy." Munsch wrote in an essay in *Canadian Children's Literature* that he "liked the kids better than anthropology. Maybe that was because I came from a family of nine children."

Munsch went through a series of jobs that involved young children, including stints in an infant day-care center and at an orphanage. He wrote on his Web site, "After I had been in day care for awhile, I decided to learn something about what I was supposed to be doing, so I went back to school for a year at the Eliot Pearson School of Child Studies at Tufts University in Medford, Massachusetts." In 1972, while working at a nursery school on a student teaching assignment, Munsch had an epiphany. He wrote in *Canadian Children's Literature,* "On the day when I was supposed to do my first circle time, I came with a lot of small containers full of corn. They made a lot of noise when rattled. I gave them to the kids and then told a sort of story-song that I made up the night before. It was about a little boy named Mortimer who did not want to go to bed.... Every time I sang it, the kids would shake their containers and a nice loud time was had by all. The story went over so well that the children kept asking for it. I even told it to my sister's children the next time I visited her. When I called her up

In his humorous picture book illustrated by Michael Martchenko, Munsch describes how a small boy's refusal to wear his snowsuit to school turns into a personal victory over educational authority. (Cover illustration by Michael Martchenko.)

later, she said that her children had taught it to the whole neighborhood and even made a play out of it. 'You should get it published,' she said." However, Munsch was not yet ready to heed his sister's advice. Threatened by the idea of publishing and hating to write because of the spelling involved, he let Mortimer's tale go undocumented for twelve years; however, it spread widely by word of mouth. By the time that Munsch published *Mortimer* in 1983, several Ontario day-care centers had already been using it as an oral story.

In 1973 Munsch received his master's degree in early childhood education from Tufts. That same year he married Ann Beeler, an educator whom he had met at a day-care center; the couple had two stillborn children, then adopted Julie, Andrew, and Tyya. After their marriage, Robert and Ann both became unemployed due to a loss of government funding for day care. They decided to move to Canada to look for work. Both husband and wife received jobs at a laboratory preschool at the University of Guelph in Guelph, Ontario. Ever since the success of his first oral story with children, Munsch continued to make up tales, usually at the rate of one per day. He wrote in *Canadian Children's Literature,* "I soon noticed that while I made up lots of stories, there were only a few that the children kept requesting to hear again. They were the good ones." When a story got repeated requests, Munsch developed its structure and presentation and made it into an interactive experience with the children. He wrote, "The more the children yelled out predictable repetition elements or imitated sound effects and gestures, the more they stayed put."

When he began working at the University of Guelph, Munsch found himself in an environment where, he noted, "people got raises and kept their jobs by publishing." The director of the laboratory school, Bruce Ryan, and his wife, Nancy, a children's librarian, both urged Munsch to write down his stories and to try and publish them. "At first," he recalled, "I made the mistake of attempting to change my stories into what I considered good writing. They were terrible. Finally I tried keeping the text as close as possible to the oral version and that worked. I think it worked because children's books are read aloud.... [T]he written text tended to lead to the same type of interactive participation that children liked in the oral version."

The first of Munsch's works to be accepted for publication were *The Mud Puddle* and *The Dark.* Both of these humorous picture books feature Julie Ann, who is called "a resourceful young woman of romper-room age" by Joan McGrath in *Canadian Children's Literature* and "a female behavior model of whom feminists will readily approve" by Carol Ann Wien in another issue of the same magazine. In the first book, an anthropomorphic mud puddle attacks Julie Ann whenever she steps outside; it waits for her behind a dog house and in a tree, among other places. Julie Ann finally realizes that in order to defeat her nemesis she must fight it with an extremely powerful element: soap. McGrath commented, "This slight, funny story is gloriously satisfactory in that Julie Ann triumphs through her own ingenuity . . . . Good (Julie Ann plus soap) triumphs over Evil (dirt), and the young reader is able to gloat with a pleasure untinged by regret for a too-sympathetic villain." In the second title, Julie Ann is pursued by the Dark, which falls out of the cookie jar and grows in size by eating shadows. After Julie Ann's father throws the Dark out of the window, the monster gobbles up shadows around the city and goes to sleep on the roof of her house until Julie Ann comes up with another clever solution to defeat it. Wien stated, "In demonstrating her self-confidence by resolving the conflicts herself [Julie Ann] conveys to young children that it is possible to cope successfully with problems." Wien concluded, "The stories work . . . as small intellectual puzzles, ideally suited to the emotional concerns of a pre-schooler. They are structurally perfect and emotionally powerful . . . . [The stories] will become standards in the repertoire of quality Canadian books."

Munsch's next book, *The Paper Bag Princess,* is one of his most well-known early works. In this story, Princess Elizabeth is engaged to be married to Prince Ronald. A fire-breathing dragon wrecks her castle, burns her clothes, and carries off Prince Ronald. Donning a large paper bag, the princess goes to rescue him. After three attempts in which, as Carol Anne Wien stated in *Canadian Children's Literature,* "the dragon obligingly demonstrates his abilities," Elizabeth is able to take Ronald back home by using her wits. However, Ronald criticizes her tangled hair and dirty paper-bag dress. Seeing Ronald's true nature, Elizabeth tells him that although he looks like a prince, he is a bum, and their upcoming marriage is called off. Michele Landsberg, writing in *Reading for the Love of It: Best Books for Young Readers,* called *The Paper Bag Princess* "a running gag that depends on the child recognizing the anachronisms, tricks, and discordancies that are slipped into the basic fairy tale." She concluded, "So basic is the fairy tale structure to our civilization, so ingrained is its accustomed tone and style, that there can hardly be a child in the country who doesn't get the joke." Although some critics accused Munsch of reverse sexism in *The Paper Bag Princess,* many have noted his clever twist on traditional fairy tales and have commended his strong female protagonist, whom *Canadian Children's Literature* critic Joan McGrath acknowledged is "becoming a cult-heroine for the skipping-rope set."

In 1983 Munsch produced the published version of his very first oral story, *Mortimer.* Initially published in a small size along with two other books, *Angela's Airplane* and *The Fire Station, Mortimer* is a considered a most unusual bedtime story. Mortimer, who is a small boy, is told by his parents, his seventeen brothers and sisters, and even the police to be quiet at bedtime. However, Mortimer insists on singing a defiant song at all of them. Finally, Mortimer becomes bored with waiting for yet another older person to come upstairs and tell him to be quiet; he falls asleep while chaos reigns below. Anne Gilmore wrote in *Quill and Quire,* "No gentle lullaby tale of a compliant sleepy child, *Mortimer* is a bedtime story with a difference." Writing in *CM: Canadian Materials,* Patricia Fry said, "It takes children

After creating chaos amongst the family members downstairs, Mortimer finally decides to quit singing his defiant song and succumb to sleep. (From Mortimer, *written by Munsch and illustrated by Michael Martchenko.)*

about two seconds to memorize Mortimer's song, and they will chant it joyfully during the telling of the tale. Also, every child identifies with the in-bed-but-not-yet-sleepy scenario. The ending is satisfying for adults and children alike." Munsch has referred to Mortimer as his personal favorite among the characters that he has created.

Thomas's Snowsuit, a picture book published in 1985, is the first of Munsch's books to win a major prize: the Ruth Schwartz Award. Thomas, a little boy on his way to school, is told by his mother that he must wear a new snowsuit that is a particularly ugly brown color. Thomas refuses, but his mother wins the resulting battle. However, she does not win the war: when his teacher says that he must wear the hideous snowsuit, Thomas again refuses. Ultimately, both his teacher and his principal end up wearing Thomas's snowsuit. Finally, Thomas chooses to put it on without being told. Calling *Thomas's Snowsuit* "the story of an adult/child confrontation with a difference," Patricia Sentance concluded in *CM: Canadian Materials* that "this little satire [is] sufficiently tongue-in-cheek to satisfy adults and kids. Fans of Robert Munsch will not be disappointed by his latest book." McGrath noted that Thomas "is at least a spiritual sibling to Robert Munsch's other absolutely little peace-destroyer, Mortimer. Pit the forces of law and order against a resolute five year old, and the establishment buckles at the knees every time—at least in Munsch's wild world."

In 1986 Munsch produced his well-known *Love You Forever*. In this picture book, the author shows how the power of unconditional parental love is transmitted from generation to generation. A mother holds her infant son and sings him a song that includes the title refrain. As the boy grows into manhood, his mother continues to sing this song to him; after he moves away, she even climbs into the window of his house in order to rock the sleeping man in her arms. When the day comes that the mother is too old and sick to sing to her son, the roles are reversed. He holds his ailing mother and rocks her while singing the familiar lullaby. The book's concluding pages show the son returning home, picking up his baby daughter, and singing to her, thus beginning the cycle again.

Based on a song that Munsch created for his two stillborn children, *Love You Forever* is regarded as a departure for its author; the book is considered more serious and introspective than Munsch's usual light-hearted fare. Thematically, *Love You Forever* expresses the enduring nature of a mother's love, a love that does not end when a child reaches adulthood. The book is also acknowledged for introducing the concepts of aging and death in an unobtrusive manner. Though it is generally praised as a sensitive and heartwarming book, *Love You Forever* is also considered by some to be a maudlin, manipulative work with little child appeal. For example, *CM: Canadian Materials* contributor Andre Gagnon labeled it "sentimentality at its worst." However, many observers find *Love You Forever* effective and reassuring. *Love You Forever,* which Munsch has called his best book, has sold more than eighteen million copies since its publication. Munsch told Mel James in the *Canada Heirloom Series* online that "this book has a nice effect on people and families and I really like that."

Munsch produced one of his most controversial titles, *I Have to Go!*, the year after the publication of *Love You Forever.* This picture book features small Andrew, who waits until he is in the car, in a snowsuit, or in bed before announcing that he has to urinate. His parents hover irritatingly over Andrew, who decides never to pee again. However, when his parents take Andrew to visit his grandparents, he has an accident in bed. When he has to go again, he tells his grandfather, and the two of them go into the bathroom together. Some teachers and librarians, who were concerned about the subject matter and Munsch's use of the word "pee," banned *I Have to Go!* from Canadian school and libraries. However, Mary Rubio concluded in *Canadian Children's Literature* that *I Have to Go!* is "very comic in the inimitable Munsch style, which includes throw-away lines for parents like when the grandmother says, 'I never had these problems with *my* children.'"

Written in a folktale style, *Giant; or Waiting for the Thursday Boat* features a giant named McKeon who wants to pound God into applesauce because St. Patrick is driving all of the giants, elves, and snakes out of Ireland. McKeon, who is named for Munsch's maternal grandfather, takes his quarrel to Heaven, where he meets God, who is in the form of a dark-skinned little girl. God tells McKeon that both he and St. Patrick are necessary—the saint to put up church bells and the giant to tear them down. At the end of the story, McKeon and St. Patrick accept each other, and an explanation for shooting stars is given: McKeon is throwing church bells out of Heaven. *Giant,* which *CM: Canadian Materials* contributor Patricia Fry called "a good addition to any library used by children," has been criticized for Munsch's portrayal of God as a little girl.

Good Families Don't is another of Munsch's works that has been protested for its content. In this picture book, young Carmen wakes up to find a huge fart on her bed. No one can rid the house of it until Carmen has a bright idea: she chases away the fart with a rose. Throughout the story, Munsch makes the subtle observation that although we are taught that nice people don't expel gas, the truth is that they do. Writing in *Emergency Librarian,* Shirley Lewis stated, "This book is no masterpiece, but if you can mentally cope with the fact that Munsch has written a real crowd-pleaser about a normally tasteless topic, I have to admit that I DID find it funny, and I have certainly noticed that from the moment the book arrived, everyone who had access to it went to the shelf and read it—often aloud—and laughed their heads off—often while giggling (I'm talking about adults here)." Munsch told Ann Vanderhoof in *Quill and Quire* that his works are "middle-of-the-road taboo." He added, "Farts are perfect; You're not supposed to talk about them, but they're not very threatening. If you tell stories about sex, for example, young children find that too threatening."

During the 1990s, Munsch regularly introduced multicultural protagonists into his works. In *Where Is Gah-Ning?* the author featured a Chinese-Canadian girl who wants to go to a nearby town on the Trans-Canada highway. Although her father refuses, Gah-Ning finds a way to achieve her goal: she floats to town on three hundred balloons. *From Far Away,* a collaboration with Saoussan Askar that is Munsch's first book of nonfiction, outlines how six-year-old Saoussan and her family left war-torn Beirut to join her family in Canada. Munsch describes how Saoussan overcomes initial difficulties with culture and language to become the best reader and speller in her class. In *Ribbon Rescue,* Jillian, a little Mohawk girl, goes to a wedding attired in the traditional ribbon dress that her grandmother made for her. While she waits for her mother, Jillian helps the wedding guests by using the long ribbons that decorate her dress. Due to her helpfulness, she is invited to be the flower girl in the wedding.

Munsch has also continued to write the humorous stories that have become his trademark. In the picture book *Something Good,* he included himself and his youngest daughter as the main characters. Clamoring for good food, small Tyya fills her father's shopping cart with ice cream and candy bars at the grocery store. After her frustrated dad orders her not to move, a clerk slaps a price tag on Tyya and she is swept up by two adults who claim that she is the nicest doll that they have ever seen. After her father gets Tyya back and pays for his daughter in the checkout line, she tells him that he has finally bought something good. Munsch used his other two children as the protagonists of two earlier books, *David's Father* and *Andrew's Loose Tooth*. In *Stephanie's Ponytail,* little Stephanie decides to wear her hair differently from the other children in her class. She comes to school in a ponytail; the next day, all the children are wearing one. Stephanie begins to wear a series of increasingly outlandish hairdos, all of which are copied by the kids. Finally, Stephanie threatens to shave her head. The next day, everyone—children and adults alike—show up bald; everyone, that is, except Stephanie, who has returned to her original ponytail.

In 1984 Munsch retired from teaching to become a full-time writer and storyteller. However, before retiring, he had become the head teacher at the Family Studies Laboratory Preschool, as well as an assistant professor at the University of Guelph. Munsch has continued to balance his dual careers of writing and storytelling; he tells stories to large crowds and small classrooms and gives workshops on storytelling to adults and teens. Munsch told David Kondo in *Canadian Children's Literature,* "I think I'm a good storyteller. I really respect kids. I'm telling stories to keep *these kids* happy." Many of Munsch's books are based on the real children that he has met on his storytelling tours and on the suggestions that they give to him both in person and in letters. Munsch wrote in *Canadian Children's Literature,* "I want my stories to mean different things to different people. I spend time getting them to do that. So the correct answer to, 'What does a Munsch story mean?' is, 'To whom?' If you are the reader then you are the arbiter of the meaning. I set it up that way. Besides, I have probably changed my mind several times about what the story meant since I wrote it down. So your own meaning is yours. You as the reader own the story. Have fun." Munsch's sense of humor comes through even in his answer to the question posed to him by Iram Khan and James Horner for *Canadian Content.* When Khan and Horner queried, "What is one question that you've always wanted to be asked?" Munsch replied, "How has being a manic-depressive, obsessive-compulsive, recovered-alcoholic nut case changed your writing?"

Biographical and Critical Sources

BOOKS

McDonough, Irma, editor, *Profiles 2,* Canadian Library Association, 1982.

Reading for the Love of It: Best Books for Young Readers, revised edition, Prentice Hall, 1987, pp. 84-85.

St. James Guide to Children's Writers, St. James Press (Detroit), 1999, pp. 772-773.

PERIODICALS

Bookbird, fall-winter, 1995, pp. 25-30.

Booklist, March 15, 1998, p. 1252; January 1, 1999, p. 889.

Canadian Children's Literature, Numbers 15 and 16, 1980, Carol Anne Wien, "Mud, Bubbles, and Dark for Early Childhood," pp. 115-119; Number 30, 1983, Joan McGrath, "Munschkinland Revisited," pp. 88-91; Number 43, 1986, David Kondo, "Robert Munsch: An Interview," pp. 26-33; Number 43, 1986, Robert Munsch, "Whatever You Make of It," pp. 22-25; Number 46, 1997, Mary Rubio, review of *I Have to Go!,* p. 108; fall, 1997, p. 60.

CM: Canadian Materials for Schools and Libraries, July, 1985, Patricia Fry, review of *Mortimer,* p. 174; January, 1986, Patricia Sentance, review of *Thomas's Snowsuit,* pp. 30-31; March, 1987, Andre Gagnon, review of *Love You Forever,* pp. 78-79.

Emergency Librarian, January-February, 1991, Shirley Lewis, review of *Good Families Don't,* p. 31; March, 1998, p. 26.

Horn Book Magazine, May-June, 1985, Sarah Ellis, "News from the North," pp. 342-345.

New York Times Book Review, November 13, 1994, M.P. Dunleavy, "Does This Book Go Too Far?"

Quill and Quire, May, 1982, Ann Vanderhoof, "The Weird and Wonderful Whimsy of Robert Munsch," p. 37; August, 1983, Anne Gilmore, review of *Angela's Airplane, The Fire Station,* and *Mortimer,* p. 34; December, 1985, Joan McGrath, review of *Thomas's Snowsuit,* p. 30; October, 1993, Kit Pearson, review of *Wait and See,* p. 37; September, 1997, Janet McNaughton, review of *Alligator Baby,* p. 72.

School Library Journal, November, 1997, p. 96.

ON-LINE

Canada Heirloom Series (in *Canada's Digital Collections*) http://collections.ic.gc.ca/ (August 22, 2000).

Canadian Content, http://track0.com/ (August 22, 2000).

CM Archive, www.umanitoba.ca/ (August 23, 2000).

The Official Robert Munsch Website, www.robert-munsch.com/ (April 3, 2000).

Amazon.com, www.amazon.com/ (August 24, 2000).

—Sketch by Gerard J. Senick

N

NORMAN, Lilith 1927-

Personal

Given name is pronounced "*Lie*-lith"; born November 27, 1927, in Sydney, New South Wales, Australia. *Education:* Studied with Library Association of Australia. *Hobbies and other interests:* Reading, cats, old movies ('30s and '40s).

Addresses

Home—21 Rhodes Ave., Naremburn, New South Wales, 2065, Australia. *Agent*—Margaret Connelly & Associates, P.O. Box 945, Warranwee, New South Wales, 2074, Australia.

Career

Newtown Municipal Library, Sydney, Australia, library assistant, 1947-49; Bonnington Hotel, London, England, telephonist, 1950-51; Angus & Robertson Books, Sydney, book shop assistant, 1951-53; Balmain District Hospital, Sydney, nursing trainee, 1953-56; City of Sydney Public Library, Sydney, library assistant, 1956-58, research officer, 1958-66, children's librarian, 1966-70; New South Wales Department of Education, *School Magazine,* Sydney, assistant editor, 1970-76, editor, 1976-78; full-time writer, 1978—. Has been a writer-in-residence at various universities; and a tutor in writing at WEA summer schools. *Member:* Children's Book Council of Australia; Australian Society of Authors.

Awards, Honors

Climb a Lonely Hill was commended as Australian Children's Book of the Year, 1970; recipient, Queen's Silver Jubilee Medal, 1977; *A Dream of Seas* was named an IBBY Honour Book by the International Board on Books for Young People, 1978; *Grandpa* was named an Honour Book by the Children's Book Council of Australia in the picture book category, 1999.

Writings

FOR CHILDREN

Climb a Lonely Hill, Collins (London), 1970, Walck, 1972.
The Shape of Three, Collins (London), 1971, Walck, 1972.
The Flame Takers, Collins (Sydney), 1973.
Mocking-Bird Man (reader), illustrated by Astra Lacis, Hodder & Stoughton (Sydney), 1977.
A Dream of Seas, illustrated by Edwina Bell, Collins (Sydney), 1978, Red Fox, 1995.
My Simple Little Brother, illustrated by David Rae, Collins (Sydney), 1979.
The Hex (collected stories), Nelson Educational, 1989.
The Laurel and Hardy Kids, Random House Australia (Sydney), 1989.
The Paddock: A Story in Praise of the Earth (picture book), illustrated by Robert Roennfeldt, Random Century Australia, 1992, Knopf (New York), 1993.
Aphanasy (picture book), illustrated by Maxim Svetlanov, Random Century Australia, 1994.
The Beetle (picture book; retelling of a Hans Christian Andersen tale), illustrated by Maxim Svetlanov, Random Century Australia, 1995.
Grandpa, illustrated by Noela Young, Margaret Hamilton Books, 1998.

FOR ADULTS

The City of Sydney: Official Guide, Sydney City Council, 1959.
Facts about Sydney, Sydney City Council, 1959.
Asia: A Select Reading List, Sydney City Council, 1959.
Some Notes on the Early Land Grants at Potts Point, Sydney City Council, 1959.
A History of the City of Sydney Public Library, Sydney City Council, 1959.
Notes on the Glebe, Sydney City Council, 1960.
Historical Notes on Paddington, Sydney City Council, 1961.
Historical Notes on Newtown, Sydney City Council, 1962.
The Brown and the Yellow: Sydney Girls' High School, 1883-1983, Oxford University Press (Melbourne), 1983.

OTHER

Also author of episode for television series, *Catch Kandy,* 1973. Short stories appear in the following anthologies: *Beneath the Sun,* edited by Patricia Wrightson, Collins, 1972; *Too True,* compiled by Anne Bower Ingram, Collins, 1974; *Stories of the City,* edited by Veronica Harvey, Evans Bros., 1977; and *Roland Harvey's Incredible Book of Almost Everything,* compiled by Roland Harvey, Five Mile Press, 1984. Contributor to *Reading Time, Encyclopaedia Britannica, Orana, Australian Library Journal, Magpies,* and *School Magazine.* Editor, *Felis,* Journal of Siamese Cat Society of New South Wales, 1965-69, and *SHSOGU News Sheet,* Journal of the Sydney High School Old Girls' Union, 1986-94.

Sidelights

Lilith Norman told *SATA:* "I didn't set out to be a children's writer—who does? No, I wanted to write the 'Great Australian Novel.' But by a serendipitous chance I happened to be a children's librarian at the time I wrote my first book, and it came to me in that form. I think ideas often dictate their own form. With Shakespeare it was plays, with Robert Frost it was poems, and so on. I could have written my children's novels as adult books by using a different viewpoint, but what came was a child's viewpoint. I write children's novels in order to explore what makes my characters tick and how they cope. I don't plan my novels in advance, so as well as being the writer I am also the first reader. I also write picture books, which are much harder: a picture book is more like a poem in that each word has to bear an enormous weight, so that finding the absolutely right word is important, and there must be no extraneous words. All our books expose our own philosophy (for want of a less pretentious word), and mine is that we all have to cope as best we can. I also think that in writing for children, no matter how difficult the situations are which we inflict on our characters, we must leave them with a smidgen of hope. There is a trend in children's books at present (at least in Australia) to show them only the seamy underside of life, and even to rub their noses in it, in the belief that this is reality. It is, but it's not the *only* reality. The world is not *only* bleak and hopeless, and if we present this to children as the only world we are selling them short, and that, I believe is to fail them and to fail ourselves as authors."

An author of diverse books ranging from realistic adventure to fantasy and, more recently, lyrical picture books, Norman creates works for children that are consistently praised for their evident love for the author's native Australian landscape and for their realistic young protagonists. Norman's first novel for children, *Climb a Lonely Hill,* is an adventure tale set in the Australian outback. Young Jack and Sue Clarke are stranded in inhospitable country when the truck they are riding in with their uncle crashes and their uncle dies. With little food and water to help them survive until they can be rescued, they have to risk a trek into the distant hills to find a water hole. What follows is a realistic depiction of their grueling journey under the unrelenting desert sun and eventual rescue. Reviewers admired the novel for its skillful characterization and faithful rendering of the Australian outback. As one *Times Literary Supplement* contributor commented, Norman is able to draw the reader into the story because "the children are real children, frail and recognizable; one cares about their fate." The critic concluded, "The book will be a sad experience for soft-hearted readers and yet a worthwhile one, for it is an honest book."

With her second novel, *The Shape of Three,* Norman examines a different type of challenge in an inhospitable environment. In this case, a newborn twin is accidentally switched with the boy of another mother while they're at the hospital. Bruce is sent home to become the only child of the wealthy Protestant Cunningham family, while Shane is taken home with Bruce's twin brother, Greg, to the large Catholic Herbert family. Greg and Shane are raised together as fraternal twins, and all seems well until Greg and Bruce meet and discover their uncanny similarity in appearance. When their mothers learn of this—and blood tests prove who the real twins are—they insist that Bruce and Shane be switched back again, which results in misery for both boys. Only after much emotional suffering is it finally decided that the boys should be returned to the families they have known since birth. Critical reaction to *The Shape of Three* was mixed. A reviewer for *Bulletin of the Center for Children's Books* stated that the "characterization and dialogue are adroit," and that Norman's comparisons of Catholic and Protestant households is well done, but added that the "book's weakness is that it smacks of the documentary approach to a case history."

With her next book, Norman began to venture into the genre of fantasy. *The Flame Takers* centers on the talented Malory family—the parents are actors and their son is a musician—who are subjected to the wicked machinations of a sadistic schoolmaster and the mysterious "flame takers, who destroy people's talent." The schoolmaster and the flame takers seek to extinguish the family's flame of talent and turn them into uninspired, materialistic members of the bourgeoisie. However, they are thwarted by a rotund German chess aficionado and by the boy's sister who, having no particular talents herself, is able to stand up to the flame takers. "Put like this," one critic in the *Times Literary Supplement* remarked, "it sounds ridiculous but it is in fact a powerful and exciting allegory."

Norman once again blends fantasy and reality in *A Dream of Seas.* Taking a much more lyrical approach to the genre than in *The Flame Takers,* Norman writes about a young Australian boy nicknamed "Seasie," whose father has recently drowned. His mother takes him to live near Bondi Beach, where Seasie becomes obsessed with the sea (thus his nickname). The story of his growing interest in the sea is paralleled by the tale of a young seal's maturation from pup to young adult. As the novel progresses, Seasie's existence among humans becomes more like a dream, while the life of the sea becomes increasingly real. Boy and seal draw closer together, and when Seasie's mother remarries and becomes pregnant, his final ties to human civilization are broken; he embraces the ocean and becomes one with the seal. The story shows "how a boy achieves independence and a separate identity," Margery Fisher indicated in *Growing Point.* As the boy matures, so does the seal, so that the ending "seems an inevitable if fantastic climax to a perfectly rational story." Melanie Guile, a contributor to *Magpies,* contended that *A Dream of Seas* "has no plot to speak of," since the focus of the story is "the boy's inner life—imaginative and spiritual," a trick the author pulls off through the force of her writing, which is "sophisticated in style and highly structured."

Norman's love for the Australian landscape, which can be seen throughout her works, is especially poignant in her picture book *The Paddock: A Story in Praise of the Earth.* Focusing on a particular plot of land in Australia ("paddock" in Australian parlance is an ordinary piece of land), the author follows its history from original formation, through the age of dinosaurs, to the first human settlements, and finally to its death from industrial usage, though the ending implies that the land will be reborn again after mankind leaves. A *Publishers Weekly* critic called this picture book a "hymn to the resilience and dominance of the land." A reviewer for *Junior Bookshelf* praised the cumulative power of the combined text and illustrations that makes its point without heavy-handedness: "A beautifully composed text and rich pictures ... point the moral of this environmental tale without undue emphasis."

Norman's next picture book, *Aphanasy,* celebrates "a sense of the explorer's wonder at the new and strange of another culture," according to *Magpies* reviewer Jan Scott. In this adventure story, the title character sets sail from medieval Russia to discover a route to India, withstanding storms and pirates, as well as the exploits of demons and evil spirits who must be warded off through the power of icons and other protective talismans. Norman turned to realism with her next book, *Grandpa,* in which the narrator, a boy of about eight, explains that his grandfather has died. His initial lack of emotion about the event is gradually replaced as he witnesses his own mother's grief over the death of her father in a scene that is "incredibly powerful," according to *Magpies* contributor Barbara James. The boy gains a more realistic recognition of what the old man had been to the family during the years in which he had lived with them. "I thought the book was outstanding," James attested in conclusion.

As Betty Gilderdale observed in *Twentieth-Century Children's Writers,* Norman's books tend to be interested in "the effect of environment on character." Whether she is writing about the influences and challenges of the natural environment on her young protagonists, or the effects of family and social pressures, her themes have often been related in at least some way to this subject. The author, however, does not like to analyze her books, believing instead that they should be self-explanatory. As she once commented, "It seems to me that a book should speak directly to the reader. If I have anything worth saying, it is there, in my books, in a far more entertaining and accessible (I hope) way than a pretentious self-analysis would provide."

Biographical and Critical Sources

BOOKS

Saxby, H.M., *A History of Australian Children's Literature, 1941-1970,* Wentworth Books, 1971.
Twentieth-Century Children's Writers, fourth edition, St. James, 1995.

PERIODICALS

Appraisal, winter, 1994, p. 5.
Booklist, January 1, 1973, p. 450; September 15, 1972, review of *Climb a Lonely Hill,* p. 101.
Bulletin of the Center for Children's Books, February, 1973, review of *The Shape of Three,* p. 96.
Growing Point, July, 1979, Margery Fisher, "Neighbourhood Tales," pp. 3539-42.
Horn Book Guide, fall, 1993, p. 270; March-April, 1995, p. 237.
Junior Bookshelf, June, 1979, p. 171; April, 1993, review of *The Paddock,* p. 61.
Kirkus Reviews, March 1, 1993, p. 303.
Library Journal, September 15, 1972, p. 2965; March 15, 1973, p. 1015.
Magpies, November, 1994, Jan Scott, review of *Aphanasy,* p. 30; May, 1995, Melanie Guilde, review of *A Dream of Seas,* p. 32; November, 1998, Barbara James, review of *Grandpa,* p. 33.
Publishers Weekly, January 1, 1973, p. 57; March 29, 1993, review of *The Paddock,* p. 55.
School Librarian, August, 1993, p. 104.
Times Literary Supplement, October 30, 1970, "Enduring All Things," pp. 1266-67; December 3, 1971, p. 1516; July 5, 1974, review of *The Flame Takers,* "Haunted Houses," p. 717.

P

PALMER, Jessica 1953-

Personal

Born June 5, 1953, in Chicago, IL; moved to England, 1988; married, 1979 (husband deceased, 1985). *Education:* Mary Mount College, degree in practical nursing, 1975; degree in alcohol counseling, 1978.

Addresses

Office—c/o Serafina Clarke, 98 Tunis Rd., London W12 7EY, England.

Career

Nurse and writer. Worked as a psychiatric nurse in Salina, KS; technical writer for oil well services company; freelance novelist, 1988—; Publishing Initiatives, Beckenham, Kent, England, editorial director, 1997—.

Writings

Dark Lullaby, Pocket Books (New York City), 1991.
Cradlesong, Pocket Books, 1993.
Healer's Quest, Point Fantasy (London), 1993.
Shadow Dance, Pocket Books, 1994.
Fire Wars, Point Fantasy, 1994.
Random Factor, Point Fantasy, 1994.
Sweet William, Pocket Books, 1995.
Return of the Wizard, Point Fantasy, 1995.
Human Factor, Point SF (London), 1996.

Contributor of short fiction to periodicals, including *Substance, Interzone,* and *London Noir.*

Sidelights

Drawing on her experiences as a psychiatric nurse, Jessica Palmer is the author of several book-length works of horror and science fiction/fantasy. In such horror novels as *Dark Lullaby,* the author illustrates the fact that the horrors of the human mind are among the most haunting of all to children, while her *Healer's Quest* and *Random Factor* explore other imaginative fictional genres. While outer space serves as a backdrop for her science-fiction novels, most of Palmer's fictional characters don't have to travel far to encounter danger. In an essay published in the *St. James Guide to Horror,* contributor Peter T. Garratt noted that "Houses are a central theme in Jessica Palmer's work: a house is supposed to be a home, but home can be treacherous, home is where the greatest horrors may lurk."

In her fictional debut, *Dark Lullaby,* Palmer tells a ghost story with a twist, as the spirit of eleven-year-old Shelley, an abused child recently killed during a fire caused by her careless parents, wants revenge. When her alcoholic mom, deadbeat dad, and younger sister move to a new home, Shelley's spirit follows, salting the family's already dysfunctional environment with a series of bizarre events. Slightly more upbeat in tone, 1993's *Cradlesong* again finds a family on the move, as fiction writer Tom Erwin moves his family into a home that, although cheap in price due to the fact that murders had occurred there, is rich in things that go bump in the night. In addition to supernatural horrors, the family must also contend with human malevolence in the form of a gang of neighborhood toughs that delights in making things unpleasant.

Palmer moves into the future in her 1994 novel *Random Factor,* as she draws readers 350 years into the future, when computers control warfare. When one of the computers aboard a warship goes on the fritz, a teen boy must use his hacker skills to discover how to regain control of the ship before his nation is forced into a destructive war. While *School Librarian* reviewer Ron Creer noted that the book is lengthy at 341 pages, he added that "the ingenuity of the [novel's] hidden twist and the denouement, and the excitement of the last 120 pages, make it worthwhile."

Biographical and Critical Sources

BOOKS

Pringle, David, editor, *St. James Guide to Horror,* St. James Press (Detroit), 1998, pp. 447-48.
Reginald, Robert, *Science Fiction and Fantasy Literature, 1975-1991,* Gale (Detroit), 1992.

PERIODICALS

Locus, June, 1991, review of *Dark Lullaby,* p. 50; July, 1993, review of *Cradlesong,* p. 44; April, 1994, review of *Shadow Dance,* p. 49.
School Librarian, November, 1994, Ron Creer, review of *Random Factor,* p. 166.*

*   *   *

PATENT, Dorothy Hinshaw 1940-

Personal

Born April 30, 1940, in Rochester, MN; daughter of Horton Corwin (a physician) and Dorothy Kate (maiden name, Youmans) Hinshaw; married Gregory Joseph Patent (a professor of zoology), March 21, 1964; children: David Gregory, Jason Daniel. *Education:* Stanford University, B.A., 1962; University of California, Berkeley, M.A., 1965, Ph.D., 1968; also studied at Friday Harbor Laboratories, University of Washington, 1965-67. *Hobbies and other interests:* Gardening, cooking, and hiking.

Addresses

Home—5445 Skyway Dr., Missoula, MT 59804.

Dorothy Hinshaw Patent

Career

Writer. Sinai Hospital, Detroit, MI, post-doctoral fellow, 1968-69; Stazione Zoologica, Naples, Italy, post-doctoral researcher, 1970-71; University of Montana, Missoula, faculty affiliate in department of zoology, 1975-90, acting assistant professor, 1977, faculty affiliate in environmental studies, 1995—. *Member:* American Institute of Biological Sciences, Authors Guild, Society of Children's Book Writers and Illustrators.

Awards, Honors

The National Science Teachers Association has cited more than forty of Patent's books as outstanding science trade books; Golden Kite Honor Book, Society of Children's Book Writers, 1977, for *Evolution Goes On Every Day,* and Golden Kite Award, 1980, for *The Lives of Spiders;* Notable Book citation, American Library Association, 1982, for *Spider Magic;* Children's Books of the Year list, Library of Congress, 1985, for *Where the Bald Eagles Gather;* Best Books of the Year list, *School Library Journal,* 1986, for *Buffalo: The American Bison Today,* Best Book for Young Adults citation, American Library Association, 1986, for *The Quest for Artificial Intelligence;* Eva L. Gordon Award, American Nature Study Society, 1987, for the body of her work; Books for the Teenage citation, New York Public Library, 1990, for *How Smart Are Animals?;* Best Books of the Year list, *School Library Journal,* and Pick of the Lists, *American Bookseller,* both 1992, and both for *Feathers;* Children's Choice Award, 1994, for *Hugger to the Rescue;* Books for the Teenage citation, New York Public Library, 1994, for *The Vanishing Feast;* AAAS Best Science Books of 1996, for *Biodiversity;* Lud Browman Award for Science Writing, Friends of the Mansfield Library, University of Montana, 1994; Best Children's Books of the Year citations, Bank Street College of Education, 1997, for *Prairies, Children Save the Rainforests,* and *Biodiversity;* Books for Young People Award, *Scientific American,* 1997, for *Pigeons;* AAAS Best Science Books of 1998, for *Apple Trees;* Best Children's Books of the Year, Bank Street College of Education, 1998, for *Back to the Wild* and *Flashy Fantastic Rain Forest Frogs,* and 1999, for *Apple Trees* and *Fire: Friend or Foe;* CBC-IRA Children's Choices selection, 1999, for *Alex and Friends: Animal Talk, Animal Thinking.* Many of Patent's books have also received state nominations and awards and have been chosen as Outstanding Science Trade Books for Children by the National Science Teachers Association.

Writings

FOR CHILDREN

Weasels, Otters, Skunks and Their Family, illustrations by Matthew Kalmenoff, Holiday House, 1973.
Microscopic Animals and Plants, Holiday House, 1974.
Frogs, Toads, Salamanders and How They Reproduce, illustrations by M. Kalmenoff, Holiday House, 1975.
How Insects Communicate, Holiday House, 1975.
Fish and How They Reproduce, illustrations by M. Kalmenoff, Holiday House, 1976.

Plants and Insects Together, illustrations by M. Kalmenoff, Holiday House, 1976.

Evolution Goes On Every Day, illustrations by M. Kalmenoff, Holiday House, 1977.

Reptiles and How They Reproduce, illustrations by M. Kalmenoff, Holiday House, 1977.

The World of Worms, Holiday House, 1978.

Animal and Plant Mimicry, Holiday House, 1978.

(With Paul C. Schroeder) *Beetles and How They Live,* Holiday House, 1978.

Butterflies and Moths: How They Function, Holiday House, 1979.

Sizes and Shapes in Nature: What They Mean, Holiday House, 1979.

Raccoons, Coatimundis and Their Family, Holiday House, 1979.

Bacteria: How They Affect Other Living Things, Holiday House, 1980.

The Lives of Spiders, Holiday House, 1980.

Bears of the World, Holiday House, 1980.

Horses and Their Wild Relatives, Holiday House, 1981.

Horses of America, Holiday House, 1981.

Hunters and the Hunted: Surviving in the Animal World, Holiday House, 1981.

Spider Magic, Holiday House, 1982.

A Picture Book of Cows, photographs by William Munoz, Holiday House, 1982.

Arabian Horses, Holiday House, 1982.

Germs!, Holiday House, 1983.

A Picture Book of Ponies, photographs by W. Munoz, Holiday House, 1983.

Whales: Giants of the Deep, Holiday House, 1984.

Farm Animals, photographs by W. Munoz, Holiday House, 1984.

Where the Bald Eagles Gather, photographs by W. Munoz, Clarion, 1984.

Baby Horses, photographs by W. Munoz, Dodd, 1985.

Quarter Horses, photographs by W. Munoz, Holiday House, 1985.

The Sheep Book, photographs by W. Munoz, Dodd, 1985.

Thoroughbred Horses, Holiday House, 1985.

Draft Horses, photographs by W. Munoz, Holiday House, 1986.

Buffalo: The American Bison Today, photographs by W. Munoz, Clarion, 1986.

Mosquitoes, Holiday House, 1986.

Maggie: A Sheep Dog (Junior Literary Guild selection), photographs by W. Munoz, Dodd, 1986.

The Quest for Artificial Intelligence, Harcourt, 1986.

Christmas Trees (Junior Literary Guild selection), Dodd, 1987.

All about Whales, Holiday House, 1987.

Dolphins and Porpoises, Holiday House, 1987.

The Way of the Grizzly, photographs by W. Munoz, Clarion, 1987.

Wheat: The Golden Harvest, photographs by W. Munoz, Dodd, 1987.

Appaloosa Horses, photographs by W. Munoz, Holiday House, 1988.

Babies!, Holiday House, 1988.

A Horse of a Different Color, photographs by W. Munoz, Dodd, 1988.

Neil Waldman depicts the meeting of conquistador Cortes and Moctezuma, the last Aztec emperor of Mexico, in Dorothy Hinshaw Patent's Quetzal: Sacred Bird of the Cloud Forest.

The Whooping Crane: A Comeback Story, photographs by W. Munoz, Clarion, 1988.

Humpback Whales, photographs by Mark J. Ferrari and Deborah A. Glockner-Ferrari, Holiday House, 1989.

Grandfather's Nose: Why We Look Alike or Different, illustrations by Diane Palmisciano, F. Watts, 1989.

Singing Birds and Flashing Fireflies: How Animals Talk to Each Other, illustrations by Mary Morgan, F. Watts, 1989.

Where the Wild Horses Roam, photographs by W. Munoz, Clarion, 1989.

Wild Turkey, Tame Turkey, photographs by W. Munoz, Clarion, 1989.

Looking at Dolphins and Porpoises, Holiday House, 1989.

Looking at Ants, Holiday House, 1989.

Seals, Sea Lions and Walruses, Holiday House, 1990.

Yellowstone Fires: Flames and Rebirth, photographs by W. Munoz, Holiday House, 1990.

An Apple a Day: From Orchard to You, photographs by W. Munoz, Cobblehill, 1990.

Flowers for Everyone, photographs by W. Munoz, Cobblehill, 1990.

Gray Wolf, Red Wolf, photographs by W. Munoz, Clarion, 1990.

How Smart Are Animals? (Junior Literary Guild selection), Harcourt, 1990.

A Family Goes Hunting, photographs by W. Munoz, Clarion, 1991.

Miniature Horses, photographs by W. Munoz, Cobblehill, 1991.

The Challenge of Extinction, Enslow, 1991.

Where Food Comes From, photographs by W. Munoz, Holiday House, 1991.

African Elephants: Giants of the Land, photographs by Oria Douglas-Hamilton, Holiday House, 1991.

Feathers, photographs by W. Munoz, Cobblehill, 1992.

Places of Refuge: Our National Wildlife Refuge System, photographs by W. Munoz, Clarion, 1992.

Nutrition: What's in the Food We Eat, photographs by W. Munoz, Holiday, 1992.

Pelicans, photographs by W. Munoz, Clarion, 1992.

Cattle: Understanding Animals, photographs by W. Munoz, Carolrhoda, 1993.

Ospreys, photographs by W. Munoz, Clarion, 1993.

Prairie Dogs, photographs by W. Munoz, Clarion, 1993.

Habitats: Saving Wild Places, Enslow, 1993.

Killer Whales, photographs by John K. B. Ford, Holiday House, 1993.

Dogs: The Wolf Within, photographs by W. Munoz, Carolrhoda Books, 1993.

Looking at Penguins, photographs by Graham Robertson, Holiday House, 1993.

Looking at Bears, photographs by W. Munoz, Holiday House, 1994.

Horses: Understanding Animals, photographs by W. Munoz, Carolrhoda, 1994.

Deer and Elk, photographs by W. Munoz, Clarion, 1994.

Patent elucidates the delicate interrelationship and interdepedence between the many life forms on earth. (Cover photo by William Munoz.)

Hugger to the Rescue, photographs by W. Munoz, Cobblehill, 1994.

The American Alligator, photographs by W. Munoz, Clarion, 1994.

The Vanishing Feast: How Dwindling Genetic Diversity Threatens the World's Food Supply, Harcourt Brace, 1994.

What Good Is a Tail?, photographs by W. Munoz, Cobblehill, 1994.

West by Covered Wagon: Retracing Pioneer Trails, photographs by W. Munoz, Walker, 1995.

Eagles of America, photographs by W. Munoz, Holiday House, 1995.

Return of the Wolf, illustrated by Hared T. Williams, Clarion, 1995.

Why Mammals Have Fur, photographs by W. Munoz, Cobblehill, 1995.

Prairies, photographs by W. Munoz, Holiday House, 1996.

Quetzal: Sacred Bird of the Cloud Forest, illustrated by Neil Waldman, Morrow, 1996.

Biodiversity, photographs by W. Munoz, Clarion, 1996.

Children Save the Rain Forest, photographs by Dan L. Perlman, Cobblehill Books, 1996.

Back to the Wild, photographs by W. Munoz, Harcourt Brace, 1997.

Pigeons, photographs by W. Munoz, Clarion, 1997.

Apple Trees, photographs by W. Munoz, Lerner, 1997.

Flashy Fantastic Rain Forest Frogs, illustrated by Kendahl Jan Jubb, Walker, 1997.

Homesteading: Settling America's Heartland, photographs by W. Munoz, Walker, 1998.

Fire: Friend or Foe, photographs by W. Munoz, Clarion, 1998.

Alex and Friends: Animal Talk, Animal Thinking, photographs by W. Munoz, Lerner, 1998.

Bold and Bright, Black-and-White Animals, illustrated by K. J. Jubb, Walker, 1998.

Mystery of the Lascaux Cave, Benchmark Books, 1998.

Secrets of the Ice Man, Benchmark Books, 1998.

Great Ice Bear: The Polar Bear and the Eskimo, illustrated by Anne Wertheim, Morrow, 1998.

Polar Bear: Sacred Bear of the Ice, illustrated by Anne Wertheim, Morrow, 1998.

In Search of Maiasaurs, Benchmark Books, 1999.

The Incredible Story of China's Buried Warriors, Benchmark Books, 1999.

Lost City of Pompeii, Benchmark Books, 1999.

Treasures of the Spanish Main, Benchmark Books, 1999.

Wild Turkeys, photographs by W. Munoz, Lerner, 1999.

Shaping the Earth, photographs by W. Munoz, Clarion, 2000.

The Bald Eagle Returns, photographs by W. Munoz, Clarion, 2000.

Polar Bears, photographs by W. Munoz, Carolrhoda, 2000.

Slinky, Scaly, Slithery Snakes, illustrated by K. J. Jubb, Walker, 2000.

Horses, photographs by W. Munoz, Lerner, 2001.

Charles Darwin: The Life of a Revolutionary Thinker, Holiday House, 2001.

A Polar Bear Biologist at Work, Franklin Watts, 2001.

Rescuing the Prairie Bandit, Franklin Watts, 2001.

FOR ADULTS

(With Diane E. Bilderback) *Garden Secrets,* Rodale Press, 1982, revised and expanded edition published as *The Harrowsmith Country Life Book of Garden Secrets: A Down-to-Earth Guide to the Art and Science of Growing Better Vegetables,* Camden House, 1991.

(With D. E. Bilderback) *Backyard Fruits and Berries,* Rodale Press, 1984.

(With Greg Patent), *A Is for Apple: More Than 200 Recipes for Eating, Munching, and Cooking America's Favorite Fruit,* Broadway Books, 1999.

Contributor to gardening and farming magazines. Has also written for *Arizoo, Camas, Falcon, Spider, Storyworks, Horn Book, The Writer, Cricket* and *The Missoulian* newspaper. Patent's photographs have appeared in *National Gardening Magazine, The Missoulian,* and in many of her children's books.

Sidelights

Dorothy Hinshaw Patent is a highly acclaimed author of over one hundred science books for young readers. A trained zoologist, Patent has written books in the biological sciences about animals from the horse to the pelican, and has examined ecological challenges in such books as *Biodiversity, Back to the Wild,* and *The Vanishing Feast.* Patent's books are geared at readers from the elementary grades through high school, and are noted for their interpretation of complex topics in concise, spirited, and informal presentations. As Zena Sutherland and May Hill Arbuthnot noted in their *Children and Books,* "Dorothy Patent has become established as an author whose books are distinguished for their combination of authoritative knowledge, detached and objective attitude, and an ability to write for the lay person with fluency and clarity .... she communicates a sense of wonder at the complexity and beauty of animal life by her zest for her subject ...."

"Many writers have known for as long as they can remember that they wanted to write. Not me," Patent noted in *Something about the Author Autobiography Series (SAAS).* "I knew that I loved animals, the woods, and exploring, and I always wanted to learn everything possible about something that interested me. But I never yearned to be a writer." Patent remarked that she grew up a tomboy, exploring the terrain around her family's homes in Minnesota and later California with her older brother. She was always more interested in catching tadpoles, playing with toads, and collecting insects than in the more conventional interests shared by girls her age. In fact, Patent remembered having trouble making girl friends in school: "To this day I'm not sure why, but maybe it was because I'd never spent much time with girls and didn't know how to act around them."

When she was in elementary school, Patent received a gift from her mother that turned her general interest in nature into a firm resolve to know all that she could of a specific subject. As a reward for practicing the piano, her mother bought her a pair of golden guppies and she recalled in *SAAS:* "The morning after we bought the

In her informational picture book, Patent not only features black-and-white animals, but explains how their coloration proves useful to their survival. (*From* Bold and Bright: Black-and-White Animals, *illustrated by Kendahl Jan Jubb.*)

fish, I peered into the bowl to check on my new pets. To my surprise, the adult fish weren't alone—three new pairs of eyes stared out at me from among the plants. I couldn't believe this miracle—the female fish had given birth during the night, and now I had five fish instead of two!" Patent's enthusiasm led her to read every book she could about tropical fish and to frequent a special Japanese fish store to learn even more.

Patent's curiosity helped her to excel in school, as did the encouragement of her family. "Learning was highly valued in my family," she commented in *SAAS.* Despite her success academically, she felt like a misfit socially. "I wanted to be like the 'in' crowd ...," she recalled. "I admired the girls who became prom queens and cheerleaders. At the time, there was no way I could understand that some of them were living the best part of their lives during high school while the best parts of my life were yet to come and would last much longer." After high school Patent went to nearby Stanford University, one of the few highly rated schools in the nation that was coeducational at the time and had a strong science program. Patent blossomed in college, where her intelligence and intellectual curiosity were valued. Despite a tragedy during her freshman year—the suicide of her roommate—which put her "into a dark emotional frame of mind that lasted the entire four years," she wrote in her autobiographical sketch that she became involved with international folk dancing, made good friends, and had interesting, challenging classes. Many of her classes emphasized writing, and "by the end of my freshman year," she recollected, "I could set an internal switch for a paper of a certain length and write it. I'm sure this discipline and training has helped me in my writing career." After a trip to Europe with a friend, Patent enrolled in graduate school at the University of California at Berkeley, where she met the man she would marry, Greg Patent, a teaching assistant in her endocrinology class.

Patent and her new husband continued their graduate work and post-doctoral research in Friday Harbor, Washington; Detroit, Michigan; and Naples, Italy; settling for a while in North Carolina before moving to Montana. Searching for a job that would allow her to spend time with her two young boys, Patent decided to try writing, and following age-old advice to write about what one knows best, she picked biology as her subject matter. Though her first two books were not published, one of them piqued the interest of an editor at Holiday House who eventually approached Patent with an idea for a book about the weasel family. Although she knew next to nothing about weasels, Patent agreed to write the book, *Weasels, Otters, Skunks and Their Family.* She spent hours doing research at the University of Montana library in Missoula, and received help from a professor at the university who happened to be one of the world's experts on weasels. Reviewing this debut volume in *Appraisal,* Heddie Kent found the book to be "fascinating and comprehensive." "[Patent's] style of writing is relaxed and enjoyable," noted a critic for *Science Books,* who also found *Weasels, Otters, Skunks and Their Family* to be a "highly interesting, readable and informative book."

Patent soon developed a pattern of careful research and organization that allowed her to write first one, then two, then three books a year. "Each book was a review," she explained in *SAAS,* "in simple language, of everything known up to that time about the subject. I chose most of the subjects myself, and they were the things that had interested me as a child—frogs, tropical fish, reptiles, butterflies." Her 1977 title, *Evolution Goes on Every Day,* and her 1980 book, *The Lives of Spiders,* were both honored by the Society of Children's Book Writers; the former title received recognition as a Golden Kite Honor Book, and the latter won the Golden Kite Award. Reviewing *The Lives of Spiders* in *Science Books and Films,* Roy T. Cunningham called it "remarkable" for "retaining a high level of scholarship and breadth of coverage" with a "minimum of esoteric vocabulary."

In the early 1980s Patent began to work with photographer William Munoz, whose name she found in a Missoula newspaper. The two would travel together to photograph the animals for a book, and became a successful team. The first few books that Patent wrote with the help of Munoz allowed her to stay in Montana, but her desire to write books on grizzly bears, whooping cranes, and wolves soon took them to Alaska, New Mexico, Texas, and other states. *Pelicans,* a 1992 addition to Patent's and Munoz's collaborative efforts, is exemplary of the tone and format of much of their work together. "The book has a well-organized text with clear, crisp, full-color photos and a thorough index," noted Susan Oliver in a *School Library Journal* review. Oliver called *Pelicans* a "high-quality nature-book on an endearing clown of a bird."

Dogs of all sorts get a similar treatment in several further titles. In *Dogs: The Wolf Within,* Patent "explores selective breeding," according to *Booklist's* Deborah Abbott, "explaining how various types of dogs have been developed to accommodate people." From Greyhounds to Border collies, Patent explores a wide variety of such breeds in a "must" book for "dog lovers and science enthusiasts," Abbott wrote. Betsy Hearne, writing in *Bulletin of the Center for Children's Books,* commented that this "author-artist team's experience with books on various species makes for a smooth production as they coordinate appealing full-color photographs with facts on the origin, domestication, behavioral characteristics, and training potential of dogs." The Newfoundland breed came into focus in *Hugger to the Rescue,* another collaborative effort with Munoz that looks at the training of Newfoundlands as rescue dogs, and at one dog in particular, Hugger. Carol Kolb Phillips, reviewing the book in *School Library Journal,* paid special attention to Patent's "conversational, anecdote-filled narrative," and to Munoz's "attractive and informative" full-color photographs. The distant relations of dogs and wolves, inspired Patent to a work of fiction in *Return of the Wolf,* which tells the story of one lone wolf, Sedra, who is forced to leave her pack, then finds a mate, and has pups to begin to form a pack of her own. "Patent entirely resists anthropomorphism," commented Roger Sutton in *Bulletin of the Center for Children's Books,* "finding drama in the instinctive drives ... that shape a wolf's life rather than in New Age sentimentality."

Horses are also dear to Patent's heart, and she has written about them in several volumes, including *Where the Wild Horses Roam* and *Horses.* Reviewing *Horses,* a contributor to *Appraisal* noted that "Patent has written a horse book that is a good read for pleasure or a source of information for reports." Deer, elk, eagles, bears, even pigeons and apples have received the collaborative treatment of Patent and Munoz. In *Looking at Bears* "Patent and Munoz have once again combined their talents to produce a stunning book about animals," wrote a reviewer for *Appraisal.* "The text is clear and straightforward, the format uncluttered, and on almost every page is a striking photograph of bears."

Reviewing *Pigeons* in *Booklist,* Carolyn Phelan noted, "This informative book offers a well-researched and readable text illustrated with clear, full-color photographs." Phelan found that the "most surprising chapter" dealt with studies of pigeon intelligence in which trained birds have been able to tell the difference between a Monet and a Picasso painting. "This excellent addition to science collections will make readers come away with a new respect for this common bird," Phelan concluded. Turning her skills to the plant kingdom, Patent has also written about America's most popular fruit in *Apple Trees,* a description of the life cycle of the apple from seed to fruit. A writer for *Kirkus Reviews* noted, "Crisp, full-color photographs highlight all phases of tree and apple growth, coupled with clear, detailed drawings that explain more difficult concepts and processes."

Working with Munoz and other illustrators, Patent has produced many books dealing with individual topics of evolutionary change and adaptation in animals. *Feathers* looks at the role of those quilled projections in flight, insulation, and camouflage in a "captivating volume" with "fact-filled pages" that is a "nonfiction bonanza," according to *Booklist*'s Abbott. Luvada Kuhn commented in *Voice of Youth Advocates,* "This small book with its handy little index will be a useful tool for the student in natural history or anyone with an interest in birds." In *What Good Is a Tail?,* Patent and Munoz teamed up "on another winning book … with a lively text, appealing color photographs, and intriguing science facts showing just how useful a tail can be," according to a writer for *Kirkus Reviews.* The two also worked together to determine *Why Mammals Have Fur,* an "eye-catching book … well designed with clear color photographs," according to a reviewer for *Appraisal.* Working with Kendahl Jan Jubb as illustrator, Patent has taken a look at animal adaptation in *Flashy Fantastic Rain Forest Frogs* and at coloration in *Bold and Bright, Black-and-White Animals.* Reviewing the former title, a writer for *Kirkus Reviews* called it a "beautiful concise look at a surprisingly varied subject." In the latter title, Patent turns her attention to fourteen animals, such as the skunk and zebra, that come in black and white and explains why. Reviewing *Bold and Bright* in *Booklist,* Shelley Townsend-Hudson noted, "There is so much to enjoy and learn in this beautiful book …. It's a standout and an outstanding book." And animal intelligence is explored in *Alex and Friends,* "a fascinating discussion," according to Elizabeth S. Watson writing in *Horn Book Guide.*

Becoming increasingly concerned with the plight of wildlife, Patent remarked in her autobiographical sketch that "wild things always seem to lose out in today's world …. We need to realize that we are part of nature, that without nature, we are not whole." To aid in such a realization, Patent has written a number of books dealing with issues of preservation, endangered species, and ecology. In *Places of Refuge* she takes a look at the National Wildlife Refuge System, while in *The Challenges of Extinction* she examines the impact of plant and animal extinction. Habitat preservation and restoration is the theme of *Habitats: Saving Wild Places,* a "brief but effective introduction," as a contributor to *Kirkus Reviews* noted, and in *The Vanishing Feast* Patent tackles the threat to the world's food supplies caused by the reduction of genetic diversity. This issue is further explored in her *Biodiversity,* a science book that is "both illuminating and inspiring," according to *Horn Book*'s Margaret A. Bush.

With *Back to the Wild,* Patent relates the successful return of animals to the wild, and in *Children Save the Rain Forest* she tells of the efforts of children around the world to raise enough money to buy a 42,000 acre tract of rain forest in Costa Rica.

Patent has also ventured into more historical and archaeological realms in such books as *West By Covered Wagon* and *Homesteading,* and also a group of books for the "Frozen in Time" series, including *In Search of Maiasaurs, Mystery of the Lascaux Cave, Secrets of the Ice Man, The Lost City of Pompeii,* and *The Incredible Story of China's Buried Warriors.* Reviewing the last two titles in *Booklist,* Hazel Rochman noted that the books "combine dramatic history with fascinating information." Such information comes in the form of text, time-lines, and a magazine-style design that "will encourage browsing," Rochman also remarked.

The majority of Patent's books, however, explain the history, breeding, growth and habits of various groups of animals, and have been widely praised for their clarity, thoroughness, and readability. Whether she is describing worms or whales, Patent's works appeal to students of all ages, from the bright eight-year-old to the curious high school student. She may use difficult vocabulary, but she explains the words used and often supplies a helpful glossary. Also, humorous examples of strange animal behavior and vivid pictures frequently combine to make her books more interesting than the ordinary textbook. Sarah Gagne, who has reviewed many of Patent's works, says that she "could probably make interesting the life and ancestors of even a garden mole."

Patent concluded in *SAAS:* "I hope that my writing can help children get in touch with the world of living things and realize how dependent we are on them, not just on the wild world but on domesticated plants and animals as well. We owe our existence to the earth, and it is the balance of nature that sustains all life; we upset that balance at our peril. I believe that well-informed children can grow up into responsible citizens capable of making the wise but difficult decisions necessary for the survival of a livable world. I plan to continue to write for those children, helping to provide them with the

In her chronicle of the late nineteenth and early twentieth centuries, Patent relates the events of the migration of settlers into the challenging American prairieland. (From Homesteading: Settling America's Heartland. *Illustrated with photographs by William Munoz.)*

information they will need in the difficult but exciting times ahead."

Biographical and Critical Sources

BOOKS

Authors of Books for Young People, 3rd edition, edited by Martha Ward et al, Scarecrow Press, 1990.
Children's Literature Review, Volume 19, Gale, 1990, pp. 147-166.
Contemporary Authors, New Revision Series, Volume 24, Gale, 1988.
Sixth Book of Junior Authors and Illustrators, edited by Sally Holmes Holtze, H. W. Wilson, 1989.
Sutherland, Zena, and May Hill Arbuthnot, *Children and Books,* seventh edition, Scott, Foresman (Chicago), 1986.

PERIODICALS

Appraisal: Science Books for Young People, fall, 1974, Heddie Kent, review of *Weasels, Otters, Skunks and Their Family,* p. 33; winter, 1976, p. 33; spring, 1979, pp. 47-48; winter, 1980, pp. 45-46; winter, 1982, p. 52; fall, 1983, p. 52; spring, 1985, p. 32; winter, 1987, pp. 55-56; spring, 1988, p. 28; fall, 1989; winter, 1993, pp. 38-40; spring, 1994, review of *Horses,* pp. 76-77; spring, 1995, review of *Looking at Bears,* p. 46; autumn, 1995, review of *Why Mammals Have Fur,* p. 36; winter, 1996, pp. 46-47; summer, 1996, p. 27; spring, 1999, p. 44.
Booklist, June 15, 1987; May 15, 1989; March 15, 1990; June 1, 1991; May 15, 1992, Deborah Abbott, review of *Feathers,* p. 1680; June 1, 1993, D. Abbott, review of *Dogs: The Wolf Within,* p. 1826; February 1, 1997, p. 943; September 1, 1997, Carolyn Phelan, review of *Pigeons,* p. 120; September 1, 1998, Shelley Townsend-Hudson, review of *Bold and Bright, Black-and-White Animals,* pp. 122-23; November 15, 1998, pp. 488, 584; December 1, 1999, p. 699; February 1, 2000, Hazel Rochman, review of *The Incredible Story of China's Buried Warriors* and *Lost City of Pompeii.*
Bulletin of the Center for Children's Books, November, 1991; February, 1993, p. 187; July-August, 1993, Betsy Hearne, review of *Dogs: The Wolf Within,* pp. 355-56; July, 1995, Roger Sutton, review of *Return of the Wolf,* p. 394; October, 1996, p. 71; September, 1997, p. 23; December, 1998, p. 141.
Horn Book, October, 1973; April, 1978; October, 1979; February, 1980; October, 1981, Sarah Gagne, review of *Horses and Their Wild Relatives,* pp. 558-559; January-February, 1995, p. 70; July-August, 1995, p. 481; January-February, 1997, Margaret A. Bush, review of *Biodiversity,* p. 78; January-February, 1999, p. 84.
Horn Book Guide, Spring, 1999, Elizabeth S. Watson, review of *Alex and Friends,* p. 107.
Kirkus Reviews, February 15, 1993, review of *Habitats,* p. 233; January 1, 1994, review of *What Good Is a Tail?,* p. 73; January 15, 1997, review of *Flashy Fantastic Rain Forest Frogs,* p. 144; February 1, 1998, review of *Apple Trees,* pp. 199-200.
Patent, Dorothy Hinshaw, article in *Something about the Author Autobiography Series,* Volume 13, Gale, 1991, pp. 137-154.
School Library Journal, February, 1977, p. 67; March, 1979, p. 150; February, 1980, p. 71; February, 1981, p. 77; November, 1984, p. 127; October, 1985, p. 186; August, 1987, p. 87; August, 1988, p. 91; January, 1989; March, 1990; December, 1992, Susan Oliver, review of *Pelicans,* p. 126; February, 1993, p. 102; July, 1993, p. 32; June, 1994, p. 141; July, 1994, Carol Kolb Phillips, review of *Hugger to the Rescue,* p. 97; July, 1995, p. 79; March, 1997, p. 180; April, 1998, p. 122; March, 1999, p. 226; October, 1999, p. 174.
Science Books: A Quarterly Review, May, 1974, review of *Weasels, Otters, Skunks and Their Family,* p. 76.
Science Books and Films, September-October, 1981, Roy T. Cunningham, review of *The Lives of Spiders,* p. 21.
Sutherland, Zena, and May Hill Arbuthnot, "Informational Books," in *Children and Books,* 7th edition, Scott, Foresman, 1986, pp. 484-548.
Voice of Youth Advocates, June, 1992, Luvada Kuhn, review of *Feathers,* pp. 131-32.

ON-LINE

Dorothy Hinshaw Patent Web site, www.dorothy-hinshawpatent.com/

—Sketch by J. Sydney Jones

*   *   *

PLATT, Richard 1953-

Personal

Born April 15, 1953, in the United Kingdom. *Education:* Studied engineering at the University of Newcastle upon Tyne, 1972-73; earned diploma in art from Newcastle College of Art and Design, 1974; Leeds Polytechnic University, B.A. (first-class honors), 1977; attended Central School of Art.

Addresses

Home—The Old Squash Court, Bayham Abbey, Tunbridge Wells, Kent TN3 8BG, England. *Agent*—Sheila Watson, Watson, Little Ltd., Capo di Monte, Windmill Hill, London NW3 6RJ, England. *E-mail*—rich@rdplatt.co.uk.

Career

Worked as a photographer and teacher of photography, 1978-80; Camerawork Gallery, London, England, 1979-80; Marshall Cavendish, sub-editor, 1980-82; Mitchell Beazley International, technical editor, 1982-83; affiliated with Applied Holographics PLC, 1984-85; freelance writer, 1985—. *Member:* Society of Authors.

Writings

Smuggler's Britain, Cassell, 1991.

Stephen Biesty's Incredible Cross-Sections Book, illustrations by Biesty, Dorling Kindersley, 1992.

Stephen Biesty's Cross-Sections Man-of-War, illustrations by Biesty, Dorling Kindersley, 1993.

Stephen Biesty's Cross-Sections Castle, illustrations by Biesty, Dorling Kindersley, 1994.

Stephen Biesty's Incredible Body, illustrations by Biesty, Dorling Kindersley, 1988.

The Smithsonian Visual Timeline of Inventions, Dorling Kindersley, 1994.

(With Brian Delf) *In the Beginning: The Nearly Complete History of Almost Everything,* Dorling Kindersley, 1995.

Stephen Biesty's Incredible Explosions, illustrations by Biesty, Dorling Kindersley, 1996.

Stephen Biesty's Incredible Everything, illustrations by Biesty, Dorling Kindersley, 1997.

Inventions Explained: A Beginner's Guide to Technological Breakthroughs, Henry Holt, 1997.

(With Brian Delf) *History: The Really Interesting Bits!,* Dorling Kindersley, 1998.

Castle Diary: The Journal of Tobias Burgess, illustrated by Chris Riddell, Candlewick, 1999.

"EYEWITNESS" SERIES

Film, 1993.

Pirate, Knopf, 1995.

Spy, Knopf/Borzoi, 1996.

Shipwreck, Dorling Kindersley, 1997.

Also author of monthly column for *SLRCamera,* 1980-82; authored one volume in the *Kodak Library of Creative Photography,* published by Mitchell Beazley in the 1980s; contributor to books and periodicals.

Sidelights

Richard Platt is the author of a growing list of informative books for young readers, and also writes for innovative multimedia projects. Some of his most popular works have been collaborations with Stephen Biesty on the *Cross-Sections* and *Incredible* series. After a failed attempt to forge a career as a photographer, Platt discovered that he had a knack for writing. He started with "how to" articles and books for budding amateur photographers, but soon determined that writing for children offered more scope and variety.

In the 1990s, Platt teamed up with popular juvenile illustrator Biesty for several books, beginning with *Stephen Biesty's Incredible Cross-Sections Book,* published in 1992. The following year, a second in the series, *Stephen Biesty's Cross-Sections Man-of-War,* proved equally interesting for late-elementary age readers, especially those enchanted by seventeenth-century battleships. Alongside Biesty's cutaway illustrations, Platt provides explanatory text that indicates the purpose and activities in each section of the ship. The hardships of life aboard such vessels for their often 800-member crews are not overlooked, either, and the drawings depict food rations crawling with maggots and a doctor's pail containing severed limbs. Ellen Mandel, writing for *Booklist,* asserted that Platt's "intriguing text" serves to

Through his eleven-year-old narrator, Richard Platt offers readers a glimpse of the life of a knight-in-training during the Middle Ages. (From Castle Diary: The Journal of Tobias Burgess, Page, *illustrated by Chris Riddell.)*

make "this meticulously presented book a treasure of factual content and visual imagery."

For *Stephen Biesty's Incredible Everything,* Platt provided more informative paragraphs to accompany the illustrations for many everyday products, such as athletic shoes and compact discs. Much of the text revolves around the manufacturing process. *Stephen Biesty's Incredible Body* is a lesson in human anatomy, with sections on each of the body's systems and several major organs. The digestive system, alone, takes up four pages. Platt has also worked with the illustrator on *Stephen Biesty's Cross-Sections Castle* and *Stephen Biesty's Incredible Explosions.*

For British publisher, Dorling Kindersley, Platt has authored several titles in their "Eyewitness" series, some of which have appeared in the United States under the Knopf/Borzoi imprint. *Pirate,* which appeared in 1996, details the world of corsairs, privateers, and crime on the seas throughout history. A reviewer for *Science Books and Films,* Richard B. Woodbury, praised the work as "a veritable miniencyclopedia or minimuseum" and "a pleasure to look at." *Spy,* issued by an American publisher in 1996, chronicles the history of espionage, and the decisive role intelligence-gathering triumphs have played in history. Of particular emphasis are the code-breaking endeavors by Allied intelligence networks during World War II. *Shipwreck,* the seventy-second in the Eyewitness series, investigates some famous sea disasters and rescues. Like the others, it is lavishly illustrated. Chris Stephenson, writing in *School Librarian,* called it "an excellent source of historical evidence and nautical information."

Platt has also written several books about inventions. His *The Smithsonian Visual Timeline of Inventions,* which appeared in 1994, won praise from reviewers for its comprehensiveness. Platt organizes his pages and the development of technology throughout the ages into five sections, including: agriculture, conquest, and communication. The timeline begins at 600,000 BCE, around the time that humans likely began using fire, and makes predictions for innovations in other areas that may arrive in the near future. Cathryn A. Camper, reviewing it for *School Library Journal,* praised Platt's skilled use of illustration and text, which Camper felt "teaches a sophisticated form of literacy similar to" that provided with multimedia learning tools—an area in which Platt already had a great deal of writing experience. "Readers will delight in the colorful pictures and the text, which gives just enough information to satisfy curiosity," opined *Voice of Youth Advocates* writer Christine Miller.

Platt has also written another work on essential technology with the 1997 tome *Inventions Explained: A Beginner's Guide to Technological Breakthroughs.* Its text explains, for elementary-age readers, some notable achievements throughout human history, and how they positively affected life. He begins with the first tools in primitive cultures, and moves on all the way to spacecraft. "The strength of the book is the way it conveys the global nature of inventions," noted a *Kirkus Reviews* assessment.

For young readers, Platt has penned some books on general history topics as well. With illustrator Brian Delf, he wrote *History: The Really Interesting Bits!,* for British publisher Dorling Kindersley in 1998. The work describes thirteen significant events that changed the course of history, including the construction of Egypt's Great Pyramid, the fall of the Roman Empire, the Russian Revolution, and World War II. Each is given a double-page spread, and Delf provides the illustrations and maps. A *Books for Keeps* review from Clive Barnes commended the writing as "accurate," and further noted that "the design is clear, colourful and enticing." Nansi Taylor, writing for *School Librarian,* termed it "a book to pore over and learn from."

In *Castle Diary: The Journal of Tobias Burgess,* Platt offers readers a glimpse into what life might have been like during the Middle Ages for an eleven-year-old boy who lives in a castle as a page, or a knight in training. Accompanied by illustrations from Chris Riddell, the 1999 title describes, in diary form, Tobias's daily life, his page friends, an illness in which he is "bled" as a cure, and a jousting tournament. Further information on medieval history is included at the back of the book. "Readers will enjoy the child's language and descriptions," stated Betsy Barnett in her *School Library Journal* review, and concluded by singling the work out as a "fresh, appealing offering."

Biographical and Critical Sources

PERIODICALS

Booklist, October 1, 1993, Ellen Mandel, review of *Stephen Biesty's Cross-Sections Man-of-War,* p. 337.

Books for Keeps, November, 1996, review of *Spy,* p. 15; May, 1998, Clive Barnes, review of *History,* p. 25.

Kirkus Reviews, September 1, 1995, review of *In the Beginning,* p. 1286; December 15, 1997, review of *Inventions Explained,* p. 1838.

Magpies, March, 1998, Lynne Babbage, review of *History,* p. 42.

School Librarian, February, 1996, Nansi Taylor, review of *In the Beginning,* p. 35; spring, 1998, Nansi Taylor, review of *History,* p. 51, and Chris Stephenson, review of *Shipwreck,* p. 41.

School Library Journal, February, 1993, Judie Porter, review of *Film,* p. 103; February, 1995, Cathryn A. Camper, review of *Smithsonian Visual Timeline,* p. 110; June, 1997, Eldon Younce, review of *Spy,* p. 142; January, 1998, Eldon Younce, review of *Stephen Biesty's Incredible Everything,* p. 128; February, 1998, Anne Chapman Callaghan, review of *Inventions Explained,* p. 115; January, 1999, Christine A. Moesch, review of *Stephen Biesty's Incredible Body,* p. 151; December, 1999, Betsy Barnett, review of *Castle Diary: The Journal of Tobias Burgess,* p. 158.

Science Books and Films, November, 1995, Richard B. Woodbury, review of *Pirate,* p. 239.

Voice of Youth Advocates, August, 1995, Christine Miller, review of *Smithsonian Visual Timeline,* p. 187.

* * *

POKEBERRY, P. J.
See MITCHELL, B(etty) J(o)

* * *

PRICEMAN, Marjorie 19(?)

Personal

Education: Rhode Island School of Design, B.F.A.; has taken graduate-level writing classes. *Hobbies and other interests:* Films.

Career

Author and illustrator.

Awards, Honors

Top Ten Picture Books of the Year citation, *Redbook* magazine, 1989, for *Friend or Frog;* Best Books of the Year selection, *Horn Book Fanfare,* 1990, for *Rachel Fister's Blister* by Amy MacDonald; ALA Notable Book selection and Best Books of the Year selection, *School Library Journal,* both 1991, for *For Laughing out Loud: Poems to Tickle Your Funnybone* by Jack Prelutsky; Best Books of the Year selection, *Horn Book*

Fanfare, 1993, for *A. Nonny Mouse Writes Again* by Jack Prelutsky; ALA Notable Book selection, Library of Congress (Children's Literature Center) Noteworthy Children's Book selection, and Bulletin for the Center for Children's Books Blue Ribbon Book citation, all 1994, for *How to Make an Apple Pie and See the World;* Parent's Choice award, 1995, for *How Emily Blair Got Her Fabulous Hair* by Susan Garrison; ALA Notable Book selection and Bulletin for the Center for Children's Books Blue Ribbon Book citation, both 1996, for *What Zeesie Saw on Delancey Street* by Elsa Okon Rael; Best Books of the Year selection, *School Library Journal* and Best Books of the Year selection, *Publishers Weekly,* both 1997, for *One of Each* by Maryann Hoberman; Sydney Taylor Award for Jewish Literature, 1997, for *When Zaydeh Danced on Eldridge Street* by Rael; Critic's Choice selection, *Family Life* magazine, 1998, for *My Nine Lives: by Clio; New York Times* Best Illustrated Children's Book award, ALA Notable Book selection, and Bulletin for the Center for Children's

Books Blue Ribbon Book citation, all 1999, for *Emeline at the Circus. Zin! Zin! Zin! A Violin,* by Lloyd Moss, was named a Caldecott Honor book in 1995. The title also received a Best Books of the Year citation from the *School Library Journal,* was named an ALA Notable book selection and received a *New York Times* Best Illustrated Children's Book award, all in 1995.

Writings

SELF-ILLUSTRATED

Friend or Frog, Houghton Mifflin(Boston), 1989.
How to Make an Apple Pie and See the World, Knopf (New York City), 1994.
My Nine Lives: by Clio, Atheneum (New York City), 1998.
Emeline at the Circus, Knopf, 1999.
(Reteller) *Froggie Went a Courting,* Little, Brown, 2000.

Evoking the character of immigrant neighborhoods of the 1930s, Marjorie Priceman illustrates Elsa Okon Rael's tale of a young Jewish girl who is taken by surprise when her stern grandfather unexpectedly breaks into dance during the holiday celebration of Simchas Torah. (From When Zaydeh Danced on Eldridge Street.*)*

ILLUSTRATOR

Amy MacDonald, *Rachel Fister's Blister,* Houghton Mifflin, 1990.

Nancy Van Laan, *A Mouse in My House,* Random House (New York City), 1990.

Jack Prelutsky, selector, *For Laughing out Loud: Poems to Tickle Your Funnybone,* Random House, 1991.

Prelutsky, selector, *A. Nonny Mouse Writes Again! Poems,* Random House, 1993.

Van Laan, *The Tiny, Tiny Boy and the Big, Big Cow: A Scottish Folk Tale,* Knopf, 1993.

Lloyd Moss, *Zin! Zin! Zin! A Violin,* Simon & Schuster (New York City), 1995.

Prelutsky, selector, *For Laughing out Louder: More Poems to Tickle Your Funnybone,* Knopf, 1995.

Susan Garrison, *How Emily Blair Got Her Fabulous Hair,* BridgeWater (New York City), 1995.

Amy MacDonald, *Cousin Ruth's Tooth,* Houghton (Boston), 1996.

Elsa Okon Rael, *What Zeesie Saw on Delancey Street,* Simon & Schuster, 1996.

Rael, *When Zaydeh Danced on Eldridge Street,* Simon & Schuster, 1997.

Wendy Gelsanliter and Frank Christian, *Dancin' in the Kitchen,* Putnam (New York City), 1998.

Mary Ann Hoberman, *One of Each,* Little, Brown, 1997.

Phyllis Theroux, *Serefina under the Circumstances,* Greenwillow (New York City), 1999.

Couric, Katie, *The Brand New Kid,* Doubleday, 2000.

Adaptations

How to Make an Apple Pie and See the World was adapted as a musical, produced by the Kennedy Center for the Performing Arts in Washington, D.C.

Sidelights

Author and illustrator Marjorie Priceman is an illustrator in great demand for her humorous and energetic artwork. Although she has illustrated the works of such authors as Jack Prelutsky, Amy MacDonald, and Nancy Van Laan, Priceman began her career with the self-illustrated *Friend or Frog.* She has gone on to pen several more original tales—including *My Nine Lives: by Clio* and *Emeline at the Circus*—that have drawn enthusiastic praise from critics. "Her picture books are rollicking and riotous," commented a *Publishers Weekly* profiler, "filled with mischievous creatures and animated household objects; it often seems as though the borders of the pages are unable to contain the energy of her artwork and creations."

Priceman's first published picture book, *Friend or Frog,* is based on the experiences of her family and friends with frogs. In the story, a young girl named Kate meets a green, spotted frog carrying a towel with the word "Hilton" on it. Naming the frog after its towel, Kate takes Hilton from Florida to live with her in New York City. The two become best friends and live happily in the city until Hilton is spotted in a guest's teacup. Then and there, Kate's unreasonable mother insists that the "creature" must go. After Kate fails to find a suitable

Beginning her nine incarnations in Mesopotamia in 3000 BC, a precocious puss named Clio invents the alphabet, names the constellations, catches a ride with Leif Eriksson, and makes the Mona Lisa smile. (From My Nine Lives, *written and illustrated by Priceman.)*

new owner for Hilton, he decides to return to Florida, and while Kate misses her friend she enjoys his postcards. Marcia Hupp praised Priceman's work in *School Library Journal* as a "rollicking romp" told with "exuberance and humor"; her opinion reflected that of the editors of *Redbook* magazine who selected *Friend or Frog* as one of the ten top picture books of the year.

Clio the cat is introduced to readers through her "autobiography" titled: *My Nine Lives.* Beginning her nine incarnations in Mesopotamia in 3000 B.C., the precocious puss names the constellations, invents the alphabet, catches a ride with Leif Eriksson, and makes the Mona Lisa smile during her nine lives. While noting that the story has more appeal to adults than younger readers, Michael Cart noted in his *Booklist* appraisal that "Priceman's hand-lettered text and illustrations rendered in various period-appropriate styles are engaging and witty." "This beguiling spoof is the cat's meow," added a *Publishers Weekly* contributor, praising the book's inclusion of several interesting and accurate historical facts.

In *Emeline at the Circus,* Priceman's 1999 picture book, she serves up what a *Horn Book* reviewer calls "a rambunctious parody of earnest and over-serious teaching" in the person of a second-grade teacher named Ms.

Splinter. Even a trip to the circus is drained of all fun by Ms. Splinter, who drones on about significant factoids. Emeline, however, gets a different learning experience after being picked up by a peanut-hungry elephant and made a part of the show under the big top. "Priceman captures the show's frenzied grace in freely painted forms that dance and swirl," noted the *Horn Book* critic, evidencing what *Booklist* reviewer Hazel Rochman called "her best, wildly exuberant style." Calling *Emeline at the Circus* "one of Priceman's most intriguing picture books," a *Publishers Weekly* contributor noted that each scene of "controlled chaos—as animals and performers in all manner of glitzy costume tumble, prance and parade about—attests to why this is called the greatest show on earth."

Priceman's *How to Make an Apple Pie and See the World* tells about a young girl who wants to make an apple pie but doesn't have all the ingredients she needs at home. Though the stores are closed, she doesn't give up; instead, she travels around the world to gather ingredients. The young pie baker journeys to Italy to find wheat for the flour, France to get a chicken and its eggs, Sri Lanka for cinnamon from the bark of a tree, England for a cow and its milk, Jamaica for sugar cane, and then to Vermont for apples. The book includes a recipe, so readers can make a pie along with the story's protagonist. A reviewer for the *Bulletin of the Center for Children's Books* described *How to Make an Apple Pie and See the World* as a "delightful contrast to more sober-sided narratives of food origins."

Other books that Priceman has both written and illustrated include *Froggie Went a Courting*, a modernized rendition of a Scottish folk tune that finds a lovestruck amphibian hopping a cab to visit the object of his affections—Ms. Mouse. The engagement and the wedding go smoothly, but during the reception a feline party crasher spoils the fun by making off with Auntie Rat. Priceman "more than matches [her] story's zip with gouache and cut-paper compositions in kicky color," noted a *Publishers Weekly* contributor of the light-hearted tale.

In addition to writing and illustrating her own stories, Priceman also collaborates with other children's book authors by matching picture book texts with her humorous illustrations. In Phyllis Theroux's *Serefina under the Circumstances*, Priceman's "bright gouache ... pictures are packed with witty details that extend the story and show a magical world," noted *Booklist* contributor Hazel Rochman, echoing praise by other critics. In *School Library Journal*, Miriam Lang Budin dubbed Priceman's paintings "clever, colorful, and energetic," and noted that they "add another dimension" to the story.

Several stories by author Elsa Okon Rael also benefit from Priceman's entertaining illustrations. *What Zeesie Saw on Delancey Street*, published in 1996, finds seven-year-old birthday girl Zeesie learning the spirit of giving when she attends a "package party" whereby money was raised to help newly arrived immigrant families. In *When Zaydeh Danced on Eldridge Street*, Rael explains

the Jewish holiday of Simchas Torah by depicting a girl and her grandfather sharing the solemn holiday celebration. Priceman's illustrations were praised by *Booklist* reviewer Rochman for "captur[ing] the Jewish immigrant neighborhood in New York City in the 1930s," while a *Publishers Weekly* contributor commented that the illustrations reflect "the sacredness and beauty of religious symbolism without abandoning her playful, deceptively casual style."

Biographical and Critical Sources

PERIODICALS

Booklist, April 15, 1989, Ilene Cooper, review of *Friend or Frog*, p. 1470; April 15, 1994, review of *How to Make an Apple Pie*, p. 1532; May 15, 1995, Julie Yates Walton, review of *Zin! Zin! Zin! A Violin*, p. 1650; October 1, 1997, Hazel Rochman, review of *When Zaydeh Danced on Eldridge Street*, p. 324; November 1, 1997, review of *One of Each*, p. 466; October 15, 1998, GraceAnne A. DeCandido, review of *Dancin' in the Kitchen*, p. 416; November 15, 1998, Michael Cart, review of *My Nine Lives: by Clio*, p. 591; April 1, 1999, H. Rochman, review of *Emeline at the Circus*, p. 1408; September 1, 1999, H. Rochman, review of *Serefina under the Circumstances*, p. 144.

Bulletin of the Center for Children's Books, July, 1989, p. 281; February, 1994, review of *How to Make an Apple Pie and See the World*, p. 199.

Horn Book, May-June, 1989, p. 363; November-December, 1993, review of *A. Nonny Nonny Mouse Writes Again!*, p. 750; September-October, 1994, p. 581; May, 1999, review of *Emeline at the Circus*, p. 320.

Publishers Weekly, December 22, 1989, Diane Roback, "Flying Starts: New Faces of 1989," pp. 26-32; April 11, 1994, p. 64; February 19, 1996, review of *Cousin Ruth's Tooth*, p. 215; February 17, 1997, "About Our Cover Artist," p. 133; June 16, 1997, review of *When Zaydeh Danced on Eldridge Street*, p. 59; August 10, 1998, review of *My Nine Lives*, p. 386; July 5, 1999, review of *Serefina under the Circumstances*, p. 20; March 8, 1999, review of *Emeline at the Circus*, p. 68; March 20, 2000, review of *Froggie Went a Courting*, p. 91.

School Library Journal, July, 1989, Marcia Hupp, review of *Friend or Frog*, p. 75; May, 1996, Anne Parker, review of *Cousin Ruth's Tooth*, p. 94; May, 1996, Sabrina L. Faunfetter, review of *For Laughing out Louder*, p. 107; December, 1996, Barbara Kiefer, review of *What Zeesie Saw on Delancey Street*, pp. 103-04; October, 1997, Susan Scheps, review of *When Zaydeh Danced on Eldridge Street*, p. 108; September, 1999, Miriam Lang Budin, review of *Serefina under the Circumstances*, p. 207; November, 1999, Veronica Schwartz, review of *Zin! Zin! Zin! A Violin*, p. 59.

PURDY, Carol 1943-

Personal

Born January 5, 1943, in Long Beach, CA; daughter of Melvin Boyce (a machinist) and Kathryn (a homemaker; maiden name, Wilbur) Slaughter; married John Purdy (a teacher), June 8, 1963; children: Laura, Mark, Sarah. *Education:* California State University, Long Beach, B.A., 1964; California State University, Sacramento, M.S.W., 1990. *Religion:* Church of Christ. *Hobbies and other interests:* Music, gardening, aerobics, drawing, water-skiing, traveling.

Addresses

Home—25310 68th Ave., Los Molinos, CA 96055. *Office*—Tehama County Mental Health, 1860 Walnut, Red Bluff, CA 96080. *Agent*—Faith Hamlin, Sanford J. Greenburger Associates, Inc., 55 Fifth Ave., New York, NY 10003.

As trouble escalates in her family, Nesuya, a Maidu Indian girl living in northern California, focuses more and more on the basket she is making for the annual memorial service held by her tribe.

Career

Orange Unified School District, Orange, CA, elementary school teacher, 1964-67; Kid Power Program, Red Bluff, CA, founder, 1988—; Tehama County Mental Health, Red Bluff, social worker, 1989—; writer. *Member:* Society of Children's Book Writers, National Association of Social Workers, American Art Therapy Association.

Awards, Honors

School Library Journal voted *Mrs. Merriwether's Musical Cat* one of the best books of 1994; *Nesuya's Basket* was named *Smithsonian Magazine* Notable Book for Children, 1997.

Writings

Iva Dunnit and the Big Wind, illustrated by Steven Kellogg, Dial, 1985.
Least of All, illustrated by Tim Arnold, Macmillan, 1987.
Kid Power: Groups of High Risk Children, Mill Creek Publishers, 1989.
Mrs. Merriwether's Musical Cat, illustrated by Petra Mathers, Putnam, 1994.
Nesuya's Basket, Robert Rinehart (Boulder, CO), 1997.

Also author of *Helping Them Heal, A Guide for Parents of Children in Play Therapy* and *Playing with Janet, A Child's Story about Play Therapy.*

Sidelights

Carol Purdy once told *SATA:* "I was not one of those children who took a flashlight to bed in order to write in my journal and knew from age three that my destiny was to be an author. While growing up in the big city of Long Beach, California, I had no idea that I would some day be a writer. My greatest interests as a child were art and music. I sang in the school choir, played several instruments, and took art classes.

"While in college I married a fellow student, and we both decided to become elementary school teachers. When we were expecting our first child, we wanted to find a country environment in which to raise a family. We moved to a seventy-five-year-old farmhouse near Red Bluff, California, and tried everything from raising pigs, horses, cattle and chickens to doing our own butchering, cheesemaking, and butter churning.

"After the birth of my third child, I thought of the advice of my high school English teacher who said I should become a writer. Six years later, after wearing out three typewriters, my book *Iva Dunnit and the Big Wind* was accepted for publication....

"With the wealth of family stories and ever-changing events of my life, there are always ideas for children's books. Finding time to write is the continual problem. I have never been a writer who devotes a certain portion of each day to the written word. Rather, I have only written when an idea became enticing to the point that I couldn't keep from developing it into a story.

"My keen interest in the problems facing children today led me to learn skills to help with those problems. My primary activities today center around my work as a psychotherapist and counselor with children and families. In addition, I lecture and train on the subjects of high-risk children, art therapy, and the Kid Power Program, which I developed early in my career, to help children from troubled families.

"My enthusiasm for writing children's books has not dimmed, and one of the most delightful aspects of my life is doing author visits at elementary schools. I also continue to be alert for that compelling idea which will start me writing the next book."

Purdy's first book, *Iva Dunnit and the Big Wind* warmed the hearts of reviewers who found in it a tall tale set in the American frontier west. Iva and her six children live by their wits and hard work and together they defeat a prairie fire and save the youngest child from hungry wolves. Then a big wind blows across the prairie and only the chickens are left outside to suffer it until Iva goes out to save them, knowing she has trained her children well to stay put out of danger when told. Unfortunately, the wind almost blows Iva away as she struggles to hold down the roof with four chickens tied to her corset strings, while her dependable children stay put inside the cabin. Iva ends up thankful when her children decide to disobey her and come to the rescue. "Tall-tale heroes like Paul Bunyan may have met their match in Iva Dunnit and her six children," declared a reviewer for *Horn Book*. In addition, Steven Kellogg's illustrations "make the prairie a striking setting for a tongue-in-cheek pioneer story with built-in child appeal," averred a contributor to *Bulletin of the Center for Children's Books*.

Purdy's next story is set in turn-of-the-twentieth-century Vermont. In *Least of All* critics found a heartwarming story about the youngest child in a large farming family who is convinced she has little to contribute until the day she teaches herself to read. At seven, Little Raven Hannah is finally allowed to churn the butter and in that way contribute to the family's welfare, while her older brothers do all the other farm work. The girl decides to take the family bible to keep her company while she performs her lonely chore and by reciting the verses she has memorized while following along with her finger, she teaches herself to read, something no one else in the family can do. Then Raven Hannah does an even better thing: she teaches her family to read too. "This is a quiet story, a fulfilling tale about the joy of accomplishment," remarked Christine Behrmann in *School Library Journal*. "The story is understated but warm," Betsy Hearne observed in *Bulletin of the Center for Children's Books*. "When the child's parents are moved by her reading, readers will be touched as well."

On a more whimsical note comes *Mrs. Merriwether's Musical Cat*, a gently humorous story about a stray cat whose metronomic tail saves Mrs. Merriwether's piano lessons from disaster until the day the cat disappears. When the cat returns with three similarly equipped kittens, joy and merriment are again restored to the houses on Mrs. Merriwether's street. "Music aficionados and cat lovers especially will find much to like here," declared a reviewer for *Publishers Weekly*.

Biographical and Critical Sources

PERIODICALS

Booklist, May 1, 1986, review of *Iva Dunnit and the Big Wind,* p. 1321; March 1, 1987, Denise M. Wilms, review of *Least of All,* pp. 1055-56; November 15, 1994, Linda Ward-Callaghan, review of *Mrs. Merriwether's Musical Cat,* p. 613.

Bulletin of the Center for Children's Books, February, 1986, review of *Iva Dunnit and the Big Wind,* p. 116; March, 1987, Betsy Hearne, review of *Least of All,* pp. 133-34.

Horn Book, March-April, 1986, review of *Iva Dunnit and the Big Wind,* p. 196; March-April, 1995, Ann A. Flowers, review of *Mrs. Merriwether's Musical Cat,* p. 188.

Kliatt, September, 1997, Sherri Forgash Ginsberg, review of *Nesuya's Basket,* p. 14.

New York Times Book Review, September 20, 1987, Jane Yolen, review of *Least of All,* p. 32.

Publishers Weekly, August 1, 1994, review of *Mrs. Merriwether's Musical Cat,* p. 78.

School Library Journal, June-July, 1987, Christine Behrmann, review of *Least of All,* p. 88; December, 1994, review of *Mrs. Merriwether's Musical Cat,* p. 26.

West Coast Review of Books, November/December, 1985, review of *Iva Dunnit and the Big Wind,* p. 51.*

*   *   *

PURNELL, Idella 1901-1982
(Idella Purnell Stone, Ikey Stone)

Personal

Born April 1, 1901, in Guadalajara, Mexico; died December 1, 1982, in Los Angeles, CA; daughter of George Edward (a dentist) and Idella (Bragg) Purnell; married Remington Stone, September 10, 1932 (deceased); children: Maryjane (Mrs. Robert Osborn), Remington P.S., Carrie (Mrs. Johnnie Ceniceros). *Education:* University of California, Berkeley, B.A., 1922; Dianetic Research Centers, H.D.A., 1950, D.Scn., 1954. *Politics:* "Middle of the road Democrat." *Religion:* Huna, Scientology, Christian.

Career

Primary school teacher in Guadalajara, Mexico, 1915; U.S. Foreign Service, secretary in American Consulate in Guadalajara, 1922-24; founder; publisher, and editor, *Palms* poetry magazine, 1923-30; Los Angeles Public Library, Los Angeles, CA, head of foreign book department, summer, 1925; University of Guadalajara,

Guadalajara, organizer and dean of first summer session, 1932; opened and operated gold mine in Ameca, Mexico, 1935-37; taught creative writing in Los Angeles, 1938-39; riveter for Douglas Aviation and for Fletcher Aviation during World War II; Dianetic Center for Dianetics and Scientology, Pasadena, CA, director, 1951-57, practitioner, 1957-66; free-lance writer. *Member:* Inter-America Society, Poetry Society of America, Science Fiction Writers Association, Mexican Congress of Fine Arts and Humanities (permanent member).

Awards, Honors

The Merry Frogs named Julia Ellsworth Ford Foundation Book, 1936; diploma from Second Mexican Congress for the Fine Arts and Humanities, 1967; *Saturday Review* poetry award.

Writings

FOR CHILDREN, EXCEPT AS NOTED

(With John M. Weatherwax) *The Talking Bird: An Aztec Story Book,* illustrated by Frances Purnell Dehlsen, Macmillan, 1930.

Tales Told to Little Paco by His Grandfather, Macmillan, 1930.

(With John M. Weatherwax) *Why the Bee Is Busy, and Other Rumanian Fairy Tales: Told to Little Marcu by Baba Maritza,* illustrated by Helen Smith, Macmillan, 1930.

The Wishing Owl: A Maya Storybook, Macmillan, 1931.

Little Yusuf: The Story of a Syrian Boy, illustrated by James L. McCreery, Macmillan, 1931.

The Lost Princess of Yucatan, Holt, 1931.

The Forbidden City, Macmillan, 1932.

(Contributor) Emma Lindsay-Squier, *Gringa* (adult nonfiction), Houghton, 1934.

Pedro the Potter, illustrated by Nils Hogner, Thomas Nelson, 1935.

The Merry Frogs, illustrated by Nadine Wenden, Suttonhouse, 1936.

(Adapter) Felix Salton, *Walt Disney's Bambi,* Health, 1944.

(Contributor) Witter Bynner, *Journey with Genius: Recollections and Reflections Concerning D. H. Lawrence* (adult nonfiction), John Day, 1951.

Luther Burbank: El Mago de las Plantas (title means "*Luther Burbank: The Magician of the Plants*"), Espasa Calpe (Argentina), 1955.

(Contributor) Edward H. Nehls, editor, *D. H. Lawrence: A Composite Biography* (adult nonfiction), three volumes, University of Wisconsin Press, 1957-59.

UNDER NAME IDELLA PURNELL STONE

(Compiler and author of introduction) *Fourteen Great Tales of ESP* (science fiction), Gold Medal Books, 1969.

(Compiler and author of introduction) *Never in This World* (science fiction), Fawcett, 1971.

Thirty Mexican Menus in Spanish and English (cookbook), Ritchie, 1971.

Stories and poems represented in children's and adult anthologies. Contributor of poetry, book reviews, short stories, and articles to literary and popular magazines for children and adults, including *Saturday Review, Saturday Evening Post, New York Post, Chatelaine, Christian Science Monitor, Child Life,* and *Torchbearer,* and to newspapers, including *New York Herald Tribune, Los Angeles Times,* and *Sierra Madre View.*

Sidelights

Before Idella Purnell's death in 1982, her career included stints as a riveter and gold mine operator, as well as a Dianetics practitioner and children's book author. She lived and worked in Mexico for many years, and spent some time teaching at the University of Guadalajara; her writing was often influenced by her experiences within the Mexican community. In addition to founding, publishing, and editing the poetry magazine *Palms* in the 1920s, she compiled two science-fiction anthologies, and produced a variety of works for young people.

Purnell drew on her familiarity with Mexican history and folklore for *The Talking Bird: An Aztec Story Book,* one of her first books for children. Co-written by John M. Weatherwax, the text follows the daily life of Paco, a boy who lives in Guadalajara with his story-telling grandfather. Through Paco's childhood adventures, Purnell narrates a series of Aztec tales that provide readers with details about (then) contemporary Mexican culture. Writing in the *Saturday Review of Literature,* Mark Van Doren maintained that Purnell's style is "as interesting as it is clear, quite as warm as it is . . . true," and noted that she depicts Paco's life in Mexico "with only enough remoteness to make the place utterly charming while it remains perfectly creditable." *New York Times Book Review* contributor Anne T. Eaton offered a favorable assessment of Frances Purnell Dehlson's illustrations. She deemed the pictures "excellent," and credited both the authors and illustrator with successfully communicating their "love for the blue skies and vivid colors of the [Mexican] country" to their readers.

Purnell turned to the Middle East for the subject of one of her next books, *Little Yusuf: The Story of a Syrian Boy.* Like *The Talking Bird, Little Yusuf* centers on the day to day life of a child, and the folktales told to him by a grandparent. While following Yusuf's daily activities, readers receive an introduction to the realities of rural existence, from food preparation to agricultural production. Eaton found that the book has a "picturesque quality," but judged *Little Yusuf* "less spontaneous than *The Talking Bird.*" In her *Saturday Review of Literature* commentary, May Lamberton Becker asserted that Purnell's text possesses "the two qualities essential to a travel book—much accurate detail and the capacity to communicate the charm of the unknown."

Purnell returned to a Mexican setting in many of her later works, including *Pedro the Potter.* In this book, she tells the story of Pedro, a young man who assumes responsibility for his family after his father is wrongly accused of murder. Pedro emerges from the experience with a new understanding of the values of individual freedom and cultural heritage. He goes on to become a celebrated painter in Mexico City, but returns to his native village to help the community with the art that he creates. In storybook form, *Pedro the Potter* outlines the political and racial conflicts between indigenous peoples and settlers of European descent in Mexico in the first half of the twentieth century. Commenting in the *New York Times Book Review,* Ellen Lewis Buell lauded *Pedro the Potter* as a book that "successfully interpret[s] the traditions and spirit of the American Indian," and observed that the "contrast between the old order and the aims of the revolutionaries is skillfully shown."

Purnell's additional work for children includes, among other titles, *Why the Bee Is Busy, and Other Rumanian Fairy Tales* and *The Merry Frogs.* Through folktales and illustrations, both of these books seek to give readers a general introduction to the culture of the lands in which they take place. While Eaton found that *Why the Bee Is Busy* does not compare favorably with *The Talking Bird,* she conceded that the former book "has something of the same charm in its descriptions of flowers and birds and outdoor life."

Purnell's body of work includes several texts for adults, along with many more books for children. In the years before her death, she focused on science fiction literature, producing several short stories and compiling two anthologies.

Biographical and Critical Sources

BOOKS

Science Fiction and Fantasy Literature: A Checklist, Volume 2, Gale, 1979.

PERIODICALS

New York Times Book Review, December 28, 1930, Anne T. Eaton, review of *The Talking Bird: An Aztec Story Book,* p. 19; January 25, 1931, Eaton, review of *Why the Bee Is Busy, and Other Rumanian Fairy Tales,* p. 16; May 17, 1931, Eaton, review of *Little Yusuf: The Story of a Syrian Boy,* p. 20; August 18, 1935, Ellen Lewis Buell, review of *Pedro the Potter,* p. 10; June 27, 1937, Eaton, review of *The Merry Frogs,* p. 11.

Saturday Review of Literature, June 13, 1931, Mark Van Doren, review of *The Talking Bird: An Aztec Story Book,* p. 902; August 22, 1931, May Lamberton Becker, review of *Little Yusuf: The Story of a Syrian Boy,* p. 78.

R

RICHARDSON, Andrew (William) 1986-

Personal

Born June 26, 1986, in Seymour, IN; son of Michael A. (an engineer) and Linda L. (a tutor) Richardson. *Education:* Attended elementary school at a Christian academy. *Religion:* Roman Catholic. *Hobbies and other interests:* Computers, coin collecting, reading, piano, clarinet, Nintendo, chorus, camping.

Addresses

Home—48 Cedar Trail, Asheville, NC 28803. *Agent*—Elaine Johnston, Steck-Vaughn Co., 4515 Seton Center Parkway, Austin, TX 78759.

Career

Writer. Piano teacher, 1995—. Duke University, member of Talent Identification Program.

Awards, Honors

Winner of Young Authors Publish a Book Contest, 1996; President's Education Award, 1998.

Writings

The Mystery of the Treasure Map, illustrated by Patrick Girouard, Raintree Steck-Vaughn (Austin, TX), 1997.

Work in Progress

Poems; programming a computer game.

Sidelights

Andrew Richardson told *SATA:* "I began writing short stories under the direction and guidance of my first-grade teacher. In second grade I attended a young author's workshop. I entered the Steck-Vaughn Young Authors Publish a Book Contest, but I did not win. In third grade I entered the contest again, and that year I won! I became a published author at the age of ten.

"The most difficult part of writing is getting that first sentence after you have outlined your story. The writing I enjoy the most is writing from personal experience. I like making treasure hunts for my younger brother and sister. I used the idea of a treasure hunt to write my book *The Mystery of the Treasure Map.*

"I think it is important to have appropriate books, videos, and video games available for kids. There are many movies and video games that my parents will not let me see because of their content. My mom checks the summary of the books I choose to make sure that they are appropriate for me.

"I thought it was fun to write a book that would be great to read at any age. I'm currently working on my computer programming skills. I'd like to develop a fun, action-packed computer game that would be appropriate for kids aged six to sixty."

Biographical and Critical Sources

PERIODICALS

Reading Teacher, October, 1998, review of *The Mystery of the Treasure Map,* p. 155.*

*   *   *

RODOWSKY, Colby 1932-

Personal

Born February 26, 1932, in Baltimore, MD; daughter of Frank M. Fossett and Mary C. Fitz-Townsend; married Lawrence Rodowsky (an appellate court judge), August 7, 1954; children: Laurie, Alice, Emily, Sarah, Gregory, Katherine. *Education:* College of Notre Dame of Maryland, B.A., 1953. *Religion:* Roman Catholic.

Addresses

Home and office—4306 Norwood Rd., Baltimore, MD 21218-1118. *Agent*—Gail Hochman, Brandt & Brandt, 1501 Broadway, NY 10036.

Career

Teacher in public schools in Baltimore, MD, 1953-55, and in a school for special education, 1955-56; Notre Dame Preparatory School, Baltimore, librarian's assistant, 1974-79; children's book reviewer, *Baltimore Sunday Sun,* 1977-84.

Awards, Honors

American Library Association Notable Book citation for *Not My Dog* and *The Gathering Room,* and Best Books for Young Adults citation for *Julie's Daughter, Hannah in Between,* and *Remembering Mog;* Hedda Seisler Mason Award, Enoch Pratt Library, for *Fitchett's Folly; School Library Journal* Best Books of the Year citations for *The Gathering Room, Julie's Daughter,* and *Sydney, Herself; Horn Book* Fanfare Award for *Not My Dog.*

Writings

FOR CHILDREN

What about Me?, F. Watts, 1976.
P.S. Write Soon, F. Watts, 1978.
Evy-Ivy-Over, F. Watts, 1978.
A Summer's Worth of Shame, F. Watts, 1980.
The Gathering Room, Farrar, Straus, 1981.
H, My Name Is Henley, Farrar, Straus, 1982.
Keeping Time, Farrar, Straus, 1983.
Fitchett's Folly, Farrar, Straus, 1987.
Dog Days, illustrated by Kathleen Collins Howell, Farrar, Straus, 1990.
Jenny and the Grand Old Great-Aunts, illustrated by Barbara Roman, Macmillan, 1992.
Hannah in Between, Farrar, Straus, 1994.
The Turnabout Shop, Farrar, Straus, 1998.
Not My Dog, illustrations by Thomas F. Yezerski, Farrar, Straus, 1999.
Spindrift, Farrar, Straus, 2000.
Jason Rat-a-Tat, illustrated by Beth Peck, Farrar, Straus, 2001.

FOR YOUNG ADULTS

Julie's Daughter (sequel to *Evy-Ivy-Over*), Farrar, Straus, 1985.
Sydney, Herself, Farrar, Straus, 1989.
Lucy Peale, Farrar, Straus, 1992.
Sydney Invincible, Farrar, Straus, 1995.
Remembering Mog, Farrar, Straus, 1996.

Rodowsky's young-adult short stories have been anthologized in *Visions,* edited by Donald Gallo, Delacorte, 1987, and in *Connections,* edited by Gallo, Delacorte, 1989.

Colby Rodowsky

OTHER

Contributor of fiction, essays, and reviews to periodicals, including *Christian Science Monitor, New York Times Book Review, Washington Post, McCall's* and *Good Housekeeping.*

Sidelights

A former teacher, Colby Rodowsky turned to writing for children when she was forty years old. The author of such award-winning books as *The Gathering Room, Julie's Daughter,* and *Remembering Mog,* Rodowsky has earned praise from critics and readers alike for her likeable empathetic protagonists and true-to-life situations. While the young people who inhabit Rodowsky's fiction live in a tough world characterized by unpredictable events and undependable authority figures, their efforts to cope with parental abandonment, poverty, and even death, are aided by warm and loving individuals. As Carol Edwards noted in the *School Library Journal,* "Rodowsky makes her readers work, never patronizing or condescending, yet always revealing inner layers that poke through the surface."

Born in 1932, Rodowsky grew up in Baltimore, Maryland. As a child she wanted to become a writer, and her mother encouraged her. "I don't know whether it was because she was a doting mother or she really thought I could write, but she was very supportive," the author once told an interviewer. Due to her parents' rocky marriage, Rodowsky spent a great deal of time at the home of her grandmother in the Chesapeake Bay, Virginia, town of Cape Charles, where she first discovered the library, and made many friends. That area, which Rodowsky recalled in an autobiographical essay for *Something about the Author Autobiography Series* (*SAAS*) was "a wonderful, almost magical place," would become the setting for several of her books.

Rodowsky's elementary-school education was completed in New York City, where she and her mother moved after her parents separated. Despite missing her friends, she loved the city; its energy inspired her to begin writing "'seriously'; pounding away on my mother's typewriter, dipping more often than not into an impassioned purple prose." She even completed her first long story, titled *The Strangons,* and confidently sent it off to a major New York publisher, although Rodowsky later recalled this childish first effort as "insignificant and forgotten."

Returning to Baltimore after her parents' divorce when she was fifteen, Rodowsky attended a prep school in Georgetown and lived with her father and his parents. After graduation, she enrolled at Maryland's College of Notre Dame, living at home and graduating with a degree in English. While there she edited the literary magazine, worked on the yearbook, and began to write vast quantities of poetry. She also met and fell in love

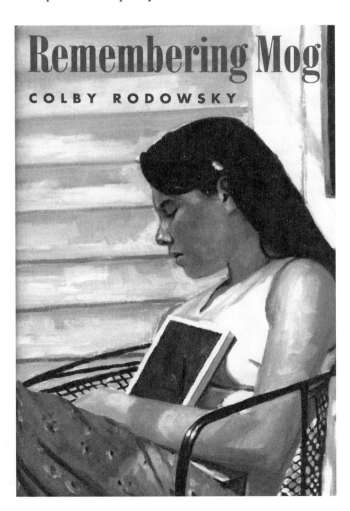

Annie's high school graduation is overshadowed by memories of her older sister's murder two years earlier, on the eve of her own graduation.

with Lawrence Rodowsky, a history major and aspiring lawyer whom she would later marry. Colby established a career as an elementary school teacher and working with children with special needs; she left teaching before the births of the couple's six children. Meanwhile, Larry Rodowsky began a successful legal career that resulted in a seat on the State of Maryland's Court of Appeals. The Rodowsky family lived in "a very noisy house," as the author once confided to *SATA*. "The house is quiet now—the children grown up and moved away," she later added. "But the family now includes five sons-in-law, one daughter-in-law, and *many* grandchildren, who all visit often (and only one dog and one cat)."

Rodowsky's writing career was inspired by a visit with one of her former teachers, Sister Maura Eichner, from Notre Dame. "We weren't talking about writing; we were just talking about books," the novelist noted. Sister Maura "finally stopped what she was saying and looked at me and said, 'Just think; you have all your writing still ahead of you.' It really kind of gives me cold chills even now when I think about it. I did not go home and write a book, but I went home thinking maybe I hadn't missed the boat on what I'd really wanted to do." She added, "I was about forty, and at that time I thought if you hadn't done anything by forty, you never would. Now I know a lot better."

In 1972 Rodowsky began a writing tutorial that forced her to return to a typewriter and, as she had done so many years before, start "banging" out a book-length manuscript. While her first effort was unsalable, it encouraged Rodowsky to attempt another ... and then another. Finally, her third effort, about a fifteen-year-old girl who has a brother with Down's syndrome, was accepted by a publisher and released in 1976 as *What about Me?*

Drawing from her experience teaching mentally handicapped children, she once explained: "I kind of backed into [*What about Me?*] because I wanted to write about a child who had a younger brother or sister with a handicap.... I didn't set out to write about a retarded child." In the novel, Rodowsky's young protagonist resents her brother Fredlet, who has Down's syndrome. Although Rodowsky generally knows how a book will end, and often writes the last page first, Fredlet's death took her, as well as her fictional characters, by surprise. Reviewing the novel for *Publishers Weekly,* Jeane Mercier called it a "profoundly moving, honest and tightly controlled, important novel." With this praise echoed by other critics, Rodowsky was encouraged to continue her literary efforts. When the first of her children left home in the late 1970s, she took over a room in the house as an office and began to feel like a "real writer," as she explained in an autobiographical sketch in *Sixth Book of Junior Authors and Illustrators.*

Rodowsky's second published novel, *P.S. Write Soon,* concerns crippled Tanner McClean, who writes an idealized version of her life to her pen-pal Jessie Lee. Tanner glosses over her handicap and the unexpected marriage of her older brother. But although she dislikes her new sister-in-law, Cheryl, the older girl teaches Tanner how to face life realistically rather than hiding in fiction. *The Gathering Room* takes place in a Baltimore cemetery. Nine-year-old Mudge's father, Ned, moves his family from the inner city and takes a job as caretaker of the old cemetery after the death of a friend. Ned teaches his son in the room where mourners used to congregate, and the boy befriends the spirits of the dead, who "provide this simple, well-wrought story with a pleasant, if melancholy sense of time and mortality," according to Jane Langton in the *New York Times Book Review*. *School Library Journal* contributor Elizabeth Holtze noted that Rodowsky "writes clear narrative and convincing dialogue.... Despite the cemetery setting and the problem posed ... this is a happy book."

A young girl with the unusual name of Slug connects three of Rodowsky's books that draw from several elements in the author's life. In *Evy-Ivy-Over,* which takes place in Rodowsky's childhood home of Cape Charles, she lives a carefree, if unorthodox, life with her grandmother, Gussie. But as Slug matures, she realizes her hand-me-down clothes are funny-looking and that Gussie herself is an odd character. She learns through contact with "normal" families, however, to appreciate Gussie. "I was very close to both of my grandmothers," Rodowsky told *CANR.* "In *Evy-Ivy-Over* ... I tried to describe the grandmother-grandchild relationship, though I must say neither of my grandmothers was at all like Gussie."

While not the main character, Slug also appears in *H, My Name Is Henley,* which deals with the plight of a young girl and her restless mother, Patti. Like Rodowsky's own mother, light-hearted, restless Patti is a bit of a dreamer; unable to stay in any one place for long, she stays until she quits her job and moves to another city. "Henley is probably the most mature and perceptive 12-year-old I've met in YA literature," stated *Voice of Youth Advocates* contributor Barbara Lenchitz Gottesman. "Rodowsky has created a masterpiece." While some reviewers pointed to some weak characterization, "The tension and conflict between mother and daughter, the strain on a child forced into adult responsibilities, and the characterization of Patti are intensely real," wrote Nancy C. Hammond in *Horn Book.*

Julie's Daughter, which won a Best Books for Young Adults award, unites Slug and her mother Julie, who abandoned her infant daughter at the bus station. Slug and Julie are brought together in caring for their neighbor, the artist Harper Tegges, who is dying of cancer. The story is seen through their three viewpoints. *Voice of Youth Advocates* contributor Debbie Earl maintained that "the differing narrations help us develop sympathy and understanding" for Rodowsky's protagonists; Earl found the novel "sensitively done and surprisingly humorous." Christine Jenkins in *Interracial Books for Children Bulletin* concluded that "*Julie's Daughter* succeeds in portraying strong women, both old and young."

Recently orphaned fifth-grader Livvy speaks to her dead mother about the adjustments she must make to find happiness and love in her new life in the care of her mother's old friend.

Rodowsky teams adventure and comedy in *Fitchett's Folly,* which takes place on Maryland's Eastern shore. The novel focuses on a motherless girl, Sarey-Ann, whose father drowns while attempting to rescue another child. Sarey-Ann has to deal with her feelings of resentment toward the foundling, Faith, who comes to live with the girl, her little brother, and her aunt. A *Horn Book* contributor noted that "Sarey's prickly dislike is convincingly portrayed in her first-person recounting.... Scrapes and adventures add to the story of Sarey's eventual acceptance of Faith."

One of Rodowsky's best-known novels, *Sydney, Herself,* features another child who has lost a parent. Sydney's Australian father died a month before she was born; blocking out his death, in a school writing assignment, Sydney decides to reinvent herself as the daughter of a rock singer, a member of the group The Boomerangs. When Sydney gives her story to a local newspaper, events snowball. A *Horn Book* reviewer lauded the novel as "fresh, humorous, and believable. Sydney is interesting—bright, gritty, and sometimes sulky." And adds that the book is "funny, poignant, and appealing."

Sydney, Herself would be followed by *Sydney, Invincible,* as Rodowsky's spunky heroine must deal with being a student in her mother's history class, working to resuscitate the school newspaper, and wait for her best friend Wally to return from boarding school in New Hampshire. Calling Sydney "a refreshingly realistic character" with problems that are "unique enough to be interesting" and solutions that are "plausible and endearing," *Voice of Youth Advocates* contributor Betsy Eubanks dubbed *Sydney, Invincible* a coming-of-age novel that shows its protagonist's "maturity evolv[ing] naturally as she deals with the accumulating stress. [Readers] are hopeful that she will succeed and gratified when she learns lessons that make her more sensitive and perceptive." "Rodowsky is an accomplished and sure-footed interpreter of what goes on in the mind of a teenaged girl," added *Washington Post Book World* critic Brigitte Weeks in praising both *Sydney, Herself* and its sequel.

In *Lucy Peale,* a love story for teens, a girl from a strict pastor's family is date-raped. Her father condemns her and she runs away to Ocean City, where she meets Jake, a kind young man, who invites her to stay with him. While the two eventually fall in love, Lucy realizes that she must find her own destiny. In the novel, Rodowsky alternates between Lucy's viewpoint and that of a narrator, a technique some reviewers found awkward. But in a starred review, a *Publishers Weekly* critic applauded the author's use of plot twists which keep Lucy and Jake's attention focused on their developing relationship, rather than on sex. *School Library Journal* contributor Jacqueline Rose appreciated "the moods created by descriptions of the sea town's atmosphere that mirror the characters' feelings." And a *Kirkus* reviewer concluded of *Lucy Peale,* that Rodowsky had penned "a heartwarming story" that is "gentle and appealing [and] written with insight and skill."

Another troubled family is portrayed in 1994's *Hannah in Between,* as twelve-year-old Hannah Brant must cope with an alcoholic parent. Avoiding bringing friends over to her house is just one way of coping with her mother's erratic behavior. Hannah also attempts to solve the problem by hiding empty bottles and, along with a father in denial, pretending that everything is "normal" at home. When her mother is injured in a car accident as a result of her drinking, Hannah must deal with her situation. *Hannah in Between* is a book that "weaves a young teen's limited understanding of the disease with her gradual acceptance that only her mother can begin to reverse her illness," according to *Horn Book* contributor Elizabeth S. Watson. "Although Rodowsky may have us following a predictable path," added *Booklist* reviewer Stephanie Zvirin, "she guides us forward with sensitivity and a sure hand."

Coping with death is the theme of several of Rodowsky's novels for young teens, among them *Remembering Mog* and *The Turnabout Shop.* In *Remembering Mog,* Annie's high school graduation is overshadowed by memories of her older sister's death two years earlier, on the eve of her own graduation. As each of her family members deal with Mog's death in their own way, Annie takes the summer to realize that she must seek professional help in coming to terms with the loss of her sister so that she can move on in her own life. Counting *Remembering Mog* as among Rodowsky's "string of solid, real-life stories, without pretense or angst," *Voice of Youth Advocates* critic Patricia J. Morrow deemed the novel "a quiet book, whose characters and dialogue bring the reader along through insights and adjustments." In *Booklist,* Stephanie Zvirin added that the novel succeeds "as a poignant, crystalline rendering of death's legacy for a parent and child."

The Turnabout Shop features a fatherless fifth-grader named Livvy, whose mother, Althea, dies and leaves her in the care of Jessie Barnes, a single friend of Livvy's mother to whom Livvy's presence is as much a surprise and adjustment as her new home is to Livvy. Slowly, the two learn to live with one another, and Livvy adapts to a move to Baltimore, a new school, new friends, and being a part of Jessie's large, close-knit family. Noting that readers will immediately identify with Rodowsky's

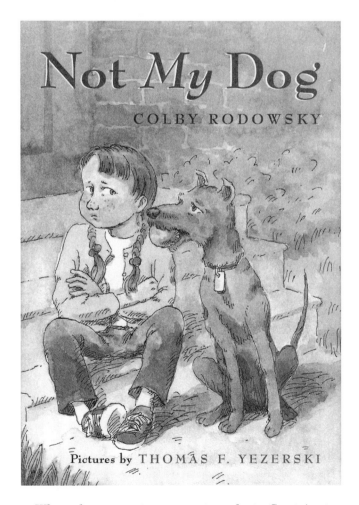

When her parents agree to adopt Great-Aunt Margaret's mutt, Ellie must face the disappointing realization that she will never get the puppy she has always wanted. (Cover illustration by Thomas F. Yezerski.)

likeable characters," a *Kirkus* reviewer added that "Jessie ... and Althea's characters burst forth from Livvy's narration as vividly as her own." A *Publishers Weekly* reviewer praised *The Turnabout Shop* as a "poignant, quiet story [that] offers a reassuring view of coming to terms with grief and unwelcome change."

In addition to her novels for older readers, Rodowsky has authored several novels for younger children. In 1990's *Dog Days*, a young girl discovers that the author of her favorite dog stories is moving in next door ... along with her famous dog. Dogs also figure prominently in *Not My Dog*, a story about a "sort of square, boring brown dog" that is inherited by nine-year-old Ellie in lieu of the bouncy puppy she had been promised by her parents—until Preston shows that he is truly the pick of the litter. 1992's *Jenny and the Grand Old Great-Aunts* is aimed at an even younger audience. In what *School Library Journal* reviewer Anna DeWind called an "appealing cross-generational story," Jenny is dropped off by herself to spend the afternoon with her great aunts in their terrifyingly quiet Victorian home. However, the home also reveals a wonderful magic, after one aunt introduces the little girl to a treasure cache in the attic. "This comforting story deftly conveys the strength of the bond that can exist between the old and the young," commented a *Publishers Weekly* contributor.

Rodowsky is perplexed by comments that imply that writing for children is easier than writing for adults. "I don't think when you write for children that you ever consciously decide you're going to make something simpler, that you ever write down in any way," she told *CANR*. "It's a challenge—a kind of balancing act," she explained to *SATA*, "and I get irritated by people who think you write for children because that's where you start, and then you work up to writing for grownups. I don't think it's any easier to write for children than for adults, but the rewards are great—particularly when I get a letter from a child whose life has been touched by a book of mine."

Biographical and Critical Sources

BOOKS

Authors and Artists for Young Adults, Volume 23, Gale, 1998, pp. 169-76.
Sixth Book of Junior Authors and Illustrators, H. W. Wilson, 1990.
Something about the Authors Autobiography Series, Volume 22, Gale, 1996, pp. 225-239.

PERIODICALS

Booklist, July, 1992, p. 1933; April 1, 1994, Stephanie Zvirin, review of *Hannah in Between*, p. 1437; April 15, 1995, S. Zvirin, review of *Sydney, Invincible*, p. 1493; February 1, 1996, S. Zvirin, review of *Remembering Mog*, p. 926; June 1, 1998, Kay Weisman, review of *The Turnabout Shop*, p. 1768; February 1, 1999, Carolyn Phelan, review of *Not My Dog*, p. 975; February 15, 2000, review of *Spindrift*, p. 1115.

Bulletin of the Center for Children's Books, February, 1984, p. 116.
Horn Book, October, 1981, p. 537; April, 1983, Nancy C. Hammond, review of *H, My Name is Henley*, p. 167; April, 1984, Mary M. Burns, review of *Keeping Time*, p. 203; July-August, 1987, review of *Fitchett's Folly*, p. 473; September-October, 1989, review of *Sydney, Herself*, p. 631; March-April, 1991, review of *Dog Days*, p. 202; May-June, 1992, p. 338; September-October, 1994, Elizabeth S. Watson, review of *Hannah in Between*, p. 601; March, 1999, Martha V. Parravano, review of *Not My Dog*, p. 212.
Kirkus Reviews, June 15, 1992, review of *Lucy Peale*, p. 784; January 15, 1998, review of *The Turnabout Shop*, p. 117.
New York Times Book Review, October 25, 1981, Jane Langton, review of *The Gathering Room*, p. 47.
Interracial Books for Children Bulletin, Vol. 17, no. 1, 1986, Christine Jenkins, review of *Julie's Daughter*, p. 7.
Publishers Weekly, January 22, 1979, review of *What About Me?*, p. 371; April 24, 1987, review of *Fitchett's Folly*, p. 70; June 9, 1989, p. 70; November 23, 1989, review of *Dog Days*, p. 65; January 6, 1992, review of *Jenny and the Grand Old Great-Aunts*, p. 66; May 4, 1992, review of *Lucy Peale*, p. 57; March 25, 1996, review of *Remembering Mog*, p. 85; January 5, 1998, review of *The Turnabout Shop*, p. 68; January 10, 2000, review of *Spindrift*, p. 69.
School Library Journal, October, 1981, Elizabeth Holtze, review of *The Gathering Room*, p. 146; January, 1983, p. 87; January, 1985, Barbara Jo McKee, review of *Keeping Time*, p. 88; September, 1985, p. 148; July, 1989, Carol A. Edwards, review of *Sidney, Herself*, p. 92; April, 1992, Anna DeWind, review of *Jenny and the Grand Old Great-Aunts*, p. 99; July, 1992, Jacqueline Rose, review of *Lucy Peale*, p. 91; August, 1995, review of *Sydney Invincible*, p. 164.
Voice of Youth Advocates, April, 1983, Barbara Lenchitz Gottesman, review of *H, My Name Is Henley*, p. 41; April, 1986, Debbie Earl, review of *Julie's Daughter*, p. 34; August, 1995, Betsy Eubanks, review of *Sydney, Invincible*, p. 164; June, 1996, Patricia J. Morrow, review of *Remembering Mog*, p. 100.
Washington Post Book World, July, 1995, Brigitte Weeks, review of *Sydney, Invincible*, pp. 16-17.
Wilson Library Bulletin, February, 1990, p. 84; May, 1990, p. 58.

* * *

ROSS, Diana
See DENNEY, Diana

* * *

ROYSTON, Angela 1945-

Personal

Born February 8, 1945, in Bridlington, Yorkshire, UK; daughter of Richard Elsworthy (a chartered accountant) and Chloe Lomas (a secretary; maiden name, Locking) Wilkinson; married Robert Royston (a psychotherapist and playwright), September 8, 1979; children: Miranda, Jack. *Education:* University of Edinburgh, M.A., 1966. *Politics:* Green Party. *Hobbies and other interests:* Literature, theater, travel.

Addresses

Home and Office—82 Tufnell Park Road, London, N7 0DT, UK. *E-mail*—roystons@dircon.co.uk.

Career

Secretary in London, England, 1967-73; Kingfisher Books/Macdonald Educational, London, children's non-fiction editor, 1973-78; Grisewood and Dempsey, London, children's nonfiction editor, 1978-82; freelance writer and editor, 1982—. *Member:* Society of Authors, UK, Amnesty International.

Writings

My First Library Road Travel, Macdonald Education, 1986.
Just Look at Road Transport, Macdonald Educational, 1988.
Monster Road-Builders, Frances Lincoln, 1989, Barron's, 1990.
Monster Building Machines, Frances Lincoln, 1989, Barron's, 1990.
Car—See How It Works, illustrated by Colin King, Frances Lincoln, 1990, published as *My Lift-the-Flap Car Book,* Putnam, 1991.
The A-to-Z Book of Cars, Barron's, 1991.
You and Your Body: 101 Questions and Answers, Hamlyn, 1993, Facts on File, 1995.
Big Machines, illustrated by Terry Pastor, Frances Lincoln, 1990, Little, Brown, 1994.
Plane, Frances Lincoln, 1994.
Whirrs, Watts and Whooshes: The Stories of 14 Inventions That Changed the World, David Bennett Books, 1994.
Incredible Facts, Henderson, 1994.
Healthy Me, illustrated by Edwina Riddell, Barron's, 1995.
(Contributor) *Marshall Cavendish Encyclopedia of Health,* M. Cavendish, 1995.
100 Greatest Women, Dragon's World, 1995.
100 Greatest Medical Discoveries, Dragon's World, 1995.
Where Do Babies Come From?, Dorling Kindersley, 1996.
Digesting: How We Fuel the Body, Grolier, 1998.
Space Station—Accident on Mir, Dorling Kindersley, 2000.

"STEPPING STONES 123" SERIES

Birthday Party, Kingfisher, 1988.
Shopping, Kingfisher, 1988.
My Family, Kingfisher, 1988.
My Friends, Kingfisher, 1988.

"FARM ANIMAL STORIES" SERIES

The Cow, illustrated by Bob Bampton, Warwick Press (New York City), 1990, Kingfisher, 1992.
The Pig, illustrated by Jim Channell, Warwick Press, 1989, Kingfisher, 1992.

The Goat, illustrated by Eric Robson, Warwick Press, 1990, Kingfisher, 1992.
The Pony, illustrated by Bampton, Warwick Press, 1990, Kingfisher, 1992.
The Hen, illustrated by Dave Cook, Warwick Press, 1989, Kingfisher, 1992.
The Sheep, illustrated by Josephine Martin, Warwick Press, 1989, Kingfisher, 1992.

FIRST READERS

The Senses, illustrated by Edwina Riddell, Barron's, 1993.
Getting Better, Frances Lincoln, 1994.
(With David Bellamy) *How Green Are You?,* Frances Lincoln, 1994.
A First Atlas, Scholastic, 1995.
Fire Fighter!, Dorling Kindersley, 1998.
Truck Trouble, Dorling Kindersley, 1998.
Space Shuttle Mission 7, Ginn, 1998.
Mighty Machines: Stories of Machines at Work, Kingfisher, 2000.

"ANIMAL LIFE STORIES" SERIES

The Deer, illustrated by Bernard Robinson, Warwick Press, 1988.
The Otter, illustrated by Robinson, Warwick Press, 1988, Kingfisher, 1988.
The Duck, illustrated by Maurice Pledger and Robinson, Warwick Press, 1988.
The Frog, illustrated by Robinson, Warwick Press, 1989, Kingfisher, 1989.
The Fox, illustrated by Robinson, Warwick Press, 1988, Kingfisher, 1988.
The Hedgehog, illustrated by Pledger, Warwick Press, 1989.
The Squirrel, illustrated by Pledger, Warwick Press, 1989, Kingfisher, 1989.
The Mouse, illustrated by Pledger, Warwick Press, 1989, Kingfisher, 1989.
The Whale, illustrated by Channell, Warwick Press, 1989, Kingfisher, 1989.
The Tiger, illustrated by Graham Allen, Warwick Press, 1988, Kingfisher, 1993.
The Elephant, Warwick Press, 1989, Kingfisher, 1989.
The Penguin, illustrated by Trevor Boyer, Warwick Press, 1988, Kingfisher, 1988.

"SEE HOW THEY GROW" SERIES

Puppy, Dorling Kindersley, 1991.
Chick, Dorling Kindersley, 1991.
Kitten, Lodestar Books (New York City), 1991.
Frog, Lodestar Books, 1991, Dorling Kindersley, 1991.
Duck, Lodestar Books, 1991, Dorling Kindersley, 1991.
Rabbit, Lodestar Books, 1992, Dorling Kindersley, 1991.
Mouse, Lodestar Books, 1992, Dorling Kindersley, 1992.
Lamb, Lodestar Books, 1992.

"WHAT'S INSIDE" SERIES

Small Animals, Dorling Kindersley, 1991.
Insects, Dorling Kindersley, 1991.
Shells, Dorling Kindersley, 1991.
Toys, Dorling Kindersley, 1991.
My Body, Dorling Kindersley, 1991.
Plants, Dorling Kindersley, 1991.

"GEOGRAPHY STARTS HERE" SERIES

Where People Live, Wayland, 1997, Raintree Steck-Vaughn (Austin, TX), 1998.
Weather around You, Wayland, 1997, Raintree Steck-Vaughn, 1998.
Maps and Symbols, Wayland, 1998, Raintree Steck-Vaughn, 1999.

"EYE OPENERS" SERIES

Diggers and Dumpers, illustrated by Jane Cradock-Watson and Dave Hopkins, Aladdin Books (New York City), 1991.
Cars, illustrated by Roger Stewart, Aladdin, 1991.
Airplanes, Aladdin, 1991.
Jungle Animals, Aladdin, 1991.
Dinosaurs, illustrated by Cradock-Watson and Hopkins, Aladdin, 1991.
Ships and Boats, illustrated by Cradock-Watson, Aladdin, 1992.
Birds, illustrated by Cradock-Watson and Hopkins, Aladdin, 1992.
Insects and Crawly Creatures, illustrated by Cradock-Watson and Hopkins, Aladdin, 1992, Dorling Kindersley, 1992.
Night-Time Animals, illustrated by Cradock-Watson and Hopkins, Aladdin, 1992, Dorling Kindersley, 1992.
Baby Animals, illustrated by Cradock-Watson and Hopkins, Little Simon (New York City), 1992.
Sea Animals, illustrated by Cradock-Watson and Hopkins, Aladdin, 1992, Dorling Kindersley, 1992.
Trains, illustrated by Cradock-Watson and Hopkins, Aladdin, 1992, Dorling Kindersley, 1992.
Minibeasts, Dorling Kindersley, 1993.

"INSIDE AND OUT" SERIES

Ships and Boats, illustrated by Cradock-Watson and Hopkins, Aladdin, 1992, Dorling Kindersley, 1992.
Flying Machines, illustrated by Sebastian Quigley, Heinemann Interactive Library, 1998.
Cars, illustrated by Roger Stewart, Heinemann, 1998.
Trucks, illustrated by Chris Forsey, Heinemann, 1998.
Emergency Rescue, illustrated by Stewart, Heinemann, 1998.
Stars and Planets, illustrated by Stephen Maturin and Stewart, Heinemann, 1998.
The Earth, illustrated by Jonathan Adams, Heinemann, 1998.
Under the Sea, Heinemann, 1998.
Pets, illustrated by Stuart Lafford, Heinemann, 1998.
Horses and Ponies, Heinemann, 1998.
Tractors, illustrated by Terry Gabbey, Heinemann, 1998.

"LIFE CYCLE" SERIES

Kangaroo, Heinemann, 1998.
Guinea Pig, Heinemann, 1998.
Frog, Heinemann, 1998.
Bean, Heinemann, 1998.
Butterfly, Heinemann, 1998.
Chicken, Heinemann, 1998.
Sunflower, Heinemann, 1998.
Salmon, Heinemann, 2000.
Mushroom, Heinemann, 2000.
Dog, Heinemann, 2000.

"ON-THE-SPOT" SERIES

Volcanoes, Reader's Digest Children's, 1999.
Pyramids, Reader's Digest Children's, 1999.

"PLANTS" SERIES

How Plants Grow, Heinemann, 1999.
Flowers, Fruits and Seeds, Heinemann, 1999.
Plants and Us, Heinemann, 1999.
Strange Plants, Heinemann, 1999.
British Plants, Heinemann, 1999.
Trees, Heinemann, 1999.

"ENVIRONMENT STARTS HERE" SERIES

Transportation, Wayland, 1998, Raintree Steck-Vaughn, 1999.
Recycling, Wayland, 1998, Raintree Steck-Vaughn, 1999.

"SAFE AND SOUND" SERIES

Fit and Strong, Heinemann, 1999.
Eat Well, Heinemann, 2000.
A Healthy Body, Heinemann, 2000.
Safety First, Heinemann, 2000.

"ON THE MOVE" SERIES

The Digger, Kingfisher, 2000.
The Truck, Kingfisher, 2000.
The Tractor, Kingfisher, 2000.
The Tugboat, Kingfisher, 2000.
The Helicopter, Kingfisher, 2000.
The Jumbo Jet, Kingfisher, 2000.

"TELL ME ABOUT" SERIES

The Human Body and How It Works, illustrated by Rob Shone and Chris Forsey, Kingfisher, 1990, Warwick, 1991.
People and Places, Kingfisher, 1991.
Buildings, Bridges and Tunnels, Warwick, 1991.
Flowers, Trees and Other Plants, Warwick, 1991.

"SCIENCE NATURE GUIDES TO NORTH AMERICA" SERIES

Wild Flowers, Thunder Bay Press (San Diego), 1994.
Trees, illustrated by David More, Thunder Bay, 1994.
Birds, Thunder Bay, 1994.
Mammals, illustrated by Jim Channell, Thunder Bay, 1995.

"A FIRST LOOK AT" SERIES

Mammals, Belitha, 1996.
Birds, Belitha, 1996.
Insects, Belitha, 1996.
Fish, Belitha, 1996.
Flowers, Belitha, 1996.
Reptiles, Belitha, 1996.
Amphibians, Belitha, 1996.

"BODY SYSTEMS" SERIES

Reproduction and Birth, Heinemann, 1997.
Eating and Digesting, Heinemann, 1997.
Thinking and Feeling, Heinemann, 1997.
Movement, Heinemann, 1997.

"HOW IT WORKS" SERIES

Levers, Heinemann, 2000.
Ramps and Wedges, Heinemann, 2000.

Wheels and Axles, Heinemann, 2000.
Pulleys and Gears, Heinemann, 2000.
Springs, Heinemann, 2000.
Screws, Heinemann, 2000.

"LEARN TO SAY NO" SERIES

Alcohol, Heinemann, 2000.
Tobacco, Heinemann, 2000.
Cannabis, Heinemann, 2000.
Inhalents, Heinemann, 2000.

OTHER

Henry VIII, Pitkin Unichrome, 1999.
The Six Wives of Henry VIII, Pitkin Unichrome, 1999.
Mary Queen of Scots, Pitkin Unichrome, 1999.
Best of York (guide), Pitkin Unichrome, 1999.
Pitkin Guide to the City of York, Pitkin Unichrome, 1999.

Several of Royston's series for young readers have been translated into Spanish.

Work in Progress

"My World of Science" series (titles include *Colour, Using Electricity, Sound and Hearing, Magnets, Materials, Solids, Liquids, and Gases, Water, Hot and Cold, Light and Shadow,* and *Forces and Motion*) and "It's Catching" series (titles include *Chickenpox, Warts and Veruccas, Colds and Flu, Conjunctivitis,* and *Head Lice*), both for Heinemann, 2001.

Sidelights

Angela Royston is the author of over a hundred and fifty nonfiction books for young readers on topics ranging from the human body to the life cycle of a kangaroo to the functioning of a lever. The British author creates books for readers from preschool to the middle grades, and as she told *Something about the Author* (SATA), "I moved into writing from editing and very much enjoy the challenge of writing about a wide variety of subjects." For Royston, it seems, no challenge is too much, and she has taken on subjects as technical as bridge building or the facts of digestion, translating such processes into age-appropriate language. "I had a broad education," Royston explained to *SATA,* "both at school and university, and feel able to tackle almost any subject, provided I can find good research material."

Born in 1945 in the north of England, in Yorkshire, she was educated at the University of Edinburgh where she earned her master's degree in 1966. After graduation, Royston migrated south to London, where she worked as a secretary for seven years, and then found work as a nonfiction editor for children's books in 1973, first with Macdonald Educational and then with Grisewood and Dempsey. This proved an excellent introduction to writing her own nonfiction books for children, and when she began her family, Royston decided to go freelance as a writer and editor full time. With many contacts in the publishing industry, she has worked mostly on commissioned books.

For preschoolers, Royston has written both stand-alone titles and series. Her *Where Do Babies Come From?* is typical Royston, as she "dishes up just the right amount" of information, according to a *Publishers Weekly* reviewer, in simplified and concise language. The same writer further noted, "Royston's matter-of-fact presentation is informative, reassuring and discreet." A contributor for *Kirkus Reviews* called the same book an "outstanding introduction for preschoolers who are already starting to ask a lot of questions about reproduction." This reviewer also commented, "A brief text and stunning full-color photographs provide just enough information to satisfy young questioners." Royston also provides preschoolers with mechanical know-how in *My Lift-the-Flap Car Book,* which kids "will adore," according to *Booklist*'s Ilene Cooper, and in *Monster Road-Builders,* which is a look at nine huge machines used in building roads. *School Library Journal*'s Susan Hepler noted, "Each page features several information-laden sentences," along with double-page spreads of the machines in question.

Royston's series titles for preschoolers include "Stepping Stones 123" and "Farm Animal Stories." Reviewing the six titles in the latter series, *The Cow, The Goat, The Hen, The Pony, The Pig,* and *The Sheep,* Diane Nunn noted in *School Library Journal* that Royston's "narration is in simple story form, relating both daily and seasonal activities of the animals from mating behaviors and birth through adulthood." Nunn felt that the "basic facts are accurate," but warned readers to "be aware that these books depict farm animals in an idyllic rural setting that has disappeared in most areas of the U.S."

The majority of Royston's books for young readers come in the five-to-seven-year-old category. Popular series for this age group include "Eye Openers," "See How They Grow," "Inside and Out," and "Animal Life Stories," among many others. In "Eye Openers," photographs and drawings are blended with simple text to illustrate and explicate topics from the area of machines such as cars and airplanes, to animals such as dinosaurs and birds. Reviewing *Cars, Diggers and Dump Trucks, Dinosaurs,* and *Jungle Animals* in *School Library Journal,* Steven Engelfried called the series a "winning visual package" with "just enough [information] to satisfy readers or listeners while they pore over the exciting illustrations." In another round-up review of *Baby Animals, Planes, Sea Animals,* and *Ships and Boats,* Dorcas Hand noted in *School Library Journal* that these are "four pleasing offerings for board-book graduates." Hand also remarked, "Each double-page spread .... offers a descriptive paragraph and a large, excellent-quality, full-color photograph of the subject." Reviewing *Baby Animals* and *Sea Animals* in *School Librarian,* Joan Hamilton Jones commented that the series "is designed to be both educational and entertaining," and does so "by combining bright photographs with large printed texts." Jones concluded, "The child is led into a world of fascinating information." Joan Feltwell, also writing in *School Librarian* noted that all the books in the series "are essentially a feast of fine photographs designed to enthrall and capture the imagination of three- to six-year-olds." *School Library Journal*'s Eldon Younce, in a review of Royston's book on trains in the series, thought that "young train enthusiasts will find this slim volume right on track." Younce went on to conclude, "Just the thing for young nonfiction readers."

Another popular Royston series for beginning readers is "See How They Grow," a group of eight books that focuses on various baby animals and show how they develop, using a story format to inform. Owen Edwards, reviewing the entire series in *Entertainment Weekly,* commented that virtual reality was still only virtual, "but until the nerds catch up with the need, there are the "See How They Grow" books," which "offer lots of pictures, information—and charm." A critic for *Kirkus Reviews* called *Rabbit,* one of the eight books in the series, "an unusually attractive informational book for the youngest." Reviewing *Lamb* and *Mouse* in *School Librarian,* Mary Crawford called the production values of the series "superb." Crawford concluded, "These books will be popular with a wide range of children as they are both informative and lovely to look at."

Royston's "Inside and Out" series, originally published in England as "A First Look Through," continues this informative look at everyday objects and animals, but with a slightly different twist. The books in this series blend short descriptive paragraphs with acetate double spreads. In "Animal Life Stories," Royston features twelve different creatures: the deer, otter, duck, frog, fox, hedgehog, squirrel, mouse, whale, tiger, elephant, and penguin, in titles named after the animal in question. *Booklist*'s Isabel Schon, in a review of the Spanish translation of *The Squirrel* (*La Ardilla*), called the entire series "an excellent introduction to the study of these animals." Schon further remarked, "Appealing and informative watercolor illustrations complement the explicit texts." A writer for *Appraisal,* reviewing *The Whale,* felt the series was "aptly named," as the "text consists of factual material, but reads like a story." The same reviewer concluded, "This book would be appropriate for the beginning reader and for reading aloud." In a round-up review of *The Elephant, The Mouse,* and *The Squirrel,* J. J. Votapka wrote in *School Library Journal,* "Charming full-color illustrations highlight these rather slight stories about the lifestyle of the animals cited in the title." Votapka further noted that the "obvious predictability" of the story format in each title "is apt to wear thin with most children." Another contributor for *Appraisal,* however, praised Royston's "very readable style" in a review of *The Fox, The Duck, The Tiger, The Otter,* and *The Penguin.* "Animals are universally the favorite science subject of the 5-8 age group," the same reviewer concluded. "These colorful, interesting books are recommended to help fill the need."

Royston has also authored, amongst others, a beginning reader series that feature flora rather than fauna, titled "Plants," and a series that takes a look at human health and well-being titled "Safe and Sound." Reviewing *Flowers, Fruits and Seeds, How Plants Grow,* and

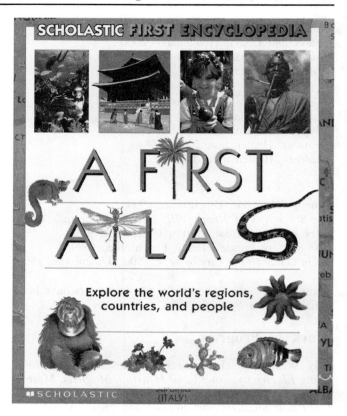

In her atlas for young readers, Royston includes not only maps, but photographs and facts about tourist sites, culture, landforms, and other pertinent topics.

Strange Plants, in *School Library Journal,* Katherine Borchert called the three titles "serviceable additions for collections in need of easy nonfiction." Kit Vaughan, also writing in *School Library Journal,* felt that two titles in the "Safe and Sound Series," *Eat Well* and *A Healthy Body,* "inform and educate readers" by the use of "short sentences and a limited vocabulary."

Additionally, Royston has penned a number of stand-alone titles as well as series for middle-grade readers. Popular individual titles include *The A-to-Z Book of Cars* and *100 Greatest Medical Discoveries.* In the former book, Royston presents a "browsing guide to automobiles," according to *Booklist*'s Julie Corsaro. Though Corsaro thought that the writing "is nothing special," she still felt that "the book is likely to burn rubber in the circulation department" because of its appealing topic. A writer for *Science Books and Films,* reviewing the same title, commented that it is a "wonderful road book." Royston covered more than a hundred medical topics in her *100 Greatest Medical Discoveries,* a book that "teems with information by both word and picture," according to a contributor for *Junior Bookshelf.* The same writer remarked that though the book was aimed at ten- to fourteen-year-olds, it could be "enjoyed by both younger and older groups."

Royston serves up series with both easy and standard reading texts for middle-grade readers. For children with reading difficulties she developed the "First Look At" series, with each title focusing on a different animal species or plant. Delvene Barnett, reviewing Royston's *Fish* in *School Librarian,* found it "inspiring," and one that "could also be used with slow learners and older less able children." Royston's "Science Nature Guides" series also presents introductions to wild flowers, trees, birds, and mammals of Great Britain and of North America in separate editions. Each book includes not only text and illustrations, but also activities, such as making a cast of animal footprints in *Mammals.* Reviewing that title in *School Librarian,* Ann Jenkin concluded, "This book is extremely good value and will be enjoyed by 8 to 12-year-olds at school or at home." The author's popular "Tell Me About" series deals with most of the topics she has written about in other series, from the human body to buildings to plants to geography and demography. Reviewing *The Human Body and How It Works,* a writer for *Appraisal* noted that it "includes detailed drawings of the human skeleton, of a developing baby, and experiments that are both appropriate for and of interest to elementary children."

Royston has made a winning combination of simplified text along with well-selected illustrations to come up with individual titles and series that both entertain and inform young readers. In doing so, she follows her own golden rule, as she explained to *SATA:* "I most like to work on books which are 'fun' and always try to find an interesting approach to explaining or describing things. I always become interested in the subjects of the books I work on, and I hope to stimulate that interest in the reader."

Biographical and Critical Sources

PERIODICALS

Appraisal: Science Books for Young People, Summer, 1989, review of *The Fox,* et al, p. 82; Summer, 1990, review of *The Whale,* pp. 46-47; Autumn, 1991, review of *The Human Body and How It Works,* p. 98.

Booklist, February 1, 1991, Isabel Schon, review of *The Squirrel (La Ardilla),* p. 1136; September 15, 1991,

Ilene Cooper, review of *My Lift-the-Flap Car Book,* p. 154; October 15, 1991, Julie Corsaro, review of *The A-to-Z Car Book,* pp. 434-35; March 15, 1994, p. 1369; April 15, 1998, p. 1449; July, 1998, p. 189.

Books for Keeps, November, 1994, p. 21.

Entertainment Weekly, April 10, 1992, Owen Edwards, review of "See How They Grow" series, p. 70.

Horn Book Guide, Fall, 1992, p. 312; Spring, 1993, p. 119; Fall, 1998, p. 420.

Junior Bookshelf, August, 1995, review of *100 Greatest Medical Discoveries,* p. 150.

Kirkus Reviews, December 15, 1991, review of *Rabbit,* pp. 1597-98; May 1, 1996, review of *Where Do Babies Come From?,* p. 692.

Observer, July 23, 1995, p. 13.

Publishers Weekly, May 27, 1996, review of *Where Do Babies Come From?,* p. 78.

School Librarian, August, 1992, Joan Hamilton Jones, review of *Baby Animals* and *Sea Animals,* p. 98; August, 1992, Mary Crawford, review of *Lamb* and *Mouse,* p. 98; November, 1992, Joan Feltwell, review of *Night-Time Animals,* p. 143; November, 1994, Ann Jenkin, review of *Mammals,* p. 158; February, 1997, Delvene Barnett, review of *Fish,* pp. 40; Summer, 1998, p. 96.

School Library Journal, February, 1990, J. J. Votapka, review of *The Elephant,* et al, p. 85; May, 1990, Susan Hepler, review of *Monster Road-Builders,* pp. 100-01; November, 1990, Diane Nunn, review of *The Cow,* et al, p. 107; January, 1992, Steven Engelfried, review of *Cars,* et al, p. 97; October, 1992, Dorcas Hand, review of *Baby Animals,* et al, p. 109; February, 1993, Eldon Younce, review of *Trains,* p. 86; November 15, 1995, p. 134; August, 1996, p. 141; October, 1997, p. 154; May, 1998, p. 137; July, 1998, p. 90; February, 1999, p. 101; January, 2000, Katherine Borchert, review of *Flowers, Fruits and Seeds,* et al, p. 126; January, 2000, Kit Vaughan, review of *Eat Well,* et al, p. 126.

Science Books and Films, June-July, 1991, review of *The A-to-Z Book of Cars,* p. 131.

—*Sketch by J. Sydney Jones*

S–T

SABUDA, Robert (James) 1965-

Personal

Born March 8, 1965, in Michigan; son of Bruce Edward (a tool-and-die maker) and Judith Elaine (a singer; maiden name, Barnes) Sabuda; companion of Dale Glenn Stine (a singer). *Education:* Pratt Institute, B.F.A. (communication design; summa cum laude), 1987.

Addresses

Home and office—260 West End Ave., #15C, New York, NY 10023-3666.

Career

Children's book author and illustrator, 1988—. *Member:* Society of Children's Book Writers and Illustrators, Moveable Book Society, New York Genealogical and Biographical Society.

Awards, Honors

Notable Children's Trade Book in the Field of Social Studies, Children's Book Council, and New York Public Library Best Children's Book of the Year, both 1990, both for *Walden;* Magic Reading Award, *Parenting Magazine,* and *Hungry Mind Review* Children's Book of Distinction, both 1992, both for *Saint Valentine; Boston Globe-Horn Book* Honor Award, 1994, for *A Tree Place;* Gold Medal winner, Dimension Illustration Awards, 1994, for *A Christmas Alphabet.*

Writings

SELF-ILLUSTRATED

Saint Valentine, Atheneum, 1992.
Tutankhamen's Gift, Atheneum, 1994.
The Christmas Alphabet (pop-up book), Orchard, 1994.
The Knight's Castle (pop-up book), Golden Books, 1994.
The Mummy's Tomb (pop-up book), Golden Books, 1994.

Help the Animals (pop-up books; 4 volumes), Reader's Digest, 1995.
Arthur and the Sword, Atheneum, 1995.
The Twelve Days of Christmas (pop-up book), Simon & Schuster, 1996.
ABC Disney (pop-up book), Disney Press, 1998.
Cookie Count: A Tasty Pop-Up, Simon & Schuster, 1998.
The Blizzard's Robe, Atheneum, 1999.
The Movable Mother Goose (pop-up), Simon & Schuster, 2000.

ILLUSTRATOR

Eugene Coco, *The Fiddler's Son,* Green Tiger Press, 1988.
Coco, *The Wishing Well,* Green Tiger Press, 1988.
Henry David Thoreau, *Walden,* text selections by Steve Lowe, Putnam, 1990.
Walt Whitman, *I Hear America Singing,* Putnam, 1991.
J. Patrick Lewis, *Earth Verses and Water Rhymes,* Atheneum, 1991.
Christopher Columbus, *The Log of Christopher Columbus,* text selections by Lowe, Putnam, 1992.
Roy Owen, *The Ibis and the Egret,* Putnam, 1993.
Constance Levy, *A Tree Place and Other Poems,* McElderry Books, 1994.
Nancy Williams, *A Kwanzaa Celebration* (pop-up book), Simon & Schuster, 1995.
Marguerite W. Davol, *The Paper Dragon,* Atheneum, 1997.

Sidelights

Robert Sabuda is an author and illustrator who has received wide-ranging acclaim as one of the foremost designers of interactive "pop-up" books. His delightful creations for the preschool set incorporate bright colors, stand-out graphics, and what a *School Library Journal* contributor termed, "striking" examples of paper engineering, in a review of *A Kwanzaa Celebration.* Sabuda has designed graphic illustrations for such classic works as the tales of Mother Goose, Henry David Thoreau's *Walden,* and a 1991 edition of nineteenth-century American poet Walt Whitman's, *I Hear America Singing.* The busy Sabuda has also built a solid reputation as a traditional illustrator by bringing to life such picture books as *The Tree Place and Other Poems,* by Constance Levy, and *The Ibis and the Egret,* by Roy Owen.

In addition to his work as an illustrator, and as a way to allow himself greater creative latitude, Sabuda has begun to pen several of his own stories, including *Saint Valentine, Tutankhamen's Gift,* and *The Blizzard's Tale,* all of which feature his unique artwork. *The Blizzard's Robe,* a story about the origin of the Northern Lights, was praised for both its text and illustrations. *School Library Journal* contributor Tina Hudak called it a "tale of survival and compassion ... [that] will warm the hearts of children and adults alike."

Born in 1965 and raised in a small, rural Michigan town, Sabuda always knew he would be an artist when he grew up; among his favorite illustrators were Tomi Ungerer, Arnold Lobel, and Norman Bridwell. "I should have known I was going to be a children's book illustrator when I presented my mom with *The Wizard of Oz* ('a pop-up book complete with cyclone!') made with my own dirty little hands," he recalled to *SATA.* "My bedroom was a mess from all my projects. Now I get paid to make messes! My mother can't believe it (but of course she's thrilled, she was sure I'd starve to death)! Sabuda credits his knack for engineering to his father, who was a mason and carpenter in addition to working as a tool-and-die maker.

Attending New York's Pratt Institute after high school, Sabuda graduated summa cum laude in 1987. With his B.F.A. in communications design in hand, he began his first illustration project for Green Tiger Press: a pair of books he designed with writer Eugene B. Coco titled *The Fiddler's Son* and *The Wishing Well.* In the late 1990s Sabuda returned to Pratt to teach a course in the craft of pop-up design. As he explained in a *Publishers Weekly* interview, "There isn't a place you can go to learn how to make pop-ups. I learned by experimenting, and looking at my favorites to see how things were done."

Sabuda's 1998 work *Cookie Count: A Tasty Pop-Up* reflects the author/illustrator's whimsical approach to his art. In the story, an ever-growing number of spatula-wielding mice stir up batch after batch of delicious cookies: everything from Linzer cookies to a gingerbread house. A reviewer for *Publishers Weekly* was impressed by Sabuda's "elaborate" two-page spreads, "each more inventive than the last." In a review of Sabuda's *The Movable Mother Goose* in *School Library Journal,* contributor John Peters could barely contain his enthusiasm, noting that Sabuda "is as much an artist as a paper engineer, capable not only of designing cutting-edge special effects, but of using them in ingeniously creative ways."

Sabuda designs pop-up history in his *The Knight's Castle* and *The Mummy's Tomb,* as relics from the past pop into the present, accompanied by simple rhyming texts and a small mouse hidden in the illustrations on each page. By opening and closing the pages, "the

Young Teune, living near the Arctic Sea, makes a robe for Blizzard when the robe is accidentally destroyed by Teune's fire in Robert Sabuda's pourquoi tale about the origin of the Northern Lights. (From The Blizzard's Robe, *written and illustrated by Sabuda.)*

figures can be made to move in amusing ways," commented *Horn Book* contributor Lolly Robinson.

Sabuda makes his home in New York City, where he works in a studio in Manhattan's Upper West Side. He lives with his boyfriend and their two cats, Tammy and Reba, "who make it a joy to work in our apartment, which is about the size of a walk-in closet. And I'd like to thank the academy and all the little people for making this possible!"

Biographical and Critical Sources

PERIODICALS

Booklist, November 15, 1992, p. 603; April 15, 1994, Ilene Cooper, review of *Tutankhamen's Gift,* p. 1537; November 1, 1995, Kathy Broderick, review of *Arthur and the Sword,* p. 478; September 1, 1996, review of *The Twelve Days of Christmas,* p. 138; October 15, 1997, Susan Dove Lempke, review of *The Paper Dragon,* p. 402; December 15, 1997, review of *Cookie Count,* p. 700; November 15, 1999, Linda Perkins, review of *The Blizzard's Robe,* p. 637; December, 1999, Ilene Cooper, review of *The Movable Mother Goose,* p. 786.

Bulletin of the Center for Children's Books, March, 1998, Deborah Stevens, review of *Cookie Count,* p. 359; December, 1998, Deborah Stevenson, review of *ABC Disney,* p. 145.

Five Owls, January, 1993, p. 63.

Horn Book Guide, spring, 1993, p. 87; spring, 1995, Lolly Robinson, review of *The Knight's Castle,* p. 53; spring, 1999, Peter D. Sieruta, review of *ABC Disney,* p. 42.

Kirkus Reviews, November 15, 1992, p. 1447; October 15, 1995, review of *Arthur and the Sword,* p. 1500.

Library Talk, January, 1993, p. 17; May, 1993, p. 26.

New Advocate, spring, 1993, p. 140.

Publishers Weekly, August 16, 1991, review of *I Hear America Singing,* p. 59; December 20, 1991, review of *The Log of Christopher Columbus,* p. 83; October 26, 1992, p. 72; October 23, 1993, review of *The Ibis and the Egret,* p. 61; October 17, 1994, review of *The Knight's Castle,* p. 80; September 18, 1995, review of *A Kwanzaa Celebration,* p. 94; September 30, 1996, review of *The Twelve Days of Christmas,* p. 88; November 25, 1996, Cindi Di Marzo, "In the Studio with Robert Sabuda," p. 30; December 1, 1997, review of *Cookie Count,* p. 55; October 25, 1999, review of *The Movable Mother Goose,* p. 79; November 29, 1999, review of *The Blizzard's Robe,* p. 70.

Reading Teacher, April, 1993, p. 592.

School Library Journal, November, 1992, p. 86; April, 1994, Meg Stackpole, review of *A Tree Place,* p. 140; October, 1995, review of *A Kwanzaa Celebration,* p. 43; November, 1997, Margaret A. Chang, review of *The Paper Dragon,* p. 79; October, 1999, Tina Hudak, review of *The Blizzard's Robe,* p. 125; February, 2000, John Peters, review of *The Moveable Mother Goose,* p. 97.*

*   *   *

SCHNEIDER, Christine M. 1972(?)-

Personal

Education: University of Kansas, graduated.

Career

Illustrator.

Writings

(Illustrator) Laura F. Nielsen, *Jeremy's Muffler,* Simon & Schuster (New York City), 1995.

(Author and illustrator) *Picky Mrs. Pickle,* Walker and Co. (New York City), 1999.

Biographical and Critical Sources

PERIODICALS

Publishers Weekly, August 30, 1999, review of *Picky Mrs. Pickle,* p. 83.

School Library Journal, September, 1999, Carol Schene, review of *Picky Mrs. Pickle,* p. 205.

ON-LINE

Amazon.com, http://www.amazon.com/ (April 5, 2000).

CNN Book News, http://cnn.com/ (February 3, 2000).*

*   *   *

SLOAN, Glenna (Davis) 1930-

Personal

Born in 1930. *Education:* Columbia University, doctorate.

Addresses

Home—26 Grove St., Garden City, NY 11530. *Office*—Department of Elementary and Early Childhood Education, Queens College of the City University of New York, Flushing, NY 11367.

Career

Queens College of the City University of New York, Flushing, NY, professor of children's literature. *Member:* International Reading Association (president-elect of Special Interest Group on Reading and Children's Literature), International Children's Literature Association (member of board of directors), National Council of Teachers of English (chairperson of Excellence in Poetry for Children Award).

Writings

The Child as Critic: Teaching Literature in the Elementary School, Teachers College Press (New York City), 1975, 2nd edition published as *The Child as Critic: Teaching Literature in Elementary and Middle Schools,* 1984, 4th edition published as *The Child as Critic: Developing Literacy through Literature,* in press.

Spotlight on Liz, Macmillan of Canada (Toronto, Ontario), 1977.

Stealing Time (juvenile novel), Royal Fireworks Publishing (Unionville, NY), 1998.

Contributor to periodicals, including *Journal of Children's Literature.*

Work in Progress

Another children's novel; research on "the possibilities of poetry and verse to enhance the child's literary development."

Biographical and Critical Sources

PERIODICALS

Children's Literature Association Quarterly, fall, 1994, Norma Bagnall, review of *The Child as Critic,* pp. 135-36.

Curriculum Review, February, 1978, review of *The Child as Critic,* p. 44; May, 1985, review of *The Child as Critic,* p. 23.

Horn Book, October, 1976, Paul Heins, review of *The Child as Critic,* p. 520.

Reading Teacher, January, 1977, review of *The Child as Critic,* p. 436.

School Library Journal, November, 1976, Margaret Mary Kimmel, review of *The Child as Critic,* p. 36.

* * *

SMITH, Jos(eph) A. 1936-

Personal

Born September 5, 1936, in Bellefonte, PA; son of George Leonard (a barber) and Frieda Regina (a beautician; maiden name, Droege) Smith; married Nancy Clare Hutchison (a family counselor), August 11, 1959 (divorced); married Charlotte Mitsua Honda (a dancer), July, 1972 (divorced); children: Kathryn (Kari) Anne, Joseph A., Emily Christian. *Education:* Attended Pennsylvania State University, summer sessions, 1955-60, New York University, New School for Social Research, Roscoe Center, and Wainwright Center for Human Resources; received B.F.A. from Pratt Institute; graduate study at Pennsylvania State University, 1960-61, and Pratt Institute, 1961-62; studied at Institute for Mind Research. *Politics:* Democrat. *Religion:* Buddhist.

Addresses

Home—159 John St., 6th Fl., New York, NY 10038-3511. *Office*—Pratt Institute, School of Art and Design, 200 Willoughby Ave., Brooklyn, NY 11205.

Career

Free-lance illustrator; Pratt Institute, School of Art and Design, Brooklyn, NY, professor of fine art, 1962—. Teacher of adult painting classes at Staten Island Museum, 1964; lecturer in drawing at Wagner College, 1965-66; teacher of a summer painting workshop for Art Alliance of Central Pennsylvania, 1969-71; teacher of the Visualization and Imagizing Workshop at Wainwright Center for Human Resources, 1975; visiting professor of fine arts at Richmond College, 1984; member of visual arts faculty at Stockton State College, Artist's and Teacher's Institute, and New Jersey Council on the Arts, summer sessions, 1987—; LaFont Painting Workshop, 1990; visiting artist at Art Institute of Chicago, 1990; visiting artist at Mississippi Art Colony, 1992. *Military service:* U.S. Army, became specialist 4.

EXHIBITIONS: Solo exhibitions include: Samuel S. Fleisher Art Memorial, Philadelphia, PA, 1961; Pratt Institute, Brooklyn, NY, 1962; Janet Nessler Gallery, New York City, 1963; Lehigh University, Bethlehem, PA, 1964; State Island Museum, Staten Island, NY, 1966; Bloomsburg State College, Bloomsburg, PA, 1968; Parsons School of Design, New York City, 1971; Chambers Gallery, Pennsylvania State University, Uni-

versity Park, 1972; Bethel Gallery, Bethel, CT, 1978; Newhouse Gallery, Snug Harbor Cultural Center, Staten Island, 1982; The Visual Arts Gallery, Adirondack Community College, Glens Falls, NY, 1988. *Group exhibitions include:* Annual Summer Exhibitions, Pennsylvania State University, 1955-60; Annual American Watercolor Society Exhibition, New York City, 1965, 1967, and 1969; "Portraits for *Time,*" New York Society of Illustrators, New York City, 1979; "Aliens," Museum of the Surreal and Art Fantastique, New York City, 1981; Carlyle Gallery, New York City, 1982 and 1983; "Separate Realities," Circlework Visions Gallery, New York City, 1986; "The Original Art," Society of Illustrators Museum of American Illustration, New York City, 1991. *Member:* Princeton Zen Society.

Awards, Honors

Dean's Medal, Pratt Institute, 1958; Mary S. Litt Award, American Watercolor Society, 1967; Juror's Choice Award, Pennsylvania State University, 1971; merit award from National Art Director's Club, 1971, New York Society of Illustrators, 1972, 1973, and 1975, American Institute of Graphic Arts, 1975, Bicentennial in Print, 1976, Art Directors Club of Metropolitan Washington, 1976, and Federal Design Council, 1976; first prize award in professional category, Pennsylvania State University, 1972; Staten Island Advance Award, Staten Island Museum, 1974; Purchase Prize in invitational section, Rutgers University, 1974; 1979 Andy Award of Merit, Advertising Club of New York; Print Club Purchase Award and merit award, University of Mississippi, 1991; *Jim Ugly* received the *Parents' Choice* Award from the Parents' Choice Foundation in 1992.

Writings

(And illustrator) *The Pen and Ink Book: Materials and Techniques for Today's Artist,* Watson-Guptill, 1992.

ILLUSTRATOR

Stan Steiner, *The Last Horse,* Holt, 1961.

Walter S. Carpenter and Philip Bluehouse, *Two Knots on a Counting Rope: A Navaho Counting Book,* Holt, 1964.

Katharine Carter (reteller), *Tales from Hans Christian Andersen,* Whitman Publishing, 1965.

Edward William Lane (reteller), *Tales from Arabian Nights,* Whitman Publishing, 1966.

The Sierra Club Survival Songbook, collected by Jim Morse and Nancy Mathews, Sierra Club, 1971.

Norman Borisoff, *Lily, The Lovable Lion,* Scholastic, 1975.

MacKinlay Kantor, *Andersonville,* Franklin Library, 1976.

Erica Jong, *Witches,* Abrams, 1981.

Joseph Conrad, *Heart of Darkness and Other Tales,* Franklin Library, 1982.

Bernard Evslin, *Hercules,* Morrow, 1984.

Deborah Hautzig (reteller), *The Wizard of Oz,* Random House, 1984.

Robin McKinley (reteller), *Tales from the Jungle Book,* Random House, 1985.

George MacDonald, *The Princess and the Goblin,* Grosset & Dunlap, 1985.

Jos. A. Smith's magical illustrations reflect the playful fantasy of Susan Cooper's tale about a young boy who goes on an adventure with the dragon from his favorite picture book. (From Matthew's Dragon.*)*

Barbara Ann Brennan, *Hand of Light*, Pleiades Books, 1987.

Susan Cooper, *Matthew's Dragon*, McElderry Books, 1991.

Helen V. Griffith, *"Mine Will," Said John*, Greenwillow (New York), 1992.

Sid Fleischman, *Jim Ugly*, Greenwillow, 1992.

Lynne Reid Banks, *The Adventures of King Midas*, Morrow, 1992.

Diana Wynne Jones, *Stopping for a Spell: Three Fantasies*, Greenwillow, 1993.

Jessie Haas, *Chipmunk!*, Greenwillow, 1993.

Mary Serfozo, *Benjamin Bigfoot*, McElderry Books, 1993.

Susan Cooper, *Danny and the Kings*, McElderry Books, 1993.

Diane Wolkstein, *Step by Step*, Morrow, 1993.

Jessie Haas, *Mowing*, Greenwillow, 1994.

Betty Levin, *Starshine and Sunglow*, Greenwillow, 1994.

Marc Gellman and Thomas Hartman, *How Do You Spell God?: Answers to the Big Questions from Around the World*, foreword by His Holiness the Dalai Lama, Morrow Junior Books, 1995.

Jessie Haas, *A Blue for Beware*, Greenwillow, 1995.

Jessie Haas, *No Foal Yet*, Greenwillow, 1995.

Nicholas Heller, *Goblins in Green*, Greenwillow, 1995.

Jessie Haas, *Sugaring*, Greenwillow, 1996.

Nancy Farmer, *Runnery Granary*, Greenwillow, 1996.

Jessie Haas, *Be Well, Beware*, Greenwillow, 1996.

Betty Levin, *Gift Horse*, Greenwillow, 1996.

Mirra Ginsburg, *Clay Boy*, Greenwillow, 1997.

Nicholas Heller, *The Giant*, Greenwillow, 1997.

Sid Fleischman, *Bandit's Moon*, Greenwillow, 1998.

Charlotte S. Huck, *A Creepy Countdown*, Greenwillow, 1998.

Nicholas Heller, *Ogres! Ogres! Ogres!: A Feasting Frenzy from A to Z*, Greenwillow, 1999.

Betty Levin, *Creature Crossing*, Greenwillow, 1999.

Jessie Haas, *Hurry!*, Greenwillow, 2000.

Nicholas Heller, *Elwood and the Witch*, Greenwillow, 2000.

Also illustrator of *European Folk Festivals,* by Sam Epstein and Beryl Epstein, 1968; *Short Takes: A Short Story Collection for Young Readers,* selected by Elizabeth Segel, 1986; *Thirteen Days of Christmas,* by Jenny Overton, 1987. Contributor to periodicals, including *Time, Newsweek, New York Times, Harper's,* and *New Times.*

Author's collections are housed at the Pennsylvania Academy of the Fine Arts, New York Stock Exchange, Lauren Rogers Museum, Library of Congress, Print Club at University of Mississippi, Rutgers University, Ministry of Education, Kassel Documenta Archive, Coeln Ludwig Museum, and Stuttgart Staatsgalerie Grafische Sammlung.

Sidelights

Jos. A. Smith told *SATA:* "I grew up in the town of State College, PA. Pennsylvania State University is located there. Although neither of my parents had had the opportunity to complete even grade school, they raised my brother and me to regard learning as the most important thing in our lives. It didn't matter what we wanted to do, they encouraged us. My brother is now chair of the industrial engineering department at Ohio State University, and I am a professor of fine art in the graduate fine art department and the undergraduate painting and drawing department at Pratt Institute in addition to my career as an artist.

"I was also fortunate to be asked by illustrator Richard Lindner to be his studio assistant while I was a student at Pratt Institute. As a result of this I had a rare opportunity to meet and listen to his friends when they visited him in his studio. These included painter Marcel Duchamp, actress Greta Garbo, artist Adja Yunkers, and cartoonist Saul Steinberg. Lindner was one of the most sensitive people I have ever known. He would stop work in the studio and we would go off for hours riding on all the elevated subway lines we could find in search of a certain red chimney that he had seen once years before, or we might go to Central Park Zoo and look at the eyes of the gorilla because of a wise expression he had. Lindner and Hobson Pittman (a painter on the faculty of the Pennsylvania Academy of the Fine Arts in Philadelphia who I studied with every summer at Pennsylvania State University until he retired and turned his studio workshops over to me) both had a profound influence on my life as an artist.

"Other important influences are related to my lifelong interest in drawing imagery from my unconscious for my drawings, sculptures, and paintings. I studied with Jean Houston at the Institute for Mind Research to learn non-drug techniques for inducing altered states. I joined the Princeton Zen Society to learn Zen meditation, and studied Jain meditation with Mouni Sri Chitrabanu, traditional shamanic trance techniques from the anthropologist Michael Harner and joined the Nyingmapa Lineage of the Tibetan Buddhists to learn their elaborate visualization techniques. I also studied biofeedback therapy and own and have used an electroencephalogram

(EEG) to record brainwave states evoked by these various methods, to understand them better. I use adaptations of all of these techniques to evoke imagery for my art, and occasionally incorporate some of the simpler forms in my art classes to enable other artists to be able to take advantage of them. Another of my lifelong interests is nature and the environment, and I have contributed my art to many environmental causes. One of the high points of my life in this area was spending one summer walking cross-country in East Africa, drawing people and photographing and filming wildlife. I have always had one or more pets, which usually included some snakes. At present I share my studio/loft, where I live, with a boa constrictor and a ball python."

Smith's affinity for the natural world is exhibited in his finely detailed, realistic illustrations for picture books such as *Chipmunk!,* by Jessie Haas, in which the family cat captures a chipmunk and brings it into the house, causing mayhem. After knocking over plants, furniture, and toys, the chipmunk lands on Dad's head, and he transports it back outside. Smith's "neatly framed color paintings capture the actions and emotions extraordinarily well," declared Deborah Abbott in *Booklist.* Likewise, Nancy A. Gifford wrote in *School Library Journal:* "The lively action and funny pictures combine to make this a good choice for story hour." Also by Haas, *Mowing* gives an account of Nora's day cutting hay in the fields with Gramps. Nora travels on foot ahead of the horse-drawn mower, keeping an eye out for the animals who live in the field and directing Gramps to mow around a killdeer nest and a young fawn. Because Smith's illustrations are often set at the eye-level of the animals, "readers see the humans and the horses as peripheral guests in the world," remarked Mary Harris Veeder in *Booklist.* In *No Foal Yet,* Nora and her grandparents endure the long wait for a new foal to be born in the stable. Using watercolor and colored pencils, Smith's illustrations "are touched with gentle, golden light, like the light of a springtime twilight," Veeder exclaimed. Smith's illustrations also convey much of the emotional element of Haas's simple tale in *Sugaring,* which details the many steps required to make maple syrup from tree sap. "This fictionalized portrayal allows Nora to take center stage in the sugaring process," observed Kay Weisman in *Booklist,* a process that is shown in minute detail to the benefit of interested young readers.

Also in a realistic vein are Smith's illustrations for *Danny and the Kings,* a heartwarming Christmas tale about a boy whose mother can't afford a Christmas tree. Offered a small tree by his friend Steve, Danny is nearly run over by a truck while dragging the tree home, and becomes the object of charity of three truckers who are known as the Kings of the Road. "Snowy winter scenes and indoor views in lovely watercolor paintings enhance the story's emotional feeling," *Booklist* reviewer Deborah Abbott remarked. For Elizabeth Devereaux and Kit Alderdice, writing in *Publishers Weekly,* Smith's illustrations carry the magical element of this modern version of the Christmas story, blurring "distinctions between what is real and what can only be hoped for."

Smith's illustrations for Diane Wolkstein's picture book *Step by Step* are also characterized as realistic with a twist of fantasy. Here, Wolkstein tells the story of an ant who ventures out one day for a visit with her grasshopper friend, stays to play a while, then slowly makes her way home. Smith's illustrations show the world from the perspective of the ant protagonist, and she and the grasshopper are realistically rendered except for one detail: the ant wears red tennis shoes and the grasshopper sports a baseball cap. Because of their size and their attire, critics deemed that small readers would likely empathize with Smith and Wolkstein's characters. "If not a show-stopper, [this is] decidedly reader-friendly," averred a reviewer for *Publishers Weekly.*

Smith's penchant for whimsy has been given free rein in a number of fantastical picture books, including *Matthew's Dragon* by Susan Cooper. In this tale, just before Matthew falls asleep he sees a dragon from one of his books come alive. The two have a snack and do battle with a neighborhood cat before growing large and flying off into the sky to frolic with all the dragons ever written about. "Smith's paintings of the dragon-crowded sky are truly breathtaking," commented a reviewer for *Publishers Weekly.* Smith created a panoply of goblins in *Goblins in Green,* an alphabet book by Nicholas Heller in which the author uses alliteration and a fantastical setting to recite the alphabet. In his illustrations, which a reviewer for *Publishers Weekly* deemed the "true treasure" of the book, Smith imbeds visual spoofs of famous paintings and films, which casts the whole project in a "zany" light, this critic continued.

The antics of goblins are again the subject in *Runnery Granary* by Nancy Farmer. In this story, no one can figure out what or who is stealing the grain from the Runnery family granary until Granny decides it must be goblins, and recites an old recipe for catching the tricky creatures. Smith's watercolor illustrations "set the story in medieval times among clean, prosperous-looking buildings and sunny woods," remarked Lolly Robinson in *Horn Book.* "And Smith's depiction of the greedy gnomes is just right," added a contributor to *Publishers Weekly:* "they're a wee bit scary, but not too much." *Booklist* reviewer Carolyn Phelan drew a similar conclusion, dubbing *Runnery Granary* "an unusual and entertaining picture book."

A Russian folk tale is the source for Mirra Ginsburg's *Clay Boy,* illustrated by Smith. Here the not-so-scary monster is cousin to the fabled Gingerbread Boy, a boy fashioned of clay by a lonely old couple who become the boy's victims. The Clay Boy is eternally hungry, and as he eats everything in sight, he grows larger and larger, until the things he eats include the old man and woman and a horse-drawn wagon. A wily goat saves the day, however, when he butts the Clay Boy in his stomach, breaking him into brittle pieces, and out pop all the people he's eaten, ready to celebrate their regained freedom. "In their play with scale, the illustrations express a wonderful combination of the monstrous and the cozy," observed Hazel Rochman in *Booklist.* Like the goblins in *Runnery Granary,* the Clay Boy is a combination of elements intended to both frighten and reassure children, though despite the boy's childlike red romper, the former response is perhaps the more likely. A reviewer for *Publishers Weekly* dubbed the Smith's rendition of the Clay Boy "deliciously creepy" and predicted that it "will no doubt deliver a mild dose of the shivers to delighted young audiences."

By the author of *Goblins in Green, The Giant* allows Smith another opportunity to portray the antics of a larger-than-life creature in ordinary circumstances. Here, a giant in purple overalls escapes from a painting, and Evan and his grandma pursue it back to the artist's studio, where the painter eventually paints the giant back into the picture. "Smith's understated illustrations play straight man to the story's energetically bizarre elements," declared a reviewer in *Publishers Weekly.* Smith teamed up with Heller for a third time in *Ogres! Ogres! Ogres!,* an alphabet book featuring a series of monsters eating their way through the alphabet. "The vibrant, detailed pictures portray the ogres caught in hilarious acts of bad manners as they play inappropriately with food," remarked Shelle Rosenfeld in *Booklist.* Charlotte Huck's *A Creepy Countdown* does a similar job for numbers with a Halloween orientation. Smith's scratchboard illustrations "capture the eerie holiday mood without being overly frightening," remarked Stephanie Zvirin in *Booklist.*

Biographical and Critical Sources

PERIODICALS

Booklist, October 15, 1993, Deborah Abbott, review of *Danny and the Kings,* p. 451, review of *Chipmunk!,* p. 452; March 15, 1994, Mary Harris Veeder, review of *Step by Step,* p. 1376; June 1, 1994, Mary Harris Veeder, review of *Mowing,* p. 1838; June 1, 1995, Mary Harris Veeder, review of *No Foal Yet,* p. 1785; September 1, 1995, Mary Harris Veeder, review of *Goblins in Green,* p. 86; June 1, 1996, Carolyn Phelan, review of *Runnery Granary,* p. 1731; November 15, 1996, Kay Weisman, review of *Sugaring,* p. 594; April 15, 1997, Hazel Rochman, review of *Clay Boy,* p. 1422; September 1, 1998, Stephanie Zvirin, review of *A Creepy Countdown,* p. 133; October 15, 1999, Shelle Rosenfeld, review of *Ogres! Ogres! Ogres!,* p. 452.

Horn Book, November-December, 1993, Ann A. Flowers, review of *Danny and the Kings,* p. 722; May-June, 1994, Elizabeth S. Watson, review of *Mowing,* p. 315; September-October, 1996, Lolly Robinson, review of *Runnery Granary,* p. 575; March-April, 1997, Ann A. Flowers, review of *Clay Boy,* p. 206; May, 1999, review of *Creature Crossing,* p. 331.

Publisher's Weekly, August 28, 1981, p. 386; July 12, 1991, review of *Matthew's Dragon,* p. 65; September 20, 1993, Elizabeth Devereaux and Kit Alderdice, review of *Danny and the Kings,* p. 39; March 14, 1994, review of *Step by Step,* p. 72; October 9, 1995, review of *Goblins in Green,* p. 86; May 20, 1996, review of *Runnery Granary,* p. 259; May 5, 1997, review of *Clay Boy,* p. 209; October 27, 1997, review of *The Giant,* p. 75.

School Library Journal, September, 1984, p. 114; April, 1992, p. 113; February, 1994, Nancy A. Gifford, review of *Chipmunk!,* p. 84.

Teacher Librarian, September, 1998, Shirley Lewis, review of *A Creepy Countdown,* p. 47.*

*   *   *

SOTO, Gary 1952-

Personal

Born April 12, 1952, in Fresno, CA; son of Manuel and Angie (Trevino) Soto; married Carolyn Sadako Oda, May 24, 1975; children: Mariko Heidi. *Education:* California State University, Fresno, B.A., 1974; University of California, Irvine, M.F.A., 1976. *Hobbies and other interests:* Travel.

Addresses

Home—43 The Crescent, Berkeley, CA 94708.

Career

University of California, Berkeley, assistant professor 1979-85; associate professor of English and ethnic studies, 1985-92, part-time senior lecturer in English department, 1992-93; University of Cincinnati, Elliston Poet, 1988; Wayne State University, Martin Luther King/Cesar Chavez/Rosa Parks Visiting Professor of English, 1990; Distinguished Professor, University of California at Riverside; full-time writer, 1993—. *Member:* Royal Chicano Navy.

Awards, Honors

Discovery/The Nation prize, 1975; United States Award, International Poetry Forum, 1976, for *The Elements of San Joaquin;* Bess Hokin Prize from *Poetry,* 1978; Guggenheim fellowship, 1979-80; National Endowment for the Arts fellowships, 1981 and 1991; Levinson Award, *Poetry,* 1984; American Book Award, Before Columbus Foundation, 1985, for *Living up the Street;* California Arts Council fellowship, 1989; Best Book for Young Adults citation, American Library Association, 1990, and John and Patricia Beatty Award, California Library Association, 1991, both for *Baseball in April and Other Stories;* George G. Stone Center Recognition of Merit, Claremont Graduate School, 1993; Andrew Carnegie Medal, 1993; National Book Award and *Los Angeles Times* Book Prize finalist, both 1995, both for *New and Selected Poems;* American Library Association Notable Book selection, and *Parents' Choice* Award, both for *Chato's Kitchen;* Literature Award, Hispanic Heritage Foundation, 1999; Author-Illustrator Civil Rights Award, National Education Association, 1999; PEN Center West Book Award, 1999, for *Petty Crimes.*

Writings

POETRY FOR ADULTS

The Elements of San Joaquin, University of Pittsburgh Press, 1977.
The Tale of Sunlight, University of Pittsburgh Press, 1978.
Where Sparrows Work Hard, University of Pittsburgh Press, 1981.
Black Hair, University of Pittsburgh Press, 1985.
Who Will Know Us?, Chronicle Books, 1990.
Home Course in Religion, Chronicle Books, 1991.
New and Selected Poems, Chronicle Books, 1995.
Junior College: Poems, Chronicle Books, 1997.
A Natural Man, Chronicle Books, 1999.

PROSE FOR ADULTS

Living up the Street: Narrative Recollections (memoirs), Strawberry Hill, 1985.
Small Faces (memoirs), Arte Publico, 1986.
Lesser Evils: Ten Quartets (memoirs and essays), Arte Publico, 1988.
(Editor) *California Childhood: Recollections and Stories of the Golden State,* Creative Arts Book Company, 1988.
A Summer Life (autobiography), University Press of New England, 1990.
(Editor) *Pieces of the Heart: New Chicano Fiction,* Chronicle Books, 1993.
Nickel and Dime (novel), University of New Mexico Press, 2000.
The Effects of Knut Hamsun on a Fresno Boy (essays), Persea Books, 2001.
Poetry Lover (novel), University of New Mexico Press, 2001.

POETRY FOR YOUNG READERS

A Fire in My Hands, Scholastic, 1991.
Neighborhood Odes, Harcourt, 1992.
Canto Familiar/Familiar Song, Harcourt, 1995.

PROSE FOR YOUNG READERS

The Cat's Meow, illustrated by Carolyn Soto, Strawberry Hill, 1987, revised edition illustrated by Joe Cepeda, Scholastic, 1995.
Baseball in April and Other Stories (short stories), Harcourt, 1990.
Taking Sides, Harcourt, 1991.
Pacific Crossing, Harcourt, 1992.
The Skirt, Delacorte, 1992.
Too Many Tamales (picture book), Putnam, 1992.
Local News (short stories), Harcourt, 1993.
The Pool Party (also see below), Delacorte, 1993.
Crazy Weekend, Scholastic, 1994.
Jesse, Harcourt, 1994.
Boys at Work, Delacorte, 1995.
Chato's Kitchen (picture book), Putnam, 1995.
Summer on Wheels, Scholastic, 1995.
The Old Man and His Door (picture book), Putnam, 1996.
Snapshots from the Wedding (picture book), Putnam, 1996.
Off and Running, illustrated by Eric Velasquez, Delacorte, 1996.
Buried Onions, Harcourt, 1997.
Novio Boy (play), Harcourt, 1997.
Petty Crimes (short stories), Harcourt, 1998.

Big Bushy Mustache (picture book), Knopf, 1998.
Nerdlandia: A Play, PaperStar, 1999.
Chato and the Party Animals (picture book), Putnam, 2000.
Jessie De La Cruz: A Profile of a United Farm Worker, Persea Books, 2000.

Soto's books have also been published in Spanish, Italian, French, and Japanese.

SHORT FILMS

The Bike, Gary Soto Productions, 1991.
The Pool Party, Gary Soto Productions, 1993.

Sidelights

Gary Soto is at heart a poet; everything he writes is overflowing with the vivid details of everyday life. Soto takes joy in the little things—remembered smells, voices in the distance, the pull of muscle when working. Growing up in a working-class Mexican-American background in Fresno, California, in the agricultural San Joaquin Valley, he has taken that milieu and that geographical region for the subject of much of his writing. Soto, in his twenty books of poetry and prose for adults, and his nearly thirty books for young readers, has demonstrated a "seemingly total recall of his youth," as Suzanne Curley remarked in the *Los Angeles Times Book Review*. Writing in the *Bloomsbury Review*, Alicia Fields commented, "Soto's remembrances are as sharply defined and appealing as bright new coins," further adding, "[h]is language is spare and simple yet vivid." Soto has garnered such prestigious honors as an American Book Award and the Andrew Carnegie Medal, and has sold over a million copies of his books.

In award-winning poetry collections for adults, such as *The Elements of San Joaquin, The Tale of Sunlight,* and *New and Collected Poems,* and in his autobiographical writings, including *Living up the Street, Small Faces, Lesser Evils,* and *A Summer Life,* Soto often presents a picture of hard-working laborers of California's Central Valley that is both hopeful and bleak. Soto, who worked as a laborer during his young adulthood, knows this literary territory firsthand. In his writing, as Raymund Paredes noted in the *Rocky Mountain Review,* "Soto establishes his acute sense of ethnicity and, simultaneously, his belief that certain emotions, values, and experiences transcend ethnic boundaries and allegiances." Writing in the *New York Times Book Review,* the critic Alan Cheuse called Soto "one of the finest natural talents to emerge" from among today's Chicano writers.

However, Soto is a writer first, a Chicano writer second. His characters and settings are often, as many critics have pointed out, Mexican-American, but his themes are large. As a reviewer for *Publishers Weekly* noted, Soto has an ability to make "the personal universal, and readers will feel privileged to share the vision of this man who finds life perplexing but a joy." With his children's fiction, which be began producing in 1990, with the short story collection, *Baseball in April and Other Stories,* Soto has created a world in which he

tracks the sometimes perilous, sometimes hilarious journey to adulthood, as his characters struggle to gain maturity and self-awareness. Soto's books for younger readers present a cornucopia of styles: there are poetry collections, such as *A Fire in My Hands, Neighborhood Odes,* and *Canto Familiar;* short stories, including *Local News* and *Petty Crimes;* middle-grade novels, such as *The Pool Party, Boys at Work, The Skirt,* and *Off and Running;* picture books, from the celebrated *Too Many Tamales* to his tales of Chato the cat; and YA novels both serious—*Taking Sides, Pacific Crossing, Jesse, Buried Onions*—and silly—*Crazy Weekend* and *Summer on Wheels.* In addition, Soto has written two plays for younger readers/performers, *Novio Boy* and *Nerdlandia,* and has filmed three short films for Spanish-speaking children. As Susan Marie Swanson noted in a *Riverbank Review* profile of the prolific author, "A child could grow up on Soto's books," starting with the picture books and graduating slowly through all the varieties he produces, coming to the adult works that he first created. "How many American authors have mapped such a journey for us to follow?" Swanson wondered. "Soto's is an extraordinary achievement."

Soto was born on April 12, 1952, in Fresno, California, the industrial center of California's fertile San Joaquin Valley. Soto's parents were American-born, but Mexican culture was strong in the home. Field work and jobs in the packing house at the local Sun-maid Raisin plant provided economic sustenance for the family. Soto, the second of three children, later also worked in the fields and as a gardener. The death of his father when Soto was five sent the family reeling, both emotionally and economically; his mother, along with the grandparents, brought up the family. Later there was a stepfather, but life was still a struggle. "I don't think I had any literary aspirations when I was a kid," Soto once told *Contemporary Authors.* "In fact we were pretty much an illiterate family. We didn't have books, and no one encouraged us to read. So my wanting to write poetry was pretty much a fluke." At various times in his youth Soto wanted to be a priest or a paleontologist—anything but a field worker picking grapes or cotton, as he did much of his youth to help out at home.

Graduating from high school in 1970, Soto first attended Fresno City College, hoping to major in geography. Quickly, however, such a dream was replaced with another: writing poetry. As Soto explained in *Contemporary Authors:* "I know the day the change began, because it was when I discovered in the library a collection of poems edited by Donald Allen called *The New American Poetry.*" In particular, Soto focused on a poem by Edward Field, "Unwanted," that seemed to describe his own sense of alienation. "I discovered this poetry and thought, This is terrific: I'd like to do something like this. So I proceeded to write my own poetry, first alone, and then moving on to take classes." Transferring to California State University, Fresno, Soto studied with noted poet Philip Levine in 1972 and 1973. Under this man's tutelage, Soto learned the nuts and bolts not only of analyzing and critiquing a poem, but also of putting one together himself. Graduating magna cum laude from California State in 1974, he married Carolyn Oda the following year while working toward a master's degree in creative writing at the University of California, Irvine. Then in 1977 he took a lecturer position at the University of California, Berkeley, in Chicano studies. That same year, his first book of poems was published.

In his first volume of poetry, *The Elements of San Joaquin,* Soto offers a grim portrait of Mexican-American life. His poems depict the violence of urban life, the exhausting labor of rural life, and the futility of trying to recapture the innocence of childhood. In the book *Chicano Poetry,* Juan Bruce-Novoa likened Soto's poetic vision to T. S. Eliot's bleak portrait of the modern world, *The Waste Land.* Soto uses wind-swept dust as a dominant image, and he also introduces such elements as rape, unflushed toilets, a drowned baby, and men "Whose arms / Were bracelets / Of burns." Soto's skill with the figurative language of poetry has been noted by reviewers throughout his career, and in *Western American Literature,* Jerry Bradley praised the metaphors in *San Joaquin* as "evocative, enlightening, and haunting." Though unsettled by the negativism of the collection, Bruce-Novoa felt the work "convinces because of its well-wrought structure, the craft, the coherence of its totality." Moreover, he thought, because it brings such a vivid portrait of poverty to the reading public, *San Joaquin* is "a social as well as a literary achievement." This first book of poems won the United States Award from the International Poetry Forum.

Many critics have also observed that Soto's writing transcends social commentary. Bruce-Novoa said that one reason why the author's work has "great significance within Chicano literature" is because it represents "a definite shift toward a more personal, less politically motivated poetry." As Alan Williamson suggested in *Poetry,* Soto avoids either idealizing the poor for their oppression or encouraging their violent defiance. Instead, he focuses on the human suffering that poverty engenders. Reviewing Soto's second volume of poetry, *The Tale of Sunlight,* in *Parnassus,* Peter Cooley praised the author's ability to temper the bleakness of *San Joaquin* with "imaginative expansiveness." The poems in *Sunlight,* many of which focus on a child named Molina or on the owner of a Hispanic bar, display both the frustrations of poverty and what Williamson called "a vein of consolatory fantasy which passes beyond escapism into a pure imaginative generosity toward life." Williamson cited as an example "the poem in which an uncle's gray hair is seen as a visitation of magical butterflies."

Other collections followed. *Where Sparrows Work Hard* and *Black Hair* both increased Soto's reputation as a poet to watch. Then in 1985, Soto's career took a change of direction. With publication of *Living up the Street,* he turned his hand to prose, writing vignette-like memoirs of growing up in Fresno.

Soto mined the experiences of his early life in Fresno in several volumes of prose memoirs, books full of

j e s s e

by gary soto

Filled with detailed images, Soto's 1994 novel depicts a young Mexican American, Jesse, who leaves home in search of a better future.

compassion, humor, and controlled anger. When Soto discusses American racial tensions in the prose collections *Living up the Street: Narrative Recollections,* and its sequel, *Small Faces,* he uses vignettes drawn from his own childhood. One vignette shows the anger the author felt upon realizing that his brown-skinned brother would never be considered an attractive child by conventional American standards. Another shows Soto's surprise at discovering that, contrary to his family's advice to marry a Mexican, he was falling in love with a woman of Japanese ancestry. In these deliberately small-scale recollections, as Paredes noted, "it is a measure of Soto's skill that he so effectively invigorates and sharpens our understanding of the commonplace." With these volumes Soto acquired a solid reputation as a prose writer as well as a poet; *Living up the Street* earned him an American Book Award. Reviewing *Living up the Street* in the *San Francisco Review of Books,* Geoffrey Dunn noted that "Soto has changed literary forms, though he returns once again to the dusty fields and industrial alleyways of his Fresno childhood" in twenty-one autobiographical short stories or vignettes. Dunn concluded that the book "is certainly a formidable work by one of America's more gifted and sensitive writers." Writing of *Small Faces,* Fields noted that the "emotional weather ranges from sunny with blue skies to dark and stormy," and the author "darts back and forth in time to form meaningful connections between past and present."

Soto's autobiographical prose continued with *Lesser Evils: Ten Quartets* and *A Summer Life.* The first of these, as Soto once explained, reflects the author's experience with Catholicism, and Soto has since declared himself a reconciled Catholic. Reviewing that collection of prose in *Western American Literature,* Gerald Haslam commented, "Gary Soto remains one of the brightest talents of his generation," and further noted that his prose sketches, written with a "universal" voice, "are adding a dimension to his reputation." *A Summer Life,* Soto's fourth collection of reminiscences, consists of thirty-nine short essays. According to Ernesto Trejo in the *Los Angeles Times Book Review,* these pieces "make up a compelling biography" of Soto's youth. As he had done in previous works, Soto here "holds the past up to memory's probing flashlight, turns it around ever so carefully, and finds in the smallest of incidents the occasion for literature." Writing in the *Americas Review,* Hector Torres compared *A Summer Life* with Soto's earlier autobiographical texts and asserted that the later book "moves with greater stylistic elegance and richer thematic coherence."

During the early 1990s Soto turned his attentions in a new direction: children's literature. A first volume of short stories for young readers, *Baseball in April and Other Stories,* was published in 1990. The eleven tales depict Mexican-American boys and girls as they enter adolescence in Hispanic California neighborhoods. In the *New York Times Book Review,* Roberto Gonzalez Echevarria called the stories "sensitive and economical." Echevarria praised Soto: "Because he stays within the teenagers' universe ... he manages to convey all the social change and stress without bathos or didacticism. In fact, his stories are moving, yet humorous and entertaining." In the *Americas Review,* Torres suggested that *Baseball in April* was "the kind of work that could be used to teach high school and junior high school English classes." Roger Sutton, reviewing this debut juvenile collection in *Bulletin of the Center for Children's Books,* noted that the stories are "told with tenderness, optimism, and wry humor." Sutton further commented that while Chicano children and their parents "will be pleased to find a book that admits larger possibilities than the stereotypes of the noble-but-destitute farmworker," kids from all cultures "will feel like part of this neighborhood."

Other short story collections by Soto include *Local News* and *Petty Crimes.* The former title consists of thirteen short stories, once again set in a Mexican-American barrio, offering insights into the Hispanic community and culture. There are tales of first jobs that end in disaster, of teenage blackmail, and of botched thespian attempts in a school play. "As always," noted a writer for *Kirkus Reviews,* "Soto shows that the concerns and triumphs of Latino children are no different from anyone's...." A reviewer for *Publishers Weekly* called the collection a "vibrant tapestry of Chicano American neighborhoods." Soto's 1998 collection, *Petty Crimes,* gathers ten "affecting short stories," according to *Booklist*'s Hazel Rochman, portraying teenagers "both swaggering and lost." Rochman concluded, "Soto is a fine writer, and in the casual talk and schoolyard confrontations, the simple words flash with poetry." A writer for *Kirkus Reviews* described the stories in *Petty Crimes* as "a kaleidoscope of Mexican-American adolescents and the bullies they confront—bullies ranging from tough, menacing teens to life's unavoidable truths."

In 1991, Soto followed up the success of his first juvenile story collection with two new juvenile publications, a young adult novel and a book of poems for younger readers. *A Fire in My Hands* consists of twenty-three poems, some of which came from his adult collection, *Black Hair.* Each poem is prefaced with a comment about how Soto came to write it, and all of them—as so much of Soto's work does—reflect his own experiences growing up Mexican American or his experiences as a father. Reviewing the collection in *School Library Journal,* Barbara Chatton felt that "Soto's poems and thoughts provide gentle encouragement to young people who are seeking to express themselves through the use of language." *Booklist*'s Rochman remarked that the collection "will attract poetry readers and writers ... for its candid, personal, undogmatic 'advice to young poets.'" Soto has since produced two more volumes of poetry for young readers, *Neighborhood Odes* (1992) and *Canto Familiar* (1995). Reviewing *Odes,* a writer for *Publishers Weekly* commented that the "Hispanic neighborhood in Soto's 21 poems is brought sharply into focus by the care with which he records images of everyday life...." Renee Steinberg, reviewing the collection in *School Library Journal,* noted, "The rewards of well-chosen words that create vivid, sensitive images await readers of this collection of poems.... Each section is an expression of joy and wonder at life's daily pleasures and mysteries." And of Soto's 1995 collection, *Canto Familiar,* Rochman commented in *Booklist,* "this collection of simple free verse captures common childhood moments at home, at school, and in the street.... This is a collection to read aloud and get kids writing about themselves."

Taking Sides, Soto's first juvenile novel, was also published in 1991. The protagonist of that book, a boy named Lincoln Mendoza, appears in both *Taking Sides* and *Pacific Crossing.* As a Mexican-American eighth-grader in *Taking Sides,* Lincoln is confronted with challenges and insecurities when he and his mother move from San Francisco's Mission District to a predominantly Anglo suburb. He works to keep his heritage intact in his new environment. Though he plays basketball for his new school, Lincoln still feels loyalty for his old team at Franklin Junior High, and when the two teams face off on the court, Lincoln learns something about friendship, loyalty, and winning. A writer for *Kirkus Reviews* felt that with this novel, Soto "creates a believable, compelling picture of the stress that racial prejudice places on minority children." Bruce Anne Shook called it a "light but appealing story" that "deals with cultural differences, moving, and basketball," in a *School Library Journal* review.

Pacific Crossing finds Lincoln and one of his friends, Tony, facing cultural challenges in another context: they embark on a voyage to Japan as exchange students. Both of them have been studying the martial art of kempo and leap at the chance to go to Japan. Once there, Lincoln comes to understand that beneath the outward differences, life with his host family in Japan is not much different than at home. Writing in the *Multicultural Review*, Osbelia Juarez Rocha called *Pacific Crossing* "cleverly crafted" and "entertaining." *Horn Book*'s Ellen Fader concluded that the novel "highlights the truisms that people are the same all over the world and that friends can be found anywhere, if one makes the effort."

With *The Skirt*, Soto turned his hand to writing novels for middle-grade readers. Miata Ramirez is heartsick because she has lost her folklorico skirt on the school bus and is desperate to get it back before the dance performance. A reviewer for *Publishers Weekly* concluded that this "short novel should find its most appreciative audience at the lower end of the intended age range." *School Library Journal*'s Ann Welton felt the book was a "fine read-aloud and discussion starter," while *Horn Book*'s Nancy Vasilakis called the book an "unpretentious story for readers new to chapter books," and "a cheery snapshot of a Mexican-American family . . . ." Miata makes another appearance in the 1996 *Off and Running*, in which she and friend Anna become running mates for class office, competing against the dreaded boys. As time runs out on the election, the two girls must figure out how to change their image and win votes. *Booklist*'s Rochman felt that this "fifth-grade comedy is as lighthearted and affectionate as ever," and that some of the chapters "will make uproarious read-alouds." A reviewer for *Publishers Weekly* called Miata a "spunky and imaginative heroine."

Miata's competitor for class president in *Off and Running* is none other than Rudy Herrera, a character who made his first appearances in *The Pool Party* and *Boys at Work*, two other middle-grade novels from Soto. In *The Pool Party*, Rudy is invited to a rich girl's party and tries to figure out what he should take as an appropriate present. Soon his whole family is offering advice, and he and friend Alex pass the time in the days before the party getting into and out of scrapes. Finally they opt for a pool toy that becomes the hit of the party. Susan Marcus, reviewing the book in *School Library Journal*, called attention to "the poetic perfection Soto exhibits both in description and in authentic dialogue," as well as to the "immersion of readers into the bosom of a loving, hard-working Mexican-American family." A writer for *Kirkus Reviews* called the novel "Engaging" and "gently humorous." Rudy and friend Alex make return appearances in *Boys at Work*. When Rudy breaks an older boy's Discman at a baseball game, he is desperate to make some money to buy a new one. Crazy money-making schemes ensue in this "easy, entertaining

read," as a *Booklist* reviewer described the book. Rosie Peasley, writing in *School Library Journal*, remarked that Soto's strength "lies in the depth, warmth, and humor of his characters," and concluded that the book's "universal growing-up themes of bully-fear, friendship, and family relationships" make the novel "a reader-friendly addition." *Boys at Work* won a Newbery Honor award.

More humor is served up in *Crazy Weekend* and *Summer on Wheels*. These comic novels for young readers both feature the blood brothers Hector and Mando, two youngsters from East Los Angeles. In *Crazy Weekend*, a "winning combination of a thriller and a comedy," according to a writer for *Publishers Weekly*, Hector and Mando, witness a robbery while visiting Hector's uncle in Fresno. Karen Williams, writing in the *Christian Science Monitor*, felt "Soto creates a rollicking adventurer of wise-cracking good-guys and accident-prone bad guys." Hector and Mando get together again in *Summer on Wheels*, in which they bike from East Los Angeles to the beach at Santa Monica, staying with relatives along the way. "Readers will quickly become caught up in the boys' many schemes and escapades which occur with humorous regularity," remarked Maura Bresnahan in a *Voice of Youth Advocates* review of the novel. Bresnahan further noted that "Soto has created two wonderfully believable friends in Hector and Mando. They are typical boys on the cusp of adolescence."

Soto has ventured as well into the arena of children's picture books. *Too Many Tamales* depicts the story of Maria, a young girl who misplaces her mother's wedding ring in tamale dough while helping to prepare a Christmastime feast. Maria—with her cousins' help—embarks on a futile effort to recover the ring by consuming vast quantities of tamales. *Booklist*'s Rochman called this first venture into picture books "a joyful success," while a writer for *Kirkus Reviews* concluded, "this one should become a staple on the holiday menu." *Chato's Kitchen* introduces a cat whose efforts to entice the local "ratoncitos"—little mice—lead him to prepare abundant portions of fajitas, frijoles, enchiladas, and other foods. In a starred review, a critic for *School Library Journal* dubbed this picture book "really cool," further noting that "Soto adeptly captures the flavor of life in el barrio in this amusing tale." A writer for *Publishers Weekly* called the book "wickedly funny." Chato makes a return appearance in the 2000 work *Chato and the Party Animals*. Further picture books from Soto include *The Old Man and His Door*, *Big Bushy Mustache*, and *Snapshots from the Wedding*, in which the festivities are seen through the camera lens of the young flower girl, Maria. "Readers will be enthralled," observed a *Publishers Weekly* reviewer.

Soto has stated that his 1994 YA novel, *Jesse*, is a personal favorite and one in which the protagonist comes close to being autobiographical. Set in the late 1960s with the Vietnam War protests, United Farm Workers movement, and promise of a better world, the novel tells the story of sixteen-year-old Jesse who has left, both home and school, escaping boredom and the abuse of his drunken stepfather. He goes to live with his older brother, struggles with poverty, and learns first-hand about discrimination. "In this vivid, muscular portrait, the title character emerges as a complex, winning young man," commented Cathryn M. Mercier in a review of the novel in *Five Owls*. In the book, Jesse finally discovers himself as an artist. "Like Soto," Mercier noted, "Jesse has the voice of a poet." *Horn Book*'s Ellen Fader called the novel "moving" and "engrossing," and concluded that it "contains strands of both humor and despair."

In Soto's 1997 *Buried Onions,* Eddie is trying to escape the poverty and gang violence of the Fresno barrio by taking vocational classes. When his cousin is killed, he is urged by his aunt to find the killer and avenge the death of his relative, but Eddie just wants to find a way out of this claustrophobic world. A job in an affluent suburb goes awry when his boss's truck is stolen while in his care. Finally, with a gang member looking for him and with his money gone, Eddie opts to join the military in hopes that he can find a better life. "In bleak sentences of whispered beauty, Eddie tells how he dropped out of vocational college and is attempting to get by with odd jobs," remarked a critic for *Kirkus Reviews*. The same reviewer noted that this "unrelenting portrait is unsparing in squalid details," concluding that the book is a "valuable tale" and "one that makes no concessions."

Meanwhile, Soto has continued with his output for adult readers, including poetry collections such as *Junior College* and *A Natural Man,* as well as his *New and Selected Poems,* a volume selected as a finalist for the National Book Award. He has also written his first adult novels, *Nickel and Dime* and *Poetry Lover.* Yet amazingly, this writer who first won over readers for his adult volumes of poetry, increasingly is becoming known as an author of books for younger readers. He has left his teaching career at Berkeley to become a full-time writer.

"This poet has gassed up his car and gone forth to meet his readers," Soto remarked in an essay posted on his internet home page, by way of explaining his success. "Over a nine-year period I have spoken to three hundred thousand teachers and students, possibly more.... In my garage sit boxes of fan letters and hand-drawn banners proclaiming me the best writer in the world. And why such a reception? Unlike most other contemporary poets and writers, I've taken the show on the road and built a name among la gente, the people. I have ventured into schools where I have played baseball and basketball with young people, sung songs, acted in skits, delivered commencement speeches, learned three chords on a Mexican guitar to serenade teachers.... I have gone to prisons and mingle with people who have done time.... My readership is strung from large cities, such as Los Angeles, to dinky Del Rey where peach trees outnumber the population by many thousands.... My business is to make readers from non-readers."

Biographical and Critical Sources

BOOKS

Bruce-Novoa, Juan, *Chicano Poetry: A Response to Chaos,* University of Texas Press, 1982.

Children's Literature Review, Volume 38, Gale, 1996.

Contemporary Literary Criticism, Gale, Volume 32, 1985; Volume 80, 1994.

Cooper-Alarcon, Daniel Francis, *The Aztec Palimpsest: Discursive Appropriations of Mexican Culture,* UMI, 1993.

Dictionary of Literary Biography, Volume 82: *Chicano Writers,* Gale, 1989, pp. 246-52.

Hispanic Literature Criticism, Gale, 1994.

St. James Guide to Young Adult Writers, 2nd edition, St. James Press, 1999.

Soto, Gary, *Elements of San Joaquin,* University of Pittsburgh Press, 1977.

PERIODICALS

Americas Review, spring, 1991, Hector Torres, reviews of *Baseball in April* and *A Summer Life,* pp. 111-15.

Bloomsbury Review, January-February, 1987, Alicia Fields, "Small But Telling Moments," p. 10.

Booklist, April 1, 1992, Hazel Rochman, review of *A Fire in My Hands,* pp. 1437-38; September 15, 1993, H. Rochman, review of *Too Many Tamales,* p. 151; June 1, 1995, review of *Boys at Work,* p. 1773; October 1, 1995, H. Rochman, review of *Canto Familiar,* p. 312; October 1, 1996, H. Rochman, review of *Off and Running,* p. 362; November 15, 1997, p. 554; March 15, 1998, H. Rochman, review of *Petty Crimes,* p. 1245; June 1, 1998, p. 1784; November 1, 1998, p. 483; February 15, 2000.

Bulletin of the Center for Children's Books, April, 1990, Roger Sutton, review of *Baseball in April,* p. 199; November, 1999, pp. 108-09.

Christian Science Monitor, March 6, 1985; May 6, 1994, Karen Williams, "Lands Real and Imagined," pp. 12-13; September 28, 1995, p. B1.

English Journal, January, 1999, pp. 122-23.

Five Owls, January-February, 1995, Cathryn M. Mercier, review of *Jesse,* p. 64.

Horn Book, November-December, 1992, Ellen Fader, review of *Pacific Crossing,* pp. 725-26; November-December, 1992, Nancy Vasilakis, review of *The Skirt,* pp. 720-21; March-April, 1995, E. Fader, review of *Jesse,* pp. 201-02.

Kirkus Reviews, September 15, 1991, review of *Taking Sides,* p. 1228; April 1, 1993, review of *Local News,* p. 464; June 15, 1993, review of *The Pool Party,* p. 792; September 1, 1993, review of *Too Many Tamales,* p. 1152; August 1, 1997, review of *Buried Onions,* p. 1229; March 1, 1998, review of *Petty Crimes,* p. 345.

Los Angeles Times Book Review, August 5, 1990, Ernesto Trejo, "Memories of a Fresno Boyhood," pp. 1, 9; August 15, 1993, Suzanne Curley, "A Better Place to Live," p. 8; April 16, 1995, p. 6; September 1, 1996, p. 11.

Nation, June 7, 1993, pp. 772-74.

New York Times Book Review, October 11, 1981, Alan Cheuse, "The Voices of Chicano," pp. 15, 36-37; May

20, 1990, p. 45; August 20, 1990, Roberto Gonzalez Echevarria, "Growing Up North of the Border," p. 45; December 19, 1993, p. 16.

Multicultural Review, June, 1993, Osbelia Juarez Rocha, review of *Pacific Crossing,* pp. 76, 78.

Parnassus, fall-winter, 1979, Peter Cooley, review of *The Tale of Sunlight.*

Poetry, March, 1980, Alan Williamson, "In a Middle Style," pp. 348-54; March, 1998, p. 339.

Publishers Weekly, March 4, 1988, review of *Lesser Evils,* p. 102; March 23, 1992, review of *Neighborhood Odes,* p. 74; August 24, 1992, review of *The Skirt,* p. 80; April 12, 1993, review of *Local News,* p. 64; August 16, 1993, p. 103; January 31, 1994, review of *Crazy Weekend,* p. 90; February 6, 1995, review of *Chato's Kitchen,* p. 84; January 20, 1997, review of *Snapshots from the Wedding,* p. 401; December 8, 1997, review of *Off and Running,* p. 74; May 25, 1998, p. 91; April, 26, 1999, p. 85; February 14, 2000, p. 175.

Riverbank Review, Fall, 1999, Susan Marie Swanson, "Gary Soto," pp. 16-18.

Rocky Mountain Review of Language and Literature, Volume 41, numbers 1-2, 1987, Raymund Paredes, "Recent Chicano Fiction," pp. 126-28.

San Francisco Review of Books, Geoffrey Dunn, review of *Living up the Street,* summer, 1986, p. 11.

School Library Journal, Susan F. Marcus, review of *The Pool Party,* p. 112; November, 1991, Bruce Anne Shook, review of *Taking Sides,* p. 124; March, 1992, Barbara Chatton, review of *A Fire in My Hands,* p. 264; May, 1992, Renee Steinberg, review of *Neighborhood Odes,* p. 128; September, 1992, Ann Welton, review of *The Skirt,* p. 255; June, 1995, Rosie Peasley, review of *Boys at Work,* p. 113; July, 1995, review of *Chato's Kitchen,* p. 69; June, 1997, p. 146; May, 1998, pp. 89, 148; September, 1998, p. 183; July, 1999, p. 55; February, 2000, p. 146.

Western American Literature, spring, 1979, Jerry Bradley, review of *The Elements of San Joaquin.;* May, 1989, Gerald Haslam, review of *Lesser Evils,* pp. 92-93.

Voice of Youth Advocates, April, 1995, Maura Bresnahan, review of *Summer on Wheels,* pp. 27-28; December, 1999, p. 339.

ON-LINE

Gary Soto Web site, http://garysoto.com/

—*Sketch by J. Sydney Jones*

*   *   *

STOBBS, William 1914-2000

OBITUARY NOTICE —See index for *SATA* sketch: Born June 27, 1914, in South Shields, England; died April 6, 2000. Administrator, illustrator, author. William Stobbs was the author and illustrator of numerous children's books featuring stories both original and retold. Head of the design department at the London School of Printing and Graphic Arts from 1948 to 1958, he also served as the principal at Maidstone College of Art in Kent, England for twenty years; he retired in 1979. Stobbs'

first picture books were retold versions of *The Story of the Three Bears* and *The Story of the Three Little Pigs,* both from 1965. However, by 1973 he was writing original material, such as his *A Mini Called Zak,* and supplying color illustrations that became increasingly intricate throughout his career as technology for color printing continued to improve. In 1958 he was awarded the Library Association's Kate Greenaway Award for illustrating *A Bundle of Ballads,* which was compiled by Ruth Manning-Sanders, and *Kashtanka,* a translated version of Anton Chekov's story.

OBITUARIES AND OTHER SOURCES:

BOOKS

Oxford Companion to Children's Literature, Oxford University Press, 1999, p. 497.

PERIODICALS

London Times, May 6, 2000.

*   *   *

STONE, Idella Purnell
See PURNELL, Idella

*   *   *

STONE, Ikey
See PURNELL, Idella

*   *   *

SVENDSEN, Mark (Nestor) 1962-

Personal

Born August 7, 1962, in Yeppoon, Australia; son of Nestor (a farmer) and Dell (a farmer; maiden name, Miller) Svendsen; married Rosamunde Anne Kneeshaw (a musician and composer), September 22, 1984; children: Thyri, Hannah. *Education:* University of Queensland, B.A., 1983; Queensland University of Technology, graduate diploma of arts administration, 1991.

Addresses

Home—Lot 2, Svendsen Rd., Emu Park, Queensland 4702, Australia. *Office*—P.O. Box 61, Emu Park, Queensland 4702, Australia. *E-mail*—svendsen@rock-net.net.au.

Career

Regional Centre of the Arts, Rockhampton, Australia, graduate administrative officer, 1991-92, administrator, 1992-95; presenter of workshops and poetry readings throughout Queensland and New South Wales, Australia, 1995—. Queensland Writers Centre, member; consultant to Regional Arts Development Fund, Livingstone Shire Council, and Gracemere Shire Council. *Member:*

Australia Council, Children's Book Council of Australia.

Awards, Honors

Writing grants, 1995, 1996, 1997, and 1998; Australia Council grant, 2000.

Writings

The Bunyip and the Night (poems for children), University of Queensland Press, 1994.

The Turtle Damns the Pursuit of Happiness (adult poems), Metro Arts Press, 1994.

Three Moon Lagoon (juvenile novella), Greater Glider Productions, 1996.

(Editor) *Songs of the East Coast,* CQU Press, 1997.

(Editor) Glenda Gabrielle and Meredyth Curlie, *True Blue Christmas,* Literacy Land, 1997.

(Editor) *Dust Road Coming,* CQU Press, 1998.

Snigger James on Grey (young adult novel), Lothian (Port Melbourne, Australia), 1999.

Poison under Their Lips (young adult novel), Lothian, 2001.

Work represented in anthologies, including *Sounds Spooky,* Greater Glider Productions, 1994; *The Girl Who Married a Fly,* Australian Association for the Teaching of English, 1997; and *Let's Jabberwocky,* edited by Jenny Poulter, Currency Press, 2001. Contributor to magazines, including *Northern Perspectives, Imago, Social Alternatives, Idiom 23,* and *Educating Young Children.*

Work in Progress

A children's picture book, *Captain Me!,* publication by Lothian expected in 2002; a collection of poetry for children, *Short and Sweet and Silly.*

Sidelights

Mark Svendsen told *SATA:* "The two most dynamic motivating forces which pervade the human psyche are fear and love. For me, these two emotions are diametrically opposed at the core of the human dialectic. What others have called the human condition is, I believe, a complex tangle of these conflicting forces in constant struggle, each vying to 'overweave' the other, to gain the ascendant. When I write I try to tap into the redemptive quality of this dynamic struggle.

"In the past I have written about bunyips—those mythic creatures said to inhabit the creeks, water holes, and billabongs of Australia—because embodied in those mythical beings is the essence of fear with which characters, through their love and acceptance, can grapple and ultimately overcome. *The Bunyip and the Night* is a picture book of six poems on the bunyip theme. Illustrated by six different illustrators, the book is not for little children but works very well for older children. Fear of the dark, adults, lonely places, and ourselves are all topics which have been raised by children when reading this book with me.

"*Three Moon Lagoon* (the euphonic name is of a real place near where I live) is a novella for nine to twelve-year-olds. It deals with the notion that our dreams, or our love for the future, *are* our future, and if we cannot dream we are stuck in the rut of today, now being what we fear most. Of course, the two children in this nightmare work out a riddle to overcome their fears and claim the future to be their own.

"*Snigger James on Grey* deals with the overcoming of fear as the growth which the adolescent must undertake to become fully adult. The child must die, and the adult must begin to grow. My new young adult novel bears the working title *Poison under Their Lips.* It traces the life of an adolescent cadet officer with Queensland's infamous Native Police Force, whose sole job was the 'dispersal of troublesome blacks.' This phrase became a euphemism for murder on sight, a directive followed with all too brutal efficiency. This force, whose activities ceased in 1901, charts the period of one of the most barbarous and callous periods of official Australian colonial history.

"Finally, *Short and Sweet and Silly* is a collection of short and sweet and silly poems. Concentrating on lyric style and nonsense verse, poetry of this type is my first love. 'I thought myself a little think / And then I thunk

Mark Svendsen

one more / I tried to thunk another think, / But thoughtless there weren't more!...'"

*   *   *

TCHEN, Richard 19(?)

Personal

Education: Swarthmore College, graduated.

Addresses

Home—Swarthmore, PA.

Career

Writer of educational materials for children and teachers, specializing in mathematics and the environment.

Writings

(With Donna Jo Napoli) *Spinners* (novel), illustrated by Donna Diamond, Dutton (New York City), 1999.

Biographical and Critical Sources

PERIODICALS

Booklist, September 1, 1999, Chris Sherman, review of *Spinners,* p. 124.
Publishers Weekly, July 19, 1999, review of *Spinners,* p. 196.

ON-LINE

Penguin Putnam Catalog, http://www.penguinputnam. com/catalog/ (April 4, 2000).*

TRAHEY, Jane 1923-2000

OBITUARY NOTICE —See index for *SATA* sketch: Born November 19, 1923, in Chicago, IL; died April 22, 2000, in Kent, CT. Advertising executive, author. Jane Trahey was the creative mind behind a wide variety of advertisements run during the 1960s and 1970s, including Blackglama Furs' "What Becomes a Legend Most" ads which featured notorious celebrities draped in the company's fur coats. For eleven years she worked within the advertising department of Nieman-Marcus, a specialty department store, and in 1958 left to begin her own advertising agency. Beginning in 1955, Trahey dedicated a fair amount of time to writing, which she considered her creative outlet. *The Taste of Texas* was published that year, and following in 1957 was her *Compleat Martini Cookbook,* which she wrote under the pseudonym Baba Erlanger with Daren Pierce. In later years she focused some attention on creating works for young people, including *Thursdays 'til 9* (published in 1980), and *Clovis Caper,* which appeared in 1983; Walt Disney optioned both titles for film production. In 1969 the American Advertising Federation named her Advertising Woman of the Year, and she was the recipient of the *Good Housekeeping* award.

OBITUARIES AND OTHER SOURCES:

PERIODICALS

Chicago Tribune, April 25, 2000, section 2, p. 7.
Los Angeles Times, May 14, 2000, p. B5.
New York Times, April 25, 2000, p. A20.

WALSH, Vivian 1960-
(V. L. Walsh)

Personal

Born October 29, 1960; daughter of Edward (a lawyer) and Gunild (von Prittwitz und Gaffron) Walsh; married J. Otto Seibold (an illustrator), February 24, 1990; children: Theadora, Amelia, Ulysses. *Education:* Attended California State University, San Francisco.

Addresses

Home—4011 25th St., San Francisco, CA 94118. *E-mail*—c/o www.jotto.com.

Career

Writer and freelance journalist.

Writings

Olive, the Other Reindeer, illustrated by husband, J. Otto Seibold, Chronicle Books (San Francisco, CA), 1997.
(Under name V. L. Walsh) *Penguin Dreams,* illustrated by Seibold, Chronicle Books, 1999.

WITH J. OTTO SEIBOLD; ILLUSTRATED BY SEIBOLD

Mr. Lunch Takes a Plane Ride, Viking (New York City), 1993.
Mr. Lunch Borrows a Canoe, Viking, 1994.
Monkey Business, Viking, 1995.
Free Lunch, Viking, 1996.
Going to the Getty: A Book about the Getty Center in Los Angeles, Getty Trust Publications (Los Angeles, CA), 1997.

Work in Progress

Gluey, a Snail Tale, illustrated by Seibold, completion expected in 2001.

Sidelights

Vivian Walsh told *SATA:* "I have always enjoyed writing. I planned on being a journalist but, writing for local magazines in San Francisco, I quickly learned that I couldn't write just the (all important) truth. Keeping the facts straight were inconvenient to a good story. My overactive imagination kept suggesting an improper amount of embellishment. I moved on to fiction. As an elderly woman I hope to step up to and through the portal of 'Poetress.'

"I collaborate with my husband, the illustrator 'J. Otto Seibold' on children's books. Our *Olive, the Other Reindeer* and the Mr. Lunch books are based on our family pets, two very real Jack Russell terriers. I admire the work of another husband-and-wife team, H. A. and

Vivian Walsh with baby Thea Walsh.

Margret Rey. Their 'Curious George' books were an inspiration for the Mr. Lunch books. Unlike the Reys, if we ever run into a thick plot problem, we can just call our dogs into the den and study them."

Biographical and Critical Sources

PERIODICALS

Booklist, September 1, 1993, Bill Ott, review of *Mr. Lunch Takes a Plane Ride,* p. 71; October 15, 1994, Janice Del Negro, review of *Mr. Lunch Borrows a Canoe,* p. 439; September 1, 1996, Stephanie Zvirin, review of *Free Lunch,* p. 145; October 15, 1997, Ilene Cooper, review of *Olive, the Other Reindeer,* p. 417; February 15, 1998, Cooper, review of *Going to the Getty,* p. 1006; September 15, 1999, John Peters, review of *Penguin Dreams,* p. 270.

Horn Book Guide, spring, 1998, Jackie C. Horne, review of *Olive, the Other Reindeer,* p. 52.

Magpies, November, 1998, review of *Olive, the Other Reindeer,* p. 4.

Newsweek, December 1, 1997, Malcolm Jones, Jr., review of *Olive, the Other Reindeer,* p. 78.

New York Times Book Review, May 17, 1998, Deborah Solomon, review of *Going to the Getty,* p. 24.

Publishers Weekly, June 28, 1993, review of *Mr. Lunch Takes a Plane Ride,* p. 75; August 29, 1994, review of *Mr. Lunch Borrows a Canoe,* p. 79; October 9, 1995, review of *Monkey Business,* p. 84; September 2, 1996, review of *Free Lunch,* p. 129; October 6, 1997, review of *Olive, the Other Reindeer,* p. 54; September 20, 1999, review of *Penguin Dreams,* p. 86.

School Library Journal, September, 1993, Liza Bliss, review of *Mr. Lunch Takes a Plane Ride,* p. 218; December, 1994, Claudia Cooper, review of *Mr. Lunch Borrows a Canoe,* p. 81; January, 1996, Heide Piehler, review of *Monkey Business,* p. 95; January, 2000, Marlene Gawron, review of *Penguin Dreams,* p. 110.

*　　　*　　　*

WALSH, V. L.
See WALSH, Vivian

*　　　*　　　*

WEBER, Bruce 1942-

Personal

Born November 20, 1942, in Brooklyn, NY; son of Paul Karl (an educator) and Miriam Lillian (a homemaker; maiden name, Goldstein) Weber; married Annette Katz (in sales), May 30, 1968; children: Allison Emma, Jonathan Russell. *Education:* University of Maryland, B.S., 1964; Pace University, M.B.A., 1968. *Politics:* Democrat. *Religion:* Jewish. *Hobbies and other interests:* Sports, music.

Addresses

Home—511 Marion Ln., Paramus, NJ 07652. *Office*—Scholastic Inc., 730 Broadway, New York, NY 10003.

Career

University of Maryland, College Park, assistant director of sports information, 1962-64; *Scholastic Coach* magazine, New York City, assistant editor, 1965-70, associate editor, 1970-81, publisher, 1981—; New York City Board of Education, Brooklyn, NY, music teacher, 1968-72; writer. *Scholastic Sports Academy* (television series), writer, 1981-84. Paramus, New Jersey Board of Education, member, 1978-87, president, 1981-83; Devonshire School Board of Governors, president, 1988-90. Director of Paramus Run, 1979—; director of Athletic Institute, 1991-93. *Member:* National Soccer Coaches Association of America, Football Writers Association of America, American Football Coaches Association.

Awards, Honors

Action for Children's Television (ACT) Award, 1982, for *Scholastic Sports Academy;* award from Sports in America, 1987, for his work for the Athletic Institute; honorary member, American Football Coaches Association, 1995.

Writings

(With William Hongash) *Questions and Answers about Baseball,* Scholastic Book Services, 1974.

The Funniest Moments in School, illustrated by Kevin Callahan, M. Evans & Company, 1973, reprinted as *School Is a Funny Place,* Scholastic Book Services, 1977.

Weird Moments in Sports, Scholastic Book Services, 1975.

The Pro Football Quiz Book, Scholastic Book Services, 1976.

The Pro Basketball Reading Kit, Bowmar, 1976.

All-Pro Basketball Stars, annual editions, Scholastic Book Services, 1976-81, Scholastic Inc., 1982-83.

The Quest for Camelot, Scholastic, Inc., 1979.

The Dynamite Animal Hall of Fame, Scholastic Book Services, 1979.

The T.V. Olympic Program Guide, Scholastic Book Services, 1980.

More Weird Moments in Sports, Scholastic Inc., 1983.

Bruce Weber's Inside Pro Football, annual editions, Scholastic Inc., 1983-92

Bruce Weber's Inside Baseball, annual editions, Scholastic Inc., 1984-92.

Athletes: Photographs by Bruce Weber, Twelvetrees, 1985.

Magic Johnson and Larry Bird, Morrow/Avon, 1986.

Sparky Anderson, edited by Michael E. Goodman, Crestwood, 1988.

The Indianapolis 500, The Creative Company, 1990.

Mickey Mantle: Classic Sports Shots, Scholastic Inc., 1993.

Lou Gehrig: Classic Sports Shots, Scholastic Inc., 1993.

Jackie Robinson: Classic Sports Shots, Scholastic Inc., 1993.

Ted Williams: Classic Sports Shots, Scholastic Inc., 1993.
Babe Ruth: Classic Sports Shots, Scholastic Inc., 1993.
Willie Mays: Classic Sports Shots, Scholastic Inc., 1993.
Baseball Trivia and Fun Book, Scholastic Inc., 1993.
Pro-Football Megastars, 1993, 1994, 1995, and *1997,* Scholastic Inc., 1993, 1994, 1995, 1997.
Pro-Basketball Megastars, 1994, 1995, and *1996,* Scholastic Inc., 1994, 1995, 1996.
Sport Shots: Barry Bonds, Scholastic Inc., 1994.
Baseball Megastars, 1994, 1995, and *1996, 1998,* Scholastic Inc., 1994, 1995, 1996, 1998.
NBA Megastars, 1997, 1998, 1999, Scholastic Inc., 1997, 1998, 1999.
You Can Yo-Yo!, Scholastic Inc., 1998.
Advanced Yo-Yo Tricks, Scholastic Inc., 1999.
Greatest Moments of the NBA, Scholastic Inc., 2000.
(With Savion Glover) *Savion: My Life in Tap,* Morrow/Avon, 2000.

Also author of *Mark McGwire: The Home-Run King,* illustrated by Thomas La Padula, 1999; and of sixty-five half-hour instructional programs for the USA Network television series *Scholastic Sports Academy,* 1981-84; contributor to *Modern Encyclopedia of Basketball,*

In Bruce Weber's instructional book, the basic steps of using a yo-yo are outlined, along with directions for more than twenty yo-yo tricks. (Cover illustration by Paul Colin.)

edited by Zander Hollander, Doubleday, 1979, and *Evetec, The McGregor Solution,* Houghton-Mifflin, 1985. Columnist for *Junior Scholastic, Science World, Voice, Scope, Dynamite, Scholastic Math, Sprint,* and *Action.* Contributor to *Teen Age* and other magazines for young people and writer under a pseudonym.

Sidelights

Bruce Weber once told *SATA:* "When I found myself sitting farther and farther away from the coach on the bench, it didn't take a genius to figure out that if I wanted to stay in sports, I'd have to find some other route than the locker-room door. I found my entrance at the press gate and I've been working my way in there every since.

"It has been wonderful. I know a great many adults who are fed up with their professional lives, doing something every day that they hate. Not me. As Garrett Morris used to say on *Saturday Night Live,* 'Baseball been very, very good to me.' The same goes for football and soccer and track and field, among other things. There is a genuine fraternity of sports, and most of my professional relationships, many of which are a quarter-century or more old, begin with sports."

Bruce Weber is an avid sports fan who has turned his avocation into his profession through writing. He has written numerous books assessing the annual performance of the nation's football, basketball, and baseball teams, and several biographies of sports figures. In Weber's annual *Inside Baseball* books, the author provides brief profiles of individual players and teams, enumerating trades, injuries, and strengths and weaknesses for each, and concludes with his choice for an all-star team, and the requisite statistics. Weber's "breezy conversational style suits baseball," contended Sherry Palmitier in her *Voice of Youth Advocates* piece on *Inside Baseball 1989,* which she dubbed "a thorough review of an exciting season." Similarly, William E. Littlefield recommended the following year's edition, *Inside Baseball 1990* in *Kliatt,* as "an easy-to-use book for the younger fan."

Among Weber's several sports biographies is the dual *Magic Johnson and Larry Bird,* which focuses on the longstanding comparisons between the two professional basketball players—one black, the other white—that reached its height when their teams competed for the NCAA championship in 1979. Weber grounds his discussion of the two players in detailed examinations of the pivotal games in the career of each, necessitating a good familiarity on the part of his audience, as Raymond L. Puffer pointed out in *Kliatt.* But Puffer noted that Weber's account of Johnson's and Bird's high school playing experiences, emphasizing how each made up his mind about college and heading off for the pros, would be of particular interest to the young adult audience. As in his annual sports round-ups, *Magic Johnson and Larry Bird* contains plenty of statistics and photographs, noted a reviewer for *Booklist,* who contended that

"Basketball buffs will welcome Weber's brisk-paced style."

Weber's other great love is music: he has a degree in instrumental music education and early in his career taught music at a school in Brooklyn. Weber once told *Contemporary Authors:* "How have I managed to combine the two seemingly distant interests? My favorite response is 'I'm probably the only sports writer in New York who can cover both the football game and the half-time show with equal facility.' My critics might debate my ability to do either well, but I'm more than willing to go one-on-one with any of them."

Weber drew upon his musical background in his biography of dancer Savion Glover, co-written by its subject, in *Savion: My Life in Tap.* Glover is a performer who first came to public attention at the age of eleven, and whose success is attributed in part to his wise choice of mentors, among them tap dance legends Honi Coles and Jimmy Slyde. *Booklist* reviewer Randy Meyer articulated his appreciation for the "deep respect and reverence Glover shows for his 'uncles' and their advice," which went far beyond the realm of the dance floor. The book's text alternates between Glover's own words and those of Weber, who, among other things, provides a concise history of the evolution of tap. He helps put in context the young dancer's phenomenal success by age twenty-six—Glover's accomplishments include the creation of the show *Bring in 'da Noise, Bring in 'da Funk,* for which he won a Tony Award for choreography. Aspiring performers will be inspired by Glover's "life, work and words," noted a reviewer in *Publishers Weekly.*

Biographical and Critical Sources

PERIODICALS

Booklist, April, 1986, review of *Magic Johnson and Larry Bird,* p. 1147; January 1, 2000, Randy Meyer, review of *Savion: My Life in Tap,* p. 896.

Kliatt, spring, 1986, Raymond L. Puffer, review of *Magic Johnson and Larry Bird,* p. 56. September, 1990, William E. Littlefield, review of *Inside Baseball 1990,* p. 52.

Publishers Weekly, December 6, 1999, review of *Savion: My Life in Tap,* p. 78.

School Library Journal, February, 1989, p. 93.

Voice of Youth Advocates, August, 1989, Sherry Palmitier, review of *Inside Baseball 1989,* pp. 181-82. *

*   *   *

WINER, Yvonne 1934-

Personal

Born July 17, 1934, in South Africa; daughter of Edwin and Antoinette (Marais) Jay; children: Kari, Sydney, Michael. *Education:* Earned diploma in teaching and M.Ed.; University of Pretoria, Ph.D. *Hobbies and other interests:* Watercolor painting, printing, gardening, bush walking.

Addresses

Home—21 Gordon Cres., Table Top Estate, Withcott, Queensland 4352, Australia. *E-mail*—winery@ icr.com.au.

Career

Charles Sturt University (Riverina College of Advanced Education), Wagga, Australia, lecturer, 1977-83; University of Southern Queensland, Toowoomba, head of department of early childhood education, 1984-97. Consultant to UNICEF Fiji, 1993.

Awards, Honors

Kath Dickson Award for excellence in teaching, Darling Downs chapter, Australian College of Education, 1993; citation for "notable Australian children's book," Australian Book Council, 1997, for *Nanangka;* Environment Award for Children's Literature, Australian Wilderness Society, for *Spiders Spin Webs.*

Writings

Finger Plays and Action Rhymes, illustrated by Frank Knight, Angus & Robertson, 1970.

Of Frogs and Snails (finger plays and action rhymes), illustrated by Lyndall Stewart, Belair Publications, 1979.

Of Beetles and Bugs (finger plays and action rhymes), illustrated by Stewart, Belair Publications, 1980.

Pocket Full of Pockets (stories for dramatization), illustrated by Nancy Renfro, Nancy Renfro Studios, 1982.

Mr. Brown's Magnificent Apple Tree, illustrated by Maya Winters, Ashton Scholastic, 1985.

Never Snap at a Bubble, illustrated by Allison McLean-Carr, Era Publications, 1987.

The Tiniest Hippo, illustrated by Donna Gynell, Era Publications, 1987.

Little Brown Monkey, illustrated by Jim Tsinganos, Era Publications, 1987.

Of Seasons and Special Days (finger plays and action rhymes), illustrated by Stewart, Belair Publications, 1988.

Timothy Toad, illustrated by Kikitsa Michalantos, Era Publications, 1988.

Herbertia the Vile, illustrated by David Kennett, Era Publications, 1990.

Twenty Magical Songs, music by Max Reeder, Sturt University Press, 1990.

Ssh, Don't Wake the Baby, illustrated by Margaret Power, Nelson, 1990, McGraw (New York City), 1993.

The Shawl, illustrated by Jim Tsinganos, Era Publications, 1991.

Moonshadow Fox, illustrated by Ilsa van Garderen, Margaret Hamilton Books, 1994.

Nanangka, illustrated by Marianne Yamagutchi, Margaret Hamilton Books, 1996.

Spiders Spin Webs, illustrated by Karen Lloyd-Jones, Margaret Hamilton Books, 1996, Charlesbridge Publishing (Watertown, MA), 1997.

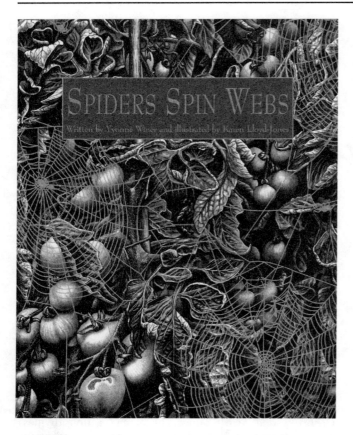

In rhyming text, Yvonne Winer explains the habits and characteristics of a wide variety of spiders and examines the structure and purpose of their webs. (Cover illustration by Karen Lloyd-Jones.)

Dream Dragon, illustrated by Stanley Wong, Margaret Hamilton Books, 1999.

Other books include *Busy Hands,* photographs by Ivan Fox, Angus & Robertson; and *Goanna and the Old Red Sun* (teacher resource book), Longman Cheshire. Work represented in anthologies, including *Voices of the Downs.*

Work in Progress

Butterflies Fly, Birds Build Their Nests, and books about frogs and sea creatures, all for Margaret Hamilton Books; research on the aesthetics of picture books and on the arts in early childhood education.

Sidelights

Yvonne Winer told *SATA:* "I was born in South Africa and grew up on a high-veld farm. It was there that I was introduced to the wealth of African music and storytelling. This was a culture rich in people from many different colorful backgrounds, each with its own music, stories, and languages. I moved to Australia in 1961, and it was here that I started writing when my children were little.

"In 1992 I returned to South Africa to complete my doctorate at the University of Pretoria, where I designed and implemented a literacy program for Ndebele children on South African farms. In 1995 I worked in Fiji as a consultant to UNICEF on emerging literacy and basic education. In 1997 I retired after thirteen years as head of early childhood education at the University of Southern Queensland, where my major focus had been emerging literacy and the arts in early childhood, especially aesthetics.

"My writing has been greatly influenced by my visits abroad to such places as Mexico, Africa, Bali, Malaysia, Thailand, Canada, and the United States. A further great influence, of course, has been the Australian outback and the tropical wilderness areas of Queensland.

"I enjoy watercolor painting, printing, gardening, and bush walking. I live at Table Top Estate, close to Toowoomba in Queensland, on five acres of bushland. My days are filled with the color and sounds of pale-headed rosellas, king parrots, rainbow lorikeets, galahs, and many other wild birds. Occasionally I have visits from wallabies, echidnas, possums, and other creatures, including joyous frogs. What bliss! I also have a very special grandchild called Bonnie Amelia."

Biographical and Critical Sources

PERIODICALS

Booklist, July, 1998, Shelley Townsend-Hudson, review of *Spiders Spin Webs,* p. 1884.
Children's Bookwatch, January, 1999, review of *Spiders Spin Webs,* p. 3.
Horn Book Guide, spring, 1999, review of *Spiders Spin Webs,* p. 110.
Kirkus Reviews, June 15, 1998, review of *Spiders Spin Webs,* p. 903-04.
Magpies, November, 1994, Maurice Saxby, review of *Moonshadow Fox,* p. 23; March, 1997, Anne Hanzl, review of *Spiders Spin Webs,* p. 24, and Annette Dale-Meiklejohn, review of *Nanangka,* p. 35.
School Library Journal, November 1, 1998, Karey Wehner, review of *Spiders Spin Webs,* p. 108.

*   *   *

WOOD, June Rae 1946-

Personal

Born September 4, 1946, in Sedalia, MO; daughter of Kenneth Sattler (a cutter and grinder), and Evelyn (a housewife; maiden name, Evans) and stepfather Olen (a railroad worker) Haggerman; married William A. Wood (a heavy equipment mechanic), December 2, 1966; children: Samantha. *Education:* Attended Central Missouri State College (now University), 1964-66. *Politics:* Republican. *Religion:* Protestant. *Hobbies and other interests:* "Quilting, reading, and granddaughter Rachel, born in 1998."

Addresses

Home—P.O. Box 337, Windsor, MO 65360.

Career

Whiteman Air Force Base, Whiteman, MO, Civil Service clerk typist, 1967-70; *Sedalia Democrat,* Sedalia, MO, staff writer for "Living Today," 1988-97. *Member:* Society of Children's Book Writers and Illustrators, Sedalia Writers' Group.

Awards, Honors

Mark Twain Award and William Allen White Award, both 1995, both for *The Man Who Loved Clowns;* Friends of American Writers Award for Juvenile Fiction, for *A Share of Freedom;* Edgar Wolfe Literary Award, Friends of the Library (Kansas City, KS).

Writings

The Man Who Loved Clowns, Putnam (New York City), 1992.
A Share of Freedom, Putnam, 1994.
When Pigs Fly, Putnam, 1995.
Turtle on a Fence Post, Putnam, 1997.
About Face, Putnam, 1999.

Contributor of articles and short stories to *Family Circle, Reader's Digest, Home Life, The Lookout, New Ways,* and *School & Community.*

Work in Progress

Another novel for young adults.

Sidelights

"My brother Richard was born [in 1948] with Down's syndrome and a heart defect," author June Rae Wood wrote in the *Sedalia Democrat* in 1995. "The doctor said he wouldn't live, and even if he did, he would never walk or talk. He advised my parents to send Richard to die in an institution, rather than take him home and let the family get attached to him." Wood, the second of what would eventually be eight children, was only two years old when her parents brought Richard, their third child, home from the hospital. Although her parents gave all their children special attention, Richard, whom Wood's mother called her little "Dickey-bird," was doted on and protected by all the family members. This was not just because he was handicapped, but also because Richard was very special to them all. He would eventually become the subject of Wood's award-winning first book, *The Man Who Loved Clowns.* "Richard was a comical little guy," Wood told Kevin Hile in an interview for *Authors and Artists for Young Adults* (*AAYA*), "friendly with everybody, even total strangers. He was, in fact, exactly like 'Punky' in the book. He really did pour out the shampoo, tell people they were fat, and fling horn bones behind the TV. He learned to walk at age four, and then he would run away from

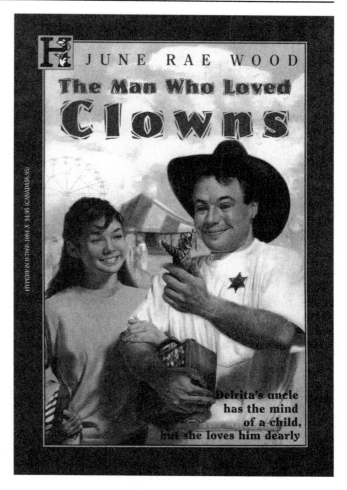

Delrita is very sensitive to the ridicule directed at her uncle who has Down's syndrome in June Rae Wood's coming-of-age novel. (Cover illustration by Dan Brown.)

home—not to be naughty, just to explore. Sometimes he'd be gone when we woke up, and we'd find him throwing dirt clods at the neighbor's chickens, just to hear them squawk. These running-away incidents, which he eventually outgrew, were the only times he was ever alone because our family was very protective of him. If we took him somewhere and people made fun, we would leave as soon as possible."

Richard died in 1985, at the age of thirty-six, when his defective heart gave out. The loss was a painful one for the entire family, but it was his sister who would end up writing about it. At the time, Wood had been writing for three years, but she had had no success publishing her works. Before that, she had not been very interested in writing, although she had always loved to read. "As a child, I enjoyed reading the life stories of Marie Curie, Thomas Edison, George Washington Carver, and many others who made great accomplishments," she told Hile. "I also loved Trixie Belden mysteries and the Laura Ingalls Wilder stories.... I remember crying my eyes out at about age twelve when I read Dale Evans' *Angel Unaware.* It was a true story about the life—and death—of a handicapped child, and unlike anything I'd ever read before. I think it touched me greatly because my own little brother had Down's syndrome."

With so many children to take care of, Wood's mother and stepfather struggled to make ends meet. (Her biological father and mother divorced when Wood was still an infant, and she was raised by her mother and stepfather, Evelyn and Olen Haggerman.) Wood described her parents: "Mom wore her straight, brown hair in a ponytail, and her usual attire was a simple housedress. She never wore makeup, and she never spent time on herself. Her 'recreation' was riding in the pickup with Dad and all of us kids to the ice cream store. Chores for her included cooking and cleaning, doing laundry with a wringer washer, caring for a huge garden, and canning hundreds of quarts of food. She was handy with a hammer, and she wasn't afraid to install a window or knock out a wall on her own. She was very creative, and could make prize-winning Halloween costumes out of old curtains, old sheets, old clothes, and a package or two of fabric dye. I used to think she never slept.

"Dad was a small man in size (about five feet, six inches) but big in my eyes. Since he worked for the railroad, his skin was brown and leathery from constant exposure to the weather, and he had a permanent squint. His summer attire was a white T-shirt and overalls, plus a railroad cap or a baseball cap to protect his balding head. In the wintertime, he couldn't wear enough clothes to keep warm. After patrolling track all day in an open motor car, he'd come home nearly frozen, his eyebrows frosted with ice. (Thus the scene in *Turtle on a Fence Post,* when Tree tells Delrita why his family doesn't have enough chairs.) Our family was close-knit and loving and was, in fact, my pattern for the Shackleford family in *The Man Who Loved Clowns.*"

While Wood and her brothers and sisters went to school, Richard stayed at home. In the 1950s there were no schools that could accommodate his special needs (although by the time he was seventeen, a school for the handicapped had opened that he attended for four years). At home, there was not much for him to do except watch television, play in the yard, and help watch over the baby of the family—sister Janie, who was born when he was nine. "Years later, Richard also kept an eye on his little nieces and nephews, just as he had with Janie. Thus the scene on page fourteen of *The Man Who Loved Clowns,*" Wood explained.

Wood recalled being a good student who graduated second out of a high school class of seventy-four in 1964. "I loved school from first grade on up, and I was very competitive. My first-quarter grade in typing class was an S-minus (same as a B-minus), and I was horrified. I bought myself a portable, manual typewriter so I could practice at home and build up speed. Since I worked evenings after school as a waitress, I started my homework about 8:30 p.m. and did my typing after that. I would type in the kitchen until Dad came thundering down the stairs because my peck-peck-pecking was keeping him awake. The payoff was that I finished the

year as the fastest typist in the class." Because of her love of reading, English class was one of her strong subjects. "English came easy for me, but I didn't particularly like writing. I wrote only what was required of me to make a good grade. In high school, I excelled in business subjects: typing, shorthand, accounting, office practice. I thought I would become a business education teacher. It never crossed my mind that I would someday be a writer. I was married and had a twelve-year-old daughter before the writing bug bit me."

While she was still attending business education classes at Central Missouri State College, the future author had a blind date with William A. Wood, an airman stationed at Whiteman Air Force Base. They quickly fell in love and married in 1966. The new Mrs. Wood left school and found work as a clerk-typist at the air force base. Four years later their daughter, Samantha, was born. Wood left her job to raise Samantha, and the family eventually moved to a rural home near Windsor, Missouri. Although Wood was happy to be a mother, she sometimes felt lonely spending all her time at home, so she decided to try her hand at writing. She read how-to books on writing and worked on short stories—for which she has three years' worth of rejection letters—and an unpublished novel called "A Summer's Worth of Trouble." This first book, the author told Hile, "is a story about a girl growing up in a large family in a small town in the 1950s. Although it's fiction, a lot of it is based on my life. One little brother, for instance, is slow about learning to walk. His nickname is 'Scooter' because he gets around by scooting on his rump, just like Richard did in real life. That book was my 'practice set.' With all those rewrites, I was learning more and more about character, dialogue, and plot—and each new version was better than the last. However, I put that manuscript aside to write *The Man Who Loved Clowns,* and it's been in the drawer ever since. I do plan to work on it again someday."

But before *The Man Who Loved Clowns,* Wood wrote an article for the magazine *Family Circle* that was her first step toward success. Published in the December 3, 1985, issue, a few months after Richard's death, the article was titled "The Boy Who Taught Love" and was about her experiences with her brother. Wood wrote how having Richard in the family was not a burden but a blessing. "God sent him not to be a *learner,* but a *teacher,*" she asserted in the article. "And without knowing it, he was the best teacher our family could have had. He taught us understanding and acceptance and compassion." The reading audience was deeply moved. "People all over the U.S. sent letters," Wood told Hile, "telling me how touched they'd been by Richard's life. However, the letters were always from grownups, and one day it occurred to me that I should try writing a story about Richard that would appeal to kids. After all, it was kids who'd been afraid of him or cruel to him, and they needed to know what he was really like. That's when I began working on *The Man Who Loved Clowns.*"

By the time she started writing the book, Wood was working part time as a staff writer for the *Sedalia*

Democrat in Sedalia, Missouri. After many hard months of writing, she submitted the manuscript to Putnam in New York City; the publisher quickly accepted the book for publication with only minor changes. One of these was to make the story's main character, Delrita, thirteen instead of twelve years old. "My editor, Refna Wilkin, said Delrita sounded thirteen and asked me to change her age in the story," Wood recalled. "Refna also said I had a 'natural thirteen-year-old voice.' Don't ask me how that came to be. I just write the way I write." *The Man Who Loved Clowns* is a fictionalization of the author's personal experiences. Instead of giving Delrita a younger brother with Down's Syndrome, Wood gives her an uncle with Down's—thirty-five-year-old "Punky." Delrita Jensen adores Uncle Punky, who is fascinated by clowns and crayons and always wears a cowboy hat—but at the same time she is embarrassed by him. She feels uncomfortable when visitors come to their house or when the family goes to church. But the novel is a coming-of-age tale, too, and not just about the difficulties of having a family member with Down's. This is Delrita's story; it deals with such issues as boyfriends, peer pressure, self-esteem, and, finally, death, as Delrita has to face her parents' tragic demise in a car accident. Punky's love and support help Delrita work through her grief, and then in a tragic twist, Punky dies, too, when his ailing heart gives out.

Critics roundly praised *The Man Who Loved Clowns* for its strong characterization and the way Wood realistically portrays difficult problems. Judith E. Landrum, writing in the *Journal of Adolescent and Adult Literacy,* noted how Wood's story challenges preconceptions of what handicapped people are really like, as well as telling the tough truth that "doing 'the right thing' does not always protect people from causing or receiving pain." A *Publishers Weekly* reviewer concluded that in this debut novel, "Wood displays a prodigious writing and storytelling talent."

"Writing *The Man Who Loved Clowns* was therapy for me," Wood told Hile. "It helped me work through my grief after the death of my brother, and the story came from my heart. Society deals with 'differences' much better today than it did when I was growing up, but we still have work to do. For instance, a lot of kids think they can 'catch' Down's syndrome and are afraid to get close to someone who has it. Since *Clowns* was published, I've made a lot of school visits, and I've heard about many methods teachers use to help promote understanding. Here are a few suggestions I'd like to pass along: 1) Invite disabled people into the classroom to talk about their specific challenges—blindness, deafness, Down's syndrome, etc. 2) Provide props such as wheelchairs, crutches, and blindfolds for the students to use while performing simple tasks. Then have them write about the difficulties they experienced. 3) For smaller groups, plan a trip to a sheltered workshop."

After *The Man Who Loved Clowns,* Wood continued to write novels for young adults about characters who face serious challenges in their families. *A Share of Freedom* is about another thirteen year old, Freedom, whose mother is an alcoholic. Because of her mother's problem, Freedom has to take care of her half-brother, Jackie. Freedom and Jackie run away after their mother is sent away for rehabilitation, but they quickly learn that they can't make it on their own and are put in a foster home. Freedom doesn't like her foster father, Martin Quincy, who is always criticizing people. The startling truth that Freedom discovers is that Martin is actually her biological father. Critics noted that *A Share of Freedom* offers many insights into family relationships. One of the main points in the novel, Wood told Hile, was that people can love each other despite their failings: "I wanted Freedom to realize that her mother did love her, in spite of the drinking." Although some reviewers thought that Martin's being Freedom's father was a bit too coincidental, many praised the novel as another strong work by the author. *Voice of Youth Advocates* contributor Bunni Union called it a "poignant story," adding that the "language reads easily and, at times, almost poetically." A *Booklist* critic said that "teens will sympathize with Freedom, cheer her determi-

Thirteen-year-old Buddy Rae faces several big challenges in her life, including a test of loyalty when her best friend accuses Buddy's Down's syndrome sister of stealing. (Cover illustration by Bart Forbes.)

nation and strength, and enjoy the promising, neatly resolved ending."

In 1995, Wood wrote another novel that included a character with Down's syndrome, *When Pigs Fly*. In this story, thirteen-year-old Buddy Richter has many problems in her life. Her father has lost his job, which has forced them to move into a run-down house in the country, away from her best friend, Jiniwin; and Buddy worries about watching over her younger sister, Reenie, who has Down's. Buddy's friends also have serious troubles. Jiniwin's parents have divorced and she has started drinking. Another friend, Dallas, has been abandoned by his father. Thus, Buddy's sister's disability is only one of many issues she must face. Although Judy Sasges wrote in *Voice of Youth Advocates* that *When Pigs Fly* is at times too "didactic" about themes such as how money doesn't buy happiness, a *Publishers Weekly* reviewer felt that the "novel treats family conflicts and social concerns with the same sensitivity of Wood's previous titles." Debbie Carton, writing in *Booklist,* also praised the "well developed and believable" characters.

Readers are reacquainted with Delrita Jensen from *The Man Who Loved Clowns* in Wood's 1997 novel, *Turtle on a Fence Post*. After her parents' deaths, Delrita and Punky had moved in with her Aunt Queenie and Uncle Bert. After Punky's death, Delrita becomes an emotional wreck, who is not ready to love other people, and she feels uncomfortable and unwanted in her new home. Her aunt, she expects, sees her as a burden on the family. Then Queenie's crabby father, Orvis, moves in. Delrita finds Orvis, who is a World War II veteran, very intimidating, and his presence makes the family situation worse. The one bright point in her life is the boy she has a crush on, Tree Shackleford, but even that seems like it will be ruined when another girl starts flirting with Tree. Delrita's life begins to turn around from two unexpected sources: a "teen buddy" program in which she helps Joey Marcum, who suffers from multiple birth defects because his mother had German measles while she was pregnant, and Orvis, who agrees to let her interview him for a school project. By the end of the book, Delrita has learned that she can love again and come out of her shell.

"Before I even thought about writing *Turtle on a Fence Post*," Wood told Hile, "I was assigned to write a story for the newspaper to commemorate the fiftieth anniversary of D-Day. I interviewed five veterans, and the stories these men told, their quiet heroism, their tears fifty years after the fact, had a profound impact on me. Their first-person accounts of the war stoked the fire of patriotism in me. In *Turtle* I wanted to pay tribute to all the veterans of World War II, and that's why I created Orvis Roebuck, Aunt Queenie's father. I needed someone who could talk first-hand about the war." A *Kirkus Reviews* critic observed how this aspect of the book comes out: "An appreciation for those who sacrifice time, effort, money, and even their lives for others infuses this memorable tale of healing." That Wood balances issues such as these, along with the subject of

disabilities and other themes, was particularly notable to *School Library Journal* contributor Carol A. Edwards. She remarked appreciatively that "this engaging story is one of a very few that shows average kids interacting enjoyably with special-needs adults without that being the focus of the story."

When asked by Hile about Edwards' comment, Wood replied, "Actually, I didn't realize I had done that until I read the *School Library Journal* review. I suppose it was a subconscious thing. When I was growing up, it was normal for us to hide the shampoo and to find chicken bones behind the TV. Why? Because we were used to Richard and his little quirks. It was no big deal. Evidently, this was in the back of my mind when I was writing about Joey. I wanted the readers to see his quirks, yes, but not as any big deal." Wood sees her characters with disabilities simply as one more aspect of her main characters' lives. "The subplots are necessary to make a believable story," she said. "Delrita would be a flat, unlikable character if she did nothing but go to school and go home again. Who cares about that? 'Cares' is the key word. I do my best to make my readers care about my protagonists. I want them to feel Delrita's love for 'Punky,' her insecurity, her grief, her anger. If they don't feel, then I have failed."

If Wood could have her books get across one message to her readers, it would be: "Happiness is not having what you want, but wanting what you have," as she told Hile. This is a direct quote from her 1999 novel, *About Face,* which features thirteen-year-old Glory Bea Goode. Glory is very shy, due to a large, red birthmark on her face. But then she meets Marvalene Zulig, whose parents work at a carnival that is in town. Marvalene is a tough girl who is bitter because she feels that her family's hard life led to her mother having a stroke and giving birth to a stillborn baby. Wood alternates viewpoints between Glory and Marvalene, showing how their friendship and emotional support help Glory gain some self-confidence and Marvalene to appreciate her life more. "Readers may not want to trade lives with either heroine," commented a *Publishers Weekly* critic, "but they will enjoy vicariously experiencing the warmth of their growing camaraderie." A reviewer for *Booklist* called *About Face* an "engaging ramble, well stocked with laughs, tears, spats, and reconciliations."

Wood is working on a sixth novel for young adults, but she's reluctant to reveal more than that. "If I talk about works in progress," she said, "I lose my steam." When getting an idea for a new book, Wood draws her stories "from real life—my own and other people's," as she told Hile. "If I hear a good story, I make a note of it. If I see an interesting 'character' on the street, I make a note of that, too. I clip newspaper articles that catch my attention. Also, the articles I wrote for the *Democrat* have proved to be a valuable resource. A case in point: I once wrote a story for the paper about a lady who cooked on a riverboat. In my most recent book, *About Face,* the character 'Pansy' used to cook on a riverboat—and because I had the newspaper story to fall back on, her dialogue is authentic." After Wood has a story in mind, she creates a short outline. "For each of my books, I've written about a three-page outline. Each outline is basically like a letter to myself. It tells me, who the characters are, what problems they will have, and how they will resolve them. The details come later with the actual writing, but I have to know how a story will end before I start."

Wood has no immediate plans to write novels for audiences other than young adult readers. "I enjoy writing for kids," she said, "but at the same time, it's an awesome responsibility. The words I write will be absorbed by young, impressionable minds, and that's why I work by a certain standard: I never write anything I'd be ashamed for my mom or my daughter to read. No foul language, no sex, and no violence just for the sake of entertainment." Not only do Wood's novels deliver their messages of the importance of appreciating what you have—love, friends, self-respect—but they serve as examples of the type of entertainment she strongly believes children and young adults need more of these days. As she pointed out in an article she wrote for the *Democrat,* "Children are great imitators. We adults must provide them with appropriate role models and wholesome books to read and movies to watch." Evidence of Wood's effect on her young readers can be seen in the letters she has received. One student wrote, "My favorite novels were *Jurassic Park* and *Mortal Kombat* until [we] read *The Man Who Loved Clowns*"; and another fan of Wood's first novel said, "I like this book because it inspired me. I had this feeling it was like burning in my fingers. I just wanted to read."

Biographical and Critical Sources

PERIODICALS

Booklist, September 1, 1994, Chris Sherman, review of *A Share of Freedom,* p. 36; December 1, 1995, Debbie Carton, review of *When Pigs Fly,* p. 638; November 15, 1997, Debbie Carton, review of *Turtle on a Fence Post,* p. 564; October 15, 1999, John Peters, review of *About Face,* p. 447.

Family Circle, December 3, 1985, June Rae Wood, "The Boy Who Taught Love," p. 24.

Journal of Adolescent and Adult Literacy, December, 1998, Judith E. Landrum, review of *The Man Who Loved Clowns,* p. 289.

Kirkus Reviews, September 1, 1997, review of *Turtle on a Fence Post,* p. 1396.

Publishers Weekly, November 9, 1992, review of *The Man Who Loved Clowns,* p. 86; September 26, 1994, review of *A Share of Freedom,* p. 71; July 24, 1995, review of *When Pigs Fly,* p. 65; October 11, 1999, review of *About Face,* p. 77.

School Library Journal, September, 1997, Carol A. Edwards, review of *Turtle on a Fence Post,* pp. 227-228.

Sedalia Democrat (Sedalia, MO), October 19, 1993, June Rae Wood, "Happiness Is 'Still a Good Book' for This Local Author," p. 4; August 4, 1994, June Rae Wood, "Some Things Are Better Left to the Imagination"; January 5, 1995, June Rae Wood, "Special Child Had Special Purpose"; May 4, 1995, June Rae Wood, "Brother Lives in Writer's Words, Kids' Thoughts."

Versailles Leader-Statesman (Versailles, MO), April 23, 1987, June Rae Wood, "To a Different Drummer," p. 5B.

Voice of Youth Advocates, April, 1995, Bunni Union, review of *A Share of Freedom,* p. 30; December, 1995, Judy Sasges, review of *When Pigs Fly,* pp. 311-312.

OTHER

Wood, June Rae, in an interview with *Authors and Artists for Young Adults,* conducted September 11, 2000.

—Sketch by Kevin Hile

Z

ZALBEN, Jane Breskin 1950-

Personal

Born April 21, 1950, in New York, NY; daughter of Murry (a certified public accountant) and Mae (a librarian; maiden name, Kirshbloom) Breskin; married Steven Zalben (an architect), December 25, 1969; children: Jonathan, Alexander. *Education:* Queens College of the City University of New York, B.A., 1971; Pratt Institute Graphic Center, graduate study in lithography, 1971-72. *Religion:* Jewish. *Hobbies and other interests:* Travel, gardening, gourmet cooking, pets.

Addresses

Home—Port Washington, NY. *Agent*—Marilyn Marlow, Curtis Brown Ltd., 10 Astor Pl., New York, NY 10003. *E-mail*—janezalben@hotmail.com.

Career

Dial Press, New York, assistant to art director of children's book department, 1971-72; Holt, Rinehart & Winston, Inc., New York, freelance book designer, 1973-74; Thomas Y. Crowell Co., New York, senior designer of children's books, 1974-75; Scribner's, New York, art director of children's books, 1975-76; writer and illustrator of children's books and novels, 1973—. School of Visual Arts, New York City, instructor of illustration, design, and writing of children's books, 1976-93; Vassar Publishing Institute, Poughkeepsie, NY, writer/artist-in-residence, 1988. *Exhibitions:* Exhibitor at individual and group shows at various institutions, including Metropolitan Museum of Art, Justin Schiller Gallery, and the American Institute of Graphics Art Show, all in New York; Every Picture Tells a Story, Los Angeles; Bush Gallery, Vermont; Books of Wonder, Beverly Hills; Elizabeth Stone Gallery, Michigan; Port Washington Library; Hecksher Museum, Long Island; Vassar College; and Findlay College. *Member:* Society of Children's Book Writers and Illustrators (judge of Golden Kite award).

Awards, Honors

AIGA award, 1978 and 1979; *Beni's First Chanukah* was named an *American Bookseller* Pick of the Lists, 1988, and a Sidney Taylor Honor Book, 1989; *Parents* magazine award, 1993; IRA Teachers' Choice award, 1993.

Writings

SELF-ILLUSTRATED

Cecilia's Older Brother, Macmillan, 1973.
Lyle and Humus, Macmillan, 1974.
Basil and Hillary, Macmillan, 1975.
Penny and the Captain, Collins, 1977.
Norton's Nighttime, Collins, 1979.
Will You Count the Stars without Me?, Farrar, Straus, 1979.
"Oh, Simple!", Farrar, Straus, 1981.
Porcupine's Christmas Blues, Philomel/Putnam, 1982.
Beni's First Chanukah, Holt, 1988.
Happy Passover, Rosie, Holt, 1990.
Leo and Blossom's Sukkah, Holt, 1990.
Goldie's Purim, Holt, 1991.
Beni's Little Library (Jewish holiday boxed set), Holt, 1991.
Buster Gets Braces, Holt, 1992.
Happy New Year, Beni, Holt, 1993.
Papa's Latkes, Holt, 1994.
Miss Violet's Shining Day, Boyds Mills Press, 1995.
Pearl Plants a Tree, Simon & Schuster, 1995.
Beni's Family Cookbook for the Jewish Holidays, Holt, 1996.
Pearl's Marigolds for Grandpa, Simon & Schuster, 1997.
Beni's Family Treasury: Stories for the Jewish Holidays, Holt, 1998.
Beni's First Wedding, Holt, 1998.
Pearl's Eight Days of Chanukah, Simon & Schuster, 1998.
To Every Season: A Family Holiday Cookbook, Simon & Schuster, 1999.

YOUNG ADULT NOVELS

Maybe It Will Rain Tomorrow, Farrar, Straus, 1982.
Here's Looking at You, Kid, Farrar, Straus, 1984.

Water from the Moon, Farrar, Straus, 1987.
Earth to Andrew O. Blechman, Farrar, Straus, 1989.
The Fortuneteller in 5B, Holt, 1991.
Unfinished Dreams, Simon & Schuster, 1996.

ILLUSTRATOR

Jan Wahl, _Jeremiah Knucklebones,_ Holt, 1974.
Jane Yolen, _An Invitation to the Butterfly Ball: A Counting Rhyme,_ Parents Magazine Press, 1976.
Lewis Carroll, _Jabberwocky,_ F. Warne, 1977.
Yolen, _All in the Woodland Early: An ABC Book,_ Collins, 1979.
Carroll, _The Walrus and the Carpenter,_ Holt, 1986.
Inner Chimes: Poems on Poetry, selected by Bobbye S. Goldstein, Wordsong/Boyds Mills Press, 1992.

OTHER

Oliver and Alison's Week, illustrated by Emily Arnold McCully, Farrar, Straus, 1980.
A Perfect Nose for Ralph, illustrated by John Wallner, Philomel, 1980.

Sidelights

Jane Breskin Zalben is an author and illustrator with numerous books to her credit, from simple counting and ABC picture books for preschoolers to young adult novels dealing with the death of a parent, Holocaust survivors, and AIDS. Since the 1983 publication of _Beni's First Chanukah,_ she has become best known as the creator of several series of picture books about the Jewish holidays that feature lovable animal characters. As an illustrator, Zalben is lauded for her warm, finely detailed watercolor renderings of anthropomorphic animals—squirrels, monkeys, penguins, and bears. Alice Digilio noted in a _Washington Post Book World_ review of _"Oh, Simple!"_ that stories "can seem too precious when small animal characters are substituted for small human ones" and praised Zalben for avoiding this problem in her "excellent tale" about two chipmunk characters. Marcia Posner, in a _School Library Journal_ appraisal of _Goldie's Purim,_ found the pictures "totally charming and accomplished," lauding the author-illustrator's "tiny, intricate patterns and ... attention to detail."

Born in 1950 in New York City, Zalben was drawing from the time she could hold a crayon. "Formal" art study began at age five when her mother took her for weekly arts lessons at the Metropolitan Museum of Art in New York City. "I just loved it," Zalben recalled of her time at the museum school, telling a _SATA_ interviewer that "it became like a comfortable second home." In sixth grade Zalben decided that when she reached the ninth grade she would apply to the High School of Music and Art; soon after she began building her portfolio.

After graduating from high school, Zalben went on to major in art at Queens College, where she was fortunate to study under several inspiring teachers. One was Marvin Bileck, a Caldecott Honor runner-up for his book _Rain Makes Applesauce._ "I still have parchment

In Jane Breskin Zalben's novel for young adults, sixth-grader Jason is inspired by his teacher, Mr. Carr, to play the violin. When Mr. Carr dies of AIDS, Jason learns the importance of following one's dreams.

and Japanese rice paper from when I was in one of his classes," she recalled. Bileck would talk about "the importance of the brushes and papers you use. It changed my life. I started thinking, gee, this would be interesting to do for a living." Another fond memory from Zalben's college years is the barn that was converted into studios for the art students. "I had my own big space," she recalled, "so it was the first time in my life I could paint until three in the morning."

Her first job after college was as a part-time assistant in the art department at New York City's Dial Press. One advantage of the job was being in the office only "three days a week, so I could do my own work the other two." But it was during this time that Zalben began to really learn about book design, and her passion for the entire process of creating children's books was developing. "I was getting advice and knowledge from people who were really the best in the field," she explained.

Nine months after finishing college, Zalben met Susan Hirschman, then editor-in-chief of children's publishing at Macmillan. Zalben credits Hirschman with having a great effect on her career. "She said certain things to me," Zalben recalled, "about writing—the clarity, the simplicity, the whole architectural concept of less is more."

A month after meeting Hirschman, Zalben published her first book, *Cecilia's Older Brother,* a tale of sibling rivalry with a twist. In this story about a family of mice, Cecilia is constantly being teased and bullied by her older brother Timothy—that is, until "something better" comes along. That something better is a baby brother, and now both Timothy and Cecilia have someone new to fight with. Zalben drew on personal memories of growing up with an older brother to create the book, which, according to a *Times Literary Supplement* critic, "has its funny moments," and is "neatly and wittily illustrated." Ethel L. Heins in *Horn Book* praised *Cecilia's Older Brother* for its "crisply detailed pictures."

With her first three books published, Zalben found herself drawn toward a different style; what she once called "the elf-and-details direction of *Butterfly Ball.*" Zalben has been developing and refining this warm, sometimes offbeat and whimsical, and, above all, richly detailed style of watercolor and pencil drawing in the more than thirty picture books she has illustrated since.

Reviewers are frequently charmed by Zalben's drawings. For example, Kristi L. Thomas's review of *"Oh, Simple!"* in *School Library Journal* praised Zalben's "exquisite tableaux of anthropomorphic animals." Carolyn K. Jenks, in her *School Library Journal* critique of *Norton's Nighttime,* commented favorably on the way

A young sheep named Pearl frets about a holiday visit from her troublesome cousins in Zalben's book of eight stories, highlighting the festivities of Chanukah. (From Pearl's Eight Days of Chanukah, *written and illustrated by Zalben.)*

"the soft, dark watercolor illustrations reflect the night-time atmosphere of the text."

After contributing to some thirteen picture books over ten years' time, Zalben also began writing young adult novels. She recalled that Sandra Jordan, then editor-in-chief at Farrar, Straus & Giroux, helped encourage this change by suggesting, "I think there's more you need to say than you're able to say in a thirty-two-page picture book." Zalben was then raising a baby and a toddler, and although she had little extra energy, she decided that naptimes would provide her the opportunity to start working on a longer story.

Her first novel, *Maybe It Will Rain Tomorrow,* was published in 1982. It is the story of Beth, a sixteen-year-old girl who must go to live with her father and his second wife after her mother's suicide. The story focuses on growing up, loss, first love, and most of all about the difficult relationship between Beth and her stepmother. Symme J. Benoff, writing in *School Library Journal,* called the book "touching" and the relationship between Beth and Linda "real [and] understandable."

Zalben went on to write three novels in a row, inspired by her experiences as a parent of teenagers. In *Water from the Moon,* teen Nicole Bernstein seems to have it all, except a love interest, which causes her to misinterpret the friendly overtures of a young man working in her father's office. The young woman's efforts to establish a secure friendship with a fellow art student are also frustrated when her friend announces her plans to leave the area when her mother changes jobs. *The Fortuneteller in 5B,* which Zalben published in 1991, focuses on Alexandria Pilaf, a teen whose anguish over the death of her own father is transferred into paranoia about an elderly woman in her apartment building. Alexandria begins to spread rumors that the woman is a vampire, because she is rarely seen during the day. Finally the truth is learned—the woman is a survivor of the concentration camps where she lost much of her family—and Alexandria finds a way to deal with her own loss. "Readers will be moved by the author's note about the concentration camp at Terezin," noted Kathy Peihl in *St. James Guide to Young Adult Writers,* "where thousands of children were sent during World War II."

The 1980s were a time of transition for Zalben. She had left the city in which she had been born and raised, and moved to the Long Island suburbs, where she felt lonely. "I hated it for the first three years," she explained, "and my first novel starts out like that about suburbia and all the houses looking the same." Although it was a difficult adjustment, her new life in the suburbs inspired her work on the "Beni" books, her illustrated series about the Jewish holidays. In her *SATA* interview, Zalben recounted the story of driving down the main street of town with her family. The streets were decorated for Christmas and her younger son Alexander wanted to know where the Chanukah decorations were. "He wanted to have a Christmas tree and the holly trailing down the banister," Zalben told *SATA.* "I said, 'Alexander, we're not going to do that, we're Jewish.' And he said, 'Well, if you don't do that then I'm going to marry a girl who's not Jewish when I grow up.'" Zalben was amused at the strong reaction she had to this situation, but it encouraged her to do a Chanukah book.

"The more I thought about it, the more I wanted to give my children, and Jewish children, a gift—something they could cuddle up with during their holiday that wasn't moralistic, pedantic and preachy," Zalben wrote in an essay in the *Miami Jewish Tribune*. She presented the idea of a picture book featuring a cuddly family of bears to her publisher, and the next six months were filled with meetings and discussions trying to answer the question, "How would Jewish people take to animals?" As Zalben wrote in her essay, the response to her idea was generally that "cute little mice were okay for Christmas books, but Jewish children shouldn't have animals."

Ultimately Zalben prevailed. She wrote the book as she had envisioned it, and the first printing of *Beni's First Chanukah*—12,500 copies—sold out in three weeks. A *Publishers Weekly* reviewer called *Beni's First Chanukah* "enchanting ... a gentle reminder that children take pleasure in simple things and that holidays need not be elaborate to be memorable." A *School Library Journal* critic termed the book "a pleasant celebration" and "a quiet story of family holiday togetherness."

The critical and popular success of *Beni's First Chanukah* led to books celebrating Passover, Sukkot, Purim, and the Jewish New Year, all featuring Beni's bear family. Zalben commented that it wasn't until the fifth book, *Happy New Year, Beni,* that she really started to feel like she "knew" the characters. *Happy New Year* was inspired by her own experience of "Tashlikh," the ritual of throwing bits of bread into a river, symbolizing the casting away of past wrongdoing to start the new year afresh. "It was so spiritual and wonderful," she remembered, "that after the holidays were over, I went home and wrote the book." A review of *Happy New Year, Beni* in *Publishers Weekly* pointed to "Zalben's sweet-natured watercolor-and-pencil illustrations" that "portray the festivities in inviting detail, from the table set with lace cloth and candles to the Torah scrolls and prayer shawls in the synagogue." Hazel Rochman, writing in *Booklist,* noted how the "sweetness is nicely undercut by pesky cousin Max, whose practical jokes and wet plastic spiders spoil Beni's fun."

Other Beni books include *Beni's Family Cookbook,* which collects recipes organized around each of the Jewish holidays. While the recipes are designed for cooks who know their way around the kitchen, the layout of the book, and its engaging illustrations, will be sure to captivate younger helpers. The young bear experiences yet another first when he hears Uncle Izzy announce his wedding plans. In *Beni's First Wedding,* readers share Beni's excitement at being a part of the wedding party, and learn about Jewish customs. Writing in *School Library Journal,* Elizabeth Palmer Abarbanel called *Beni's First Wedding* "a wonderful selection for children anticipating a family wedding, and a must for libraries serving Jewish communities."

In addition to her Beni character, Zalben has introduced a young sheep named Pearl who, with her little brother Avi in tow, explores the Jewish tradition from a female perspective. In *Pearl's Eight Days of Chanukah,* published in 1998, Pearl's twin cousins, Sophie and Harry, come to spend the holidays, allowing readers to share in the crafts, ceremonies, and festivities that comprise Chanukah. Noting that the book's strength "lies in the depiction of Chanukah as a time to celebrate and enjoy the company of friends and family," a *School Library Journal* contributor praised the colored pencil and watercolor illustrations as "warm and appealing." While noting that Zalben's "cozy, finely detailed" illustrations are the strength of this book, a *Publishers Weekly* contributor warned that the crafts described in *Pearl's Eight Days of Chanukah* required more craft supplies than are readily available in the average home.

Pearl Plants a Tree describes the "environmental" holiday of Tu B'shvat, as Pearl and her grandfather discuss his first home in America and the tree he once planted there. Pearl decides to follow the tradition by raising an apple tree seedling; the following spring she and her grandfather celebrate the tree-planting holiday together. In the poignant *Pearl's Marigolds for Grandpa,* the young sheep must cope with the loss of her beloved grandfather, in a story that *School Library Journal* contributor Susan Scheps noted "will be comfortably reassuring to children who have lost a beloved grandparent." The book also contains information on the mourning customs for six major religious traditions.

Although Zalben's primary fame rests on her "Beni" books, she continues exploring the many different projects that have allowed her to express herself. A recent young adult novel, 1996's *Unfinished Dreams,* focuses on sixth grade student Jason Glass and his relationship with his middle school principal, Mr. Carr, who ultimately dies of AIDS. It is also about music—Mr. Carr had inspired Jason to learn to play the violin—and Zalben's story explores the healing power of art. "Zalben has written an introspective novel, with real people who have real conversations," commented *Voice of Youth Advocates* contributor Ann Bouricius. The critic added that the book "will be savored by those who enjoy a subtly rich and quiet read."

In addition to writing books about friendship, feelings, warmth, and family, Zalben travels around the world, speaking to young fans about her writing and her art. Her experiences with her readers, her family, and others in her life, continue to fuel her passion for her work. "Sometimes you need to rewrite things that you haven't had, and you also need to duplicate things you have had. If I've had bad times in my life, I don't stop my art. I get closer to it and go into it more. The art is a friend."

Biographical and Critical Sources

BOOKS

St. James Guide to Young Adult Writers, St. James Press, 1997.

PERIODICALS

Booklist, December 15, 1975, p. 583; December 15, 1988; March 15, 1990, p. 1464; September 15, 1990; January 1, 1992; July, 1993, Hazel Rochman, review of *Happy New Year, Beni;* August, 1995, Kathy Broderick, review of *Miss Violet's Shining Day,* p. 1958; November 15, 1995, Stephanie Zvirin, review of *Pearl Plants a Tree,* p. 566; June 1, 1996, Susan Dove Lempke, review of *Unfinished Dreams,* p. 1704; September 15, 1996, Stephanie Zvirin, review of *Beni's Family Cookbook,* p. 236; November 1, 1997, Ilene Cooper, review of *Pearl's Marigolds for Grandpa,* p. 485.

Bulletin of the Center for Children's Books, November, 1973; February, 1979; November, 1982; October, 1984; December, 1991, p. 111.

Hadassah Magazine, August-September, 1993, Rahel Musleah, "Love Pictures," pp. 38-39.

Horn Book, June, 1973, Ethel L. Heins, review of *Cecilia's Older Brother,* pp. 263-264; October, 1978, p. 511; March-April, 1990, p. 197; January-February, 1992, p. 77; September-October, 1996, Elizabeth Watson, review of *Unfinished Dreams,* p. 603.

Miami Jewish Tribune, December 22, 1989, Jane Breskin Zalben, "Chanukah Story."

Publishers Weekly, November 3, 1975, p. 72; June 26, 1978, p. 117; October 15, 1979, p. 67; December 12, 1980, p. 47; July 3, 1981, p. 146; April 30, 1982; October 15, 1982; April 10, 1987, p. 95; November 11, 1988, review of *Beni's First Chanukah,* p. 55; October 27, 1989, p. 70; January 19, 1990; October 26, 1990, p. 69; January 18, 1991, p. 57; September 20, 1991, p. 135; May 18, 1992, p. 68; August 16, 1993, p. 49; September 20, 1993, review of *Happy New Year, Beni;* October 14, 1996, review of *Beni's Family Cookbook,* p. 85; September 28, 1998, review of *Pearl's Eight Days of Chanukah,* p. 52.

School Library Journal, December, 1975, p. 65; September, 1979, Carolyn K. Jenks, review of *Norton's Nighttime,* p. 125; November, 1981, Kristi L. Thomas, review of *"Oh, Simple!",* p. 84; May, 1982, Symme J. Bennoff, review of *Maybe It Will Rain Tomorrow,* p. 76; October, 1988, review of *Beni's First Chanukah;* November, 1989, p. 116; April, 1990, p. 101; February, 1991, p. 77; May, 1991, Marcia Posner, review of *Goldie's Purim,* p. 86; December, 1991, p. 120; April, 1992, p. 102; December, 1993, p. 97; January 1, 1996, Marcia W. Posner, review of *Pearl Plants a Tree,* p. 99; February, 1997, Susan Scheps, review of *Beni's Family Cookbook,* p. 126; September, 1997, Susan Scheps, review of *Pearl's Marigolds for Grandpa,* p. 198; May, 1998, Elizabeth Palmer Abarbanel, review of *Beni's First Wedding,* pp. 128-29; October, 1998, review of *Pearl's Eight Days of Chanukah,* p. 39; February, 2000, Augusta R. Malvagno, review of *To Every Season,* p. 116.

Times Literary Supplement, November 23, 1973, review of *Cecilia's Older Brother,* p. 1436.

Voice of Youth Advocates, August, 1996, Ann Bouricius, review of *Unfinished Dreams,* p. 164.

Washington Post Book World, August 9, 1981, Alice Digilio, "Young Bookshelf."*